Not For Tourists Guide to

SAN FRANCISCO

Get more on
notfortourists.com

Keep connected with:

Twitter:
twitter/notfortourists

Facebook:
facebook/notfortourists

iPhone App:
nftiphone.com

www.notfortourists.com

Not For Tourists Inc

Skyhorse Publishing

designed by:
Not For Tourists, Inc
NFT$_{TM}$—Not For Tourists$_{TM}$ Guide to San Francisco
www.notfortourists.com

Publisher
Skyhorse Publishing

Co-Founders
Jane Pirone
Rob Tallia

City Editor
Barbara Rockwell

Information Design
Jane Pirone
Rob Tallia
Scot Covey

Director
Stuart Farr

Managing Editors
Craig Nelson
Rob Tallia

Sales & Marketing Director
Sarah Hocevar

Production Manager
Aaron Schielke

Printed in China
ISBN# 978-1-61608-531-5 $16.95

9th Edition

Every effort has been made to ensure that the information in this book is as up-to-date as possible at press time. However, many details are liable to change—as we have learned.
Not For Tourists cannot accept responsibility for any consequences arising from the use of this book.

Not For Tourists does not solicit individuals, organizations, or businesses for listings inclusion in our guides, nor do we accept payment for inclusion into the editorial portion of our book; the advertising sections, however, are exempt from this policy. We always welcome communications from anyone regarding ANYTHING having to do with our books; please visit us on our website at www.notfortourists.com for appropriate contact information.

www.skyhorsepublishing.com

10 9 8 7 6 5 4 3 2 1

Dear NFT User,

Well, 2011 was quite a year! San Franciscans learned to live without Happy Meals, preparations began for the upcoming America's Cup, and for the first time ever the San Francisco Giants began the baseball season as the reigning World Series Champs (the last time the club won a World Series was in 1954 as the New York Giants).

And despite the country's sagging economy, here in San Francisco things have stayed relatively stable. Our economy was in the compost heap long before the rest of the country caught up. Always on the cutting edge, that's our Frisco.

The wheezing, bedridden economy has had some positive effect on the citay by the bay, as rent has actually gone down in the first time since forever. It's also getting too uncomfortable for speculator types looking to exploit the brain-shaped city's wealth of ideas. No gold here, boys! Take it to ______ (wherever the gold is).

But we at NFT know where the gold is, and we're going to tell you! It's in your hands. That's right, on pages 15-18 we reveal the location of a fairly large amount of gold. It's up to you to decode our complex language of map symbols, words, and page numbers. While you're working on that, check out the rest of the book for the latest in listings, maps, tips, and all-around expert NFT guidance. We've got our team of local writers and scourges-about-town back to let you know what's going on, and where—all in a compact, sharp-looking volume that's easy to check when you're going from place to place.

Speaking of keeping things mobile, we've launched an award-winning series of city-by-city iPhone apps, crammed with thousands of listings. With geo-location to tell you everything you need to know about wherever you are, it's the newest way to get up-to-the-minute tips, the minute you want them. And if you're into the whole Twitter and Facebook thing, you can seek us out there, too.

Here's hoping you find what you need in the fog…

Rob, Jane, Barbara, Craig, Sarah, etc

Central

Richmond

Sunset

Upper Market and Beyond

Map 1 • Marina / Cow Hollow (West)

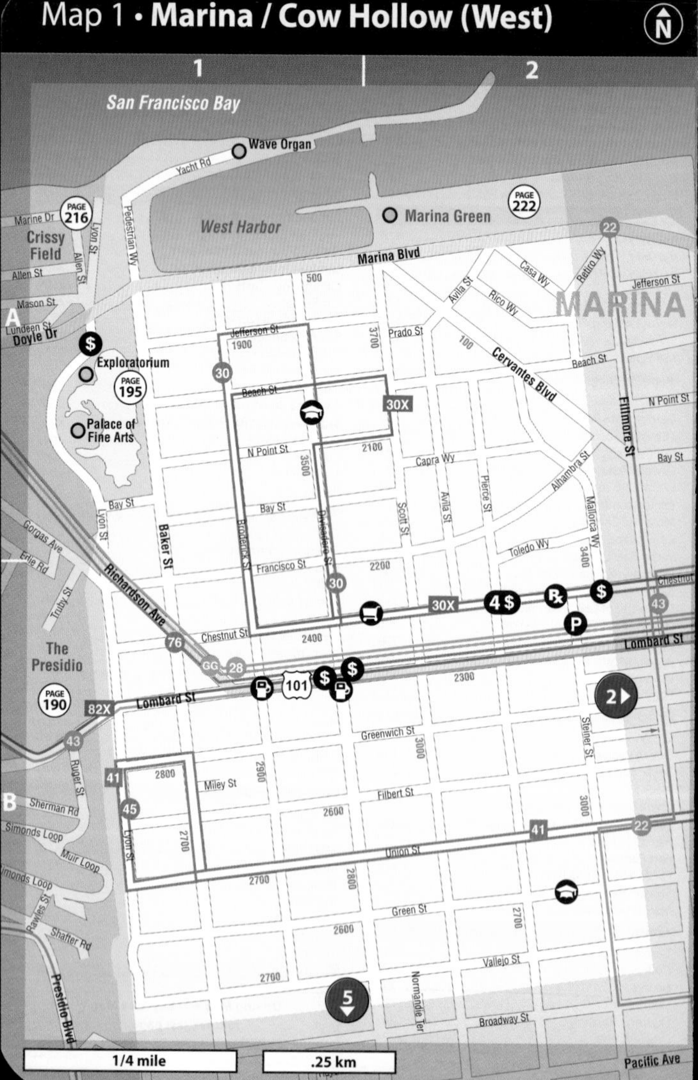

Flanked by the Presidio to the west and the Bay to the north, this neighborhood has some of the best sea-level strolling and views in the city, particularly from Marina Boulevard along the shore of Marina Green. Main drags Chestnut Street and Union Street offer shopping and a mix of bars and restaurants. Busy Lombard Street has motels, drugstores, fast food, and other necessities.

Banks

- **Bank of America** • 2200 Chestnut St
- **Bank of America (ATM)** • 3601 Lyon St
- **Chase** • 2166 Chestnut St
- **Citibank** • 2198 Chestnut St
- **US (ATM)** • Walgreens • 3201 Divisadero St
- **Wachovia** • 2197 Chestnut St
- **Wells Fargo** • 2055 Chestnut St

Gas Stations

- **76** • 2498 Lombard St
- **Valero** • 2601 Lombard St

Landmarks

- **Exploratorium** • 3601 Lyon St
- **Marina Green** • Marina Blvd b/w Scott St & Webster St
- **Palace of Fine Arts** • 3301 Lyon St
- **Wave Organ** • Yacht Rd

Parking

Pharmacies

- **Walgreens** • 2141 Chestnut St

Schools

- **Claire B Lilienthal Elementary** • 3630 Divisadero St
- **St Vincent De Paul** • 2350 Green St

Supermarkets

- **Marina Supermarket** • 2323 Chestnut St

Map 1 • Marina / Cow Hollow (West)

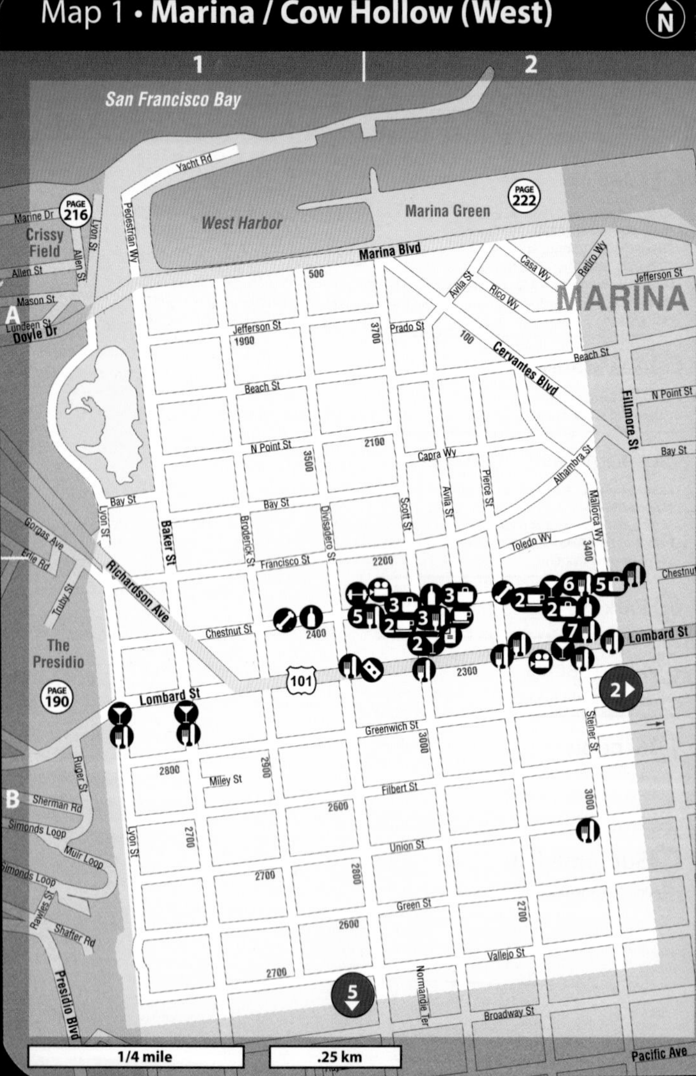

Throngs of twenty-something professionals bar hop along lively Chestnut Street. Shoppers will find old standbys like Lucky Brand as well as a freckling of unique boutiques. For dinner on the fancy side, Isa is a good bet. For something different, hit Liverpool Lil's pub next to the Presidio gates.

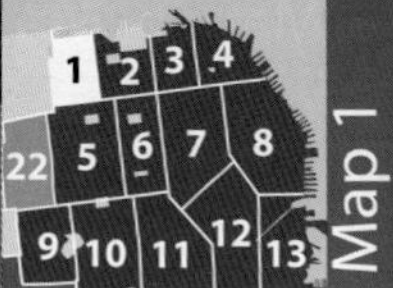

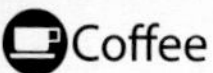

Coffee

- **Bechelli's Coffee Shop** • 2346 Chestnut St
- **Coffee Roastery** • 2331 Chestnut St
- **Grove Cafe** • 2250 Chestnut St
- **Peet's** • 2156 Chestnut St
- **Starbucks** • 2132 Chestnut St

Copy Shops

- **The UPS Store** • 2269 Chestnut St

Gyms

- **Crunch** • 2324 Chestnut St

Liquor Stores

- **California Wine Merchant** • 2113 Chestnut St
- **Marina Delicatessen & Liquors** • 2299 Chestnut St
- **United Liquor & Deli** • 2401 Chestnut St

Movie Theaters

- **Marina Theatre** • 2149 Chestnut St
- **Presidio Theatre** • 2340 Chestnut St

Nightlife

- **Bin 38** • 3232 Scott St
- **The Final Final** • 2990 Baker St
- **Gravity Room** • 3251 Scott St
- **Liverpool Lil's** • 2942 Lyon St
- **Marina Lounge** • 2138 Chestnut St

Pet Shops

- **Animal Connection II** • 2419 Chestnut St
- **Catnip & Bones** • 2220 Chestnut St

Restaurants

- **A16** • 2355 Chestnut St
- **Ace Wasabi's Rock and Roll Sushi** • 3339 Steiner St
- **Amici's East Coast Pizzeria** • 2200 Lombard St
- **Baker Street Bistro** • 2953 Baker St
- **Barney's Gourmet Hamburger** • 3344 Steiner St
- **Bechelli's Coffee Shop** • 2346 Chestnut St
- **Bistro Aix** • 3340 Steiner St
- **Blue Barn** • 2105 Chestnut St
- **Chilayo** • 2150 Chestnut St
- **Circa** • 2001 Chestnut St
- **Dragon Well** • 2142 Chestnut St
- **E'Angelo** • 2234 Chestnut St
- **The Grove** • 2250 Chestnut St
- **Home Plate** • 2274 Lombard St
- **IHOP** • 2299 Lombard St
- **Isa** • 3324 Steiner St
- **Izzy's Steak and Chops** • 3345 Steiner St
- **Liverpool Lil's** • 2942 Lyon St
- **Los Hermanos** • 2026 Chestnut St
- **Mamacita** • 2317 Chestnut St
- **Mel's Drive-In** • 2165 Lombard St
- **Mezes** • 2373 Chestnut St
- **Original Buffalo Wings** • 2499 Lombard St
- **Pluto's** • 3258 Scott St
- **Ristorante Parma** • 3314 Steiner St
- **Rose's Café** • 2298 Union St
- **Squat and Gobble** • 2263 Chestnut St
- **Terzo** • 3011 Steiner St
- **Yukol Place Thai Cuisine** • 2380 Lombard St

Shopping

- **Benefit** • 2219 Chestnut St
- **Books Inc** • 2251 Chestnut St
- **Chadwick's of London** • 2068 Chestnut St
- **City Optix** • 2154 Chestnut St
- **Fiori** • 2314 Chestnut St
- **Fleet Feet** • 2076 Chestnut St
- **Lucca Delicatessen** • 2120 Chestnut St
- **Lucky Brand** • 2301 Chestnut St
- **Miette** • 2109 Chestnut St
- **Pure Beauty** • 2085 Chestnut St
- **Rabat** • 2080 Chestnut St
- **Smash Shoes** • 2030 Chestnut St

Video Rental

- **Blockbuster** • 2460 Lombard St

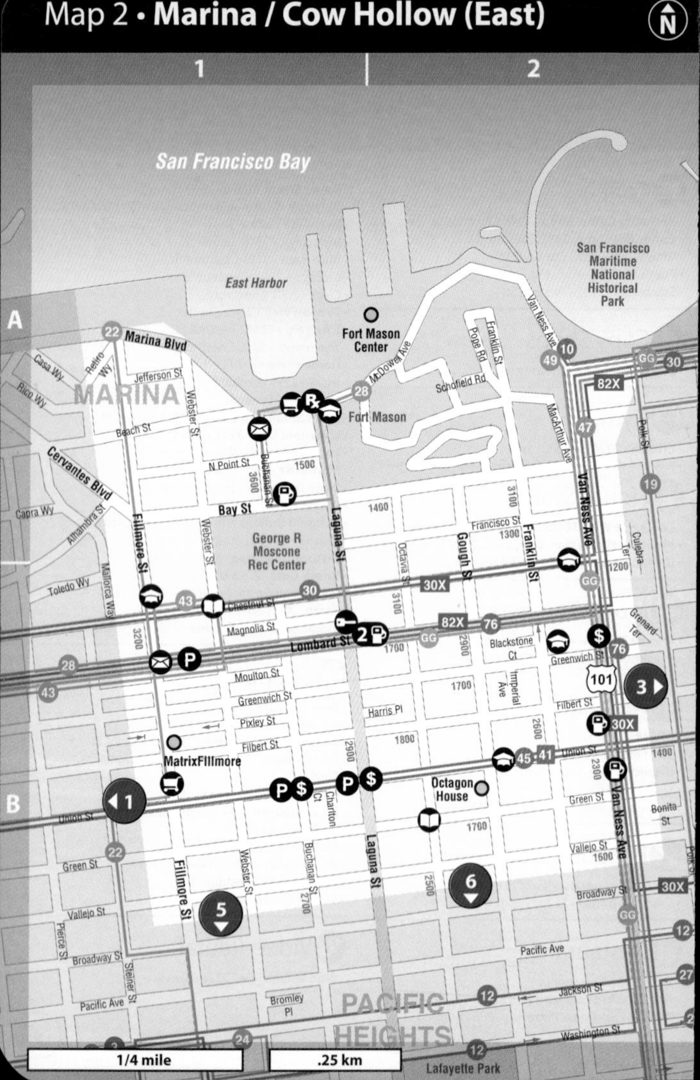

N
1
2
A
B
San Francisco Bay
East Harbor
Fort Mason Center
Fort Mason
San Francisco Maritime National Historical Park
MARINA
PACIFIC HEIGHTS
George R Moscone Rec Center
MatrixFillmore
Octagon House
Lafayette Park
Marina Blvd
Jefferson St
Beach St
N Point St
Bay St
Chestnut St
Magnolia St
Lombard St
Moulton St
Greenwich St
Pixley St
Filbert St
Union St
Green St
Vallejo St
Broadway St
Pacific Ave
Jackson St
Washington St
Fillmore St
Webster St
Buchanan St
Laguna St
Octavia St
Gough St
Franklin St
Van Ness Ave
Polk St
Cervantes Blvd
Casa Wy
Rico Wy
Retiro Wy
Capra Wy
Alhambra St
Toledo Wy
Mallorca Way
Steiner St
Pierce St
McDowell Ave
Pope Rd
Franklin St
Schofield Rd
MacArthur Ave
Francisco St
Blackstone Ct
Imperial Ave
Harris Pl
Charlton Ct
Bromley Pl
Culebra Ter
Greenwich St
Grenard Ter
Bonita St
101
1/4 mile
.25 km

Life is simply fabulous—and clean—in the Marina and Cow Hollow, SF's enclave for young adult professionals. Fort Mason, a onetime military outpost, is now a cultural destination with museums, experimental theater, and acres of open space.

Banks

- **Bank of America** • 1995 Union St
- **Chase** • 2750 Van Ness Ave
- **Wells Fargo** • 1900 Union St

Car Rental

- **Car Enterprises** • 1800 Lombard St

Gas Stations

- **76** • 2559 Van Ness Ave
- **Chevron** • 1598 Bay St
- **Chevron** • 1790 Lombard St
- **Chevron** • 2465 Van Ness Ave
- **Shell** • 1800 Lombard St

Landmarks

- **Fort Mason Center** • Buchanan St & Marina Blvd
- **MatrixFillmore** • 3138 Fillmore St
- **Octagon House** • 2645 Gough St

Libraries

- **Golden Gate Valley Library** • 1801 Green St
- **Marina Branch Library** • 1890 Chestnut St

Parking

Pharmacies

- **Safeway** • 15 Marina Blvd

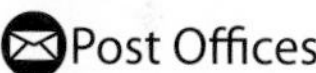

Post Offices

- **Marina Green Retail Store** • 3749 Buchanan St
- **Marina Station** • 2055 Lombard St

Schools

- **CCSF (Fort Mason Campus)** • Laguna St & Marina Blvd
- **Hergl** • 1570 Greenwich St
- **Marina Middle** • 3500 Fillmore St
- **San Francisco School of Massage** • 1327 Chestnut St
- **Sherman Elementary** • 1651 Union St

Supermarkets

- **Real Food Company** • 3060 Fillmore St
- **Safeway** • 15 Marina Blvd

Map 2 • Marina / Cow Hollow (East)

Cow Hollow's stylish main drag is Union Street, brimming with boutiques, salons, trendy restaurants, and pickup bars. Like Chestnut Street in the Marina, it's an ideal destination for preening, strolling, window shopping, and flirting over the evening's first lemon drop (especially at Betelnut Pejiu Wu, the Balboa, or Eastside West).

Coffee

- **Coffee Roastery** • 2191 Union St
- **Espresso Roma Cafe** • 3130 Fillmore St
- **First Cup** • 2911 Van Ness Ave
- **Notes from Underground** • 2399 Van Ness Ave
- **Starbucks** • 1899 Union St
- **Starbucks** • 3735 Buchanan St

Copy Shops

- **FedEx Office** • 3225 Fillmore St

Farmers Markets

- **San Francisco Marina (Tues, 11:30am–4pm)** • Fillmore St & Chestnut St

Gyms

- **24 Hour Fitness** • 3741 Buchanan St ㉔
- **Curves (women only)** • 2529 Van Ness Ave
- **Crunch** • 1725 Union St

Hardware Stores

- **Fredericksen Hardware** • 3029 Fillmore

Liquor Stores

- **Albertino's** • 1897 Lombard St
- **Michaelis Wine & Spirits** • 2198 Union St
- **PlumpJack Wines** • 3201 Fillmore St
- **Silver Platter Delicatessen** • 2501 Van Ness Ave
- **Winestyles** • 2118 Union St

Nightlife

- **Balboa Cafe** • 3199 Fillmore St
- **Bar None** • 1980 Union St
- **Black Magic Voodoo Lounge** • 1400 Lombard St
- **The Brazen Head** • 3166 Buchanan St
- **Bus Stop** • 1901 Union St
- **City Tavern** • 3200 Fillmore St
- **Comet Club** • 3111 Fillmore St
- **HiFi** • 2125 Lombard St
- **Horseshoe Tavern** • 2024 Chestnut St
- **Kelley's Tavern** • 3231 Fillmore St
- **MatrixFillmore** • 3138 Fillmore St
- **Mauna Loa** • 3009 Fillmore St
- **Ottimista Enoteca Café** • 1838 Union St
- **Silver Cloud** • 1994 Lombard St

Pet Shops

- **Marina Pet Hospital** • 2024 Lombard St

Restaurants

- **Abigail's** • 2120 Greenwich St
- **Alegrias Spanish Restaurant** • 2018 Lombard St
- **Balboa Cafe** • 3199 Fillmore St
- **Betelnut Pejiu Wu** • 2030 Union St
- **Boboquivari's** • 1450 Lombard St
- **The Brazen Head** • 3166 Buchanan St
- **Eastside West** • 3154 Fillmore St
- **Greens Restaurant** • Ft Mason, Bldg A
- **Helmand Palace** • 2424 Van Ness Ave
- **Jake's Steaks** • 3301 Buchanan St
- **La Boulange at Union** • 1909 Union St
- **La Cucina** • 2136 Union St
- **Mas Sake Freestyle Sushi** • 2030 Lombard St
- **Matterhorn Swiss Restaurant** • 2323 Van Ness Ave
- **Pacific Catch** • 2027 Chestnut St
- **Pane e Vino** • 1715 Union St
- **Perry's** • **1944 Union St**
- **What's Up Dog!** • 2211 Filbert St

Shopping

- **Ambiance** • 1864 Union St
- **American Apparel** • 2174 Union St
- **Artesanias Showroom** • 1711 Greenwich St
- **The Bar Method** • 3333 Fillmore St
- **Canyon Beachwear** • 1728 Union St
- **Chan's Trains & Hobbies** • 2450 Van Ness Ave
- **CocoaBella Chocolates** • 2102 Union St
- **Enchanted Crystal** • 1895 Union St
- **Jest Jewels** • 1869 Union St
- **Krimsa** • 2190 Union St
- **Lush** • 2116 Union St
- **Mingle** • 1815 Union St
- **Mudpie** • 1694 Union St
- **PlumpJack Wines** • 3201 Fillmore St
- **Real Food Company** • 3060 Fillmore St

Video Rental

- **Choi's Home Video** • 1410 Lombard St

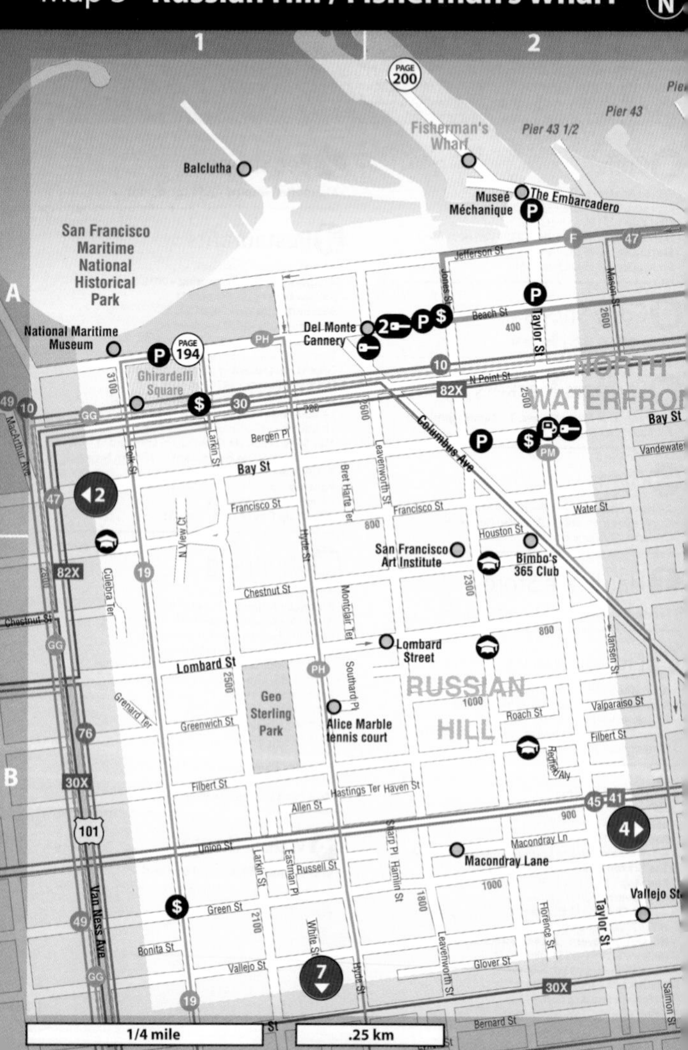

N
1
2
PAGE 200
Pier 43
Pier 43 1/2
Fisherman's Wharf
Balclutha
Museé Méchanique
The Embarcadero
San Francisco Maritime National Historical Park
Jefferson St
Beach St
Jones St
Taylor St
Mason St
National Maritime Museum
PAGE 194
Ghirardelli Square
Del Monte Cannery
N Point St
NORTH WATERFRONT
Columbus Ave
Bay St
Larkin St
Bergen Pl
Polk St
Leavenworth St
Bret Harte Ter
Hyde St
Francisco St
N View Ct
Vandewater
Water St
Houston St
San Francisco Art Institute
Bimbo's 365 Club
Culebra Ter
MacArthur Ave
Chestnut St
Montclair Ter
Lombard Street
Lombard St
Jansen St
RUSSIAN HILL
Geo Sterling Park
Southard Pl
Alice Marble tennis court
Grenard Ter
Greenwich St
Roach St
Valparaiso St
Filbert St
Redfield Aly
Hastings Ter
Haven St
Allen St
Van Ness Ave
Union St
Macondray Ln
Macondray Lane
Eastman Pl
Russell St
Sharp Pl
Hamlin St
Green St
Florence St
Vallejo St
White St
Bonita St
Glover St
Salmon St
Bernard St
1/4 mile
.25 km

Join your sweetheart in a romp through romantic Russian Hill. Steep, tree-lined hills dotted with stately apartment buildings give way to leafy enclaves offering unbeatable views of the city and the Bay. Down along the waterfront, tourists swarm over Fisherman's Wharf, Ghirardelli Square, and the Cannery at Del Monte Square.

Banks

- **Bank of America (ATM)** • 2325 Polk St
- **Bank of America (ATM)** • 900 North Point St
- **US (ATM)** • Walgreens • 2801 Jones St
- **Wells Fargo (ATM)** • 501 Bay St

Car Rental

- **Avis** • 500 Beach St
- **Budget** • 495 Bay St
- **Electric Time Car Rental** • 2800 Leavenworth St
- **Hertz** • 500 Beach St

Gas Stations

- **76** • 490 Bay St

Landmarks

- **Alice Marble tennis court** • Greenwich St & Hyde St
- **Balclutha** • Hyde St Pier
- **Bimbo's 365 Club** • 1025 Columbus Ave
- **Del Monte Cannery** • 2801 Leavenworth St
- **Fisherman's Wharf** • Embarcadero b/w Aquatic Park & Pier 39
- **Ghirardelli Square** • 900 North Point St
- **Lombard Street** • Lombard St b/w Hyde St & Leavenworth St
- **Macondray Lane** • Jones St b/w Green St & Union St
- **Museé Mécanique** • Fisherman's Wharf
- **National Maritime Museum** • 900 Beach St
- **San Francisco Art Institute** • 800 Chestnut St
- **Vallejo Steps** • Vallejo St & Mason St

Parking

Schools

- **CCSF (Chinatown/North Beach Campus)** • 940 Filbert St
- **Galileo High** • 1150 Francisco St
- **San Francisco Art Institute** • 800 Chestnut St
- **Yick Wo Elementary** • 2245 Jones St

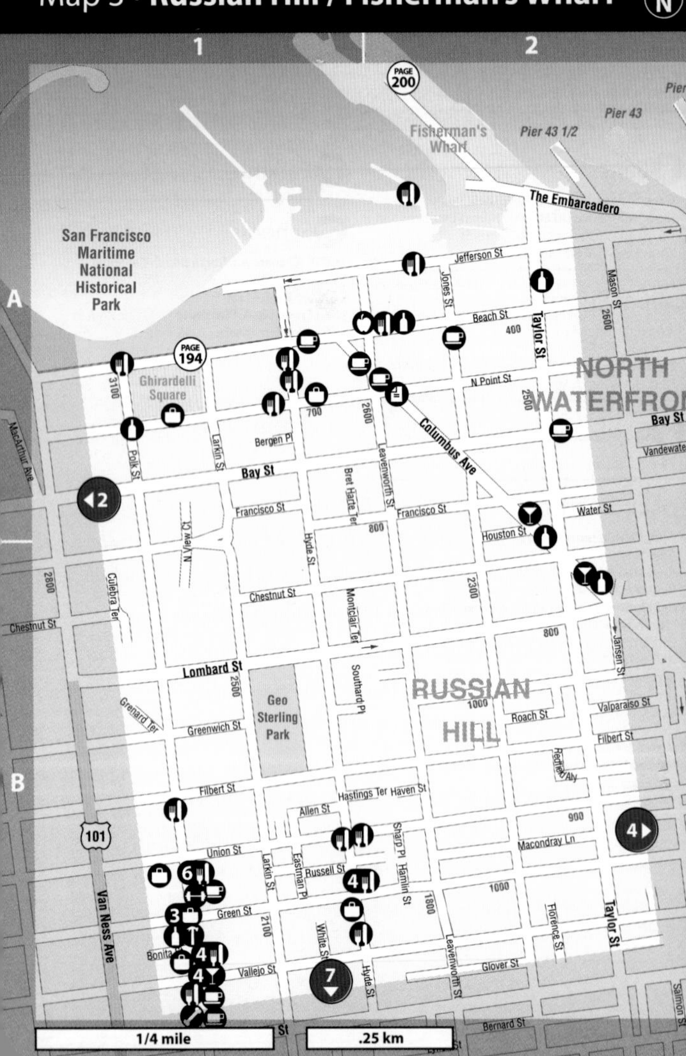
N
1
2
PAGE 200
Pier
Pier 43
Pier 43 1/2
Fisherman's Wharf
The Embarcadero
San Francisco Maritime National Historical Park
A
Jefferson St
Jones St
Mason St
2600
Beach St
400
Taylor St
PAGE 194
NORTH WATERFRONT
3100
Ghirardelli Square
N Point St
2500
Bay St
700
2600
Columbus Ave
MacArthur Ave
Polk St
Larkin St
Bergen Pl
Vandewater
Bay St
2
Bret Harte Ter
Leavenworth St
Francisco St
Francisco St
Water St
800
Houston St
N View Ct
Hyde St
2800
Culebra Ter
Chestnut St
Chestnut St
Montclair Ter
2300
800
Jansen St
Lombard St
2500
Geo Sterling Park
Southard Pl
RUSSIAN HILL
1000
Roach St
Valparaiso St
Grenard Ter
Greenwich St
Filbert St
Redfield Aly
B
Filbert St
Hastings Ter
Haven St
Allen St
900
4
101
Sharp Pl
Macondray Ln
Union St
Larkin St
Eastman Pl
Russell St
Hamlin St
1000
Van Ness Ave
Green St
2100
1800
Florence St
Taylor St
White St
Bonita
Vallejo St
7
Hyde St
Leavenworth St
Glover St
Salmon St
Bernard St
1/4 mile
.25 km

Sundries / Entertainment

Head to Hyde and Polk Streets for the eclectic mix of cafés, restaurants, boutiques, and bars. On both streets, outposts for the posh set mingle with longtime local businesses. On sunny days, grab an ice cream from Swensen's and watch tourist-packed cable cars grind to and from the Wharf below.

Coffee

- **Boulange de Polk** • 2310 Polk St
- **Coffee Adventures** • 1331 Columbus Ave
- **Pergamino** • 1321 Columbus Ave
- **Starbucks** • 2801 Jones St
- **Starbucks** • 499 Bay St
- **Starbucks** • 680 Beach St
- **Starbucks** • 2165 Polk St

Copy Shops

- **The UPS Store** • 1288 Columbus Ave

Farmers Markets

- **The Cannery @ Del Monte Sq (open daily 10am–8pm; Sun, 11am)** • Leavenworth St & Columbus St

Gyms

- **Crunch** • 2330 Polk St

Hardware Stores

- **Cole Hardware** • 2254 Polk St

Liquor Stores

- **Anchorage Liquor** • 561 Beach St
- **Golden 7** • 940 Columbus Ave
- **SF Liquor** • 3098 Polk St
- **Wharf Liquors & Deli** • 2730 Taylor St
- **William Cross Wine Merchants** • 2253 Polk St
- **Willie's Liquor** • 1018 Columbus Ave

Nightlife

- **Bimbo's 365 Club** • 1025 Columbus Ave
- **The Buccaneer** • 2155 Polk St
- **The Buena Vista Cafe** • 2765 Hyde St
- **Cresta's 2211 Club** • 2211 Polk St
- **Fiddler's Green** • 1333 Columbus Ave
- **The Greens Sports Bar** • 2239 Polk St
- **Kennedy's Irish Pub & Indian Curry House** • 1040 Columbus Ave
- **La Rocca's Corner** • 957 Columbus Ave
- **Tonic** • 2360 Polk St

Pet Shops

- **Bow Wow Meow & Co** • 2150 Polk St

Restaurants

- **Ana Mandara** • 891 Beach St
- **Aux Delices** • 2327 Polk St
- **Boudin** • 160 Jefferson St
- **Boulange de Polk** • 2310 Polk St
- **Buena Vista** • 2765 Hyde St
- **Frascati** • 1901 Hyde St
- **Gary Danko** • 800 North Point St
- **Grandeho's Kamekyo** • 2721 Hyde St
- **In-N-Out Burger** • 333 Jefferson St
- **Kara's Cupcakes** • 900 N Point St
- **La Folie** • 2316 Polk St
- **Lemongrass Thai Cuisine** • 2348 Polk St
- **Luella** • 1896 Hyde St
- **Nick's Crispy Tacos** • 1500 Broadway
- **Okoze Sushi** • 1207 Union St
- **Pesce** • 2227 Polk St
- **Polker's** • 2226 Polk St
- **Rex Café** • 2323 Polk St
- **Scoma's** • Pier 47
- **Sushi Groove** • 1916 Hyde St
- **Swensen's Ice Cream** • 1999 Hyde St
- **Yabbies Coastal Kitchen** • 2237 Polk St
- **Za Pizza** • 1919 Hyde St
- **Zarzuela** • 2000 Hyde St

Shopping

- **Aimee, Andrew & Company** • 2238 Polk St
- **Atelier des Modistes** • 1903 Hyde St
- **The Candy Store** • 1507 Vallejo St
- **Cole Hardware** • 2254 Polk St
- **Ghirardelli Square** • 900 North Point St
- **Lavande Nail Spa** • 2139 Polk St
- **Patagonia** • 770 N Point St
- **Russian Hill Bookstore** • 2234 Polk St
- **Smoke Signals** • 2223 Polk St
- **William Cross Wine Merchants** • 2253 Polk St

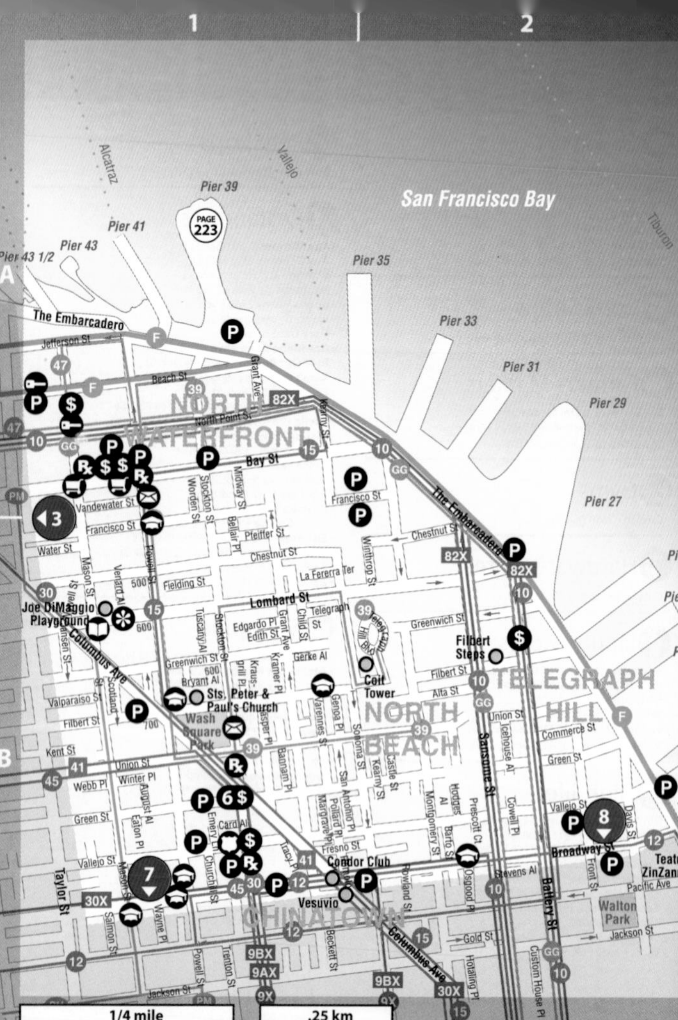

1
2
A
B
San Francisco Bay
Alcatraz
Vallejo
Tiburon
Pier 39
PAGE 223
Pier 41
Pier 43
Pier 43 1/2
Pier 35
Pier 33
Pier 31
Pier 29
Pier 27
The Embarcadero
Jefferson St
Beach St
North Point St
NORTH WATERFRONT
Bay St
Francisco St
Vandewater St
Water St
Chestnut St
La Fererra Ter
Lombard St
Greenwich St
Filbert St
Alta St
Union St
Commerce St
Green St
Vallejo St
Broadway St
Pacific Ave
Jackson St
Gold St
Stevens Al
Fresno St
Card Al
Valparaiso St
Kent St
Webb Pl
Winter Pl
Eaton Pl
Mason St
Powell St
Stockton St
Grant Ave
Kearny St
Midway St
Worden St
Bellair Pl
Pfeiffer St
Winthrop St
Fielding St
Edgardo Pl
Edith St
Child St
Gerke Al
Telegraph Hill Blvd
Tuscany Al
Bryant Al
Varennes St
Genoa Pl
Jasper Pl
Kraus-grill Pl
Kramer Pl
Sonoma St
Castle St
Baanam Pl
San Antonio Pl
Pollard Pl
Margrave Pl
Montgomery St
Hodges Al
Barto St
Prescott Ct
Osgood Pl
Sansome St
Battery St
Icehouse Al
Cowell Pl
Front St
Davis St
Custom House Pl
Hotaling Pl
Rowland St
Beckett St
Trenton St
Emery Ln
Churchill St
Wayne Pl
Salmon St
Taylor St
August Al
Venard Al
Scotland St
Columbus Ave
Tracy Pl
Joe DiMaggio Playground
Sts. Peter & Paul's Church
Wash Square Park
Coit Tower
Filbert Steps
TELEGRAPH HILL
NORTH BEACH
CHINATOWN
Condor Club
Vesuvio
Walton Park
Teatro ZinZanni
500
600
700
1/4 mile
.25 km

With its lively cafés, dark watering holes, and artistic flair, North Beach holds a rare appeal for both tourists and locals. Once an Italian enclave and later the cradle of the Beat Movement, the area's narrow alleys and hectic thoroughfares teem with people night and day. Parking is a nightmare.

Banks

- **Bank of America** • 1455 Stockton St
- **Bank of America (ATM)** • 330 Bay St
- **Bank of the West** • 480 Columbus Ave
- **Citibank** • 580 Green St
- **Citibank (ATM)** • 2650 Mason St
- **GBC International Bank** • 1355 Stockton St
- **US** • 1435 Stockton St
- **US (ATM)** • Walgreens • 1344 Stockton St
- **Wells Fargo** • 350 Bay St
- **Wells Fargo** • 468 Columbus Ave
- **Wells Fargo (ATM)** • 1255 Battery St

Car Rental

- **Dollar** • 2500 Mason St
- **Enterprise** • 350 Beach St

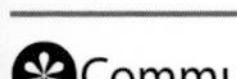

Community Gardens

Landmarks

- **Coit Tower** • 1 Telegraph Hill Blvd
- **Condor Club** • 560 Broadway
- **Filbert Steps** • Filbert St & Sansome St
- **Joe DiMaggio Playground** • 651 Lombard St
- **Sts Peter and Paul's Church** • 666 Filbert St
- **Teatro ZinZanni** • The Embarcadero & Pier 5

Libraries

- **North Beach Branch Library** • 2000 Mason St

Parking

Pharmacies

- **North East Medical Pharmacy** • 1520 Stockton St
- **Safeway** • 350 Bay St
- **Walgreens** • 1344 Stockton St
- **Walgreens** • 320 Bay St

Police

- **Central Police Station** • 766 Vallejo St

Post Offices

- **North Beach (Carrier) Station** • 2200 Powell St
- **North Beach (Finance) Station** • 1640 Stockton St

Schools

- **Francisco Middle** • 2190 Powell St
- **Garfield Elementary** • 420 Filbert St
- **John Yehall Chin Elementary** • 350 Broadway
- **Parker Elementary** • 840 Broadway St
- **St Mary's Chinese Day** • 910 Broadway
- **Sts Peter & Paul** • 660 Filbert St

Supermarkets

- **Safeway** • 350 Bay St
- **Trader Joe's** • 401 Bay St

1 2

A

B

San Francisco Bay
Alcatraz
Vallejo
Tiburon
Pier 39
PAGE 223
Pier 41
Pier 43
Pier 43 1/2
Pier 35
Pier 33
Pier 31
Pier 29
Pier 27
The Embarcadero
Jefferson St
Beach St
North Point St
Grant Ave
Kearny St
NORTH WATERFRONT
Bay St
Stockton St
Worden St
Midway St
Bellair Pl
Francisco St
Vandewater St
Water St
Pfeiffer St
Chestnut St
La Ferrera Ter
Winthrop St
Mason St
Powell St
Venard Al
Fielding St
Lombard St
Telegraph Pl
Edgardo Pl
Edith St
Child St
Telegraph Hill Blvd
Greenwich St
Jansen St
Columbus Ave
Tuscany Al
Gerke Al
Kramer Pl
Kraus-grill Pl
Bryant Al
Filbert St
Alta St
TELEGRAPH HILL
Valparaiso St
Scotland St
Wash Square Park
Jasper Pl
Genoa Pl
Varennes St
NORTH BEACH
Union St
Icehouse Al
Commerce St
Sansome St
Kent St
Green St
Webb Pl
Winter Pl
August Al
Eaton Pl
Bannam Pl
San Antonio Pl
Sonoma St
Kearny St
Castle St
Montgomery St
Hodges Al
Prescott Ct
Cowell Pl
Vallejo St
Davis St
Margrave Pl
Pollard Pl
Fresno St
Romolo
Tracy Pl
Emery Ln
Broadway St
Front St
Churchill St
Taylor St
Howland St
Barto St
Osgood Pl
Stevens Al
Battery St
Pacific Ave
Walton Park
Jackson St
CHINATOWN
Salmon St
Wayne Pl
Beckett St
Gold St
Columbus Ave
Hotaling Pl
Custom House Pl
Trenton St
Powell St
Jackson St
500
600
700
1/4 mile
.25 km

Old-school favorites Caffe Trieste, Gino & Carlo, Mara's Bakery, and North Beach Restaurant peacefully coexist with hordes of tourists and porn palaces. Boutiques dot Grant Street up the hill. At dusk, try a leisurely stroll through dog-friendly Washington Square Park.

Coffee

- **Bocce Café** • 478 Green St
- **Caffe Puccini** • 411 Columbus Ave
- **Caffe Roma Coffee Roasting** • 526 Columbus Ave
- **Caffe Trieste** • 601 Vallejo St
- **Cavalli Cafe & Imports** • 1441 Stockton St
- **Coffee Roastery** • 950 Battery St
- **Curly's Coffee Shop** • 1624 Powell St
- **Melt** • 700 Columbus Ave
- **San Francisco Coffee Roasting** • Pier 39
- **Starbucks** • 1255 Battery St
- **Tan's Cafe** • 155 Francisco St

Copy Shops

- **Pip Printing** • 2041 Powell St

Gyms

- **24 Hour Fitness** • 350 Bay St ⓦ
- **San Francisco Bay Club** • 150 Greenwich St

Liquor Stores

- **Broadway Cigars & Liquors** • 550 Broadway St
- **Broadway Liquors** • 460 Broadway
- **Dee Vine Wines** • Pier 19

Nightlife

- **15 Romolo** • 15 Romolo Pl
- **Bamboo Hut** • 479 Broadway St
- **Broadway Studios** • 435 Broadway
- **Dragon Bar** • 473 Broadway
- **Fuse** • 493 Broadway
- **Gino and Carlo** • 548 Green St
- **Grant & Green Saloon** • 1371 Grant Ave
- **Hawaii West** • 729 Vallejo St
- **La Trappe** • 800 Greenwich St
- **Northstar Café** • 1560 Powell St
- **O'Reilly's** • 622 Green St
- **Pier 23 Café** • Pier 23
- **The Red Jack Saloon** • 131 Bay St
- **Rogue Ales Public House** • 673 Union St
- **Rosewood** • 732 Broadway
- **The Saloon** • 1232 Grant Ave
- **Savoy Tivoli** • 1434 Grant Ave
- **Sip Bar & Lounge** • 787 Broadway
- **Steps of Rome Caffe** • 348 Columbus Ave
- **Suede** • 383 Bay St
- **Tony Nik's Café** • 1534 Stockton St

Pet Shops

- **Hung Ming Aquarium** • 660 Broadway St
- **North Beach Pet Supply** • 801 Greenwich St

Restaurants

- **Burgermeister** • 759 Columbus Ave
- **Buster's** • 366 Columbus Ave
- **Butterfly** • Pier 33 & Bay St
- **Café Jacqueline** • 1454 Grant Ave
- **The Caffe Sport** • 574 Green St
- **Capp's Corner** • 1600 Powell St
- **Coi** • 373 Broadway
- **Da Flora** • 701 Columbus Ave
- **El Raigon** • 510 Union St
- **Enrico's Sidewalk Café** • 504 Broadway St
- **Fog City Diner** • 1300 Battery St
- **Forbes Island** • H dock, b/w Pier 39 & 41
- **Firenze by Night** • 1429 Stockton St
- **Golden Boy Pizza** • 542 Green St
- **Henry's Hunan** • 924 Sansome St
- **The House** • 1230 Grant Ave
- **Houston's** • 1800 Montgomery St
- **Hunan** • 924 Sansome St
- **Il Fornaio** • 1265 Battery St
- **Il Pollaio** • 555 Columbus Ave
- **Iluna Basque** • 701 Union St
- **Impala** • 501 Broadway
- **International House of Pancakes** • 200 Beach St
- **Joe DiMaggio's** • 601 Union St
- **L'Osteria del Forno** • 519 Columbus Ave
- **La Boulange** • 543 Columbus Ave
- **Mama's on Washington Square** • 1701 Stockton St
- **Mario's Bohemian Cigar Store Café** • 566 Columbus Ave
- **Mo's Grill** • 1322 Grant Ave
- **North Beach Pizza** • 1462 Grant Ave
- **North Beach Pizza** • Pier 39
- **North Beach Restaurant** • 1512 Stockton St
- **Panta Rei** • 431 Columbus Ave
- **Pasta Pomodoro** • 655 Union St
- **Pier 23 Café** • Pier 23
- **Piperade** • 1015 Battery St
- **Ristorante Ideale** • 1315 Grant Ave
- **Rose Pistola** • 532 Columbus Ave
- **Steps of Rome Caffe** • 348 Columbus Ave
- **The Stinking Rose** • 325 Columbus Ave
- **Sushi Hunter** • 1701 Powell St
- **Trattoria Contadina** • 1800 Mason St
- **Victoria Pastry Co** • 1362 Stockton St
- **Washington Square Bar & Grill** • 1707 Powell St

Shopping

- **101 Music** • 1414 Grant Ave
- **AB Fits** • 1519 Grant Ave
- **Alla Prima Lingerie** • 1420 Grant Ave
- **Biordi** • 412 Columbus Ave
- **Eastwind Books & Trading** • 1435 Stockton St
- **Goorin Hats Shop** • 1612 Stockton St
- **Graffeo Coffee Roasting Co** • 735 Columbus Ave
- **Liguria Bakery** • 1700 Stockton St
- **Lola of North Beach** • 1415 Grant Ave
- **Mara's Bakery** • 503 Columbus Ave
- **Mee Mee Bakery** • 1328 Stockton St
- **Ooma** • 1422 Grant Ave
- **Schein & Schein** • 1435 Grant Ave

Video Rental

- **Film Yard Video** • 1610 Stockton St
- **Tak Tat (Chinese)** • 1341 Stockton St

The Presidio
PAGE 190
Lyon Street Stairs
Mrs. Doubtfire house
Alta Plaza Park
PACIFIC HEIGHTS
KPOO Mural
Hamilton Rec Ctr
The Fillmore
Kimball Playground
St John Coltrane African Orthodox Church
WESTERN ADDITION
The Painted Ladies
Alamo Square
HAIGHT ASHBURY
Geary Blvd
Fillmore St
Divisadero St
California St
Bush St
Sutter St
Turk St
Golden Gate Ave
Fulton St
Masonic Ave
1/4 mile
.25 km

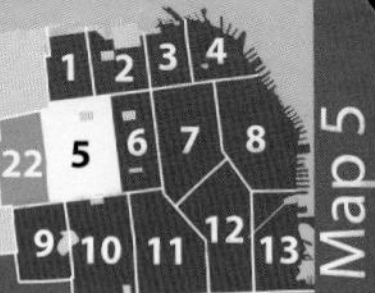

Aside from boasting the city's most manicured mansions, Pac Heights is also home to one of the steepest hills (Fillmore between Green and Broadway), scenic vistas at Alta Plaza Park, and the Lyon Street Stairs. Down in the Western Addition, ornate Victorian triplexes mingle with low-income housing.

Banks

- **Bank of America** • 2310 Fillmore St
- **Bank of America (ATM)** • 1700 Fillmore St
- **Chase** • 1720 Fulton St
- **Citibank** • 3296 Sacramento St
- **US (ATM)** • Walgreens • 1363 Divisadero St
- **Wells Fargo** • 1750 Divisadero St
- **Wells Fargo** • 2100 Fillmore St
- **Wells Fargo (ATM)** • 1750 Fulton St
- **Wells Fargo (ATM)** • 3150 California St

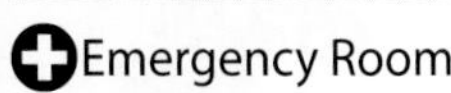

Emergency Rooms

- **Kaiser Permanente Medical Center** • 2425 Geary Blvd

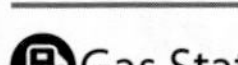

Gas Stations

- **76** • 1301 Divisadero St
- **Chevron** • 2500 California St
- **Shell** • 2501 California St

Landmarks

- **Alamo Square** • Fulton St & Scott St
- **Alta Plaza Park** • Clay St & Steiner St
- **The Fillmore** • 1805 Geary Blvd
- **KPOO Mural** • Post St & Steiner St
- **Lyon Street Stairs** • Lyon St & Broadway St
- **Mrs. Doubtfire house** • 2640 Steiner St
- **The Painted Ladies** • 720 Steiner St
- **St John Coltrane African Orthodox Church** • 1286 Fillmore St

Libraries

- **Presidio Branch Library** • 3150 Sacramento St
- **Western Addition Library** • 1550 Scott St

Parking

Pharmacies

- **B & B Pharmacy** • 1727 Filmore St
- **Charlie's Pharmacy** • 1101 Fillmore St
- **Kaiser Permanente Medical Center—Pediatric Pharmacy** • 2200 O'Farrell St
- **Kaiser Permanente Medical Center Pharmacy** • 2238 Geary Blvd
- **Post & Divisadero Pharmacy** • 2299 Post St
- **Sav-On Drugs** • Albertsons • 1750 Fulton St
- **Sutter Professional Pharmacy** • 2300 Sutter St
- **Walgreens** • 1363 Divisadero St
- **Walgreens** • 1899 Fillmore St

Police

- **Northern Police Station** • 1125 Fillmore St

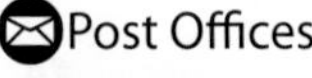

Post Offices

- **Steiner Street Station** • 1849 Geary Blvd

Schools

- **Convent of the Sacred Heart High** • 2222 Broadway St
- **Drew College Preparatory** • 2901 California St
- **Gateway Charter** • 1430 Scott St
- **Golden Gate Elementary** • 1601 Turk St
- **Hearing and Speech Center of Northern California** • 1234 Divisadero St
- **Hillwood Academic Day** • 2521 Scott St
- **Jewish Community High School of the Bay** • 1835 Ellis St
- **Kipp San Francisco Bay Academy** • 1430 Scott St
- **Raoul Wallenberg Alternative High** • 40 Vega St
- **San Francisco University High** • 3065 Jackson St
- **San Francisco Waldorf** • 2938 Washington St
- **St Dominic's Elementary** • 2445 Pine St
- **Sterne** • 2690 Jackson St
- **Town School for Boys** • 2750 Jackson St
- **William L Cobb Elementary** • 2725 California St

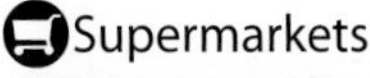

Supermarkets

- **Mollie Stone's** • 2435 California St

Map 5 • Pacific Heights / Western Addition

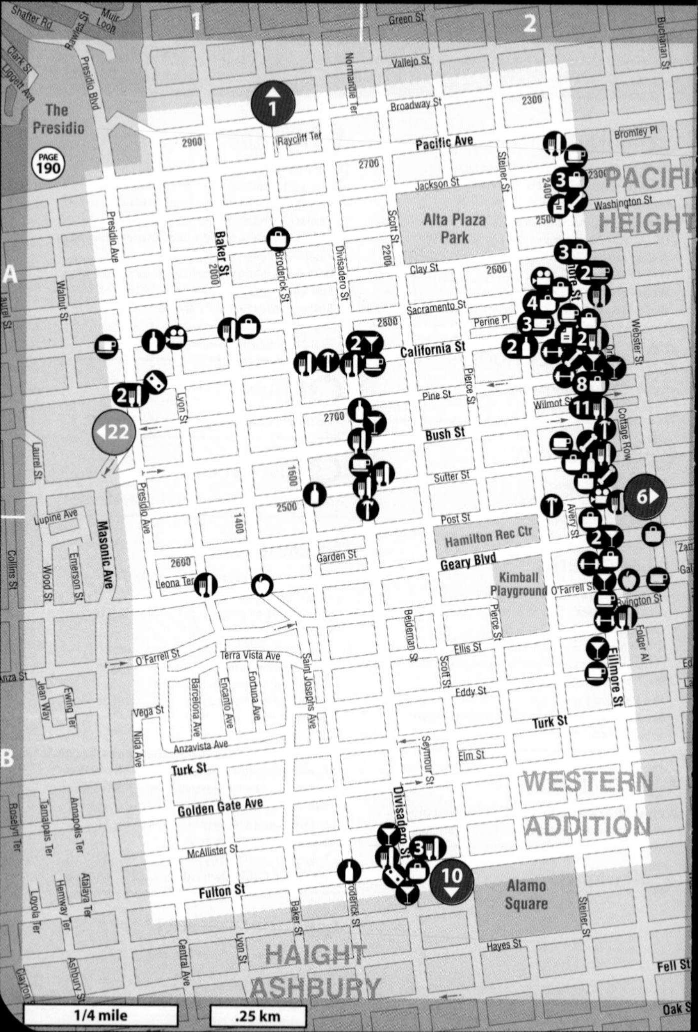

Shafter Rd
Rawles St
Muir Loop
Clark St
Liggett Ave
Presidio Blvd
The Presidio
PAGE 190
Green St
Vallejo St
Normandie Ter
Broadway St
2300
Buchanan St
Bromley Pl
2900
Raycliff Ter
Pacific Ave
2700
Steiner St
Jackson St
2400
PACIFIC HEIGHTS
Washington St
2500
Alta Plaza Park
Presidio Ave
Baker St
2000
Broderick St
Divisadero St
Scott St
2200
Clay St
2600
Walnut St
Laurel St
Sacramento St
2800
Perine Pl
Webster St
California St
Pierce St
Pine St
Wilmot St
Lyon St
2700
Cottage Row
Bush St
Laurel St
1600
Sutter St
Presidio Ave
2500
Avery St
1400
Post St
Hamilton Rec Ctr
Lupine Ave
Masonic Ave
Garden St
Geary Blvd
Collins St
Wood St
Emerson St
2600
Leona Ter
Kimball Playground
O'Farrell St
Byington St
Beideman St
Pierce St
Folger Al
Ellis St
O'Farrell St
Terra Vista Ave
Saint Josephs Ave
Scott St
Fillmore St
Jean Way
Ewing Ter
Barcelona Ave
Encanto Ave
Fortuna Ave
Eddy St
Vega St
Turk St
Nida Ave
Anzavista Ave
Seymour St
Elm St
Turk St
WESTERN ADDITION
Roselyn Ter
Tamalpais Ter
Annapolis Ter
Golden Gate Ave
Divisadero St
McAllister St
Loyola Ter
Hemway Ter
Atalaya Ter
Fulton St
Baker St
Broderick St
Alamo Square
Steiner St
Central Ave
Lyon St
HAIGHT ASHBURY
Hayes St
Clayton St
Ashbury St
Fell St
Oak St
1/4 mile
.25 km

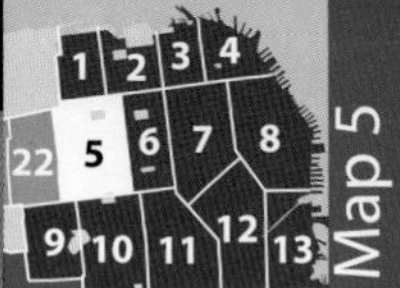

Fillmore Street flows from a trendy boutique and restaurant belt in the north to don't-leave-anything-in-the-car around Geary Boulevard. In exchange for living dangerously, that area is top notch in musical choices with the classic Fillmore Auditorium and blues venue Boom Boom Room. The single screen Clay Theatre shows great independent films.

Coffee

- **Café Luna** • 3313 Sacramento St
- **Coffee Bean & Tea Leaf** • 2201 Fillmore St
- **Fillmore Street Café** • 1301 Fillmore St
- **Martha & Bros** • 2800 California St
- **Peet's** • 2197 Filmore St
- **Royal Ground Coffee** • 2060 Fillmore St
- **Starbucks** • 1335 Webster St
- **Starbucks** • 1501 Fillmore St
- **Starbucks** • 1750 Divisadero St
- **Starbucks** • 2222 Fillmore St
- **Starbucks** • 2435 California St
- **Tully's Coffee** • 2455 Fillmore St

Copy Shops

- **Copy Net** • 2404 California St
- **The UPS Store** • 2443 Fillmore St

Farmers Markets

- **Fillmore San Francisco (May—Nov; Sat, 9 am—1 pm)** • Fillmore St & O'Farrell St
- **Kaiser Hospital-San Francisco (Wed, 10 am—2 pm)** • 2425 Geary Blvd

Gyms

- **24 Hour Fitness** • 2434 California St ㉔
- **Club One** • 1455 Fillmore St
- **Pacific Heights Health Club** • 2356 Pine St

Hardware Stores

- **Central Ace Hardware** • 1949 Post St
- **Divisadero Lock & Hardware** • 1649 Divisadero St
- **Fillmore Hardware** • 1930 Fillmore St
- **Pacific Heights True Value Hardware** • 2828 California St

Liquor Stores

- **A A Market** • 667 Broderick St
- **D&M Wine & Liquor** • 2200 Fillmore St
- **Friends Liquor** • 1758 Fillmore St
- **Stewart's Grocery** • 2498 Sutter St
- **VINO Inc** • 2425 California St
- **WC Liquor** • 1836 Divisadero St
- **Wilking Wine & Liquor** • 3273 Sacramento St

Movie Theaters

- **Clay Theatre** • 2261 Filmore St
- **Kabuki Cinema** • 1881 Post St
- **Vogue Theatre**• 3290 Sacramento St

Nightlife

- **Bar 821** • 821 Divisadero St
- **Boom Boom Room** • 1601 Fillmore St
- **The Fillmore** • 1805 Geary Blvd
- **Fly Bar** • 762 Divisadero St
- **Frankie's Bohemian Café** • 1862 Divisadero St
- **Harry's Bar** • 2020 Fillmore St
- **Lion Pub** • 2062 Divisadero St
- **Rasselas Jazz Club** • 1534 Fillmore St
- **Solstice** • 2801 California St
- **Yoshi's Jazz Club & Japanese Restaurant** • 1330 Fillmore St

Pet Shops

- **Aqua Forest Aquarium** • 1718 Fillmore St
- **Barry for Pets** • 1840 Fillmore St
- **George** • 2411 California St
- **Pets Unlimited** • 2343 Fillmore St

Restaurants

- **Café Abir** • 1300 Fulton St
- **Candybar** • 1335 Fulton St
- **The Cheese Steak Shop** • 1716 Divisadero St
- **Dino's Pizzeria** • 2101 Fillmore St
- **Dosa** • 1700 FIllmore St
- **Elite Café** • 2049 Fillmore St
- **Eliza's** • 2877 California St
- **Ella's** • 500 Presidio Ave
- **Florio** • 1915 Fillmore St
- **Fresca** • 2114 Fillmore St
- **Garibaldi's on Presidio** • 347 Presidio Ave
- **The Grove** • 2016 Fillmore St
- **Jackson Fillmore** • 2506 Fillmore St
- **King Lee's Chinese** • 1426 Fillmore St
- **La Mediterranee** • 2210 Fillmore St
- **Little Star Pizza** • 846 Divisadero St
- **Noah's Bagels** • 2213 Fillmore St
- **Osaka** • 1923 Fillmore St
- **SPQR** • 1911 Fillmore St
- **Stelladoro Pizza** • 808 Divisadero St
- **Takara** • 22 Peace Plz
- **Ten-Ichi** • 2235 Fillmore St
- **Tony's Cable Car Restaurant** • 2500 Geary Blvd
- **Tortilla Heights** • 1750 Divisadero St
- **Woodhouse Fish Company** • 1914 Fillmore St

Shopping

- **Benefit** • 2117 Fillmore St
- **Betsey Johnson** • 2031 Fillmore St
- **Crossroads Trading Company** • 1901 Fillmore St
- **The Firm** • 2999 Washington St
- **George** • 2411 California St
- **Gimme Shoes** • 2358 Fillmore St
- **Goodwill Boutique** • 1669 Fillmore St
- **HeidiSays Collections** • 2426 Fillmore St
- **In Water Flowers** • 2132 Fillmore St
- **Juicy News** • 2453 Fillmore St
- **Jurlique** • 2136 Fillmore St
- **Katsura Garden** • 1825 Post St
- **Kiehl's** • 2360 Fillmore St
- **La Boulange** • 2325 Pine St
- **L'Occitane** • 2207 Fillmore St
- **Marcus Books** • 1712 Fillmore St
- **Margaret O'Leary** • 2400 Fillmore St
- **Mrs Dewson's Hats** • 2050 Fillmore St
- **Narumi** • 1902 Fillmore St
- **Nest** • 2300 Fillmore St
- **Paper Source** • 1925 Fillmore St
- **Shu Uemura** • 1971 Fillmore St
- **Sue Fisher King** • 3067 Sacramento St
- **Sunhee Moon** • 1833 Fillmore St
- **Toujours** • 2484 Sacramento St
- **Winterbranch Gallery** • 2119 Fillmore St
- **Zinc Details** • 1905 Fillmore St

Video Rental

- **Film Yard Video** • 803 Divisadero St
- **Hollywood Video** • 3150 California St

Map 6 • Pacific Heights / Japantown

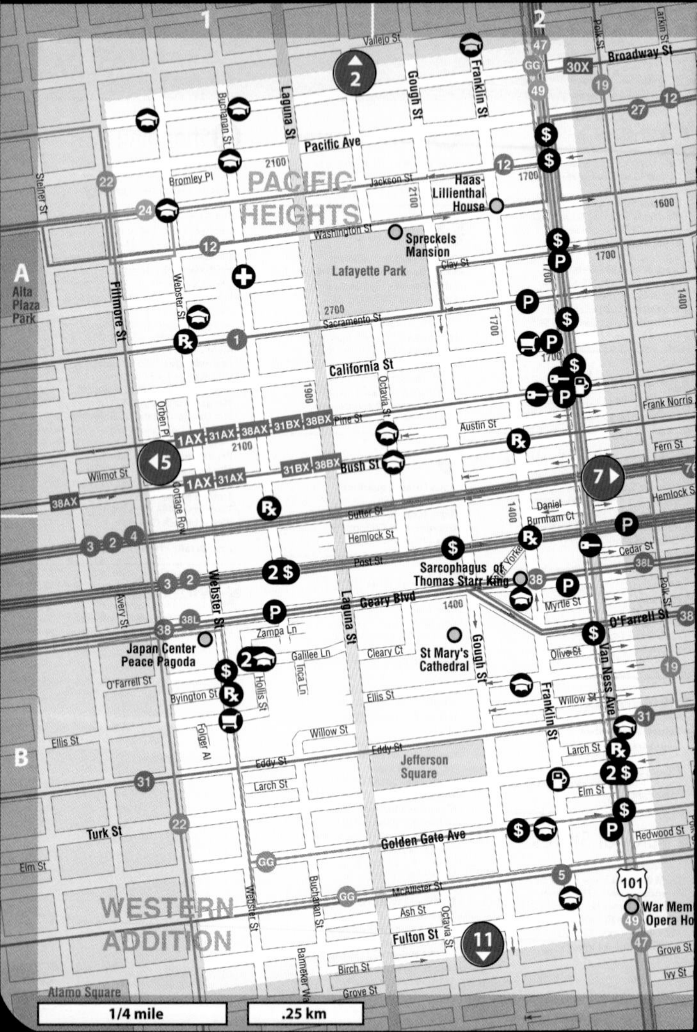

Dogs, children, and sunbathers love Lafayette Park, the crown of this part of Pacific Heights. The Japan Center Peace Pagoda anchors the few blocks that make up Japantown. Sluggish Van Ness Avenue marks the eastern border of the neighborhood. The modern interior of St. Mary's Cathedral makes for a study of light's visible spectrum.

Banks

- **Bank of America** • 1640 Van Ness Ave
- **Bank of America (ATM)** • 1000 Van Ness Ave
- **Bank of America (ATM)** • 601 Van Ness Ave
- **California** • 1696 Post St
- **Citibank** • 1399 Post St
- **Citibank** • 1801 Van Ness Ave
- **First Republic** • 2001 Van Ness Ave
- **San Francisco Federal CU** • 770 Golden Gate Ave
- **Sterling** • 2045 Van Ness Ave
- **Union** • 1675 Post St
- **United Commercial** • 711 Van Ness Ave
- **US** • 540 Van Ness Ave
- **Wells Fargo** • 1335 Webster St
- **Wells Fargo** • 1560 Van Ness Ave

Car Rental

- **City Rent A Car** • 1500 Van Ness Ave
- **Enterprise** • 1133 Van Ness Ave
- **Hertz** • 1644 Pine St

Emergency Rooms

- **California Pacific Medical Center Pacific Campus** • 2333 Buchanan St

Gas Stations

- **Chevron** • 1501 Van Ness Ave
- **Shell** • 800 Turk St

Landmarks

- **Haas-Lillienthal House** • 2007 Franklin St
- **Japan Center Peace Pagoda** • Geary Blvd & Webster St
- **Sarcophagus of Thomas Starr King** • Geary Blvd & Franklin St
- **Spreckels Mansion** • 2080 Washington St
- **St Mary's Cathedral** • 1111 Gough St
- **War Memorial Opera House** • 301 Van Ness Ave

Parking

Pharmacies

- **1000 Cranes Pharmacy** • 1832 Buchanan St
- **Franklin Pharmacy** • 1508 Franklin St
- **Safeway** • 1335 Webster St
- **Walgreens** • 1301 Franklin St
- **Walgreens** • 2100 Webster St
- **Walgreens** • 790 Van Ness Ave

Schools

- **Alternative/Opportunity** • 555 Franklin St
- **CCSF (Alemany Campus)** • 750 Eddy St
- **Hamlin** • 2120 Broadway St
- **John Swett Alternative Elem** • 727 Golden Gate Ave
- **La Mel** • 1801 Bush St
- **Montessori House of Children** • 1187 Franklin St
- **Newcomer High** • 2340 Jackson St
- **Pacific School of Dentistry** • 2155 Webster St
- **Raphael Weill Childrens Center** • 1501 O'Farrell St
- **Rosa Parks Elementary** • 1501 O'Farrell St
- **Sacred Heart Cathedral Preparatory** • 1055 Ellis St
- **St Brigid** • 2250 Franklin St
- **Stuart Hall for Boys** • 2252 Broadway St
- **Stuart Hall High** • 1715 Octavia St

Supermarkets

- **Safeway** • 1335 Webster St
- **Whole Foods Market** • 1765 California St

N
1
2
A
B
Vallejo St
Broadway St
Polk St
Larkin St
Buchanan St
Laguna St
Gough St
Franklin St
Pacific Ave
2100
Bromley Pl
PACIFIC
HEIGHTS
Jackson St
1700
1600
Steiner St
Washington St
Lafayette Park
Clay St
Alta
Plaza
Park
Fillmore St
Webster St
2700
Sacramento St
1400
California St
1900
Octavia St
Frank Norris
Orben Pl
Pine St
Austin St
Fern St
2100
Bush St
Wilmot St
Cottage Row
Hemlock
Sutter St
Daniel
Burnham Ct
Hemlock St
Peter Yorke Way
Cedar St
Post St
Geary Blvd
Myrtle St
O'Farrell St
Avery St
Zampa Ln
Galilee Ln
Cleary Ct
Olive St
Van Ness Ave
Inca Ln
Hollis St
O'Farrell St
Byington St
Ellis St
Willow St
Folger Al
Willow St
Larch St
Ellis St
Eddy St
Jefferson
Square
Eddy St
Larch St
Elm St
Turk St
Golden Gate Ave
Redwood St
Elm St
101
McAllister St
Ash St
WESTERN
ADDITION
Fulton St
Grove St
Ivy St
Birch St
Bammeker Way
Grove St
Alamo Square
1/4 mile
.25 km

Van Ness Avenue is a giant, traffic-packed big box strip. Alternatively, head to Post Street in Japantown, where seemingly nondescript buildings hold an interior treasure of Japanese grocery stores, noodle shops, sushi, imported furniture, and the largest Japanese language bookstore in the US (Kinokuniya Bookshop).

Coffee

- **Café Lavender** • 1610 Post St
- **Macha Café** • 1355 Sutter St
- **Murata's Cafe Hana** • 1737 Post St
- **Peet's** • 601 Van Ness Ave
- **Philz Coffee** • 748 Van Ness Ave
- **Starbucks** • 1401 Van Ness Ave
- **Starbucks** • 1560 Van Ness Ave
- **Tully's Coffee** • 1661 Pine St
- **Van Ness Bakery & Café** • 1122 Van Ness Ave

Copy Shops

- **Colour Drop** • 727 Van Ness Ave
- **Copy Mill** • 780 Van Ness Ave
- **FedEx Office** • 1 Daniel Burnham Ct
- **FedEx Office** • 1800 Van Ness Ave
- **Magnacopia Printing Center** • 1111 Geary Blvd
- **Staples** • 1700 Van Ness Ave
- **The UPS Store** • 1770 Post St
- **The UPS Store** • 601 Van Ness Ave

Gyms

- **24 Hour Fitness** • 1200 Van Ness Ave
- **Cathedral Hill Plaza Athletic Club** • 1333 Gough St
- **Crunch** • 1000 Van Ness Ave
- **YMCA** • 1530 Buchanan St

Hardware Stores

- **Soko Hardware** • 1698 Post St

Liquor Stores

- **A&M Liquor** • 1600 Sutter St
- **Beverages & More** • 1301 Van Ness Av
- **Sutter-Franklin Liquors** • 1400 Sutter St
- **Van Ness Liquors** • 1846 Van Ness Ave

Movie Theaters

- **AMC Van Ness 14** • 1000 Van Ness Ave
- **Opera Plaza Cinema** • 601 Van Ness Ave
- **Viz** • 1746 Post St @ New People

Nightlife

- **Crimson Lounge** • 687 McAllister St
- **Koko Cocktails** • 1060 Geary St
- **Route 101** • 1332 Van Ness Ave

Restaurants

- **Harris'** • 2100 Van Ness Ave
- **House of Prime Rib** • 1906 Van Ness Ave
- **Iroha** • 1728 Buchanan St
- **Juban** • 1581 Webster St
- **Korea House** • 1640 Post St
- **May's Coffee Shop** • 1737 Post St
- **Mel's Drive-In** • 1050 Van Ness Ave
- **Mifune** • 1737 Post St
- **Sapporo-ya** • 1581 Webster St
- **Tommy's Joynt** • 1101 Geary Blvd

Shopping

- **Books Inc** • 601 Van Ness Ave
- **Kinokuniya Bookshop** • 1581 Webster St
- **Rosebowl Florist & Wine Shop** • 601 Van Ness Ave
- **Whole Foods Market** • 1765 California St

Video Rental

- **Blockbuster** • 1493 Webster St
- **Hollywood Video** • 2025 Van Ness Ave
- **Japan Video & Media** • 1737 Post St
- **JBC Rental Video (Japanese)** • 1748 Buchanan St
- **Nihonmachi Video Rental (Japanese)** • 1832 Buchanan St
- **People Video Rental (Japanese)** • 1740 Buchanan St

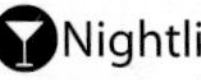

Chinatown
Nob Hill
Tenderloin
South of Market
Union Square
Golden Gate Fortune Cookie
Chambord Apartments
Pacific Union Club
Grace Cathedral
Melvin M Swig Interfaith Memorial
Masonic Auditorium
Huntington Hotel
450 Sutter Medical Bldg
Fleur de Lys
Bohemian Club
Heart Sculpture
Ocean Aquarium
Great American Music Hall
Glide Memorial United Methodist Church
Powell St Cable Car Turn Around
Asian Art Museum
SF Main Library
Civic Center Farmers Market
City Hall
Civic Center
Van Ness Ave
Polk St
Larkin St
Hyde St
Leavenworth St
Jones St
Taylor St
Mason St
Powell St
Stockton St
Grant Ave
Broadway St
Pacific Ave
Jackson St
Washington St
Clay St
Sacramento St
California St
Pine St
Bush St
Sutter St
Post St
Geary St
O'Farrell St
Ellis St
Eddy St
Turk St
Golden Gate Ave
McAllister St
Grove St
Hayes St
Market St
Mission St
Howard St
Columbus Ave
1/4 mile
.25 km

Elegant hotels with commanding views, old money old-timers, and prominent landmarks define Nob Hill. Nearby, Chinatown beckons with pulsating streets, the aroma of Chinese herbs, and an abundance of food spots and gift shops. Union Square is bordered by bustling department stores as well as the watch-your-back Tenderloin.

Banks

- **Bank of America** • 1 Powell St
- **Bank of America** • 445 Powell St
- **Bank of America** • 865 Market St
- **Bank of America** • 944 Stockton St
- **Bank of America (ATM)** • 335 Powell St
- **Bank of the Orient** • 1023 Stockton St
- **Chase** • 1201 Market St
- **Chase** • 1500 Polk St
- **Citibank (ATM)** • 945 Market St
- **East West** • 1241 Stockton St
- **First Republic** • 1088 Stockton St
- **GBC International Bank** • 1226 Stockton St
- **Oceanic** • 447 Sutter St
- **San Francisco Federal CU (ATM)** • 1 Dr Carlton B Goodlett Pl
- **United Commercial** • 1301 Stockton St
- **US (ATM)** • Walgreens • 135 Powell St
- **US (ATM)** • Walgreens • 2120 Polk St
- **US (ATM)** • Walgreens • 459 Powell St
- **Wells Fargo** • 1015 Stockton St
- **Wells Fargo** • 1266 Market St
- **Wells Fargo** • 460 Sutter St
- **Wells Fargo (ATM)** • 374 Golden Gate Ave
- **Wells Fargo (ATM)** • 84 Ellis St

Car Rental

- **A-One Rent-A-Car** • 434 O'Farrell St
- **Alamo** • 320 O'Farrell St
- **Alamo** • 750 Bush St
- **Avis** • 675 Post St
- **Budget** • 321 Mason St
- **Convertibles-City Rent-A-Car** • 1433 Bush Street
- **Discount Rentals** • 349 Mason St
- **Dollar** • 364 O'Farrell St
- **Enterprise** • 222 Mason St
- **Enterprise** • 819 Ellis St
- **Hertz** • 335 Powell St
- **Hertz** • 433 Mason St
- **Hertz** • 500 Post St
- **Hertz** • 55 4th St
- **Hertz** • 55 Cyril Magnin St
- **Hertz** • 950 Mason St
- **National** • 320 O'Farrell St
- **National** • 750 Bush St
- **Reliable Rent-A-Car** • 349 Mason St
- **Thrifty** • 350 O'Farrell St

Car Washes

- **Woody and Sons' Auto Detailing** • 843 Polk St

Community Gardens

Emergency Rooms

- **Chinese Hospital** • 845 Jackson St
- **Saint Francis Memorial** • 900 Hyde St

Landmarks

- **450 Sutter Medical Building** • 450 Sutter St
- **Asian Art Museum** • 200 Larkin St
- **Bohemian Club** • 624 Taylor St
- **Chambord Apartments** • 1298 Sacramento St
- **City Hall** • 1 Dr Carlton Goodlett Pl
- **Civic Center** • Grove St b/w Franklin St & Leavenworth St
- **Civic Center Farmers Market (Wed & Sun, 7am–5:30pm)** • Market St b/w 7th St & 8th St
- **Fleur De Lys** • 777 Sutter St
- **Glide Memorial United Methodist Church** • 330 Ellis St
- **Golden Gate Fortune Cookie Company** • 56 Ross Aly
- **Grace Cathedral** • 1100 California St
- **Great American Music Hall** • 859 O'Farrell St
- **Heart Sculpture** • Post & Powell St
- **The Huntington Hotel** • 1075 California St
- **Masonic Auditorium** • 1111 California St
- **Melvin M Swig Interfaith Memorial Labyrinth** • Taylor St & California St
- **Ocean Aquarium** • 120 Cedar St
- **Pacific Union Club** • 1000 California St
- **Powell St Cable Car Turn Around** • Powell St & Market St
- **San Francisco Main Library** • 100 Larkin St
- **Union Square** • Geary St & Powell St

Libraries

- **Chinatown Branch Library** • 1135 Powell St
- **San Francisco Law Library** • 401 Van Ness Ave
- **San Francisco Main Library** • 100 Larkin St

Parking

Pharmacies

- **450 Sutter Pharmacy** • 450 Sutter St
- **Chinatown Medical Pharmacy** • 823 Jackson St
- **Chinese Hospital Pharmacy** • 845 Jackson St
- **Clay Medical Pharmacy** • 929 Clay St
- **Ellis Pharmacy** • 468 Ellis St
- **Rite Aid** • 1300 Bush St
- **St Francis Pharmacy** • 901 Hyde St
- **Walgreens** • 1301 Market St
- **Walgreens** • 135 Powell St
- **Walgreens** • 1524 Polk St
- **Walgreens** • 2120 Polk St
- **Walgreens** • 459 Powell St
- **Walgreens** • 500 Geary St
- **Walgreens** • 825 Market St
- **Wellman's Pharmacy** • 1053 Stockton St

Police

- **Tenderloin Police Station** • 301 Eddy St

Post Offices

- **Chinatown Station** • 867 Stockton St
- **Civic Center Box Unit / Pacific Center** • 101 Hyde St
- **Federal Building** • 450 Golden Gate Ave
- **Macy's Union Square Station** • 170 O'Farrell St
- **Pine Street Station** • 1400 Pine St

Schools

- **California Art Institute** • 1170 Market St
- **Cathedral School for Boys** • 1275 Sacramento St
- **De Marillac Middle** • 175 Golden Gate Ave
- **Fashion Institute of Design and Merchandising** • 55 Stockton St
- **Gordon J Lau Elementary** • 950 Clay St
- **Hastings College of the Law** • 200 McAllister St
- **Redding Elementary** • 1421 Pine St
- **San Francisco Christian Academy** • 230 Jones St
- **Spring Valley Elementary** • 1451 Jackson St
- **Tenderloin Community** • 627 Turk St

Supermarkets

- **Cala Foods** • 1095 Hyde St
- **Real Food Company** • 2140 Polk St

Map 7 • Nob Hill /
loin
N
1
2
3
6
8
12
A
B
Union St
Green St
Bonita St
Vallejo St
Glover St
Broadway St
Bernard St
Lynch St
Morrell St
Taylor St
Salmon St
Wayne Pl
Churchill St
Columbus Ave
CHINATO
Trenton St
John St
Jackson St
Stone St
1500
Pacific Ave
Polk St
Southard Pl
1400
Leavenworth St
Jones St
Van Ness Ave
Jackson St
Wetmore St
Spofford St
Grant Ave
1700
Washington St
Hyde St
Priest St
Clay St
Sproule Ln
Collier St
Pl
Pagoda
Stockton St
Pleasant St
Clay St
NOB HILL
1700
Sacramento St
1600
Joice St
1700
1400
California St
1000
Powell St
Dashiell Hammett
Pine St
Jones St
900
Frank Norris St
Bush St
Campton Pl
Larkin St
Hyde St
800
Fern St
700
Cosmo Pl
Union Square
Stockton St
Maide
Sutter St
Daniel Burnham Ct
Hemlock St
800
Shannon St
Post St
Cedar St
101
Geary St
O'Farrell St
Taylor St
Cyril Magnin
St
Olive St
Ellis St
Cohen Pl
TENDERLOIN
Mason St
Franklin St
Willow St
Powell St
Eddy St
Wagner Al
Turk St
Polk St
Larch St
Larkin St
Mint St
SOUTH
Turk St
Elm St
Dale Pl
5th St
MARKE
Golden Gate Ave
Breen Pl
6th St
Redwood St
Stevenson St
Jessie St
McAllister St
Van Ness Ave
Tehama St
Clementina St
Jevyssie St
Mission St
Grove St
Civic Center
Ivy St
Julia St
7th St
Russ St
Moss St
Hayes St
Natoma St
Howard St
8th St
1/4 mile
.25 km

n general, the closer you are to the top of Nob Hill or Union Square, the itzier the shops and services. The theater district and Tenderloin to the vest is a sometimes seedy grab-bag of bare-bones food spots, nightclubs, esidential hotels, rare booksellers, drug deals, and liquor stores.

Coffee

- **All Day Café** • 1105 Market St
- **Bob's Donut & Pastry Shop** • 1621 Polk St
- **Borders** • 400 Post St
- **Borders** • 845 Market St
- **Cable Car Coffee** • 900 Market St
- **Café Bean** • 800 Sutter St
- **Café Encore** • 488 Post St
- **Café La Taza** • 470 Post St
- **Café Madeleine** • 43 O'Farrell St
- **Café Prima Fila** • 891 Bush St
- **Café Royale** • 800 Post St
- **Caffe Espresso** • 462 Powell St
- **Coffee Bean & Tea Leaf** • 773 Market St
- **Coffee Cabin** • 899 Hyde St
- **Cup a Joe Coffee House** • 608 Geary St
- **Cup a Joe Coffee House** • 896 Sutter St
- **Double Team Coffee** • 882 Bush St
- **Emile's Coffee & Tea** • 614 Polk St
- **Farm:table** • 754 Post St
- **Gallery Café** • 1200 Mason St
- **Gateway Croissant** • 390 Golden Gate Ave
- **Golden Coffee House** • 901 Sutter St
- **H2O Café** • 1330 Polk St
- **It's A Grind** • 1800 Polk St
- **Java Xpress** • 1095 Market St
- **Little Paris Coffee Shop** • 939 Stockton St
- **Picnic** • 1808 Polk St
- **Quetzal** • 1234 Polk St
- **Quickly** • 709 Larkin St
- **Quickly** • 1170 Powell St
- **Quickly** • 1733 Polk St
- **Royal Ground Coffee** • 1605 Polk St
- **Cafe Bellini** • 865 Market St
- **Starbucks** • 201 Powell St
- **Starbucks** • 222 Mason St
- **Starbucks** • 390 Stockton St
- **Starbucks** • 442 Geary St
- **Starbucks** • 1231 Market St
- **Taylor Street Coffee Shop** • 375 Taylor St
- **What A Grind** • 881 Post St

Copy Shops

- **Copy Action** • 29 Grove St
- **Copy Circle** • 1701 Polk St
- **Faithful Fools Copying** • 230 Hyde St
- **FedEx Office** • 333 O'Farrell St
- **K K Copying & Printing** • 500 Larkin St
- **The UPS Store** • 1819 Polk St
- **The UPS Store** • 588 Sutter St

Farmers Markets

- **Civic Center Farmers Market (Wed & Sun, 7am–5:30pm)** • Market St b/w 7th St & 8th St

Gyms

- **Club One** • 450 Golden Gate Ave
- **Club One** • 535 Mason St
- **Club One** • 950 California St

Hardware Stores

- **Brownie's Ace Hardware** • 1563 Polk St
- **Cole Hardware** • 70 4th St
- **Haji's Hardware** • 1170 Sutter St
- **Peerless General Supply** • 156 Leavenworth St
- **Polk Home Hardware** • 1630 Polk St

Liquor Stores

- **Civic Center Market** • 1292 Market St
- **Empire Liquors** • 399 Eddy St
- **Fox Liquor & Delicatessen** • 570 Larkin St
- **Fred's Liquor Store** • 300 Mason St
- **G&H Liquors** • 201 Jones St
- **Gng Liquors** • 40 5th St
- **Grand Liquor Market** • 67 Taylor St
- **Haz Liquors** • 1401 Polk St
- **Imperial Square Liquors** • 251 Ellis St
- **International House** • 395 Geary St
- **J&D Liquor** • 1042 Polk St
- **Jug Shop** • 1590 Pacific Ave
- **King Liquor and Deli** • 693 Post St
- **Le Beau Nob Hill Market** • 1263 Leavenworth St
- **Liquor & Deli On Union Square** • 423 Stockton St
- **Marine Club Liquor & Deli** • 615 Sutter St
- **Marty's Liquor & Gourmet** • 657 Sutter St
- **Mason Liquor & Deli** • 530 Mason St
- **Napa Valley Winery Exchange** • 415 Taylor St
- **Nob Hill Liquors** • 1000 Hyde St
- **O'Farrell Liquors** • 405 O'Farrell St
- **Polk Clay Liquor** • 1700 Polk St
- **Royal Liquors** • 1400 Polk St
- **San Francisco Deli & Liquor** • 810 Mission St
- **Sonoma Liquor** • 65 6th St
- **Spencer & Daniel's Wine Outlet** • 1541 Polk St
- **Tenderloin Liquors** • 62 Turk St
- **Traveler's Liquors** • 22 7th St
- **Woerner's Liquors** • 901 Geary St

Nob Hill / Tenderloin
CHINATOWN
NOB HILL
TENDERLOIN
SOUTH OF MARKET
Union Square
Civic Center
Powell St
Green St
Bonita St
Vallejo St
Glover St
Broadway St
Bernard St
Lynch St
Pacific Ave
Jackson St
Washington St
Clay St
Pleasant St
Sacramento St
California St
Pine St
Frank Norris St
Bush St
Fern St
Sutter St
Hemlock St
Post St
Cedar St
Geary St
Myrtle St
O'Farrell St
Olive St
Ellis St
Willow St
Eddy St
Turk St
Larch St
Elm St
Golden Gate Ave
Redwood St
McAllister St
Grove St
Ivy St
Hayes St
Van Ness Ave
Franklin St
Polk St
Larkin St
Hyde St
Leavenworth St
Jones St
Taylor St
Mason St
Powell St
Stockton St
Grant Ave
Columbus Ave
Mission St
Howard St
Market St
Daniel Burnham Ct
Campton Pl
Cosmo Pl
Cyril Magnin St
Mint St
Stevenson St
Jessie St
5th St
6th St
7th St
8th St
Natoma St
Tehama St
Clementina St
Russ St
Moss St
1/4 mile
.25 km

The choices for entertainment in this neighborhood offer something for every taste and budget. Sip amazing cocktails at Bourbon & Branch followed by exemplary French cuisine at Fleur De Lys. Or go low-brow with a whisky at Edinburgh Castle, oysters at Swan Depot, then a cold beer in the back room at the Hemlock where you can see an excellent live show.

Movie Theaters

- **Lumiere Theater** • 1572 California St

Nightlife

- **222 Hyde** • 222 Hyde St
- **Aunt Charlie's Lounge** • 133 Turk St
- **The Big Four** • Huntington Hotel • 1075 California St
- **Bigfoot Lodge** • 1750 Polk St
- **Blur** • 1121 Polk St
- **Bourbon & Branch** • 501 Jones St
- **The Brown Jug Saloon** • 496 Eddy St
- **Chelsea Place** • 641 Bush St
- **The Cinch** • 1723 Polk St
- **Club Six** • 60 6th St
- **Edinburgh Castle** • 950 Geary St
- **Etiquette Lounge** • 1108 Market St
- **Great American Music Hall** • 859 O'Farrell St
- **Ha-Ra Club** • 875 Geary St
- **Harry Denton's Starlight Room** • Sir Francis Drake Hotel • 450 Powell St
- **Hemlock Tavern** • 1131 Polk St
- **The Hidden Vine** • 620 Post St
- **High Tide** • 600 Geary St
- **The Hyde Out** • 1068 Hyde St
- **Kimo's** • 1351 Polk St
- **Le Colonial** • 20 Cosmo Pl
- **Lefty O'Doul's** • 333 Geary St
- **Lush Lounge** • 1221 Polk St t
- **Mezzanine** • 444 Jessie St
- **Mr Smith's** • 34 7th St
- **Owl Tree** • 601 Post St
- **R Bar** • 1176 Sutter St
- **Red Devil Lounge** • 1695 Polk St
- **Redwood Room** • Clift Hotel • 495 Geary St
- **Rrazz Room** • Hotel Nikko • 222 Mason St
- **Ruby Skye** • 420 Mason St
- **Shanghai Kelly's** • 2064 Polk St
- **Slide** • 430 Mason St
- **Soluna** • 272 McAllister St
- **Suite One8one** • 181 Eddy St
- **Swig** • 561 Geary St
- **Tonga Room & Hurricane Bar** • Fairmont Hotel • 950 Mason St
- **Top of the Mark** • 1 Nob Hill
- **Tunnel Top** • 601 Bush St
- **The Warfield** • 982 Market St
- **Whiskey Thieves** • 839 Geary St
- **Zeki's Bar** • 1319 California St

Pet Shops

- **Animal Connection II** • 1677 Washington St
- **Ocean Aquarium** • 120 Cedar St

Restaurants

- **A La Turca** • 869 Geary St
- **Acquerello** • 1722 Sacramento St
- **Allegro Romano** • 1701 Jones St
- **Ananda Fuara** • 1298 Market St
- **The Bagelry** • 2139 Polk St
- **The Bell Tower** • 1900 Polk St
- **The Big 4 Restaurant** • Huntington Hotel • 1075 California St
- **Biscuits and Blues** • 401 Mason St
- **Brenda's French Soul Food** • 652 Polk St
- **Campton Place** • Campton Place Hotel • 340 Stockton St
- **Canteen** • 817 Sutter St
- **Cantina** • 580 Sutter St
- **Chutney** • 511 Jones St
- **Colibri** • 438 Geary St
- **Crustacean** • 1475 Polk St
- **Dining Room at the Ritz-Carlton** • 600 Stockton St
- **Dottie's True Blue Café** • 522 Jones St
- **Farallon** • 450 Post St
- **farmerbrown** • 25 Mason St
- **Fifth Floor** • Hotel Palomar • 12 4th St
- **Fleur De Lys** • 777 Sutter St
- **Golden Era** • 572 O'Farrell St
- **Grand Café** • 501 Geary St
- **Hana Zen** • 115 Cyril Magnin St
- **Hidden Vine** • 620 Post St
- **Hyde Street Bistro** • 1521 Hyde St
- **Hyde Street Seafood House & Raw Bar** • 1509 Hyde St
- **Indonesia Restaurant** • 678 Post St
- **Jai Yun** • 923 Pacific Ave
- **Katana-Ya** • 430 Geary St
- **Kuleto's** • 221 Powell St
- **Lalola Bar de Tapas** • 1358 Mason St
- **Le Colonial** • 20 Cosmo Pl
- **Lotta's** • 1720 Polk St
- **Lucky Creation** • 854 Washington St
- **Mangosteen** • 601 Larkin St
- **Masa's** • 648 Bush St
- **Michael Mina** • Westin St Francis • 335 Powell St
- **Millennium** • Hotel California • 580 Geary St
- **Morty's** • 280 Golden Gate Ave
- **Nook** • 1500 Hyde St
- **Olive Bar and Restaurant** • 743 Larkin St
- **Ozone Thai** • 1160 Polk St
- **Pakwan** • 501 O'Farrell St
- **Pearl's Deluxe Burgers** • 708 Post St
- **Persimmon** • 582 Sutter St
- **Piccadilly Fish & Chips** • 1348 Polk St
- **Postrio** • 545 Post St
- **Ristorante Milano** • 1448 Pacific Ave
- **Rotunda** • Neiman Marcus • 150 Stockton St
- **Rue St Jacques** • 1098 Jackson St
- **Saha** • 1075 Sutter St
- **Saigon Sandwich Shop** • 560 Larkin St
- **Scala's Bistro** • Sir Francis Drake Hotel • 432 Powell St
- **Sears Fine Food** • 439 Powell St
- **Shalimar** • 532 Jones St
- **Straits Restaurant** • 845 Market St
- **Street** • 2141 Polk St
- **Sushi Rapture** • 1400 Leavenworth St
- **Swan Oyster Depot** • 1517 Polk St
- **Tai Chi Restaurant** • 2031 Polk St
- **Taqueria Can-Cun** • 1003 Market St
- **Thai Spice** • 1730 Polk St
- **Tu Lan** • 8 6th St
- **Turtle Tower** • 631 Larkin St
- **U-Lee Restaurant** • 1468 Hyde St
- **Venticello** • 1257 Taylor St
- **Victor's Pizza** • 1411 Polk St

Shopping

- **Alessi** • 424 Sutter St
- **Apple Store** • 1 Stockton St
- **Argonaut Book Shop** • 786 Sutter St
- **Betsey Johnson** • 160 Geary St
- **Cheese Plus** • 2001 Polk St
- **City Discount** • 1542 Polk St
- **Clarion Music Center** • 816 Sacramento St
- **Cocoa Bella Chocolates** • 865 Market St
- **Cris** • 2056 Polk St
- **DSW Shoe Warehouse** • 111 Powell St
- **European Book Co** • 925 Larkin St
- **Foot Worship** • 1214 Sutter St
- **Ghirardelli** • 42 Stockton St
- **Goodwill Boutique** • 822 Geary St
- **Good Vibrations** • 1620 Polk St
- **Kayo Books** • 814 Post St
- **L'Occitane** • 865 Market St
- **The Levi's Store** • 300 Post St
- **Lombardi's Sports** • 1600 Jackson St
- **Lush** • 240 Powell St
- **The North Face** • 180 Post St
- **One Half** • 1837 Polk St
- **Out of the Closet** • 1498 Polk St
- **Picnic** • 1808 Polk St
- **Pink** • 255 Post St
- **Public Barber Salon** • 571 Geary St
- **Rasputin Music** • 69 Powell St
- **Real Food Company** • 2140 Polk St
- **Velvet da Vinci** • 2015 Polk St
- **Venus Superstar** • 1112 Sutter St
- **Westfield San Francisco Centre** • 865 Market St

Video Rental

- **Anna's Video (Vietnamese)** • 406 Ellis St
- **Blockbuster** • 1098 Bush St
- **Front Lyne** • 1259 Polk St
- **Gramophone Video** • 1538 Polk St
- **Power Vision** • 1048 Market St
- **Sa Vanh Video (Thai)** • 651 Larkin St
- **US Video Rental** • 720 Geary St
- **Video Wave** • 1651 Polk St
- **Video Zone** • 786 Bush St

FINANCIAL DISTRICT
EMBARCADERO
SOMA
SOUTH BEACH
SOUTH OF MARKET
City Lights Bookstore
Specs' Twelve Adler Museum Cafe
Portsmouth Square
Sentinel Building
Transamerica Pyramid
Redwood Park
Walton Park
Embarcadero Center
Justin Herman Plaza
Vaillancourt Fountain
Ferry Building
555 California
Sing Buildings
Hallidie Building
Hunter-Dulin Building
VC Morris Building
Lotta's Fountain
Rincon Center
Cupid's Span
Yerba Buena Center
SF MoMA
Tree Sculpture
Moscone Center
South Park
Historic Interpretive Signage
AT&T Park
Powell St
Montgomery St
Embarcadero
City Hall
Market St
Mission St
Howard St
Folsom St
Harrison St
Bryant St
Brannan St
Townsend St
The Embarcadero
Sansome St
Battery St
Front St
Davis St
Drumm St
Kearny St
Montgomery St
Columbus Ave
Broadway St
Pacific Ave
Jackson St
Washington St
Clay St
Merchant St
Commercial St
Sacramento St
California St
Pine St
Bush St
Sutter St
Post St
Geary St
O'Farrell St
Ellis St
Maiden Ln
Campton Pl
Tillman Pl
Halleck St
Stevenson St
Jessie St
New Montgomery St
Minna St
Natoma St
Tehama St
1st St
2nd St
3rd St
4th St
5th St
Fremont St
Beale St
Main St
Spear St
Steuart St
Delancy St
Hawthorne St
Shipley St
Clara St
Welsh St
Freelon St
Zoe St
Ritch St
Jack London Aly
S Park St
Stillman St
Lapu Lapu St
Rizal St
Bonifacio St
Mabini St
Gallagher Ln
Essex St
Lansing St
Guy Pl
Federal St
King St
Embarcadero Ctr
PAGE 208
PAGE 310
PAGE 199
PAGE 196
PAGE 235
1/4 mile
.25 km

With the Ferry Building's popular farmers market and the ballpark's success, development dollars funnel into South Beach along the Embarcadero in the form of condos. During the daytime, the Financial District teems with workers among the Transamerica Pyramid and other historic buildings.

Banks

- **America California** • 417 Montgomery St
- **Bank of America** • 1 Market St
- **Bank of America** • 33 New Montgomery St
- **Bank of America** • 345 Montgomery St
- **Bank of America** • 50 California St
- **Bank of America** • 500 Battery St
- **Bank of America** • 701 Grant Ave
- **Bank of America (ATM)** • 100 1st St
- **Bank of America (ATM)** • 163 Brannan St
- **Bank of America (ATM)** • 345 3rd St
- **Bank of America (ATM)** • 4 Embarcadero Ctr
- **Bank of America (ATM)** • 785 Market St
- **Bank of America (ATM)** • Ferry Bldg • Embarcadero & Market St
- **Bank of East Asia** • 520 Montgomery St
- **Bank of Guam** • 404 Montgomery St
- **Bank of the Orient** • 233 Sansome St
- **Bank of the West** • 1 Front St
- **Bank of the West** • 295 Bush St
- **Bank of the West** • 505 Montgomery St
- **California** • 465 California St
- **California Pacific** • 250 Montgomery St
- **Chase** • 100 Pine St
- **Chase** • 1040 Grant Ave
- **Chase** • 2 Embarcadero Ctr
- **Chase** • 401 California St
- **Chase** • 700 Market St
- **Citibank** • 1000 Grant Ave
- **Citibank** • 245 Market St
- **Citibank** • 260 California St
- **Citibank** • 451 Montgomery St
- **Citibank** • 590 Market St
- **Citibank** • 845 Grant Ave
- **Citibank** • 99 Post St
- **Citibank (ATM)** • 1 Embarcadero Ctr
- **Citibank (ATM)** • 1 Sansome St
- **Citibank (ATM)** • 217 Sutter St
- **Citibank (ATM)** • 43 Drumm St
- **Citibank (ATM)** • 564 Market St
- **Citibank (ATM)** • 711 Market St
- **City National** • 150 California St
- **County** • 595 Market St
- **Far East National** • 500 Montgomery St
- **First** • 1143 Grant Ave
- **First** • 550 Montgomery St
- **First National Northern** • 65 Post St
- **First Republic** • 1 Embarcadero Ctr
- **First Republic** • 101 Pine St
- **First Republic** • 44 Montgomery St
- **Golden Gate** • 225 Bush St
- **Mechanics** • 343 Sansome St
- **Northern Trust** • 580 California St
- **Oceanic** • 130 Battery St
- **Pacific National Bank** • 300 Montgomery St
- **Sterling** • 600 Montgomery St
- **Trans Pacific National** • 55 2nd St
- **Union** • 350 California St
- **Union** • 400 California St
- **Union** • 44 Montgomery St
- **United Commercial** • 1066 Grant Ave
- **United Commercial** • 555 Montgomery St
- **United Commercial** • 743 Washington St
- **United Commercial** • 900 Kearny St
- **US** • 101 California St
- **US** • 201 Montgomery St
- **US** • 525 Market St
- **US (ATM)** • Walgreens • 100 Sansome St
- **US (ATM)** • Walgreens • 141 Kearny St
- **US (ATM)** • Walgreens • 275 Sacramento St
- **US (ATM)** • Walgreens • 730 Market St
- **US (ATM)** • Walgreens • 88 Spear St
- **Wachovia** • 75 1st St
- **Wells Fargo** • 1 California St
- **Wells Fargo** • 1 Montgomery St
- **Wells Fargo** • 100 Spear St
- **Wells Fargo** • 1160 Grant Ave
- **Wells Fargo** • 2 Grant Ave
- **Wells Fargo** • 225 Bush St
- **Wells Fargo** • 292 Battery St
- **Wells Fargo** • 439 Washington St
- **Wells Fargo** • 464 California St
- **Wells Fargo (ATM)** • 120 Kearny St
- **Wells Fargo (ATM)** • 201 3rd St
- **Wells Fargo (ATM)** • 425 Market St
- **Wells Fargo (ATM)** • 544 Market St
- **Wells Fargo (ATM)** • 760 Market St
- **Westamerica** • 214 California St

Car Rental

- **Alamo** • 687 Folsom St
- **Budget** • 5 Embarcadero Ctr
- **Enterprise** • 727 Folsom St
- **Hertz** • 101 The Embarcadero
- **National** • 687 Folsom St

Gas Stations

- **76** • 390 1st St
- **Shell** • 551 3rd St
- **Shell** • 598 Bryant St

Landmarks

- **555 California** • 555 California St
- **City Lights** • 261 Columbus Ave
- **Cupid's Span** • Embarcadero & Folsom St
- **Embarcadero Center** • 301 Clay St
- **Ferry Building** • Embarcadero & Market St
- **Hallidie Building** • 130–150 Sutter St
- **Historic Interpretive Signage Project** • Embarcadero & King St
- **Hunter-Dulin Building** • 111 Sutter St (at Montgomery)
- **Justin Herman Plaza** • Market St & Embarcadero
- **Lotta's Fountain** • Kearny St b/w Geary Blvd & Market St
- **One Rincon Hill** • 511 Harrison St
- **Portsmouth Square** • Kearny St b/w Clay St & Washington St
- **Redwood Park** • 600 Montgomery St
- **Rincon Center** • 101 Spear St
- **Sea Change Sculpture** • Townsend St & 2nd St
- **Sentinel Building** • 916 Kearny St
- **SFMOMA** • 151 3rd St
- **Sing Chong and Sing Fat Buildings** • Grant St & California St
- **South Park** • 2nd St & Brannan St
- **Spec's Twelve Adler Museum Cafe** • 12 William Saroyan Pl
- **Transamerica Pyramid** • 600 Montgomery St
- **Transamerica Redwood Park** • 600 Montgomery St
- **Tree Sculpture** • 747 Howard St
- **Vaillancourt Fountain** • 4 Embarcadero Ctr
- **VC Morris Building (Circle Gallery)** • 140 Maiden Ln
- **Vesuvio** • 255 Columbus Ave
- **Yerba Buena Center for the Arts** • 701 Mission St

Libraries

- **Foundation Center, San Francisco** • 312 Sutter St
- **Mechanics' Institute Library** • 57 Post St
- **San Francisco Law Library Financial District Branch** • 685 Market St

Parking

Pharmacies

- **Ping Yuen Drug Store** • 750 Pacific Ave
- **Republic Pharmacy CO** • 704 Grant Ave
- **Rite Aid** • 776 Market St
- **Walgreens** • 100 Sansome St
- **Walgreens** • 116 New Montgomery St
- **Walgreens** • 141 Kearny St
- **Walgreens** • 275 Sacramento St
- **Walgreens** • 300 Montgomery St
- **Walgreens** • 33 Drumm St
- **Walgreens** • 456 Mission St
- **Walgreens** • 730 Market St
- **Walgreens** • 88 Spear St
- **Wellman's Pharmacy** • 728 Pacific Ave

Post Offices

- **Brannan Street Finance** • 460 Brannan St
- **Embarcadero Postal Center** • 226 Harrison St
- **Gateway Station** • 1 Embarcadero Ctr
- **Rincon Finance** • 180 Steuart St
- **Sutter Street Postal Store** • 150 Sutter St

Schools

- **Academy of Art College** • 79 New Montgomery St
- **Brandon College** • 25 Kearny St
- **CCSF (Downtown Campus)** • 88 4th St
- **Chinese Education Center** • 657 Merchant St
- **Dharma Realm Buddhist University-Gold Mountain Monastery** • 800 Sacramento St
- **Notre Dame Des Victoires** • 659 Pine St
- **San Francisco Institute of Architecture** • 1366 Mission St
- **Sonoma College** • 301 Howard St
- **UC Berkeley Extension Downtown** • 425 Market St
- **Wharton (West)** • 101 Howard St

- **Safeway** • 145 Jackson St
- **Whole Foods Market** • 399 4th St

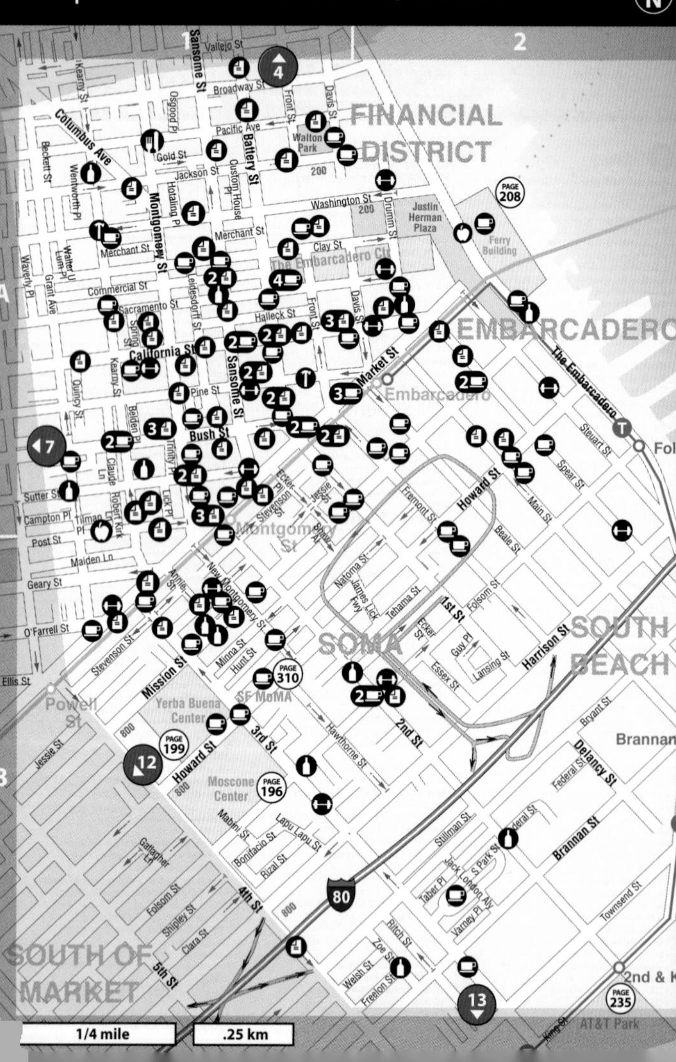

1
2
A
B
FINANCIAL DISTRICT
EMBARCADERO
SOUTH BEACH
SOMA
SOUTH OF MARKET
Vallejo St
Broadway St
Pacific Ave
Gold St
Jackson St
Washington St
Merchant St
Clay St
Commercial St
Sacramento St
Halleck St
California St
Pine St
Bush St
Sutter St
Campton Pl
Tillman Pl
Post St
Maiden Ln
Geary St
O'Farrell St
Ellis St
Kearny St
Columbus Ave
Beckett St
Wentworth Pl
Walter U Lum Pl
Waverly Pl
Grant Ave
Sansome St
Osgood Pl
Hotaling Pl
Montgomery St
Custom House Pl
Battery St
Front St
Davis St
Drumm St
Leidesdorff St
Spring St
Quincy St
Belden Pl
Trinity Pl
Claude Ln
Robert Kirk Ln
Lick Pl
Walton Park
Justin Herman Plaza
Ferry Building
The Embarcadero Ctr
The Embarcadero
Market St
Embarcadero
Steuart St
Spear St
Main St
Beale St
Fremont St
Howard St
Ecker Pl
Stevenson St
Jessie St
Shaw Al
Montgomery St
New Montgomery St
Annie St
Minna St
Hunt St
Mission St
Natoma St
James Lick Fwy
Tehama St
1st St
Folsom St
Ecker St
Guy Pl
Lansing St
Essex St
Harrison St
Bryant St
Brannan
Delancy St
Federal St
Brannan St
Stillman St
Jack London Aly
S Park St
Taber Pl
Varney Pl
Townsend St
Ritch St
Zoe St
Welsh St
Freelon St
2nd St
3rd St
4th St
5th St
Hawthorne St
Powell St
Yerba Buena Center
SF MoMA
Moscone Center
Mabini St
Bonifacio St
Rizal St
Lapu Lapu St
Gallagher Ln
Folsom St
Shipley St
Clara St
Stevenson St
Jessie St
Howard St
King St
AT&T Park
2nd & K
Fols
200
800
80
4
7
12
13
PAGE 208
PAGE 310
PAGE 199
PAGE 196
PAGE 235
1/4 mile
.25 km

coffee shop or a big-bank ATM is most certainly on every corner, and there no shortage of happy hour bars. For downtown lunch enjoyment there e hole-in-the-walls and fancy restaurants for all, whether a Downtown ll-timer, a Moscone Center convention attendee, or a visitor to SFMOMA n free first Tuesday of the month.

Coffee

- **Cafe Algiers** • 50 Beale St
- **Café Dolci** • 740 Market St
- **Café Madeleine** • 149 New Montgomery St
- **Café Madeleine** • 300 California St
- **Caffe Centro** • 102 S Park St
- **Caffe Trieste** • 199 New Montgomery St
- **Coffee Bean & Tea Leaf** • 4 Embarcadero Ctr
- **Coffee Roaster** • 536 Davis St
- **Coffee Roastery** • 180 Howard St
- **Daly Habit** • 1 Maritime Plaza
- **Golden Gate Perk Internet Café** • 401 Bush St
- **Java House** • Pier 40
- **Latte Express** • 600 Kearny St
- **Martha & Bros** • 50 1st St
- **Nas Coffee** • 101 Spear St
- **Nazdak Café** • 221 Main St
- **Peet's** • 1 California St
- **Peet's** • Ferry Bldg • Embarcadero & Market St
- **Peet's** • 2 Embarcadero Ctr
- **Peet's** • 217 Montgomery St
- **Peet's** • 22 Battery St
- **Peet's** • 298 Market St
- **Peet's** • 405 Howard St
- **Peet's** • 595 Mission St
- **Peet's** • 680 Mission St
- **Peet's** • 595 Market St
- **Powersource Juice Bar** • 81 Fremont St
- **Samovar Tea Lounge** • 730 Howard St
- **Sausalito Espresso** • 100 1st St
- **Starbucks** • 299 2nd St @ Courtyard Marriott
- **Starbucks** • 201 3rd St
- **Starbucks** • 1 Market Plz
- **Starbucks** • 425 Battery St
- **Starbucks** • 295 California St
- **Starbucks** • 123 Mission St
- **Starbucks** • 199 Fremont St
- **Starbucks** • 201 Spear St
- **Starbucks** • 264 Kearny St
- **Starbucks** • 27 Drumm St
- **Starbucks** • 333 Market St
- **Starbucks** • 340 Mission St
- **Starbucks** • 343 Sansome St
- **Starbucks** • 359 Grant Ave
- **Starbucks** • 36 2nd St
- **Starbucks** • 44 Montgomery St
- **Starbucks** • 359 Grant Ave
- **Starbucks** • 455 Market St
- **Starbucks** • 505 Sansome St
- **Starbucks** • 52 California St
- **Starbucks** • 555 California St
- **Starbucks** • 565 Clay St
- **Starbucks** • 7 3rd St
- **Starbucks** • 701 Battery St
- **Starbucks** • 74 New Montgomery St
- **Starbucks** • 99 Jackson St
- **Tasili Caffe** • 345 Spear St
- **Tea Garden** • 515 Mission St
- **Tully's Coffee** • 2 Embarcadero Ctr
- **Tully's Coffee** • 225 Bush St
- **Tully's Coffee** • 275 Battery St
- **Tully's Coffee** • 303 2nd St
- **Tully's Coffee** • 425 Market St
- **Tully's Coffee** • Hilton • 750 Kearny St

Copy Shops

- **ABC Legal Copying** • 234 Bush St
- **American Legal Copy** • 333 Bush St ㉔
- **Better Choice** • 654 Sacramento St
- **BPS Reprographics** • 201 Jackson St
- **Capitol Reprographics** • 500 Sansome St ㉔
- **Copy America** • 115 Sansome St
- **Copy Central** • 110 Sutter St
- **Copy Central** • 120 Montgomery St
- **Copy Central** • 4 Embarcadero Ctr
- **Copy Central** • 650 California St
- **Copy Central** • 705 Market St
- **Copy Central** • 71 Stevenson St
- **Copy Central** • 9 Maritime Plaza
- **Copy Edge** • 163 Jessie St
- **Copy Edge Printing** • 354 Sansome St
- **Copy Edge Printing** • 9 Columbus Ave
- **Copy Mat** • 120 Howard St
- **Copy Mat** • 455 Market St
- **Copy Service** • 385 Bush St
- **Copy Station** • 199 2nd St
- **Copy Station** • 44 Montgomery St
- **Copy Station** • 441 California St
- **Copymat** • 191 Battery St
- **Direct Copy** • 50 Post St
- **Document Services Unlimited** • 65 Battery St
- **FedEx Office** • 100 California St
- **FedEx Office** • 120 Bush St
- **FedEx Office** • 127 Kearny St
- **FedEx Office** • 3 Embarcadero Ctr
- **FedEx Office** • 303 2nd St
- **FedEx Office** • 369 Pine St
- **FedEx Office** • 50 Fremont St
- **FedEx Office** • 555 California St
- **FedEx Office** • 585 Kearny St
- **FedEx Office** • 71 Spear St
- **FedEx Office** • 724 Battery St
- **FedEx Office** • 726 Market St
- **Ford Graphics** • 850 Battery St
- **Gill Reprographics** • 603 Commercial St
- **J Solutions** • 155 Main St
- **Krishna Copy and Printing** • 45 Kearny St
- **Let Us Copy** • 235 California St
- **Metro Copy** • 225 Bush St
- **Midnight Run Copy** • 98 Battery St ㉔
- **Minuteman Press** • 529 Commercial St
- **Office Depot** • 33 3rd St
- **Print One** • 11 Spear St
- **Professional Copy & Print** • 603 Mission St
- **Rapid Reprographics** • 564 Market St
- **Ready Copy** • 731 Sansome St
- **San Francisco Legal** • 100 California St ㉔
- **Speedway Copy Systems** • 227 Front St
- **Speedway Copy Systems** • 300 Pine St
- **Speedway Copy Systems** • 47 Belden Pl
- **Speedway Copy Systems** • 524 Washington St
- **Speedway Copy Systems** • 610 3rd St
- **Speedway Typesetting & Design** • 475 4th St
- **Staples** • 300 California St
- **Techno Reprographics** • 465 California St
- **The UPS Store** • 110 Pacific Ave
- **The UPS Store** • 182 Howard St

Farmers Markets

- **Crocker Galleria (Thurs 11 am–3 pm)** • Crocker Galleria • 50 Post St
- **Ferry Plaza (Tues 10 am–2 pm, Sat 8 am–2 pm)** • Ferry Bldg • Embarcadero & Market St

Gyms

- **24 Hour Fitness** • 100 California St ㉔
- **24 Hour Fitness** • 303 2nd St ㉔
- **24 Hour Fitness** • 45 Montgomery St ㉔
- **Bay Club - Bank of America Center** • 555 California St
- **Club One** • 1 Sansome St
- **Club One** • 2 Embarcadero Ctr
- **Club One** • 350 3rd St
- **Crunch** • 345 Spear St
- **Crunch** • 61 New Montgomery St
- **Embarcadero YMCA** • 169 Steuart St
- **Equinox Fitness Club** • 301 Pine St
- **Golden Gateway Fitness** • 370 Drumm St
- **The Sports Club/LA** • 747 Market St

Hardware Stores

- **Ace Hardware** • 140 Pine St
- **New City Hardware** • 809 Kearny St

Liquor Stores

- **Bacar** • 448 Brannan St
- **Diablo Grande Wine Gallery** • 669 Mission St
- **Drumm Liquor & Deli** • 15 Drumm St
- **Ferry Plaza Wine Merchant** • Ferry Bldg • Embarcadero & Market St
- **Fine Wines International** • Pier 19
- **Hennesseys Wines And Spec** • 545 2nd St
- **John Walker & Co** • 175 Sutter St
- **London Wine Bar** • 415 Sansome St
- **Neill's Grocery & Liquor** • 521 3rd St
- **Wayne's Liquor** • 911 Kearny St
- **The Whiskey Shop / Hector Russell Scottish Imports** • 360 Sutter St
- **Zain's Fine Wine** • 246 2nd St

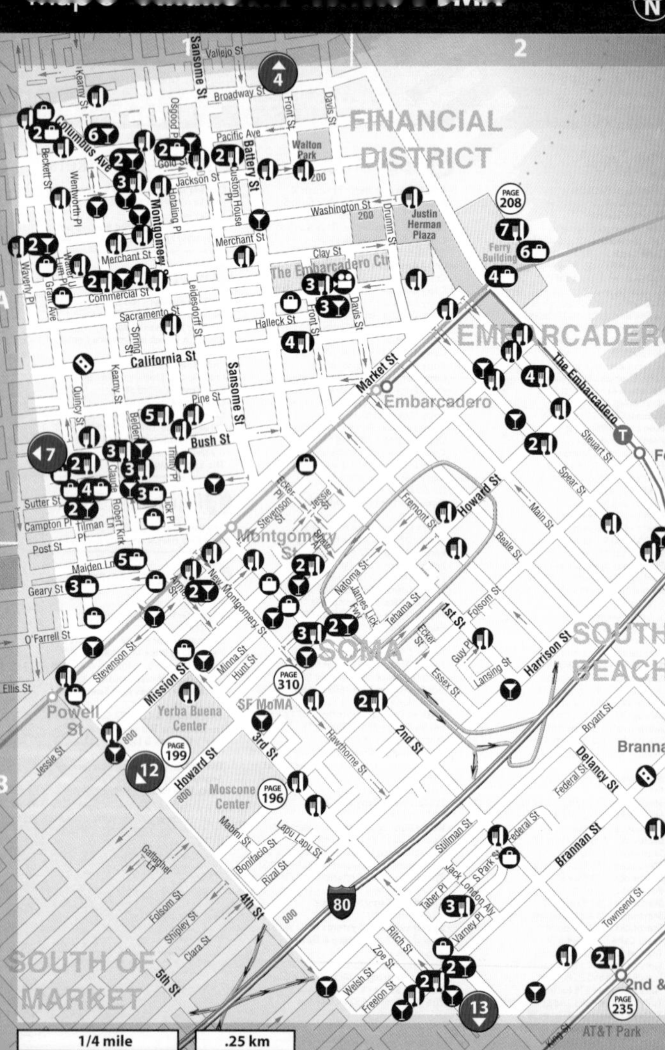

N
1
2
A
B
FINANCIAL DISTRICT
EMBARCADERO
SOMA
SOUTH BEACH
SOUTH OF MARKET
Walton Park
Justin Herman Plaza
Ferry Building
The Embarcadero Ctr
Embarcadero
Montgomery St
Powell St
Yerba Buena Center
SF MoMA
Moscone Center
AT&T Park
2nd &
Branna
PAGE 208
PAGE 310
PAGE 199
PAGE 196
PAGE 235
Vallejo St
Broadway St
Pacific Ave
Jackson St
Washington St
Merchant St
Clay St
Commercial St
Sacramento St
Halleck St
California St
Pine St
Bush St
Sutter St
Campton Pl
Tilman Pl
Post St
Maiden Ln
Geary St
O'Farrell St
Ellis St
Kearny St
Columbus Ave
Beckett St
Wentworth Pl
Waverly Pl
Walter U Lum Pl
Grant Ave
Osgood Pl
Gold St
Hotaling Pl
Montgomery St
Sansome St
Custom House Pl
Battery St
Front St
Davis St
Drumm St
Leidesdorff St
Spring St
Quincy St
Belden Pl
Trinity Pl
Claude Ln
Robert Kirk Ln
Lick Pl
Annie St
Market St
The Embarcadero
Steuart St
Spear St
Main St
Beale St
Fremont St
Howard St
Ecker Pl
Stevenson St
Jessie St
Shaw Al
New Montgomery St
Natoma St
James Lick Fwy
Tehama St
1st St
Folsom St
Ecker St
Guy Pl
Lansing St
Essex St
Harrison St
Bryant St
Delancy St
Federal St
Brannan St
Mission St
Minna St
Hunt St
3rd St
Hawthorne St
2nd St
Mabini St
Lapu Lapu St
Bonifacio St
Rizal St
4th St
Gallagher Ln
Folsom St
Shipley St
Clara St
5th St
Stillman St
Jack London Aly
S Park St
Taber Pl
Varney Pl
Ritch St
Zoe St
Welsh St
Freelon St
Townsend St
King St
80
200
800
4
7
12
13
1/4 mile
.25 km

Enjoy early morning coffee and a sticky bun while perusing the delicious wares at the Ferry Building Market. Join in a demonstration or live concert on Justin Herman Plaza. Celebrate Bastille Day in one of the bistros on French-accented Belden Place. Imbibe stellar cocktails at a slick hotel bar. Then, nap time.

Movie Theaters

- **Embarcadero Center Cinema** • 1 Embarcadero Ctr

Nightlife

- **111 Minna Gallery** • 111 Minna St
- **Azul** • 1 Tillman Pl
- **Bacar** • 448 Brannan St
- **Bix** • 56 Gold St
- **The Bubble Lounge** • 714 Montgomery St
- **Buddha Bar** • 901 Grant Ave
- **The Cigar Bar and Grill** • 850 Montgomery St
- **Club NV** • 525 Howard St
- **The Cosmopolitan** • 121 Spear St
- **Dave's** • 29 3rd St
- **Eddie Rickenbacker's** • 133 2nd St
- **EZ5** • 684 Commercial St
- **Fluid Ultra Lounge** • 662 Mission St
- **Fourth Street Bar & Deli** • 55 4th St
- **Glas Kat** • 520 4th St
- **Gordon Biersch** • 2 Harrison St
- **Harrington's Bar & Grill** • 245 Front St
- **House of Shields** • 39 New Montgomery St
- **The Irish Bank** • 10 Mark Ln
- **Jillian's** • 101 4th St
- **Kate O'Briens** • 579 Howard St
- **L'Amour Nightclub** • 600 Jackson St
- **The Lusty Lady** • 1033 Kearny St
- **Mr. Bing's** • 201 Columbus Ave
- **The Pied Piper Bar & Maxfield's** • Palace Hotel • 2 New Montgomery St
- **Punch Line** • 444 Battery St
- **Rickhouse** • 246 Kearny St
- **Royal Exchange** • 301 Sacramento St
- **San Francisco Brewing Company** • 155 Columbus Ave
- **Seasons Bar & Lounge** • 757 Market St
- **Spec's Twelve Adler Museum Cafe** • 12 William Saroyan Pl
- **Sugar Cafe** • 679 Sutter St
- **Sutter Station** • 554 Market St
- **Temple Nightclub** • 540 Howard St
- **Thirsty Bear** • 661 Howard St
- **Tosca Café** • 242 Columbus Ave
- **Vesuvio** • 255 Columbus Ave
- **XYZ** • W Hotel • 181 3rd St
- **Zeke's** • 600 3rd St

Restaurants

- **5A5 Steak Lounge** • 244 Jackson St
- **21st Amendment** • 563 2nd St
- **Alfred's Steak House** • 659 Merchant St
- **Americano** • 8 Mission St
- **B44** • 44 Belden Pl
- **Bacar** • 448 Brannan St
- **Baladie Gourmet Café** • 337 Kearny St
- **Banana House** • 321 Kearny St
- **Birley's Sandwiches** • 4 Embarcadero Ctr
- **Bix** • 56 Gold St
- **B & M Mei Sing Restaurant** • 62 2nd St
- **Bocadillos** • 710 Montgomery St
- **Boulevard** • 1 Mission St
- **Boxed Foods** • 245 Kearny St
- **Brandy Ho's Hunan Food** • 217 Columbus Ave
- **Brickhouse Café and Bar** • 426 Brannan St
- **Brindisi Cucina di Mare** • 88 Belden Pl
- **The Butler and The Chef Bistro** • 155 S Park St
- **Café Bastille** • 22 Belden Pl
- **Cafe Claude** • 7 Claude Ln
- **Cafe Venue** • 70 Leidesdorff St
- **Cafe Venue** • 218 Montgomery St
- **Caffe Centro** • 102 S Park St
- **Caffe Macaroni Sciue Sciue** • 124 Columbus Ave
- **Cane Rosso** • 1 Ferry Building
- **Chaat Café** • 320 3rd St
- **Chaya Brasserie** • 132 The Embarcadero
- **Chef Jia's** • 925 Kearny St
- **Ciao Bella Gelato** • 1 Ferry Building
- **Crossroads Café** • 699 Delancey St
- **Delica** • 1 Ferry Bldg •
- **Globe** • 290 Pacific Ave
- **Golden Flower Vietnamese Restaurant** • 667 Jackson St
- **Golden Star Vietnamese Restaurant** • 11 Walter U Lum Pl
- **Gott's Roadside** • 1 Ferry Building
- **Henry's Hunan** • 110 Natoma St
- **Hog Island Oyster Company** • 1 Ferry Bldg
- **House of Nanking** • 919 Kearny St
- **Hunan** • 110 Natoma St
- **Jai Yun** • 680 Clay St
- **Koh Samui and the Monkey** • 415 Brannan St
- **Kokkari Estiatorio** • 200 Jackson St
- **Kyo-Ya** • Palace Hotel • 2 New Montgomery St
- **Le Central Bistro** • 453 Bush St
- **Local Kitchen & Wine Merchant** • 330 1st St
- **MarketBar** • 1 Ferry Bldg
- **Maya** • 303 2nd St
- **Mel's Drive-In** • 801 Mission St
- **Mijita** • Market St & The Embarcadero
- **Mixt Greens** • 560 Mission St
- **MoMo's** • 760 2nd St
- **Naan-N-Curry** • 533 Jackson St
- **One Market** • 1 Market St
- **Out the Door** • 1 Ferry Bldg
- **Ozumo** • 161 Steuart St
- **Paladar Cafe Cubano** • 329 Kearny St
- **Pazzia Caffe & Pizzeria** • 337 3rd St
- **Perbacco** • 230 California St
- **Plouf** • 40 Belden Pl
- **Quince** • 470 Pacific Ave
- **R&G Lounge** • 631 Kearny St
- **Red's Java House** • Pier 30 & Bryant St
- **Salt House** • 545 Mission St
- **Sam Wo Restaurant** • 813 Washington St
- **Sam's Grill & Seafood Restaurant** • 374 Bush St
- **San Buena Taco Truck** • 375 Pacific Ave
- **The Sentinel** • 37 New Montgomery St
- **Slanted Door** • Ferry Bldg • Embarcadero & Market St
- **South Park Café** • 108 S Park St
- **Sweet Joanna's Café** • 101 Howard St
- **Tadich Grill** • 240 California St
- **The Toaster Oven** • 3 Embarcadero Ctr
- **The Toaster Oven** • 145 2nd St
- **The Toaster Oven** • 201 Spear St
- **Tommaso's** • 1042 Kearny St
- **Tommy Toy's Cuisine Chinoise** • 655 Montgomery St
- **Town Hall** • 342 Howard St
- **Tres Agaves** • 130 Townsend St
- **Tropisueño** • 75 Yerba Buena Ln
- **What's Up Dog!** • 28 Trinity Pl
- **Yank Sing** • 101 Spear St
- **Zare** • 606 Folsom St

Shopping

- **AG Ferrari Foods** • 688 Mission St
- **Acme Bread** • 1 Ferry Bldg • Marketplace Shop #15
- **Adolph Gasser** • 181 2nd St
- **Ambassador Toys** • 2 Embarcadero Ctr
- **American Apparel** • 363 Grant Ave
- **Camper** • 39 Grant Ave
- **Candelier** • 33 Maiden Ln
- **City Lights** • 261 Columbus Ave
- **Container Store** • 26 4th St
- **Cowgirl Creamery Artisan Cheese** • 1 Ferry Bldg
- **Discount Camera** • 33 Kearny St
- **Eastern Bakery** • 720 Grant Ave
- **Far West Fungi** • 1 Ferry Bldg
- **Ferry Plaza Wine Merchant** • Ferry Building • Embarcadero & Market St
- **Fiona's Sweetshoppe** • 214 Sutter St
- **Fog City News** • 455 Market St
- **Frette** • 124 Geary St
- **Frog Hollow Farm** • 1 Ferry Bldg
- **Golden Gate Bakery** • 1029 Grant Ave
- **Goorin Hat Shop** • 111 Geary St
- **Gump's** • 135 Post St
- **Hermes** • 125 Grant Ave
- **Hog Island Oyster Co.** • 1 Ferry Bldg
- **Indie Industries** • 218 Columbus Ave
- **Jeffrey's Toys** • 685 Market St
- **Japonesque** • 824 Montgomery St
- **Jeremy's** • 2 S Park St
- **John Walker & Co** • 175 Sutter St
- **Katz Bagels** • 606 Mission St
- **Loehmann's** • 222 Sutter St
- **Loehmann's Mens** • 211 Sutter St
- **Ma Maison** • 592 3rd St
- **Marina Morrison** • 30 Maiden Ln
- **Miette** • 1 Ferry Bldg
- **North Bay Photographer's Supply** • 436 Bryant St
- **Recchiuti** • 1 Ferry Bldg
- **Red Blossom Tea Co** • 831 Grant Ave
- **Stonehouse California Olive Oil** • 1 The Ebarcadero
- **Sur La Table** • 1 Ferry Bldg •
- **Teuscher Chocolate** • 307 Sutter St
- **Torso Vintages** • 272 Sutter St
- **William Stout Architectural Books** • 804 Montgomery St
- **Yves Saint Laurent** • 166 Maiden Ln

Video Rental

- **South Beach Video** • 151 Brannan St
- **Starsight Video Entertainment (Chinese)** • 766 Sacramento St

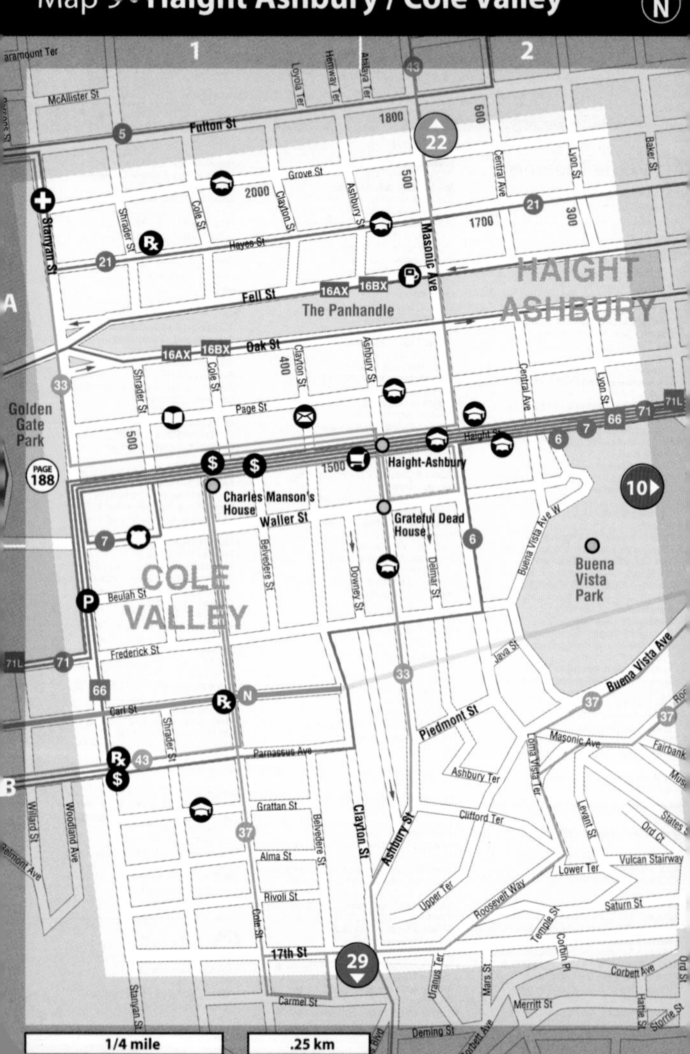

N
1
2
A
B
Paramount Ter
McAllister St
Loyola Ter
Hemway Ter
Atalaya Ter
Fulton St
1800
600
Grove St
2000
500
Central Ave
Lyon St
Baker St
Stanyan St
Shrader St
Cole St
Clayton St
Ashbury St
Masonic Ave
1700
300
Hayes St
HAIGHT
ASHBURY
Fell St
16AX
16BX
The Panhandle
Oak St
400
Page St
Golden
Gate
Park
500
Haight St
1500
Haight-Ashbury
Charles Manson's
House
Waller St
Grateful Dead
House
Belvedere St
Downey St
Delmar St
Buena Vista Ave W
Buena
Vista
Park
COLE
VALLEY
Beulah St
Frederick St
Java St
Buena Vista Ave
Carl St
Piedmont St
Masonic Ave
Parnassus Ave
Ashbury Ter
Loma Vista Ter
Fairbank
Clifford Ter
Levant St
Grattan St
Willard St
Woodland Ave
Belmont Ave
Alma St
Ord Ct
Vulcan Stairway
Lower Ter
Upper Ter
Roosevelt Way
Rivoli St
Saturn St
Temple St
Corbin Pl
17th St
Carmel St
Uranus Ter
Mars St
Corbett Ave
Ord St
Merritt St
Hattie St
Storrie St
Deming St
1/4 mile
.25 km

PAGE 188

Hippies and anything free left the Haight when the housing prices soared. Expect to find gutter punk teens panhandling and selling eighths of oregano shake. Fashionable boutiques and expensive vintage clothing shops abound. Nearby Cole Valley is clean-cut, subdued, and a fully self-sufficient neighborhood.

Banks

- **US (ATM)** • Walgreens • 199 Parnassus Ave
- **Wells Fargo** • 1726 Haight St
- **Wells Fargo (ATM)** • 1653 Haight St

Emergency Rooms

- **St Mary's Medical Center** • 450 Stanyan St

Gas Stations

- **Chevron** • 1698 Fell St

Landmarks

- **Buena Vista Park** • Haight St & Buena Vista Ave
- **Charles Manson's House** • 636 Cole St
- **Grateful Dead House** • 710 Ashbury St
- **Haight-Ashbury** • Haight St & Ashbury St

Libraries

- **Park Branch Library** • 1833 Page St

Parking

Pharmacies

- **Pharmaca Integrative Pharmacy** • 925 Cole St
- **Saint Mary's Prescription Pharmacy** • 2166 Hayes St
- **Walgreens** • 199 Parnassus Ave

Police

- **Park Police Station** • 1899 Waller St

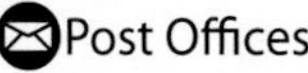

Post Offices

- **Clayton Street Station** • 554 Clayton St

Schools

- **Aim High Academy** • 1351 Haight St
- **CCSF (John Adams Campus)** • 1860 Hayes St
- **Grattan Elementary** • 165 Grattan St
- **Lycee Francais** • 755 Ashbury St
- **New Traditions Elementary** • 2049 Grove St
- **Urban School of San Francisco** • 1563 Page St
- **William R De Avila Elementary** • 1351 Haight St

Supermarkets

- **Haight Street Market** • 1530 Haight St

Map 9 • Haight Ashbury / Cole Valley
N
1
2
A
B
Fulton St
Grove St
Hayes St
Fell St
The Panhandle
Oak St
Page St
Haight St
Waller St
Beulah St
Frederick St
Carl St
Parnassus Ave
Grattan St
Alma St
Rivoli St
17th St
Carmel St
Stanyan St
Shrader St
Cole St
Clayton St
Ashbury St
Masonic Ave
Central Ave
Lyon St
Baker St
Belvedere St
Downey St
Delmar St
Golden Gate Park
HAIGHT ASHBURY
COLE VALLEY
Buena Vista Park
Buena Vista Ave
Buena Vista Ave W
Piedmont St
Java St
Masonic Ave
Ashbury Ter
Clifford Ter
Loma Vista Ter
Levant St
Vulcan Stairway
Lower Ter
Upper Ter
Roosevelt Way
Saturn St
Temple St
Corbin Pl
Corbett Ave
Merritt St
Uranus Ter
Mars St
Deming St
Hattie St
Ord Ct
McAllister St
Paramount Ter
Parsons St
Loyola Ter
Hemway Ter
Atalaya Ter
Willard St
Woodland Ave
Belmont Ave
PAGE 188
22
10
29
1/4 mile
.25 km

Aside from vestiges of the '60s, shopping is the draw. Hunt for records at Amoeba Music, outfit your feet at Villains. Catch an indie or cult film at the Red Vic. Stroll to Hama-Ko for hardcore sushi, a very cheap drink at Gold Cane, or someting fancier to sip at Alembic.

Coffee

- **Café Reverie** • 848 Cole St
- **Cantata Coffee Company** • 1708 Haight St
- **Central Coffee Tea & Spice** • 1696 Hayes St
- **Coffee To The People** • 1206 Masonic Ave
- **Cole Valley Café** • 701 Cole St
- **Emma's Coffee House** • 1901 Hayes St
- **Lava Java** • 852 Stanyan St
- **Red Victorian Peace Café** • 1665 Haight St
- **Rockin' Java Coffee House** • 1821 Haight St
- **Sacred Grounds Coffee House** • 2095 Hayes St
- **Tully's Coffee** • 919 Cole St

Gyms

- **Cole Valley Fitness** • 957 Cole St
- **Curves (women only)** • 638 Stanyan St

Hardware Stores

- **Cole Hardware** • 956 Cole St
- **Roberts Hardware** • 1629 Haight St

Liquor Stores

- **Ashbury Market** • 205 Frederick St
- **Haight & Cole Liquors** • 1699 Haight St
- **Liquid Experience** • 1589 Haight St
- **Seventeenth & Cole St Market** • 1400 Cole St
- **Sunshine Wine & Liquor** • 1754 Haight St
- **Van de Cole Liquors** • 906 Cole St

Movie Theaters

- **Red Vic** • 1727 Haight St

Nightlife

- **The Alembic Bar** • 1725 Haight St
- **Club Deluxe** • 1511 Haight St
- **Finnegan's Wake** • 937 Cole St
- **Gold Cane Cocktail Lounge** • 1569 Haight St
- **Hobson's Choice** • 1601 Haight St
- **Kezar Pub** • 770 Stanyan St
- **Magnolia Pub and Brewery** • 1398 Haight St
- **Martin Macks** • 1568 Haight St
- **Milk Bar** • 1840 Haight St
- **Murio's Trophy Room** • 1811 Haight St
- **Persian Aub Zam Zam** • 1633 Haight St
- **Trax** • 1437 Haight St

Pet Shops

- **Cole Valley Pets** • 910 Cole St

Restaurants

- **All You Knead** • 1466 Haight St
- **Burgermeister** • 86 Carl St
- **Best of Thai Noodle** • 1418 Haight St
- **Blue Front Café** • 1430 Haight St
- **Boulange de Cole Valley** • 1000 Cole St
- **Cha Cha Cha** • 1801 Haight St
- **Citrus Club** • 1790 Haight St
- **El Balazo** • 1654 Haight St
- **Eos Restaurant & Wine Bar** • 901 Cole St
- **Escape From New York Pizza** • 1737 Haight St
- **Grandeho's Kamekyo** • 943 Cole St
- **Hama-Ko Sushi** • 108 Carl St
- **Home Service Market** • 1700 Hayes St
- **Kan Zaman** • 1793 Haight St
- **North Beach Pizza** • 800 Stanyan St
- **Panhandle Pizza** • 2077 Hayes St
- **Parada** • 22 1805 Haight St
- **People's Cafe** • 1419 Haight St
- **Ploy II** • 1770 Haight St
- **Pork Store Café** • 1451 Haight St
- **Red Victorian Peace Café** • 1665 Haight St
- **Squat and Gobble** • 1428 Haight St
- **Zazie** • 941 Cole St

Shopping

- **Ambiance** • 1458 Haight St
- **American Apparel** • 1615 Haight St
- **Amoeba Music** • 1855 Haight St
- **Aqua Surf Shop** • 1742 Haight St
- **Ashbury Tobacco Center** • 1524 Haight St
- **Buffalo Exchange** • 1555 Haight St
- **Cal Surplus** • 1541 Haight St
- **Ceiba Records** • 1364 Haight St
- **City Optix** • 1685 Haight St
- **Cold Steel America** • 1783 Haight St
- **Cole Hardware** • 956 Cole St
- **Crossroads Trading Company** • 1519 Haight St
- **Daljeets** • 1773 Haight St
- **Discount Fabrics** • 2315 Irving St.
- **Egg** • 85 Carl St
- **FTC** • 1632 Haight St
- **Giant Robot** • 618 Shrader St
- **Haight Ashbury Music Center** • 1540 Haight St
- **Haight Ashbury Tattoo & Piercing** • 1525 Haight St
- **Held Over** • 1543 Haight St
- **Ideele** • 1600 Haight St
- **Isabel Shoes** • 1529 Haight St
- **John Fluevog** • 1697 Haight St
- **Kidrobot** • 1512 Haight St
- **La Rosa Vintage** • 1711 Haight St
- **Loyal Army Clothing** • 1728 Haight St
- **Mendel's Art Supplies** • 1556 Haight St
- **New York Apparel** • 1772 Haight St
- **Occasions Boutique** • 858 Cole St
- **Pharmaca** • 925 Cole St
- **Piedmont Boutique** • 1452 Haight St
- **Positively Haight Street** • 1400 Haight St
- **Ruby** • 1431 Haight St
- **Say Cheese** • 856 Cole St
- **SFO Snowboard Shop** • 1630 Haight St
- **Shoe Biz II** • 1553 Haight St
- **Skates on Haight** • 1818 Haight St
- **Super Shoe Biz** • 1420 Haight St
- **Villains** • 1672 Haight St
- **Villains Vault** • 1653 Haight St
- **Wasteland** • 1660 Haight St
- **X Generation 2** • 1401 Haight St
- **Zoe Bikini** • 3386 18th St

Video Rental

- **Into Video** • 1439 Haight St
- **Video Nook** • 842 Cole St

Fulton St
Alamo Square
Shoe Garden
Grove St
Hayes
Fell St
Oak St
Page St
Haight St
Laussat St
Waller St
Germania St
Hermann St
Duboce Park
Duboce Ave
Duboce Bikeway Mural
Reservoir St
14th St
Henry St
15th St
Beaver St
16th St
17th St
Ford St
18th St
Hancock St
19th St
Cumberland St
Divisadero St
Fillmore St
Webster St
Buchanan St
Castro St
Market St
Church St
Dolores St
Noe St
Sanchez St
Steiner St
Scott St
Broderick St
Baker St
Lyon St
Pierce St
Potomac St
Carmelita St
Lloyd St
Alpine Ter
Buena Vista Ter
Buena Vista Ave
Buena Vista Ave E
Buena Vista Park
Park Hill Ave
Roosevelt Way
Corona Heights
Masonic Ave
Fairbanks St
Randall Museum Dog Run
Randall Museum
De Forest Way
Flint St
Museum Way
States St
Ord Ct
Vulcan Stairway
Levant St
Saturn St
Ord St
Corbett Ave
Hattie St
Storrie St
Clover St
Clover Ln
Thorp Ln
Lamson Ln
Douglass St
Eureka St
Diamond St
Collingwood St
Hartford St
Seward St
Carson St
Market St Railway Mural
Harvey Milk Memorial Plaza
Castro Theatre
Harvey's
Eureka Valley Harvey Milk Memorial Library
Café Du Nord
Mission Dolores
Dolores Park
Chula Ln
Abbey St
Alert Aly
Landers St
Hidalgo Ter
Rosemont Pl
Ramona Ave
Dorland St
Oakwood St
Boynton Ct
Belcher St
Sharon St
Harlow St
Dehon St
Pond St
Prosper St
Walter St
Birch St
Ivy St
Hayes St
Linden St
Hickory St
Lily St
Banneker Way
HAIGHT ASHBURY
DMV
Abner Phelps House
PAGE 212
1/4 mile
.25 km

Rainbow flags, leather bars, men with lap dogs, men in cutoffs, boys dancing it up at the Café— that's just the side of the Castro that is living up to the reputation. The tamer side is the restored Victorians bought up in the '60s and '70s by those who didn't flee.

Banks

- **Bank of America** • 1275 Fell St
- **Bank of America** • 501 Castro St
- **Bank of America (ATM)** • 45 Castro St
- **Citibank** • 444 Castro St
- **Citibank (ATM)** • 3998 18th St
- **Sterling** • 2122 Market St
- **US** • 443 Castro St
- **US (ATM)** • Walgreens • 2145 Market St
- **Wells Fargo** • 2020 Market St
- **Wells Fargo** • 557 Castro St
- **Wells Fargo (ATM)** • 2308 Market St
- **Wells Fargo (ATM)** • 425 Divisadero St
- **Wells Fargo (ATM)** • 498 Castro St

Car Rental

- **Enterprise** • 2001 Market St
- **Ford Rent-A-Car** • 2001 Market St

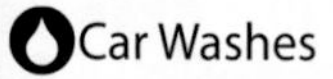

Car Washes

- **Divisadero Touchless Car Wash** • 444 Divisadero St

Community Gardens

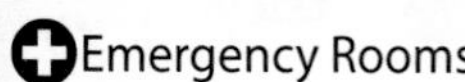

Emergency Rooms

- **California Pacific Medical Center Davies Campus** • Castro St & Duboce St

Gas Stations

- **76** • 2175 Market St
- **76** • 443 Divisadero St
- **Arco** • 1175 Fell St
- **Chevron** • 2399 Market St
- **Shell** • 1070 Oak St

Landmarks

- **Abner Phelps House** • 1111 Oak St
- **Café du Nord** • 2170 Market St
- **Castro Theatre** • 429 Castro St
- **Corona Heights** • Roosevelt Wy & Museum Wy
- **DMV** • 1377 Fell St
- **Dolores Park** • Dolores St b/w 18th St & 20th St
- **Duboce Bikeway Mural** • Duboce b/w Market St & Church St
- **Harvey Milk Memorial Plaza** • 400 Castro St
- **Harvey's** • 500 Castro St
- **Market St Railway Mural** • 300 Church St
- **Mission Dolores** • 3321 16th St
- **Randall Museum** • 199 Museum Wy
- **Randall Museum Dog Run** • Roosevelt Wy & Museum Wy
- **Shoe Garden** • Steiner St & Grove St

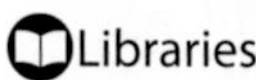

Libraries

- **Eureka Valley / Harvey Milk Memorial Library** • 3555 16th St

Pharmacies

- **Castro Street Pharmacy** • 45 Castro St
- **Safeway** • 2020 Market St ㉔
- **Stadtlanders Pharmacy** • 445 Castro St
- **Statscript Pharmacy** • 2262 Market St
- **Walgreens** • 2145 Market St
- **Walgreens** • 4129 18th St
- **Walgreens** • 498 Castro St ㉔
- **Walgreens** • 499 Haight St

Post Offices

- **18th Street Station** • 4304 18th St

Schools

- **Burt Children's Center** • 940 Grove St
- **Children's Day** • 333 Dolores St
- **Everett Middle** • 450 Church St
- **Harvey Milk Civil Rights Academy** • 4235 19th St
- **Holy Family Day Home** • 299 Dolores St
- **Ida B Wells High** • 1099 Hayes St
- **John Muir** • 380 Webster St
- **McKinley Elementary** • 1025 14th St
- **Mission Dolores** • 3321 16th St
- **Mission High** • 3750 18th St
- **Pacific Primary** • 1500 Grove St
- **Sacred Heart Elementary** • 735 Fell St
- **San Francisco Friends** • 117 Diamond St
- **Sanchez** • 325 Sanchez St

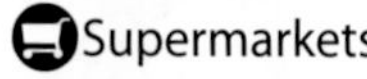

Supermarkets

- **DeLano's IGA** • 4201 18th St
- **Safeway** • 2020 Market St ㉔

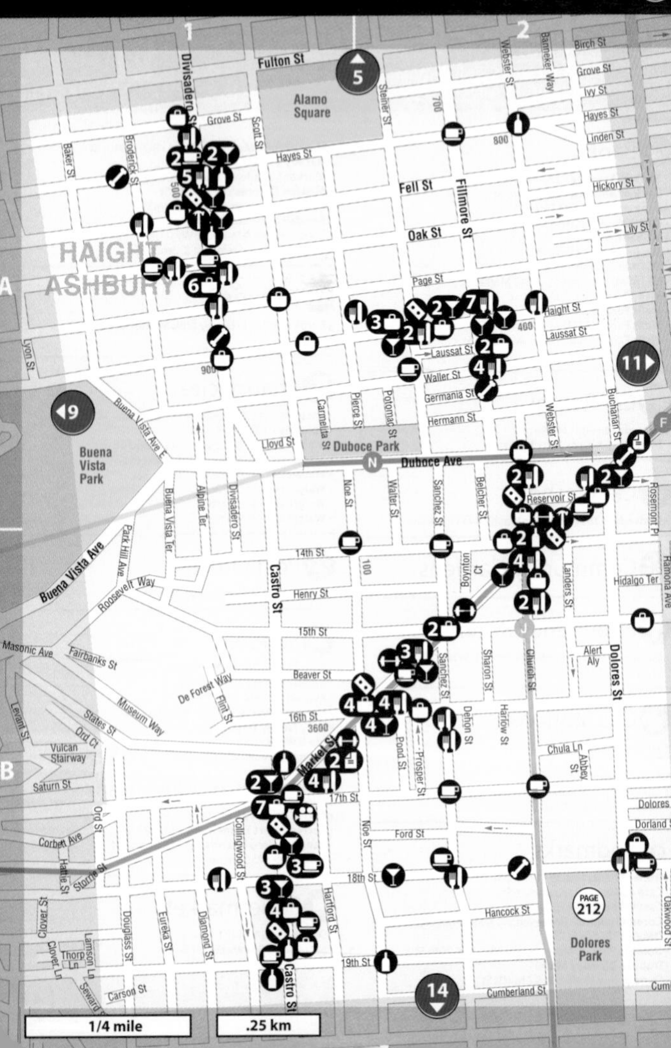

Fulton St
Alamo Square
Grove St
Hayes St
Fell St
Oak St
Page St
Haight St
Lausaat St
Waller St
Germania St
Hermann St
Duboce Park
Duboce Ave
Fillmore St
Divisadero St
Broderick St
Baker St
Scott St
Steiner St
Webster St
Buchanan St
Birch St
Grove St
Ivy St
Hayes St
Linden St
Hickory St
Lily St
HAIGHT ASHBURY
Lyon St
Buena Vista Park
Buena Vista Ave E
Buena Vista Ave
Lloyd St
Reservoir St
14th St
15th St
Henry St
Beaver St
16th St
17th St
18th St
19th St
Market St
Castro St
Noe St
Sanchez St
Church St
Dolores St
Dolores Park
Hancock St
Cumberland St
Masonic Ave
Roosevelt Way
Vulcan Stairway
Saturn St
Corbett Ave
Douglass St
Eureka St
Diamond St
Collingwood St
Hartford St
PAGE 212
1/4 mile
.25 km

The Castro supplies one of the biggest assets of a sleepless city: 24-hour food (Orphan Andy's, Sparky's). Local live music is fresh at Café du Nord and the brave can make their own music with karaoke at The Mint. Lower Haight is brunch central at Kate's Kitchen and Café du Soleil by morning and beer heaven at Toronado by night.

Coffee

- **Bean Bag Coffee House** • 601 Divisadero St
- **Bean There** • 201 Steiner St
- **Café** • 2369 Market St
- **Castro Cheesery** • 427 Castro St
- **Castro Tarts** • 564 Castro St
- **Cup a Joe Coffee House** • 3801 17th St
- **Church Street Cafe** • 260 Church St
- **Dolores Park Cafe** • 501 Dolores St
- **Duboce Park Café** • 2 Sanchez St
- **Five Star Truffles & Coffee** • 411 Divisadero St
- **Jumpin' Java Coffee House** • 139 Noe St
- **Morning Due Café** • 3698 17th St
- **Oakside Café** • 1195 Oak St
- **Peet's** • 2257 Market St
- **Peet's** • 310 Broderick St
- **Philz Coffee** • 4023 18th St
- **Samovar Tea Lounge** • 498 Sanchez St
- **Spike's Coffee & Tea** • 4117 19th St
- **Starbucks** • Safeway • 2020 Market St
- **Starbucks** • 2018 Market St
- **Starbucks** • 4094 18th St

Copy Shops

- **Copy Central** • 2336 Market St
- **FedEx Office** • 1967 Market St
- **The UPS Store** • 2370 Market St

Gyms

- **24 Hour Fitness** • 2145 Market St (24)
- **Gold's Gym** • 2301 Market St
- **The Gym SF (men only)** • 2275 Market St

Hardware Stores

- **Handy Handyman Hardware** • 2075 Market St
- **SF Hardware** • 512 Divisadero St

Liquor Stores

- **Castro Village Wine** • 4121 19th St
- **George's Market & Deli** • 702 14th St
- **H&W Liquors** • 801 Hayes St
- **KD'S Grog n' Groc** • 2416 Market St
- **New Star Ell Liquors** • 501 Divisadero St
- **Noe Hill Market** • 4001 19th St
- **Rikker's Liquors** • 2077 Market St

Movie Theaters

- **Castro Theatre** • 429 Castro St

Nightlife

- **The Bar on Church** • 198 Church St
- **Blackbird** • 2124 Market St
- **Café du Nord** • 2170 Market St
- **Café Flore** • 2298 Market St
- **Club Waziema** • 543 Divisadero St
- **Harvey's** • 500 Castro St
- **The Independent** • 628 Divisadero St
- **Last Call Bar** • 3988 18th St
- **Lime** • 2246 Market St
- **Lucky 13** • 2140 Market St
- **Mad Dog in the Fog** • 530 Haight St
- **Madrone Lounge** • 500 Divisadero St
- **The Midnight Sun** • 4067 18th St
- **The Mint** • 1942 Market St
- **Mojo Bicycle Café** • 639 Divisadero St
- **Molotov's** • 582 Haight St
- **Nickies** • 466 Haight St
- **The Page** • 298 Divisadero St
- **Pilsner Inn** • 225 Church St
- **Q Bar** • 456 Castro St
- **San Francisco Badlands** • 4121 18th St
- **Toad Hall** • 4146 18th St
- **Toronado** • 547 Haight St
- **The Twin Peaks Tavern** • 401 Castro St
- **Uva Enoteca** • 568 Haight St

Pet Shops

- **Best in Show** • 300 Sanchez St
- **Health Wize for Pets** • 157 Fillmore St
- **Jeffrey's Natural Pet Food** • 3809 18th St
- **Osso & Co** • 501 Broderick St
- **Pet Food Express** • 1975 Market St

Restaurants

- **2223 Restaurant** • 2223 Market St
- **Alamo Square Seafood Grill** • 803 Fillmore St
- **Ali Baba's Cave** • 531 Haight St
- **Anchor Oyster Bar** • 579 Castro St
- **Axum Café** • 698 Haight St
- **Bar Crudo** • 655 Divisadero St
- **Bi-Rite Creamery** • 3692 18th St
- **Burgermeister** • 138 Church St
- **Café du Soleil** • 200 Fillmore St
- **Café Flore** • 2298 Market St
- **Catch** • 2362 Market St
- **Cathay Express Restaurant** • 720 14th St
- **Chilli Cha Cha** • 494 Haight St
- **Chow** • 215 Church St
- **Club Waziema** • 543 Divisadero St
- **Crepevine** • 216 Church St
- **Cuco's** • 488 Haight St
- **Da Pitt** • 705 Divisadero St
- **Eiji** • 317 Sanchez St
- **El Castillito** • 136 Church St
- **Estela's Fresh Sandwiches** • 250 Fillmore St
- **Frances** • 3870 17th St
- **Home** • 2100 Market St
- **Indian Oven** • 233 Fillmore St
- **Jay's Cheesesteak** • 553 Divisadero St
- **Kate's Kitchen** • 471 Haight St
- **La Fajita** • 2312 Market St
- **La Mediterranee** • 288 Noe St
- **Lily's BBQ** • 705 Divisadero St
- **The Little Chihuahua** • 292 Divisadero St
- **Love N Haight Deli & Café** • 553 Haight St
- **M & L Market** • 691 14th St
- **Marcello's Pizza** • 420 Castro St
- **Memphis Minnie's BBQ Joint** • 576 Haight St
- **Metro Caffe** • 247 Fillmore St
- **Nickies** • 466 Haight St
- **Nizario's Pizza** • 4077 18th St
- **NOPA** • 560 Divisadero St
- **Nopalito** • 306 Broderick St
- **Oakside Cafe** • 1195 Oak St
- **Orphan Andy's** • 3991 17th St (24)
- **Red Jade Restaurant** • 245 Church St
- **RNM** • 598 Haight St
- **Rosamunde Sausage Grill** • 545 Haight St
- **Rotee** • 400 Haight St
- **Samovar Tea Lounge** • 498 Sanchez St
- **Sausage Factory** • 517 Castro St
- **Sparky's** • 242 Church St (24)
- Starbelly • 3583 16th St
- **Tangerine** • 3499 16th St
- **Thep Phanom Thai Cuisine** • 400 Waller St
- **Woodhouse Fish Company** • 2073 Market St
- **Ziryab** • 528 Divisadero St

Shopping

- **A Different Light Bookstore** • 489 Castro St
- **AG Ferrari Foods** • 468 Castro St
- **Backspace** • 351 Divisadero St
- **The Bead Store** • 417 Castro St
- **Books Inc** • 2275 Market St
- **Citizen** • 536 Castro St
- **Cliff's Variety Store** • 479 Castro St
- **Comix Experience** • 305 Divisadero St
- **Cookin'** • 339 Divisadero St
- **Costumes on Haight** • 735 Haight St
- **Country Cheese, Inc** • 415 Divisadero St
- **Crossroads Trading Company** • 2123 Market St
- **De La Sole Footwear** • 549 Castro St
- **Delessio Market** • 302 Broderick St
- **Doe** • 629 Haight St
- **Edo Salon** • 601 Haight St
- **Faye's Video & Espresso Bar** • 3614 18th St
- **Gamescape** • 333 Divisadero St
- **Golden Produce** • 172 Church St
- **Groove Merchant** • 687 Haight St
- **Harvest Ranch Market** • 2285 Market St
- **Imaginknit** • 3897 18th St
- **Jack's Record Cellar** • 254 Scott St
- **Karizma** • 213 Church St
- **Katz Bagels** • 663 Haight St
- **L'Occitane** • 556 Castro St
- **Life** • 604 Haight St
- **Mickey's Monkey** • 218 Pierce St
- **Needles and Pens** • 3253 16th St
- **Other Shop** • 327 Divisadero St
- **Out of the Closet** • 100 Church St
- **Plant'It Earth** • 661 Divisadero St
- **Rolo** • 2351 Market St
- **Salon Baobao** • 2041 Market St
- **Sam's Smoke Shop** • 250 Divisadero St
- **Streetlight Records** • 2350 Market St
- **Studio 3579** • 499 Dolores
- **Sui Generis** • 2265 Market St
- **Swirl on Castro** • 572 Castro St
- **Tan Bella** •2185 Market St
- **Tim's Market** • 667 Fillmore St
- **Thorough Bread and Pastry** • 248 Church St
- **Three Twins Ice Cream** •254 Fillmore St
- **Under One Roof** • 518 Castro St
- **Upper Playground** • 220 Fillmore St
- **Wak Shack Salon** • 782 Haight St
- **Zip Zap Hair** • 245 Fillmore St

Video Rental

- **Blockbuster** • 160 Church St
- **Castro Video** • 525 Castro St
- **Gramophone Video & DVD** • 2095 Market St
- **Naked Eye News & Video** • 607 Haight St
- **Superstar Satellite** • 474 Castro St

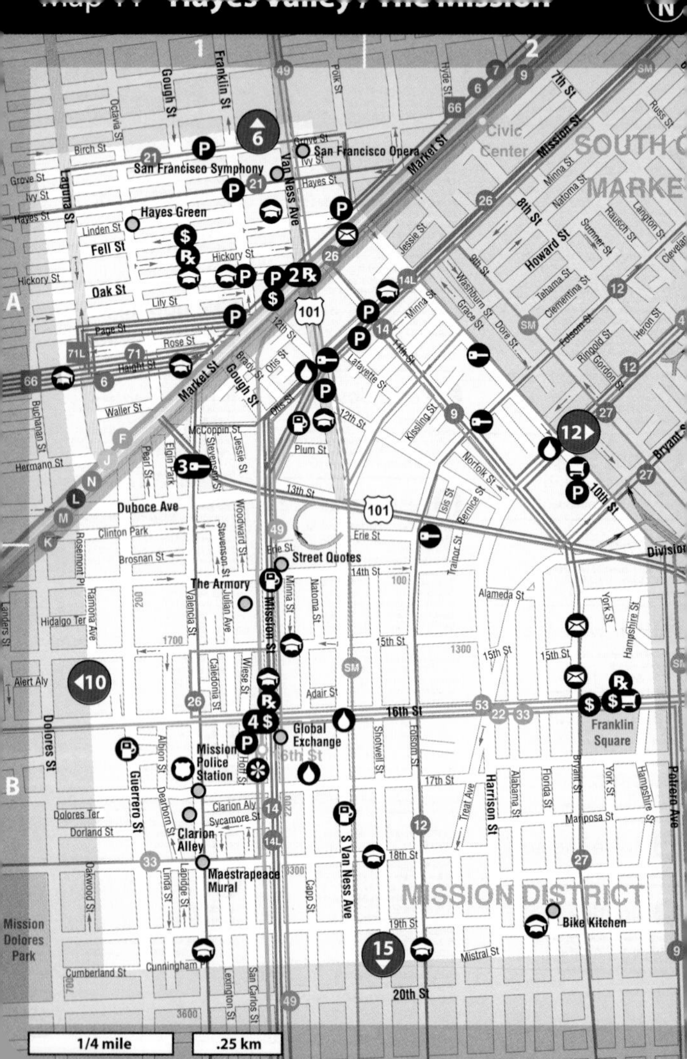
San Francisco Symphony
San Francisco Opera
Hayes Green
Civic Center
SOUTH OF MARKET
Street Quotes
The Armory
Global Exchange
Mission Police Station
Clarion Alley
Maestrapeace Mural
MISSION DISTRICT
Bike Kitchen
Franklin Square
Mission Dolores Park
Market St
Mission St
Van Ness Ave
S Van Ness Ave
Gough St
Franklin St
Octavia St
Laguna St
Buchanan St
Dolores St
Guerrero St
Valencia St
Howard St
Folsom St
Harrison St
Bryant St
Potrero Ave
Duboce Ave
16th St
20th St
1/4 mile
.25 km

's two great neighborhoods in one—slightly more fashionable Hayes alley to the north of Market and the beginning of the Mission to the outh. This area has tons of mass transit, highway on/off ramps, festivals, arades, old buildings, new lofts, and everything else thrown in. You won't e bored.

Banks

Bank of America • 1525 Market St
Bank of America (ATM) • 2017 Mission St
Chase • 2300 16th St
Mission National • 3060 16th St
Pacific National Bank • 2001 Mission St
US (ATM) • Walgreens • 300 Gough St
Wells Fargo • 2300 16th St
Wells Fargo • 3027 16th St

Car Rental

Alamo • 150 Valencia St
Bargain Rent-A-Car • 1748 Folsom St
Enterprise • 1480 Folsom St
Enterprise • 1600 Mission St
Hertz • 241 10th St
National • 150 Valencia St
Specialty Car Rentals • 150 Valencia St

Car Washes

Auto City Brushless Car Wash • 505 S Van Ness Ave
Oscar's Auto Detail • 145 Capp St
Tenth & Harrison Car Wash • 1394 Harrison St
Tower Hand Car Wash • 1601 Mission St

Community Gardens

Gas Stations

Arco • 1798 Mission St
Chevron • 1601 Mission St
Gas and Shop • 599 S Van Ness Ave
Shell • 400 Guerrero St

Landmarks

The Armory • 1800 Mission St
Bike Kitchen • 650 Florida St
Clarion Alley • 17th St & Valencia St
Global Exchange • 2017 Mission St
Hayes Green • Octavia Blvd b/w Hayes St & Fell St
Maestrapeace Mural • 18th St & Valencia St
Mission Police Station • 630 Valencia St
San Francisco Opera • 301 Van Ness Ave
San Francisco Symphony • 201 Van Ness Ave
Street Quotes • 14th St & Mission St

Parking

Pharmacies

- **Rite Aid** • 1496 Market St
- **Safeway** • 2300 16th St ㉔
- **Walgreens** • 1979 Mission St
- **Walgreens** • 300 Gough St

Police

- **Mission Police Station** • 630 Valencia St

Post Offices

- **Bryant Street Station** • 1600 Bryant St
- **Fox Plaza Finance Station** • 1390 Market St
- **Potrero Retail Store** • 1655 Bryant St

Schools

- **Bay High** • 1950 Mission St
- **California Institute of Integral Studies** • 1453 Mission St
- **Chinese American International** • 150 Oak St
- **French American International** • 150 Oak St
- **John O'Connell Alternative High** • 2355 Folsom St
- **Marshall Elementary** • 1575 15th St
- **Mission Language & Vocational** • 2929 19th St
- **New College of California** • 777 Valencia St
- **San Francisco Conservatory of Music** • 50 Oak St
- **San Francisco Law** • 20 Haight St
- **St Charles** • 3250 18th St
- **The Walden School** • 214 Haight St

Supermarkets

- **Costco** • 450 10th St
- **Safeway** • 2300 16th St
- **Ted's Market** •1530 Howard St

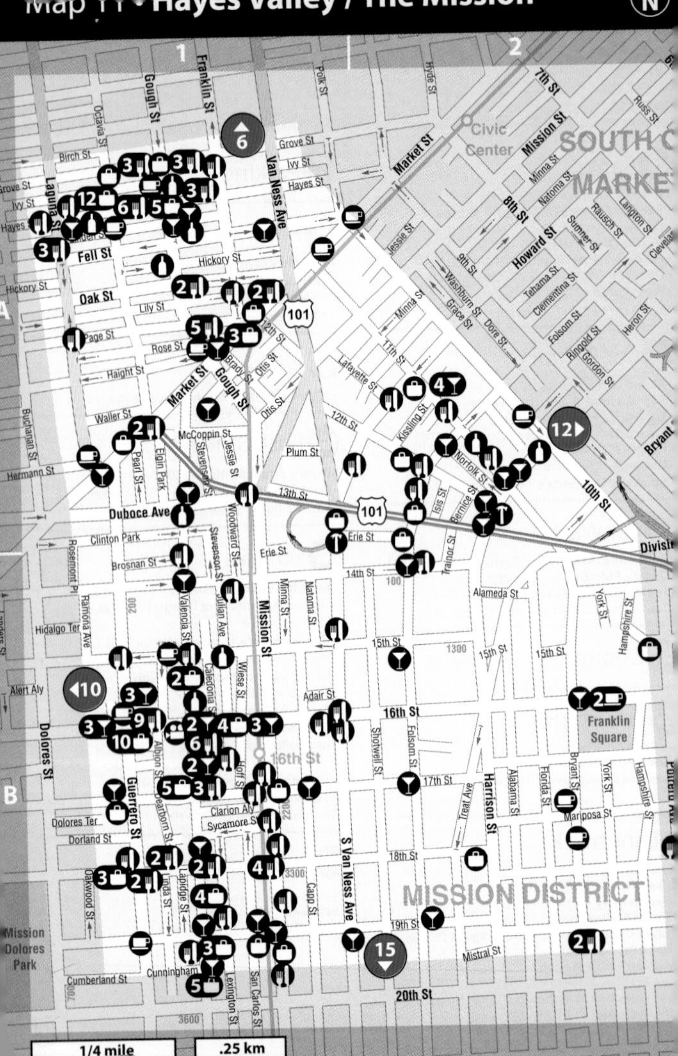

Map 11 • Hayes Valley / The Mission
N
1
2
A
B
Franklin St
Gough St
Octavia St
Polk St
Hyde St
7th St
Russ St
Civic Center
Mission St
SOUTH OF MARKET
Market St
Grove St
Ivy St
Hayes St
Birch St
Laguna St
Van Ness Ave
Minna St
Natoma St
8th St
Langton St
Rausch St
Sumner St
Cleveland
Jessie St
Howard St
9th St
Tehama St
Clementina St
Fell St
Hickory St
Washburn St
Grace St
Dore St
Folsom St
Ringold St
Heron St
Gordon St
Oak St
Lily St
101
12th St
Page St
Rose St
Brady St
Otis St
Lafayette St
11th St
Haight St
Buchanan St
Waller St
McCoppin St
Kissling St
Bryant
Hermann St
Pearl St
Elgin Park
Stevenson St
Jessie St
Plum St
Norfolk St
10th St
13th St
Isis St
Bernice St
Duboce Ave
Woodward St
Erie St
Division
Clinton Park
Rosemont Pl
Brosnan St
Trainor St
14th St
Alameda St
York St
Hampshire St
Hidalgo Ter
Ramona Ave
Valencia St
Julian Ave
Mission St
Minna St
Natoma St
15th St
1300
Alert Aly
Caledonia St
Wiese St
Adair St
16th St
Franklin Square
Dolores St
Albion St
16th St
Hoff St
Shotwell St
Folsom St
Guerrero St
Dearborn St
17th St
Harrison St
Alabama St
Florida St
Bryant St
York St
Hampshire St
Potrero Ave
Clarion Aly
Sycamore St
Treat Ave
Dolores Ter
Dorland St
Mariposa St
S Van Ness Ave
18th St
Oakwood St
Lapidge St
Linda St
3300
Capp St
MISSION DISTRICT
Mission Dolores Park
19th St
Mistral St
Cunningham
Cumberland St
Lexington St
San Carlos St
20th St
3600
1/4 mile
.25 km

You'll never go hungry, whether you've got $5 or $500 to spend on food—everything from Pancho Villa and Limon to Delfina and Slow Club and dozens of places in between. Shopping is equally stellar—from the fashionable shops on Hayes to Valencia institutions such as 826 Valencia, Paxton Gate, and Good Vibrations.

Coffee

- **Blue Bottle Coffee Co.** • 315 Linden St
- **Café La Vie** •514 Octavia St
- **Caffe Trieste** • 1667 Market St
- **Cafico Café** • 1475 Market St
- **Capricorn Coffees & Teas** • 353 10th St
- **Coffee Bar** • 1890 Bryant St
- **Four Barrel Coffee** • 375 Valencia St
- **It's Tops Coffee Shop** • 1801 Market St
- **Java Supreme** • 703 Guerrero St
- **Muddy Waters Coffee House** • 521 Valencia St
- **Peet's** • 2300 16th St
- **Starbucks** • 1390 Market St
- **Starbucks** • 2300 16th St
- **Starbucks** • 2727 Mariposa St

Hardware Stores

- **City Door & Hardware** • 165 13th St
- **Post Tool** • 245 S Van Ness Ave

Liquor Stores

- **Arlequin Wine Merchant** • 384 Hayes St
- **Fred's Liquor & Delicatessen** • 200 Valencia St
- **Garage Café** • 320 11th St
- **K&H Liquors** • 501 Valencia St
- **True Sake** • 560 Hayes St
- **Victoria Liquors & Sandwiches** • 201 Gough St
- **Wines Of California Gifts** • 415 10th St

Movie Theaters

- **Roxie Theater** • 3117 16th St

Nightlife

- **500 Club** • 500 Guerrero St
- **Absinthe** • 398 Hayes St
- **Amnesia** • 853 Valencia St
- **Beauty Bar** • 2299 Mission St
- **Bender's Bar and Grill** • 806 S Van Ness Ave
- **Blondie's Bar and No Grill** • 540 Valencia St
- **Butter** • 354 11th St
- **Casanova Lounge** • 527 Valencia St
- **Cav** • 1666 Market St
- **Dalva** • 3121 16th St
- **Delirium** • 3139 16th St
- **DNA Lounge** • 375 11th St
- **Double Dutch** • 3192 16th St
- **Double Play** • 2401 16th St
- **The Eagle Tavern** • 398 12th St
- **Elbo Room** • 647 Valencia St
- **Elixir** • 3200 16th St
- **Esta Noche** • 3079 16th St
- **Gestalt Haus** • 3159 16th St
- **Homestead** • 2301 Folsom St
- **Kilowatt** • 3160 16th St
- **Lexington Club** • 3464 19th St
- **Little Baobab** • 3388 19th St
- **Marlena's** • 488 Hayes St
- **Martuni's** • 4 Valencia St
- **Nihon Whiskey Lounge** • 1779 Folsom St
- **Orbit Room** • 1900 Market St
- **Phoenix Bar** • 811 Valencia St
- **Place Pigalle** • 520 Hayes St
- **Rickshaw Stop** • 155 Fell St
- **Rite Spot Cafe** • 2099 Folsom St
- **Roxie Theater** • 3117 16th St
- **Skylark** • 3089 16th St
- **Slim's** • 333 11th St
- **Sugar Lounge** • 377 Hayes St
- **Thieves Tavern** • 496 14th St
- **Truck** • 1900 Folsom St
- **Uptown** • 200 Capp St
- **Wish Bar & Lounge** • 1539 Folsom St
- **Zeitgeist** • 199 Valencia St

Restaurants

- **Absinthe** • 398 Hayes St
- **Andalu** • 3198 16th St
- **Arinell Pizza** • 509 Valencia St
- **Bar Jules** • 609 Hayes St
- **Bar Tartine** • 561 Valencia St
- **Basil Canteen** • 1489 Folsom St
- **Big Lantern** • 3170 16th St
- **Big Nate's Barbeque** • 1665 Folsom St
- **Blowfish Sushi** • 2170 Bryant St
- **Blue Muse** • 370 Grove St
- **Bodhi Vietnamese Cuisine** • 211 Valencia St
- **Burger Joint** • 807 Valencia St
- **Caffe Delle Stelle** • 395 Hayes St
- **Canto do Brasil** • 41 Franklin St
- **Cav** • 1666 Market St
- **Cha Cha Cha** • 2327 Mission St
- **Cha-Ya** • 762 Valencia St
- **Charanga** • 2351 Mission St
- **Chez Spencer** • 82 14th St
- **Christopher Elbow Chocolates** • 401 Hayes St
- **La Cumbre** • 515 Valencia St
- **DeLessio Market** • 1695 Market St
- **Delfina** • 3621 18th St
- **Destino** • 1815 Market St
- **Domo** • 511 Laguna St
- **Double Decker** • 465 Grove St
- **El Toro Taqueria** • 598 Valencia St
- **Espetus Churrascaria** • 1686 Market St
- **Farina** • 3560 18th St
- **Flipper's** • 482 Hayes St
- **Frjtz** • 581 Hayes St
- **Go Getters Pizza** • 69 Gough St
- **Hayes Street Grill** • 320 Hayes St
- **Hotel Biron** • 45 Rose St
- **Irma's Pampanga Restaurant** • 2901 16th St
- **It's Tops Coffee Shop** • 1801 Market St
- **Jardiniere** • 300 Grove St
- **Kenny's Restaurant** • 518 S Van Ness Ave
- **La Oaxaquena** • 2128 Mission St
- **Limon** • 524 Valencia St
- **Little Star Pizza** • 400 Valencia St
- **Luna Park** • 694 Valencia St
- **Manora's Thai Cuisine** • 1600 Folsom St
- **Maverick** • 3316 17th St
- **Minako** • 2154 Mission St
- **Moisehe's Pippic** • 425A Hayes St
- **Momi Toby's Revolution Café** • 528 Laguna St
- **The Monk's Kettle** • 3141 16th St
- **Pakwan** • 3182 16th St
- **Pancho Villa Taqueria** • 3071 16th St
- **Paramount Piroshki** • 585 Potrero Ave
- **Patxi's Chicago Pizza** • 511 Hayest St
- **paul k** • 199 Gough St
- **Pauline's Pizza and Wine Bar** • 260 Valencia St
- **Picaro** • 3120 16th St
- **Pizzeria Delfina** • 3611 18th St
- **Poc Chuc** • 2886 16th St
- **Pork Store Café** • 3122 16th St
- **Range** • 842 Valencia St
- **The Sage Cafe** • 340 Grove St
- **Samovar Tea Lounge** • 297 Page St
- **Slow Club** • 2501 Mariposa St
- **Stacks'** • 501 Hayes St
- **Sunflower Restaurant** • 3111 16th St
- **Suppenkuche** • 525 Laguna St
- **Suriya Thai Restaurant** • 1532 Howard St
- **Sushi Groove South** • 1516 Folsom St
- **Taqueria Cancun** • 2288 Mission St
- **Taqueria El Buen Sabor** • 699 Valencia St
- **Tartine Bakery** • 600 Guerrero St
- **Tartine Café Francais** • 244 Gough St
- **Thrill of the Grill** • 535 Valencia St
- **Tokyo Go Go** • 3174 16th St
- **Truly Mediterranean** • 3109 16th St
- **Universal Café** • 2814 19th St
- **Walzwerk** • 381 S Van Ness Ave
- **What's Up Dog!** • 1599 Howard St
- **Woodward's Garden** • 1700 Mission St
- **Yamo** • 3406 18th St
- **Zuni Café** • 1658 Market St

Shopping

- **ADS Hats** • 418 Valencia St
- **Alla Prima Lingerie** • 539 Hayes St
- **Amore Animal Supply** • 696 Valencia St
- **The Apartment** • 3469 18th St
- **Arlequin Wine Merchant** • 384 Hayes St
- **Artist Xchange** • 3169 16th St
- **Azalea Boutique** • 411 Hayes St
- **Bell Jar** • 3187 16th St
- **Bi-Rite Market** • 3639 18th St
- **Black and Blue Tattoo** • 381 Guerrero St
- **Bombay Ice Creamery** • 552 Valencia St
- **Botanica Yoruba** • 3423 19th St
- **British American Imports** • 726 15th St
- **Bulo** • 418 Hayes St
- **Candystore Collective** • 3153 16th St
- **Chamalyn** • 3491 19th St
- **Claudia Kussano** • 591 Guerrero St
- **Clothes Contact** • 473 Valencia St
- **Community Thrift Store** • 623 Valencia St
- **The Curiosity Shoppe** • 855 Valencia St
- **Currents** • 911 Valencia St
- **Dark Garden** • 321 Linden St
- **DeLessio Market** • 1695 Market St
- **Density** • 593 Valencia St
- **Discount Fabrics** • 201 11th St
- **Dish** • 541 Hayes St
- **Evelyn's** • 2088 Oakdale Ave
- **F. Dorian** • 370 Hayes St
- **Five and Diamond** • 510 Valencia St
- **Flax** • 1699 Market St
- **Flight 001** • 525 Hayes St
- **Gimme Shoes** • 416 Hayes St
- **Good Vibrations** • 603 Valencia St
- **Harrington Galleries** • 599 Valencia St
- **Hideo Wakamatsu** • 563 Valencia St
- **Idol Vintage** • 3162 16th St
- **Katz Bagels** • 3147 16th St
- **La Library** • 380 Guerrero St
- **Lava9** • 542 Hayes St
- **Lavish** • 508 Hayes St
- **Little Otsu** • 849 Valencia St
- **Lost Art Salon** • 245 S Van Ness Ave
- **Martin's 16th Street Emporium** • 3248 16th St
- **Miette** • 449 Octavia St
- **The Mission Statement** • 3458 18th St
- **Mission Thrift** • 2330 Mission St
- **Monument** • 573 Valencia St
- **Multikulti** • 539 Valencia St
- **Nomads** • 556 Hayes St
- **Oxenrose Salon** • 448 Grove St
- **The Painted Lady Tattoo** • 491 Guerrero St
- **Paxton Gate** • 824 Valencia St
- **Paxton Gate's Curiosities For Kids** • 766 Valencia St
- **Propeller** • 555 Hayes St
- **Rainbow Grocery** • 1745 Folsom St
- **The San Francisco Chocolate Factory** • 286 12th St
- **Schauplatz** • 791 Valencia St
- **Self Edge** • 714 Valencia St
- **Seventh Heart** • 1592 Market St
- **Shoe Biz** • 877 Valencia St
- **Soundworks** • 228 Valencia St
- **Sports Authority** • 1690 Folsom St
- **Sunhee Moon** • 3167 16th St
- **Therapy** • 545 Valencia St
- **Thrift Town** • 2101 Mission St
- **Timbuk2** • 506 Hayes St
- **Retrospect Furniture Design** • 1649 Market St
- **True Sake** • 560 Hayes St
- **Weston Wear** • 569 Valencia St
- **Zeni** • 567 Hayes St

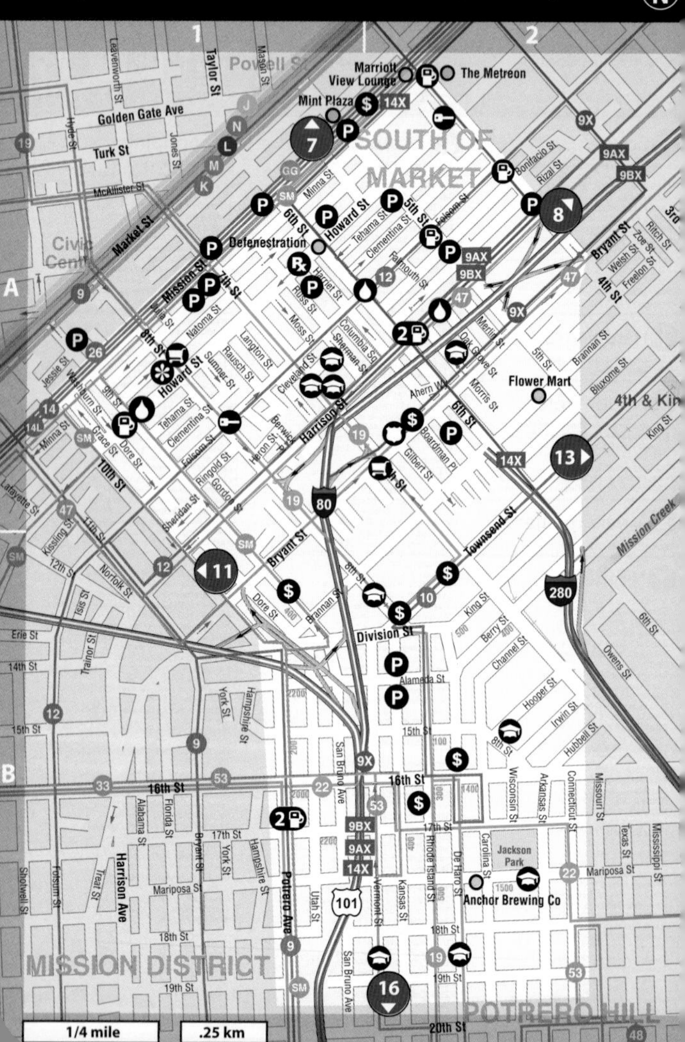

SOUTH OF MARKET
MISSION DISTRICT
POTRERO HILL
Civic Center
Marriott View Lounge
The Metreon
Mint Plaza
Defenestration
Flower Mart
Jackson Park
Anchor Brewing Co
Market St
Mission St
Howard St
Folsom St
Harrison St
Bryant St
Brannan St
Townsend St
King St
Division St
16th St
17th St
18th St
19th St
20th St
Mariposa St
Potrero Ave
Harrison Ave
1/4 mile
.25 km

The not-long-for-this-world witty sculpture "Defenestration," which features a bunch of apartment furniture freeze-framed in mid-suicide, marks a city seam where urban tenements meet industrial glamor. Make a vist to Anchor Brewing headquarters for a glimpse inside a local company that actually still makes amazing beer in small batches.

Banks

- **Bank of America** • 680 8th St
- **Citibank** • 350 Rhode Island St
- **San Francisco Federal CU (ATM)** • 850 Bryant St
- **Union** • 640 Townsend St
- **Wells Fargo** • 555 9th St
- **Wells Fargo (ATM)** • 300 De Haro St
- **Wells Fargo (ATM)** • 833 Mission St

Car Rental

- **Avis** • 821 Howard St
- **Enterprise** • 312 8th St

Car Washes

- **Apex Hand Car Washing and Detailing** • 301 6th St
- **San Francisco Car Wash** • 1298 Howard St

Community Gardens

Gas Stations

- **76** • 401 Potrero Ave
- **76** • 800 Folsom St
- **Chevron** • 1000 Harrison St
- **Chevron** • 1298 Howard St
- **Shell** • 1201 Harrison St
- **Shell** • 300 5th St
- **Shell** • 377 6th St
- **Shell** • 388 Potrero Ave

Landmarks

- **Anchor Brewing Company** • 1705 Mariposa St
- **Defenestration** • 6th St & Howard St
- **Flower Mart** • 640 Brannan St
- **Marriott View Lounge** • 55 4th St
- **The Metreon** • 101 4th St
- **Mint Plaza** • Jessie St & Mint St

Parking

Pharmacies

- **AHF Pharmacy** • 1025 Howard St

Police

- **Southern Police Station** • 850 Bryant St

Schools

- **Bessie Carmichael Elementary** • 375 7th St
- **Bessie Carmichael Elementary** • 55 Sherman St
- **California College of Arts** • 1111 8th St
- **Enola Maxwell Middle** • 655 De Haro St
- **Five Keys Charter** • 70 Oak Grove St
- **International Studies Academy** • 693 Vermont St
- **Life Learning Academy** • 651 8th St
- **Live Oak** • 1555 Mariposa St
- **San Francisco County Special Education** • 1098 Harrison St

Supermarkets

- **Harvest Urban Market** • 191 8th St
- **Trader Joe's** • 555 9th St

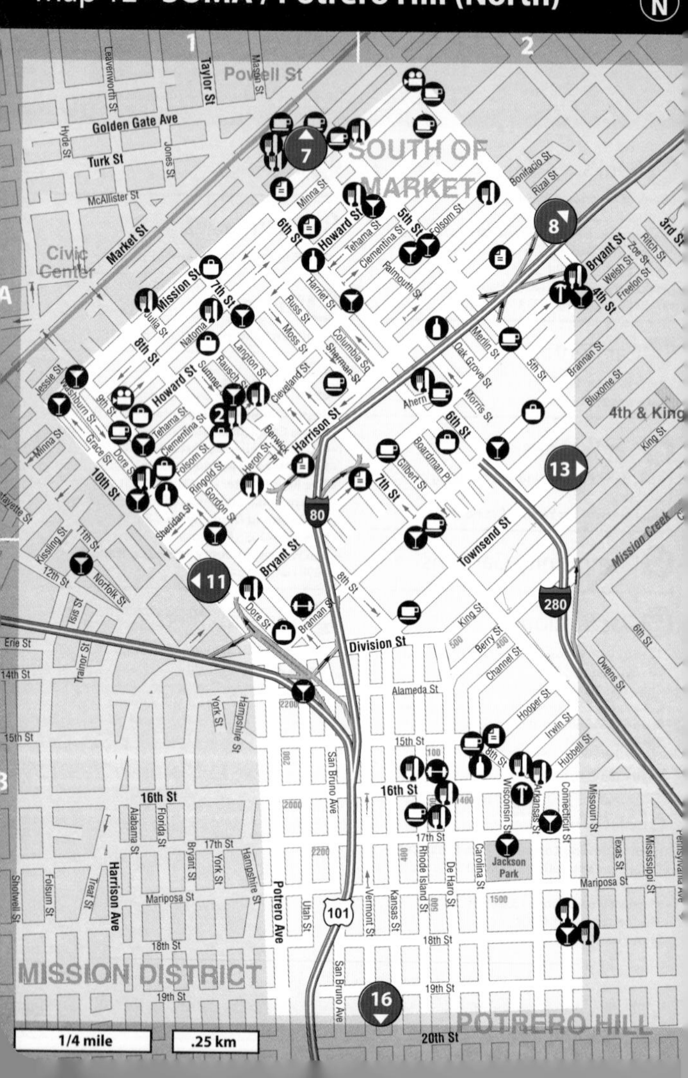

SOUTH OF MARKET
Civic Center
4th & King
MISSION DISTRICT
POTRERO HILL
Jackson Park
1/4 mile
.25 km
Market St
Mission St
Howard St
Folsom St
Harrison St
Bryant St
Brannan St
Townsend St
Division St
16th St
Potrero Ave
Harrison Ave

The sun always shines on the Hill, but the bar scene is better in its shadow. Visit Hotel Utah and channel your inner Barbary Coast longshoreman. Mighty makes industrial space pulsate with beats demanding you get footloose. At the incline to Potrero, shopping gets serious and food becomes cuisine.

Coffee

- **A2 Café** • 1111 8th St
- **Blue Bottle Coffee Co.** • 66 Mint St
- **Café Annalita** • 845 Howard St
- **Caffe Roma Coffee Roasting** • 885 Bryant St
- **Grab N Go** • 480 6th St
- **Java Trading** • 100 5th St
- **Latte Express** • 48 5th St
- **SF Coffee Company** • 70 13th St
- **Starbucks** • 120 4th St
- **Starbucks** • 1298 Howard St
- **Starbucks** • 350 Rhode Island St
- **Starbucks** • 689 Townsend St
- **Susie's Café** • 603 7th St

Copy Shops

- **BPS Reprographic** • 945 Bryant St
- **FedEx Office** • 1155 Harrison St
- **Ford Graphics** • 981 Mission St
- **Graphic Reproduction** • 496 Natoma St
- **Staples** • 855 Harrison St
- **Vogue Graphics** • 1111 8th St

Gyms

- **Gold's Gym** • 1001 Brannan St
- **World Gym Fitness Center** • 290 De Haro St

Hardware Stores

- **Belmont Hardware** • 115 Wisconsin St
- **EM Hundley Hardware** • 617 Bryant St

Liquor Stores

- **Diana Market** • 282 9th St
- **Fred's Liquor & Groceries** • 151 6th St
- **Wine Club** • 953 Harrison St
- **Wine House Limited** • 129 Carolina St

Movie Theaters

- **AMC Loews Metreon 16/IMAX** • 101 4th St
- **San Francisco Cinematheque** • 145 9th St

Nightlife

- **1015 Folsom** • 1015 Folsom St
- **Annie's Social Club** • 917 Folsom St
- **AsiaSF** • 201 9th St
- **Brainwash Cafe & Laundromat** • 1122 Folsom St
- **Cat Club** • 1190 Folsom St
- **The Chieftain Irish Pub** • 198 5th St
- **The City Beer Store & Tasting Bar** • 1168 Folsom St
- **Club 93** • 93 9th St
- **Club 6ix** • 60 6th St
- **Connecticut Yankee** • 100 Connecticut St
- **The Endup** • 401 6th St
- **Hole in the Wall Saloon** • 1369 Folsom St
- **Holy Cow** • 1535 Folsom St
- **Hotel Utah Saloon** • 500 4th St
- **Il Pirata** • 2007 16th St
- **Mars Bar & Restaurant** • 798 Brannan St
- **Mighty** • 119 Utah St
- **Shine** • 1337 Mission St
- **The Stud** • 399 9th St
- **Thee Parkside** • 1600 17th St

Restaurants

- **54 Mint** •16 Mint Plaza
- **AK Subs** • 397 8th St
- **AsiaSF** • 201 9th St
- **Axis Café & Gallery** • 1201 8th St
- **Basil Thai** • 1175 Folsom St
- **Brainwash Café & Laundromat** • 1122 Folsom St
- **Cafe Venue** • 67 5th St
- **Chez Maman** • 1453 18th St
- **Chez Papa** • 4 Mint St
- **The Chieftain Irish Pub** • 198 5th St
- **Custom Burger** • 121 7th St
- **Dos Pinas** • 251 Rhode Island St
- **Goat Hill Pizza** • 300 Connecticut St
- **Grab 'N Go** • 480 6th St
- **Heaven's Dog & Noodle Shop** • 1148 Mission St
- **Henry's Hunan** • 1016 Bryant St
- **Orson** • 508 4th St
- **Out the Door** • 845 Market St
- **Restaurant LuLu** • 816 Folsom St
- **Sally's** • 300 De Haro St
- **Triptych** • 1155 Folsom St
- **What's Up Dog!** • 300 De Haro St
- **Wolfe's Lunch** • 1220 16th St

Shopping

- **Flower Mart** • 640 Brannan St
- **General Bead** • 637 Minna St
- **Off the Wall** • 281 9th St
- **Out of the Closet** • 1295 Folsom St
- **Podesta Baldocchi** • 410 Harriet St
- **REI** • 840 Brannan St
- **SF Design Center** • 2 Henry Adams St
- **Stormy Leather** • 1158 Howard St
- **Trader Joe's** • 555 9th St

South Beach Harbor
China Basin
McCovey Cove
AT&T Park
PAGE 235
Pier 46B
Pier 48C
Pier 48
Mission Rock Terminal
CalTrain Depot
4th & King
Mission Rock
MISSION BAY
UCSF Mission Bay
Mariposa
POTRERO HILL
House featured in the movie Pacific Heights
Pier 52
Pier 54
Pier 64
Central Basin
Pier 68
Port of SF Northern Cargo Terminals
Mission Creek
Brannan St
Bluxome St
Townsend St
4th St
3rd St
King St
5th St
Berry St
Channel St
China Basin St
Mission Rock St
Owens St
6th St
7th St
Illinois St
Michigan St
Alameda St
El Dorado St
16th St
17th St
Mariposa St
18th St
19th St
20th St
Hubbell St
Daggett St
Missouri St
Texas St
Mississippi St
Pennsylvania Ave
Iowa St
Indiana St
Minnesota St
Tennessee St
1/4 mile
.25 km

Besides Giants fans that frequent AT&T Park, blame area congestion on Caltrain comings and goings. Either end of the neighborhood can offer noshing opportunities or shopping. Better yet, explore the piers that penetrate South Beach Harbor. Some are commercial docks, while others house hidden gems.

Banks

- **Bank of America** • 501 Brannan St
- **Bank of America (ATM)** • 24 Willie Mays Plaza
- **US (ATM)** • Walgreens • 670 4th St
- **Washington Mutual** • 255 King St
- **Wells Fargo** • 286 King St
- **Wells Fargo** • 490 Brannan St
- **Wells Fargo (ATM)** • 737 3rd St

Landmarks

- **AT&T Park** • 24 Willie Mays Plaza
- **House featured in the movie Pacific Heights** • 1243 19th St

Libraries

- **Mission Bay Branch Library** • 960 4th St

Parking

Pharmacies

- **Safeway** • 298 King St
- **Walgreens** • 670 4th St

Schools

- **University of Phoenix** • 185 Berry St
- **Webster Elementary** • 465 Missouri St

Supermarkets

- **Safeway** • 298 King St

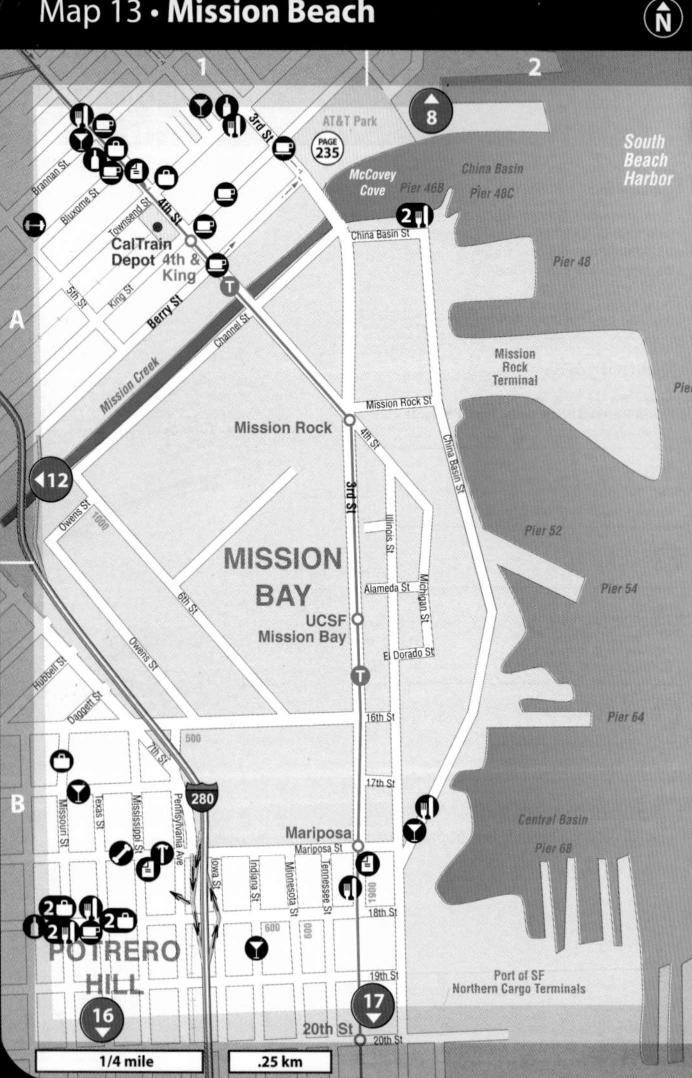
N
1
2
AT&T Park
8
PAGE 235
South Beach Harbor
China Basin
McCovey Cove
Pier 46B
Pier 48C
China Basin St
Pier 48
3rd St
4th St
Brannan St
Bluxome St
Townsend St
CalTrain Depot
4th & King
5th St
King St
Berry St
Channel St
A
Mission Creek
Mission Rock Terminal
Mission Rock St
Mission Rock
12
Owens St
1000
MISSION BAY
6th St
Illinois St
Pier 52
Alameda St
Michigan St
Pier 54
UCSF Mission Bay
El Dorado St
Owens St
Hubbell St
Daggett St
16th St
Pier 64
500
7th St
17th St
280
B
Missouri St
Texas St
Mississippi St
Pennsylvania Ave
Central Basin
Mariposa
Mariposa St
Pier 68
Iowa St
Indiana St
Minnesota St
Tennessee St
1900
18th St
POTRERO HILL
600
19th St
Port of SF Northern Cargo Terminals
16
17
20th St
1/4 mile
.25 km

Oenophiles can breathe a sigh of relief if they ever find themselves sober in this neck of the woods. Between K&L's wall to wall bottle selection and Ruby Wine's boutique finds, there's room to tempt temperance and then some.

Coffee

- **Borders** • 200 King St
- **Farley's** • 1315 18th St
- **Latte Express** • 648 4th St
- **Philz Coffee** • 201 Berry St
- **Starbucks** • Safeway • 298 King St
- **Starbucks** • 490 Brannan St

Copy Shops

- **Copyworld** • 2001 3rd St
- **Direct Mail Center** • 1099 Mariposa St
- **The UPS Store** • 660 4th St

Gyms

- **San Francisco Tennis Club** • 645 5th St

Hardware Stores

- **Center Hardware & Supply** • 999 Mariposa St

Liquor Stores

- **K&L Wine Merchants** • 638 4th St
- **Ruby Wine** • 1419 18th St
- **Third & Townsend Liquor** • 698 3rd St

Nightlife

- **330 Ritch** • 360 Ritch St
- **Bottom of the Hill** • 1233 17th St
- **Café Cocomo** • 650 Indiana St
- **The Ramp** • 855 Terry Francois St

Pet Shops

- **Pawtrero Hill Bathhouse & Feed** • 199 Mississippi St

Restaurants

- **Aperto** • 1434 18th St
- **Chez Papa Bistrot** • 1401 18th St
- **Fringale** • 570 4th St
- **Hazel's Kitchen** • 1319 18th St
- **Moshi Moshi** • 2092 3rd St
- **Primo Patio Café** • 214 Townsend St
- **The Ramp** • 855 Terry Francois St

Shopping

- **Arch** • 99 Missouri St
- **Bell and Trunk Flowers** • 1411 18th St
- **Christopher's Books** • 1400 18th St
- **Collage Gallery** • 1345 18th St
- **K&L Wine Merchants** • 638 4th St
- **Limn** • 290 Townsend St
- **Ruby Wine** • 1419 18th St

NOE VALLEY
DIAMOND HEIGHTS
Dolores Park
Glen Canyon Park
Sparky
PAGE 212
10
15
29
32
Castro St
Market St
Noe St
Church St
Dolores St
24th St
Clipper St
30th St
Diamond Heights Blvd
Sanchez St
Diamond St
Douglass St
Eureka St
Hoffman Ave
Grand View Ave
Alvarado St
Elizabeth St
Jersey St
25th St
26th St
Army St
27th St
Duncan St
28th St
Valley St
29th St
Day St
20th St
Liberty St
21st St
Hill St
22nd St
23rd St
18th St
19th St
17th St
Cumberland St
Hancock St
Ford St
Chula Ln
Dolores Ter
Dorland St
Vicksburg St
Comerford St
1/4 mile
.25 km

Protected from the fog by Twin Peaks on one side and the Mission on the other, Noe Valley's clear weather and nicer homes attract a proud population of young families, lesbians, and well-heeled ex-hippies. The Noe Valley Voice dishes out the inside scoop on the neighborhood.

Banks

- **Bank of America** • 4098 24th St
- **Chase** • 3998 24th St
- **Sterling** • 3800 24th St
- **Wells Fargo** • 4045 24th St

Community Gardens

Landmarks

- **Sparky** • 20th St & Church St

Libraries

- **Noe Valley Branch Library** • 451 Jersey St

Pharmacies

- **Rx Unlimited Pharmacy** • 3895 22nd St
- **Walgreens** • 1333 Castro St

Post Offices

- **Noe Valley** • 4083 24th St

Schools

- **Alvarado Elementary** • 625 Douglass St
- **CCSF (Castro/Valencia Campus)** • 1220 Noe St
- **Edison Charter Academy** • 3531 22nd St
- **Eureka Learning Center** • 464 Diamond St
- **Immaculate Conception Academy** • 3625 24th St
- **James Lick Middle** • 1220 Noe St
- **St James** • 321 Fair Oaks St
- **St Philip's** • 665 Elizabeth St

NOE VALLEY
DIAMOND HEIGHTS
Dolores Park
Glen Canyon Park
Market St
Castro St
24th St
Noe St
Church St
Dolores St
Clipper St
Diamond Heights Blvd
1/4 mile
.25 km

You should be able to find everything you need on either 24th Avenue or Church Street. Highlights include the farmers market, Tuggey's Hardware, PlumpJack Wines, Bliss Bar, Savor (brunch), Lovejoy's Tea Room, and Noe Valley Bakery. It's all good.

Coffee

- **Bernie's Coffee** • 3966 24th St
- **Lovejoy's Tea Room** • 1351 Church St
- **Luv A Java** • 1300 Dolores St
- **Martha & Bros** • 1551 Church St
- **Martha & Bros** • 3868 24th St
- **Starbucks** • 3995 24th St
- **Tully's Coffee** • 3966 24th St

Copy Shops

- **Jensen's Mail & Copy** • 5214 Diamond Heights Blvd

Farmers Markets

- **Noe Valley (Sat, 8am—1pm)** • 24th St & Sanchez St

Gyms

- **24 Hour Fitness** • 3800 24th St
- **Purely Physical Fitness** • 1300 Church St

Hardware Stores

- **Tuggey's Hardware** • 3885 24th St

Liquor Stores

- **J&J Grocery & Liquor** • 3751 24th St
- **Mama's Market** • 3500 22nd St
- **PlumpJack Wines** • 4011 24th St
- **Shufat Market** • 3807 24th St
- **St Clair Liquors** • 3900 24th St

Nightlife

- **Bliss Bar** • 4026 24th St
- **The Dubliner** • 3838 24th St
- **Noe's Bar** • 1199 Church St
- **Valley Tavern** • 4054 24th St

Pet Shops

- **Animal Company** • 4298 24th St
- **Noe Valley Pet** • 1451 Church St

Restaurants

- **Barney's Gourmet Hamburger** • 4138 24th St
- **Chloe's Café** • 1399 Church st
- **Fattoush** • 1361 Church St
- **Firefly** • 4288 24th St
- **Fresca** • 3945 24th St
- **Hamano Sushi** • 1332 Castro St
- **Happy Donuts** • 3801 24th St
- **Incanto** • 1550 Church St
- **Le Zinc** • 4063 24th St
- **Lovejoy's Tea Room** • 1351 Church St
- **Pasta Pomodoro** • 4000 24th St
- **Ristorante Bacco** • 737 Diamond St
- **Savor** • 3913 24th St

Shopping

- **24th Street Cheese Company** • 3893 24th St
- **Ambiance** • 3985 24th St
- **Apple Blossom** • 1303 Castro St
- **Astrid's Rabat Shoes** • 3909 24th St
- **Church Nails** •1211 Church St
- **Flowers of the Valley** • 4077 24th St
- **French Tulip** • 3903 24th St
- **Holey Bagel** • 3872 24th St
- **Joshua Simon** • 3915 24th St
- **Just for Fun** • 3982 24th St
- **Lehr's German Specialties** • 1581 Church St
- **Noe Valley Bakery** • 4073 24th St
- **Noe Valley Pet** • 1451 Church St
- **Omnivore Books on Food** • 3885 Cesar Chavez St
- **PlumpJack Wines** • 4011 24th St
- **Rabat** • 4001 24th St
- **See Jane Run** • 3910 24th St
- **Shoe Biz** • 3810 24th St
- **Wink SF** • 4107 24th St
- **Xela Imports** • 3925 24th St

Video Rental

- **Noe Valley Video** • 3936 24th St
- **Video Wave of Noe Valley** • 1431 Castro St

MISSION DISTRICT
16th St
17th St
18th St
19th St
20th St
21st St
22nd St
23rd St
24th St
25th St
26th St
Cesar Chavez St
Guerrero St
Valencia St
Mission St
S Van Ness Ave
Harrison St
Potrero Ave
Dolores St
Balmy Alley
Garfield Square
Precita Ave
Bernal Heights Park
1/4 mile
.25 km

One of the city's sunniest neighborhoods is also one of its most diverse, as post-college neophytes rub shoulders with recent Latin American immigrants. Mission Street is a corridor of cheap taquerias and stores selling an array of random goods. One block over, Valencia Street brims with coffee shops, bookstores, fusion restaurants, and a vibrant nightlife.

Banks

- **Bank of America** • 2701 Mission St
- **Bank of America (ATM)** • 2850 24th St
- **Bank of the West** • 2812 Mission St
- **Chase** • 2900 Mission St
- **Mission National** • 2773 Mission St
- **US** • 2601 Mission St
- **Wells Fargo** • 2595 Mission St

Community Gardens

Gas Stations

- **American Gas** • 2831 Cesar Chavez

Landmarks

- **Balmy Alley** • Balmy St b/w 24th & 25th St

Libraries

- **Mission Branch Library** • 300 Bartlett St

Parking

Pharmacies

- **A-G Pharmacy** • 3636 Cesar Chavez
- **Community Pharmacy** • 2462 Mission St
- **Farmacia Remedios** • 2400 Mission St
- **Internacional-Farmacia** • 2481 Mission St
- **Walgreens** • 2690 Mission St

Post Offices

- **CPU World Pioneer** • 2830 24th St
- **Mission Station** • 1198 S Van Ness Ave

Schools

- **Bryant** • 1050 York St
- **CCSF (Mission Campus)** • 160 Bartlett St
- **Cesar Chavez** • 825 Shotwell St
- **Downtown High** • 110 Bartlett St
- **Flynn Elementary** • 3125 Cesar Chavez
- **George R Moscone Elementary** • 2576 Harrison St
- **Hilltop** • 1325 Florida St
- **Horace Mann Middle** • 3351 23rd St
- **Katherine Michiels** • 1335 Guerrero St
- **Leadership Public Schools Oakland** • 2601 Mission St
- **Sand Paths Academy** • 1218 S Van Ness Ave
- **St Peter's Parish** • 1266 Florida St
- **Synergy Elementary** • 1387 Valencia St

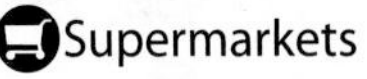

Supermarkets

- **Delano's IGA** • 1245 S Van Ness Ave

MISSION DISTRICT
16th St
17th St
18th St
19th St
20th St
21st St
22nd St
23rd St
24th St
25th St
26th St
Cesar Chavez St
Army St
27th St
Duncan St
28th St
Valley St
29th St
Guerrero St
Valencia St
Mission St
S Van Ness Av
Harrison St
Potrero Ave
Dolores St
Dolores Ter
Dorland St
Albion St
Dearborn St
Oakwood St
Cumberland St
Liberty St
Hill St
Alvarado St
Quane St
Ames St
San Jose Ave
Elizabeth St
Fair Oaks St
Poplar St
Juri St
Orange Aly
Bartlett St
Osage Aly
Lilac St
Capp St
Cypress St
Virgil St
Shotwell St
Horace St
Folsom St
Lucky St
Treat Ave
Balmy St
Alabama St
Florida St
Bryant St
York St
Hampshire St
Utah St
Mariposa St
Mistral St
Brice Ter
Garfield Square
Precita Ave
Bessie St
Mirabel Ave
Montezuma St
Manchester St
Aztec St
Stoneman St
Norwich St
Powers Ave
Coso Ave
Fair Ave
Peters Ave
Coleridge St
Lundys Ln
Prospect Ave
Bonview St
Esmeralda Ave
Bernal Hts Blvd
Ripley St
Bernal Heights Park
Tiffany Ave
Mullen Ave
Montcalm St
Rutledge St
Massasoit St
Samoset St
Brewster St
Costa St
Faith St
Joy St
Peralta Ave
Macedonia St
Holladay Ave
Wright
1/4 mile
.25 km

Taquerias proliferate here, with 24th Street hosting some of the best in the city, including El Farolito (open very late) and El Tonayense. Coffee is huge here, too; try Ritual, Sugarlump, and Atlas. Aquarius Records and Dog Eared Books are de rigueur shopping. Humphry Slocombe is ice cream heaven.

Coffee

- **Atlas Café** • 3049 20th St
- **Café La Boheme** • 3318 24th St
- **Café La Taza** • 2475 Mission St
- **Javalencia** • 920 Valencia St
- **Jump Start Coffee & Grocery** • 1192 Guerrero St
- **Little Spot Café** • 1199 S Van Ness Ave
- **Medjool** • 2522 Mission St
- **Mission Creek Café** • 968 Valencia St
- **Muddy's Coffee House** • 1304 Valencia St
- **Paisanos Café** • 3017 Mission St
- **Philz Coffee** • 3101 24th St
- **Progressive Grounds** • 2301 Bryant St
- **Ritual Coffee** • 1026 Valencia St
- **Sugarlump Coffee** • 2862 24th St
- **Sweet Chinito Coffee** • 3100 Mission St

Hardware Stores

- **House of Color** • 2850 24th St
- **Workingman's Headquarters** • 2871 Mission St

Liquor Stores

- **ABC Market** • 2801 Bryant St
- **Ed & Danny's Market & Liquor** • 999 S Van Ness Ave
- **Garcia Liquor** • 2592 Mission St
- **Lucca Ravioli** • 1100 Valencia St
- **Mike's Liquors & Groceries** • 2499 Mission St
- **P&S Liquor Store** • 3100 24th St
- **Red Dragon Liquors** • 2397 Mission St
- **Samy's Liquor & Groceries** • 2847 24th St
- **That's It Market** • 2699 Mission St
- **Tony' s Market and Liquor** • 2751 24th St

Movie Theaters

- **Foreign Cinema** • 2534 Mission St

Nightlife

- **The Attic Club** • 3336 24th St
- **Bluesix** • 3043 24th St
- **Bruno's** • 2389 Mission St
- **Dirty Thieves** • 3050 24th St
- **Doc's Clock** • 2575 Mission St
- **Dovre Club** • 1498 Valencia St
- **Foreign Cinema** • 2534 Mission St
- **Latin American Club** • 3286 22nd St
- **The Liberties** • 998 Guerrero St
- **Lone Palm** • 3394 22nd St
- **Make-Out Room** • 3225 22nd St
- **Medjool** • 2522 Mission St
- **Mission Bar** • 2695 Mission St
- **Phone Booth** • 1398 S Van Ness Ave
- **Pop's** • 2800 24th St
- **The Red Poppy Art House** • 2698 Folsom St
- **Savanna Jazz** • 2937 Mission St

Restaurants

- **Atlas Café** • 3049 20th St
- **Big Mouth Burger** • 3392 24th St
- **Boogaloo's** • 3296 22nd St
- **Buffalo Exchange** • 1210 Valencia St
- **Café Gratitude** • 2400 Harrison St
- **Dosa** • 995 Valencia St
- **Dynamo Donuts** • 2760 24th St
- **El Farolito** • 2779 Mission St
- **El Mahajual** • 1142 Valencia St
- **El Metate** • 2406 Bryant St
- **El Nuevo Fruitilandia** • 3077 24th St
- **El Tonayense** • 3150 24th St
- **El Valenciano Restaurant and Bar** • 1153 Valencia St
- **flour + water** • 2401 Harrison St
- **Foreign Cinema** • 2534 Mission St
- **Garcon** • 1101 Valencia St
- **Herbivore** • 983 Valencia St
- **Jay's Cheesesteak** • 3285 21st St
- **La Taqueria** • 2889 Mission St
- **La Taqueria Guadalajara** • 3146 24th St
- **Lolo** • 3230 22nd St
- **Los Jarritos** • 901 S Van Ness Ave
- **Medjool** • 2522 Mission St
- **Mission Pie** • 2901 Mission St
- **Old Jerusalem Restaurant** • 2976 Mission St
- **Papalote** • 3409 24th St
- **Pete's Barbeque** • 2399 Mission St
- **Phat Philly** • 3388 24th St
- **Revolution Café** • 3248 22nd St
- **Roosevelt's Tamale Parlor** • 2817 24th St
- **Schmidt's** • 2400 Folsom St
- **Serrano's Pizza** • 3274 21st St
- **Sidewalk Juice** • 3287 21st St
- **St Francis Fountain** • 2801 24th St
- **Tao Café** • 1000 Guerrero St
- **Udupi Palace** •1007 Valencia St
- **Velvet Cantina** • 3349 23rd St

Shopping

- **Aquarius Records** • 1055 Valencia St
- **Back to the Picture** • 934 Valencia St
- **Casa Bonampak** • 1051 Valencia St
- **Casa Lucas Market** • 2934 24th St
- **Dema** • 1038 Valencia St
- **Dianda's Italian American Pastry** • 2883 Mission St
- **Dog Eared Books** • 900 Valencia St
- **Dynamo Donuts** • 2760 24th St
- **Encantada Gallery** • 908 Valencia St
- **Fabric 8** • 3318 22nd St
- **Gypsy Honeymoon** • 3599 24th St
- **Hair Candy Salon** • 3387 22nd St
- **House of Hengst** • 924 Valencia St
- **Humphry Slocombe** • 2790 Harrison St
- **Janet Moyer Landscaping** • 1031 Valencia St
- **Laku** • 1069 Valencia St
- **Lucca Ravioli** • 1100 Valencia St
- **Modern Times Bookstore** • 2919 24th St
- **Retro Fit** • 910 Valencia St
- **Room 4** • 904 Valencia St
- **Ruby** • 3602 20th St
- **Scarlet Sage Herb Co** • 1173 Valencia St
- **The Touch** • 956 Valencia St
- **Valencia Whole Foods** • 999 Valencia St
- **Vanilla, Saffron imports** • 949 Valencia St

Video Rental

- **Lost Weekend Video** • 1034 Valencia St
- **US Video** • 2969 Mission St
- **World Pioneer Video** • 2830 24th St

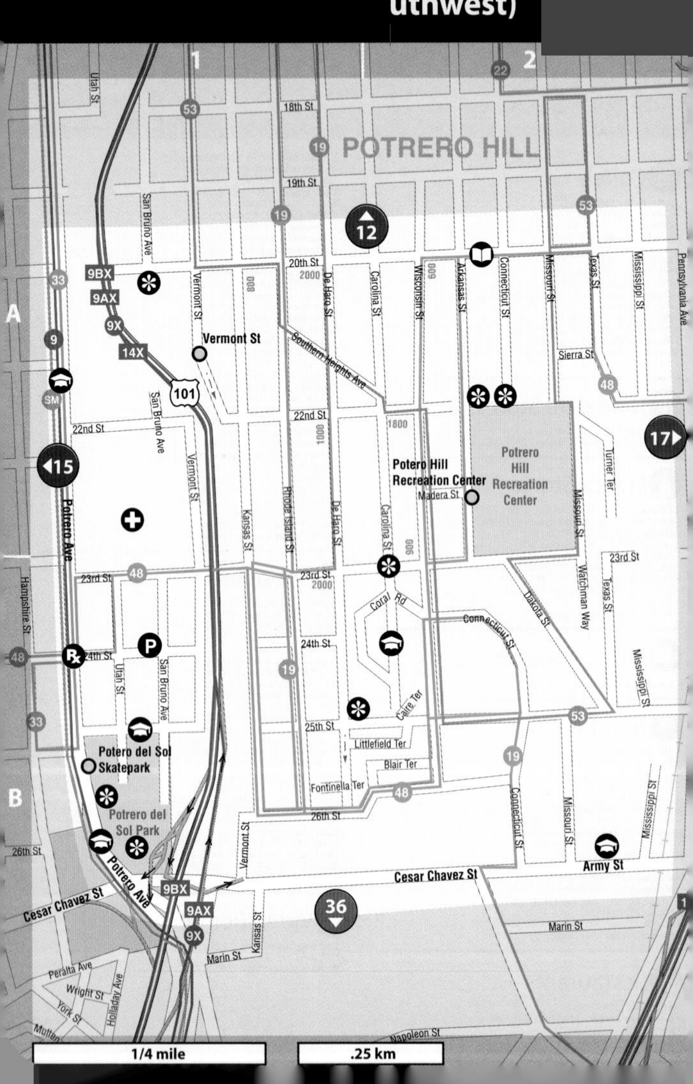

1
2
POTRERO HILL
18th St
19th St
20th St
22nd St
23rd St
24th St
25th St
26th St
Utah St
San Bruno Ave
Vermont St
Kansas St
Rhode Island St
De Haro St
Carolina St
Wisconsin St
Arkansas St
Connecticut St
Missouri St
Texas St
Mississippi St
Pennsylvania Ave
Sierra St
Southern Heights Ave
Turner Ter
Vermont St
Potero Hill Recreation Center
Madera St
Potrero Hill Recreation Center
Watchman Way
Dakota St
Coral Rd
Caire Ter
Littlefield Ter
Blair Ter
Fontinella Ter
Potrero Ave
Hampshire St
Potero del Sol Skatepark
Potrero del Sol Park
Cesar Chavez St
Army St
Marin St
Peralta Ave
Wright St
York St
Holladay Ave
Mullen
Napoleon St
A
B
1/4 mile
.25 km

This part of Potrero Hill is predominantly residential, but it's worth an urban hike here up 20th Street to Connecticut or Missouri Streets to take in the postcard-perfect views of downtown and the Bay. The weather here is some of the best in San Francisco, so pickup ball games are often in play at the Potrero Hill Rec Center.

Community Gardens

Emergency Rooms

- **San Francisco General** • 1001 Potrero Ave

Landmarks

- **Potrero del Sol/La Raza Skatepark** • 25th St & Utah St
- **Potrero Hill Recreation Center** • 801 Arkansas St
- **Vermont St** • 20th St & Vermont St

Libraries

- **Potrero Library** • 1616 20th St

Parking

Pharmacies

- **Walgreens** • 1189 Potrero Ave (24)

Schools

- **Buena Vista Annex** • 2641 25th St
- **Meadows-Livingstone** • 1499 Potrero Ave
- **Rise Institute** • 1760 Cesar Chavez St
- **Seneca Center** • 887 Potrero Ave
- **Starr King Elementary** • 1215 Carolina St

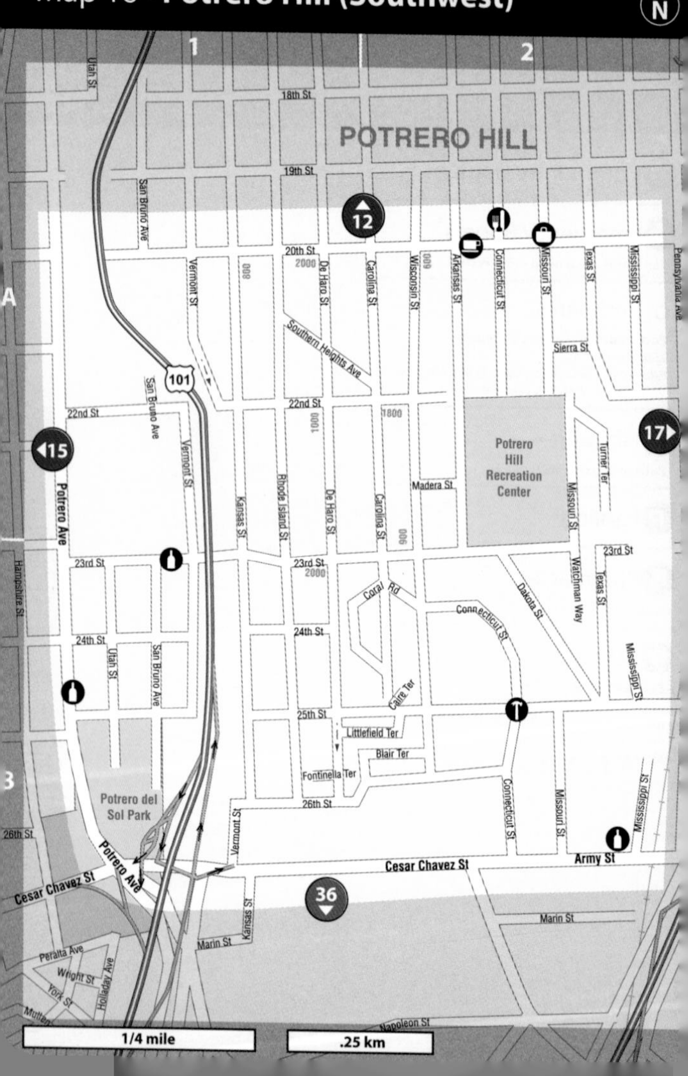

Map 16 • Potrero Hill (Southwest)
N
1
2
A
B
POTRERO HILL
18th St
19th St
20th St
22nd St
23rd St
24th St
25th St
26th St
Utah St
San Bruno Ave
Vermont St
Kansas St
Rhode Island St
De Haro St
Carolina St
Wisconsin St
Arkansas St
Connecticut St
Missouri St
Texas St
Mississippi St
Pennsylvania Ave
Southern Heights Ave
Sierra St
Turner Ter
Madera St
Potrero Hill Recreation Center
Watchman Way
Dakota St
Coral Rd
Caire Ter
Littlefield Ter
Blair Ter
Fontinella Ter
Potrero Ave
Hampshire St
Potrero del Sol Park
Cesar Chavez St
Army St
Marin St
Peralta Ave
Wright St
York St
Holladay Ave
Napoleon St
101
12
15
17
36
2000
800
600
1800
1000
900
1/4 mile
.25 km

The restaurant and bar scene is almost nonexistent, but Thinkers Café is a fortunate outpost for residents. If you want a stiff drink or higher-end dining, head to 18th Street on the northern part of Potrero Hill (Map 12).

Coffee

- **Thinkers Café** • 1631 20th St

Hardware Stores

- **Heieck Supply** • 1111 Connecticut St

Liquor Stores

- **Grand Seven Liquor & Valley** • 1740 Cesar Chavez St
- **L&L Liquors** • 2449 23rd St
- **Potrero Market & Deli** • 1298 Potrero Ave

Restaurants

- **Jay's Deli** • 501 Connecticut St

Shopping

- **Good Life Grocery** • 1524 20th St

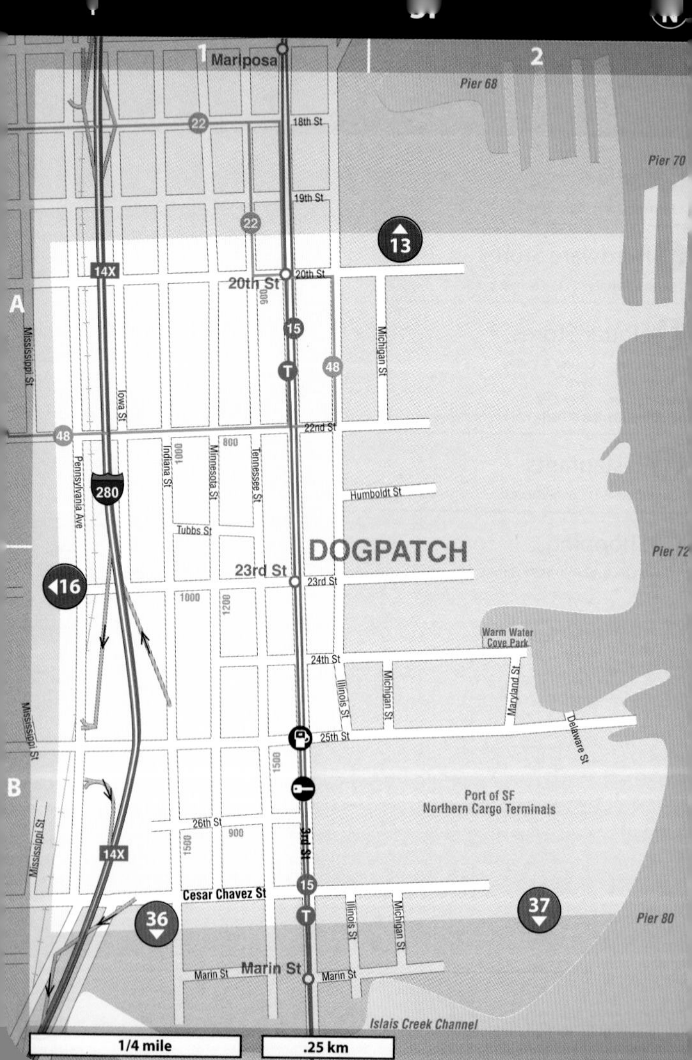

Mariposa
Pier 68
Pier 70
18th St
19th St
20th St
13
20th St
14X
A
Mississippi St
Michigan St
Iowa St
22nd St
Indiana St
Minnesota St
Tennessee St
Pennsylvania Ave
280
Humboldt St
Tubbs St
DOGPATCH
Pier 72
23rd St
23rd St
16
Warm Water Cove Park
24th St
Illinois St
Michigan St
Maryland St
Delaware St
25th St
B
Port of SF Northern Cargo Terminals
26th St
3rd St
Cesar Chavez St
36
37
Pier 80
Marin St
Marin St
Marin St
Islais Creek Channel
1/4 mile
.25 km

A former working-class/industrial neighborhood in the midst of transformation, this area will look completely different in five years. The impetus for change is largely due to the new Third Street Light Rail and the trickle-down effect of the Mission Bay improvement projects taking place nearby. For the time being, though, there's still not much here.

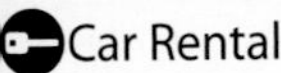

Car Rental

- **Rent-A-Wreck** • 2955 3rd St

Gas Stations

- **Shell** • 2890 3rd St

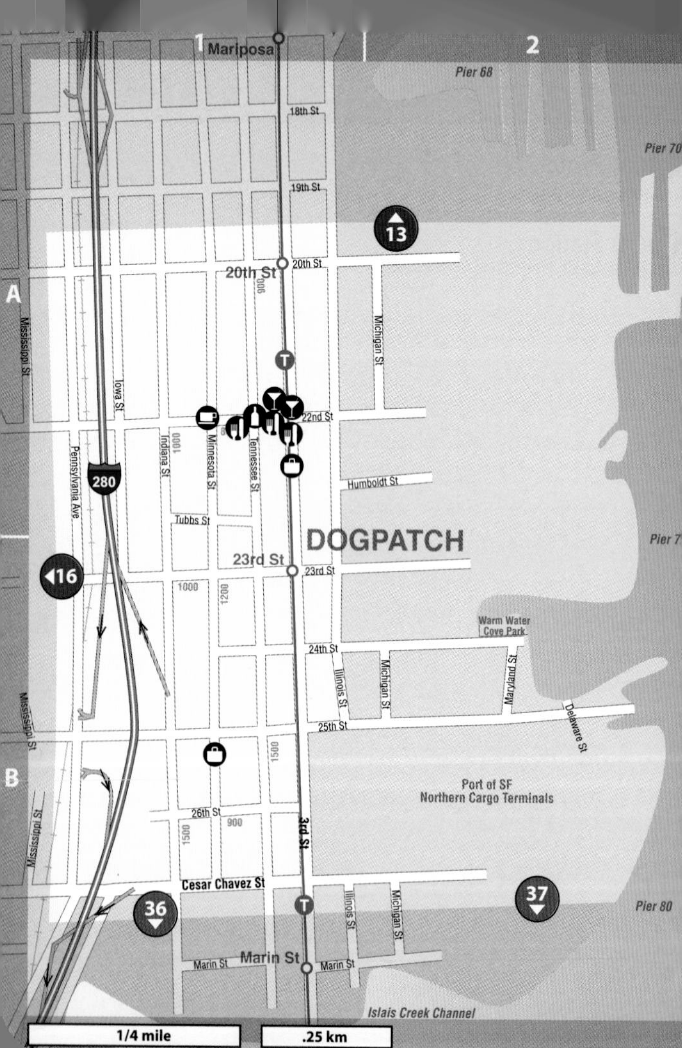

1
2
A
B
Mariposa
Pier 68
18th St
Pier 70
19th St
13
20th St
20th St
900
Michigan St
Mississippi St
Iowa St
22nd St
Indiana St
1000
Minnesota St
Tennessee St
280
Pennsylvania Ave
Humboldt St
Tubbs St
DOGPATCH
Pier 7
23rd St
23rd St
16
1000
1200
Warm Water
Cove Park
24th St
Illinois St
Michigan St
Maryland St
Delaware St
Mississippi St
25th St
1500
Port of SF
Northern Cargo Terminals
B
Mississippi St
26th St
900
1500
3rd St
Cesar Chavez St
36
37
Illinois St
Michigan St
Pier 80
Marin St
Marin St
Marin St
Islais Creek Channel
1/4 mile
.25 km

f the ongoing land-grab is any indication, this neighborhood will soon see a boom in restaurants, bars, and and shops. Hopefully not, though, as the kicked-back neighborhood is just the right size right now. Grab a hearty brunch at Just For You Café, dive into some soul food and beers at the Hard Knox Café, or head to the Dogpatch Saloon on Sunday afternoon to hear live jazz.

Coffee

- **Cup of Blues** • 900 22nd St

Liquor Stores

- **Reno's Liquor Store** • 728 22nd St

Nightlife

- **Dogpatch Saloon** • 2496 3rd St
- **Yield Wine Bar** • 2490 3rd St

Restaurants

- **Hard Knox Café** • 2526 3rd St
- **Just for You Café** • 732 22nd St
- **Piccino** • 801 22nd St

Shopping

- **Crushpad** • 2573 3rd St
- **Pro Camera** • 1405 Minnesota St

1
2
A
B
Pacific Ocean
Lincoln Park
PAGE 193
Palace of the Legion of Honor
El Camino Del Mar
Fort Miley
Veterans Affairs Medical Center
Point Lobos
Land's End
Seal Rock Dr
Clement St
Merrie Way
Alta Mar Way
Sutro Heights Park
Sutro Baths
Point Lobos Ave
Geary Blvd
7900
Cliff House
Sutro Heights Park
48th Ave
47th Ave
46th Ave
45th Ave
44th Ave
43rd Ave
42nd Ave
41st Ave
40th Ave
39th Ave
Anza St
Seal Rocks State Beach
Camera Obscura
5500
Sutro Heights Ave
Upper Great Hwy
Balboa St
4200
La Playa St
Cabrillo St
4600
Golden Gate National Recreation Area
Fulton St
North Lake
PAGE 188
Golden Gate Municipal Golf Course
John F Kennedy Dr
Chain Of Lakes Dr W
Chain Of Lakes Dr E
Great Hwy
Middle
1/4 mile
.25 km

Residential and mellow, the periphery of this area is home to some of the city's most regal spots. The Sutro Baths ruins echo a bygone time. Stately in form and locale, the Palace of the Legion of Honor brims with art from a bygone time. Just north of Ocean Beach is the newly minted Cliff House featuring the beloved Camera Obscura.

Banks

- **Wells Fargo** • 850 La Playa St

Emergency Rooms

- **San Francisco VA Medical Center** • 4150 Clement St

Landmarks

- **Camera Obscura** • 1096 Point Lobos Ave
- **Cliff House** • 1090 Point Lobos Ave
- **Fort Miley** • El Camino Del Mar & Clement St
- **Land's End** • El Camino del Mar & Seal Rock Dr
- **Palace of the Legion of Honor** • 34th Ave & Clement St
- **Sutro Baths** • Point Lobos Ave & Great Hwy
- **Sutro Heights Park** • Point Lobos Ave & 48th Ave

Pharmacies

- **Safeway** • 850 La Playa St
- **Walgreens** • 25 Point Lobos Ave

Schools

- **St Thomas the Apostle** • 3801 Balboa St

Supermarkets

- **Safeway** • 850 La Playa St

1
2
A
B
Pacific Ocean
Lincoln Park
PAGE 193
El Camino Del Mar
Veteran Affairs Medical Center
Point Lobos
Clement St
Seal Rock Dr
Merrie Way
Alta Mar Way
Point Lobos Ave
Point Lobos Ave
Geary Blvd
7900
500
500
Sutro Heights Park
48th Ave
47th Ave
46th Ave
45th Ave
44th Ave
43rd Ave
42nd Ave
41st Ave
40th Ave
39th Ave
400
Anza St
5500
600
Seal Rocks State Beach
Sutro Heights Ave
Upper Great Hwy
Balboa St
700
4200
La Playa St
Cabrillo St
4600
Golden Gate National Recreation Area
Fulton St
North Lake
PAGE 188
Golden Gate Municipal Golf Course
John F Kennedy Dr
Chain Of Lakes Dr W
Chain Of Lakes Dr E
Great Hwy
1/4 mile
.25 km

Not much in the way of commercial activity here at the ocean's edge, but you can visit the Beach Chalet for a beer and some tasty food. Balboa Street features some good neighborhood options such as the authentically Chinese KL Restaurant. All in all, it's a quiet corner of the city.

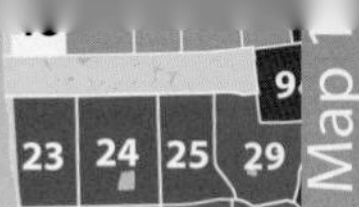

Restaurants

- **Al-Masri Egyptian Restaurant** • 4031 Balboa St
- **Beach Chalet Brewery** • 1000 Great Hwy
- **Hunan Café #2** • 4450 Cabrillo St
- **Louis' on Sutro Baths** • 902 Point Lobos Ave
- **Seal Rock Inn** • 545 Point Lobos Ave

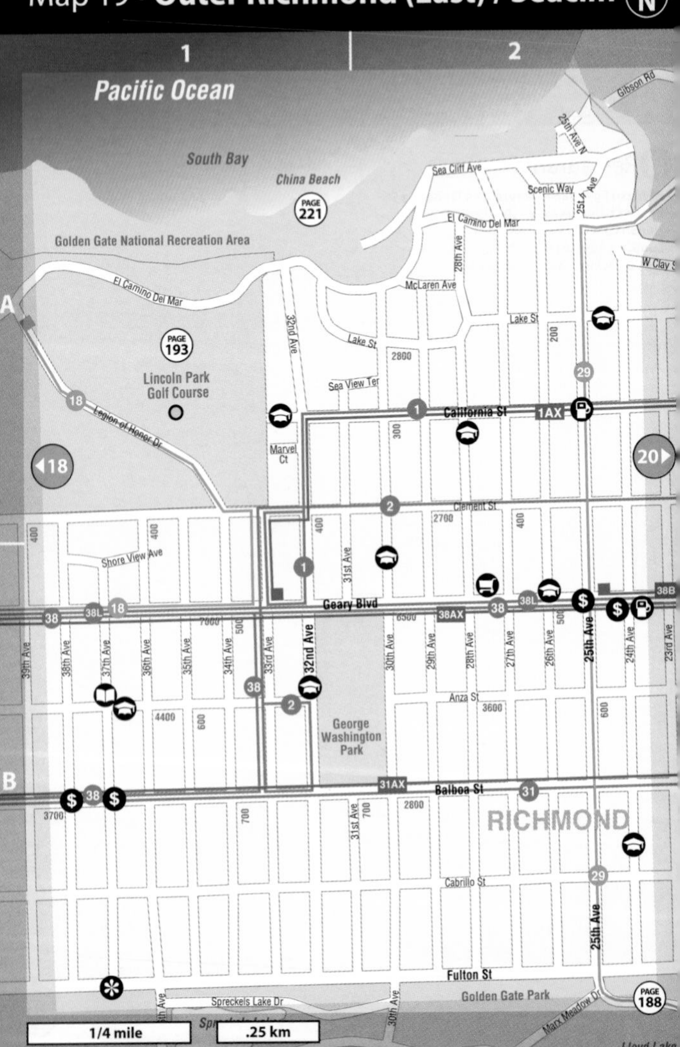

Pacific Ocean
South Bay
China Beach
PAGE 221
Golden Gate National Recreation Area
El Camino Del Mar
PAGE 193
Lincoln Park Golf Course
Legion of Honor Dr
Sea Cliff Ave
Scenic Way
25th Ave N
Gibson Rd
El Camino Del Mar
28th Ave
McLaren Ave
W Clay St
Lake St
32nd Ave
Lake St
Sea View Ter
California St
1AX
Marvel Ct
Clement St
Shore View Ave
Geary Blvd
38AX
38B
39th Ave
38th Ave
37th Ave
36th Ave
35th Ave
34th Ave
33rd Ave
32nd Ave
31st Ave
30th Ave
29th Ave
28th Ave
27th Ave
26th Ave
25th Ave
24th Ave
23rd Ave
Anza St
George Washington Park
31AX
Balboa St
RICHMOND
Cabrillo St
Fulton St
Spreckels Lake Dr
Golden Gate Park
Marx Meadow Dr
PAGE 188
Lloyd Lake
1/4 mile
.25 km

Seacliff is old money, and that money buys you a mansion with a bridge view. Lincoln Park also has beautiful views (and they're free). Walk from the park's public golf course down to the Lands End Coastal Trail for a dramatic stroll complete with stunning scenery, or find hidden China Beach.

Banks

- **Bank of America** • 3701 Balboa St
- **Citibank** • 6100 Geary Blvd
- **United Commercial** • 3601 Balboa St

Community Gardens

Gas Stations

- **76** • 301 25th Ave
- **Chevron** • 6000 Geary Blvd

Landmarks

- **Lincoln Park Golf Course** • 300 34th Ave

Libraries

- **Anza Branch Library (closed for renovations)** • 550 37th Ave

Schools

- **Cabrillo Elementary** • 735 24th Ave
- **George Washington High** • 600 32nd Ave
- **Katherine Delmar Burke** • 7070 California St
- **Kittredge** • 2355 Lake St
- **Lafayette Elementary** • 4545 Anza St
- **Presidio Middle** • 450 30th Ave
- **St John of SF Orthodox Academy** • 6210 Geary Blvd

Supermarkets

- **Delano's IGA** • 6333 Geary Blvd

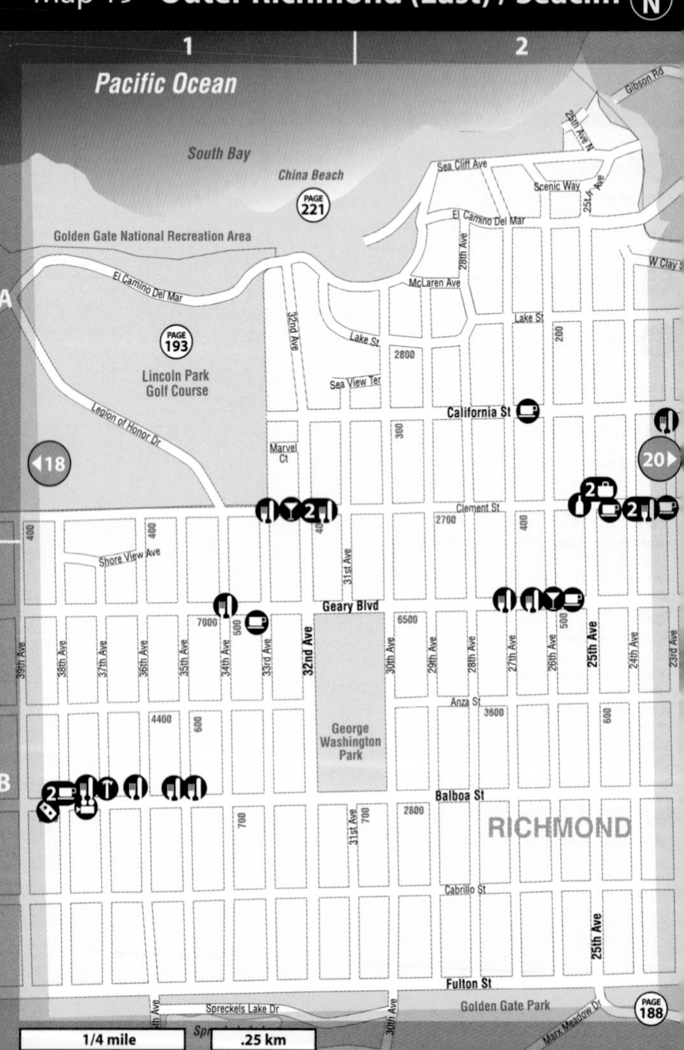
N
1
2
A
B
Pacific Ocean
South Bay
China Beach
PAGE 221
Golden Gate National Recreation Area
El Camino Del Mar
PAGE 193
Lincoln Park Golf Course
Legion of Honor Dr
18
20
Gibson Rd
25th Ave N
Sea Cliff Ave
Scenic Way
25th Ave
El Camino Del Mar
28th Ave
W Clay St
McLaren Ave
Lake St
200
32nd Ave
Lake St
2800
Sea View Ter
California St
Marvel Ct
300
Clement St
2700
400
Shore View Ave
31st Ave
Geary Blvd
7000
500
6500
39th Ave
38th Ave
37th Ave
36th Ave
35th Ave
34th Ave
33rd Ave
32nd Ave
30th Ave
29th Ave
28th Ave
27th Ave
26th Ave
25th Ave
24th Ave
23rd Ave
Anza St
3600
4400
600
George Washington Park
Balboa St
700
2800
RICHMOND
Cabrillo St
25th Ave
Fulton St
Spreckels Lake Dr
30th Ave
Golden Gate Park
Marx Meadow Dr
PAGE 188
1/4 mile
.25 km

The Richmond District gets pretty sleepy out here. Catch a double feature at the Balboa Theater; go to Simple Pleasures Café for a pre-flick cup and the Sweet House for tapioca. End the evening with a scorpion bowl at Trad'r Sam or a pint at the Tee Off.

Coffee

- **Joe's Coffee Shop** • 6134 Geary Blvd
- **Quickly** • 2201 Clement St
- **Quickly** • 6901 Geary Blvd
- **Royal Ground Coffee** • 2342 Clement St
- **Tal-Y-Tara Tea & Polo Shoppe** • 6439 California St
- **Zephyr Caffe** • 3643 Balboa St

Hardware Stores

- **Crown Lock & Hardware** • 3615 Balboa St

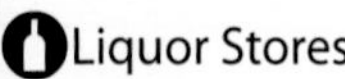

Liquor Stores

- **Twenty-Five and Clement Liquors** • 2400 Clement St

Movie Theaters

- **Balboa Theater** • 3630 Balboa St

Nightlife

- **Tee Off Bar & Grill** • 3129 Clement St
- **Trad'r Sam** • 6150 Geary Blvd

Restaurants

- **Bill's Place** • 2315 Clement St
- **Chino's Taqueria** • 3416 Balboa St
- **Drunken Sushi** • 2311 Clement St
- **El Mansour** • 3119 Clemnt St
- **Mayflower** • 6255 Geary Blvd
- **Oyaji Restaurant** • 3123 Clement St
- **Pacific Café** • 7000 Geary Blvd
- **Pizzetta 211** • 211 23rd Ave
- **Simple Pleasures Café** • 3434 Balboa St
- **The Sweet House** • 3512 Balboa St
- **Zephyr Caffe** • 3643 Balboa St

Shopping

- **AK Meats** • 2346 Clement St
- **Gaslight & Shadows Antiques** • 2335 Clement St

Video Rental

- **Poppa Opp's** • 3739 Balboa St

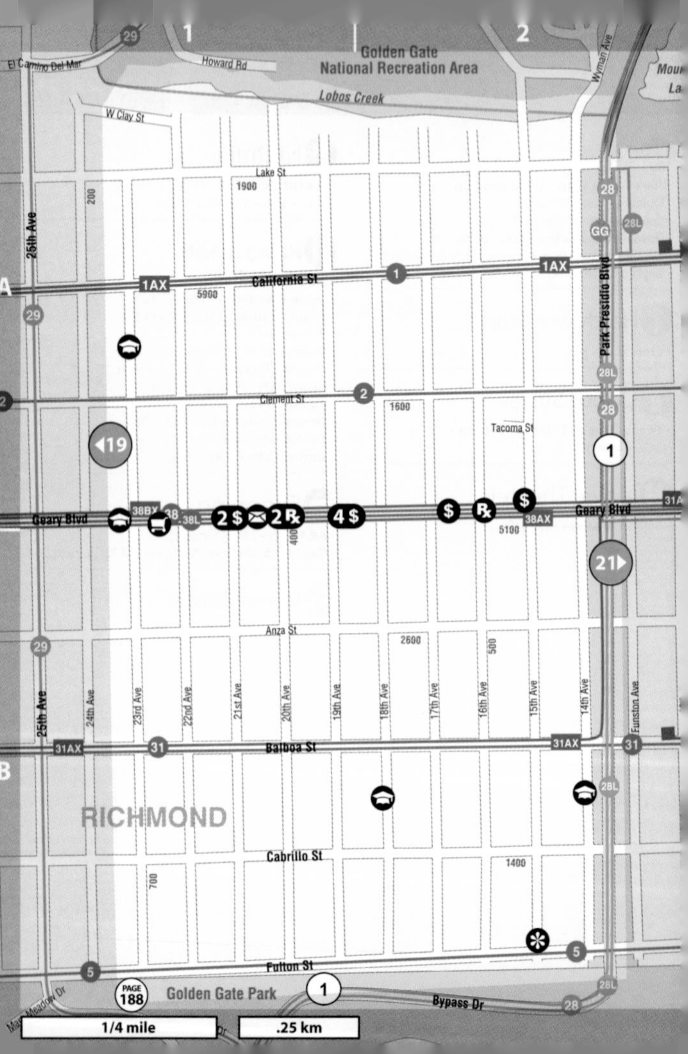

Golden Gate
National Recreation Area
Lobos Creek
El Camino Del Mar
Howard Rd
W Clay St
Lake St
1900
200
25th Ave
California St
1AX
5900
Park Presidio Blvd
Clement St
1600
Tacoma St
Geary Blvd
38BX
38L
38AX
5100
31A
Anza St
2600
500
400
25th Ave
24th Ave
23rd Ave
22nd Ave
21st Ave
20th Ave
19th Ave
18th Ave
17th Ave
16th Ave
15th Ave
14th Ave
Funston Ave
Balboa St
31AX
RICHMOND
Cabrillo St
1400
700
Fulton St
PAGE 188
Golden Gate Park
Bypass Dr
Middle West Dr
1/4 mile
.25 km

eary is where the action is in this ethnically diverse zone. Avoid roblematic parking by taking the 38-Geary (the most-used city bus). eary and 25th is the center of the SF Russian immigrant community; score pierogi at a grocery and shop for cheap fruits and veggies at the plentiful sian markets.

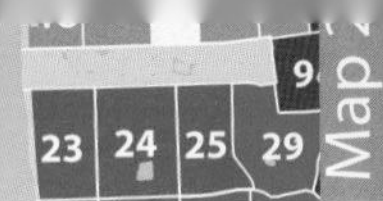

Banks

- **Bank of America** • 5500 Geary Blvd
- **California** • 5255 Geary Blvd
- **Chase** • 5655 Geary Blvd
- **Citibank (ATM)** • 5100 Geary Blvd
- **First Republic** • 5628 Geary Blvd
- **Sterling** • 5498 Geary Blvd
- **United Commercial** • 5501 Geary Blvd
- **Wells Fargo** • 5455 Geary Blvd

Community Gardens

Pharmacies

- **Evergreen Pharmacy** • 5601 Geary Blvd
- **Joe's Pharmacy** • 5199 Geary Blvd
- **Torgsyn Discount Pharmacy** • 5614 Geary Blvd

Post Offices

- **Geary Station** • 5654 Geary Blvd

Schools

- **Alamo Elementary** • 250 23rd Ave
- **Argonne Elementary** • 680 18th Ave
- **Hebrew Academy** • 645 14th Ave
- **St Monica's** • 5950 Geary Blvd

Supermarkets

- **Thom's Natural Foods** • 5843 Geary Blvd

1
2
A
B
Golden Gate
National Recreation Area
El Camino Del Mar
Howard Rd
Lobos Creek
Wyman Ave
W Clay St
Lake St
1900
200
25th Ave
California St
5900
Park Presidio Blvd
Clement St
1600
Tacoma St
19
1
Geary Blvd
4
3
2
400
5100
Geary Blvd
21
Anza St
2600
500
25th Ave
24th Ave
23rd Ave
22nd Ave
21st Ave
20th Ave
19th Ave
18th Ave
17th Ave
16th Ave
15th Ave
14th Ave
Funston Ave
Balboa St
RICHMOND
Cabrillo St
700
1400
Fulton St
PAGE 188
Golden Gate Park
1
Bypass Dr
1/4 mile
.25 km

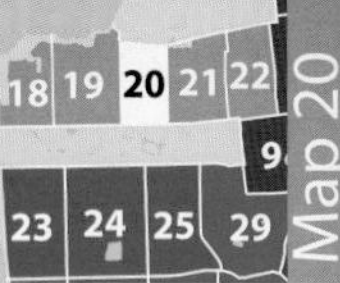

This area is primarily an eating destination as the presence of various immigrant communities has led to numerous sushi, Vietnamese, and Russian options. Popular Kabuto serves fresh well-presented sushi. Afterwards, satisfy your sweet tooth at the Creations Dessert House.

Coffee

- **Emma's Coffee House** • 5549 Geary Blvd
- **Peet's** • 5201 Geary Blvd
- **Starbucks** • Wells Fargo • 5455 Geary Blvd
- **Thanh Thanh** • 2205 Clement St

Copy Shops

- **The UPS Store** • 5758 Geary Blvd

Gyms

- **YMCA** • 360 18th Ave

Hardware Stores

- **Creative Paint & True Value** • 5435 Geary Blvd

Liquor Stores

- **Blackwell's Wines** • 5620 Geary Blvd
- **Liberty Market** • 5851 Geary Blvd
- **Martell's Liquors & Groceries** • 5615 Geary Blvd

Movie Theaters

- **Four Star Theater** • 2200 Clement St

Nightlife

- **Blarney Stone** • 5625 Geary Blvd
- **Tommy's Mexican Restaurant** • 5929 Geary Blvd

Pet Shops

- **Cal's Pet Supply** • 5950 California St

Restaurants

- **Aziza** • 5800 Geary Blvd
- **Creations Dessert House** • 5217 Geary Blvd
- **Kabuto Sushi** • 5121 Geary Blvd
- **Khan Toke Thai House** • 5937 Geary Blvd
- **Kitaro** • 5723 Geary Blvd
- **La Vie** • 5830 Geary Blvd
- **Mescolanza** • 2221 Clement St
- **Tia Margarita** • 300 19th Ave
- **Tommy's Mexican Restaurant** • 5929 Geary Blvd
- **Ton Kiang** • 5821 Geary Blvd
- **Yet Wah** • 2140 Clement St

Shopping

- **Blackwell's Wines** • 5620 Geary Blvd
- **Hobby Company of San Francisco** • 5150 Geary Blvd
- **Kawaii Corner** • 5406 Geary Blvd
- **Purple Skunk** • 5820 Geary Blvd
- **San Francisco Brewcraft** • 1555 Clement St

Video Rental

- **Blockbuster** • 5240 Geary Blvd
- **Video Café** • 5700 Geary Blvd

1
2
PRESIDIO
PAGE 190
Presidio Golf Course
Park Blvd
West Pacific Ave
Hays St
Belles St
Brown St
Wyman Ave
Mountain Lake
Mountain Lake Park
West Pacific Ave
Presidio Ter
Arguello Blvd
Cherry St
PRESIDIO HEIGHTS
Lake St
500
100
Temple Emanu-El
A
California St
1AX
1BX
Cornwall St
4900
200
Park Presidio Blvd
22
Euclid
Clement St
Palm Ave
Jordan Ave
100
38BX
Geary Blvd
38AX
3900
15th Ave
14th Ave
Funston Ave
12th Ave
11th Ave
10th Ave
9th Ave
8th Ave
7th Ave
6th Ave
5th Ave
4th Ave
3rd Ave
2nd Ave
Almaden Ct
Loraine Ct
Anza St
1700
500
20
Edward St
B
Balboa St
31BX
1000
Golden Gate Ave
Cabrillo St
700
McAllister St
N Willard St
Fulton St
Golden Gate Park
Conservatory
Conservatory Dr W
PAGE 188
John F Kennedy Dr
1/4 mile
.25 km

This neighborhood has grown to be one of the city's premier eating and drinking destinations, so always allow extra time for parking. Lower rents have brought an influx of the young and hip looking for their San Francisco Days. Bordered by GGP to the south and the Presidio and Mountain Lake Park to the north, outdoor activities (and fog) abound.

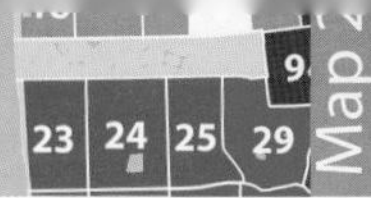

Banks

- **Bank of America** • 600 Clement St
- **Bank of America (ATM)** • 4141 Geary Blvd
- **Bank of East Asia** • 622 Clement St
- **Bank of the Orient** • 317 6th Ave
- **Bank of the West** • 801 Clement St
- **Chase** • 301 Clement St
- **Citibank** • 4455 Geary Blvd
- **Citibank (ATM)** • 900 Clement St
- **East West** • 4355 Geary Blvd
- **Gateway Bank FSB** • 919 Clement St
- **San Francisco Federal CU** • 4375 Geary Blvd
- **United Commercial** • 498 Clement St
- **US (ATM)** • Walgreens • 745 Clement St
- **Wells Fargo (ATM)** • 599 Clement St

Car Rental

- **Enterprise** • 4250 Geary Blvd
- **Hertz** • 3928 Geary Blvd
- **Toyota** • 3800 Geary Blvd

Gas Stations

- **76** • 3898 California St
- **Chevron** • 3675 Geary Blvd
- **Shell** • 4501 Geary Blvd

Landmarks

- **Temple Emanu-El** • 2 Lake St

Libraries

- **Richmond Branch Library** • 351 9th Ave

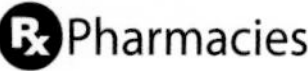

Pharmacies

- **Kaiser Permanente Medical Center—Outpatient Pharmacy** • 4141 Geary Blvd
- **Walgreens** • 745 Clement St

Police

- **Richmond Police Station** • 461 6th Ave

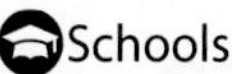

Schools

- **Frank McCoppin** • 651 6th Ave
- **George Peabody Elementary** • 251 6th Ave
- **Laurel** • 350 9th Ave
- **Olympia Institute** • 950 Clement St
- **Roosevelt Middle** • 460 Arguello Blvd
- **Star of the Sea Grammar** • 360 9th Ave
- **Sutro Elementary** • 235 12th Ave
- **Zion Lutheran Church** • 495 9th Ave

1
2
PRESIDIO
PAGE 190
Presidio Golf Course
Park Blvd
West Pacific Ave
Hays St
Belles St
Brown St
Wyman Ave
Mountain Lake
Mountain Lake Park
West Pacific Ave
Presidio Ter
Arguello Blvd
Cherry St
PRESIDIO HEIGHTS
A
Lake St
500
100
100
California St
Cornwall St
California St
4900
200
200
Park Presidio Blvd
Arguello Blvd
22
Euclid
Palm Ave
Jordan Ave
Clement St
1
Geary Blvd
Geary Blvd
400
3900
15th Ave
14th Ave
Funston Ave
12th Ave
11th Ave
10th Ave
9th Ave
8th Ave
7th Ave
6th Ave
5th Ave
4th Ave
3rd Ave
2nd Ave
Almaden Ct
Loraine Ct
Anza St
500
1700
500
Arguello Blvd
20
Edward St
Balboa St
B
1000
100
Golden Gate Ave
Cabrillo St
McAllister St
N Willard St
700
Fulton St
Golden Gate Park
Conservatory Dr
Conservatory Dr W
PAGE 188
John F Kennedy Dr
Garden Dr
1/4 mile
.25 km

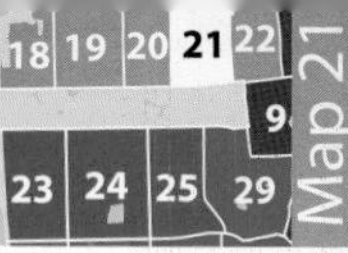

ts all here, everything from coffee shops, liquor stores, hardware stores, bookstores (Green Apple), and pet shops to several Irish pubs, several Irish pubs, rocknroll dives (540 Club), more-than-edible pizza (Giorgio's), and some of the city's best ethnic eateries—Burma Superstar, Spices I & II, Cinderella Russian Bakery and Brother's Korean BBQ.

Coffee

- **Blue Danube Coffee House** • 306 Clement St
- **Café Muse** • 785 8th Ave
- **Coffee Break** • 4601 Geary Blvd
- **Haig's Delicacies** • 642 Clement St
- **Java Source** • 343 Clement St
- **Javaholics** • 449 Balboa St
- **Martha & Bros** • 200 Clement St
- **Quickly** • 331 Clement St
- **Velo Rouge Café** • 798 Arguello Blvd

Copy Shops

- **Copy Max** • 3700 Geary Blvd

Hardware Stores

- **Home Hardware** • 335 Clement St
- **Standard Plumbing-Ace Hardware** • 1019 Clement St

Liquor Stores

- **Drink Liquor** • 601 2nd Ave
- **Pyramid Liquors** • 4401 Geary Blvd

Nightlife

- **540 Club** • 540 Clement St
- **Abbey Tavern** • 4100 Geary Blvd
- **The Bitter End** • 441 Clement St
- **Buckshot Restaurant, Bar and Gameroom** • 3848 Geary Blvd
- **Dirty Trix** • 408 Clement St
- **The Dogs Bollix** • 408 Clement St
- **Ireland's 32** • 3920 Geary Blvd
- **The Plough and the Stars** • 116 Clement St
- **Rockit Room** • 406 Clement St
- **Would You Believe** • 4652 Geary Blvd

Pet Shops

- **B&B Pet Supplies** • 4820 Geary Blvd
- **Lucky Ocean Aquarium** • 109 Balboa St
- **Sixth Avenue Aquarium** • 425 Clement St

Restaurants

- **B Star Bar** • 127 Clement St
- **Bella Trattoria** • 3854 Geary Blvd
- **Brother's Korean BBQ** • 4128 Geary Blvd
- **Burma Superstar** • 309 Clement St
- **Chapeau!** • 126 Clement St
- **Cinderella Russian Bakery and Café** • 436 Balboa St
- **Coriya Hot Pot City** • 852 Clement St
- **Giorgio's Pizza** • 151 Clement St
- **Katia's Russian Tea Room** • 600 5th Ave
- **King of Thai** • 346 Clement St
- **King of Thai** • 639 Clement St
- **Le Soleil** • 133 Clement St
- **Little Vietnam Café** • 309 6th Ave
- **Mandalay** • 4348 California St
- **Q** • 225 Clement St
- **The Richmond** • 615 Balboa St
- **Spices I** • 294 8th Ave
- **Spices II** • 291 6th Ave
- **Star India** • 3721 Geary Blvd
- **Sushi Bistro** • 445 Balboa St
- **Tawan's Thai** • 4403 Geary Blvd
- **Tong Palace** • 933 Clement St
- **Toy Boat Dessert Café** • 401 Clement St
- **Velo Rouge Café** • 798 Arguello Blvd
- **Wing Lee Bakery** • 503 Clement St

Shopping

- **April in Paris** • 55 Clement St
- **Arguello Super Market** • 782 Arguello Blvd
- **First Korean Market** • 4625 Geary Blvd
- **Green Apple Books & Music** • 506 Clement St
- **Heroes Club** • 840 Clement St
- **Kamei Restaurant Supply** • 547 Clement St
- **Kumquat** • 147 Clement St
- **New Sunny Land** • 538 Clement St
- **Park Life** • 220 Clement St
- **Richmond New May Wah Supermarket**• 707 Clement St
- **Schubert's Bakery** • 521 Clement St
- **Sloat Garden Center** • 327 3rd Ave
- **Super Tokio** • 251 Clement St

Video Rental

- **Jeong Eum Sa** • 4050 Geary Blvd
- **Richmond Video & Laser (Hong Kong)** • 837 Clement St

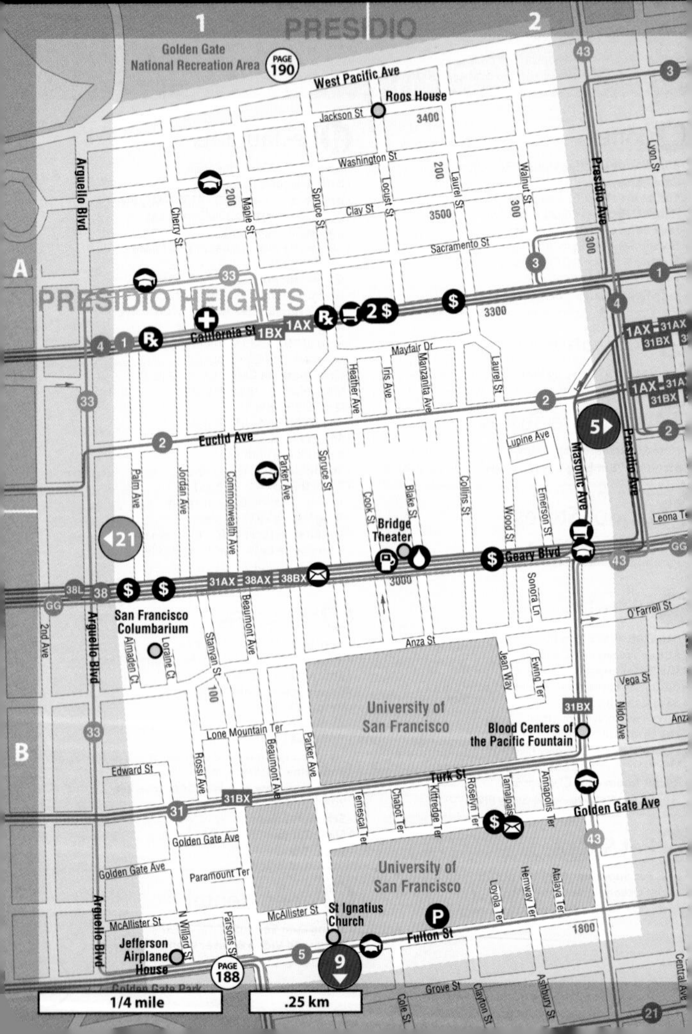

1
2
A
B
PRESIDIO
Golden Gate National Recreation Area
PAGE 190
West Pacific Ave
Roos House
Jackson St
3400
Washington St
Clay St
3500
Sacramento St
Arguello Blvd
Cherry St
Maple St
Spruce St
Locust St
Laurel St
Walnut St
Presidio Ave
Lyon St
PRESIDIO HEIGHTS
California St
3300
Mayfair Dr
Heather Ave
Iris Ave
Manzanita Ave
Euclid Ave
Lupine Ave
Masonic Ave
Palm Ave
Jordan Ave
Commonwealth Ave
Parker Ave
Cook St
Blake St
Collins St
Wood St
Emerson St
Leona Ter
Bridge Theater
Geary Blvd
3000
Sonora Ln
O'Farrell St
San Francisco Columbarium
Almaden Ct
Loraine Ct
Stanyan St
Beaumont Ave
Anza St
Jean Way
Ewing Ter
Vega St
2nd Ave
University of San Francisco
Blood Centers of the Pacific Fountain
Nido Ave
Lone Mountain Ter
Rossi Ave
Edward St
Turk St
Temescal Ter
Chabot Ter
Kittredge Ter
Roselyn Ter
Tamalpais Ter
Annapolis Ter
Golden Gate Ave
Paramount Ter
Loyola Ter
Hemway Ter
Atalaya Ter
McAllister St
St Ignatius Church
Fulton St
1800
Jefferson Airplane House
N Willard St
Parsons St
PAGE 188
Golden Gate Park
Grove St
Cole St
Clayton St
Ashbury St
Central Ave
1/4 mile
.25 km

This upscale part of the city features distinctive neighborhoods. Mansions border the Presidio in the Pacific Heights section (visit the Roos House), while Laurel Heights, south of California Street, is a quiet mix of apartments and town houses. University of San Francisco's medical offices provide outstanding care.

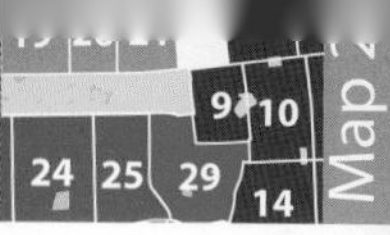

Banks

- **Bank of America** • 2835 Geary Blvd
- **Bank of America** • 3565 California St
- **Bank of America (ATM)** • 2345 Golden Gate Ave
- **First Republic** • 3533 California St
- **US** • 3550 Geary Blvd
- **Wells Fargo** • 3431 California St
- **Wells Fargo** • 3624 Geary Blvd

Car Washes

- **Shell** • 3035 Geary Blvd

Emergency Rooms

- **California Pacific Medical Center California Campus** • 3700 California St

Gas Stations

- **Shell** • 3035 Geary Blvd

Landmarks

- **Blood Centers of the Pacific Fountain** • 270 Masonic Ave
- **Bridge Theater** • 3010 Geary Blvd
- **Jefferson Airplane House** • 2400 Fulton St
- **Roos House** • 3500 Jackson St
- **San Francisco Columbarium** • 1 Loraine Ct
- **St Ignatius Church** • 650 Parker Ave

Parking

Pharmacies

- **Walgreens** • 3601 California St
- **Walgreens** • 3838 California St

Post Offices

- **CPU University of SF** • 2299 Golden Gate Ave
- **Golden Gate Station** • 3245 Geary Blvd

Schools

- **Claire Lillenthal** • 3950 Sacramento St
- **One Fifty Parker Ave** • 150 Parker Ave
- **Presidio Hill** • 3839 Washington St
- **San Francisco Day** • 350 Masonic Ave
- **University of San Francisco** • 2130 Fulton St

Supermarkets

- **Cal-Mart Supermarket** • 3585 California St
- **Trader Joe's** • 3 Masonic Ave

1
2
A
B
PRESIDIO
Golden Gate National Recreation Area
PAGE 190
West Pacific Ave
Jackson St
3400
Washington St
Clay St
3500
Sacramento St
Arguello Blvd
Cherry St
Maple St
Spruce St
Locust St
Laurel St
Walnut St
Presidio Ave
Lyon St
PRESIDIO HEIGHTS
California St
3300
Mayfair Dr
Heather Ave
Iris Ave
Manzanita Ave
Euclid Ave
Lupine Ave
Masonic Ave
Palm Ave
Jordan Ave
Commonwealth Ave
Parker Ave
Cook St
Blake St
Collins St
Wood St
Emerson St
Leona Ter
Geary Blvd
3000
Sonora Ln
O'Farrell St
Beaumont Ave
Stanyan St
Almaden Ct
Loraine Ct
2nd Ave
Anza St
Jean Way
Ewing Ter
Vega St
Nido Ave
University of San Francisco
Lone Mountain Ter
Rossi Ave
Edward St
Turk St
Temescal Ter
Chabot Ter
Kittredge Ter
Roselyn Ter
Tamalpais Ter
Annapolis Ter
Golden Gate Ave
Paramount Ter
Loyola Ter
Hemway Ter
Atalaya Ter
McAllister St
N Willard St
Parsons St
Fulton St
1800
PAGE 188
Grove St
Cole St
Clayton St
Ashbury St
Central Ave
1/4 mile
.25 km

California and Sacramento Streets are the destination for boutique shopping and specialty foods. Try Bryan's for excellent meat and fish. Geary Street has the bargains and the down-to-earth shopping (and of course Mel's).

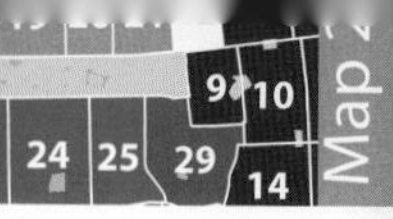

Coffee

- **Earth's Coffee** • 3400 Geary Blvd
- **Nani's Coffee** • 2739 Geary Blvd
- **Peet's** • 3419 California St
- **Starbucks** • 1799 Fulton St
- **Starbucks** • 3595 California St

Copy Shops

- **FedEx Office** • 25 Stanyan St
- **Geary Print Shop** • 3000 Geary Blvd
- **Office Depot** • 2675 Geary Blvd
- **Pro Image Printing** • 3216 Geary Blvd
- **The UPS Store** • 3145 Geary Blvd

Gyms

- **Curves (women only)** • 2675 Geary Blvd

Hardware Stores

- **Hardware Unlimited** • 3326 Sacramento St
- **Standard 5 & 10 Ace** • 3545 California St

Liquor Stores

- **Beverages & More** • 3445 Geary Blvd
- **Wine Impressions** • 3461 California St

Movie Theaters

- **Bridge Theater** • 3010 Geary Blvd

Nightlife

- **The Pig & Whistle** • 2801 Geary Blvd

Pet Shops

- **Drew's K-9 Korner** • 3518 Geary Blvd
- **Pet Source** • 2900 Geary Blvd

Restaurants

- **Asqew Grill** • 3415 California St
- **Lucky Penny** • 2670 Geary Blvd
- **Mel's Drive-In** • 3355 Geary Blvd
- **Pancho's Salsa Bar & Grill** • 3440 Geary Blvd
- **Papalote** • 1777 Fulton St
- **Rigolo** • 3465 California St
- **Sociale** • 3665 Sacramento St
- **Twilight** • 2600 McAllister St

Shopping

- **AG Ferrari Foods** • 3490 California St
- **Bedroom Outlet** • 2901 Geary Blvd
- **Books Inc** • 3515 California St
- **Bryan's Quality Meats** • 3473 California St
- **Button Down** • 3415 Sacramento St
- **Day One** • 3490 California St
- **The Grocery Store** • 3625 Sacramento St
- **Kendall Wilkinson** • 3419 Sacramento St
- **Kindersport** • 3566 Sacramento St
- **Mom's the Word** • 3385 Sacramento St
- **The Ribbonerie** • 3695 Sacramento St
- **Threshold** • 3419 Sacramento St
- **Trader Joe's** • 3 Masonic Ave

Video Rental

- **One Stop Video** • 3416 Geary Blvd

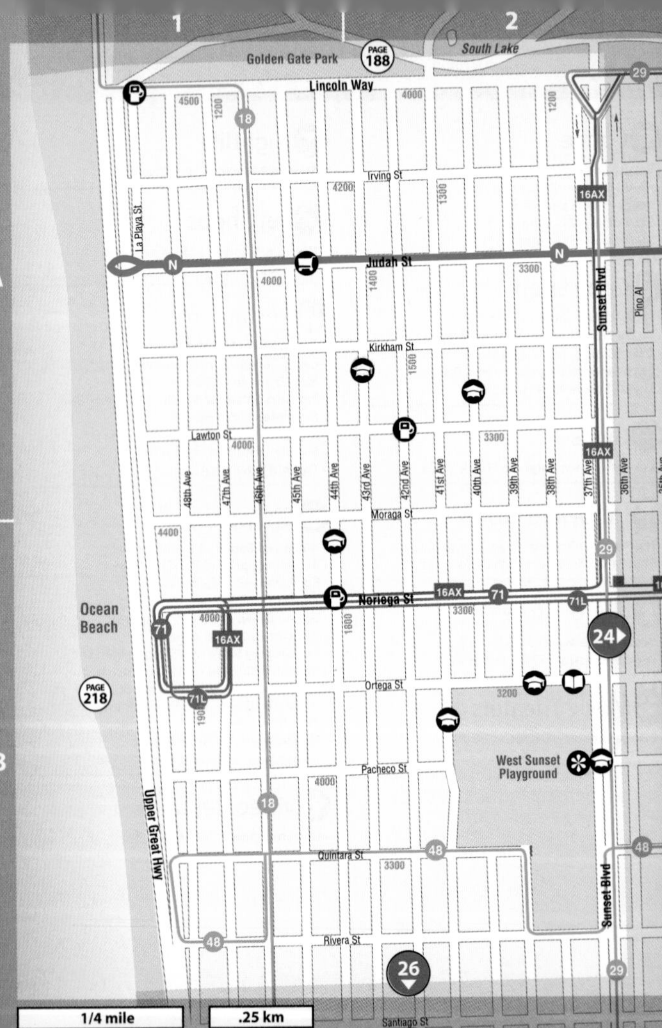
1
2
A
B
Golden Gate Park
PAGE 188
South Lake
Lincoln Way
4500
1200
4000
1200
29
18
Irving St
4200
1300
16AX
La Playa St
Judah St
N
4000
1400
3300
Sunset Blvd
Pino Al
Kirkham St
1500
Lawton St
4000
3300
16AX
48th Ave
47th Ave
46th Ave
45th Ave
44th Ave
43rd Ave
42nd Ave
41st Ave
40th Ave
39th Ave
38th Ave
37th Ave
36th Ave
35th Ave
Moraga St
4400
29
Noriega St
16AX
71
71L
3300
Ocean Beach
71
4000
16AX
1800
24
PAGE 218
71L
1900
Ortega St
3200
West Sunset Playground
Pacheco St
4000
18
Upper Great Hwy
48
Quintara St
3300
48
Sunset Blvd
Rivera St
48
26
29
1/4 mile
.25 km
Santiago St

Year-round, hardcore surfers hold ground (and water) at Ocean Beach, while bikers and joggers frequent the seaside paths on Great Highway. The eternal fog gives the residential Outer Sunset a stigma that is refuted by sunny beach days during Indian Summer. Residents here like to live on the edge—of the contiguous United States, that is.

Community Gardens

Gas Stations

- **76** • 1200 La Playa St
- **76** • 3601 Lawton St
- **76** • 3701 Noriega St

Libraries

- **Ortega Branch Library** • 3223 Ortega St

Schools

- **AP Giannini Middle** • 3151 Ortega St
- **Francis Scott Key Elementary** • 1530 43rd Ave
- **Holy Name Elementary** • 1560 40th Ave
- **Independence Continuation** • 1717 44th Ave
- **St Ignatius College Preparatory** • 2001 37th Ave
- **Sunset Elementary** • 1920 41st Ave

Supermarkets

- **Other Avenues** • 3930 Judah St

1
2
Golden Gate Park
PAGE 188
South Lake
Lincoln Way
Irving St
La Playa St
Judah St
Sunset Blvd
Pino Al
Kirkham St
Lawton St
48th Ave
47th Ave
46th Ave
45th Ave
44th Ave
43rd Ave
42nd Ave
41st Ave
40th Ave
39th Ave
38th Ave
37th Ave
36th Ave
35th Ave
Moraga St
Noriega St
Ocean Beach
24
PAGE 218
Ortega St
West Sunset Playground
Pacheco St
Upper Great Hwy
Quintara St
Sunset Blvd
Rivera St
26
1/4 mile
.25 km
Santiago St
A
B

Sprinkled among boxy, pastel-colored, single-family homes are playgrounds and dollar stores. The N-Judah streetcar will take passengers from downtown all the way out to the beach, and ethnic restaurant gems such as the venerated Thanh Long are found at the end of Noriega and Judah Streets.

Coffee

- **Corner Cup** • 3655 Lawton St
- **Java Beach Café** • 1396 La Playa St
- **Kaila's Corner Cup** • 3655 Lawton St

Gyms

- **Liberty Fitness Center (women only)** • 3725 Noriega St

Hardware Stores

- **Chu Supply Hardware** • 3644 Lawton St
- **Sunset True Value Hardware** • 3126 Noriega St

Liquor Stores

- **JM Liquors** • 3801 Noriega St
- **Lawton Liquors** • 3645 Lawton St

Nightlife

- **Flanahan's Pub** • 3805 Noriega St
- **Pittsburgh's Pub** • 4207 Judah St

Restaurants

- **El Beach Burrito** • 3914 Judah St
- **Golden Gate Pizza and Indian Cuisine** • 4038 Judah St
- **Java Beach Café** • 1396 La Playa St
- **Outerlands** • 4001 Judah St
- **Pisces** • 3414 Judah St
- **The Pizza Place on Noriega** • 3901 Noriega St
- **Polly Ann Ice Cream** • 3138 Noriega St
- **Sea Biscuit Café** • 3815 Noriega St
- **Sea Breeze Café** • 3940 Judah St
- **Thanh Long** • 4101 Judah St

Shopping

- **Other Avenues** • 3930 Judah St

Metson Lake
Stow Lake
Middle Dr W
Metson Rd
Martin Luther King Jr Dr
Mallard Lake
Golden Gate Park
Lincoln Way
Irving St
Judah St
Kirkham St
Lawton St
SUNSET
Moraga St
Noriega St
Ortega St
Pacheco St
Sunset Reservoir
Quintara St
Santiago St
PARKSIDE
Sunset Blvd
Pino Al
37th Ave
36th Ave
35th Ave
34th Ave
33rd Ave
32nd Ave
31st Ave
30th Ave
29th Ave
28th Ave
27th Ave
26th Ave
25th Ave
24th Ave
23rd Ave
22nd Ave
21st Ave
20th Ave
19th Ave
38th Ave

This gridded neighborhood—'The Avenues'—houses much of San Francisco's middle-class and envelopes them in fog during the summer. Many of the family homes were built after World War II by Henry Doelger, who favored uniformity. Some residents have even been known to try their keys on the wrong house.

Banks

- **Bank of America** • 1945 Irving St
- **Bank of America** • 2325 Noriega St
- **Bank of America (ATM)** • 1450 Noriega St
- **Bank of East Asia** • 1250 Noriega St
- **Bank of the Orient** • 2001 Irving St
- **Chase** • 1811 19th Ave
- **Chase** • 2323 Irving St
- **Citibank** • 1900 Noriega St
- **Citibank** • 2000 Irving St
- **Far East National** • 2309 Noriega St
- **First Republic** • 1809 Irving St
- **Sterling** • 2501 Irving St
- **United Commercial** • 1301 Noriega St
- **United Commercial** • 2219 Irving St
- **United Commercial** • 2533 Noriega St
- **US** • 1850 Irving St
- **US (ATM)** • Walgreens • 1750 Noriega St
- **Wells Fargo** • 2300 Irving St

Gas Stations

- **76** • 1400 19th Ave
- **76** • 1700 Noriega St
- **76** • 2525 Pacheco St
- **Chevron** • 1288 19th Ave
- **Chevron** • 1890 19th Ave
- **Shell** • 1200 19th Ave

Pharmacies

- **Ace Pharmacy** • 2505 Noriega St
- **Golden Gate Pharmacy** • 1844 Noriega St
- **Greenhouse Pharmacy** • 1516 Noriega St
- **Safeway** • 2350 Noriega St
- **Walgreens** • 1750 Noriega St
- **Walgreens** • 2050 Irving St

Post Offices

- **Sunset Finance Station** • 1314 22nd Ave

Schools

- **Abraham Lincoln High** • 2162 24th Ave
- **Adda Clevenger Junior Prep** • 1577 34th Ave
- **Cornerstone Academy-Kindergarten Annex** • 1925 Lawton St
- **Lawton Alternative School** • 1570 31st Ave
- **Lawton Elementary** • 1570 31st Ave
- **Robert Louis Stevenson Elementary** • 2051 34th Ave
- **Russian American International** • 1250 Quintara St
- **Sunset Bible** • 1690 21st Ave

Supermarkets

- **Safeway** • 2350 Noriega St

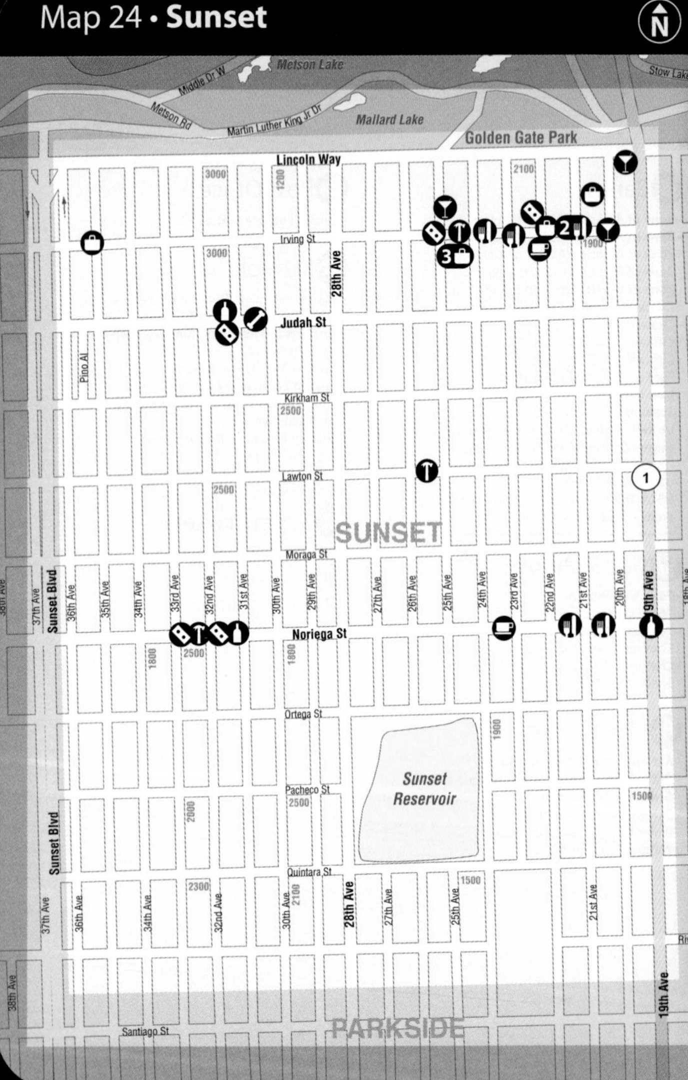
N
Metson Lake
Middle Dr W
Stow Lake
Metson Rd
Martin Luther King Jr Dr
Mallard Lake
Golden Gate Park
Lincoln Way
Irving St
Judah St
Kirkham St
Lawton St
SUNSET
Moraga St
Noriega St
Ortega St
Pacheco St
Sunset Reservoir
Quintara St
Santiago St
PARKSIDE
Pino Al
Sunset Blvd
38th Ave
37th Ave
36th Ave
35th Ave
34th Ave
33rd Ave
32nd Ave
31st Ave
30th Ave
29th Ave
28th Ave
27th Ave
26th Ave
25th Ave
24th Ave
23rd Ave
22nd Ave
21st Ave
20th Ave
19th Ave
18th Ave
3000
2100
1200
1900
2500
1800
2000
2300
1500

Irving Street past 19th Avenue is the main drag where you'll find an eclectic mix of Asian restaurants, Irish pubs, and coffee shops. For above-average fare, locals head to Marnee Thai and Micado for sushi. Neighborhood booze fanciers wet their whistle at Durty Nelly's and the Chug Pub.

Coffee

- **Henry's House of Coffee** • 1618 Noriega St
- **Quickly** • 2116 Irving St
- **Starbucks** • 1800 Irving St

Hardware Stores

- **9 PM Ace Hardware** • 2526 Noriega St
- **U Save Plumbing & Hardware** • 1928 Lawton St
- **Win Long Hardware & Supply** • 2244 Irving St

Liquor Stores

- **Nineteenth Avenue Liquors** • 1800 19th Ave
- **Quarts & Pints Liquor Store** • 2434 Noriega St
- **Sunset Strip Liquor** • 2601 Judah St

Nightlife

- **Chug Pub** • 1849 Lincoln Wy
- **Durty Nelly's Irish Pub** • 2328 Irving St
- **The Taco Shop at Underdogs** • 1824 Irving St

Pet Shops

- **Animal Connection** • 2550 Judah St

Restaurants

- **Café Bakery** • 1345 Noriega St
- **Marnee Thai** • 2225 Irving St
- **Micado** • 2126 Irving St
- **Shangri-La** • 2026 Irving St
- **Sunrise Deli & Café** • 2115 Irving St

Shopping

- **The Hard Ware Store** • 2401 Irving St
- **Jazz Quarter** • 1267 20th Ave
- **Sunset Music Company** • 2311 Irving St
- **Sunset Soccer Supply** • 3401 Irving St
- **Wonderful Foods Co** • 2035 Irving St
- **Yes Variety** • 2345 Irving St

Video Rental

- **Blockbuster** • 2400 Irving St
- **Kukjea Video (Korean)** • 2600 Judah St
- **Noriega Tapes Video & Trading Co** • 1443 Noriega St
- **Sunlight Video (Korean, Japanese, Chinese)** • 2560 Noriega St
- **Tam's Laser (Chinese)** • 2102 Irving St

Golden Gate Park
PAGE 188
Stow Lake Dr
Bowling Green Dr
Lincoln Way
Hugo St
Irving St
Judah St
Parnassus Ave
Kirkham St
Lawton St
Moraga St
Noriega St
Ortega St
Pacheco St
FOREST HILL
19th Ave
18th Ave
17th Ave
16th Ave
15th Ave
14th Ave
Funston Ave
12th Ave
11th Ave
10th Ave
9th Ave
8th Ave
7th Ave
6th Ave
5th Ave
4th Ave
3rd Ave
2nd Ave
Lurline St
Aloha Ave
Lomita Ave
Encinal Walk
Sheldon Ter
Mount Ln
Selma Way
Cascade Walk
Aerial Way
Ortega Way
Oriole Way
Radio Ter
Mandalay Ln
Cragmont Ave
Rockridge Dr
Fanning Way
Gateview Ct
Mendosa Ave
Rivera St
Cecilia Ave
San Marcos Ave
Castenada Ave
Montalvo Ave
Dorantes Ave
Auto Dr
Locksley Ave
Warren Dr
Devonshire Way
Lake Forest Ct
Laguna Honda Res Street
Laguna Honda Blvd
Clarendon Ave
Clarendon Woods Ave
Linares Ave
Ventura Ave
Alton Ave
Sotelo Ave
Magellan Ave
Mesa Ave
Santa Rita Ave
Lopez Ave
Marcela Ave
Sola Ave
Path St
Plaza St
Anglo Al
20th Ave
Woods
1/4 mile
.25 km

UCSF's proximity guarantees a young-ish crowd, bars, and ample cheap food, but simultaneously keeps things quiet—cozy side streets and reliable fog make it easy to stay in and study. Runners and picnickers love the short jaunt to Golden Gate Park's trails and meadows.

Banks

- **Bank of America** • 800 Irving St
- **Citibank** • 701 Irving St
- **Sterling** • 825 Irving St
- **US** • 1200 Irving St
- **Wells Fargo** • 725 Irving St

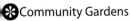

Community Gardens

Gas Stations

- **Shell** • 601 Lincoln Wy

Libraries

- **Helen Crocker Russell Library** • 9th Ave & Lincoln Wy
- **Sunset Branch Library** • 1305 18th Ave

Pharmacies

- **Reliable Pharmacy** • 801 Irving St

Post Offices

- **Irving Street Postal Store** • 821 Irving St

Schools

- **Alice Fong Yu Elementary** • 1541 12th Ave
- **Gateway High** • 1350 7th Ave
- **Herbert Hoover Middle** • 2290 14th Ave
- **Jefferson Elementary** • 1725 Irving St
- **Oakes Children's Center** • 1348 10th Ave
- **St Anne's** • 1320 14th Ave
- **Woodside International** • 1555 Irving St

Supermarkets

- **Andronico's** • 1200 Irving St
- **Europa Express** • 1342 Irving St

Stow Lake Dr
1
2
Golden Gate Park
PAGE 188
Bowling Green Dr
Lincoln Way
1200
Hugo St
2nd Ave
Irving St
900
3rd Ave
Parnassus Ave
Judah St
A
19th Ave
18th Ave
1400
17th Ave
16th Ave
15th Ave
14th Ave
Funston Ave
12th Ave
11th Ave
10th Ave
9th Ave
8th Ave
7th Ave
6th Ave
5th Ave
4th Ave
Kirkham St
Lurline St
Lawton St
Aloha Ave
Lomita Ave
Locksley Ave
FOREST
HILL
Lawton St
Locksley Ave
Warren Dr
Auto Dr
15th Ave
14th Ave
Encinal Walk
Moraga St
Noriega St
Sheldon Ter
Noriega St
Noriega St
Ortega St
Selma Way
Noriega St
29
Devonshire Way
Lake Forest Ct
Christopher
Mount Ln
1800
Warren Dr
20th Ave
24
16th Ave
15th Ave
14th Ave
Cascade Walk
Aerial Way
Laguna Honda Res Street
Ortega Way
Ortega St
Clarendon Woods Ave
Angio Al
Funston Ave
12th Ave
Pacheco St
Linares Ave
Pacheco St
Oriole Way
Laguna Honda Blvd
Clarendon Ave
B
Pacheco St
Mandalay Ln
Radio Ter
8th Ave
Ventura Ave
2000
12th Ave
Cragmont Ave
Alton Ave
Castenada Ave
Rockridge Dr
Fanning Way
Pacheco St
Sotelo Ave
Magellan Ave
Plaza St
9th Ave
Gateview Ct
Funston Ave
Mendosa Ave
Mesa Ave
Santa Rita Ave
Marcela Ave
Sola Ave
Lopez Ave
Magellan Ave
Rivera St
Castenada Ave
30
San Marcos Ave
Woodside
Cecilia Ave
Path St
Castenada Ave
Montalvo Ave
Dorantes Ave
San Marcos Ave
1/4 mile
.25 km

he action is on 9th Avenue and Irving Street. Try Ebisu for sushi and izmendi Bakery for superb scones. Get a buzz at the Beanery or play unken backgammon at Little Shamrock. For shopping, check out ishbone's novelty knick-knacks. Parking is scarce—try Bowling Green ive across Lincoln Way.

Coffee

- Alvin's Scrumptious Coffees & Teas • 1708 Irving St
- Beanery • 1307 9th Ave
- Beanery • 602 Irving St
- Secret Garden Tea House • 721 Lincoln Wy
- Starbucks • 744 Irving St

Copy Shops

- Lauretta Printing & Copy • 1600 Irving St
- The UPS Store • 1032 Irving St

Gyms

- Golden Gate Fitness • 1247 9th Ave

Hardware Stores

- Progress Hardware • 724 Irving St

Liquor Stores

- Judah Ninth Avenue Liquors • 1400 9th Ave
- Stand-By Market • 1400 8th Ave

Nightlife

- Blackthorn Tavern • 834 Irving St
- Fireside Bar • 603 Irving St
- The Little Shamrock • 807 Lincoln Wy
- Mucky Duck • 1315 9th Ave
- Yancy's Saloon • 734 Irving St

Restaurants

- **Arizmendi Bakery** • 1331 9th Ave
- **Art's Cafe** • 747 Irving St
- **Crepevine** • 624 Irving St
- **Ebisu** • 1283 9th Ave
- **Enjoy Vegetarian Restaurant** • 754 Kirkham St
- **Gordo Taqueria** • 1239 9th Ave
- **Hahn's Hibachi** • 535 Irving St
- **Hotei** • 1290 9th Ave
- **Irving Street Cafe** • 716 Irving St
- **Kiki** • 1269 9th Ave
- **L'Avenida** • 511 Irving St
- **Marnee Thai** • 1243 9th Ave
- **Milano Pizzeria** • 1330 9th Ave
- **Naan-N-Curry** • 642 Irving St
- **New Eritrea Restaurant** • 907 Irving St
- **Pacific Catch** • 1200 9th Ave
- **Park Chow** • 1240 9th Ave
- **Peasant Pies** • 1039 Irving St
- **Pluto's** • 627 Irving St
- **San Tung Chinese Restaurant** • 1031 Irving St
- **Wing Sing Bakery** • 339 Judah St
- **Yumma's** • 721 Irving St

Shopping

- **Amazing Fantasy** • 650 Irving St
- **Andronico's** • 1200 Irving St
- **Cheese Boutique** • 1298 12th Ave
- **The Great Overland Book Company** • 345 Judah St
- **Crossroads Trading Company** • 630 Irving St
- **Great Stuff** • 1377 9th Ave
- **Holy Gelato!** • 1392 9th Ave
- **Irving Variety** • 647 Irving St
- **Le Video** • 1231 9th Ave
- **Misdirections Magic Shop** • 1236 9th Ave
- **On the Run** • 1310 9th Ave
- **Paragraph** • 1234 9th Ave
- **Tutti Frutti** • 718 Irving St
- **Wishbone** • 601 Irving St

Video Rental

- **Golden Gate Video** • 1799 10th Ave
- **Le Video** • 1231 9th Ave

Santiago St
48th Ave
47th Ave
46th Ave
45th Ave
44th Ave
43rd Ave
42nd Ave
41st Ave
40th Ave
39th Ave
38th Ave
37th Ave
Sunset Blvd
Great Hwy
Taraval St
Ulloa St
Vicente St
Wawona St
South Sunset Playground
Ocean Beach
Sloat Blvd
Yorba Ln
San Francisco Zoo
Zoo Rd
Skyline Blvd
Lake Merced
Lancaster Ln
Lakeshore Dr
Country Club Dr
Brookhaven Ln
Berkshire Wy
Huntington Dr
Bonnie Brae Ln
Lake Merced Blvd
1/4 mile
.25 km

PAGE 218

The zoo is the main attraction in this part of town, and a baby gorilla is currently its biggest star. Taraval Street along the Metro L line has some action, but the urban landscape becomes almost entirely residential as the road approaches ocean sand. The Doggie Diner head suspended at Sloat and 45th adds a hallucinatory touch to a quiet corner of the city.

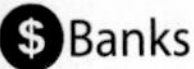

Banks

- **US (ATM)** • Walgreens • 3001 Taraval St

Landmarks

- **San Francisco Zoo** • 1 Zoo Rd

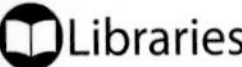

Libraries

- **United Irish Cultural Center** • 2700 45th Ave

Pharmacies

- **Walgreens** • 3001 Taraval St

Schools

- **Japanese Bilingual West** • 3045 Santiago St
- **St Gabriel** • 2550 41st Ave
- **Ulloa Elementary** • 2650 42nd Ave

1
2
23
Santiago St
3600
48th Ave
47th Ave
46th Ave
45th Ave
44th Ave
43rd Ave
42nd Ave
41st Ave
2300
40th Ave
39th Ave
38th Ave
37th Ave
Sunset Blvd
36th Ave
Great Hwy
Taraval St
3500
2400
2400
PAGE 218
A
Ocean Beach
Ulloa St
4300
2500
Vicente St
3400
2600
2700
South Sunset Playground
27
Wawona St
3000
41st Ave
Yorba Ln
Sloat Blvd
San Francisco Zoo
B
Lancaster Ln
Lakeshore Dr
Country Club Dr
Brookhaven Ln
Ocean A
Berkshire Wy
Huntington Dr
Zoo Rd
Skyline Blvd
Bonnie Brae Ln
Lakeshore Dr
Lake Merced Blvd
Lake Merced
1/4 mile
.25 km

At the Riptide, enjoy a fireside drink, knotty pine décor, and eclectic music. Satisfy your curiosity as to just what Chinese Muslim food is at Old Mandarin Islamic. Feel your green thumb start twitching in the vicinity of Sloat Garden Center, one of the best places in the city to buy house plants. Have the quintessential Asian grocery store experience at Sunset Super.

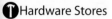

Hardware Stores

- **Lakeside Hardware & Lumber** • 3401 Taraval St

Liquor Stores

- **Glass & Bottles Liquors** • 3150 Vicente St
- **Seabee Liquor** • 3000 Taraval St

Restaurants

- **Bashful Bull Too!** • 3600 Taraval St
- **North Beach Pizza** • 3054 Taraval St
- **Old Mandarin Islamic** • 3132 Vicente St

Shopping

- **Aqua Surf Shop** • 2830 Sloat Blvd
- **Sloat Garden Center** • 2700 Sloat Blvd
- **Sunset Supermarket** • 2801 Vicente St

Video Rental

- **New Video Corner (Chinese)** • 3008 Taraval St

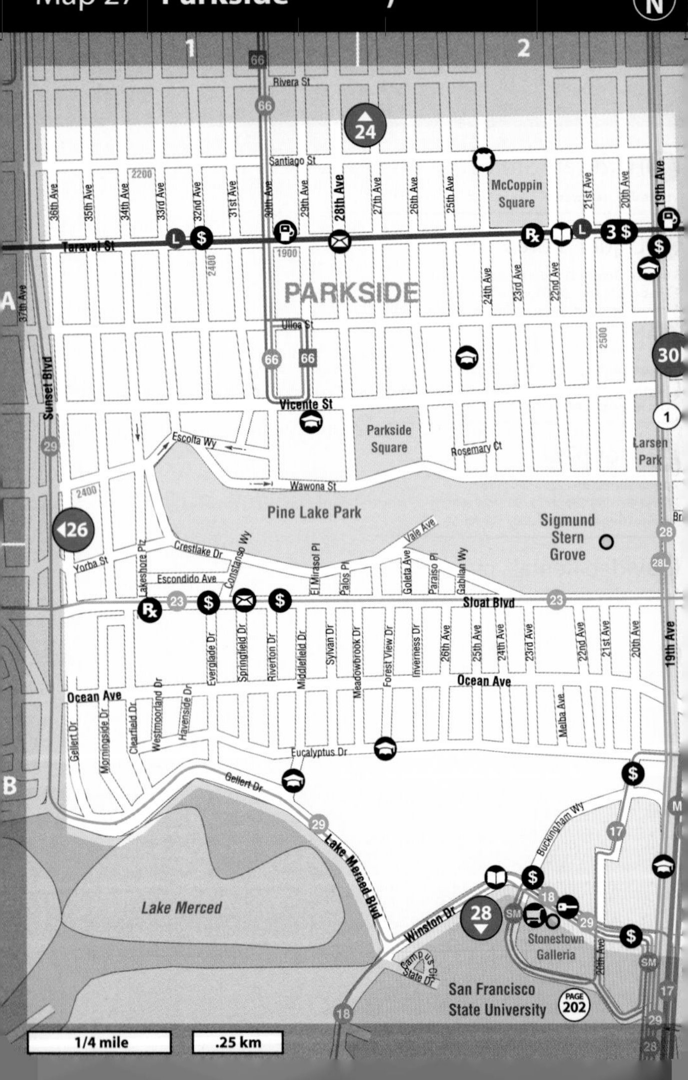
Map 27 • Parkside
N
1
2
A
B
Rivera St
Santiago St
Taraval St
Ulloa St
Vicente St
Escolta Wy
Wawona St
Rosemary Ct
PARKSIDE
McCoppin Square
Parkside Square
Larsen Park
Pine Lake Park
Sigmund Stern Grove
36th Ave
35th Ave
34th Ave
33rd Ave
32nd Ave
31st Ave
30th Ave
29th Ave
28th Ave
27th Ave
26th Ave
25th Ave
24th Ave
23rd Ave
22nd Ave
21st Ave
20th Ave
19th Ave
37th Ave
Sunset Blvd
2200
2400
1900
2500
Crestlake Dr
Constanso Wy
Vale Ave
Yorba St
Lakeshore Plz
Escondido Ave
El Mirasol Pl
Palos Pl
Goleta Ave
Paraiso Pl
Gabilan Wy
Sloat Blvd
Everglade Dr
Springfield Dr
Riverton Dr
Middlefield Dr
Sylvan Dr
Meadowbrook Dr
Forest View Dr
Inverness Dr
Ocean Ave
Melba Ave
Gellert Dr
Morningside Dr
Clearfield Dr
Westmoorland Dr
Havenside Dr
Eucalyptus Dr
Lake Merced Blvd
Lake Merced
Winston Dr
Buckingham Wy
Campus Cir
State Dr
Stonestown Galleria
San Francisco State University
PAGE 202
1/4 mile
.25 km

Essentials

This is a quiet and modest neighborhood with Stern Grove at its heart. During summer Sundays, the area is jammed with people going to the Grove's free concerts. Parking is usually decent in the neighboring affluent St Francis Wood.

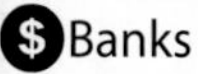

Banks

- **Bank of America** • 1007 Taraval St
- **Bank of America** • Albertsons • 1515 Sloat Blvd
- **Bank of America** • 245 Winston Dr
- **Chase** • 926 Taraval St
- **Citibank** • 2400 19th Ave
- **Citibank** • 3146 20th Ave
- **Citibank (ATM)** • 2222 Taraval St
- **First** • 1000 Taraval St
- **Wachovia** • 1595 Sloat Blvd

Car Rental

- **Enterprise** • Stonestown Mall, Winston Dr

Gas Stations

- **76** • 1855 Taraval St
- **Shell** • 2399 19th Ave

Landmarks

- **Sigmund Stern Grove** • 19th Ave & Sloat Blvd
- **Stonestown Galleria** • 3251 20th Ave

Libraries

- **Parkside Branch Library** • 1200 Taraval St
- **Sutro Library** • 480 Winston Dr

Pharmacies

- **Sav-On Drugs** • Albertsons • 1515 Sloat Blvd
- **Walgreens** • 1201 Taraval St

Police

- **Taraval Police Station** • 2345 24th Ave

Post Offices

- **Lakeshore Plaza Station** • 1543 Sloat Blvd
- **Parkside Station** • 1800 Taraval St

Schools

- **Dianne Feinstein Elementary** • 2550 25th Ave
- **Edgewood Center for Children** • 1801 Vicente St
- **Lakeshore Elementary** • 220 Middlefield Dr
- **Lakeside Presbyterian** • 201 Eucalyptus Dr
- **Lowell High** • 1101 Eucalyptus Dr
- **Mercy High** • 3250 19th Ave
- **Parkside Preschool & Kindergarten** • 2425 19th Ave
- **St Stephen's** • 401 Eucalyptus Dr

Supermarkets

- **Trader Joe's** • 265 Winston Dr

N
1
2
Rivera St
24
Santiago St
36th Ave
35th Ave
34th Ave
33rd Ave
32nd Ave
31st Ave
30th Ave
29th Ave
28th Ave
27th Ave
26th Ave
25th Ave
McCoppin Square
21st Ave
20th Ave
19th Ave
Taraval St
2200
2400
1900
2
PARKSIDE
24th Ave
23rd Ave
22nd Ave
A
37th Ave
Ulloa St
2500
30
Sunset Blvd
Vicente St
1
Parkside Square
Escolta Wy
Rosemary Ct
Larsen Park
Wawona St
2400
Pine Lake Park
Sigmund Stern Grove
26
Crestlake Dr
Constanso Wy
Vale Ave
Yorba St
Lakeshore Plz
Escondido Ave
El Mirasol Pl
Palos Pl
Goleta Ave
Paraiso Pl
Gabilan Wy
Sloat Blvd
Everglade Dr
Springfield Dr
Riverton Dr
Middlefield Dr
Sylvan Dr
Meadowbrook Dr
Forest View Dr
Inverness Dr
26th Ave
25th Ave
24th Ave
23rd Ave
22nd Ave
21st Ave
20th Ave
19th Ave
Ocean Ave
Ocean Ave
Gellert Dr
Morningside Dr
Clearfield Dr
Westmoorland Dr
Havenside Dr
Melba Ave
Eucalyptus Dr
B
Gellert Dr
Buckingham Wy
3
Lake Merced Blvd
Lake Merced
Winston Dr
28
Campus Cir
State Dr
Stonestown Galleria
20th Ave
San Francisco State University
PAGE 202
1/4 mile
.25 km

You'll find most of what you need on Taraval Street and Sloat Boulevard. Stonestown Galleria is a popular mall; it's got all your nicer chain stores. On Taraval, try El Burrito Express for burritos or Ming's for Chinese.

Coffee

- **Quickly** • 1050 Taraval St
- **Starbucks** • 3251 20th Ave
- **Tully's Coffee** • 1509 Sloat Blvd

Copy Shops

- **Copy Circle** • 959 Taraval St
- **FedEx Office** • 1597 Sloat Blvd
- **The UPS Store** • 1559 Sloat Blvd

Gyms

- **Curves (women only)** • 2453 Taraval St
- **Curves (women only)** • 555 Buckingham Wy
- **Fitness USA Supercenters** • 3251 20th Ave
- **YMCA** • 333 Eucalyptus Dr

Hardware Stores

- **Great Wall Hardware** • 1821 Taraval St

Liquor Stores

- **Gene's Liquor** • 2201 Taraval St
- **Linda's Liquor** • 1026 Taraval St
- **Liquor Locker** • 1223 Taraval St
- **Sevan Liquor & Deli** • 1508 Taraval St

Nightlife

- **Costello's Four Deuces** • 2319 Taraval St
- **Grandma's Saloon** • 1016 Taraval St
- **Shannon Arms** • 915 Taraval St

Pet Shops

- **Pet Food Express** • 3160 20th Ave
- **Petco** • 1591 Sloat Blvd
- **Sunset Pet Supply** • 2226 Taraval St
- **Tropical Reef Aquarium** • 1732 Taraval St

Restaurants

- **Eight Immortals** • 1433 Taraval St
- **El Burrito Express** • 1601 Taraval St
- **King of Thai** • 1541 Taraval St
- **Ming's Diner** • 2129 Taraval St
- **Ristorante Marcello** • 2100 Taraval St
- **Shin Toe Bul Yi** • 2001 Taraval St

Shopping

- **Apple Store** • 3251 20th Ave
- **L'Occitane** • 3251 20th Ave
- **Marco Polo Italian Ice Cream** • 1447 Taraval St
- **Stonestown Galleria** • 3251 20th Ave

Video Rental

- **Blockbuster** • 1503 Sloat Blvd
- **International Video (Arabic)** • 1850 Taraval St
- **Just Another Video Depot** • 1038 Taraval St
- **Lam's Video & Laser** • 1043 Taraval St

Escolta Wy
Wawona St
Pine Lake Park
Vale Ave
Crestlake Dr
Escondido Ave
Yorba St
Lakeshore Plz
Sunset Blvd
36th Ave
37th Ave
38th Ave
39th Ave
40th Ave
41st Ave
Sloat Blvd
Ocean Ave
Lakeshore Dr
Country Club Dr
Huntington Dr
Zoo Rd
Berkshire Wy
Lake Merced Blvd
Gellert Dr
Morningside Dr
Clearfield Dr
Westmoorland Dr
Havenside Dr
Everglade Dr
Springfield Dr
Riverton Dr
Middlefield Dr
Sylvan Dr
Meadowbrook Dr
Forest View Dr
Inverness Dr
26th Ave
25th Ave
24th Ave
23rd Ave
22nd Ave
21st Ave
20th Ave
Melba Ave
Eucalyptus Dr
Lake Merced
Winston Dr
Stonestown Galleria
Buckingham Wy
Campus
State Dr
PAGE 202
San Francisco State University
Stonecrest Dr
Wyton Ln
Denslowe Dr
Stratford Dr
Banbury Dr
Harding Rd
Harding Park Golf Course
Font Blvd
Tapia Dr
Arellano Ave
Pinto Ave
Acevedo Ave
Serrano Dr
Fuente Ave
Cardenas Ave
Crespi Drive
Grijalva Dr
Varela Ave
Gonzalez Dr
Higuera Ave
Juan Bautista Cir
Diaz Ave
Castelo Ave
Cambon Dr
Felix Ave
Vidal Dr
Arballo Dr
Gonzalez Dr
Bucareli Dr
Rivas Ave
Garces Dr
Josepha Ave
Brotherhood Wy
Chumasero Dr
Thomas More
Fort Funston
PAGE 224
John Muir Dr
Skyline Blvd
N Lake Merced Hls
S Lake Merced Hls
San Francisco
San Mateo
Congo St
Wilshire Ave
Westdale Ave
Westlawn Ave
Lake Vista Ave
S Mayfair Ave
1/2 mile
.5 km

San Francisco State University, Lake Merced (great for running, biking, and boating), and the renovated Harding Park Golf Course dominate this area. Fort Funston is also nearby; take your puppy for play dates above the beach and watch the hang gliders. Aside from college parties, the area is quiet at night.

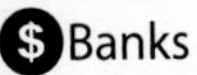

Banks

- **Bank of America (ATM)** • 1650 Holloway Ave
- **Chase (ATM)** • 1650 Holloway Ave
- **Wells Fargo (ATM)** • 1650 Holloway Ave
- **Wells Fargo (ATM)** • 35 Cambon Dr

Landmarks

- **Fort Funston** • Skyline Blvd & John Muir Dr

Schools

- **Brandeis Hillel Day** • 655 Brotherhood Wy
- **Bridgemont Jr & Sr High** • 777 Brotherhood Wy
- **Holy Trinity Orthodox** • 999 Brotherhood Wy
- **Krouzian Zekarian Armenian** • 825 Brotherhood Wy
- **San Francisco State University** • 1600 Holloway Ave
- **St Thomas More Elementary** • 50 Thomas More Wy

Escolta Wy
Wawona St
Pine Lake Park
Vale Ave
41st Ave
40th Ave
39th Ave
38th Ave
37th Ave
36th Ave
Sunset Blvd
Yorba St
Lakeshore Plz
Crestlake Dr
Escondido Ave
Sloat Blvd
Lakeshore Dr
Country Club Dr
Huntington Dr
Everglade Dr
Springfield Dr
Riverton Dr
Middlefield Dr
Sylvan Dr
Meadowbrook Dr
Forest View Dr
Inverness Dr
26th Ave
25th Ave
24th Ave
23rd Ave
22nd Ave
21st Ave
20th Ave
Ocean Ave
Melba Ave
Zoo Rd
Berkshire Wy
Gellert Dr
Morningside Dr
Clearfield Dr
Westmoorland Dr
Havenside Dr
Eucalyptus Dr
Lakeshore Dr
Lake Merced Blvd
Gellert Dr
27
Lake Merced
Lake Merced
Lake Merced Blvd
Winston Dr
Stonestown Galleria
20th Ave
Campus
State Dr
Buckingham Wy
Stonecrest Dr
PAGE 202
Harding Rd
Harding Park Golf Course
Lake Merced Blvd
Font Blvd
San Francisco State University
Wyton Ln
35
Tapia Dr
Arellano Ave
Denslowe Dr
Stratford Dr
3
Pinto Ave
Acevedo Ave
Tapia Dr
Serrano Dr
Fuente Ave
Cardenas Ave
Varela Ave
Crespi Dr
Grijalva Dr
Gonzalez Dr
Banbury Dr
PAGE 224
Lake Merced
Higuera Ave
Juan Bautista Cir
Diaz Ave
Vidal Dr
Arballo Dr
Gonzalez Dr
Bucareli Dr
Castelo Ave
Cambon Dr
Felix Ave
Garces Dr
Rivas Ave
Grijalva Dr
Josepha Ave
Font Blvd
Vidal Dr
Garces Dr
Brotherhood Wy
John Muir Dr
Skyline Blvd
Chumasero Dr
Thomas More Wy
N Lake Merced Hls
S Lake Merced Hls
San Francisco
San Mateo
Congo St
Lake Merced Blvd
Wilshire Ave
Westdale Ave
Westlawn Ave
Lake Vista Ave
S Mayfair Ave
1/2 mile
.5 km

Sundries / Entertainment

It's common to find backpackers hanging out at SFSU. The activist-happy campus is an oasis of green amid beige surroundings. Cheap eats, including a pub, can be found inside the Cesar Chavez student center and around campus.

Gyms

- **Village Fitness Center** • 750 Font Blvd

Movie Theaters

- **Stonestown Twin 2** • 501 Buckingham Wy

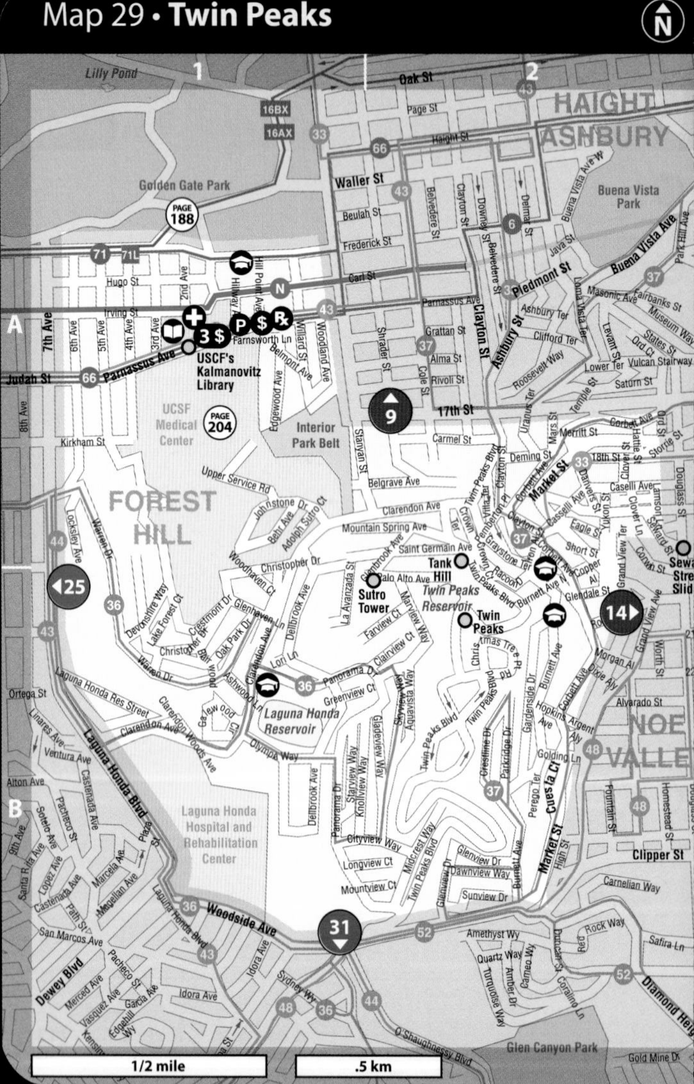

Map 29 • Twin Peaks
N
Lilly Pond
Oak St
Page St
HAIGHT ASHBURY
Haight St
Waller St
Beulah St
Frederick St
Carl St
Golden Gate Park
PAGE 188
Buena Vista Park
Buena Vista Ave W
Buena Vista Ave
Belvedere St
Clayton St
Downey St
Delmar St
Java St
Piedmont St
Masonic Ave
Fairbanks St
Museum Way
Park Hill Ave
Hugo St
Irving St
7th Ave
6th Ave
5th Ave
4th Ave
3rd Ave
2nd Ave
Hillway Ave
Hill Point Ave
Parnassus Ave
Farnsworth Ln
Willard St
Woodland Ave
Belmont Ave
Judah St
USCF's Kalmanovitz Library
Shrader St
Grattan St
Alma St
Rivoli St
Cole St
Ashbury St
Ashbury Ter
Clifford Ter
Roosevelt Way
Loma Vista Ter
Levant St
Ord Ct
States St
Vulcan Stairway
Lower Ter
Saturn St
Temple St
17th St
Uranus Ter
Mars St
Merritt St
Corbett Ave
Ord St
Hattie St
Storrie St
UCSF Medical Center
PAGE 204
Edgewood Ave
Interior Park Belt
Stanyan St
Carmel St
Kirkham St
8th Ave
Upper Service Rd
Belgrave Ave
Deming St
Market St
18th St
Danvers St
Clover St
Douglass St
Caselli Ave
FOREST HILL
Johnstone Dr
Behr Ave
Adolph Sutro Ct
Clarendon Ave
Mountain Spring Ave
Twin Peaks Blvd
Villa Ter
Clayton St
Pemberton Pl
Crown Ter
Eagle St
Yukon St
Clover Ln
Seward St
Locksley Ave
Warren Dr
Woodhaven Ct
Christopher Dr
Glenbrook Ave
Saint Germain Ave
Tank Hill
Graystone Ter
Short St
Copper Al
Grand View Ter
Corwin St
Palo Alto Ave
Sutro Tower
Twin Peaks Reservoir
Racoon Dr
Burnett Ave N
Glendale St
La Avanzada St
Dellbrook Ave
Marview Way
Twin Peaks
Devonshire Way
Lake Forest Ct
Crestmont Dr
Glenhaven Ln
Farview Ct
Clairview Ct
Christmas Tree Pt Rd
Grand View Ave
Worth St
Christopher Dr
Oak Park Dr
Lori Ln
Panorama Dr
Morgan Al
Dixie Aly
Warren Dr
Ashwood Ln
Greenview Ct
Skyview Way
Aquavista Way
Gardenside Dr
Burnett Ave
Corbett Ave
Alvarado St
Ortega St
Laguna Honda Res Street
Clarendon Ave
Laguna Honda Reservoir
Twin Peaks Blvd
Hopkins Ave
Argent Aly
NOE VALLEY
Linares Ave
Ventura Ave
Laguna Honda Blvd
Clarendon Woods Ave
Olympia Way
Gladeview Way
Starview Way
Knollview Way
Crestline Dr
Parkridge Dr
Golding Ln
Alton Ave
Castenada Ave
Dellbrook Ave
Panorama Dr
Perego Ter
Cuesta Ct
Fountain St
Homestead St
Laguna Honda Hospital and Rehabilitation Center
Pacheco St
Sotelo Ave
9th Ave
Santa Rita Ave
Lopez Ave
Marcela Ave
Plaza St
Cityview Way
Midcrest Way
Twin Peaks Blvd
Glenview Dr
Dawnview Way
Market St
High St
Clipper St
Castenada Ave
Magellan Ave
Longview Ct
Mountview Ct
Sunview Dr
Carnelian Way
Path St
San Marcos Ave
Woodside Ave
Laguna Honda Blvd
Amethyst Wy
Rock Way
Safira Ln
Dewey Blvd
Pacheco St
Idora Ave
Quartz Way
Cameo Wy
Duncan St
Coralino Ln
Turquoise Way
Amber Dr
Diamond Heights
Merced Ave
Vasquez Ave
Garcia Ave
Idora Ave
Sydney Wy
Edgehill Wy
O'Shaughnessy Blvd
Glen Canyon Park
Gold Mine Dr
1/2 mile
.5 km

Forest Hill and Twin Peaks are hilltop residential islands far removed from the neighborhood buzz down the hill. Smack dab in the middle of the city, the view from Twin Peaks can be the best in town—but strong winds often bring in thick fog in the evening.

Banks

- **Bank of America (ATM)** • 350 Parnassus Ave
- **Bank of America (ATM)** • 500 Parnassus Ave
- **Wells Fargo (ATM)** • 400 Parnassus Ave
- **Wells Fargo (ATM)** • 510 Parnassus Ave

Emergency Rooms

- **UCSF Medical Center at Parnassus** • 505 Parnassus Ave

Landmarks

- **Seward Street Slides** • Douglass St & Seward St
- **Sutro Tower** • 250 Palo Alto Ave
- **Tank Hill** • Twin Peaks Blvd & Crown Ter
- **Twin Peaks** • Twin Peaks Blvd
- **UCSF's Kalmanovitz Library** • 530 Parnassus Ave

Libraries

- **Library & Center for Knowledge** • 530 Parnassus Ave

Parking

Pharmacies

- **PH Pharmacy** • 350 Parnassus Ave

Schools

- **The Circus Center** • 755 Frederick St
- **Clarendon Elementary** • 500 Clarendon Ave
- **Rooftop Elementary** • 445 Burnett Ave
- **Rooftop Middle** • 500 Corbett Ave

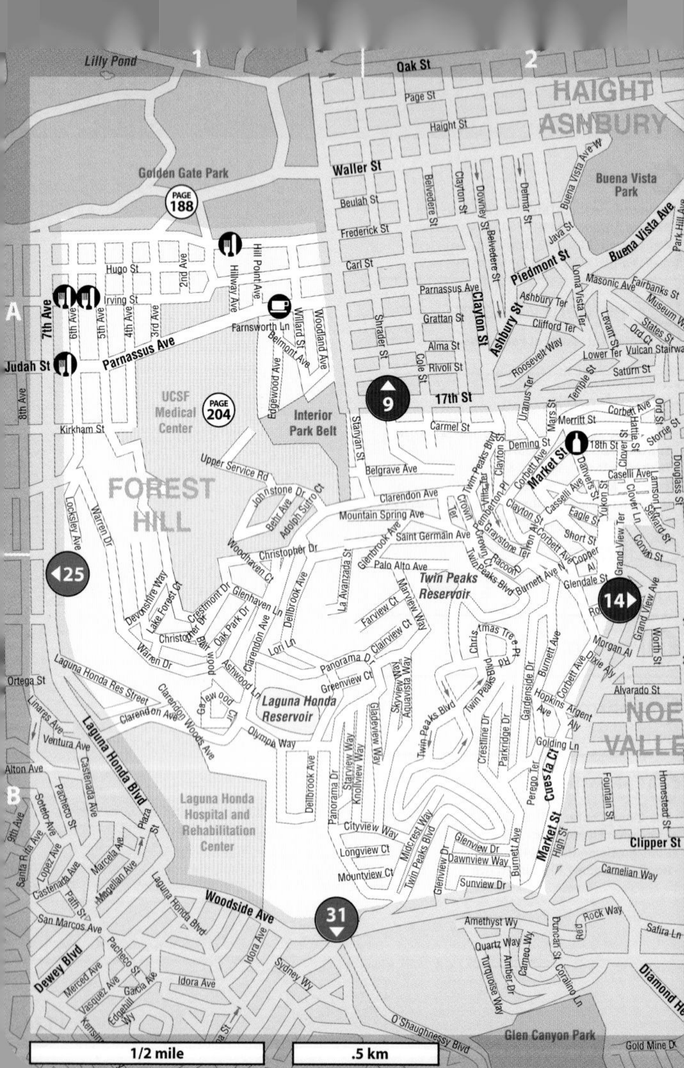
1
2
A
B
Lilly Pond
Oak St
Page St
Haight St
HAIGHT ASHBURY
Buena Vista Park
Buena Vista Ave W
Buena Vista Ave
Park Hill Ave
Golden Gate Park
PAGE 188
Waller St
Beulah St
Frederick St
Carl St
Belvedere St
Clayton St
Downey St
Delmar St
Java St
Piedmont St
Masonic Ave
Fairbanks St
Museum Way
Ashbury Ter
Clifford Ter
Loma Vista Ter
Levant St
States St
Ord Ct
Lower Ter
Vulcan Stairway
Roosevelt Way
Saturn St
Temple St
Hugo St
Irving St
7th Ave
6th Ave
5th Ave
4th Ave
3rd Ave
2nd Ave
Hillway Ave
Hill Point Ave
Farnsworth Ln
Willard St
Woodland Ave
Belmont Ave
Parnassus Ave
Grattan St
Alma St
Rivoli St
Shrader St
Cole St
Ashbury St
Judah St
8th Ave
UCSF Medical Center
PAGE 204
Edgewood Ave
Interior Park Belt
9
17th St
Carmel St
Uranus Ter
Mars St
Corbett Ave
Merritt St
18th St
Market St
Danvers St
Hattie St
Ord St
Storrie St
Douglass St
Kirkham St
Stanyan St
Upper Service Rd
Belgrave Ave
Deming St
Twin Peaks Blvd
Clayton St
Caselli Ave
FOREST HILL
Johnstone Dr
Behr Ave
Adolph Sutro Ct
Clarendon Ave
Mountain Spring Ave
Pemberton Pl
Villa Ter
Crown Ter
Eagle St
Yukon St
Clover Ln
Lamson Ln
Seward St
Locksley Ave
Warren Dr
Woodhaven Ct
Christopher Dr
Glenbrook Ave
Saint Germain Ave
Graystone Ter
Short St
Copper Al
Grand View Ter
Corwin St
25
Palo Alto Ave
La Avanzada St
Marview Way
Twin Peaks Reservoir
Racoon Dr
Burnett Ave N
Glendale St
14
Grand View Ave
Devonshire Way
Lake Forest Ct
Crestmont Dr
Glenhaven Ln
Dellbrook Ave
Farview Ct
Oak Park Dr
Clarendon Ave
Lori Ln
Clairview Ct
Christmas Tree Pt Rd
Burnett Ave
Morgan Al
Worth St
Dixie Aly
Warren Dr
Panorama Dr
Greenview Ct
Corbett Ave
Alvarado St
Ortega St
Laguna Honda Res Street
Ashwood Ln
Laguna Honda Reservoir
Skyview Way
Aquavista Way
Twin Peaks Blvd
Gardenside Dr
Hopkins Ave
Argent Aly
NOE VALLEY
Linares Ave
Clarendon Ave
Clarendon Woods Ave
Olympia Way
Gladeview Way
Crestline Dr
Parkridge Dr
Golding Ln
Ventura Ave
Laguna Honda Blvd
Starview Way
Knollview Way
Dellbrook Ave
Panorama Dr
Perego Ter
Cuesta Ct
Fountain St
Homestead St
Alton Ave
Castenada Ave
Laguna Honda Hospital and Rehabilitation Center
Pacheco St
Soteio Ave
9th Ave
Plaza St
Cityview Way
Midcrest Way
Glenview Dr
Dawnview Way
Burnett Ave
Market St
High St
Clipper St
Santa Rita Ave
Lopez Ave
Marcela Ave
Magellan Ave
Castenada Ave
Longview Ct
Mountview Ct
Twin Peaks Blvd
Sunview Dr
Carnelian Way
Path St
Laguna Honda Blvd
Woodside Ave
31
Amethyst Wy
Rock Way
Safira Ln
San Marcos Ave
Idora Ave
Quartz Way
Duncan St
Cameo Way
Dewey Blvd
Pacheco St
Sydney Wy
Turquoise Way
Amber Dr
Coralino Ln
Diamond Heights Blvd
Merced Ave
Vasquez Ave
Garcia Ave
Idora Ave
Edgehill Wy
O'Shaughnessy Blvd
Glen Canyon Park
Gold Mine Dr
1/2 mile
.5 km

If your idea of fun involves fantastic views, exploring streets you never knew existed, and making out in secluded woods, this may be the place. Otherwise, look to the nearby Inner Sunset, Castro, or the Haight for cafés, nightlife, shopping, or necessities.

Coffee

- **Starbucks** • 350 Parnassus Ave

Liquor Stores

- **Holsum Market** • 4686 18th St

Restaurants

- **Lime Tree** • 450 Irving St
- **New Ganges Restaurant** • 775 Frederick St
- **Pomelo** • 92 Judah St
- **Yellow Submarine** • 503 Irving St

WEST PORTAL
ST. FRANCIS WOOD
INGLESIDE
Taraval St
Ulloa St
Vicente St
Wawona St
Sloat Blvd
Ocean Ave
19th Ave
West Portal Ave
Portola Dr
Junipero Serra Blvd
Monterey Blvd
Santa Clara Ave
Dewey Blvd
Claremont Blvd
Larsen Park
Sigmund Stern Grove
Stonestown Galleria
Cerritos Ave
Miramar Ave
Westgate Dr
1/4 mile
.25 km

his is the west end of the old tunnel burrowed underneath Twin Peaks that starts out at the Castro. The "Main Street" is a classic strip of shops and restaurants catering to the quiet, laid-back, conservative, middle-class residents. To the south is the exclusive, mansion-studded enclave of St. Francis Wood.

Banks

- **Bank of America** • 288 West Portal Ave
- **Bank of the West** • 2606 Ocean Ave
- **Chase** • 98 West Portal Ave
- **Citibank** • 130 West Portal Ave
- **Citibank** • 2499 Ocean Ave
- **San Francisco Federal CU** • 2645 Ocean Ave
- **US** • 2656 Ocean Ave
- **Wells Fargo** • 145 West Portal Ave
- **Wells Fargo (ATM)** • 730 Taraval St

Gas Stations

- **76** • 800 Ulloa St

Libraries

- **Merced Branch Library** • 155 Winston Dr
- **West Portal Branch Library** • 190 Lenox Wy

Pharmacies

- **Rite Aid** • 200 West Portal Ave
- **Safeway** • 730 Taraval St
- **Walgreens** • 2 West Portal Ave
- **Walgreens** • 2550 Ocean Ave

Post Offices

- **West Portal Station** • 317 West Portal Ave

Schools

- **Aptos Middle** • 105 Aptos Ave
- **Commodore Sloat Elementary** • 50 Darien Wy
- **St Cecilia** • 660 Vicente St
- **West Portal Elementary** • 5 Lenox Wy
- **West Portal Lutheran** • 200 Sloat Blvd

Supermarkets

- **Eezy Freezy Market** • 25 West Portal Ave
- **Safeway** • 730 Taraval St
- **St Francis Market** • 16 West Portal Ave
- **West Portal Produce Market** • 222 West Portal Ave

WEST PORTAL
ST. FRANCIS WOOD
INGLESIDE
Larsen Park
Sigmund Stern Grove
Stonestown Galleria
19th Ave
Taraval St
Ulloa St
Vicente St
Wawona St
Sloat Blvd
Portola Dr
West Portal Ave
Claremont Blvd
Dewey Blvd
Santa Clara Ave
Monterey Blvd
Ocean Ave
Junipero Serra Blvd
Westgate Dr
Miramar Ave
Cerritos Ave
Saint Francis Blvd
San Marcos Ave
1/4 mile
.25 km

Clustered around the train station are some great diners, restaurants, and old-fashioned store front shops along West Portal Avenue. When you're done trying to eat cheap (try Submarine Center), the Philosopher's Club offers an ongoing symposium about the ravages of long term alcoholism.

Coffee

- **Manor Coffee Shop** • 321 West Portal Ave
- **Peet's** • 54 West Portal Ave
- **Starbucks** • 100 West Portal Ave

Copy Shops

- **The UPS Store** • 236 West Portal Ave

Gyms

- **24 Hour Fitness** • 1850 Ocean Ave ㉔

Hardware Stores

- **Papenhausen Hardware** • 32 West Portal Ave

Liquor Stores

- **San Francisco Wine Trading** • 250 Taraval St
- **Stop & Save Liquor** • 755 Taraval St

Movie Theaters

- **CineArts at the Empire** • 85 West Portal Ave

Nightlife

- **Joxer Daly's** • 46 West Portal Ave
- **Philosopher's Club** • 824 Ulloa St
- **Portals Tavern** • 179 West Portal Ave
- **Que Syrah** • 230 W Portal Ave

Pet Shops

- **Happy Pet** • 709 Taraval St

Restaurants

- **Ambrosia Bakery** • 2605 Ocean Ave
- **Bulls Head Restaurant** • 840 Ulloa St
- **Bursa** • 60 West Portal Ave
- **Café for All Seasons** • 150 West Portal Ave
- **El Toreador** • 50 West Portal Ave
- **Fresca** • 24 West Portal Ave
- **Manor Coffee Shop** • 321 West Portal Ave
- **Mozzarella di Bufala** • 69 West Portal Ave
- **Raintree Café** • 118 West Portal Ave
- **Submarine Center** • 820 Ulloa St

Shopping

- **Ambassador Toys** • 186 West Portal Ave
- **Goodwill Boutique** • 2605 Ocean Ave
- **Growing Up** • 240 West Portal Ave
- **Guerra Quality Meats** • 490 Taraval St
- **Little Fish Boutique** • 320 W Portal Ave

Video Rental

- **Diamond Video** • 99 West Portal Ave

Laguna Honda Hospital and Rehabilitation Center
Portola Dr
Glen Canyon Park
DIAMOND HEIGHTS
Mount Davidson Park
Mt Davidson Cross
Monterey Blvd
Miramar Ave
1/4 mile
.25 km

Standing at 938 feet, Mt. Davidson is the highest point in San Francisco. Covered in eucalyptus and blackberry on the sea-side and dry grass to the east, the hill is topped by a 103-foot-high cross commemorating the Armenian genocide—you'll recognize it from Dirty Harry. In between here and Glen Canyon is a residential neighborhood spilling down the hillside.

Banks

- **First National Northern** • 699 Portola Dr
- **US (ATM)** • Walgreens • 685 Portola Dr

Gas Stations

- **Coast** • 701 Portola Dr
- **Independent** • 598 Portola Dr

Landmarks

- **Mt Davidson Cross** • Dalewood Wy & Myra Wy

Pharmacies

- **Walgreens** • 689 Portola Dr

Schools

- **Archbishop Riordan High** • 175 Phelan Ave
- **Maria Montessori** • 678 Portola Dr
- **Miraloma Elementary** • 175 Omar Wy
- **San Francisco County Court Woodside Learning Center** • 375 Woodside Ave
- **School of the Arts High** • 555 Portola Dr
- **St Brendan's Elementary** • 940 Laguna Honda Blvd
- **St Finn Barr Catholic** • 419 Hearst Ave
- **Sunnyside Elementary** • 250 Foerster St
- **Wen Jian Ying School** • 259 Judson Ave

Supermarkets

- **Mollie Stone's** • 635 Portola Dr
- **Safeway** • 625 Monterey Blvd
- **Viglizzo's Tower Market** • 635 Portola Dr

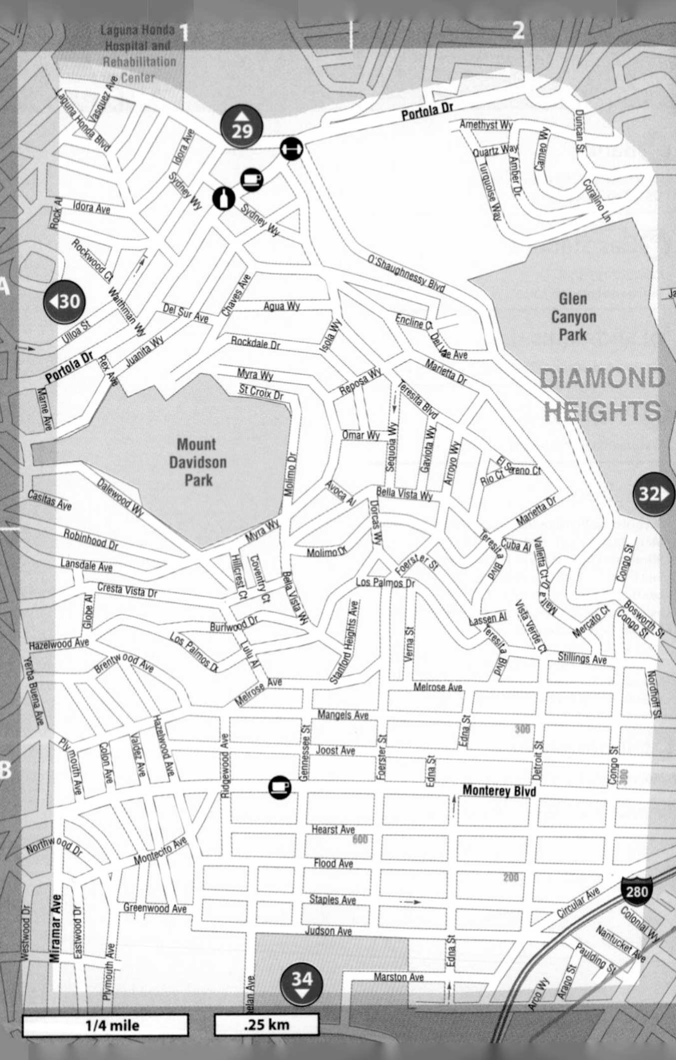

Laguna Honda Hospital and Rehabilitation Center
1
2
A
B
29
30
32
34
280
Portola Dr
Amethyst Wy
Quartz Way
Turquoise Way
Amber Dr
Cameo Wy
Duncan St
Coralino Ln
O'Shaughnessy Blvd
Glen Canyon Park
DIAMOND HEIGHTS
Mount Davidson Park
Laguna Honda Blvd
Vasquez Ave
Idora Ave
Sydney Wy
Rock Al
Rockwood Ct
Waithman Wy
Del Sur Ave
Chaves Ave
Agua Wy
Isola Wy
Ulloa St
Juanita Wy
Rex Ave
Marne Ave
Rockdale Dr
Myra Wy
St Croix Dr
Reposa Wy
Encline Ct
Marietta Dr
Teresita Blvd
Omar Wy
Sequoia Wy
Gaviota Wy
Arroyo Wy
El Sereno Ct
Rio Ct
Molimo Dr
Avoca Al
Bella Vista Wy
Dorcas Wy
Casitas Ave
Dalewood Wy
Robinhood Dr
Lansdale Ave
Cresta Vista Dr
Hillcrest Ct
Coventry Ct
Foerster St
Los Palmos Dr
Cuba Al
Vallejo Ct
Congo St
Globe Al
Burlwood Dr
Lulu Al
Stanford Heights Ave
Verna St
Lassen Al
Vista Verde Ct
Mercato Ct
Bosworth St
Hazelwood Ave
Brentwood Ave
Melrose Ave
Stillings Ave
Yerba Buena Ave
Nordhoff St
Mangels Ave
Edna St
Joost Ave
Plymouth Ave
Colon Ave
Valdez Ave
Ridgewood Ave
Gennessee St
Detroit St
Monterey Blvd
Hearst Ave
Northwood Dr
Montecito Ave
Flood Ave
Staples Ave
Circular Ave
Colonial Wy
Nantucket Ave
Paulding St
Greenwood Ave
Judson Ave
Marston Ave
Westwood Dr
Miramar Ave
Eastwood Dr
Phelan Ave
Arco Wy
Arano St
300
600
200
1/4 mile
.25 km

Sundries / Entertainment

All commercial activity is concentrated along the stretch of Monterey that leads to the freeway and the strip mall on Portola. Miraloma Liquor Store is a one-stop-shop with cheap sandwiches and a nice little taqueria inside.

Coffee

- **Railroad Expresso** • 705 Monterey Blvd
- **Starbucks** • 675 Portola Dr

Gyms

- **Curves (women only)** • 608 Portola Dr

Liquor Stores

- **Miraloma Liquor Store** • 691 Portola Dr

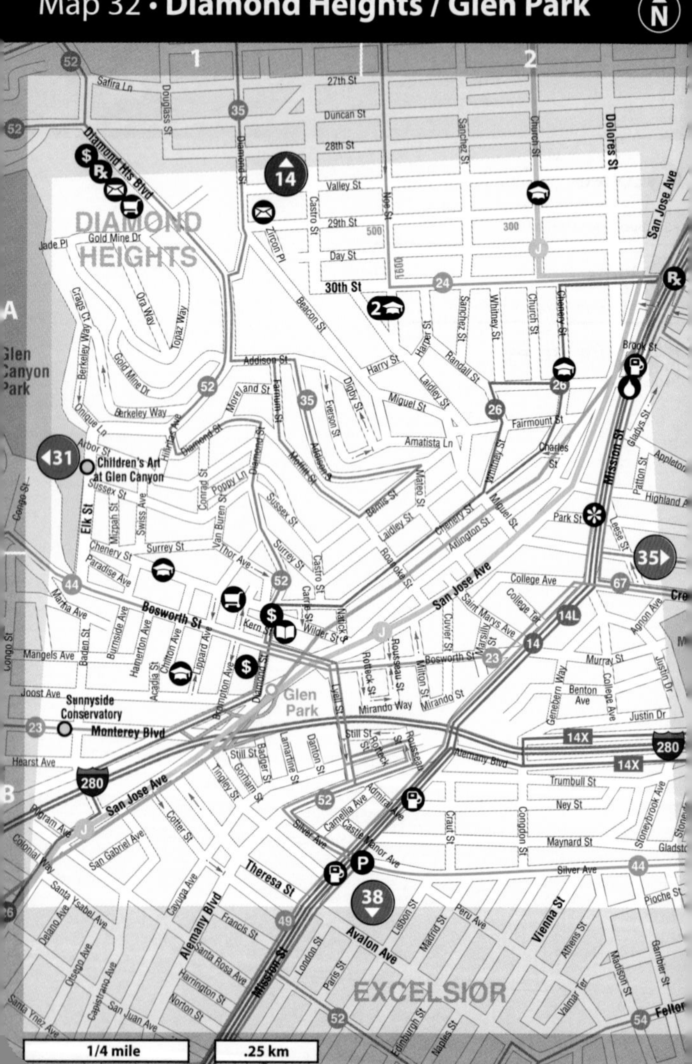
DIAMOND HEIGHTS
Glen Canyon Park
Children's Art at Glen Canyon
Sunnyside Conservatory
Glen Park
EXCELSIOR
Diamond Hts Blvd
Bosworth St
San Jose Ave
Monterey Blvd
Alemany Blvd
Mission St
30th St
Dolores St
1/4 mile
.25 km

Though adjacent, these neighborhoods are worlds apart in vibe and weather. Diamond Heights, with its ho-hum apartments and contemporary homes, is frequently foggy but offers unbeatable views. Sunny Glen Park in the valley below is a friendly 'village' with narrow, winding streets and charming, older homes. BART and the lovely Glen Canyon Park are close to both.

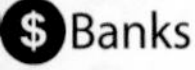

Banks

- **Bank of America** • 5268 Diamond Heights Blvd
- **Bank of America (ATM)** • 2810 Diamond St
- **Citibank** • 2895 Diamond St

Car Washes

- **Shell** • 3550 Mission St

Community Gardens

Gas Stations

- **Shell** • 3550 Mission St
- **Shell** • 4298 Mission St
- **Speedy** • 4199 Mission St

Landmarks

- **Children's Art at Glen Canyon** • Glen Canyon
- **Sunnyside Conservatory** • 236 Monterey Blvd

Libraries

- **Glen Park Branch Library** • 2825 Diamond St

Parking

Pharmacies

- **Walgreens** • 5260 Diamond Heights Blvd

Post Offices

- **Diamond Heights Finance** • 5262 Diamond Heights Blvd

Schools

- **Fairmount Elementary** • 65 Chenery St
- **Glen Park Elementary** • 151 Lippard Ave
- **Kate Kennedy Children's Center** • 1670 Noe St
- **Mission Education Center** • 1670 Noe St
- **St John's** • 925 Chenery St
- **St Paul's** • 1690 Church St

Supermarkets

- **Canyon Market** • 2815 Diamond St
- **Safeway** • 5290 Diamond Heights Blvd

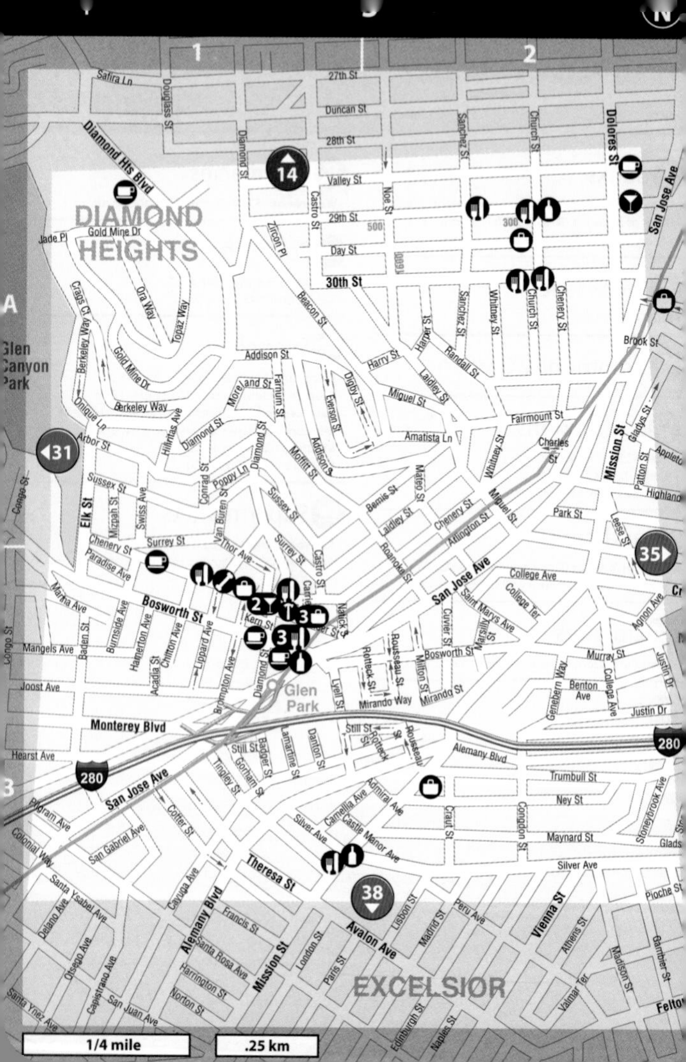

1
2
A
B
DIAMOND HEIGHTS
Glen Canyon Park
Glen Park
EXCELSIOR
14
31
35
38
280
Safira Ln
Douglass St
27th St
Duncan St
28th St
Valley St
29th St
Day St
30th St
Diamond Hts Blvd
Diamond St
Castro St
Noe St
Sanchez St
Church St
Dolores St
San Jose Ave
Zircon Pl
Jade Pl
Gold Mine Dr
Ora Way
Topaz Way
Crags Ct
Berkeley Way
Beacon St
Whitney St
Chenery St
Harper St
Randall St
Harry St
Laidley St
Miguel St
Brook St
Addison St
Moreland St
Farnum St
Everson St
Digby St
Fairmount St
Amatista Ln
Charles St
Mission St
Gladys St
Appleton
Onique Ln
Arbor St
Hiliritas Ave
Moffitt St
Sussex St
Poppy Ln
Conrad St
Congo St
Elk St
Mizpah St
Swiss Ave
Van Buren St
Bemis St
Mateo St
Arlington St
Patton St
Highland
Park St
Leese St
Chenery St
Surrey St
Thor Ave
Roanoke St
Paradise Ave
College Ave
College Ter
Saint Marys Ave
Marsilly St
Agnon Ave
Bosworth St
Carrie St
Kern St
Natick St
Marsily St
Cuvier St
Mangels Ave
Baden St
Burnside Ave
Hamerton Ave
Chilton Ave
Lippard Ave
Acadia St
Brompton Ave
Rotteck St
Rousseau St
Milton St
Murray St
Justin Dr
Genebern Way
Benton Ave
Joost Ave
Lyell St
Mirando Way
Mirando St
Monterey Blvd
Still St
Hearst Ave
Badger St
Lamartine St
Dalton St
Alemany Blvd
Trumbull St
Tingley St
Gorham St
Ney St
Admiral Ave
Camellia Ave
Castle Manor Ave
Craut St
Congdon St
Stoneybrook Ave
Maynard St
Silver Ave
Pilgrim Ave
Cotter St
San Gabriel Ave
Colonial Way
Theresa St
Cayuga Ave
Santa Ysabel Ave
Delano Ave
Otsego Ave
Capistrano Ave
Francis St
Santa Rosa Ave
Harrington St
Norton St
San Juan Ave
Santa Ynez Ave
Mission St
London St
Paris St
Avalon Ave
Lisbon St
Madrid St
Peru Ave
Vienna St
Athens St
Valmar Ter
Madison St
Gambier St
Pioche St
Edinburgh St
Naples St
1/4 mile
.25 km

The homey Glen Park 'downtown' around Chenery and Diamond Streets has excellent restaurants, a bar, an upscale market, and a cozy library. Diamond Heights offers a Safeway and a few utilitarian stores. Over the hill is Noe Valley's yuppie-friendly 24th Street and the decidedly more ethnic Outer Mission.

Coffee

- **Café Bello** • 2885 Diamond St
- **Higher Grounds Coffee House** • 691 Chenery St
- **Pebble's Café** • 2852 Diamond St
- **Starbucks** • Safeway • 5290 Diamond Heights Blvd

Hardware Stores

- **Glen Park Hardware** • 685 Chenery St

Liquor Stores

- **Glen Park Liquor** • 2900 Diamond St
- **Mission Silver Market** • 4304 Mission St
- **Veteran's Liquor Store** • 1710 Church St

Nightlife

- **Glen Park Station** • 2816 Diamond St
- **O'Greenberg's** • 1600 Dolores St

Pet Shops

- **Critter Fritters Pet Foods** • 670 Chenery St

Restaurants

- **Alice's** • 1599 Sanchez St
- **Chenery Park** • 683 Chenery St
- **Eggettes** • 2810 Diamond St
- **Joe's Cable Car** • 4320 Mission St
- **La Ciccia** • 291 30th St
- **La Corneta Taqueria** • 2834 Diamond St
- **Le P'tit Laurent** • 699 Chenery St
- **Pomelo** • 1793 Church St
- **Regent Thai** • 1700 Church St
- **Tyger's** • 2798 Diamond St

Shopping

- **Artesanias Unique Home Furnishings** • 1747 Church St
- **Canyon Market** • 2815 Diamond St
- **Cheese Boutique** • 666 Chenery St
- **Destination Bakery** • 598 Chenery St
- **Manila Oriental Market** • 4175 Mission St
- **Modernpast** • 677 Chenery St
- **Thrillhouse Records** • 3422 Mission St

INGLESIDE
Ingleside Terraces Sundial
Ocean View Playground
San Francisco Co
San Mateo Co
Ocean Ave
Cerritos Ave
Cedro Ave
Mercedes Way
Lunado Ct
Lunado Way
Lyndhurst Dr
Junipero Serra Blvd
Entrada Ct
Borica St
Corona St
De Soto St
Victoria St
Urbano Dr
Estero Ave
Aliviso St
Head St
Pinehurst Way
Manor Dr
Lakewood Ave
Fairfield Way
Keystone Way
Dorado Ter
Legion Ct
Pico Ave
De Montfort Ave
Holloway Ave
Jules Ave
Faxon Ave
Granada Ave
Garfield St
Grafton Ave
Banbury Dr
19th Ave
Beverly St
Monticello St
Byxbee St
Ralston St
Vernon St
Bright St
Ashton Ave
Capitol Ave
Miramar Ave
Plymouth Ave
Brighton Ave
Shields St
Lakeview Ave
Thrift St
Orizaba Ave
Felix Ave
Montana St
Sargent St
Minerva St
Arch St
Ramsell St
Lobos St
Chester Ave
Saint Charles Ave
Randolph St
Farallones St
Broad St
Brotherhood Wy
Stanley St
Payson St
Sadowa St
Hampton
Alemany
Worcester Ave
Sagamore St
Palmetto Ave
St Charles
Panama St
Niantic Ave
Crystal St
De Long St
Regent St
San Luis Ave
Belle Ave
Liebig St
Goethe St
Rhine St
Wilson St
Rice St
Lessing St
San Jose Ave
Flournoy St
San Mateo Ave
Santa Cruz Ave
San Diego Ave
Cayuga
1/4 mile
.25 km

Ingleside Terraces, to the west, is more upscale; in Ingleside proper you're more likely to see single-family homes and street corners decorated with discarded mattresses and dudes on milk crates. It's still relatively safe, though—just not particularly exciting.

Banks

- **Bank of America (ATM)** • 1649 Ocean Ave
- **Citibank (ATM)** • 2000 Ocean Ave
- **Citibank (ATM)** • 3080 San Jose Ave
- **Sterling** • 3951 Alemany Blvd

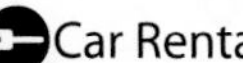

Car Rental

- **Enterprise** • 4050 19th Ave

Gas Stations

- **76** • 1490 Ocean Ave
- **Chevron** • 1100 Junipero Serra Blvd
- **Chevron** • 2998 San Jose Ave
- **Valero** • 1101 Junipero Serra Blvd
- **Valero** • 1799 Ocean Ave

Landmarks

- **Ingleside Terraces Sundial** • Borcia St & Entrado Ct

Libraries

- **Ingleside Branch Library** • 1298 Ocean Ave
- **Ocean View Branch Library** • 345 Randolph St

Pharmacies

- **Rite Aid** • 1830 Ocean Ave
- **Walgreens** • 1630 Ocean Ave

Schools

- **City Arts and Technology** • 301 De Montfort Ave
- **Jose Ortega Elementary** • 400 Sargent St
- **Sheridan Elementary** • 431 Capitol Ave
- **Voice of Pentecost Academy** • 1970 Ocean Ave

1
2
A
B
30
34
28
INGLESIDE
Mercedes Way
Cedro Ave
Cerritos Ave
Pinehurst Way
Manor Dr
Lakewood Ave
Fairfield Way
Keystone Way
Dorado Ter
Lunado Ct
Lunado Way
Urbano Dr
Entrada Ct
Borica St
Corona St
De Soto St
Victoria St
Legion Ct
Pico Ave
Lyndhurst Dr
Junipero Serra Blvd
Estero Ave
Alviso St
De Montfort Ave
Ocean Ave
Head St
Holloway Ave
19th Ave
Jules Ave
Faxon Ave
Granada Ave
Banbury Dr
Garfield St
Grafton Ave
Beverly St
Monticello St
Byxbee St
Ralston St
Vernon St
Bright St
Ashton Ave
Capitol Ave
Miramar Ave
Plymouth Ave
Brighton Ave
Shields St
Lakeview Ave
Orizaba Ave
Thrift St
Felix Ave
Montana St
Sargent St
Minerva St
Ocean View Playground
Arch St
Ramsell St
Chester Ave
Lobos St
Randolph St
Saint Charles Ave
Farallones St
Broad St
Brotherhood Wy
Stanley St
Sadowa St
Payson St
Kempton Ave
Worcester Ave
Sagamore St
San Francisco Co
San Mateo Co
Alemany
Palmetto Ave
St Charles Ave
280
Crystal St
Cayuga
Panama St
Niantic Ave
De Long St
Regent St
Liebig St
San Luis Ave
Goethe St
Rhine St
Wilson St
Rice St
Lessing St
San Jose Ave
San Mateo Ave
Santa Cruz Ave
San Diego Ave
Flournoy St
Belle Ave
200
500
100
1/4 mile
.25 km

Sundries / Entertainment

Ocean Avenue is the main commercial street. Affordable restaurants, a few cafés, drugstores, and hair salons serve City College students and Ingleside residents alike. Better shopping and entertainment, however, is five minutes away on West Portal Avenue.

Coffee

- **Caffe D Melanio** • 1314 Ocean Ave
- **Java on Ocean** • 1700 Ocean Ave
- **King's Coffee Shop** • 1901 Ocean Ave

Copy Shops

- **Copy Edge** • 1508 Ocean Ave
- **The UPS Store** • 1728 Ocean Ave

Gyms

- **Bally Total Fitness** • 3951 Alemany Blvd

Liquor Stores

- **A&N Liquors** • 1521 Ocean Ave
- **Homran Liquors** • 1551 Ocean Ave
- **Nora's Market** • 454 Capitol Ave
- **Normas Liquor** • 733 Randolph St
- **RC Package House** • 98 Broad St

Nightlife

- **The Ave** • 1607 Ocean Ave

Pet Shops

- **Aquatic Central** • 1963 Ocean Ave

Restaurants

- **Ocean Taqueria** • 1941 Ocean Ave
- **Yama Sushi** • 850 Holloway Ave

Video Rental

- **Oceanview Video (English)** • 1720 Ocean Ave

Map 34 • Oceanview

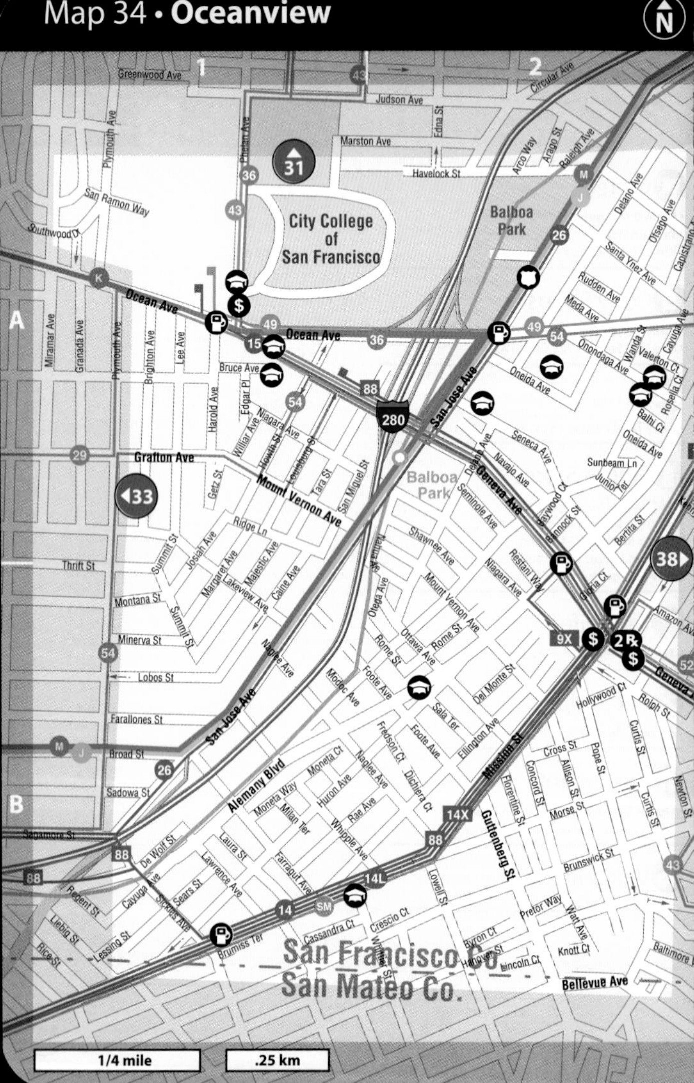

an Francisco City College dominates this residential, working-class eighborhood. A collection of various high schools contributes to the emographic, which includes the stretching greens of Balboa Park and the ART station. With I-280 and some large thoroughfares, Oceanview (which oesn't really have an ocean view) is a well-connected transit hub.

Banks

Bank of America • 5150 Mission St
US (ATM) • Walgreens • 965 Geneva Ave
Wells Fargo (ATM) • 50 Phelan Ave

Gas Stations

76 • 999 Ocean Ave
Arco • 5898 Mission St
Independent • 2099 San Jose Ave
Independent • 5098 Mission St
Shell • 2200 Alemany Blvd

Pharmacies

Daniel's Pharmacy • 943 Geneva Ave
Walgreens • 965 Geneva Ave

Police

Ingleside Police Station • 1 John Young Ln

Schools

Balboa High • 1000 Cayuga Ave
Bethel Center • 2557 Alemany Blvd
City College of San Francisco • 50 Phelan Ave
Independence High • 1000 Cuyuga Ave
James Denman Middle • 241 Oneida Ave
Leadership High • 300 Seneca Ave
Lick Wilmerding High • 755 Ocean Ave
Longfellow Elementary • 755 Morse St
San Francisco Christian • 25 Whittier St
San Francisco Junior Academy • 66 Geneva Ave

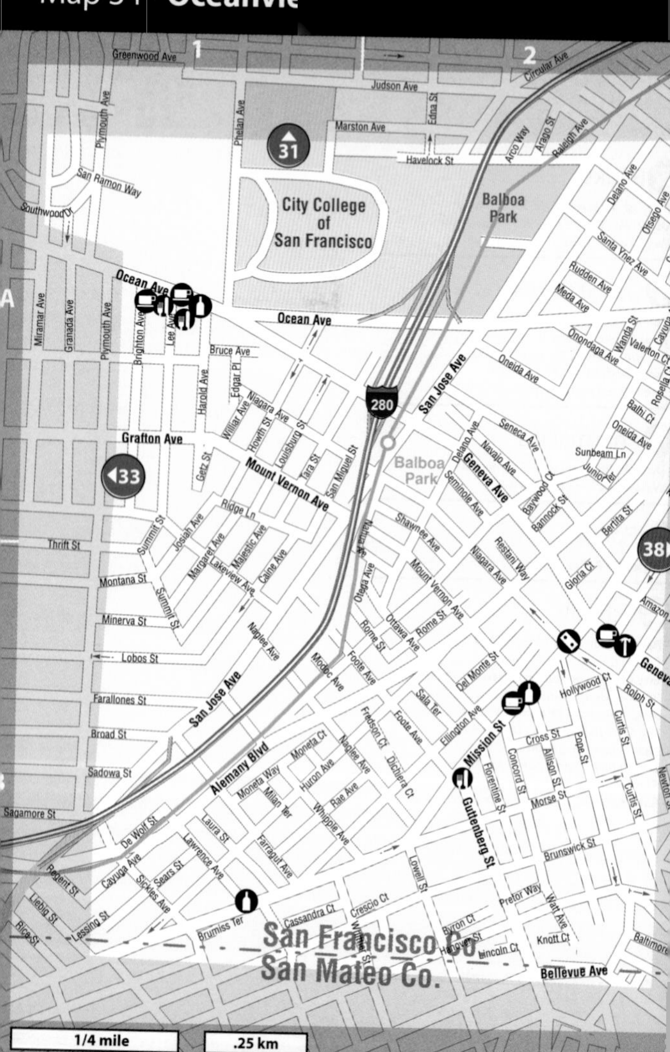

Greenwood Ave
Judson Ave
Circular Ave
Marston Ave
Edna St
Havelock St
Phelan Ave
Plymouth Ave
San Ramon Way
Southwood Dr
31
City College of San Francisco
Balboa Park
Arco Way
Arago St
Raleigh Ave
Delano Ave
Otsego Ave
Santa Ynez Ave
Rudden Ave
Meda Ave
Ocean Ave
Miramar Ave
Granada Ave
Plymouth Ave
Brighton Ave
Lee Ave
Bruce Ave
Edgar Pl
Harold Ave
Onondaga Ave
Wanda St
Valerton Ct
Oneida Ave
San Jose Ave
280
Niagara Ave
Willar Ave
Howth St
Louisburg St
Tara St
San Miguel St
Grafton Ave
Getz St
33
Mount Vernon Ave
Balboa Park
Delano Ave
Geneva Ave
Seminole Ave
Navajo Ave
Seneca Ave
Baywood Ct
Bannock St
Sunbeam Ln
Junior Ter
Bertita St
Oneida Ave
Balhi Ct
Rosella Ct
Ridge Ln
Summit St
Josiah Ave
Margaret Ave
Majestic Ave
Lakeview Ave
Caine Ave
Thrift St
Montana St
Summit St
Minerva St
Lobos St
Naglee Ave
Ottega Ave
Shawnee Ave
Mount Vernon Ave
Niagara Ave
Restani Way
Gloria Ct
38
Amazon
Rome St
Ottawa Ave
Rome St
Foote Ave
Modoc Ave
Del Monte St
Hollywood Ct
Rolph St
Geneva
Farallones St
San Jose Ave
Broad St
Sala Ter
Ellington Ave
Mission St
Fredson Ct
Foote Ave
Alemany Blvd
Moneta Ct
Naglee Ave
Dichiera Ct
Cross St
Pope St
Curtis St
Allison St
Concord St
Florentine St
Sadowa St
Moneta Way
Milan Ter
Huron Ave
Rae Ave
Whipple Ave
Morse St
Curtis St
Newton St
Sagamore St
De Wolf St
Laura St
Farragut Ave
Guttenberg St
Brunswick St
Lawrence Ave
Regent St
Cayuga Ave
Sears St
Sickles Ave
Lowell St
Prefor Way
Watt Ave
Liebig St
Lessing St
Rice St
Brumiss Ter
Cassandra Ct
Crescio Ct
Whittier St
Byron Ct
Hanover St
Lincoln Ct
Knott Ct
Baltimore
San Francisco Co.
San Mateo Co.
Bellevue Ave
1/4 mile
.25 km

Most of the commerce lies along Mission Street. At the intersection with Geneva Avenue is the center of a San Francisco left alone and thriving. Along the K streetcar tracks on Ocean Avenue, small cafés attract foreign and local students from City College and hordes of kids from around the block.

Coffee

- **Claddagh Coffee** • 951 Geneva Ave
- **Java Creperie** • 1125 Ocean Ave
- **Quickly** • 5301 Mission St
- **Quickly** • 1039 Ocean Ave

Hardware Stores

- **J&J True Value Hardware** • 929 Geneva Ave

Liquor Stores

- **Mike's Liquors** • 5084 Mission St
- **United Liquor Market** • 5298 Mission St
- **Willey's Den** • 1015 Ocean Ave
- **Woody's Liquor Store** • 5799 Mission St

Restaurants

- **Beep's Burgers** • 1051 Ocean Ave
- **Java Jitters** • 1125 Ocean Ave
- **Reinas Restaurant** • 5479 Mission St

Video Rental

- **Mission Video** • 5188 Mission St

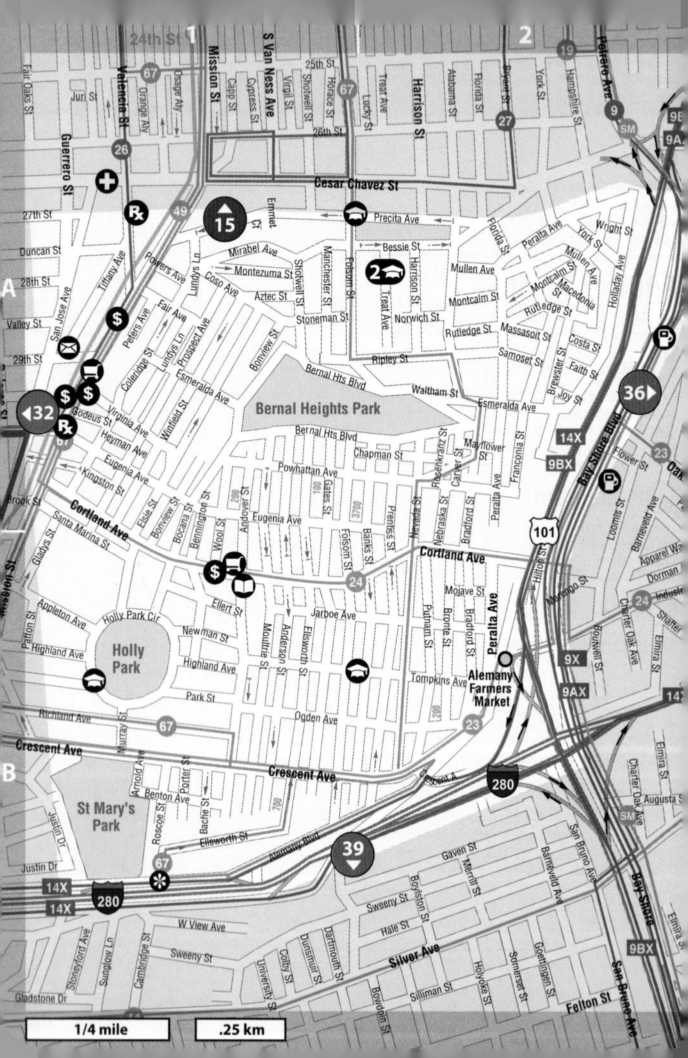

24th St
1
2
Mission St
S Van Ness Ave
Valencia St
Guerrero St
Harrison St
Potrero Ave
Cesar Chavez St
Precita Ave
15
32
36
39
Bernal Heights Park
Bernal Hts Blvd
Cortland Ave
Holly Park
St Mary's Park
Alemany Farmers Market
Crescent Ave
Alemany Blvd
Silver Ave
Bay Shore Blvd
Peralta Ave
Folsom St
Mission St
A
B
1/4 mile
.25 km

Tucked away beneath Bernal Heights Park and its commanding views of downtown and the Bay, Bernal Heights is perhaps San Francisco's best-kept neighborhood secret. Cortland Avenue has everything a lazy afternoon-into-evening could require: bookshops, hair salons, gourmet restaurants, and even an overgrown back-yard beer garden. Nice.

Banks

- **Bank of America** • 3250 Mission St
- **Bank of America** • 433 Cortland Ave
- **US (ATM)** • Walgreens • 3398 Mission St
- **Wells Fargo (ATM)** • 3350 Mission St

Community Gardens

Emergency Rooms

- **California Pacific Medical Center St. Luke's Campus** • 3555 Cesar Chavez

Gas Stations

- **Chevron** • 101 Bay Shore Blvd
- **Shell** • 319 Bay Shore Blvd

Landmarks

- **Alemany Farmers Market (Sat, 6am–5pm)** • 100 Alemany Blvd

Libraries

- **Bernal Heights Branch Library** • 500 Cortland Ave

Pharmacies

- **Walgreens** • 1580 Valencia St
- **Walgreens** • 3398 Mission St

Post Offices

- **Bernal Heights Finance Station** • 189 Tiffany Ave

Schools

- **Junipero Serra Elementary** • 625 Holly Park Cir
- **Metropolitan Arts & Tech** • 1550 Treat Ave
- **Paul Revere Elementary** • 555 Tompkins Ave
- **St Anthony / Immaculate Conception** • 299 Precita Ave

Supermarkets

- **Good Life Grocery** • 448 Cortland Ave
- **Safeway** • 3350 Mission St ㉔

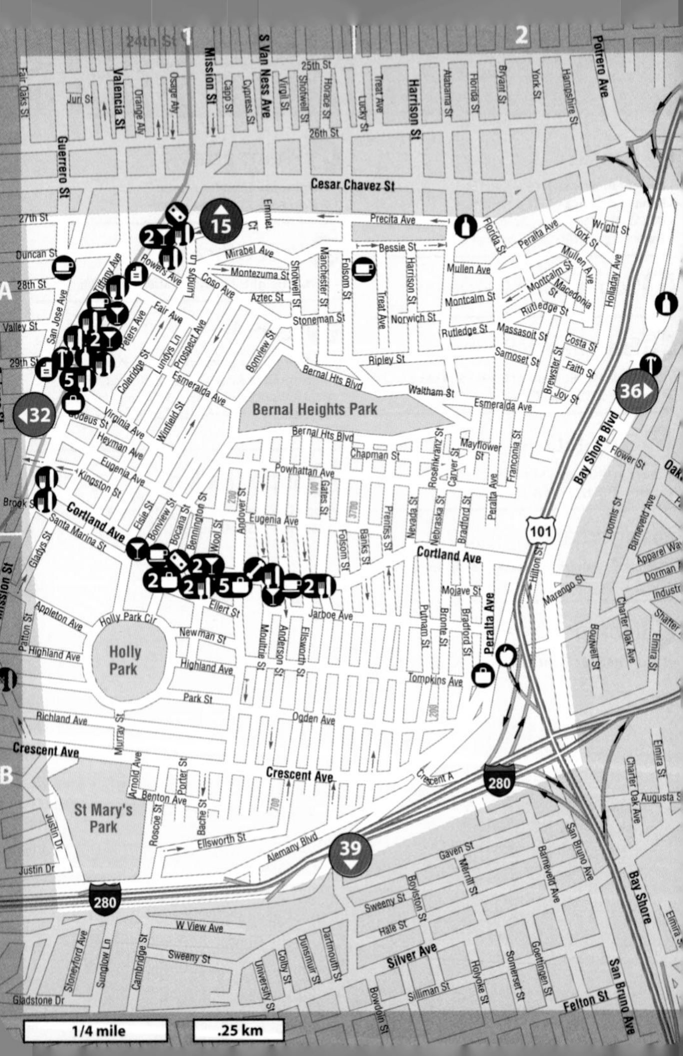
1
2
A
B
24th St
25th St
26th St
Cesar Chavez St
27th St
28th St
29th St
Fair Oaks St
Juri St
Valencia St
Orange Aly
Osage Aly
Mission St
Capp St
Cypress St
S Van Ness Ave
Virgil St
Shotwell St
Horace St
Lucky St
Treat Ave
Harrison St
Alabama St
Florida St
Bryant St
York St
Hampshire St
Potrero Ave
Guerrero St
Duncan St
Valley St
San Jose Ave
Tiffany Ave
Powers Ave
Lundys Ln
Coso Ave
Emmet Ct
Precita Ave
Mirabel Ave
Montezuma St
Aztec St
Manchester St
Folsom St
Bessie St
Mullen Ave
Montcalm St
Norwich St
Stoneman St
Rutledge St
Massasoit St
Samoset St
Ripley St
Peralta Ave
Wright St
Macedonia St
Holladay Ave
Costa St
Faith St
Brewster St
Joy St
Fair Ave
Peters Ave
Coleridge St
Prospect Ave
Esmeralda Ave
Bonview St
Bernal Hts Blvd
Waltham St
Bernal Heights Park
Virginia Ave
Winfield St
Heyman Ave
Eugenia Ave
Kingston St
Brook St
Cortland Ave
Santa Marina St
Chapman St
Powhattan Ave
Gates St
Rosenkranz St
Carver St
Mayflower St
Franconia St
Elsie St
Bocana St
Bennington St
Wool St
Andover St
Prentiss St
Banks St
Nevada St
Nebraska St
Bradford St
Bay Shore Blvd
Flower St
Loomis St
Barneveld Ave
Apparel Way
Dorman Ave
Industrial
Shafter
Hilton St
Marengo St
Gladys St
Mission St
Ellert St
Jarboe Ave
Mojave St
Putnam St
Bronte St
Appleton Ave
Holly Park Cir
Newman St
Patton St
Highland Ave
Holly Park
Moultrie St
Anderson St
Ellsworth St
Tompkins Ave
Bouwell St
Charter Oak Ave
Elmira St
Park St
Richland Ave
Ogden Ave
Murray St
Crescent Ave
Arnold Ave
Porter St
Benton Ave
Roscoe St
Bache St
St Mary's Park
Justin Dr
Alemany Blvd
Gaven St
Merrill St
Augusta St
San Bruno Ave
Boylston St
Sweeny St
Hale St
W View Ave
Stoneyford Ave
Sunglow Ln
Cambridge St
University St
Colby St
Dunsmuir St
Dartmouth St
Silver Ave
Holyoke St
Somerset St
Goettingen St
Silliman St
Bowdoin St
Felton St
Gladstone Dr
Bay Shore
101
280
15
32
36
39
1/4 mile
.25 km

ernal brims with restaurants for every taste and budget: from gourmet omfort food at Blue Plate to Taqueria Cancun or Zante's Indian Pizza. After linner, treat yourself to some tropical ice cream at Mitchell's, see live music t El Rio, or tie one on at the lesbian-friendly Wild Side West.

Coffee

- **Cup of Java** • 1600 Guerrero St
- **Martha & Bros** • 745 Cortland Ave
- **Cafe Seventy8** • 78 29th St
- **Park Bench Cafè** • 3214 Folsom St
- **Progressive Grounds** • 400 Cortland Ave

Copy Shops

- **Copy Central** • 3181 Mission St
- **The UPS Store** • 60 29th St

Farmers Markets

- **Alemany Farmers Market (Sat, 6am—5pm)** • 100 Alemany Blvd

Hardware Stores

- **Cole Hardware** • 3312 Mission St
- **Sartor Saw Works** • 250 Bay Shore Blvd

Liquor Stores

- **Beverages & More** • 201 Bay Shore Blvd
- **DJ Liquors** • 3278 Mission St
- **Sam's Liquor** • 580 Precita Ave

Nightlife

- **3300 Club** • 3300 Mission St
- **Argus Lounge** • 3187 Mission St
- **El Rio** • 3158 Mission St
- **The Knockout** • 3223 Mission St
- **Roccapulco** • 3140 Mission St
- **Skip's Tavern** • 453 Cortland Ave
- **Stray Bar** • 309 Cortland Ave
- **Vino Rosso** • 629 Cortland Ave
- **The Wild Side West** • 424 Cortland Ave

Pet Shops

- **Bernal Beast** • 509 Cortland Ave

Restaurants

- **Angkor Borei** • 3741 Mission St
- **Baby Blues BBQ** • 3149 Mission St
- **Blue Plate** • 3218 Mission St
- **El Patio** • 3193 Mission St
- **El Zocalo** • 3230 Mission St
- **Emmy's Spaghetti Shack** • 18 Virginia Ave
- **The Front Porch** • 65A 29th St
- **Goood Frikin' Chicken** • 10 29th St
- **Jasmine Tea House** • 3253 Mission St
- **Liberty Café**• 410 Cortland Ave
- **Little Nepal** • 925 Cortland Ave
- **Mitchell's Ice Cream** • 688 San Jose Ave
- **Moki's Sushi & Pacific Grill** • 615 Cortland Ave
- **Nervous Dog Coffee** • 3438 Mission St
- **Taqueria Cancun** • 3211 Mission St
- **Zante's Indian Cuisine & Pizza** • 3489 Mission St

Shopping

- **Bernal Beast** • 509 Cortland Ave
- **Chloe's Closet** • 451 Cortland Ave
- **Cole Hardware** • 3312 Mission St
- **East & West Gourmet Afghan Foods** • 108 Medburn St.
- **Heartfelt** • 436 Cortland Ave
- **Red Hill Books** • 401 Cortland Ave

Video Rental

- **Blockbuster** • 3125 Mission St
- **Four Star Videos** • 402 Cortland Ave

Cesar Chavez
Army St
Marin St
Napoleon St
Jerrold Ave
Toland St
Galvez Ave
Hudson Ave
Evans Ave
Innes Ave
Kirkwood Ave
Oakdale Ave
Palou Ave
Quint St
Flora Grubb Gardens
Bayview Opera House
Silver Ave
Bay Shore Blvd
Thornton Ave
Williams Ave
3rd St
Industrial St
Evans
Hudson Innes
Kirkwood/ Lasalle
Oakdale/ Palou
Revere/ Shafter
Williams
BAYVIEW
1/4 mile
.25 km

While the rumors are true—this area is sketchy at night—it's also one of the city's only under-commercialized neighborhoods. A visit with mostly friendly residents who know the local history will introduce you to the fine art and community events at the Bayview Opera House.

Banks

- **Bank of America** • 2090 Jerrold Ave
- **Bank of America** • 5000 3rd St
- **Union** • 3801 3rd St
- **US** • 4947 3rd St
- **US (ATM)** • Walgreens • 3801 3rd St
- **Wells Fargo** • 3801 3rd St

Car Rental

- **Enterprise** • 445 Charter Oak Ave

Gas Stations

- **76** • 3800 3rd St
- **76** • 975 Bay Shore Blvd
- **Arco** • 2190 Carroll Ave
- **Shell** • 3750 3rd St

Landmarks

- **Bayview Opera House** • 4705 3rd St
- **Flora Grubb Gardens** • 1634 Jerrold Ave

Libraries

- **Bayview - Anna E Waden** • 5075 3rd St

Pharmacies

- **Walgreens** • 5300 3rd St
- **Walgreens Drug Store** • 3801 3rd St

Post Offices

- **Napoleon Street Carrier Complex** • 180 Napoleon St

Schools

- **Big City Montessori** • 240 Industrial St
- **CCSF (Southeast Campus)** • 1800 Oakdale Ave
- **Drew Elementary** • 50 Pomona St
- **Joshua Marie Cameron Academy** • 3801 3rd St
- **Thurgood Marshall High** • 45 Conkling St
- **Willie Brown College Prep** • 2055 Silver Ave

N
Cesar Chavez
Army St
Marin St
Napoleon St
Jerrold Ave
Toland St
Evans Ave
Oakdale Ave
Quint St
Silver Ave
Thornton Ave
Williams Ave
Bay Shore Blvd
3rd St
Evans
Hudson/Innes
Kirkwood/Lasalle
Oakdale/Palou
Revere/Shafter
Williams
BAY VIEW
16
35
37
40
101
280
1/4 mile
.25 km

Sundries / Entertainment

Even if you're not a vegetarian, it's worth a trip to the gigantic Bayview Farmers Market. They have a large selection of organic, ethnic, and specialty produce. For cheap eats, head to La Laguna for Mexican or Soo Fong for Chinese. Dance-aholics frequent Space 550, a cavernous club known for slammin' electronic music events.

Coffee

- **America's Best Coffee Roasting** • 1500 Davidson Ave
- **Javalencia** • 3900 3rd St
- **Ritual Coffee** • 1634 Jerrold Ave
- **Road House Coffee** • 5191 3rd St

Copy Shops

- **Bay Copy Plus** • 3801 3rd St
- **Pressworks** • 111 Toland St
- **The Print Shop** • 2132 Oakdale Ave

Farmers Markets

- **Bayview (May—Oct, Wed, 8:30am—12:30pm)** • Walgreens • 3rd & Galvez Ave

Gyms

- **Curves (women only)** • 3801 3rd St

Hardware Stores

- **Bay Area Builders Hardware** • 33 Elmira St
- **Bay Tool & Supply** • 1650 Evans Ave
- **G Mazzei & Sons Hardware** • 5166 3rd St
- **Lumberland Builders Supply** • 2590 Oakdale Ave
- **Safeco Electric and True Value** • 301 Toland St

Liquor Stores

- **Bayview Liquors** • 4700 3rd St

Nightlife

- **Space 550** • 550 Barneveld Ave

Restaurants

- **La Laguna** • 3906 3rd St
- **Old Clam House** • 299 Bayshore Blvd
- **Soo Fong** • 3801 3rd St

Shopping

- **San Francisco Wholesale Produce Market** • 2095 Jerrold Ave
- **Scrap** • 801 Toland St

1
2
Pier 80
17
Marin St
Islais Creek Channel
Amador St
Pier 94
Port of SF
Southern Cargo Terminals
Burke Ave
Cargo Way
Evans Ave
Evans Ave
Mendell St
15
19
Newhall St
Hudson/Innes
A
36
Fairfax Ave
Newhall St
Jennings St
Pier 96
Hudson Ave
Kirkwood/Lasalle
Bowman Ct
Rebecca Ln
Keith St
54
44
Heron's
Head
Park
Innes Ave
Kirkwood Ave
Dukes Ct
Dedman Ct
Reuel Ct
Hunters Point Blvd
Middle Point Rd
Wills St
La Salle Ave
Youngs Ct
Mabrey Ct
Cashmere St
India Basin
Mckinnon Ave
Westbrook Ct
Newcomb Ave
Hilltop
Park
Skatebowl
Hare St
Hudson Ave
Oakdale Ave
Ardath Ct
Oakdale/
Palou
Hilltop
Park
Harbor Rd
Innes Ave
Marist St
Griffith St
Dormer Ct
Hudson Ave
Hudson Ct
Rosie Lee Ln
Hayes St
Garlington Ct
La Salle Ave
Osceola Ln
Beatrice Ln
Palou Ave
Whitfield Ct
Ingalls St
Northridge Rd
Fitch St
Earl St
Quesada Ave
George Ct
Kiska Rd
Keith St
Revere Ave
23
Oakdale Ave
Baldwin Ct
Reardon Rd
Dormitory Rd
Kirkwood Ave
19
Hudson Ave
Donahue St
English St
54
McKinnon Ave
Albatross Ct
Cleo Rand Ln
Innes Ave
Galvez Ave
McCann St
Lockwood St
Griffith St
Navy Rd
Earl St
Friedell St
Robinson St
Hunter's Point
Ingalls St
Crisp Rd
Atoll Cir
Nautilus Ct
Jerrold Ave
Coleman St
Hill Dr
Galvez Ave
La Salle Ave
Marlin Ct
La Salle Ave
Fischer Ave
Van Keuren Ave
Hawes St
Crisp Rd
Hill Dr
Horn Ave
D St
Spear Ave
Nimitz Ave
Blandy St
C St
Griffith St
Spear Ave
19
B
Fitch St
E St
Spear Ave
6th Ave
I St
H St
Hussey St
Cochrane St
Morrell St
40
19
Manseau St
J St
South Basin
Mahan St
PAGE
239
Candlestick Park
1/2 mile
.5 km

Formerly a working shipyard and the site of the US's first dry dock, Hunter's Point is currently being redeveloped to provide affordable housing and attract businesses into this economically-deprived sector of the city. The Hunter's Point Artist Community is here as well, providing affordable studio space for local artists.

Landmarks

- **Hilltop Park Skatebowl** • Hilltop Park

Community Gardens

Post Offices

- **Diamond Heights Carrier Annex** • 151 Mendell St
- **San Francisco P+DC** • 1300 Evans Ave

Schools

- **Burnett Nursery & School-Age** • 1520 Oakdale Ave
- **CCSF (Evans Campus)** • 1400 Evans Ave
- **George Washington Carver Elementary** • 1360 Oakdale Ave
- **Gloria R Davis Middle** • 1195 Hudson Ave
- **Joshua Marie Cameron Academy** • 100 Whitney Young Cir
- **Malcolm X Academy** • 350 Harbor Rd

N
1
2
A
B
Pier 80
17
Marin St
Islais Creek Channel
Amador St
Port of SF
Southern Cargo Terminals
Pier 94
Burke Ave
Cargo Way
Evans Ave
Evans Ave
Mendell St
Newhall St
Hudson/Innes
36
Fairfax Ave
Hudson Ave
Newhall St
Jennings St
Pier 96
Kirkwood/Lasalle
Bowman Ct
Rebecca Ln
Keith St
Innes Ave
Kirkwood Ave
Dukes Ct
Dedman Ct
Reuel Ct
La Salle Ave
Youngs Ct
Mabrey Ct
Cashmere St
Middle Point Rd
Wills St
Hunters Point Blvd
Heron's Head Park
India Basin
Mckinnon Ave
Newcomb Ave
Westbrook Ct
Lindsay Cir
Jakey Ct
Hare St
Hudson Ave
Innes Ave
Oakdale Ave
Oakdale/Palou
Bell Ct
Bass Ct
Hilltop Park
Hudson Ave
Harbor Rd
Marist St
Griffith St
Hayes St
Commer Ct
La Salle Ave
Osceola Ln
Garlington Ct
Whitfield Ct
Beatrice Ln
Rosie Lee Ln
Hudson Ct
Ingalls St
Northridge Rd
Fitch St
Earl St
Palou Ave
Keith St
Quesada Ave
Revere Ave
George Ct
Oakdale Ave
Baldwin Ct
Kiska Rd
Reardon Rd
Dormitory Rd
Kirkwood Ave
Hudson Ave
Innes Ave
Donahue St
English St
McCann St
Lockwood St
Galvez Ave
Friedell St
McKinnon Ave
Navy Rd
Earl St
Cleo Rand Ln
Albatross Ct
Atoll Cir
Nautilus Ct
La Salle Ave
Coleman St
Hill Dr
Galvez Ave
Robinson St
Hunter's Point
Crisp Rd
Griffith St
Ingalls St
Hawes St
Griffith St
Fitch St
Crisp Rd
Horn Ave
Fischer Ave
Van Keuren Ave
Spear Ave
D St
C St
Blandy St
Nimitz Ave
Spear Ave
Spear Ave
6th Ave
I St
H St
Hussey St
Cochrane St
Morrell St
E St
40
Manseau St
J St
South Basin
Mahan St
PAGE 239
Candlestick Park
1/2 mile
.5 km

City planners had this nabe poised for radical change after the opening of the 3rd Street Light Rail, but nothing much new happened after the economy's free fall. If anything, we've seen more closings than openings in recent years. Speakeasy Ales is still here, though, and on Friday evenings opens its brewery doors to the thirsty.

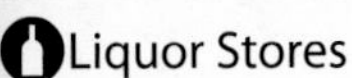

Liquor Stores

- **Speakeasy Ales & Lagers** • 1195 Evans Ave
- **Surfside Liquors** • 950 Innes Ave

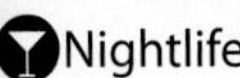

Nightlife

- **Speakeasy Ales & Lagers** • 1195 Evans Ave

Restaurants

- **Evans Street Post Office Cafeteria** • 1300 Evans Ave
- **Wok-In Cafeteria** • 50 Mendell St

Shopping

- **Building Resources** • 701 Amador St

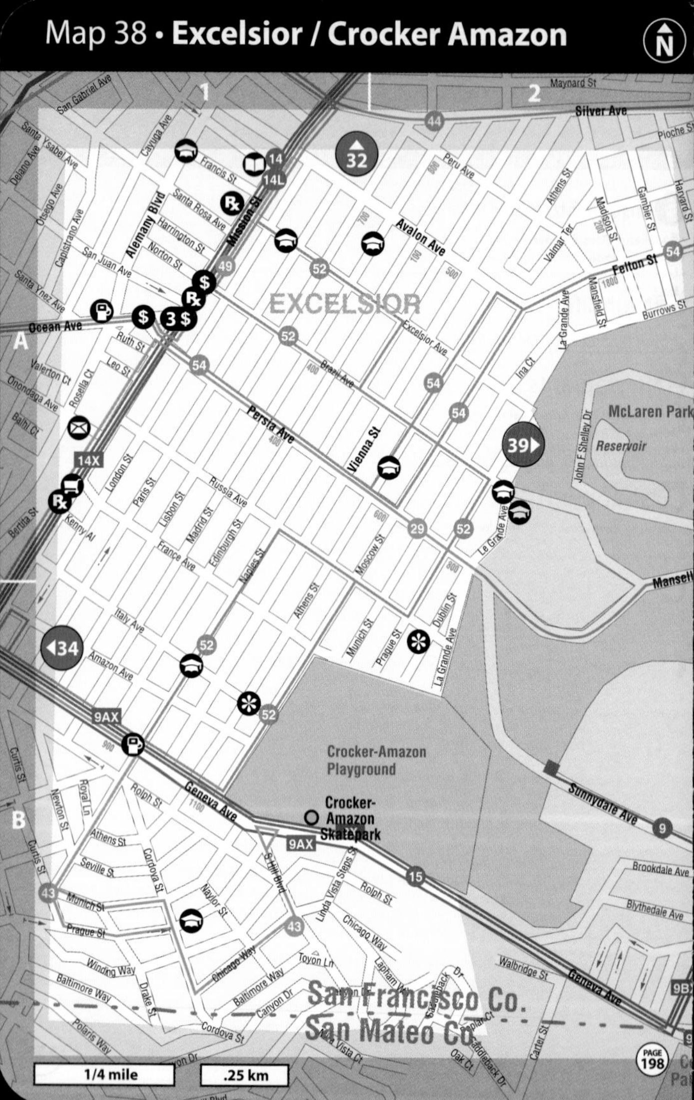
N
EXCELSIOR
McLaren Park
Reservoir
Crocker-Amazon Playground
Crocker-Amazon Skatepark
San Francisco Co.
San Mateo Co.
Mission St
Alemany Blvd
Ocean Ave
Geneva Ave
Persia Ave
Avalon Ave
Excelsior Ave
Brazil Ave
Russia Ave
France Ave
Italy Ave
Amazon Ave
Silver Ave
Maynard St
Felton St
Burrows St
Peru Ave
Athens St
Madison St
Gambier St
Harvard St
Pioche St
Valmar Ter
Mansfield St
La Grande Ave
Ina Ct
John F Shelley Dr
Mansell
Sunnydale Ave
Brookdale Ave
Blythedale Ave
Walbridge St
Carter St
Vienna St
Moscow St
Munich St
Prague St
Dublin St
London St
Paris St
Lisbon St
Madrid St
Edinburgh St
Naples St
Francis St
Santa Rosa Ave
Harrington St
Norton St
San Juan Ave
Cayuga Ave
San Gabriel Ave
Santa Ysabel Ave
Delano Ave
Otsego Ave
Capistrano Ave
Santa Ynez Ave
Ruth St
Leo St
Valerton Ct
Onondaga Ave
Rosella Ct
Baltic Ct
Berlita St
Kenny Al
Curtis St
Royal Ln
Newton St
Rolph St
Athens St
Seville St
Cordova St
Naylor St
Munich St
Prague St
Winding Way
Baltimore Way
Drake St
Polaris Way
Cordova St
Chicago Way
Canyon Dr
Toyon Ln
S Hill Blvd
Linda Vista Steps
Lapham Way
Saddleback Dr
Oak Ct
1
2
A
B
32
39
34
14
14L
14X
9AX
9
9BX
15
29
43
44
49
52
54
3
1/4 mile
.25 km

PAGE 198

The neighborhood where Jerry Garcia grew up is one of the city's lesser-known areas. Don't let that stop you from visiting, though, as Mission Street is chock-full of ethnic groceries and restaurants, and McLaren Park provides a choice playground for all.

Banks

- **Bank of America** • 15 Ocean Ave
- **Citibank** • 4638 Mission St
- **US** • 4610 Mission St
- **US (ATM)** • Walgreens • 4645 Mission St
- **Wells Fargo** • 4648 Mission St

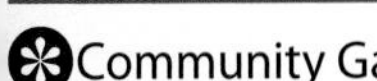

Community Gardens

Gas Stations

- **76** • 1798 Alemany Blvd
- **Arco** • 1200 Geneva Ave

Landmarks

- **Crocker Amazon Skatepark** • 1600 Geneva Ave

Libraries

- **Excelsior Branch Library** • 4400 Mission St

Pharmacies

- **Central Drug San Francisco** • 4494 Mission St
- **Safeway** • 4950 Mission St
- **Walgreens** • 4645 Mission St

Post Offices

- **Excelsior Finance Station** • 15 Onondaga St

Schools

- **Cleveland Elementary** • 455 Athens St
- **Corpus Christi** • 75 Francis St
- **Epiphany** • 600 Italy Ave
- **Excelsior** • 325 La Grande Ave
- **Guadalupe Elementary** • 859 Prague St
- **June Jordan School for Equity** • 325 La Grande Ave
- **Monroe Elementary** • 260 Madrid St
- **San Francisco Community** • 125 Excelsior Ave

Supermarkets

- **Safeway** • 4950 Mission St

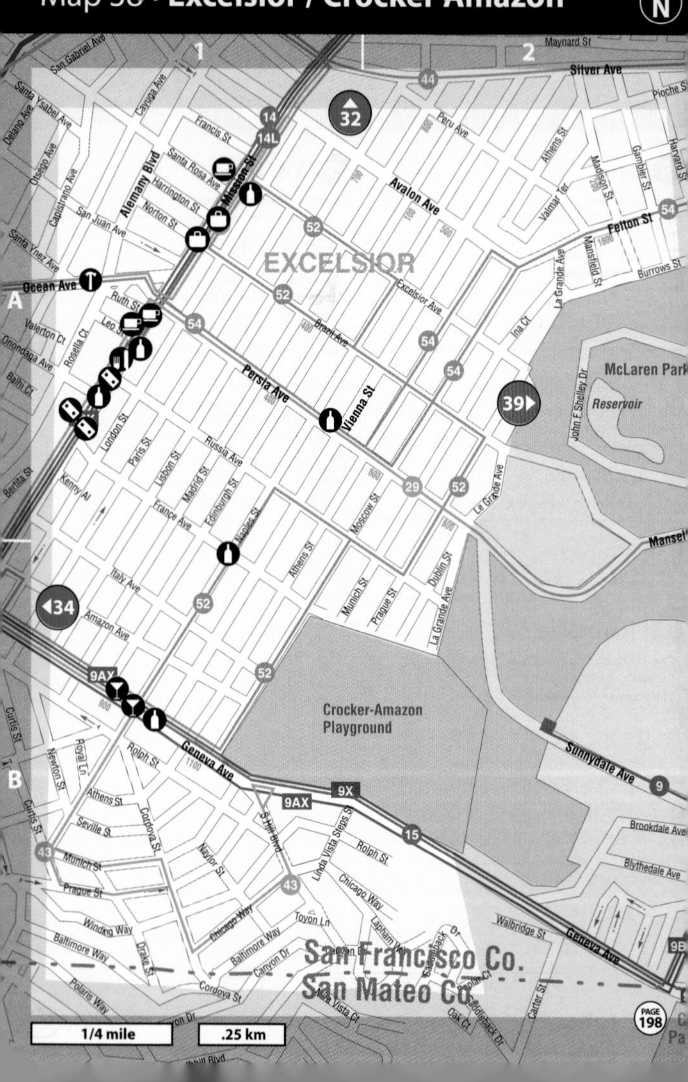
N
1
2
A
B
Maynard St
Silver Ave
Pioche St
San Gabriel Ave
Santa Ysabel Ave
Delano Ave
Cayuga Ave
Otsego Ave
Capistrano Ave
Francis St
Santa Rosa Ave
Alemany Blvd
Harrington St
Mission St
Norton St
San Juan Ave
Santa Ynez Ave
Ocean Ave
Ruth St
Leo St
Valerton Ct
Onondaga Ave
Rosella Ct
Balhi Ct
Peru Ave
Athens St
Madison St
Gambier St
Harvard St
Avalon Ave
Valmar Ter
Felton St
Mansfield St
Burrows St
EXCELSIOR
Excelsior Ave
Brazil Ave
La Grande Ave
Ina Ct
McLaren Park
Reservoir
John F Shelley Dr
Persia Ave
Vienna St
Russia Ave
London St
Paris St
Lisbon St
Madrid St
Edinburgh St
Naples St
Moscow St
Le Grande Ave
Mansell
Kenny Al
France Ave
Bertita St
Athens St
Munich St
Prague St
Dublin St
La Grande Ave
Italy Ave
Amazon Ave
Crocker-Amazon Playground
Sunnydale Ave
Geneva Ave
Rolph St
Curtis St
Newton St
Royal Ln
Athens St
Seville St
Cordova St
S Hill Blvd
Linda Vista Steps
Rolph St
Brookdale Ave
Blythedale Ave
Munich St
Prague St
Naylor St
Chicago Way
Toyon Ln
Lapham Way
Walbridge St
Winding Way
Baltimore Way
Drake St
Chicago Way
Baltimore Way
Canyon Dr
San Francisco Co.
San Mateo Co.
Polaris Way
Cordova St
Carter St
Oak Ct
Saddleback Dr
1/4 mile
.25 km
PAGE 198
32
34
39
14
14L
44
52
54
29
43
15
9
9X
9AX
9B
100
200
400
500
600
700
800
900
1000
1100
1800

Sundries / Entertainment

While you wouldn't travel this far down Mission Street for the nightlife, shopping at some of the produce and meat markets here will yield some unexpected bargains. Dining options are varied, too—grab a burrito or stop in for a real Italian sandwich at Sorrento's Delicatessen. Grab a drink at neighborhood spot Broken Record.

Coffee

- **Cones N' Cakes** • 4482 Mission St
- **Mama Café** • 4754 Mission St
- **Martha & Bros** • 4726 Mission St

Hardware Stores

- **Shic Hardware** • 58 Ocean Ave

Liquor Stores

- **D&D Liquor & Deli** • 1231 Geneva Ave
- **D's Corner** • 700 Naples St
- **Excelsior Liquors** • 4501 Mission St
- **Frank's Market & Liquors** • 4799 Mission St
- **Snack & Bottle Shop** • 644 Persia Ave
- **Sorrento Delicatessen (wine only)** • 4763 Mission St

Nightlife

- **The Broken Record** • 1166 Geneva Ave
- **Geneva Pub** • 1196 Geneva Ave

Restaurants

- **North Beach Pizza** • 4787 Mission St

Shopping

- **Casa Lucas Market** • 4555 Mission St
- **El Chico Produce No 2** • 4600 Mission St

Video Rental

- **F&M Video (Filipino)** • 4790 Mission St
- **Hong Kong Video & Trading (Chinese and Spanish)** • 4907 Mission St
- **Movie Magic** • 4877 Mission St

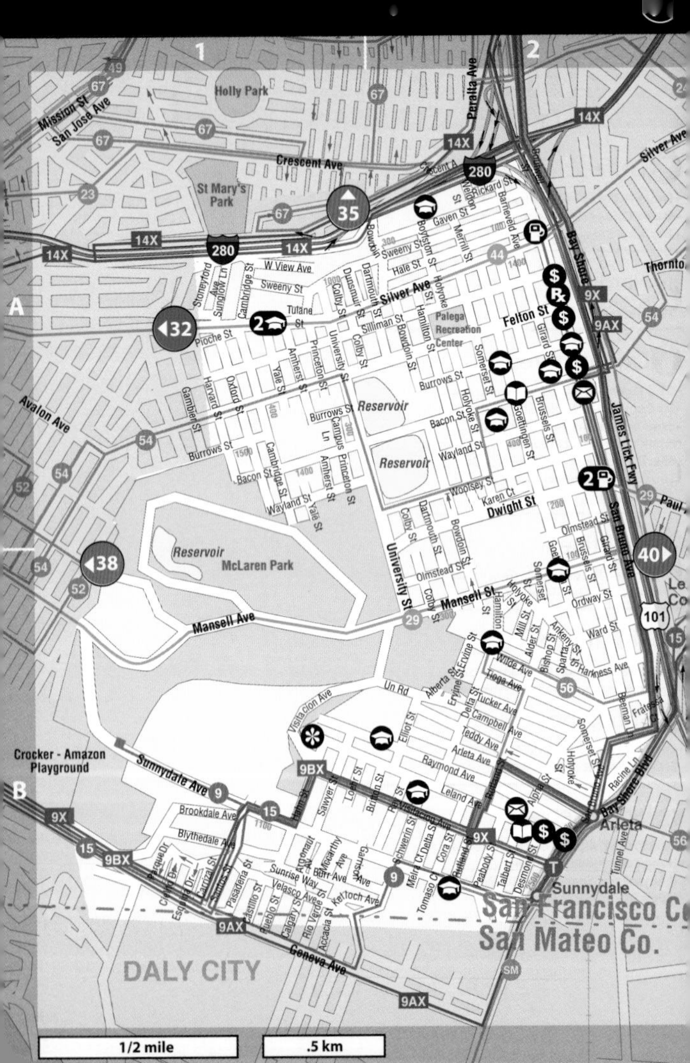

1
2
A
B
Holly Park
St Mary's Park
McLaren Park
Reservoir
Palega Recreation Center
Crocker - Amazon Playground
DALY CITY
San Francisco Co.
San Mateo Co.
Sunnydale
Arleta
Mission St
San Jose Ave
Crescent Ave
Silver Ave
Felton St
Burrows St
Bacon St
Wayland St
Woolsey St
Dwight St
Olmstead St
Mansell St
Mansell Ave
University St
Sunnydale Ave
Visitacion Ave
Geneva Ave
Bay Shore
James Lick Fwy
San Bruno Ave
Bay Shore Blvd
Avalon Ave
Peralta Ave
Paul Ave
Thornton
280
101
1/2 mile
.5 km

Protection from the fog makes this place enticing, but the ever-so-reliable 3rd Street Light Rail has yet to deliver much. Smaller homes contribute to lower prices, which have attracted a large immigrant population from all corners of the world. McLaren Park boasts some of the best views of SF's least-considered neighborhoods.

Banks

- **Bank of America** • 2485 San Bruno Ave
- **Bank of America** • 6 Leland Ave
- **Bank of the West** • 2675 San Bruno Ave
- **US (ATM)** • Walgreens • 2494 San Bruno Ave

Community Gardens

Gas Stations

- **Art's Valerio** • 2985 San Bruno Ave
- **Independent** • 2990 San Bruno Ave
- **Shell** • 2380 San Bruno Ave

Libraries

- **Portola Library** • 380 Bacon St
- **Visitacion Valley Library** • 45 Leland Ave

Pharmacies

- **Walgreens** • 2494 San Bruno Ave

Post Offices

- **McLaren Station** • 2755 San Bruno Ave
- **Visitacion Station** • 68 Leland Ave

Schools

- **Cornerstone Academy** • 801 Silver Ave
- **Edward R Taylor** • 423 Burrows St
- **El Dorado Elementary** • 70 Delta St
- **Hillcrest Elementary** • 810 Silver Ave
- **Martin Luther King Jr Middle** • 350 Girard St
- **Our Lady of the Visitacion** • 795 Sunnydale Ave
- **Phillip Burton Academic** • 400 Mansell St
- **San Francisco** • 300 Gaven St
- **SR Martin College Preparator** • 2660 San Bruno Ave
- **St Elizabeth's Elementary** • 450 Somerset St
- **Visitacion Valley Elementary** • 55 Schwerin St
- **Visitacion Valley Middle** • 450 Raymond Ave

You can see McLaren Park from the freeway—it's a big, 317-acre, tree-covered hilltop—the ideal place for a car chase. But if you don't own your own car, check out the movie *Bullit* and you can catch a glimpse of the park during the famous car chase scene.

Coffee

- **Café and Restaurant Monte Cristo** • 2101 Geneva Ave
- **Lolocup** • 2527 San Bruno Ave
- **Quickly** • 2763 San Bruno Ave

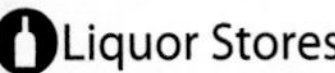

Liquor Stores

- **Bus Stop Liquors & Deli** • 2698 San Bruno Ave
- **Easy Stop Market** • 2203 Geneva Ave
- **M&M Shortstop** • 2145 Geneva Ave
- **White Palace Liquor Store** • 1524 Silver Ave

Restaurants

- **Café and Restaurant Monte Cristo** • 2101 Geneva Ave

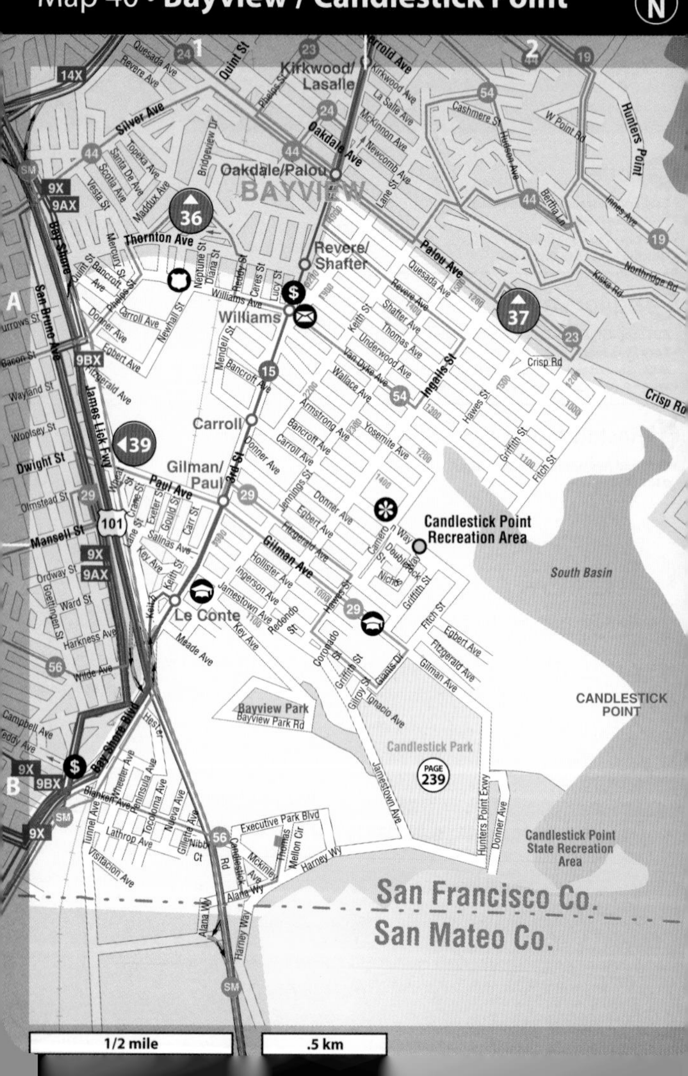
BAYVIEW
Kirkwood/ Lasalle
Oakdale/Palou
Revere/ Shafter
Williams
Carroll
Gilman/ Paul
Le Conte
Candlestick Point Recreation Area
South Basin
CANDLESTICK POINT
Bayview Park
Candlestick Park
PAGE 239
Candlestick Point State Recreation Area
San Francisco Co.
San Mateo Co.
1/2 mile
.5 km

The new MUNI rail line that now runs along 3rd Street has made this area more accessible, but it has not as yet lured more visitors here from other parts of the city—except for those watching the 49ers at Monster Park and the windsurfers off Candlestick Point.

Banks

- **Citibank (ATM)** • 2200 Bay Shore Blvd
- **US (ATM)** • Walgreens • 5300 3rd St

Community Gardens

Landmarks

- **Candlestick Point Recreation Area** • 1150 Carroll Ave

Police

- **Bayview Police Station** • 201 Williams Ave

Post Offices

- **Bayview Station** • 2111 Lane St

Schools

- **Bret Harte Elementary** • 1035 Gilman Ave
- **Kipp Bayview Academy** • 1060 Key Ave

BAYVIEW
Kirkwood/ Lasalle
Oakdale/Palou
Revere/ Shafter
Williams
Carroll
Gilman/ Paul
Le Conte
South Basin
CANDLESTICK POINT
Candlestick Park
Candlestick Point State Recreation Area
Bayview Park
San Francisco Co.
San Mateo Co.
PAGE 239
36
37
39
101
1/2 mile
.5 km

retend you're a local by sitting at the counter at B & J 1/4 lb Burgers. El zteca: huge burritos and wall-to-wall murals. There are some bars to isit before watching the 49ers at Monster Park. If you want a work out, andlestick Point State Recreation Area is popular with windsurfers.

Coffee

Bayside Coffee Shop • 2011 Bay Shore Blvd
Candlestick Coffee & Espresso • 2155 Bay Shore Blvd

Liquor Stores

Friendly Liquor • 1499 Thomas Ave
H&K Liquor & Deli • 1300 Fitzgerald Ave
Smitty's Market • 2610 Bay Shore Blvd

Nightlife

Monte Carlo • 1705 Yosemite Ave

Restaurants

B&J 1/4 lb Burgers • 6202 3rd St
El Azteca Taqueria • 5298 3rd St

Shopping

Leeling Imports & Exports • 5534 3rd St

Ashbury Ave
EL CERRITO
Sunset View Cemetery
KENSINGTON
Summit Reservoir
Charles Lee Tilden Regional Park
El Cerrito Plaza
Fairmount Ave
San Pablo Ave
Canyon Rd
Contra Costa Co
Alameda Co
Arlington Ave
Grizzly Peak Blvd
Albany Hill Park
Key Route Blvd
Colusa Ave
Lake Anza
Marin Ave
Solano Ave
ALBANY
Tilden Regional Golf Co
Marin Ave
Spruce St
Sutter St
Golden Gate Fields Racetrack
University of California
Berkeley (East)
Hopkins St
PAGE 174
Gilman St
Oxford St
San Pablo Ave
Cedar St
80
North Berkeley
UC Berkeley
580
University Ave
PAGE 206
6th St
Berkeley
Bancroft Wy
Durant Ave
123
Shattuck Ave
Clark Ke Campus
Berkeley (West)
Grove St
PAGE 172
Dwight Wy
Sacramento St
Aquatic Park
Grove Park
13
San Pablo Park
College Ave
Claremont Ave
Ashby Ave
Ashby
Adeline St
Telegraph Ave
Alcatrez Ave
Rockridge
Stanford Ave
San Francisco Bay
Powell St
24
Broadway
EMERYVILLE
OAKLAND
1 mile
1 km

Overview

The city of Berkeley, famous for its university and seismically-sensitive land, has a long history of positive town/gown relations and community activism. And while the memory of radical ideas still permeates the air, as you get closer to the center and its many academic establishments (besides the UC, there are also the Graduate Theological Union, Vista Community College, and various vocational schools), you're now more likely to encounter a Starbucks than a protest. Shattuck Avenue, at the center of the city, hosts a staggering array of restaurants and bars (but beware; prices increase as you move further north). Telegraph Avenue, extending southward from campus, is where the out-of-towners shop, the punks beg, and the freshmen eat. Most of the properties in North Berkeley are occupied by studious grad students who don't even have time to enjoy their fabulous views; West Berkeley is a residential mecca; and artistic creativity thrives in gritty South Berkeley. Each neighborhood has a different feel, but the city has an almost unmatched cohesive pride.

Berkeley coffee shops, once hotbeds of activism, have made a seamless transition into 21st-century café culture: Brewed Awakenings (1807 Euclid Ave) is filled with students typing papers; at Au Coquelet (2000 University Ave) you can play scrabble and get a hot meal until 1am; at the Free Speech Movement Café (Moffit Undergraduate Library, UC Berkeley Campus) you can learn about Berkeley's most famous social movement and sip a great latte; and you can sit and blog away your concerns at Caffe Strada (2300 College Ave). Visit the original Peet's Coffee & Tea (2124 Vine St) for a strong cup of joe and a taste of a true Berkeley institution.

For cultural experiences, there is no shortage of activity: La Peña (3105 Shattuck Ave) hosts performing arts showcases, poetry slams, and documentaries with a focus on Latin American politics and culture. Next door, Starry Plough slams poetry on Wednesdays over a pint of Guinness. At Ashkenaz (1317 San Pablo Ave) you can rock your body to world and roots music. The Pacific Film Archive, located on campus, screens rare and rediscovered prints of movie classics, new and historic works by great international film directors, restored silent films, and indie fiction and documentaries. On-stage entertainment in this town ranges from neighborhood theater companies like the Shotgun Players and the nationally renowned Berkeley Repertory Theatre to original punk rock at 924 Gilman.

Food

Famous for both its fancy eateries like Chez Panisse and its cheap on-the-go bites like La Burrita, Berkeley offers the palate variety that mirrors the diversity of the town's population. Visit the Farmers Market (Sat, Tues, Thurs; check www.ecologycenter.org/bfm for locations) for organic veggies, tree-ripened fruits, and handmade artisan breads. Sit on the grass and have delicious mango sticky rice at Thai Temple's popular Sunday Brunch (Russell St & MLK Jr Wy). Order a slice of gourmet vegetarian pizza at The Cheese Board (1504 Shattuck Ave), or try the Chicago-style deep dish at Zachary's (1853 Solano Ave). If you're looking for a sandwich or salad (of massive proportions), try Café Intermezzo (2442 Telegraph Ave) and don't forget to sample the homemade honey-wheat bread. While you're at it, ask any of the college kids, and they won't deny: no outing is complete without a cheap, low-fat indulgence at Yogurt Park (2433 Durant Ave).

Outdoors

To get away from the rumble, walk up Euclid Avenue. Extraordinary views of San Francisco across the Bay will accompany you on your stroll. Less than a mile uphill sits the Rose Garden, and then through the tunnel, you'll discover Cordonices Park's playground and picnic area. Just a bit higher is the expanse of Tilden Park: there's hiking, a golf course, and even Lake Anza with a beach (yes, it's fake). Climbers and sunset lovers prefer the crags of Indian Rock at the northern end of Shattuck Avenue. For more of the bay's magnificent views, take a relaxing hike or run up the fire trail behind the stadium, past Strawberry Canyon, and pick blackberries on the side of the road (when you get to the bench at the top, continue to Lawrence Berkeley Labs on 1 Cyclotrone Road, or head back down). On the other side of town, you can rollerblade or bike from North Berkeley BART all the way to Richmond on Ohlone Greenway.

How to Get There

With BART stations at Ashby, Downtown, and North Berkeley, and AC Transit running from San Francisco and Oakland, getting to Berkeley on public transportation is easy. However, be aware that BART trains stop running around midnight, and AC Transit service runs on a limited schedule in the late night/early morning hours. If you insist on driving, exit on University Avenue from I-80 E, or follow Hwy 13 into town from the east. Street parking is tough around campus and on the main drags of Telegraph and Shattuck Avenues, but patience and persistence often pay off. For lot parking the UC Berkeley parking lots or the Telegraph/Channing Lot (2431 Channing Wy) are always good options, but be sure to get your ticket validated or prices will be steep.

ALBANY
Solano Ave
Marin Ave
Key Route Blvd
Golden Gate Fields Racetrack
University of California
Berkeley Skatepark
Harrison St
Gilman St
Camelia St
Page St
Jones St
Dartmouth St
Hopkins St
Cedar St
North Berkeley
San Pablo Ave
University Ave
Sacramento St
Martin Luther King Jr Wy
Berkeley Marina
Dwight Wy
Aquatic Park
San Pablo Park
Grove Park
Ashby Ave
Alcatraz Ave
San Francisco Bay
80
580
123
1/2 mile
.5 km

Festivals & Events

For more information about city-sponsored events, and for individual links for the events listed below, visit www.ci.berkeley.ca.us.

Cal Day—Saturday in mid-April. Annual UC Berkeley open house for the community; performances, exhibits, lectures, tours, sports events, etc. Contact Visitor Services at 510-642-5215.
Earth Day—Saturday closest to April 22. Festival and Eco-Motion Parade downtown. 510-548-2220.
Berkeley Bay Festival—Saturday in late April or May. Food, music, entertainment, boat tours, and free sailing at the Berkeley Marina. 510-644-8623.
People's Park Anniversary Street Fair & Concert— Late April or early May at the People's Park. 510-644-7729.
Berkeley Arts Festival—First two weeks in May. 510-665-9496.
Fourth of July Celebration—July 4th at the Berkeley Marina. 510-548-5335
Berkeley Kite Festival—Last weekend in July at the Cesar Chavez North Waterfront Park. 510-235-5483.
"How Berkeley Can You Be?" Parade/Festival—Fourth Sunday in September in downtown and North Berkeley. 510-849-4688.
Berkeley Artisans Holiday Open Studios— Four weekends, Thanksgiving into December. 510-845-2612

Landmarks

- **The Berkeley Marina** • University Ave & Frontage Rd
- **Berkeley Skatepark** • 5th St & Harrison St

Coffee

- **Broom Bush Café** • 2725 San Pablo Ave
- **Café Fanny** • 1603 San Pablo Ave
- **Caffe Trieste** • 2500 San Pablo Ave
- **Coffee Conscious** • 1312 Gilman St
- **Espresso Roma Café** • 1549 Hopkins St
- **Fellini Coffeebar** • 1401 University Ave
- **Jimmy Beans** • 1290 6th St
- **Peet's** • 1776 4th St
- **Peet's** • 1825 Solano Ave
- **Starbucks** • 1799 Solano Ave
- **Uncommon Café** • 2813 7th St

Movie Theaters

- **Oaks** • 1875 Solano Ave

Nightlife

- **924 Gilman** • 924 Gilman St
- **Albatross Pub** • 1822 San Pablo Ave
- **Ashkenaz** • 1317 San Pablo Ave
- **Lanesplitter** • 2033 San Pablo Ave
- **Missouri Lounge** • 2600 San Pablo Ave
- **Pyramid Alehouse & Brewery** • 901 Gilman St

Pet Shops

- **East Bay Vivarium** • 1827 5th St

Restaurants

- **900 Grayson** • 900 Grayson St
- **Bacheeso's Garden** • 2501 San Pablo Ave
- **Bette's Oceanview Diner** • 1807 4th St
- **Cactus Taqueria** • 1881 Solano Ave
- **Cafe M** • 1799 4th St
- **Café Rouge** • 1782 4th St
- **Casa Latina** • 1805 San Pablo Ave
- **Everett and Jones in Berkeley** • 1955 San Pablo Ave
- **Gioia Pizzeria** • 1586 Hopkins St
- **Gregoire** • 2109 Cedar St
- **Juan's Place** • 941 Carleton St
- **The Kabana** • 1106 University Ave
- **King Tsin** • 1699 Solano Ave
- **Picante Berkeley** • 1328 6th St
- **Spenger's Fresh Fish Grotto** • 1919 4th St
- **Tacubaya** • 1788 4th St
- **T-Rex Barbecue** • 1300 10th St
- **Vanessa's Bistro** • 1715 Solano Ave
- **Viks Chaat Corner** •2390 4th St
- **Zachary's Pizza** • 1853 Solano Ave
- **Zaki Kabob** • 1101 San Pablo Ave

Shopping

- **Acme Bread Company** • 1601 San Pablo Ave
- **Berkeley Bowl** • 920 Heinz Ave
- **Berkeley Horticultural Nursery** • 1310 McGee Ave
- **Fourth Street Shopping District** • Cedar St & 4th St
- **George** • 1844 4th St
- **La Farine Bakery** • 1820 Solano Ave
- **Magnet** • 2508 San Pablo Ave
- **Mignonne** • 2447 San Pablo Ave
- **Monterey Market** • 1550 Hopkins St
- **The North Face Outlet** • 1238 5th St
- **Ohmega Salvage** • 2407 San Pablo Ave
- **Pegasus Books** • 1855 Solano Ave
- **Photolab** • 2235 5th St
- **Sweet Adeline Bakeshop** • 3350 Adeline St
- **Tokyo Fish Market** • 1220 San Pablo Ave
- **Urban Ore** • 900 Murray St

Berkeley Rose Garden
Codornices Park
Live Oak Park
Eunice St
Hopkins St
Spruce St
Berryman St
Rose St
Vine St
Oxford St
Cedar St
Arch St
Scenic Ave
Hawthorne Ter
Euclid Ave
Le Roy Ave
La Loma Ave
Buena Vista Wy
Hilgard Ave
Le Conte Ave
Ridge Rd
Virginia St
Francisco St
Deleware St
Hearst Ave
Berkeley Wy
University Ave
Addison St
Center St
Allston Wy
Kittredge
Bancroft Wy
Durant Ave
Channing Wy
Haste St
Dwight Wy
Shattuck Ave
Berkeley
UC Berkeley
MAP 206
University Dr
S Hall Rd
Campanile Wy
Sather Rd
Barrow Ln
Bowditch St
Stadium Rim Wy
Centennial Dr
Cyclotron Rd
People's Park
Warring St
Prospect St
Tilden Regional Park Golf Course
Grizzly Peak Blvd
Fairlawn Dr
Queens Rd
Northgate Ave
Hill Rd
Summit Rd
Glendale Ave
Campus Dr
Parnassus Rd
Olympus Ave
Roosevelt Ave
McKinley Ave
Blake St
Parker St
McGee Ave
Grant St
Martin Luther King Jr Wy
Milvia St
Berkeley Iceland
Grove Park
Fulton St
Ellsworth St
Dana St
Regent St
Hillegass Ave
Benvenue Ave
College Ave
Etna St
Piedmont Ave
Clark Kerr Campus
Carleton St
Derby St
Ward St
Stuart St
Oregon St
Russell St
Forest Ave
Garber St
Cherry St
Kelsey St
Avalon Ave
Pine Ave
Magnolia St
Belrose Ave
Claremont Blvd
Domingo Ave
Tunnel Rd
Ashby Ave
Webster St
Emerson St
Essex St
Wheeler St
Deakin St
Telegraph Ave
Prince St
Woolsey St
Colby St
Lewinston Ave
Eton Ave
Claremont Ave
Brookside Ave
Plaza Dr
Parkside Dr
Hillcrest Rd
Chabolyn Ter
Mystic St
Florio St
King St
Ellis St
Harper St
Adeline St
Ashby
66th St
63rd St
Alcatraz Ave
1/2 mile
.5 km

Landmarks

- **Berkeley Rose Garden** • 1200 Euclid Ave
- **Berkeley Iceland** • 2727 Milvia St
- **People's Park** • 2556 Haste St

Coffee

- **A'Cuppa Tea** • 3202 College Ave
- **Addison Annex Café** • 2107 Addison St
- **All Star Café** • 2172 Shattuck Ave
- **Au Coquelet Café** • 2000 University Ave
- **Berkeley Espresso** • 1900 Shattuck Ave
- **Brewed Awakening** • 1807 Euclid Ave
- **Café Espresso Experience** • 2440 Bancroft Wy
- **Café Milano** • 2522 Bancroft Wy
- **Café Sienna** • 2490 Bancroft Wy
- **Caffe Strada** • 2300 College Ave
- **Coffee Spot** • 2475 Bancroft Wy
- **Espresso Roma Cafe** • 2960 College Ave
- **Fertile Grounds** • 1796 Shattuck Ave
- **French Hotel Café** • 1540 Shattuck Ave
- **International House Café** • 2299 Piedmont Ave
- **Le Bateau Ivre** • 2629 Telegraph Ave
- **Love at First Bite** • 1510 Walnut St
- **Masse's Pastries** • 1469 Shattuck Ave
- **Paragon Bar & Café** • 41 Tunnel Rd
- **Peet's** • 2124 Vine St
- **Peet's** • 2501 Telegraph Ave
- **Peet's** • 2255 Shattuck Ave
- **Peet's** • 2916 Domingo Ave
- **Starbucks** • 2128 Oxford St
- **Starbucks** • 2224 Shattuck Ave
- **Sweetheart Café** • 2523 Durant Ave
- **Tully's Coffee** • 2150 Shattuck Ave
- **Venus Restaurant** • 2327 Shattuck Ave
- **Yali's Oxford St Café** • 1920 Oxford St

Movie Theaters

- **California Theater** • 2113 Kittredge St
- **Elmwood Theatre** • 2966 College Ave
- **PFA** • 2575 Bancroft Wy
- **Shattuck Cinemas** • 2230 Shattuck Ave
- **United Artists Cinemas 7** • 2274 Shattuck Ave

Nightlife

- **Beckett's Irish Pub** • 2271 Shattuck Ave
- **Black Repertory Theatre** • 3201 Adeline St
- **Blakes on Telegraph** • 2367 Telegraph Ave
- **Epic Arts** • 1923 Ashby Ave
- **Jupiter** • 2181 Shattuck Ave
- **La Peña Cultural Center** • 3105 Shattuck Ave
- **Shattuck Down Low** • 2284 Shattuck Ave
- **The Starry Plough** • 3101 Shattuck Ave
- **Thalassa Bar & Billiards** • 2367 Shattuck Ave
- **Triple Rock Brewery** •1920 Shattuck Ave

Restaurants

- **Angeline's Louisana Kitchen** • 2261 Shattuck Ave
- **Blondie's Pizza** • 2340 Telegraph Ave
- **Brazil Café** • 1983 Shattuck Ave
- **Cancun Taqueria** • 2134 Allston Wy
- **César** • 1515 Shattuck Ave
- **Cha Am Thai** • 1543 Shattuck Ave
- **The Cheese Board** • 1512 Shattuck Ave
- **Chez Panisse** • 1517 Shattuck Ave
- **Crepes A Go-Go** • 2125 University Ave
- **Fat Apples** • 1346 Martin Luther King Jr Wy
- **House of Curries** • 2984 College Ave
- **Jayakarta** • 2026 University Ave
- **Joshu-ya Sushi** • 2441 Dwight Way
- **Jupiter** • 2181 Shattuck Ave
- **Kirala** • 2100 Ward St
- **La Burrita** • 1832 Euclid Ave
- **La Cascada** • 2164 Center St
- **La Note** • 2377 Shattuck Ave
- **Long Life Vegi House** • 2129 University Ave
- **Manpuku** • 2977 College Ave
- **Mitama** • 3201 College Ave
- **Revival Bar + Kitchen** • 2102 Shattuck Ave
- **Rick & Ann's Restaurant** • 2922 Domingo Ave
- **Saul's Deli and Restaurant** • 1475 Shattuck Ave
- **Shen Hua** • 2914 College Ave
- **The Smokehouse** • 3155 Telegraph Ave
- **Sushi Ko** • 64 Shattuck Sq
- **Top Dog** • 2534 Durant Ave
- **Udupi Palace** • 1901 University Ave
- **Yogurt Park** • 2433 Durant Ave

Shopping

- **Amoeba Music** • 2455 Telegraph Ave
- **Annapurna** • 2416 Telegraph Ave
- **Berkeley Bowl** • 2020 Oregon St
- **Berkeley Flea Market** • 1937 Ashby Ave
- **Buffalo Exchange** • 2585 Telegraph Ave
- **The Cheese Board** • 1512 Shattuck Ave
- **Crossroads Trading Company** • 2338 Shattuck Ave
- **Jeremy's** • 2967 College Ave
- **Looking Glass Photo** • 2848 Telegraph Ave
- **Mars Mercantile** • 2398 Telegraph Ave
- **Moe's Books** • 2476 Telegraph Ave
- **Pegasus Books** • 2349 Shattuck Ave
- **Rasputin Music** • 2401 Telegraph Ave
- **Sweet Dreams** • 2901 College Ave
- **Whole Foods Market** • 3000 Telegraph Ave

Supermarkets

- **Star Grocery** • 3068 Claremont Ave

North Oakland / Emeryville
Downtown Oakland / Lake Merritt
OAKLAND
PIEDMONT
ALAMEDA
BAY FARM ISLAND
PAGE 180
PAGE 178
PAGE 236
PAGE 246

Powell St
Stanford Ave
Ashby
Claremont Ave
Rockridge
College Ave
Telegraph Ave
Shattuck Ave
San Pablo Ave
Martin Luther King Jr Wy
Telegraph St
MacArthur
Broadway
Claremont Country Club
Mountain View Cemetery
Morcom Amphitheatre of Roses
Oakland Ave
Grand Ave
Lake Merritt
Park Blvd
13th Ave
Lincoln Ave
Fruitvale Ave
Foothill Blvd
Peralta Hacienda Historical Park
35th Ave
29th Ave
Fruitvale
MacArthur Blvd
High St
Seminary Ave
San Leandro St
73rd Ave
Coliseum
Coliseum Complex
Oakland International Airport
Alameda Municipal Golf Course
Doolittle Dr
San Leandro Bay
San Francisco Bay
Broadway
Park St
Otis Dr
Central Ave
Grand St
Webster St
Buena Vista Ave
Lincoln Ave
Decatur St
Naval Supply Center (Alameda Oakland)
Naval Airstation Alameda Nimitz Field
Main St
Oakland Inner Harbor
US Naval Supply Center
Oakland West
Peralta St
Maritime St
7th St
Oakland Army Base
Viaduct
W Grand Ave
Market St
19th St/ Oakland
Oakland City Center/12th St

1 mile
1 km

Overview

San Francisco may be the first place you think of when you hear 'city by the bay' but it certainly isn't the only place. Oakland, with its adorable neighborhoods, ethnic diversity, radical history, and eclectic architecture, is as much of a destination out here as Brooklyn is in New York City. Travel through Oakland's neighborhoods and you'll find everything from near-ghetto conditions to gentrified warehouse districts, cute bungalow neighborhoods to hillside mansions, city streets, pools, art centers, and a beautiful regional park system in the Oakland hills—perfect for hiking, biking and all things nature.

If you are looking for a day out through some 'Oaktown' neighborhoods filled with craftsman bungalows and Victorian homes, boutiques, cafés, bookstores, and the like, try the Rockridge,Temescal, or Piedmont Ave neighborhoods in North Oakland. Check out places like Bittersweet Chocolate Café (everything chocolate), Diesel Books (both in Rockridge), Piedmont Stationery, Piedmont Cinema, and the new hip store Issues (Piedmont Ave), or Bakesale Betty, Lanesplitter and Your #1 Black Muslim Bakery (Temescal) for a unique taste of some of the best Oakland has to offer. Get your art on at the newly renovated Studio One Arts Center (on 45th Street between Broadway and Shafter) where you can find a range of art classes for adults at great prices. For a park-like stroll and a significant history lesson, take the dog for a walk in Mountainview Cemetery (founded in 1863, and designed by none other than Frederick Law Olmsted). Walk by the mansion-like tombs of famous San Franciscans who are the namesakes for such streets as Powell and Stanyan. Famous architect Julia Morgan is buried here alongside common and famous people of all ethnicities, races, and religions.

Oakland's incredible diversity can be found in many of its neighborhoods, including the pan-Asian Chinatown's center at 8th and Webster, the hub of downtown. Since it gets much less tourism than San Francisco's famous Chinatown, this neighborhood has a few less 'junk' stores and is perhaps on the more authentic-side. This is the neighborhood to find the best fake-meat restaurants, including the Golden Lotus (on Franklin and 13th), New World Vegetarian (9th and Broadway), and the Layonna Vegetarian Health Food Market, that sells all the kinds of fake meat you might ever want to try. The Fruitvale neighborhood in East Oakland is home to the cities growing Hispanic community, once named after... you guessed it, fruit orchards. Along International Boulevard between Lake Merritt and Fruitvale are a variety of excellent (and cheap) ethnic restaurants; here you'll find everything from Korean barbeque to carnitas and empanandas. Plan your visit to coincide with the celebrations of Cinco de Mayo or Dia de los Muertos and you'll be in for a real treat.

East of downtown but west of Fruitvale is the hamlet 'hood of Lake Merritt. It is a quick fifteen-minute walk from downtown, and cozy shops and restaurants can be found tucked away in sloping streets overlooking the water. Looking up at the hills, you can mistake it for a small Mediterranean city. Joggers can be found rounding the lake all day and you'll often see small sail boats, kayaks, and rowboats forging the waters. And once you've made your way around the lake, take a stroll down Lakeshore or Grand Avenues, home to a farmers market every Saturday, and a plethora of restaurants, cafes (check out the workers' co-op Arizmendi Bakery or Walden Pond Bookstore), and shops. The Easy Lounge is a perfect place for fresh cocktails post-farmers market. Visit the beautifully restored Lake Merritt movie theater on a Saturday night to hear the organ played before your movie, or get some pizza and a beer while watching a movie at the Parkway Theater just east of the Lake.

In recent years, downtown Oakland has seen an increase in activity, with notable restaurants, cafés, and cultural centers flourishing along its streets. The Malonga Casquelourd Center, formerly Alice Arts Center, hosts a variety of performances and cultural events. The Center is also home to the Jahva House, where one of the best open mics in Oakland takes place weekly. Jack London Square is a typical tourist trap and it continues to undergo lofty renovations and overall expansion. Just east of this area is the city's new and obtuse warehouse district, where expensive lofts now exist in old warehouses. A loft community of artists, bohemians, intellectuals, and yuppies has colonized the area. You'll find Oakland's best ribs and cornbread at Everett and Jones in Jack London Square and Oakland's best DIY museum/store at Oaklandish (411 2nd St). Despite what you may have heard, Oakland also has a thriving and varied nightlife scene. While you may want to steer clear of some West Oakland and far East Oakland neighborhoods after dark, the rest of the city can and should be explored. For the upscale set, @Seventeeth (510 17th St) and Air Lounge (492 9th St) rival San Francisco's swankiest lounges. Café Van Kleef's (1621 Telegraph Ave), the White Horse Inn (the country's 2nd oldest gay bar) at 6551 Telegprah, and Luka's Taproom & Lounge (2221 Broadway) for a good night out with or without music.

Coffee

- **Peet's** • 2066 Antioch Ct

Landmarks

- **Morcom Rose Garden** • 600 Jean St
- **Peralta Hacienda Historical Park** • 2465 34th Av

Nightlife

- **Kingman's Lucky Lounge** • 3332 Grand Ave

Shopping

- **The Food Mill** • 3033 MacArthur Blvd
- **Nuherbs** • 3820 Penniman Ave
- **Walden Pond Books** • 3316 Grand Ave

Restaurants

- **Brown Sugar Kitchen** • 2534 Mandela Pkwy
- **Camino** • 3917 Grand Ave
- **El Farolito** • 3646 International Blvd
- **El Taco Zamorano** • 4345 International Blvd
- **Jalisco** • 1721 International Blvd
- **Los Cocos** • 1449 Fruitvale Ave
- **Powderface Café** • 3411 E 12th St
- **Quinn's Lighthouse** • 1951 Embarcadero

Downtown Oakland / Lake Merritt

Downtown Oakland / Lake Merritt

Landmarks

- **African-American Museum and Library** • 659 14th St
- **Cathedral of Christ the Light** • 180 Grand Ave
- **Children's Fairyland** • 699 Bellevue Ave
- **Creative Growth Art Center** • 355 24th St
- **Malonga Casquelourd Center for the Arts** • 1428 Alice St
- **The Museum of African-American Technology Science Village** • 408 14th St
- **Museum of Children's Art** • 538 9th St
- **Oakland Asian Cultural Center** • 388 9th St
- **Oakland Museum of California** • 1000 Oak St
- **Oakland Public Library - Main Branch** • 125 14th St
- **The Paramount Theatre** • 2025 Broadway St
- **Pro Arts** • Clay St & 2nd St

Supermarkets

- **Trader Joe's** • 3250 Lakeshore Ave

Coffee

- **Awaken Cafe** • 414 14th St
- **Caffe 817** • 817 Washington St
- **L'amyx Tea Bar** • 3437 Lakeshore Ave
- **Mama Buzz** • 2318 Telegraph Ave
- **Peet's** • 1111 Broadway
- **Peet's** • 2501 Telegraph Ave
- **Peet's** • 3258 Lakeshore Ave
- **Starbucks** • 1200 Clay St
- **Starbucks** • 1211 Embarcadero
- **Starbucks** • 315 1/2 20th St
- **Starbucks** • 3347 Lakeshore Ave
- **Starbucks** • 801 Broadway
- **Tully's Coffee** • 102 Frank H Ogawa Plz

Movie Theaters

- **Grand Lake Theater** • 3200 Grand Ave
- **Jack London Stadium 9** • 100 Washington St

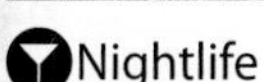

Nightlife

- **Air Lounge** • 492 9th St
- **Baggy's by the Lake** • 288 E 18th St
- **Café Van Kleef** • 1621 Telegraph Ave
- **EASY** • 3255 Lakeshore Ave
- **Heinold's First and Last Chance Bar** • 48 Webster St
- **Kincaid's Bayhouse** • 1 Franklin St
- **La Estrellita** • 446 E 12th St
- **Luka's Taproom & Lounge** • 2221 Broadway St
- **Radio Bar** • 435 13th St
- **The Ruby Room** • 132 14th St
- **@Seventeenth** • 510 17th St
- **Stork Club** • 2330 Telegraph Ave
- **The Trappist** • 460 8th St
- **Uptown Nightclub** • 1928 Telegraph Ave
- **Yoshi's** • 510 Embarcadero W

Restaurants

- **Arizmendi** • 3265 Lakeshore Ave
- **Battambang** • 850 Broadway St
- **BC Deli Sandwiches** • 818 Franklin St
- **Holy Land Kosher** • 677 Rand Ave
- **House of Chicken 'n Waffles** • 444 Embarcadero W
- **Flora** • 1900 Telegraph Ave
- **Golden Lotus** • 1301 Franklin St
- **Kincaid's** • 1 Franklin St
- **Le Cheval** • 1007 Clay St
- **Luka's Taproom & Lounge** • 2221 Broadway St
- **Lynn and Lu's** • 3353 Grand Ave
- **Pho Ga Huong Que Café** • 1228 7th Ave
- **Smart Alec's Intelligent Food** • 2355 Telegraph Ave
- **Tamarindo Antojeria** • 468 8th St
- **Yoshi's** • 510 Embarcadero W

Shopping

- **AK Press** • 674 23rd St
- **Bibliomania** • 1816 Telegraph Ave
- **Country Cheese** • 2101 San Pablo Ave
- **Fiveten Studio** • 831 Broadway
- **Juniper Tree** • 3303 Lakeshore Ave
- **Mannequin Madness** • 430 Orange St
- **Pican** • 2295 Broadway
- **Rock, Paper, Scissors** • 2278 Telegraph Ave
- **Verse** • 461 9th St

How to Get There

From San Francisco, Highway 80 east over the beautiful Bay Bridge leads to Highways 580, 880, and 980, which go to east, west, and downtown Oakland respectively.

From Contra Costa County, Highway 24 through the Caldecott Tunnel leads to north Oakland.

From the northern part of the East Bay, and from all points east, Highway 80 W leads directly to Oakland.

Almost all entries to Oakland go through the MacArthur Maze. There's terrible commuter traffic, so it's best to avoid it from 7 am to 10 am and 4 pm to 8 pm.

BART and AC Transit have service to Oakland as well. And though you can't ride a bike across the Bay Bridge, Caltran runs a bike shuttle during commute hours between the Transbay Terminal Building in San Francisco and MacArthur BART.

North Oakland / Emeryville

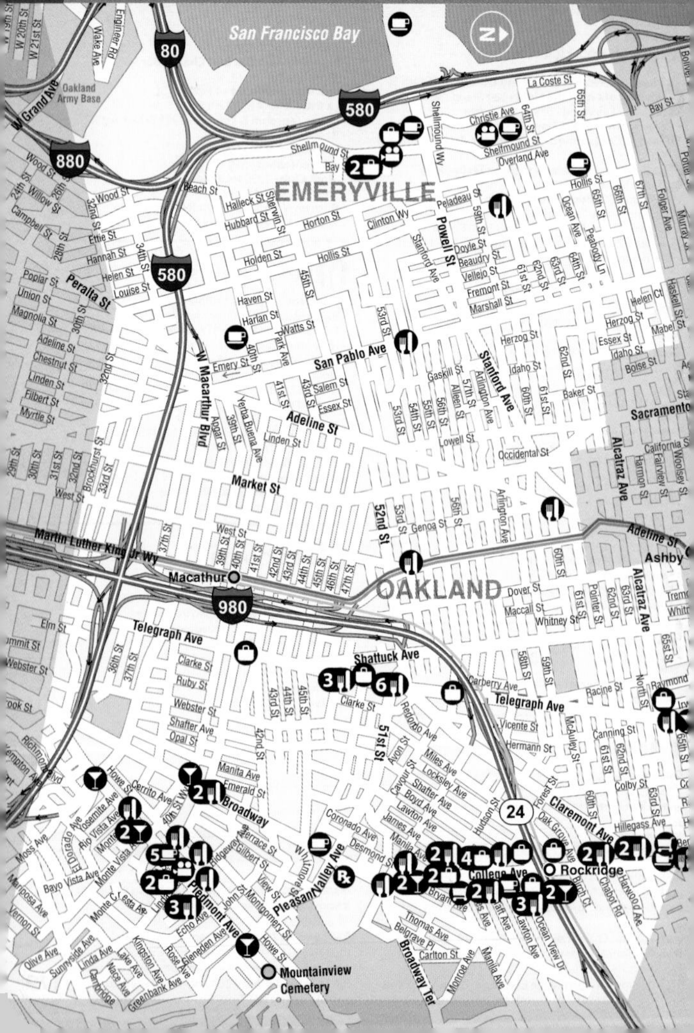

North Oakland / Emeryville

Landmarks

- **Mountain View Cemetery** • 5000 Piedmont Ave

Supermarkets

- **Trader Joe's** • 5727 College Ave
- **Yasai Produce Market** • 6301 College Ave

Coffee

- **Bittersweet Café** • 5427 College Ave
- **Cole Coffee** • 6255 College Ave
- **Gaylord's Caffe Espresso** • 4150 Piedmont Ave
- **L'amyx Tea Bar** • 4179 Piedmont Ave
- **Peet's** • 4050 Piedmont Ave
- **Peet's** • 5959 Shellmound St
- **Starbucks** • 1405 65th St
- **Starbucks** • 2200 Powell St
- **Starbucks** • 3839 Emery St
- Starbucks • 4098 Piedmont Ave
- **Starbucks** • 5132 Broadway
- **Starbucks** • 5765 Christie Ave

Movie Theaters

- **AMC Bay Street 16** • 5614 Shellmound St
- **Piedmont Theatre** • 4186 Piedmont Ave
- **Emery Bay Stadium 10** • 6330 Christie Ave

Nightlife

- **Ben & Nick's** • 5612 College Ave
- **Bill McNally's Irish Pub** • 5352 College Ave
- **Cato's Ale House** • 3891 Piedmont Ave
- **Conga Lounge** • 5422 College Ave
- **Egbert Souse's** • 3758 Piedmont Ave
- **George and Walt's** • 5445 College Ave
- **George Kaye's** • 4044 Broadway St
- **Kerry House** • 4092 Piedmont Ave
- **Kona Club** • 4401 Piedmont Ave
- **The White Horse Inn** • 6551 Telegraph Ave

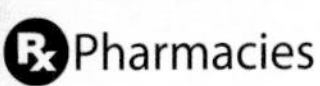

Pharmacies

- **Long's Drugs** • 5100 Broadway

Restaurants

- **À Côté** • 5478 College Ave
- **Art's Crab Shak** • 4031 Broadway St
- **Asmara** • 5020 Telegraph Ave
- **Bakesale Betty's** • 5098 Telegraph Ave
- **Barney's Gourmet Burgers** • 5819 College Ave
- **Ben & Nick's** • 5612 College Ave
- **Bucci's** • 6121 Hollis St
- **Burma Superstar** • 4721 Telegraph Ave
- **Café Colucci** • 6427 Telegraph Ave
- **César** • 4039 Piedmont Ave
- **Crepevine** • 5600 College Ave
- **Dona Tomas** • 5004 Telegraph Ave
- **Dopo** • 4293 Piedmont Ave
- **Fentons Creamery** • 4226 Piedmont Ave
- **Genova Delicatessen and Ravioli** • 5095 Telegraph Ave
- **J's Mexican American Food** • 4063 Piedmont Ave
- **La Calaca Loca** • 5199 Telegraph Ave
- **Lanesplitter's** • 4799 Telegraph Ave
- **Little Shin Shin** • 4258 Piedmont Ave
- **Lois the Pie Queen** • 851 60th St
- **Los Cantaros** • 5412 San Pablo Ave
- **Mama's Royal Café** • 4012 Broadway St
- **Nan Yang** • 6048 College Ave
- **Noodle Theory** • 6099 Claremont Ave
- **Oliveto Café and Restaurant** • 5655 College Ave
- **Pizzaiolo** • 5008 Telegraph Ave
- **Sabuy Sabuy** • 5231 College Ave
- **Shangri-La Vegan Restaurant** • 4001 Linden St
- **Soi Four** • 5421 College Ave
- **Somerset** • 5912 College Ave
- **Sura** • 4869 Telegraph Ave
- **Tropix** • 3814 Piedmont Ave
- **Wood Tavern** • 6317 College Ave
- **Zachary's Pizza** • 5801 College Ave

Shopping

- **Ancient Ways** • 4075 Telegraph Ave
- **Apple Store** • 5656 Bay St
- **Article Pract** • 5010 Telegraph Ave
- **Atomic Garden** • 5453 College Ave
- **Café Mariposa & Bakeshop** • 5427 Telegraph Ave
- **Crossroads Trading Company** • 5636 College Ave
- **Diesel Bookstore** • 5433 College Ave
- **Fenton's Creamery** • 4226 Piedmont Ave
- **Issues** • 20 Glen Ave
- **Itsy Bitsy** • 5520 College Ave
- **Maison d'etre** • 5640 College Ave
- **Pendragon Books** • 5560 College Ave
- **Rockridge Market Hall** • 5655 College Ave
- **Rockridge Rags** • 5711 College Ave
- **Saturn Records** • 1501 Powell
- **Siobhan Van Winkel** • 6371 Telegraph Ave
- **Teacake Bake Shop** • 5615 Bay St
- **Trader Joe's** • 5700 Christie Ave

Things to Do

Oakland Museum of California • 1000 Oak St at 10th; Lake Merritt BART station, 510-238-2200; www.museumca.org
A wonderful museum dedicated to the art, history, and culture of California.

Joaquin Miller Park
Joaquin Miller Rd (entrance about 1 mile from Highway 13), 510-238-3481; www.oaklandnet.com/parks/facilities/parks_joaquin_miller.asp
A beautiful park in the Oakland Hills, it has some of the oldest redwood groves in the East Bay.

Grand Lake Theatre
3200 Grand Ave (near MacArthur and 580); 510-452-3556; www.renaissancerialto.com/current/grandlake.htm
This theater, built in 1926, shows first-run movies. The political statements on the marquee are definitely worth driving by for as is the spectacular sign.

Parkway Theatre
1834 Park Blvd, 510-814-2400; www.picturepubpizza.com
California's first speakeasy now shows older movies to movie-goers sitting on large comfy couches and lounge chairs.

Children's Fairyland
699 Bellevue Ave, 510-452-2259; www.fairyland.org/info.html
Amazing playground destination for kids right on Lake Merritt.

Old Oakland Farmers Market
9th St (b/w Broadway & Clay St), 510-745-7100
Every Friday, 8 am–2 pm. Get your fresh fruits, veggies, and prepared foods.

Pro Arts East Bay Open Studios
510-763-4361; www.proartsgallery.org
The East Bay's longest-running and largest open studios event. Take a self-guided tour of hundreds of Oakland artists' studios the first weekends in June.

Woodminster Amphitheatre
3300 Joaquin Miller Rd, 510-531-9597; www.woodminster.com
This outdoor amphitheater sits deep in the Oakland Hills in Joaquin Miller Park, and has been home to the annual Woodminster Summer Musicals for the last 40 years. Pack a picnic and blanket and visit Oakland's theater under the stars.

General Information

Websites: www.ci.sausalito.ca.us
www.sausalito.org

Overview

Just over the Golden Gate lies picturesque Sausalito. With a mere 7,500 residents, by most standards it's a small town. However, its numbers swell during the summertime as tourists arrive by the ferryload and day-trippers fill the narrow sidewalks.

Sausalito is a beautiful spot, enjoying unsurpassed views of the city across the bay. The southern part of town along Bridgeway is chockablock with souvenir shops, boutiques, galleries, and overpriced cafés, as well as two terrific bars, the No Name and Paterson's; the local scene can be found a short walk away on Caledonia Street, which is full of great restaurants like Sushi Ran (107 Caledonia St, 415-332-3620), a favorite of many Bay Area foodies.

Sausalito is host to many street fairs and festivals throughout the year, from art shows to chili cook-offs. The town is also home to a unique community of floating homes—approximately 400 houseboats in all—some of them tiny one-room abodes, others magnificent mansions on the water.

How to Get There

Head north on US 101 over the Golden Gate Bridge, and take the first exit (Alexander Ave). Follow Alexander 1.5 miles downhill into town. Better yet, take a ferry: the Blue & Gold fleet (415-705-5555; www.blueandgoldfeet.com) from Fisherman's Wharf or Golden Gate Ferry (415-455-2000; www.goldengateferry.org) from the Ferry Building in downtown San Francisco. Even better, ride a bike—the ride across the bridge is thrilling (for its views and for its close encounters with tourists on rental bikes), and the descent into Sausalito is fast. Most casual riders prefer to take the ferry back instead of climbing back out.

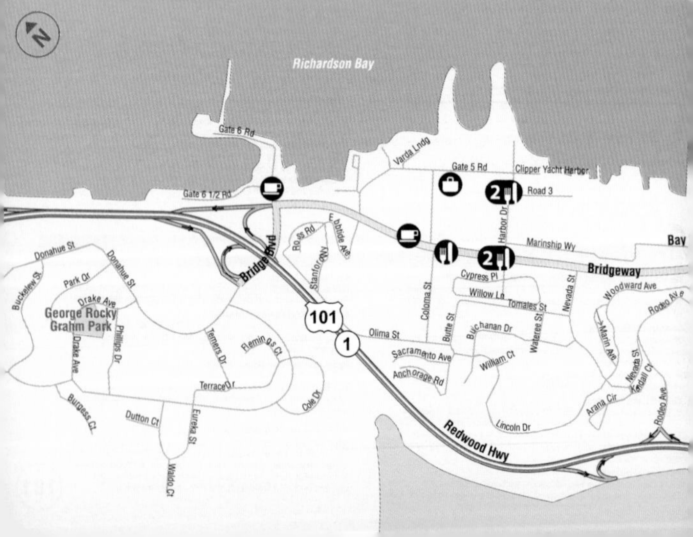

Landmarks

- **Bay Model Visitor Center** • 2100 Bridgeway

Banks

- **Bank of America** • 750 Bridgeway
- **Citibank (ATM)** • 1901 Bridgeway
- **Wells Fargo** • 715 Bridgeway

Coffee

- **Bayside Café** • 1 Gate 6 Rd
- **Bridgeway Bagel** • 3001 Bridgeway
- **Bridgeway Café** • 633 Bridgeway
- **Café Tutti** • 12 El Portal
- **Caffe DiVino** • 37 Caledonia St
- **Lappert's Ice Cream** • 689 Bridgeway
- **Lappert's Ice Cream** • 817 Bridgeway
- **Lighthouse Café** • 1311 Bridgeway
- **Sausalito Bakery & Café** • 571 Bridgeway
- **Starbucks** • 14 Princess St
- **Winship Restaurant** • 670 Bridgeway

Movie Theaters

- **Century Theatres Marin** • 101 Caledonia St

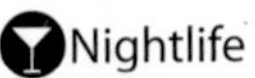

Nightlife

- **No Name Bar** • 757 Bridgeway
- **Paterson's Bar** • 739 Bridgeway
- **Smitty's Bar** • 214 Caledonia St

Restaurants

- **Avatars** • 2656 Bridgeway
- **Feng-Nian Chinese Restaurant** • 2650 Bridgeway
- **Fish.** • 350 Harbor Dr
- **Fred's Coffee Shop** • 1917 Bridgeway
- **Paradise Bay** • 1200 Bridgeway
- **Poggio Ristorante** • 777 Bridgeway
- **Sushi Ran** • 107 Caledonia St

Shopping

- **Flying Oliver Books** • 215 Caledonia St
- **Heath Ceramics** • 400 Gate 5 Rd
- **Pinestreet Papery** • 2 1/2 Caledonia St
- **Sausalito Ferry Company** • 688 Bridgeway

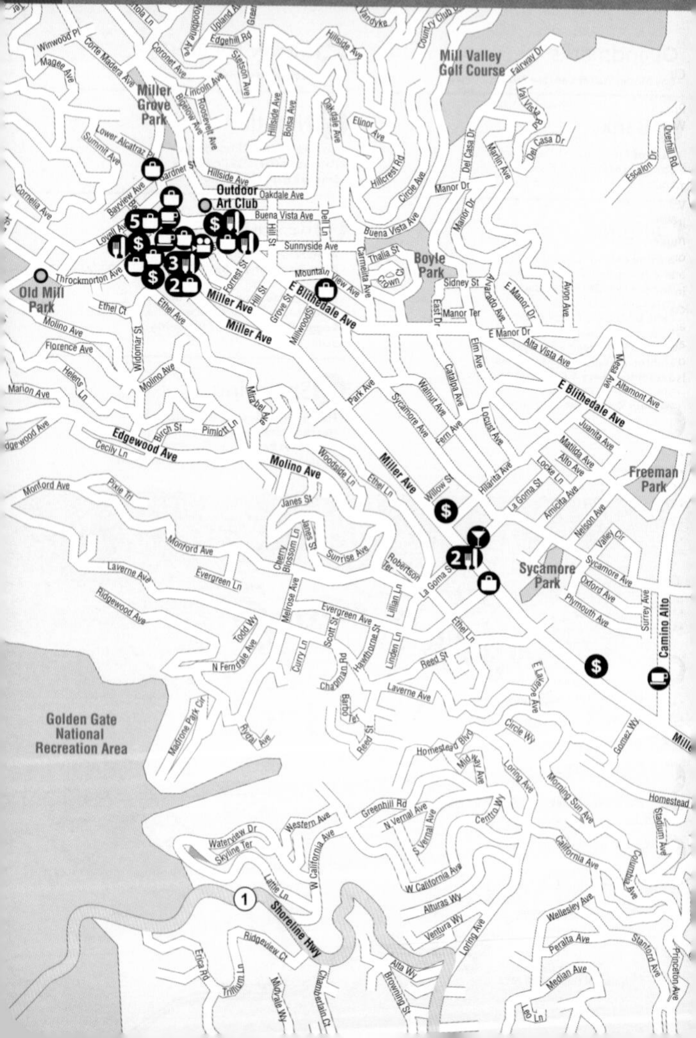

Mill Valley Golf Course
Miller Grove Park
Outdoor Art Club
Boyle Park
Old Mill Park
Freeman Park
Sycamore Park
Golden Gate National Recreation Area
Winwood Pl
Magee Ave
Corte Madera Ave
Coronet Ave
Woodbine Ave
Upland Ave
Edgehill Rd
Stetson Ave
Vandyke
Hillside Ave
Country Club Dr
Fairway Dr
Val Vista Pl
Del Casa Dr
Overhill Rd
Escalon Dr
Lincoln Ave
Bigelow Ave
Roosevelt Ave
Hillside Ave
Boisa Ave
Oakdale Ave
Elinor Ave
Hillcrest Rd
Circle Ave
Manor Dr
Marlin Ave
Lower Alcatraz Pl
Summit Ave
Gardner St
Cornelia Ave
Bayview Ave
Oakdale Ave
Buena Vista Ave
Dell Ln
Hill St
Sunnyside Ave
Lovell Ave
Throckmorton Ave
Forrest St
Mountain View Ave
Carmelita Ave
Thalia St
Crown Ct
Sidney St
Alvarado Ave
E Manor Dr
Avon Ave
East Dr
Manor Ter
E Blithedale Ave
Miller Ave
Grove St
Millwood St
Ethel Ct
Ethel Ave
Molino Ave
Florence Ave
Widomar St
Helens Ln
Marion Ave
Edgewood Ave
Cecily Ln
Birch St
Pimlott Ln
Mirabel Ave
Park Ave
Sycamore Ave
Walnut Ave
Catalpa Ave
Elm Ave
Alta Vista Ave
Mesa Ave
Altamont Ave
Juanita Ave
Matilda Ave
Alto Ave
Locust Ave
Fern Ave
Hilarita Ave
Locke Ln
La Goma St
Amicita Ave
Nelson Ave
Valley Cir
Woodside Ln
Ethel Ln
Willow St
Monford Ave
Pixie Trl
Janes St
Sunrise Ave
Robertson Ter
Cherry Blossom Ln
Laverne Ave
Evergreen Ln
Ridgewood Ave
Todd Wy
Melrose Ave
Evergreen Ave
Scott St
Hawthorne St
Lillian Ln
Linden Ln
La Goma St
Oxford Ave
Plymouth Ave
Surrey Ave
Camino Alto
N Ferndale Ave
Curry Ln
Chapman Rd
Reed St
Barbo Ter
Laverne Ave
E Laverne Ave
Madrone Park Cir
Rydal Ave
Reed St
Circle Wy
Gomez Wy
Homestead Blvd
Midway Ave
Loring Ave
Morning Sun Ave
Homestead
Stadium Ave
Greenhill Rd
N Vernal Ave
S Vernal Ave
Centro Wy
Western Ave
Waterview Dr
Skyline Ter
W California Ave
California Ave
Columbia Ave
Lattie Ln
Shoreline Hwy
W California Ave
Alturas Wy
Ventura Wy
Loring Ave
Wellesley Ave
Peralta Ave
Stanford Ave
Princeton Ave
Median Ave
Ridgeview Ct
Erica Rd
Trillium Ln
Midvale Wy
Chamberlain Ct
Alta Wy
Browning St
Leo Ln

General Information

City Hall:	26 Corte Madera Ave Mill Valley, CA 94941
Phone:	415-388-4033
Website:	www.cityofmillvalley.org

Overview

Tucked at the foot of Mt Tamalpais in Marin County, Mill Valley makes a delightful day trip from San Francisco. In its early days, the town's plentiful redwoods provided much of the lumber that built San Francisco. Later on, Mill Valley was famous for its creek-fed canyons and superb hiking as well as "the crookedest railroad in the world," a steam-and gravity-powered train that connected the town with the top of the mountain and nearby Muir Woods. Although the invasion of the automobile and the great fire of 1929 put the railroad out of business 75 years ago, the town's natural beauty is as seductive as ever.

Downtown Mill Valley is delineated by Throckmorton and Miller Avenues. Depot Plaza and adjacent Lytton Square form the center of the action. Though the town's present reputation rests on the tiny boutiques and galleries that wouldn't seem out of place on Rodeo Drive, there are also quality restaurants nearby, such as the famously romantic El Paseo, tucked into a brick-lined street. Nightlife is more attractive here than in most shopping meccas, too—the Throckmorton Theater offers theater, music, and performance in a gorgeous old building, and the Sweetwater is your best bet to catch one of Marin County's many reclusive rock stars in an intimate, sometimes unannounced set. Rest your head at the Mill Valley Inn and get a massage the next morning at the Tea Garden Springs Day Spa around the corner.

Banks

- **Bank of America** • 60 Throckmorton Ave
- **Citibank** • 130 Throckmorton Ave
- **Citibank (ATM)** • 349 Miller Ave
- **Wells Fargo** • 18 Miller Ave
- **Wells Fargo** • 525 Miller Ave
- **The Old Mill** • Throckmorton Ave & Old Mill St

Landmarks

- **Old Mill Park** • Throckmorton Ave & Old Mill St
- **Outdoor Art Club** • 1 W Blithedale Ave

Coffee

- **LaCoppa** • 2 Miller Ave
- **Peet's** • 88 Throckmorton Ave
- **Starbucks** • 45 Camino Alto

Movie Theaters

- **CineArts Sequoia** • 25 Throckmorton Ave

Nightlife

- **2 AM Club** • 380 Miller Ave

Restaurants

- **Avatars Punjab Burritos** • 15 Madrona St
- **Buckeye Roadhouse** • 15 Shoreline Hwy
- **Bungalow 44** • 44 E Blithedale Ave
- **Fruit Stand** • Shoreline Hwy & Tennessee Valley Rd
- **Ino** • 25 Miller Ave
- **Joe's Taco Lounge** • 382 Miller Ave
- **La Ginestra** • 127 Throckmorton Ave
- **Mama's Royal Café** • 393 Miller Ave
- **Pearl's Phatburgers** • 8 E Blithedale Ave
- **Piazza D'Angelo** • 22 Miller Ave

Shopping

- **All Wrapped Up** • 38 Miller Ave
- **Alphadog** • 6 Miller Ave
- **Benefit** • 35 Throckmorton Ave
- **The Depot Bookstore & Café** • 87 Throckmorton Ave
- **Mill Valley Hat Box** • 118 Throckmorton Ave
- **Mill Valley Market** • 12 Corte Madera Ave
- **Pharmaca** • 230 E Blithedale Ave
- **Strawbridges** • 86 Throckmorton Ave
- **Tea Garden Springs Day Spa** • 38 Miller Ave
- **Tony's Shoe Repair** • 38 Corte Madera Ave
- **Two Neat** • 111 Throckmorton Ave
- **Village Music** • 31 Sunnyside
- **Vintage Wine & Spirits** • 67 Throckmorton Ave
- **Whole Foods Market** • 414 Miller Ave

Landmarks

- **The Old Mill** • Old Mill Park, Throckmorton Ave & Old Mill St • Built in the 1830s and used for 15 years (what you see now is a reconstruction), this landmark is the town's namesake. Mill Valley's beautiful glass-and-redwood library is nearby at the edge of the park.

- **Outdoor Art Club** • 1 W Blithedale Ave • Founded by civic-minded women in 1902 who wanted to preserve Mill Valley's unique natural environment, the Club later became a champion of conservation efforts in surrounding areas as well. Beautifully designed by Bernard Maybeck in a charming garden setting.

Festivals & Events

- **Mill Valley Film Festival** (mid-Oct) • Various venues • The Sequoia Theatre at 25 Throckmorton Avenue is the festival's main venue, but events take place throughout Marin County. The festival is highly regarded within independent film circles and features seminars, panel discussions, and in-person tributes as well as films from around the world. For more information, call 415-383-5256 or visit www.mvff.com.

- **Dipsea Race** (mid-June) • The 7.1-mile course stretching from downtown Mill Valley over Mt. Tamalpais to Stinson Beach includes the grueling 676 Dipsea Steps and is run by 1,500 competitors every summer. This is the second-oldest footrace in the country after the Boston Marathon. For more information, visit www.dipsea.org.

- **Mill Valley Wine & Gourmet Food Tasting** (late June) • Lytton Sq b/w Miller Ave & Sunnyside Ave • Wineries from nearby Napa and Sonoma bring their wares to be sampled alongside the town's delectable food offerings. $30 in advance (or $35 the day of) buys you all the wine you can taste. Visit www.millvalley.org/wine_intro.html to preorder tickets.

- **Concerts in the Plaza** (Summer Thursdays) • Lytton Sq b/w Miller Ave & Sunnyside Ave • Local talent covering a variety of genres entertains the crowds for free.

- **Paint-off in the Plaza** (Late July) • The City Arts commission presents the annual paint-off competition in the Plaza. You can go see the artists working beginning at 10 am or check out the finished masterpieces after 3 pm. For more information visit www.cityofmillvalley.org/boards-art-paint-off.pdf.

- **Mill Valley Fall Arts Festival** (late Sept) • Old Mill Park, Throckmorton Ave & Old Mill St • Two days of art, entertainment, and food among the redwoods. Visit www.mvfaf.org for more information.

- **Mountain Play at the Mountain Theatre** (a.k.a. The Cushing Memorial Theatre) (May and June) • Mt Tamalpais State Park • This stunning outdoor amphitheater seats 3,750 people and has been the dramatic setting for different plays every year since 1913; walking the six miles down the mountain after the performance is part of the fun. Visit www.mountainplay.org for schedule and ticket information.

Outdoors

- **Mt. Tamalpais State Park** • Headquarters at 801 Panoramic Hwy • Visit over 50 miles of hiking and biking trails, scenic vistas, and campgrounds. 415-388-2070.

- **Tennessee Beach** • End of Tennessee Valley Trail • Hiking, horseback riding, and picnic tables on the black sand beach. 415-331-1540.

How to Get There

Mill Valley is approximately ten miles north of San Francisco across the Golden Gate Bridge. Take 101 to the Mill Valley/Stinson Beach exit and head west on what becomes Shoreline Highway. After about a mile, veer right at the stoplight by the gas station (left takes you onto Highway 1 and over to the coast). The road becomes Miller Avenue and leads you right into the heart of downtown.

Alternately, take the Tiburon/E Blithedale exit, two off-ramps along 101 after the Mill Valley/Stinson Beach exit. Head west and follow your nose for about three miles. East Blithedale Avenue is the other main thoroughfare into downtown Mill Valley.

Golden Gate Transit offers minimal bus service to Mill Valley, mostly serving commuters. Change buses at Marin City. Visit www.goldengate.org for more details.

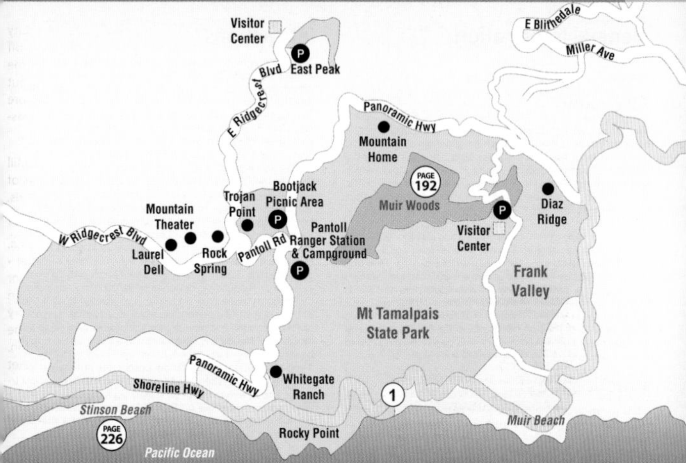

General Information

Address:	801 Panoramic Hwy Mill Valley, CA 94941
Phone:	415-388-2070
Website:	www.parks.ca.gov/?page_id=471 www.mttam.net
Open:	Daily 7am–sunset year round
Entry:	Free to enter, $8 per car to park, camping costs start at $25

Overview

Easy access from San Francisco makes Marin County's Mt Tamalpais State Park a popular day trip for restless city dwellers and nature lovers. Once thought to be a remnant of an extinct volcano, geologists now believe that Mt Tam was created during millenniums of shifts in the nearby San Andreas Fault. The park's 6,300 acres contain oak woodlands, grassy meadows, chaparral, and even redwoods. These mini-ecosystems are teeming with flora, with more than 750 plant species cataloged thus far. For most visitors, however, the highlight is the panoramic view from the 2,571-foot peak, which (on a clear day) looks out over San Francisco, Ocean Beach, Angel Island, Mt. Diablo, the Marin Headlands, and a vast expanse of the Pacific Ocean. On those rare exceptionally clear days, visibility can extend all the way to the Sierra Nevada mountains (150 miles to the east), and to the Farallon Islands 25 miles offshore. Originally, explorers named the peak La Sierra de Nuestro Padre de San Francisco. That proved to be too long, and so the mountain was renamed Tamalpais, a Miwok Indian word. To the locals it's simply (and affectionately) called Mt Tam.

Considered the birthplace of mountain biking, Mt Tam is still a favorite among Bay Area riders. Not all trails are open to cyclists, but there are plenty of twisting and technical roads along the mountain's flank and up to its peak. Hikers can sweat it out on 50 miles of trails within the park (watch out for the prevalent poison oak), which connect to a 200-mile network on adjacent land. The steep trails can be dangerous for both bikers and hikers, so caution is advised. Climbers have an option of four 25- to 45-foot slabs, in the Northern Formation to propel, and geocachers will be sure to find plenty of hidden treasures throughout the park (www.geocaching.com). Campers who think showering is overrated or are frightened by the sound of a flushing toilet can throw down a bedroll at a first-come, first-serve tent site, or call a few months in advance to reserve one of the 10 rustic cabins (415-388-2070). (The Steep Ravine camp sites and cabins are closed every October.) Day-trippers who enjoy running water can picnic in the Bootjack Picnic Area, which has tables, grills, potable water, and toilets that actually flush.

If it is your first excursion to Mt Tamalpais, you should check out the visitor center on the East Peak Summit. There's also a refreshment stand open daily during the summer. If you're not in the woods to escape civilization, you can use the phones, picnic tables, wireless Internet access (hmmm), and fully accessible restrooms there.

The Mountain Theater (also called The Cushing Memorial Theater) has been in use since the early 1900s. In the 1930s, the Civilian Conservation Corps added seating, improved the stage, and landscaped the area. The stone amphitheater seats 3,750 and stages the Mountain Play each spring, an annual event since 1913.

Practicalities

During the summer months, when the weather heats up and the vegetation dries out, park authorities sometimes close parts of Mt Tam due to the high risk of fire. You can get an update on park closures by calling the Pantoll Ranger Station at 415-388-2070.

How to Get There—Driving

From the south, take Highway 101-North, then take Highway 1 to the Stinson Beach exit and follow signs up the mountain. If you're distracted by the incredible scenery and the curvy roads, then let someone else do the driving so you can enjoy the view without any risk of steering yourself off a cliff. And please watch out for the many cyclists.

General Information

Phone: 415-831-2700
Website: http://sfrecpark.org

Overview

One of the city's finest features, this swath of urban greenery is home to treasures that can surprise and delight even the most jaded San Franciscan. Each Sunday (and Saturdays during the spring and summer months), John F. Kennedy Drive, which snakes through the heart of the park, is closed to auto traffic, so cyclists, joggers, skaters, and even swing dancers have the pavement to themselves.

Bigger than New York City's Central Park, Golden Gate Park takes up 1,013 acres and is about 3 miles long and 1/2-mile wide. William Hammond Hall designed the park in 1870 and chose John McLaren to succeed him in 1887. McLaren worked for fifty years to improve the green by adding trees and plants from all over the world to beautify the vast recreational area. McLaren lived at McLaren Lodge (35), built in 1896, until he died at age 96 in 1943. The park boasts more than fifty ways to spend your day, from buffalo watching (5) and paddle boating (15) to horticultural museums (34) and barbecue pits (12).

Practicalities

If it is summery and sunny in the rest of the city, there is still a chance of dreary mist in the park. Bordered by the fog line of Stanyan Street to the east, Great Highway to the west, Lincoln Way to the south, and Fulton Street to the north, the park is most easily accessed from 19th Avenue. Since parking is often difficult, public transportation is the best way to go. For bus, streetcar, and cable car service to Golden Gate Park, take the Muni 5, 7, 16AX, 16BX, 18, 21, 28, 28L, 29, 33, 44, 66, 71, and 71L. The Golden Gate Shuttle ($2 for all-day pass, exact change required) picks up passengers at 15 locations throughout the park every 15 minutes on weekends and holidays from from 9am-6pm year round. There is also a parking structure just inside the park at 10th Avenue.

Smokers (of all kinds) should note the new city ordinance banning smoking from city parks. Light up here, and you may end up getting fined.

Attractions

The Dutch Windmill (1) is one of two originally constructed to irrigate the park. The M.H. de Young Memorial Museum (21), renowned for its vast collection of old and contemporary American art, reopened on October 15, 2005 (50 Hagiwara Tea Garden Dr, 415-750-3600; http://deyoung.famsf.org.asp) after four years of planning and renovations. It's one of the coolest buildings not just in SF, but in America, period. The Sharon Art Studio (31) is a terrific community resource for art classes and education with programs for all ages and abilities (next to the Children's Playground, accessed by Bowling Green Drive between Kennedy and King drives, 415-753-7004; www.sharonartstudio.org). The Buffalo Paddock, created in 1892, has been newly renovated, and the furry residents seem to enjoy the new digs that offer visitors more upfront and personal views of the beasts (5). The California Academy of Sciences has been in the park since 1916, but damage from the 1989 earthquake prompted the Academy to rebuild. Like a phoenix rising from the ashes, the new building, designed by Renzo Piano and touted as the greenest museum in the world, is completed. It still features a library, research laboratory, planetarium, aquarium, and natural history museum, but now boasts a rainforest dome and living roof. Fans of Claude, the albino alligator, will be glad to know that he made the move unscathed. Tickets are $29.95, with 3 bucks off if you take public transportation. Despite the price tag, the CAS is hugely popular. When you go, expect long lines and not just to get in. The aquarium has been known get more crowded than a Who concert, especially on Free Days; check www.calacademy.org for more. The new building is located across the Music Concourse (22) from the de Young (21).

Nature

The Conservatory of Flowers (34), the oldest surviving conservatory in the Western Hemisphere, houses huge palm trees, exotic orchids, and water lilies from around the world (JFK Dr, 415-831-2090; www.conservatoryofflowers.org). The Shakespeare Garden (24) is a sweet-smelling tribute to the plants and flowers mentioned in the Bard's poems and plays. The San Francisco Botanical Garden at Strybing Arboretum (18) entices the senses with more than 6,000 plant species (9th Ave and Lincoln Wy, 415-661-1316; www.sfbotanicalgarden.org). The arboretum is located near the Japanese Tea Garden (19), which features Asian foliage. In the middle of Stow Lake (15) is an island called Strawberry Hill (16), which is 428 feet high and makes for a nice city hike.

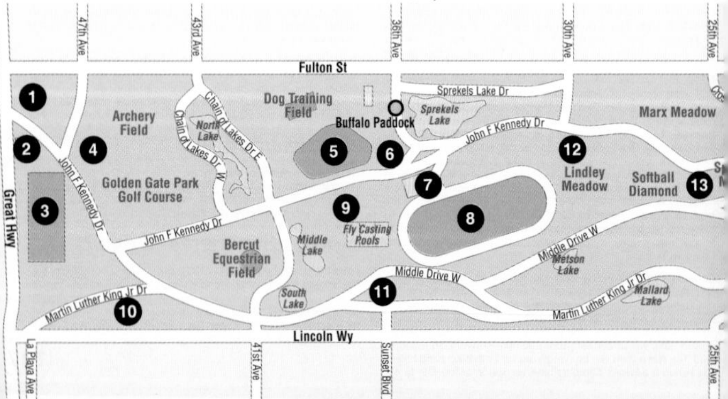

Architecture & Sculpture

The Japanese Tea Garden (19) was developed by Makato Hagiwara, a famed Japanese landscape designer (who is also said to be the inventor of the fortune cookie), and features a meditative teahouse, native Japanese and Chinese plants, and beautiful sculptures and bridges. The Conservatory of Flowers (34) is a great piece of Victorian architecture modeled after London's Kew Gardens. McLaren Lodge (35), built in 1896, is one of the oldest Mission-style buildings in San Francisco and it still remains a gorgeous sight. The two-story Beach Chalet (2) features some of the most beautiful murals in the city and also houses the park's visitor's center (1000 Great Hwy at Ocean Beach, 415-831-2700; www.beachchalet.com).

Open Spaces

Take your dog to romp in one of the park's two dog runs (11, 37). Most of the picnic tables are first-come, first-serve, but if you've got some meat to heat, reserve a barbecue pit ahead of time at the Pioneer Log Cabin (20) or by calling 415-831-5500.

Performance

Paid concerts, including Now and Zen and Outside Lands, are held in different meadows throughout the park, as well as free events like Shakespeare in the Park and the sprawling Hardly Strictly Bluegrass Festival. Always free is the big roller boogie held every Sunday at 6th Ave. and JFK.

Sports

The San Francisco 49ers played in Kezar Stadium (32) from 1946 to 1970. Now it's used for high school, amateur, and recreational sports. An archery field lies just north of the public nine-hole golf course (4). The Fly Casting Pools (9) draw aspiring and expert fishermen alike. The park has two main soccer fields (3, 8) and pick-up games wherever there is green space. Not to be left out, handball players have their choice of indoor or outdoor amusement (26). The San Francisco Lawn Bowling Club offers beginner lessons on the Bowling Greens (28) most Wednesdays and Saturdays at noon (call 415-487-8787" to confirm). If we're going to count handball and lawn bowling as sports, why not pull out your old skates and groove with the roller dancers off JFK Drive. There are twenty-one tennis courts (33) located at the eastern side of the park, available weekdays on a first-come, first-served basis. Reservations for courts are required on weekends and holidays (415-831-6301). Playing fields and times must be reserved for most team sports. Call 415-831-5510 (for soccer, football, baseball, and softball) for pricing and available times.

Landmarks of Golden Gate Park

1. Dutch Windmill & Queen Wilhelmina Tulip Garden
2. Beach Chalet
3. Soccer Fields
4. Golf Course & Clubhouse
5. Bison Paddock
6. Model Yacht Club
7. Equestrian Center & Police Stables
8. Golden Gate Park Stadium Soccer & Polo Fields
9. Anglers Lodge & Fly Casting Pools
10. Playground
11. Dog Run
12. Barbecue Pits
13. Picnic Area
14. Rose Garden
15. Stow Lake Boathouse / Boat Rentals
16. Strawberry Hill
17. Playground
18. Botanical Garden and Strybing Arboretum
19. Japanese Tea Garden
20. Pioneer Log Cabin
21. M.H. de Young Memorial Museum
22. Music Concourse
23. County Fair Building & Horticultural Library
24. Shakespeare Garden
25. Baseball Field
26. Handball Courts
27. De Laveaga Dell & AIDS Memorial Grove
28. Lawn Bowling Greens
29. Carousel
30. Children's Playground
31. Sharon Art Studio
32. Kezar Stadium
33. Tennis Courts
34. Conservatory of Flowers
35. McLaren Lodge
36. Horseshoe Pits
37. Dog Run
38. Official City Tree
39. Park Police Station

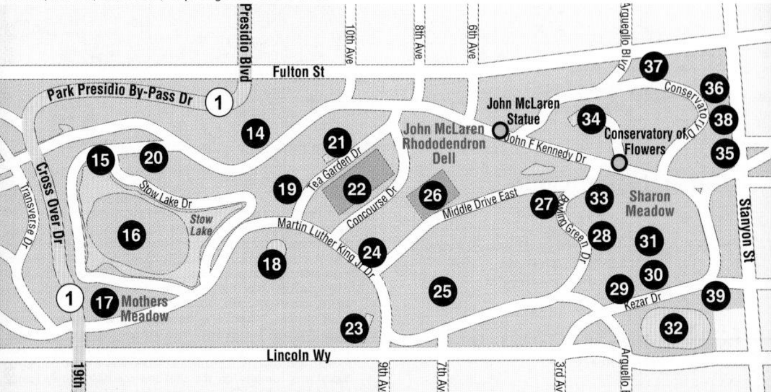

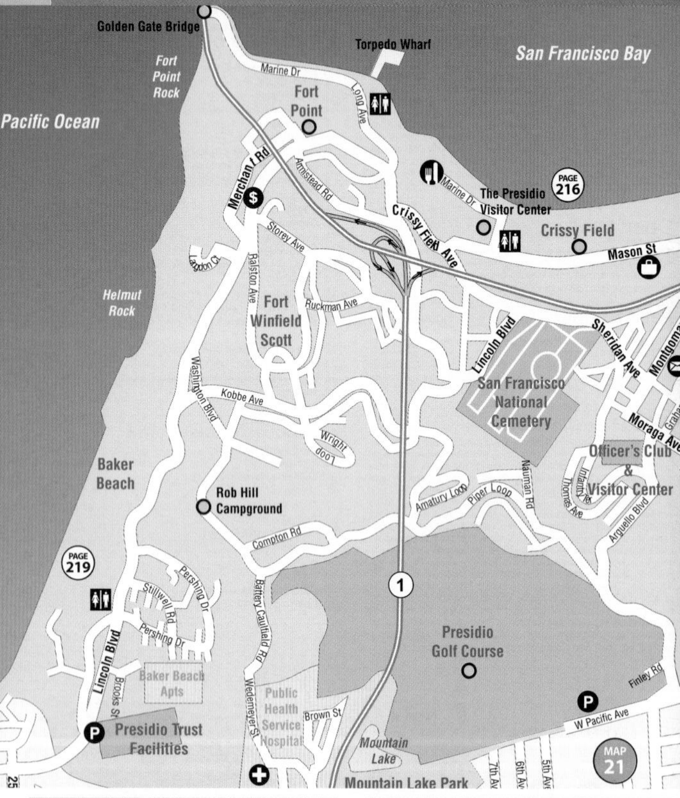

General Information

Website:	www.presidio.gov www.nps.gov/prsf
Mailing Address:	Golden Gate National Recreation Area Bldg 201, Fort Mason San Francisco, CA 94123
Visitor Center:	415-561-4323
Non-Emergency Park Police:	415-561-5505
Open:	24 hours a day, year-round
Entry:	Free

Overview

As if a heartbreakingly beautiful location, a trend-setting cultural aesthetic, and endless charming architecture weren't enough, San Franciscans can also boast of having a national park in their city. A former military outpost, the Presidio's 1,491 acres contain more than 500 historic buildings, old coastal defense fortifications, a national cemetery (the only cemetery within San Francisco city limits), forests, beaches, dramatic coastal bluffs, and miles and miles of trails. It comes as no surprise that everyone jumped when the base was decommissioned and the land was made available for development. The Presidio's new tenants are real movers and shakers. Lucasfilm Ltd. operates a 1,500-employee digital arts complex on the site, and the Walt Disney Family Foundation opened The Walt Disney Family Museum, a museum

dedicated to the animator, in 2009. Twenty-one distinct residential neighborhoods also sprawl over the Presidio—monthly rental options range from $1800 for a one-bedroom apartment to $15,000 for a seven-bedroom house. The Presidio is federal property and does not have to abide by San Francisco laws, such as rent control. Despite the construction and development on the grounds, nothing has marred the beauty of this green-tipped peninsula.

The people of the Ohlone Native American tribe are the first known residents of this land, and the area was named by the Spanish soldiers and missionaries who arrived to conquer and convert in 1776. The Presidio went on to serve as a military post under the flags of Spain, Mexico, and the United States at different points in its military career. It has played a logistical role in every major US military conflict over the last 150 years. In 1994, the old military hero finally retired and became a part of the Golden Gate National Recreation Area.

As proof of its historic, scenic, and recreational value, the residential neighborhoods that border the Presidio are some of the more expensive locales in the city. Part of what these residents pay for is easy access to this welcoming chunk of nature—the 11 miles of hiking trails include the Golden Gate Promenade, the Coastal Trail, an ecology trail, and portions of the Bay Area Ridge Trail, the Bay Trail, and the Anza National Historic Trail. 14 miles of paved roads provide smooth—albeit mostly hilly—biking for cyclists. There are also some unpaved parts of the Bay Area Ridge Trail if off-road is more your style. The park also contains numerous sports facilities, including a golf course, bowling alley, tennis courts, athletic fields, and a campground. Baker Beach, the site of the first Burning Man in 1989, features a clothing-optional section, north of the hazardous surf sign (don't get excited: the nudists are mostly old dudes). Offering flat terrain and sweeping views of the Golden Gate, Crissy Field (named for Major Dana H. Crissy, not a Marina chick) is a popular spot for dog walkers, swimmers, bikers, hikers, and kite fliers.

How to Get There—Driving

The Presidio can be reached from the north by crossing the Golden Gate Bridge (Highways 1 and 101); from the east by way of Lombard Street (Highway 101); and from the south via Highway 1.

How to Get There—Mass Transit

San Francisco Municipal Railway (Muni) buses serve the Presidio via the 28, 29, 43, and 76 lines. Bus service from the North Bay to the Golden Gate Bridge toll plaza is available through Golden Gate Transit. Commercial cable car buses are available from Fisherman's Wharf. The Presidio Trust provides free shuttle service within the Presidio and to nearby public transit stops.

Banks

- **First Republic** • 210 Lincoln Blvd

Landmarks

- **Andy Goldsworthy Spire** • Bay Ridge Trail near Arguello Blvd
- **Crissy Field** • Mason St
- **Fort Point** • Long Ave & Marine Dr
- **Golden Gate Bridge** • US Hwy 101
- **Presidio Bowling Center** • 93 Moraga Ave
- **Presidio Golf Course** • 300 Finley Rd
- **The Presidio Visitor Center** • temporarily at Bldg 105, Montgomery St
- **Rob Hill Campground** • Washington Blvd & Central Magazine Rd

Post Offices

- **Presidio Station** • 950 Lincoln Blvd, Bldg 210

Gyms

- **YMCA - Presidio Community** • 63 Funston Ave

Restaurants

- **Crissy Field Warming Hut** • 983 Marine Dr

Shopping

- **Sports Basement** • 610 Mason St

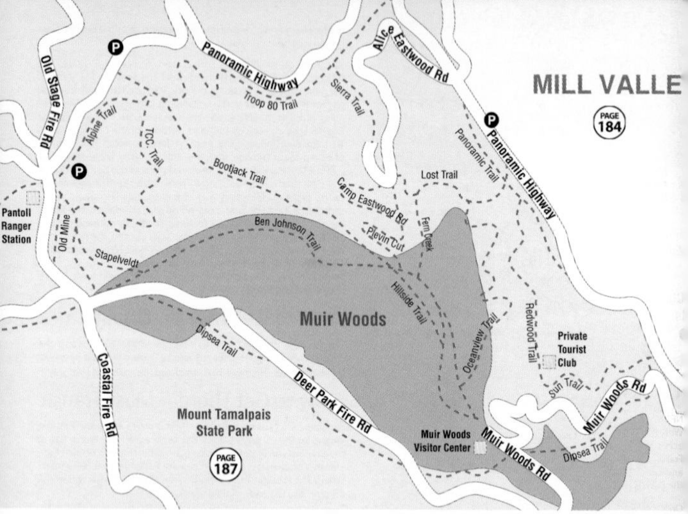

General Information

Address:	Muir Woods National Monument Mill Valley, CA 94941
Phone:	415-388-2596
Website:	http://www.nps.gov/muwo
Hours:	Daily, 8 am to sunset, including holidays.
Admission:	$5 day fee or $20 for an annual pass.

Overview

During California's rapid industrialization and the beginning of the Gold Rush in 1849, Marin County, once covered in redwoods, was laid bare by development. The land that is now Muir Woods was spared from logging only because of its inaccessibility—and thank God! This sanctuary of old-growth redwood trees is a little piece of heaven. The land was purchased in 1905 by Congressman William Kent, who paid $45,000 for 295 acres of gargantuan redwood trees (they are the tallest trees that grow on earth). To protect his trees, he donated the land to the federal government and President Theodore Roosevelt declared it a national monument in 1908. Although Roosevelt offered to name the area after Kent, the modest congressman decided instead to memorialize conservationist John Muir (thus earning him another gold star in our book).

The monument, which preserves the last redwood forest in the Bay Area, sees about 750,000 visitors annually making weekend parking very difficult. Most visitors stick to the main trail, an easy two-mile round-trip stroll along Redwood Creek; this paved path is accessible for strollers and wheelchairs. Several other dirt trails (totaling six miles) wind their way through the monument, and especially ambitious hikers can connect to an even larger network of paths on contiguous land in Mt Tamalpais State Park. Park rangers lead daily guided walks through the woods; it's best to call ahead for scheduling information. The fact that a place as unspeakably beautiful as Muir Woods can be so close to a major city like SF just makes life just a bit more bearable, don't you think?

Picnicking is not allowed in Muir Woods, but the Muir Woods Café, which serves sandwiches, salads, and sausages, is located near the entrance. Pets are prohibited, with the exception of service dogs. Bikes are allowed only on designated fire roads surrounding Muir Woods. For obvious reasons, smoking is not permitted anywhere near the sacred forest.

How to Get There—Driving

From the south, take Highway 101 N across the Golden Gate Bridge. Exit Highway 1/Stinson Beach (there will be a sign for Muir Woods at this exit) and drive about 0.5 miles. At the stoplight, turn left. Drive about 2.7 miles. At the top of the hill, turn right towards Muir Woods/Mount Tamalpais. Follow posted signs to Muir Woods.

How to Get There—Mass Transit

Golden Gate Transit (415-921-5858) offers a free shuttle service (bus 66) to Muir Woods on summer weekends and holidays. From San Francisco, Golden Gate Transit buses 10, 70 and 80 will take you to the shuttle stop. Bus 63 also runs on weekends and holidays and makes stops at the Mountain Home Inn, Pantoll Station, and Bootjack on Panoramic Highway. From any of these stops, it is a one- to two-mile hike down to Muir Woods.

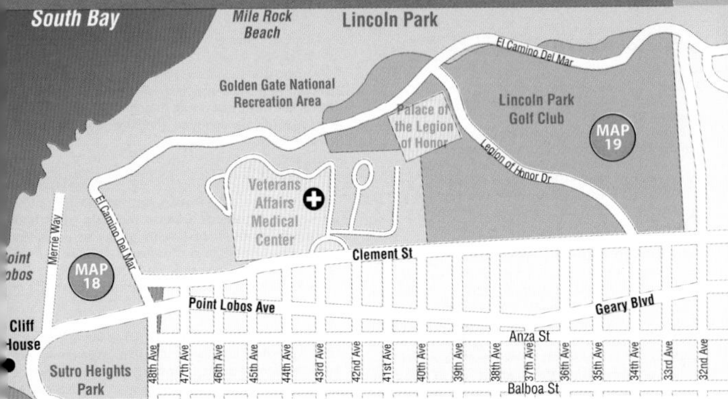

Overview

NFT Maps: 18 & 19

With views of the Golden Gate Bridge and the Marin Headlands, 193-acre Lincoln Park is one of the most spectacular park spaces in San Francisco. It's also probably the only one where visitors can play golf and then stroll over to one of the finest art collections in the country, the Palace of the Legion of Honor.

Originally the site of the Golden Gate cemetery, city commissioners developed Lincoln Park in 1908, turning the Gold Rush graveyard into a posh 18-hole golf course. Many of the corpses were exhumed and moved as the plot was transformed, but hundreds of bodies remain buried beneath this picturesque park.

Practicalities

The park can be easily accessed by car from 34th Avenue or El Camino del Mar. There is parking near the golf course (does this sound like a bad idea, anyone?) and the Legion of Honor museum. Muni bus 18 stops right at the Legion of Honor (and anyone with a Muni pass or a bus transfer receives a $2 discount on admission to the museum).

Lincoln Park Golf Course

34th Ave & Clement St; 415-221-9911;
http://sfrecpark.org/Rec-Golf.aspx

The par-68 public golf course, where you can putt atop bluffs overlooking the Golden Gate, is one of the park's most popular attractions. The layout is not as challenging as the other two public 18-hole courses in town, Harding Park and the Presidio, nor has it benefited from a renovation like the others (even though the course dates back to 1908). The back nine at Lincoln offer challenges for even the most confident golfer, including the 17th hole, a 240-yard par-3 that offers spectacular views of the Golden Gate Bridge. An automated phone system allows non-residents to make reservations six days ahead of time (415-750-4653). Locals can save $13–14 on green fees by picking up a Resident Golf Card at City Hall. 18 holes cost about $37 on weekdays and $41 on weekends. There is no driving range at Lincoln Park, and the putting green is a little lumpy, but the pro shop is fully equipped.

Palace of the Legion of Honor

100 34th Ave; 415-750-3600;
http://legionofhonor.famsf.org/

This grand Beaux-Arts building, a 3/4-scale replica of Paris's 18th-century Palais de la Légion d'Honneur, houses a notable collection of ancient and European art. The museum was given to San Francisco by the city's grandmother of Art and Culture, Alma de Bretteville Spreckels, who filled it with many sculptures she bought from Rodin himself, including an early cast of *The Thinker*. During construction, music-loving Alma had a Skinner organ (not as dirty as it sounds) built right the architecture. The Skinner can be experienced at Public Organ Concerts (also not dirty) held Saturdays and Sundays at 4 pm. Hours: Tues–Sun, 9:30 am–5:25 pm. General admission is $11, Seniors are $8, Youth (13–17) $7, and children under 13 are free (with additional surcharges for special exhibitions), but the first Tuesday of every month is free! The museum has an excellent café and a well-stocked museum store.

Lincoln Park is also home to George Segal's controversial Holocaust Memorial sculpture, located near the Palace of the Legion of Honor. Installed in 1984, Segal's chilling work depicts a pile of emaciated, dead bodies next to one lone survivor gazing out over the Pacific.

Lands End and the Coastal Trail

www.parksconservancy.org/visit/park-sites/lands-end.html

The newly paved Coastal Trail runs along the cliffside at Lincoln Park, and is hands-down the best way to get out of the city without leaving San Francisco. The trail begins on the east side of the park, where a small platform with benches looks out over the Marin Headlands. If you're coming from the Legion of Honor, just walk straight down through the golf course and you'll hit it. Continue west along the coastline, and the trail eventually reaches Lands End, a rocky outcropping with an odd gravel maze art piece and priceless views of the Golden Gate. There is no food or water along the trail, but if you bring a picnic you can nestle down and eat at one of the secluded rock beaches. If you continue walking (watch out for hardy trail-runners!) you'll end up in beautiful Sutro Heights Park, which has a great view of the coast on those exceptional clear days. Below that, in the rocky inlet below the Cliff House, you can find the ruins of Sutro Baths, a giant, heated, seawater swimming complex built in 1896. The structure that housed the Baths was destroyed by a fire in 1966, but the remains of the huge public pools can still be explored. Both places are named after Adolph Sutro, an affluent early citizen and the 24th mayor of San Francisco. (Newsom you've got your work cut out for you.) Warning—this is a San Francisco trail, there are hills, and it can be bone-freezing if the fog is in. The best part about it? Crowds are rare.

General Information

NFT Map:	3
Address:	900 North Point St San Francisco, CA 94109
Phone:	415-775-5500
Website:	www.ghirardellisq.com
Summer Hours:	Mon—Sat: 10 am—9 pm; Sun: 10 am—6 pm (June—Sept)
Winter Hours:	Mon—Thurs: 11 am—7 pm; Fri—Sun: 11 am—6 pm (Sept—Apr)

Overview

Right next to Fisherman's Wharf, Ghirardelli Square (pronounced with a hard "g") boasts scores of chocolate-starved travelers every day of the year. Among the tourists, a new creature emerges--the part-time resident. The top floor of the square has been turned into Fairmount Heritage Place, a partial-ownership condominium complex that offers 5 weeks a year of top-of-the-world living. Prices start at about $262,000. Yes, San Franciscans admit to sometimes visiting the square even when they're not entertaining out-of-towners. When the weather is warm, the big steps facing the bay and Alcatraz offer world-class people-watching opportunities for both tourists and locals.

So who, you ask, is this mysterious Ghirardelli? Domenica "Domingo" Ghirardelli, Italian goldrusher-cum-chocolatier, and his chocolate-loving, entrepreneurial sons bought a block of property on North Point Street overlooking the San Francisco Bay in 1893, after two of those many relentless San Francisco fires destroyed his first lot on Jackson Street. By 1915, the North Point Street property featured manufacturing plants, offices, employee housing, and a prominent clock tower. Together, the buildings formed...Ghirardelli Square.

In the 1960s, Ghirardelli Chocolate was purchased by the Golden Grain Macaroni Company and moved across the bay to San Rafael. The new Ghirardelli Square officially opened in 1964. The brick-terraced courtyard of fine shops and restaurants has been granted National Historic Register status. The original 1860 cast-iron chocolate grinder is located in the Lower Plaza, and other chocolate-making equipment still operates on a small scale in the Ghirardelli Chocolate Manufactory. The famous "Ghirardelli" sign, 25 feet tall and 125 feet wide, brightly welcomes ships into the Bay and has become a San Francisco landmark.

Practicalities

Everything at Ghirardelli Square is easy to locate, but if you need help, an information booth is located at Fountain Plaza, which sells souvenirs, film, chocolate, Muni passes, and gives out free maps (as if ours aren't enough for you!).

The seven principal buildings that make up the Square are: the Clock Tower, the Mustard Building, the Cocoa Building, the Chocolate Building, Woolen Mill, Wurster, and the Power House—all part of the original Ghirardelli factory.

Parking is available at a garage on Beach Street between Larkin at Polk streets. Discounted parking is available with merchant validation. Rates are $2.25 per twenty minutes, with a $32 maximum for up to 24 hours. But with all the traffic that comes through here, your best bet is to avoid the parking issue altogether and take public transportation.

Activities

The annual Chocolate Festival, held on the 1st or 2nd weekend in September, features chocolate treats from Ghirardelli Square establishments, as well as prominent restaurants, bakeries, and chocolatiers from around the Bay Area. Not to be missed is the "Earthquake" ice cream sundae-eating contest, where the winner receives his or her weight in Ghirardelli Chocolate.

Holidays are a time for family fun at Ghirardelli Square. On the Fourth of July, there is live musical entertainment and kid-related festivities. Christmas celebrations include the annual Tree Lighting Ceremony in late November, when there are a variety of caroling performances, a local celebrity emcee, and a visit from the Clauses. The 50-foot tree is decorated with, as you've probably guessed, chocolate bars.

Where to Eat Food Besides Chocolate

On the Fountain Plaza you will still find the nostalgic favorite Lori's Diner for your burger and five-dollar-shake needs. McCormick & Kuleto's offers seafood and sea views in the Wurster Building along Beach Street. Ana Mandara, located in the Power House, serves up modern Vietnamese cuisine. Cellar 360, a wine and tapas bar in the Woolen Mill building, caters to a gourmet crowd. And when all the eating is done, don't forget about dessert. Kara's Cupcakes offers an organic assortment of this ever popular sweet treat, while Crown and Crumpet offers an English tea time experience seven days a week. And of course, there is the chocolate. After all, this is Ghirardelli Square. A hot fudge sundae from the Ghirardelli Ice Cream and Chocolate Shop in the Fountain Plaza is a classic, ooey-gooey favorite.

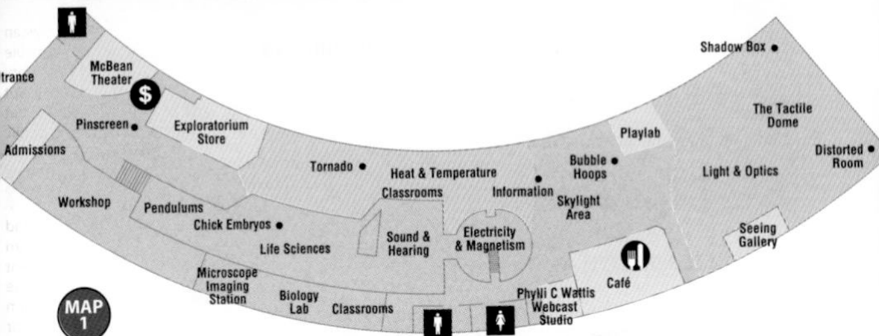

General Information

Map:	Use this current floor plan as a guide: http://www.exploratorium.edu/visit/plan_your_visit/floor_map.php
Address:	3601 Lyon St San Francisco, CA 94123
Phone:	415-561-0360
Website:	www.exploratorium.edu
Hours:	Tues—Sun: 10 am—5 pm, closed Mondays (except for select holidays), Thanksgiving & Christmas Day
Entry:	$15 for adults; $12 for youth (13-17), seniors (65+) and students; $10 for children aged 4-12; free for children 3 and under; free for all first Wednesday of each month. Tactile Dome is $20 for ages 7 and up, general admission included.

Overview

Want to see what happens to a building during an earthquake? How about charging your body with enough static electricity to give you a Don King 'do? The Exploratorium, located in San Francisco's Palace of Fine Arts, includes over 650 science, art, and human perception exhibits. Founded in 1969 by Dr. Frank Oppenheimer, who was director until his death in 1985, the Exploratorium is a learning center that combines science and technology with nature and art.

No one is a passive visitor here. Interactive exhibits explore how humans perceive light, color, sound, motion, electricity, heat, language, weather, and more. Don't worry: each exhibit has a "How Does It Work?" card for anyone who can't remember their high school science (yes, we're talking about you). The not-to-be-missed Tactile Dome lets you crawl, climb, and slide through unusual textures in darkness, guided only by touch (which is not that different from a typical night on the town in San Francisco). The experience requires an extra fee with admission and a reservation. We highly recommend making a reservation in advance of your visit by calling 415-561-0362. The museum also hosts regular film screenings. The Exploratorium has been celebrating an International Geek Holiday of its own creating for over 20 years now. Pi Day, which just happens to fall on Einstein's birthday, occurs on 3/14 at 1:59 pm. It is celebrated with Pi, and also with pie.

The stately, classical-looking Palace of Fine Arts (built in 1915 for the international expo) might seem like an odd place to locate a science museum, but not when you consider that for many years its annual lease with the city was $1. Now that the lease is expired and space is at a premium, the museum is developing a new location at Piers 15 and 17. Meanwhile, the Exploratorium continues to keep pace with the rapidly changing technological world. Its facilities include a multimedia Learning Center, wired classrooms, a Microscope Imaging Station, the 150-seat McBean Theater, and the Phyllis C. Wattis Webcast Studio. It can only get better. The museum will be relocating to Piers 15 and 17 in 2013.

How to Get There—Driving

From the North Bay, cross the Golden Gate Bridge, following signs indicating downtown San Francisco. Take the Marina exit on the left. (You'll see the Marina exit sign overhead.) Pass the Lyon Street entrance and proceed straight on Marina Boulevard. Then turn right on Divisadero Street, right on Jefferson Street, right on Broderick Street, and left on Marina Boulevard. Move immediately into the right lane, turn right on Yacht Road and follow signs for Exploratorium parking; the lot is next to the St. Francis Yacht Club.

From the East Bay, cross the Bay Bridge. Follow the signs to the Ninth Street exit. Stay in the right-hand lane. Go one block and turn right onto Ninth. Stay in the left-hand lane. Immediately after Market Street, veer left onto Hayes Street. Make a right turn onto Van Ness Avenue. Take Van Ness to Lombard. (Look for signs to the Golden Gate Bridge.) Turn left onto Lombard. Once on Lombard, get into the right-hand lane. Turn right on Divisadero Street, left on Marina Boulevard, and then immediately move into the right lane. Turn right on Yacht Road and follow signs for Exploratorium parking (lot is next to the St. Francis Yacht Club).

From the South Bay or the Peninsula, take 101 N to the Market Street/Van Ness exit. Take Van Ness to Lombard. (Look for signs to the Golden Gate Bridge.) Then follow directions from East Bay.

How to Get There—Mass Transit

The Exploratorium has convenient access to public transportation. San Francisco Muni buses 30, 43, 28, and 29 go right to the door, and Muni bus lines 22, 41, and 45 stop nearby. If you're taking BART, get off at the Montgomery Street station, walk half a block up Market Street to Third Street, and catch the 30 Stockton bus on the corner. Practically all downtown-bound Golden Gate Transit buses stop near the Exploratorium.

How to Get There—Biking

The Exploratorium is a little over two miles from the Embarcadero BART station or the Golden Gate Ferry terminal at the foot of Market Street. Follow signs to Fort Mason until you pass the Marina Yacht Club. The Palace of Fine Arts will be across the boulevard on your left.

North Building and South Building

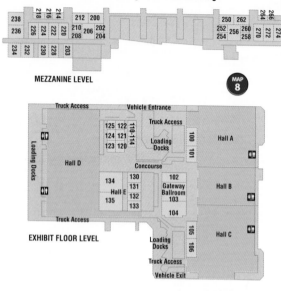

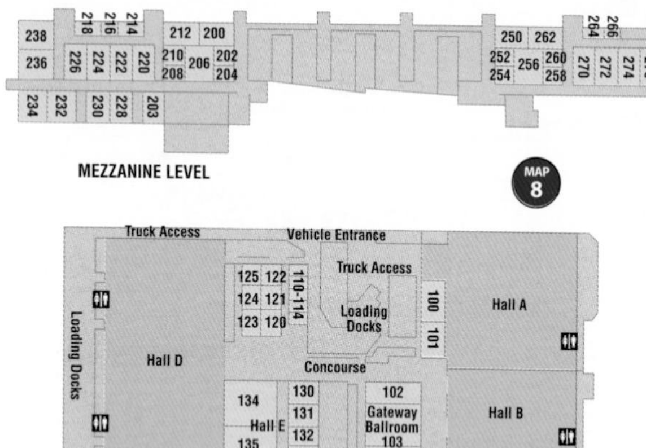

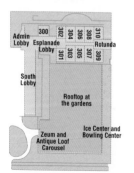

Center for the Arts
Galleries and Forum Building
Theatre
Yerba Buena Gardens Esplanade
North Lobby
Sony Metreon
300
302
304
306
308
310
Admin Lobby
Esplanade Lobby
Rotunda
301
303
305
307
309
South Lobby
Rooftop at the gardens
Ice Center and Bowling Center
Zeum and Antique Loof Carousel

STREET LEVEL

West Building

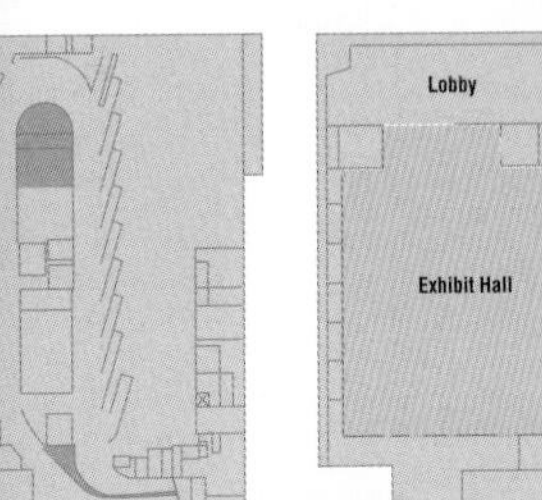

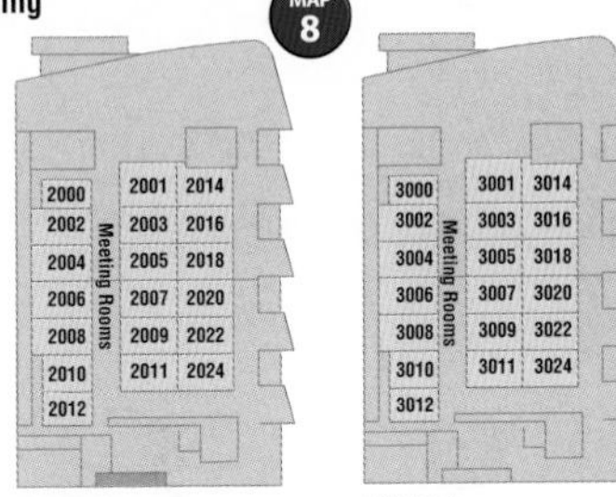

General Information

NFT Map: 8
Address: 747 Howard St,
San Francisco, CA 94103
Phone: 415-974-4000
Fax: 415-974-4073
Website: http://www.moscone.com/mtgplanners/floorplans/index.shtml

Overview

Notice a lot of bag-laden, name-tag-emblazoned people in "business casual" ambling around the streets? They're called conventioneers, and they're a form of wildlife typical to a habitat known as the Moscone Center. The Moscone Center hosts the majority of San Francisco's trade shows, conventions, and corporate banquets. The center is conveniently located in the heart of downtown San Francisco, which affords great dining, shopping, nightlife, and lodging options.

The Moscone complex is composed of three main buildings (Moscone South, Moscone North, and Moscone West) that cover more than twenty acres of building space and 700,000 square feet of exhibit space. All three buildings blend energy-efficient technology and unique designs, including Moscone South's dramatic 16-post-tensioned steel and concrete arches arranged in pairs to support its roof. To maximize light dispersal, large expanses of glass were used for the exterior. Skylights also extend as much natural light as possible. The center has won a series of awards for its environmental efforts, notably for the 60,000 square-foot solar panel project on top of Moscone South.

In addition to the ample interior space, the Moscone Center takes great advantage of its outdoor space. On top of Moscone South is the Rooftop at Yerba Buena Gardens. It features a kid's outdoor jungle gym and Zeum, an educational center that teaches children about technology and the arts with hands-on activities. The complex also features the Yerba Buena Ice Skating and Bowling Center, a unique 1906 carousel, a café, and concession stands. Across the street, on top of Moscone North, the Yerba Buena Gardens include an expansive grassy knoll and a memorial to Martin Luther King, Jr. To the left and right of the gardens sit the Yerba Buena Center for the Arts and the Metreon respectively—a balancing act of non-profit arts and commercial entertainment.

How to Get There—Driving

Head north on Interstate 101, then take 80 E. Take the Fourth Street exit. Make a left on Bryant, a left on Third, and a left on Howard. The Moscone Center is located on the 700 block of Howard Street. You'll find Moscone South on your left and Moscone North on your right.

Via the Bay Bridge, take the Fremont Street exit to Howard Street and turn left on Howard.

Via the Golden Gate Bridge, take the Lombard Street exit to Van Ness Avenue. Turn right on Van Ness. Travel south to Grove. This will be approximately two miles. Turn left on Grove Street. Continue to Market Street. Cross Market Street and travel south on Eighth Street to Folsom. Turn left on Folsom, left on Third, and left on Howard.

How to Get There—Mass Transit

If you're taking BART or Muni Metro, disembark at the Powell Street Station. Exit to Fourth and Market Streets and turn right onto Fourth. Walk two blocks south to Howard and turn left. The Moscone Center is located on the 700 block of Howard Street. You'll find Moscone South on your right and Moscone North on your left.

If CalTrain is more your speed, get off at Fourth and Townsend. Cross Fourth Street from the train station and catch the 15, 30, or 45 lines. Get off at Third and Folsom. Walk one block north up towards Howard Street. Turn left onto Howard.

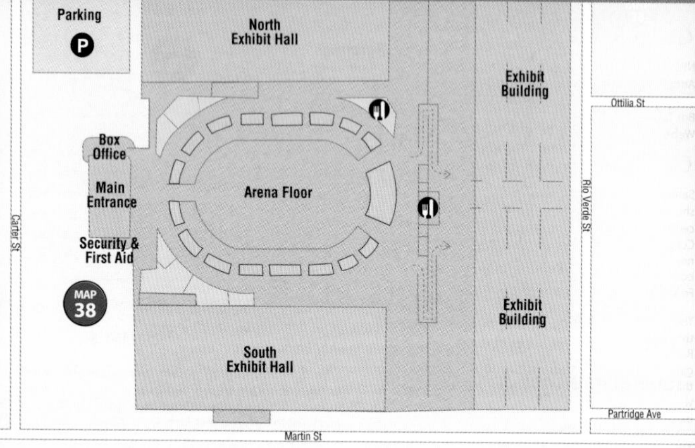

General Information

NFT Map:	38
Address:	2600 Geneva Ave Daly City, CA 94014
Phone:	415-404-4111
Website:	www.cowpalace.com

Overview

There was once a time when stepping on manure in the Cow Palace was a valid concern. The center gained its unusual name from the popular livestock exhibition it once held. After a brief stint as an Army base during World War II, the center has been functioning as a major events arena since the late 1940s. The first athletic event hosted by the Cow Palace was the U.S. Heavyweight Boxing Championship in 1949. Other sports-related shows that followed were roller derby, tennis, wrestling, professional basketball, martial arts, and ice hockey. Of perhaps more interest, the Grateful Dead unveiled the greatest P.A. system ever—the "Wall of Sound"—here in 1974. Today, the Palace hosts political conventions, ice shows, rodeo, Ringling Bros. Barnum & Bailey Circus, the San Francisco Sport & Boat Show, the Golden Gate Kennel Club Dog Show, and the new Body Art Expo featuring over 200 artists tattooing and piercing onsite. Hopefully, the Governator won't make good on his threat to sell the Cow Palace. Maybe he'll decide to have a bake sale instead.

Some epic Cow Palace concerts have included the Beatles, the Rolling Stones, Elvis Presley, the Grateful Dead, Santana, ZZ Top, Paul McCartney & Wings, Neil Diamond, Elton John, U2, and Prince. Notable celebrity appearances include the Royal Canadian Mounted Police, Liberace, the Billy Graham Crusade (with attendance of 696,525), John F. Kennedy, and Evel Knievel.

How to Get There—Driving

From the Golden Gate Bridge, follow Hwy 1 (19th Ave) past SF State University. Take the Cow Palace/Alemany Boulevard loop and continue to Alemany Boulevard. Turn left onto Alemany and continue to Geneva Avenue. Turn right onto Geneva and follow the signs. The Cow Palace is on the right. Get on the 9X at Harrison and 5th St and it will take you right there...express-like.

From 101 N, take the Brisbane/Cow Palace exit and go straight to Geneva and turn left. The Cow Palace is located ten blocks up on the left.

From 101 S, take the Cow Palace/Third Street exit and immediately merge to the right onto Bayshore. Follow Bayshore and turn right onto Geneva. The Cow Palace is located ten blocks up on the left.

From 280 N, take the Geneva/Ocean exit and turn right onto Geneva Avenue. Follow for a few miles and the Cow Palace will be on the right.

From 280 S, take the Geneva/Ocean exit and turn left onto Geneva Avenue. Follow for a few miles and the Cow Palace will be on the right.

How to Get There—Mass Transit

Take the San Francisco/Daly City BART line to Balboa Park station. From Balboa Park station, take the 15 Muni bus to the Cow Palace bus stop at Santos Street.

A good alternative to mass transit is the Daly City Cab service. Call 650-992-8865 for taxi transportation to or from the Cow Palace or to schedule taxi pickups at Balboa Park BART station.

General Information

NFT Map:	8
Address:	701 Mission St San Francisco, CA 94103
Box Office & Information:	415-978-ARTS (2787)
Website:	www.ybca.org

Overview

Sandwiched between the wacky retail world of the Metreon shopping center and the even wackier world of 20th-century modern art displayed at the SFMOMA, Yerba Buena Center for the Arts is a bright spot in San Francisco's SOMA neighborhood. The Center is comprised of two landmark buildings, both run by the nonprofit center: the Galleries and Forum Building and the Theater.

The YBCA complex features a state-of-the-art 755-seat theater, a 6,700-square-foot space known as the Forum Building, and a 94-seat Screening Room. The Center's galleries present contemporary art exhibits in every medium that are usually worth a look-see. You can visit the Center's website for a schedule of upcoming events, as well as information on current and future gallery exhibitions.

YBCA is located next to the Yerba Buena Gardens Esplanade, a lovely urban oasis that serves as a prime picnicking spot for the downtown lunch crowd. Outdoor live music animates the space from May to October. The Gardens' centerpiece is the 50-foot-high, 20-foot-wide waterfall that leads to the impressive Martin Luther King, Jr. Memorial. Twelve glass sections behind the waterfall are engraved with quotes from Dr. King's writings and speeches. Visit www.yerbabuenagardens.com for more information.

The Gardens include a Butterfly Garden that provides a peaceful habitat for a number of different butterflies, as well as a sanctuary for humans (i.e., weary shoppers, stressed-out cubicle-land refugees, and anyone else seeking urban relief). *Oché Wat Té Ou (Reflection)*, a work that honors the native Ohlone Indians, is a semicircular, wood wall decorated with Ohlone basket designs and set behind a curved pool. The artists created the piece intending for it to be used as a stage for performances by poets, storytellers, and others adept at the oral tradition. The Sister City Gardens feature flowering plants from thirteen of San Francisco's sister cities around the world. Food and drink are available here in stylish surroundings at Samovar Tea Lounge (415-227-9400). The greenspace also has several pieces of sculpture on display, such as *Shaking Man*, a freaky, life-sized bronze statue of a segmented businessman (he looks like he's been run through a paper shredder and glued back together) extending a handshake to visitors.

Got kids? Head across the street to Zeum (415-820-3320; www.zeum.org), an art and technology museum for young people. In the same complex, there is an historic carousel, a bowling alley, an ice-skating rink, and a children's play area.

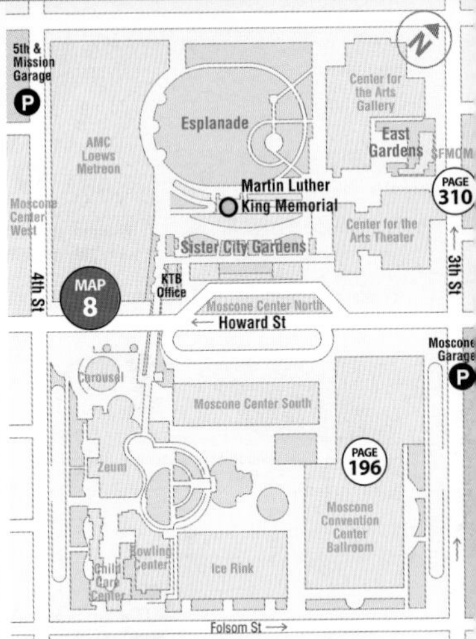

How to Get There—Driving

From the East Bay, take I-80 and exit at Fremont Street. Turn left onto Fremont at the end of the ramp, and another left onto Howard. Turn right on Fifth Street. Follow Fifth to Mission and turn right. Follow Mission to YBCA, between Fourth and Third Streets. From the South Bay, take 101 N and follow signs for I-80 E. Exit on Fourth Street, which will lead to Bryant. Turn left on Third Street. The Theater is on your left at the intersection of Third and Howard. The Galleries and Forum building is on your left at the intersection of Third and Mission. From the North Bay, take 101 S to the Lombard Street exit. Follow Lombard to Van Ness, turning right on Van Ness. Follow Van Ness until you reach Golden Gate then turn left. Golden Gate will take you across Market Street onto Sixth Street. Turn left onto Mission. Follow Mission to YBCA, between Fourth and Third Streets.

How to Get There—Mass Transit

If you're taking BART, exit at the Montgomery Street Station or the Powell Street Station. Muni bus users can take all Market Street lines, as well as 5 Fulton, 9 San Bruno, 14 Mission, 15 Third, 30 Stockton, 38 Geary, or 45 Union. If you're a Muni Metro rider, exit at either the Powell or Montgomery Street Station.

Golden Gate Transit buses 10, 20, 50, 60, 70, and 80 stop on Mission Street at Third Street. The Caltrain stop closest to the YBCA is at Fourth and Townsend Streets.

Fisherman's Wharf / Pier 39

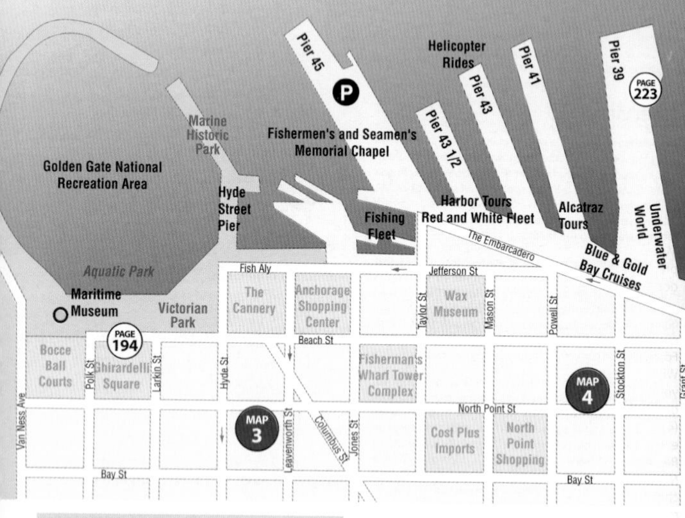

General Information

NFT Maps:	3 & 4
Address:	Northpoint St b/w Van Ness Ave & Grant St
Phone:	415-391-2000
Website:	www.fishermanswharf.org

Overview

A local's take: Fisherman's Wharf is a tightly encapsulated, overly commercial tourist bubble where every third person is wearing pastel-colored "SF"fleece. Fine—but who cares? Sure, the ubiquitous postcard-and-shot-glass shops make it seem slightly tacky, but the Wharf is not without its hidden charms. After all, the area boasts a rich history, Ghirardelli chocolate, sweeping bay views, holiday celebrations, and quality seafood. Aside from the stigma attached to this place, what's not to like? And one mustn't forget the sea lions. You'll find them basking in all their smelly, noisy glory on the K-dock adjacent to Pier 39. The sea lion population is highest in winter, when it can grow to as many as 900. During summer months, a stalwart crew of dedicated dock loungers stays behind while the majority of the animals migrate to the Channel Islands.

The Wharf economy is not driven solely by tourism—it's been a continuously functioning fishing port since the days of the California Gold Rush.

Attractions

Alcatraz Cruises is the exclusive operator of ferry service to Alcatraz Island, the prison-turned-museum (415-981-ROCK or 415-981-7625). Trips depart about every half-hour, but sell out quickly in the summer—book as far in advance as possible. To spice it up, take the night tour to the island, or combine the regular tour with a visit to Angel Island for an all-day outing. The Red & White Fleet (Pier 43) has been open since 1892 and takes passengers sailing underneath the Golden Gate Bridge and around Angel Island (415-673-2900). For an aquatic adventure that doesn't require leaving dry land, the Aquarium of the Bay's clear underwater tunnels, tanks, and touch pools offer a window into the Bay habitat and the its over 23,000 sea creatures (415-623-5300). Thrill-seekers can perform aerial feats on the Frequent Flyers bungee trampoline (415-981-6300); soar over San Francisco on a seaplane ride (415-332-4843); or brave Turbo Ride, which uses 3D and hydraulic seats to put you right in the action: a roller coaster, log ride or even smack dab in SpongeBob's square pants. Located at the end of Pier 39 by the Bay, the hand-painted San Francisco Carousel with its 1,800 twinkling lights is a hit with kids. Kids of all ages will have bunches of fun at the part-arcade, part-museum Musée Mécanique, Pier 45, especially those old enough to remember when it was housed at Ocean Beach's Playland at the Beach. And yes, Laughing Sal is still there. The Wax Museum (800-439-4305) has Hollywood celebrities, presidents, and scientists all looking their best—don't miss the museum's Chamber of Horrors.

Shopping

For the most part, the shops surrounding Fisherman's Wharf aren't reason enough for locals to visit (unless you've got some inexplicable hankering to stock up on kitschy San Fran trinkets). The Anchorage Square (415-775-6000) houses two dozen shops that sell everything from Russian crafts to personalized hats. Residents often brave the crowds here to feast at In-N-Out Burger (333 Jefferson St, 800-786-1000), the chain's only location within city limits. Though slightly more upscale than the Anchorage, The Cannery (2801 Leavenworth St, 415-771-3112) doesn't offer much in the way of shopping outside of the usual tourist fare. The largest shopping center is Pier 39 (2 Beach St, 415-705-5500), with 110 specialty shops. Again, most are only cool if you're a tourist, or between the ages of 12 and 16. At scenic Ghirardelli Square (page 194), galleries, souvenir shops, and a variety of restaurants surround an attractively laid-out square. The real attraction here is the chocolate sold at the Ghirardelli Ice Cream and Chocolate Shop.

Restaurants

Alioto's Restaurant offers great food with a great view (#8 Fisherman's Wharf, 415-673-0183). For the penny-pinchers, free parking is included at the Franciscan Crab Restaurant (Pier 43 1/2, 415-362-7733) and Scoma's (Pier 47, 415-771-4383). Cheap eats can be had at Joe's Crab Shack (245 Jefferson St, 415-673-2266). Other notable restaurants include Fior d'Italia (2237 Mason St, 415-986-1886), which claims to be the oldest Italian restaurant in the country, Ana Mandara (Ghirardelli Square, 415-771-6800), a Vietnamese restaurant owned by actor Don Johnson, and Pompei's Grotto (340 Jefferson St, 415-776-9265), a family-owned and operated seafood favorite since 1946. No man is an island, but an exclusive dining experience can be just that. Forbes Island (415-951-4900) is the world's only man-made floating *isla* and boasts port-holed dining rooms underwater or those overlooking Alcatraz and the Golden Gate Bridge.

Lodging

- **Argonaut Hotel** • 495 Jefferson St • 415-563-0800
- **Best Western Tuscan Inn** • 425 North Point St • 415-561-1100
- **Courtyard by Marriott** • 580 Beach St • 415-775-3800
- **Heritage Marina Hotel** • 2550 Van Ness Ave • 415-776-7500
- **Hilton** • 2620 Jones St • 415-885-4700
- **Holiday Inn** • 1300 Columbus Ave • 1-800-942-7348
- **Hyatt** • 555 North Point St • 415-563-1234
- **Marriott** • 1250 Columbus Ave • 415-775-7555
- **Radisson Hotel** • 250 Beach St • 415-392-6700
- **Sheraton** • 2500 Mason St • 1-888-393-6809
- **Wharf Inn** • 2601 Mason St • 415-673-7411

How to Get There—Driving

From the south, take the 101 N towards San Francisco. Take 280 N towards downtown San Francisco. Exit at King Street. Follow King Street past AT&T Park where it becomes the Embarcadero. Continue down the Embarcadero, staying in the middle lane. Turn left onto Bay Street, right onto Mason Street, then left onto Northpoint Street.

From East Bay via the Bay Bridge, take 80 W to San Francisco, crossing the Bay Bridge. Exit at Harrison Street/Embarcadero (this exit is on the left side). At the bottom of the exit, turn right onto Harrison Street. At the end of Harrison Street, take a left onto the Embarcadero. Continue down the Embarcadero, staying in the middle lane. Turn left onto Bay Street, right onto Mason Street, then left onto Northpoint Street.

How to Get There—Mass Transit

Muni lines 19-Polk, 47-Van Ness, 30-Stockton, 10-Townsend, 15-Third Street, and 39-Coit serve the area. From the shared BART/Muni Embarcadero station, take the F-line streetcar. A fun alternative is the Powell-Hyde cable car to Beach Street or the Powell-Mason cable car to Bay Street.

San Francisco State University

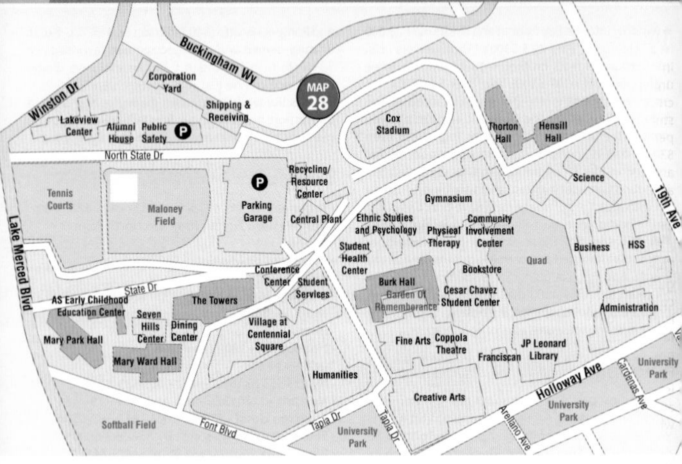

General Information

NFT Map:	28
Mailing Address:	1600 Holloway Ave San Francisco, CA 94132
Location:	1600 Halloway Ave b/w Cardenas Ave & Varela Ave
Phone:	415-338-1111
Website:	www.sfsu.edu
Established:	1899
Present Enrollment:	29,628 (80% undergraduates)
Type of School:	Public

Overview

Located near the city's posh and sylvan St. Francis Wood neighborhood, San Francisco State University's campus is an academic oasis bordered by the Stonestown Shopping Mall to the north, Lake Merced to the west, and tree-lined residential areas south and east. Walk around SFSU's sizeable campus and you'll notice perhaps the school's most admirable trait: an incredibly diverse student body that includes virtually every ethnic group and culture (not to mention age). In fact, SFSU enrolls more international students than any master's degree-granting institution in the country. SFSU ranks tenth in the nation in awarding degrees to minorities.

At SFSU, students don't just learn in classrooms and laboratories—they learn in the Bay Area itself. We sound like we're taking this stuff straight out of their brochure, don't we? But we're not. It's actually true. The school is committed to incorporating learning with service, and SFSU students have always worked to improve city housing projects, bring music instruction to city schools, help immigrants prepare for citizenship tests, and support health care for low-income residents.

Tuition

In the 2010–2011 academic year, resident undergraduate students who took up to six units of credit paid $2,507 per semester. Graduate resident students who enrolled in up to six units paid $2,999 per semester. Out-of-state students paid an extra $372 per unit for semester fees. On-campus room and board cost around an additional $12,000 for the academic year.

Parking

The Lot 20 garage offers general paid public, visitor/guest, and student parking. It's open 24/7 and costs $3 for 2 hours or $6 for the day; exact change is required. The roof level is restricted to staff and faculty weekdays between 7 am and 5 pm. Lot 25 is open daily to the general public from 7 am to 10 pm. For those who bike to campus, the (free!) Bike Barn is open from 7:30 am to 10 pm weekdays and closes at 5 pm on Fridays (note that the Bike Barn is closed when class is not in session).

Cultural Events

In addition to regular music performances and exhibits at the Cesar Chavez Student Center, the University offers a number of annual cultural and arts-related events. Each May, the University's Cinema Department presents its Film Finals Showcase, a one-night gala event showcasing the work of young Bay Area filmmakers. Most of the films in the showcase go on to the national and international film festival circuit. Most performances are free for faculty, staff, and students, and very cheap for community members. The school also hosts community service programs, such as the annual African-American Community Health Fair, usually held in the spring.

Sports

SFSU competes in the NCAA's Division II in 11 different sports, and in the California Collegiate Athletic Association in every sport except wrestling. SFSU currently sponsors men's and women's basketball, cross-country, soccer, track & field, and swimming. Baseball and wrestling have men's teams, while indoor track & field, softball, tennis, and volleyball have women's squads. The varsity teams have piled up 140 NCAA Championship trophies over the years. Intramural leagues, tournaments, and special events exist for students during the academic year. Workout facilities are available in the gym at noon and during certain evening hours for students, faculty, and staff.

Intercollegiate athletics are an integral component of the academic experience at SFSU. On-campus athletic facilities include Cox Stadium, Main Gymnasium, Maloney Field, Stephenson Field, the main pool, and tennis courts. Also, the Gator Conditioning Center is a fitness facility available to all student athletes.

Intramural leagues, tournaments, and special events are offered in the fall and spring semesters. The program consists of men's, women's, and co-ed sports including basketball, volleyball, indoor soccer, swimming, bowling, ultimate Frisbee, water polo, softball, badminton, tennis, and flag football.

Department Contact Info

Undergraduate Studies. 415-338-2206
Graduate Studies 415-338-2234
College of Behavioral & Social Studies 415-338-1846
College of Business 415-338-1276
College of Creative Arts 415-338-2467
College of Education 415-338-2687
College of Ethnic Studies 415-338-1693
College of Extended Learning 415-405-7700
College of Health & Human Services . . 415-338-3326
College of Humanities. 415-338-1541
College of Science and Engineering . . 415-338-1571
Division of Information Technology . . . 415-338-1420
Disability Resource Center. 415-338-2472
Interdisciplinary Studies. 415-338-6927
Lost and Found 415-338-2306
Recreation Program. 415-338-2218
Student Health Center 415-338-1251

University of California, San Francisco

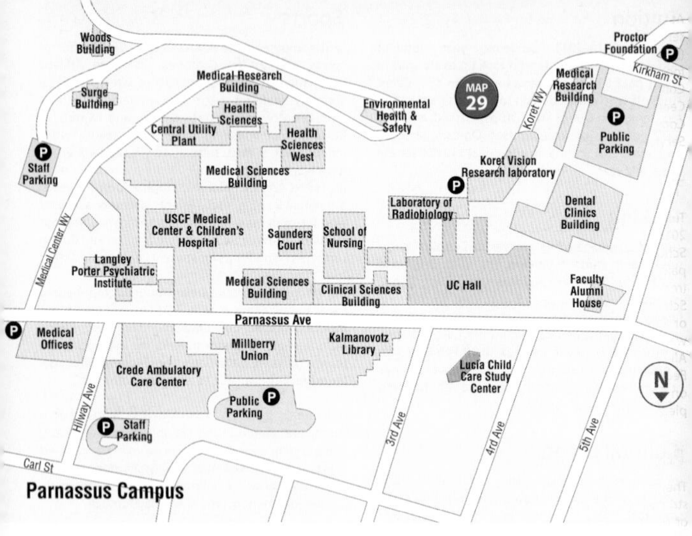

General Information

NFT Map:	29
Mailing Address:	The University of California San Francisco, CA 94143
Parnassus Location:	505 Parnassus Ave
General Phone:	415-476-9000
Website:	www.ucsf.edu

Overview

The University of California, San Francisco (UCSF) offers graduate and professional programs in health sciences, education, and patient care, and has been part of the UC system for 138 years. With over 18,000 faculty and staff, the university is the second largest employer in San Francisco. UCSF places a strong emphasis on the diversity of its student body, as well as a commitment to public service amongst its students. The UCSF Homeless Clinic, which provides free medical care to homeless people in San Francisco, is run completely by UCSF students. They also run a free dental clinic. The Medical Effectiveness Research Center for Diverse Populations (MERC) conducts research on the barriers that impede various ethnic and economic groups' access to quality health care.

UCSF students train at three main teaching hospitals in the city: San Francisco General Hospital, UCSF-Mount Zion Medical Center, and the Department of Veterans Affairs Medical Center.

The 43-acre campus at Mission Bay (16th St and Owens St) is the newest addition to UCSF and part of the overall Mission Bay urban development project. In 2003, the first researchers moved into Genentech Hall. By May 2004, 1,200 faculty, staff, and students were working and studying on the campus and, in 15 years, they expect the campus population to grow ninefold. Future plans for the campus include a child-care center, a 1,400-space parking garage, and a 2.2-acre site for a public school. The latest information on the campus may be found at www.ucsf.edu/mission-bay.

University of California, San Francisco

At the main Parnassus Campus, many student services are located in the Millberry Union building (500 Parnassus Ave). There you'll find the bookstore; food services, such as the Courtyard Café, Palio Coffee Bar, and Panda Express; the Recreation Fitness Center; Golden 1 Credit Union; Reprographics/Quick Copy; conference centers; The Source Computer Services; and faculty housing.

Tuition

Tuition varies by school and program. For the 2010–2011 academic year, California-resident Medical School students paid $27,129 and non-residents paid $39,374. Dental School students paid $30,612 (residents) or $42,857 (non-residents). For the School of Pharmacy, tuition was $26,060 (residents) or $38,305 (non-residents). Nursing School tuition was $14,695 (residents) or $26,940 (non-residents). All fees are estimates and do not include housing. Fees for the Graduate Division vary depending on field of study. For the most up-to-date figures, please visit the school's website.

Parking

The university's advice when it comes to parking is striaghtforward: "parking is often difficult at many of our campus locations," reads their website, and we couldn't agree more. There are, however, some limited parking options if public transportation is not an option. Servicing the Parnassus Heights Campus is the Millberry Union Public Garage, located at 500 Parnassus Avenue and Irving Street. The first four hours cost $3 each (totaling $12 for up to four hours). The 24-hour maximum is $24). The Westside/Kirkham Surface Lot is located behind the School of Dentistry at 707 Parnassus Avenue, and the rates are the same as Millberry Union, but are only in effect from 7 am to 6 pm on weekdays. At all other times, a 24-hour flat rate of $2 is in effect. At Beckman/Koret Surface Lot, fees are the same as above, with the same hours as Westside/Kirkham. After 6 pm and on weekends, the lot is for permit parking only.

For parking information at the other four campuses, visit www.campuslifeservices.ucsf.edu/transportation/parking/.

UCSF provides shuttles at some locations on the campuses, including the student apartments on Turk Street, the 16th and Mission BART, and the transportation station at Powell Street.

Sports

UCSF does not have competitive sports teams, but does offer a wide variety of recreational sports including clubs, leagues, and drop-in practices. The Millberry Recreation & Fitness Center is located in Millberry Union, 500 Parnassus Avenue, I Level East. There is also a brand new center, Bakar Fitness & Recreation at Mission Bay, which has both indoor and glamorous rooftop swimming pools.

Department Contact Info

Dentistry 415-476-2737
Graduate Studies 415-476-2310
Nursing............................. 415-476-1435
Pharmacy............................ 415-476-2732
Physical Therapy (academic).......... 415-476-3147
Physical Therapy (clinic) 415-476-3451
Medicine 415-476-4044

Other Campuses

- **Laurel Heights** · 3333 California St
- **UCSF/Mount Zion Medical Center** · 1600 Divisadero St
- **Buchanan Dental Center** · 100 Buchanan St
- **San Francisco General Hospital** · 1001 Potrero Ave
- **Hunters Point Facility** · 900 Palou Ave
- **Veterans Affairs Medical Center** · 4150 Clement St
- **Mission Bay** · 16th St & Owens St

University of California, Berkeley

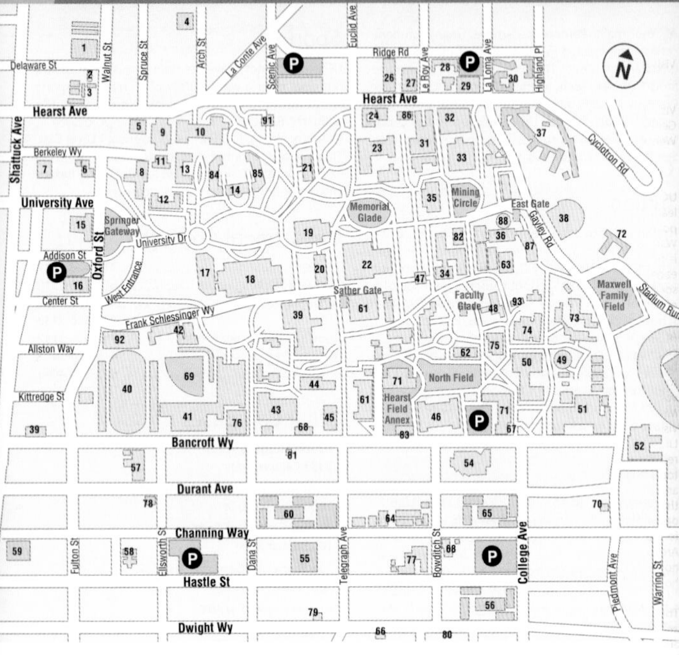

1. Oxford Research Unit
2. Natural Resources Laboratory
3. Insectary
4. McEnerney
5. Barker
6. University Garage
7. UC Press
8. Warren
9. Koshland
10. Tolman
11. Genetics and Plant Biology
12. Mulford
13. Morgan
14. Wellman
15. University Hall/ Visitor Services
16. UC Printing Services
17. Life Sciences
18. Valley Life Sciences
19. Moffitt Library
20. California
21. Haviland
22. Main Library/Bancroft Library
23. McCone Earth Sciences
24. North Gate Hall
26. Etcheverry
27. Soda
28. Cloyne Court
29. Tennis
30. Foothill Student Housing
31. Davis
32. Cory
33. Hearst Mining
34. Birge
35. Evans
36. Latimer
37. Stern
38. Hearst Greek Theatre
39. Career Center
40. Edwards Stadium/Goldman Field
41. Recreational Sports Facility
42. Callaghan
43. Zellerbach
44. Cesar E Chavez Student Center
45. King Student Union
46. Hearst Gym
47. Sather Tower
48. Faculty Club
49. Calvin Laboratory
50. Wurster
51. Law Building
52. International House
53. California Memorial Stadium
54. UC Berkeley Art Museum
55. Haste/Channing Student Housing
56. Residence Halls Unit 2
57. Tang Center/ University Health Services
58. Jones Child Study Center
59. Manville Apartments
60. Residence Halls Unit 3
61. Wheeler
62. Hildebrand
63. Senior Hall
64. Parking and Transit Operations Office
65. Residence Halls Unit 1
66. Dwight Way House
67. Hearst Museum
68. Community Living Office
69. Evans Field
70. Casa Joaquin Murieta
71. Froeber
72. Bowles
73. Haas
74. Minor
75. Hertz
76. Spieker Aquatics Com
77. 2536-38
78. 2298
79. 2427
80. 2600
81. 2440 Bancroft Wy
82. Campbell
83. PFA Thatre
84. Hilgard
85. Giannini
86. Naval Architechture
87. Stanley
88. Donner
89. Banway 2111
90. Eshleman
91. University House
92. Hellman Tennis Cente

University of California, Berkeley

General Information

Visitor's Services: 101 Sproul Hall
2200 University Ave
Berkeley, CA 94720

Visitor's Services: 510-623-5215
General Info: 510-642-6000
Website: www.berkeley.edu

Overview

UC Berkeley, or Cal for short, is not only one of the world's leading intellectual centers, but it also has a history of political and social activism that few can rival. The Vietnam War protesters on Sproul Plaza are long gone, but there is no shortage of speaking out on campus. Students are eager to speak their mind on international, local, and social issues, thereby upholding the university's legacy of free speech.

At Berkeley, each department has its own library collection. When the Gardner Stacks of Doe Library, which holds all humanities, arts, and social science-related tomes, opened in 1994, the transportation of its 1.5 million volumes was dubbed "the biggest book move west of the Mississippi." Entry into Doe requires a student ID, but visitors unaffiliated with the university can enter the Valley Life Sciences Building Library, where a giant dinosaur replica guards the main hallway. Best views are from the top of the Campanile, from the lounge in 1015 Evans Hall, and from the affiliated Berkeley National Laboratory up the hill. Lectures with guest speakers are usually free and open to the public—call the department of your interest for information on upcoming talks. The Pacific Film Archive and the Berkeley Art Museum on campus have noteworthy exhibits and showcases. The Greek Theatre hosts popular summer concerts.

The campus itself is a beautiful assortment of architectural and historic landmarks scattered amidst green glades and hidden woodsy paths. You can walk across campus in 15 minutes (watch out for bike dismount areas markings—tickets from security are quite common), and if you're late to a meeting on the hour—no worries, as on "Berkeley time," classes start at ten after. The amazing East Bay weather demands hanging out outside. Students cooperate by playing Frisbee on Memorial Glade, bouldering the stone wall at Davis Hall, or seeking out the eccentric markers. They call South Hall the "Mary Poppins Building," as the roof looks like the scene of the chimney sweep's dance; there is a bizarre stain on the stone on Sather Gate that is said to look like Jimi Hendrix. Check out the Free Speech Movement Café of Moffitt Library: plaques and posters there depict the movement's history and origins on campus. (Ironically, back in the 1960s, university authorities were the biggest opponent of the developments.)

Tuition

In the 2010–2011 academic year, undergraduate tuition cost $6230.75 per semester for California residents, and $17,670.25 for non-residents. Add another average $1,000 per month for room and board (dorms are more expensive than co-op houses around campus, and apartments vary), another $3,000 a year for books, incidentals, and transportation (though full-time students get an Alameda County bus sticker with tuition). Nonetheless, compared to some unnamed here schools, where one semester's tuition is more than all this put together, you're getting yourself a bargain!

Sports

The Golden Bears have many nationally-ranked top-ten teams in various men's and women's sports. For schedules and tickets, visit the Cal athletics website, www.calbears.com. The biggest game of the season is the annual football game against Stanford University, held at the beautiful home stadium every other year. The university also offers a comprehensive intramural and club sports program, and the lap pools and the Recreational Sports Facility are open to students for a nominal fee.

Parking

As in any busy, bustling city, street parking is a total nightmare. Northside is usually more flexible than Southside, but watch for big events such as football games, concerts at the Greek Theatre, and graduations; during high-traffic events, you could be circling the block for hours. Parking on campus requires a permit, and the campus police are vigilant about ticketing non-permit holders. Consider the public lots (Oxford St & Allston Wy, Durant Ave & Telegraph Ave, Bancroft Wy & Telegraph Ave, and Center St & Shattuck Ave). The best thing to do, for your sanity, is to leave the car at home and take BART. Exit at the Downtown Berkeley station, located just a short walk from campus.

Department Contact Info

Undergraduate Admissions................510-642-3175
Graduate Admissions......................510-642-7405
Boalt Hall Law School......................510-642-2274
College of Letters & Science................510-642-1483
College of Chemistry.......................510-642-5060
College of Engineering.....................510-642-5771
College of Natural Resources...............510-642-7171
Graduate School of Education..............510-642-5345
Graduate School of Journalism.............510-642-3383
Haas School of Business....................510-642-1421
The Richard & Rhoda Goldman School of Public Policy.............510-642-4670
School of Information & Management Systems....................510-642-1464
School of Optometry.......................510-642-9537
School of Public Health.....................510-642-6531
School of Social Welfare~...................510-642-4341

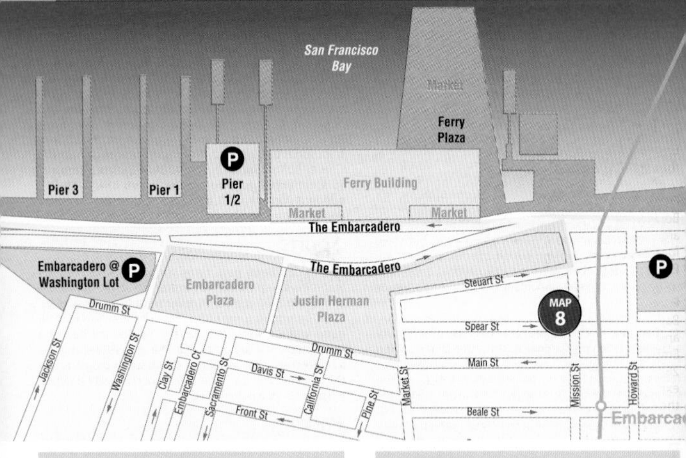

General Information

NFT Map: 8
Address: One Ferry Building
San Francisco, CA 94111
Phone: 415-693-0996
Website: www.ferrybuildingmarketplace.com
Hours: Mon–Fri: 10 am–6 pm,
Thursday 10 am–2 pm (year-round)
Sat: 9 am–6 pm, Sun: 11 am–5 pm
Hours for individual businesses may vary

Ferry Plaza Farmers Market

Phone: 415-291-3276
Website: www.cuesa.org
Hours: Tues: 10 am–2 pm (year-round)
Sat: 8 am–2 pm (year-round)

Ferry Information

www.transitinfo.org
www.goldengateferry.org
www.baylinkferry.com
www.sfport.com
www.blueandgoldfleet.com

Overview

The Ferry Building is a jewel of the San Francisco waterfront and a testament to San Francisco's survivor spirit. In 1898, the Ferry Building opened over the older, wooden Ferry House. Its foundation is the largest for an over-water building. Ferry Building architect A. Page Brown was wise to have used steel to frame the new construction—the structure has survived two major earthquakes, the first in 1906 and the second in 1989. During the '89 earthquake, the neighboring, old Embarcadero freeway crumbled, but the mighty Ferry Building stood firm.

One of our favorite Saturday morning activities is to go down to the recently renovated Ferry Building, grab a cup of coffee, and celebrate our favorite thing...*food*! Saturdays offer two great reasons to visit the Ferry Building: amazing food stores and restaurants inside the Marketplace and the bustling Ferry Plaza Farmers Market outside. Be prepared to battle hoards of tourists and locals for access to the market's fresh, organic produce, beautiful flowers, meat, cheeses, breads, and of course, amazing bay views. Believe us, it's a worthwhile fight.

Oh yeah...the Ferry Building also operates as a ferry terminal. Since well before the building of the Golden Gate and Bay Bridges, the Ferry Building has been an embarkation point for transport to the East Bay, Marin, and Contra Costa County. There are still plenty of ferry commuters that pass through the building, the tide rising at rush hour when the cafés start to fill up. Try a ferry for your next visit to Oakland or Sausalito.

How to Get There—Driving

From the Bay Bridge, take the Main Street/ Embarcadero exit, turn right onto Harrison Street then turn left onto the Embarcadero.

From the Golden Gate Bridge, take the Marina Boulevard exit, and proceed on Marina Boulevard around the Safeway. Turn left onto Bay Street, driving for approximately 2 miles, then turn right onto the Embarcadero.

From the South Bay, take Highway 101 towards the Bay Bridge (I-80), then take the Fourth Street exit and stay right on Bryant Street. Turn left onto the Embarcadero. The alternative is to take Highway 280 towards downtown and take the Sixth Street exit, staying right on Brannan Street. Turn left on the Embarcadero.

Parking

Parking is available in two lots located at the north end of the Ferry Building, at Pier 1/2 and at the Embarcadero & Washington lot directly across from Pier 1/2. IParking garages are also located beneath each of the four Embarcadero Center buildings, accessible via Drumm, Davis, Front and Battery Streets, between Sacramento and Clays streets. On weekends only, you can also park in the 75 Howard Street Garage for a $4 flat rate good for up to four hours from 6 am to 6 pm. Valet parking is also available in front of the building all day Monday–Friday and on weekend evenings. Hey, if you're lucky, you might even hit the jackpot and snag a metered space on the street. Just remember to come with a roll (or two) of quarters.

How to Get There—Mass Transit

The F Market above-ground vintage streetcar line goes right to the Ferry Building. If you're taking the Muni or Bart underground, get off at the Embarcadero stop and take the escalators to Market Street. The Ferry Building is about a block and a half away.

Ferry Building Marketplace Merchants

Bread & Cheese
Acme Bread Company
Cowgirl Creamery's Artisan Cheese Shop

Books & Ferry Tickets
Bay Crossings (Ferry Tickets, Maps & Guides)
Book Passage (Books & Literary Events)

Cafés & Small Eateries
Boulette's Larder
DELICA
Hog Island Oyster Company
Il Cane Rosso
MIJITA
Out the Door

Coffee & Tea
Blue Bottle Coffee
Imperial Tea Court
Peet's Coffee & Tea

Cookware & Tableware
The Gardener
Heath Ceramics
Sur La Table

Farm Produce, Flowers & Garden
Benedetta
Farm Fresh to You
Far West Fungi
Ferry Plaza Farmers Market (CUESA)
Kingdom of Herbs

Meat, Poultry, & Fish
Boccalone Salumeria
Ferry Plaza Seafood
Golden Gate Meat Company
Hog Island Oyster Company
Prather Ranch Meat Co.
San Francisco Fish Company

Pastry, Ice Cream, & Chocolate
Ciao Bella Gelato
Frog Hollow Farm
Mariposa Baking Company
Miette
Recchiuti Confections
Scharffen Berger Chocolate Maker

Restaurants
Gott's Roadside
MarketBar
Slanted Door (NFT pick!)

Specialty Grocery & Prepared Foods
McEvoy Ranch Olive Oil
Stonehouse California Olive Oil
Village Market

Wine & Spirits
Ferry Plaza Wine Merchant

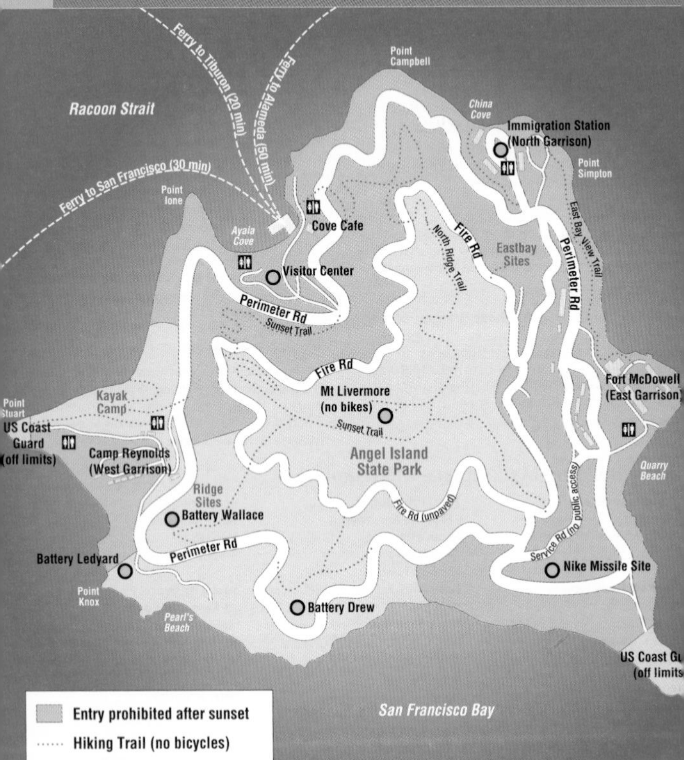

General Information

Phone:	415-435-5390
Website:	www.angelisland.org, www.angelisland.com www.parks.ca.gov/?page_id=468
Hours:	8 am to sunset, year-round
Entry:	Free

Overview

Angel Island is the largest island in San Francisco Bay, covering 740 acres. Visitors can now take a guided tour of the newly renovated United States Immigration Station, including the Dentention Barracks. The tours run Wednesday through Sunday at 11 am, 12:30 pm, and 2 pm and costs $7 for adults, $5 for children ages 5-11. It sits as an oasis of natural beauty rich in historical significance, just a ferry ride from the city. Across the centuries, it's been a hunting ground for the Miwok Indians, a Civil War encampment, a quarantine station, a POW camp, and an immigration station referred to as "the Ellis Island of the West." In reality it was quite different, as immigrants (97% Chinese) were detained rather than welcomed at "the Guardian of the Western Gate." During the Cold War it was used as a Nike Missile Base, and by 1963 the entire island had become State of California parkland, with the exception of the Coast Guard stations on Point Blunt and Point Stuart (still in operation).

Practicalities

Tourist season runs from March through November, with all services in full swing on a daily basis. The off-season sees some activity; however, tours and ferries are limited.

Activities

While no dogs, roller blades, skateboards, or scooters are allowed, there is still fun to be had. Over thirteen miles of foot trails and fire roads ring the island, along with eight miles of cycling trails, making for great hiking and biking fun (bring your own or rent on-site). Follow the Perimeter Road to access the historical sights such as the Immigration Station and Fort McDowell, as well as the island's beaches. The sandy shores are not for swimming—these are the same rough, cold waters shared with Alcatraz.

A trail leads up to the 788-foot summit of Mount Livermore (so it's not *quite* a mountain). When the Nike Missile Base was built, the top of the peak was shaved down 15 feet to accommodate a helicopter landing pad and a control booth. The dirt was only pushed over to the side and not removed, and recently the top has been reshaped to its original contours. Here you'll find a panoramic view and, on a clear day, you can see all five Bay Area bridges.

Tours of the historic sights are given by volunteer docents on weekends and holidays. Motorized one-hour TramTours are also presented through the Angel Island Company and feature an audio guide that highlights the island's military and cultural history ($13.50 for adults, $12.50 for seniors, $9.50 for students, and free for kids 5 & under). The island's Cove Café, located near the ferry dock, offers sandwiches, soups, coffee, beer, and wine for sale.

When the families, tourists, and commotion depart on that last ferry, the island is yours. Nine campsites are available for reservation at $15–20 a night depending on the time of year (8 people maximum; 800-444-PARK; www.reserveamerica.com). Amenities at each site include barbeques, tables, running water, pit toilets, and food lockers. Pack light and leave the Duraflame in the fireplace as you will have to carry your gear at least two miles to the sites and no wood fires are allowed. Expect to book a weekend night a few months in advance. There is also a slightly more expensive kayak-accessible site (holds up to 20 people) for $30 a night. Sea Trek Kayaks (415-488-1000; www.seatrekkayak.com) leads kayak tours around the island. Visit their website for rates and class information.

How to Get There—Ferry

Blue & Gold Fleet

(415-705-8200; www.blueandgoldfleet.com) runs a 15–20 minute ferry service from Fisherman's Wharf to Ayala Cove with one-way tickets that cost $8.50 for adults and $4.50 for children aged 6–12 years.

The Angel Island-Tiburon Ferry

(415-435-2131; www.angelislandferry.com) runs from Tiburon (we kid you not). A round-trip ticket to ride with admission is $13.50 for adults and seniors, $11.50 for children 6–10 years old, $3.50, free for children 2 and younger, and you can even take your bike along for an extra $1 fee.

The Alameda/Oakland Ferry

(510-749-5972; www.eastbayferry.com) runs on summer weekends at a cost of $14.50 for adults, $11.25 for students and seniors, $8.50 for children 5–12 years old, and free for children under five. Visit the respective websites for a detailed operating schedule and don't forget that ferries have abbreviated service during the off-peak season. But that's okay. The San Francisco Bay gets so choppy and sharky in the winter, it's best to stay inland.

How to Get There—Boat

If you're lucky enough to know someone with their own yacht, private slips 30' to 50' are available year-round on a first-come, first-served basis. Fees are changed according to season, with day fees ranging from $10–15 and overnight fees ranging from $15–$20.

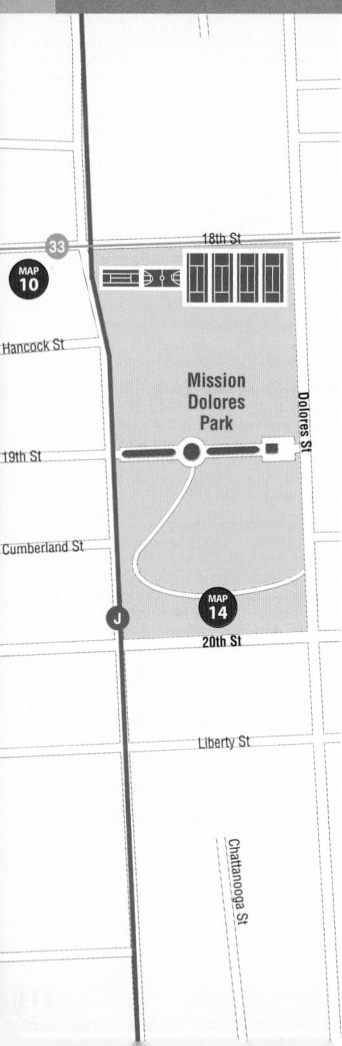

Overview

NFT Maps: 10 & 14

Built on top of a cemetery (don't worry, the last body laid to rest here went under way back in 1894), Mission Dolores Park is a popular haunt for locals from surrounding neighborhoods like the Castro, the Mission, and Noe Valley. On clear, sunny days, groups spread out on the grassy hills while dogs romp and children toddle around the playground area. Casual birthday parties and get-togethers commonly occupy picnic tables on the weekends. Outdoor fitness groups, as well as Tai Chi practitioners and personal trainers with clients in tow, are regular early morning fixtures. When temperatures rise in the city, you can expect Dolores Park to be peppered with bikini-clad bodies starved for sun. Park facilities include six public tennis courts, one basketball court, two soccer fields (often unusable after heavy rains), a clubhouse, public restrooms (prepare to hold your nose), water fountains, and paved pathways frequently used for jogging, walking, and promenading with baby carriages. A new playground is scheduled to open in 2012.

Established as a city park in 1905, the sloping area takes its name from Mission Dolores, founded by Spanish colonists in 1776. The Mission Dolores buildings still stand near the intersection of Dolores Street and 16th Street and house an active Catholic church. One of the few areas unscathed by the great 1906 earthquake and ensuing fires, the park became the site of a temporary refugee camp for San Franciscans whose homes had been destroyed during the natural disaster.

Directly across the street from the park at Dolores and 18th Street is the popular outdoor spot, the Dolores Park Café. Across the street from the cafe is the Bi-Rite Creamery (3692 18th St) featuring delicious, if pricey, organic, exotic-flavored ice creams—think honey lavender, balsamic strawberry, and brown sugar with ginger caramel swirl.

How to Get There—Driving

Dolores Park is bounded by Dolores, Church, 18th, and 20th Streets. From Highway 101, take the Cesar Chavez West exit. Follow Cesar Chavez to Dolores St. Turn right on Dolores Street. Follow until you reach the park. From the Golden Gate Bridge, follow the signs to downtown San Francisco, which take you along Lombard Street. Turn right on Van Ness Ave and follow to Market Street. Turn right on Market. Turn left on Dolores and follow to the park.

How to Get There—Mass Transit

San Francisco Municipal Railway (Muni) J-Church line stops right in the park as does the 33-Stanyan bus line. Alternatively, you can ride the 26 Valencia bus to the Valencia/16th St stop. Then walk west two blocks and up another two blocks to the park.

General Information

Address:	1 Bear Valley Rd Pt. Reyes Station, CA 94956
Phone:	415-464-5100
Website:	www.nps.gov/pore/
Open:	Sunrise till sunset daily, overnight camping available with a permit, but post-midnight beach fires and overnight parking are prohibited

Overview

Point Reyes National Seashore is a lush, dramatically beautiful, 100-square-mile wilderness preserve abundant with beaches, marshes, forests, grazing lands, and a wider array of land, sea, and airborne critters than you can find practically nowhere else. (Twenty-three endangered species and nearly half of North America's bird species hang out on Point Reyes.) Eighty miles and 32,000 acres of undeveloped coastland host elephant seals, sea lions, mountain lions, coho salmon, steelhead trout, sardines, anchovies, and the occasional shark, and the inland forests and grasslands are abundant with deer, rabbit, mink, beaver, a black bear or two, and tule elk, which flourish in their own 2,600-acre reserve at Tomales Point.

The area's first inhabitants were the Coast Miwok, who lived and thrived for thousands of years in over a hundred villages within the Seashore alone. (A re-created Miwok village, Kule Loklo, is open to the public, and every summer the tribe's descendants throw a Big Time festival out on the coast that is not unlike the get-togethers of the past, www.kuleloklo.com.) British buccaneer Sir Francis Drake (probably) landed here in 1579, claiming the area for Elizabeth I. During and after the Gold Rush, failed miners turned their attention to the verdant grasslands of West Marin and brought dairy ranching to Point Reyes, still one of the region's defining aspects.

The area became a federally protected National Seashore in 1962, and today Point Reyes is a popular getaway destination for birders, bikers, kayakers, tidepoolers, and anyone who loves the natural abundance of this magical place. Hikers can satisfy their itch with over 147 miles of trails, and four campgrounds are available with picnic tables, food lockers, and charcoal braziers for hike-in camping (no cars allowed; permit required from Bear Valley Visitor Center, 415-464-5100). Whale watching is also popular during migration season (peak times are mid-January and mid-March) and free ranger-led excursions and field seminars are a fun and always informative way to spend an afternoon.

Points of Interest

Bear Valley Visitor Center – Exhibits of both environmental and historical interest as well as an auditorium for educational programs.
Info: 415-464-5100.

Mount Wittenberg – At 1300 feet, this is the highest point on the seashore, with expectedly gorgeous vistas.

Point Reyes Lighthouse – Situated on a cliff 300 feet above the ocean, this cast-iron tower has saved many a mist-shrouded mariner from shipwreck since 1870 (Point Reyes not only juts 10 miles into the Pacific, it's the second-foggiest spot in North America and the windiest place on the Pacific Coast). Open to the public Thursdays through Mondays. Info: 415-669-1534.

RCA/Marconi Wireless Stations – In 1913 Guglielmo Marconi, the father of wireless radio, commissioned the building of the wireless telegraphy transmitting station in Bolinas and the receiving station in Marshall, the most powerful on the Pacific Rim. It was replaced 20 years later with an Art Deco receiving station. In 2000 park staff and volunteers set about to restore the original RCA/Marconi stations to their original luster.

Miwok Archeological Preserve of Marin – Offers classes in arrow-making, basket-weaving, hide-tanning, flint-knapping, and other time-honored skills. Info: www.mapom.org.

Pierce Dairy Ranch and Morgan Horse Ranch – Working ranches open to the public for self-guided tours. Check out the breeding grounds for America's first horse breed: the Morgan horse.
Info: 415-464-5169.

Point Reyes Bird Observatory – Point Reyes is a birder's paradise, and this is the place to get started. Includes visitor's center and nature trail. Open 365 days a year. Info: www.prbo.org, 707-781-2555.

Five Brooks Stables - Explore the Seashore on horseback. Info: 415-663-1570 or www.fivebrooks.com.

Drake's Bay Family Farms - Stop by for a fresh half-dozen harvested right out of Drakes Estero. Info: 415-669-1149.

Point Reyes Outdoors Sea Kayaking Tours - Get up close and personal with harbor seals and leopard sharks. Kayaking is permitted at Drakes Estero and Limantour Estero from July through February and at Tomales Bay year-round. Info: 415-663-8192 or www.pointreyesoutdoors.com.

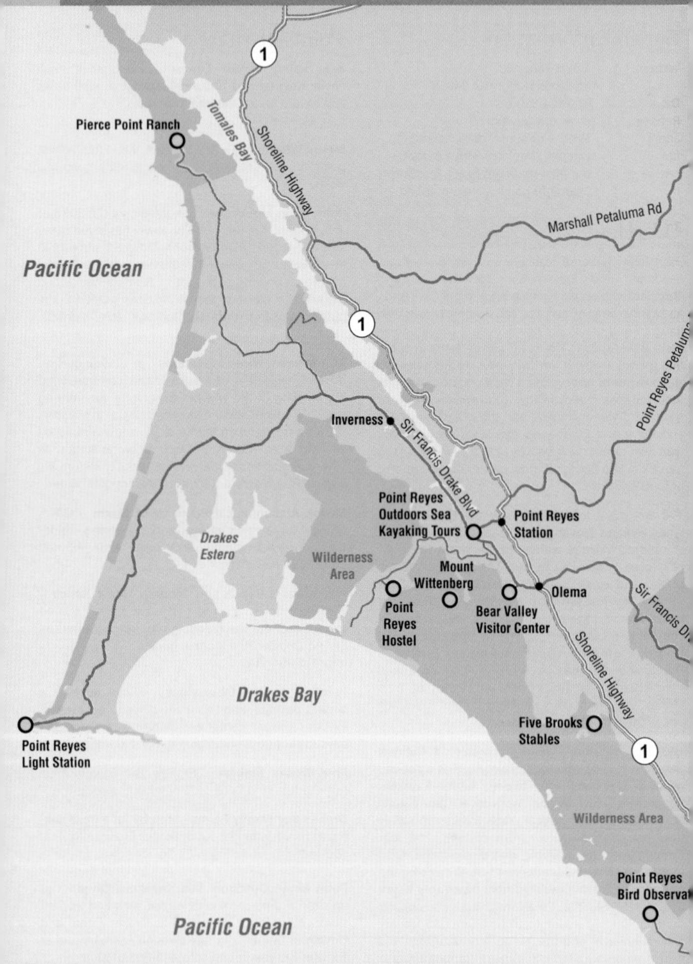
1
Pierce Point Ranch
Tomales Bay
Shoreline Highway
Marshall Petaluma Rd
Pacific Ocean
1
Point Reyes Petaluma
Inverness
Sir Francis Drake Blvd
Point Reyes
Outdoors Sea
Kayaking Tours
Point Reyes
Station
Drakes
Estero
Wilderness
Area
Mount
Wittenberg
Point
Reyes
Hostel
Bear Valley
Visitor Center
Olema
Sir Francis Dr
Shoreline Highway
Drakes Bay
Five Brooks
Stables
1
Point Reyes
Light Station
Wilderness Area
Point Reyes
Bird Observa
Pacific Ocean

Food, Drink, Etc.

Website: www.cafereyes.net

Drake's Bay Oyster Farm - The best meal in Point Reyes is the farm-fresh oysters you purchase here and grill over a wood fire right on the beach. (Beach fires can only burn pine, almond, or driftwood, and require a permit.) 17171 Sir Francis Drake Blvd, Inverness, CA 94937, 415-669-1149.

Tony's Seafood - Fresh local seafood in a casual roadhouse setting along Tomales Bay. 18863 Highway 1, Marshall, CA 94940, 415-663-1107.

Toby's Feed Barn - A general store that carries hay, tack, and feed for livestock on one side, and fancy jams, country gifts, and souvenirs for visitor-stock on the other. It sits in the center of town and serves as a hangout, hosting the weekly organic farmers market June–Oct. 11250 Highway 1, Point Reyes Station, CA 94940, 415-663-1223, http://www.tobysfeedbarn.com/.

Pine Cone Diner - Diner food taken to an ethereal new level. Fourth & B Sts, Point Reyes Station, CA 94956, 415-663-1536, www.5happy.com/pineconediner/.

Bovine Bakery - The most delectable sticky buns, bear claws, and breadstuffs within at least 100 miles. 11315 Shoreline Highway, Point Reyes Station, CA 94956, 415-663-9420.

Cowgirl Creamery - A wide and excellent array of artisan cheeses made from locally produced organic milk. Fresh produce and picnic items too. 80 Fourth St, Point Reyes Station, CA 94956, 415-663-9335, www.cowgirlcreamery.com.

Station House Café - Serving breakfast, lunch, and dinner everyday except Wednesdays, SHC is a Point Reyes staple. With a wide array of gourmet options from burgers and seafood to pastas, there is something for everyone. 11180 Highway 1, Point Reyes Station, CA 94956, 415.663.1515, www.stationhousecafe.com.

Point Reyes Books - A great small bookstore with good local maps, guides, readings, etc. 11315 State Route 1, Point Reyes Station, CA 94956, 415-663-1542, www.ptreyesbooks.com.

Café Reyes - On the corner as you turn into the 3-block town is this restaurant featuring an outdoor patio, full bar, and big-screen TV, with oversized plates of fresh Mexican and California cuisine. 11101 Highway 1, Point Reyes Station, CA 94956, 415-663-9493, www.cafereyes.net.

Accommodations

Point Reyes Hostel - Ideal for the low-cost, big-backpack crowd. 415-663-8811.
http://www.norcalhostels.org/reyes/

Inns of Marin - Free lodging service representing 35 area bed and breakfasts. www.innsofmarin.com.

How to Get There—Public Transit

West Marin Stagecoach's Route 68 bus runs between San Rafael, Inverness, and Point Reyes Station Mondays through Saturdays. Call 415-526-3239 for schedules. San Rafael is as close as Golden Gate Transit's frequent Route 70 and 80 buses from downtown San Francisco get. Call 511 for schedules.

How to Get There—Driving

Point Reyes National Seashore is 30 miles north of San Francisco along the coast highway. Head across the Golden Gate Bridge and stay on 101 until the Sir Francis Drake-San Anselmo exit. Remain on Sir Francis Drake Boulevard as it meanders for 21 miles through San Anselmo, Fairfax, and West Marin until it ends at Highway 1 in Olema. Go right on Highway 1, continue about 100 yards, and take the first left onto Bear Valley Road. In just under a half mile, go left past the big, red barn to the Bear Valley Visitor Center. Or veer off 101 at the Mount Tamalpais-Stinson Beach exit just past Sausalito and take Highway 1 from there instead; it takes longer, but the scenery is lovely.

General Information

Crissy Field Center: 415-561-7690
Address: 603 Mason St & Halleck St
Presidio, CA 94129
Interim location at 1199 East Beach, Presidio, CA
Website: www.crissyfield.org

Overview

Looking out over Crissy Field, it's impossible to tell that from 1919 to 1936 it was an Army Air Corps airstrip. Vast environmental restoration projects (including the planting of 100,000 native plants) have been undertaken with an eye towards heavy human use, and have turned the area into either a mellow ecological showcase or a park on steroids. Either way, Crissy Field has something for everyone.

Crissy Field's 1.5 miles of shoreline are marked by several small beaches, which are shared by windsurfers, waders, and San Franciscans' beloved dogs. Directly behind the shoreline, the Golden Gate Promenade leads a continuous stream of walkers, runners, and rollerbladers past windswept sand spits, picnic areas, footpaths, huge fields of native bunchgrasses (unsuitable for field sports), and a reconstructed tidal marsh with wildflowers and migratory birds. All of the action is framed by postcard views of the Golden Gate Bridge (particularly from Fort Point, directly underneath), sailboats and cargo ships dotting the bay, the wooded hills of the Presidio and Marin Headlands, and Angel Island views across the water.

Sunny days, even in the winter, will draw large crowds of locals and tourists alike, but the ample space allows everyone to do their thing in perfect harmony. How very San Francisco.

Amenities

If you're interested in environmental stewardship in an urban environment, the Crissy Field Center (415-561-7752) offers environmental education programming, an activity area, a teaching kitchen, a library, an information center, and a bookstore (415-561-7761). The Crissy Field Center Café (415-561-7756), overlooking the marsh, offers local, organic food with a view. The Center is open everyday from 9 am to 5 pm. Closer to Fort Point

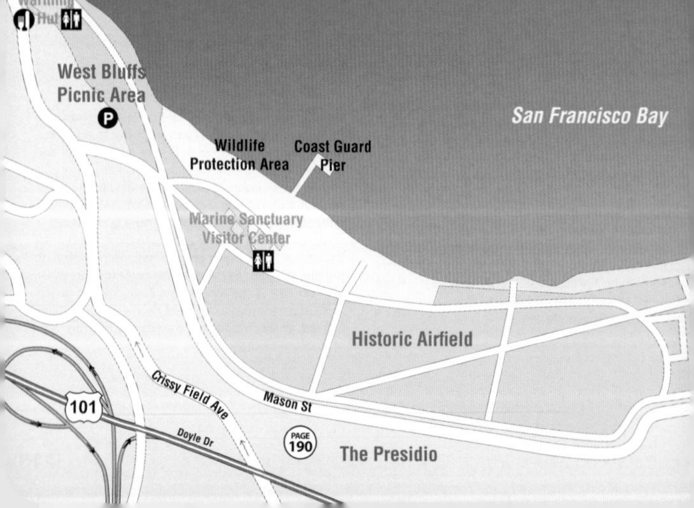

is the Warming Hut (415-561-3042), a smaller organic food café and bookstore, which was closed due to fire damage at the time this book was published.

All-terrain wheelchairs are available for rent at the Crissy Field Center. If you're planning on hosting a big group event (50+ people), you'll need to acquire a permit from the National Park Service (415-561-4300).

There are several restrooms around Crissy Field—when you have to go, there are many places to go. See the map below for specific locations, or make friends with a bush.

Activities

Crissy Field is part of the popular bike route that runs from Aquatic Park near Fisherman's Wharf, across Golden Gate Bridge, to the seaside town of Tiburon. Along the Golden Gate Promenade, you can enjoy views of the Golden Gate and boats on the Bay while strolling, jogging, or rollerblading. The strong winds along the bay front make windsurfing, kite-surfing, and flying kites popular activities. The West Bluffs Picnic Area, next to the Warming Hut, is an excellent place to crash seven-year-olds' birthday parties. Fishing is allowed, but don't try to trap any of the orange Dungeness crabs that use the Bay as a nursery—it's illegal to even touch them.

How to Get There

If you're driving, enter the Presidio from Marina Boulevard as it merges with 101 N toward the Golden Gate Bridge. Parking is available in a lot near East Beach, near the Warming Hut at the west end of Crissy Field, or at the Main Post parking area.

Muni routes 28-19th Avenue, 29-Sunset, and 43-Masonic come directly into the Presidio and drop off at the Main Post parking area, from which you can walk to Crissy Field.

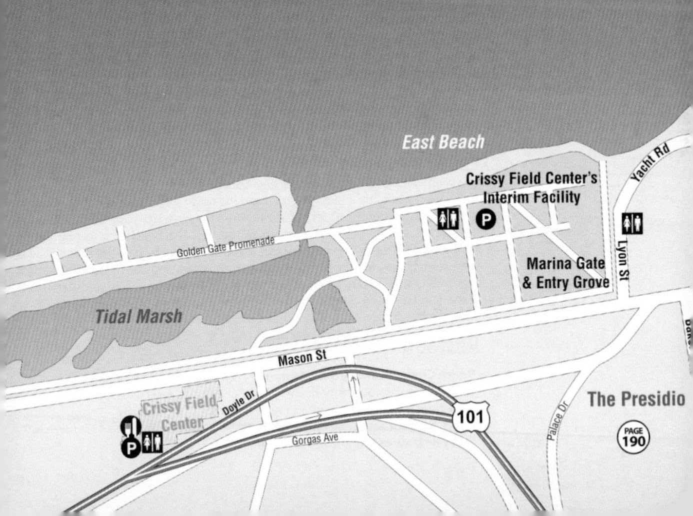

General Information

NFT Map:	23 & 26
Park Services:	415-561-4700
Website:	www.nps.gov

Overview

At four miles long, this is the city's largest beach, but cold waters, harsh winds, dangerous rip tides, strong currents, summer fog, and a total absence of lifeguards make it less than a hot spot for beachgoers looking for a little r & r. Many people have drowned here just wading in the water. If that's not enough to keep the bronzed bods out of the salt drink, great white sharks are occassionally spotted in the vicinity. The awesome currents and marine wildlife, however, are no deterrent for Bay Area surfers (pop crooner Chris Isaak is known to be a regular). Despite the blustery weather, this beach is usually filled with joggers, dog walkers, and, on warm days, sunbathers. Bonfires may be lit in special fire rings installed throughout the beach (call the Ocean Beach Hotline for details at 415-561-4741), making it a popular spot for picnicking, cookouts, and nighttime bonfire festivities. Sea lions can be spotted by Seal Rock—that's the big one white-washed in bird shit.

Practicalities

The beach is part of the Golden Gate National Recreation Area, and is free and open to the public at all times. It is conveniently located along the Great Highway, and there are several free parking lots along the road. Although the park service allows dogs on the beach, there is a leash policy to protect the population of endangered western snowy plovers, which inhabit the beach ten months out of the year. To get there, take bus 38-Geary, 31-Balboa, 5-Fulton, or the N-Judah Muni.

Restrooms

Although scarce, there are a few restrooms and changing rooms located along the beach, mostly around the southern end near the zoo, as well as on the residential side of the Great Highway, which parallels the main thoroughfare. Most surfers simply change in and out of their wetsuits right in the parking lot, which only adds to the view at Ocean Beach. Outdoor showers are located at Sloat Boulevard. And nobody will know (or care) if you pee in the ocean.

Sports

This is an extremely popular and scenic spot for surfing, especially during the fall and winter, when the winds die down and the north swells start producing world-class waves. Fledgling surfers take caution—the currents have been known to sweep the unwary out to the mouth of the bay. The beach is also popular for fishing, and the path that runs parallel to the shore and next to the highway is an ideal stretch for walking, running, and biking. Many popular runs end up at the beach (Bay to Breakers on the third Sunday of May every year), and the course of the San Francisco Marathon (July) and the Nike Women's Marathon (October) traverses the stretch from JFK to the zoo and back.

Restaurants & Cafés

- **Beach Chalet Brewery & Restaurant** • 1000 Great Hwy • 415-386-8439
- **Cliff House** (Seafood, American) • 1090 Point Lobos Ave • 415-386-3330
- **Java Beach Café** (American) • 1396 La Playa St • 415-665-5282
- **Louis' Restaurant** (Breakfast, American) • 902 Point Lobos Ave • 415-387-6330
- **Win's Restaurant** (Chinese) • 3040 Taraval St • 415-759-1818

Overview

Nestled between Sea Cliff and the Golden Gate Bridge along the Presidio's western edge, Baker Beach is one of the most popular beaches among locals and tourists alike. In fact, it's one of the most popular urban beaches in the country. Less windy than Ocean Beach, this stretch of sandy real estate is the premier spot for catching some rays, and we're talking serious sun worship here—bathing suits are optional at the northern end of the shore. (The nude area begins near the brown and yellow "Hazardous Surf" sign.) On some days you'll see more gawkers than nudists, but if the weather is particularly warm, be prepared for a major flesh parade.

Although the undertow is extremely dangerous, San Franciscans flock to Baker Beach for the beautiful views, surfing, nude bathing, and hiking trails. But the undertow isn't the only danger here—in 1959, Baker Beach was the site of the Bay Area's first shark attack. There haven't been any there since, however.

The shoreline is dotted with several interesting rock formations, some of which can be climbed, and some of which are rather dangerous to scale, depending on the tide (think slippery surface, jagged rocks, and treacherous slopes). The nearby gun batteries are a great (and safer) spot to explore a bit of local history. Built in 1904 to protect the harbor's minefields, they offer a stellar view of the beach and the bay. Baker Beach also has picnicking facilities with tables and grills at the east end of the parking lot. Beyond the northern tip of Baker Beach and over the rocky hill, is another beach alternately known as North Baker Beach, Golden Gate Bridge Beach, and the Gay Beach—the nudity is more prevalent here, as are various x-rated shenanigans that we'll leave to the imagination.

Activities / Practicalities

Swimming is discouraged, but surfing and boardsailing are very popular at this beach. The surrounding water becomes very deep very quickly, providing a great spot for fishing. Aside from water activities, this beach is famous for its winding hiking trails around the sloping cliffs off the Presidio. The area is filled with indigenous vegetation (including poison oak, so be careful what you touch). There are also rare birds and amazing views. The main trail, called Lands End, is 5.5 miles long and is pretty hilly, so be sure to wear appropriate hiking shoes. Restrooms are located near the parking lot and beach hours are from 9 am to 7 pm during the winter (October to April), and 9 am to 10 pm the rest of the year.

How to Get There

Driving from San Francisco, follow the signs for Baker Beach on Lincoln Boulevard. The beach is located between the Sea Cliff neighborhood and the Golden Gate Bridge. The parking lot on Bowley Street (off Lincoln Boulevard) is free, but fills up very quickly in the summertime. If you must drive, be prepared to look for parking blocks away from the main parking lots. Try your luck by heading north on 25th Avenue to Lincoln Boulevard. Turn right on Lincoln then take the second left on Bowley Street. Take Bowley to Gibson Road and turn right. Gibson will lead you straight to the east parking lot. If you're biking it, there are ample bike racks located around the parking areas. If you'd rather take public transportation, hop on the 29-Sunset Muni bus that stops nearby.

Please note that clothing is required in the parking lot and may only be shed in specified areas.

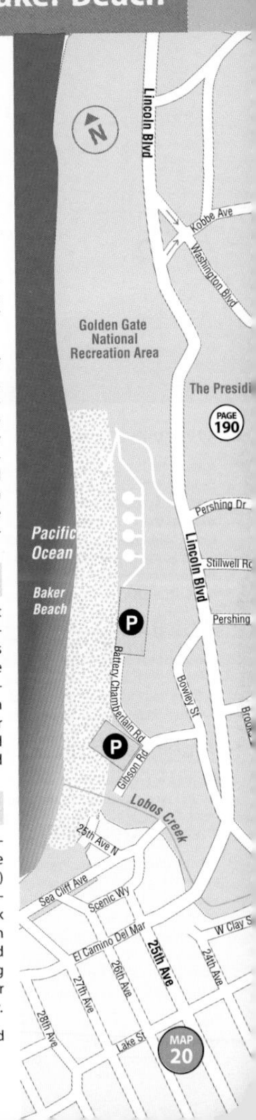

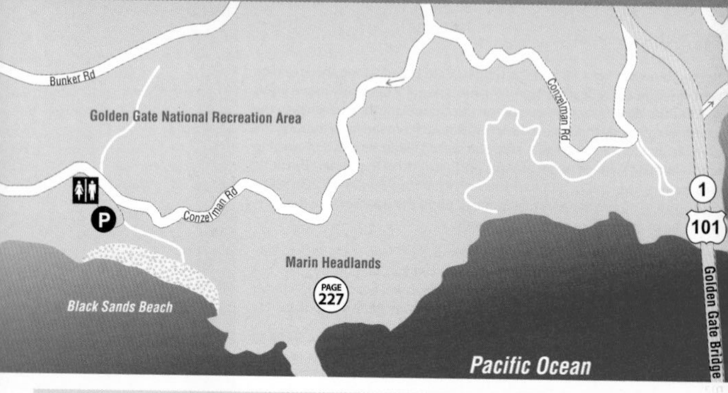

Overview

Just across the Golden Gate Bridge from San Francisco, and (on a clear day) within view of Baker Beach, Black Sands Beach offers a more exclusive retreat for those who enjoy nude sunbathing, magnificent views, and a stretch of sand largely to themselves. This 100-foot-wide beach's black volcanic sand is coarser and harder to walk on than the more traditional sand found on Baker, but the overall vibe at Black Sands is distinctly more casual and low-key. Unlike Baker Beach, Black Sands takes some effort to visit. Parking is limited, off-road vehicles are strictly forbidden, and the steep, poison oak-lined trail leading down to the beach is a challenge. However, once you arrive, the treacherous trek will have been well worth it. Just make sure you stay on the main path—the cliffs are steep and can be dangerous if you veer away from the well-worn trail.

Activities

You won't see many surfers at Black Sands Beach (probably because the trail down is too hard to navigate with a surfboard in hand), but fishermen do frequent the area. The most popular activities here, however, are nude sunbathing and Frisbee-throwing. If you decide to brave the cold water, note that the beach largely faces the channel between Marin and San Francisco, where currents through the Golden Gate are strong and can be very dangerous.

Amenities / Practicalities

The nearest restaurants, hotels, motels, and other amenities are in Sausalito. There are restrooms in the parking lot and picnic areas along the road that leads away from Black Sands Beach.

How to Get There

Driving directions to trailhead: Cross the Golden Gate Bridge toward Marin and take the Alexander Avenue exit off Highway 101. (The exit will come up quickly on the right as soon as you cross the bridge.) Turn left, away from Sausalito, go through the tunnel that runs under the highway, and then turn right and follow Conzelman Road up to the Marin Headlands. When you come to some old military fortifications, the road becomes one-way and runs steeply downhill (offering amazing views of the Golden Gate). Once the road begins to flatten at about 3.6 miles, look for a small parking area and restrooms on the left. The lot is easy to miss, so keep your eyes peeled. Note: The trailhead at the parking area is blocked by a sign that reads "Trail Closed." Fear not, the rangers have assured us that this posting simply translates to "Trail Not Maintained." Passage is allowed.

There is no public transit available to Black Sands Beach. You can bike into the Marin Headlands, but do so with care, and wear protective gear—the roads there are incredibly steep and potentially dangerous for bikers. A coastal hiking trail passes 100 feet beyond the parking lot.

China Beach / Mile Rock Beach

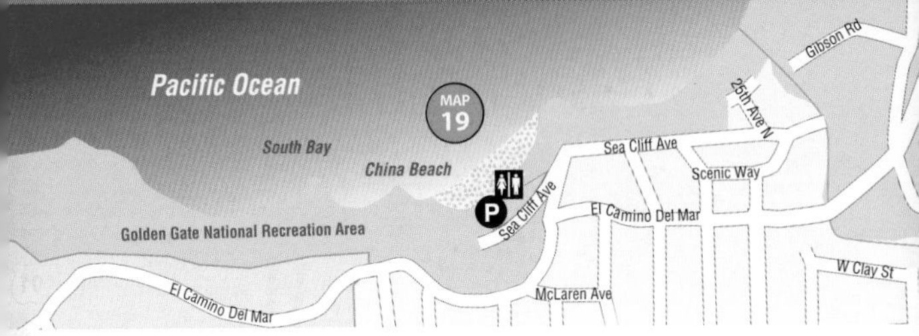

Overview

NFT Map: 19

Locals originally called this area China Beach, in reference to the Chinese fishermen who docked their junks and camped at this spot during Gold Rush times. It was briefly renamed Phelan Beach after former San Francisco mayor and US Senator James D. Phelan, who was responsible for banning all Chinese immigrants from the beach and the local fishing industry in the 1880s and '90s. Some maps still refer to China Beach as Phelan State Beach, but most locals refer to the quaint patch of shore by its original name. In 1981, a stone marker was placed at the trailhead leading down the steep steps to the beach. Phelan might roll over in his grave to know that the marker celebrates the contributions of the Chinese fishermen to a critical industry and a young city.

China Beach offers great views of the Golden Gate Bridge and the Marin Headlands. A large part of its appeal stems from its unlikely placement—it's tucked into one of the city's most exclusive residential neighborhoods. The beach occupies a small cove bounded by cliffs and overlooked by mansions that enjoy the same stunning views. As with many Bay Area beaches, the unpredictable surf near Baker Beach and China Beach makes swimming risky, so if you do go out, don't go alone. Located west of Baker Beach, between Baker Beach and Land's End, China Beach has changing rooms, barbeque pits, and an enclosed sundeck.

Activities

The beach is small, and visitors mostly sunbathe (clothed) and picnic. Other recreational activities include surfing and fishing. There are some opportunities for rock scrambling at either end of the beach when the tide is low, but caution is advised. For many photographers this is a favorite place to capture iconic images of the Golden Gate Bridge.

Large waves from the northwest provide excellent surfing conditions, but swimming and wading are generally discouraged due to the strong tidal currents. A lifeguard is on duty from April to October, and a ranger is often on-site as well.

Amenities/Practicalities

Restrooms and showers are located in the changing area at China Beach Station, where you'll also find the enclosed sun deck. On Clement Street, facing Lincoln Park, you'll find restaurants and a grocery store to suit all of your dining and picnicking needs.

How to Get There

Driving directions: The beach is accessible from a parking lot at Sea Cliff and 28th Avenues, near El Camino del Mar. A ramp, along with a more direct but steeper trail, leads downhill to the beach.

Mass transit: The Muni 29 bus, which goes to Baker Beach, will drop you off at 25th Avenue and Camino Del Mar. From there, it's about a four-block walk west to Sea Cliff Avenue, then down the slope to the beach.

San Francisco Marina & Marina Green

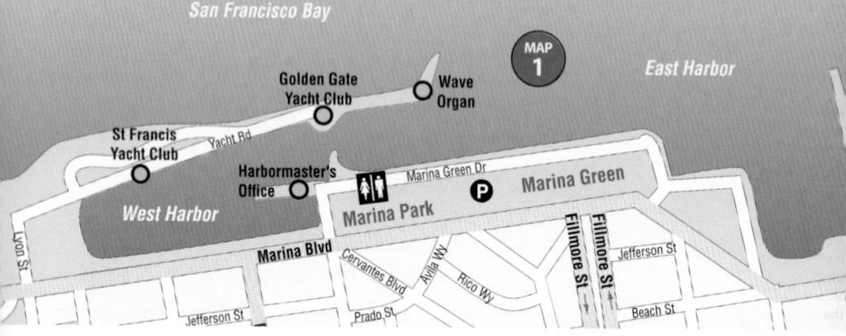

Overview

Until 1912, the Marina Green area was primarily underwater, its shore dominated by sand dunes, fishermen's hovels, and power plants. After the area was destroyed by the 1906 earthquake, 635 acres were filled with sand, mud, and quake detritus to create the grounds for the 1915 Panama-Pacific International Exposition. Today the area is occupied by three exclusive yacht clubs (are there any other kind?) and a public park. The San Francisco Marina is overseen by the San Francisco Parks & Recreation Department and is composed of two harbors, West Harbor and East Harbor (a.k.a. Gashouse Cove). The Marina Green, a popular spot for locals and tourists alike, separates the two harbors.

The Marina Green is San Francisco's front lawn. A half-mile strip of grass with a seawall on its bayside, the Green is lined with the opulent, glass-fronted mansions of the Marina district with their remarkable views of the Bay. The Green itself is usually dotted with kite flyers and is sometimes used for organized athletic activities. There's a paved walkway with benches along the seawall, or you can venture out onto the jetty to contemplate the magnificent views of Alcatraz, Russian Hill, and the Golden Gate Bridge.

A controversial proposal to build two new breakwaters in the Bay has created some heat in the community—environmentalists and locals believe that the barriers would disrupt tidal patterns and increase sedimentation and erosion of the shore, not to mention ruining the view of the bay from the Green. The cynics in the group claim that the whole project is orchestrated by the owners of expensive boats who are concerned only with sailing conditions.

One of the Marina's most unique sites is the Wave Organ, located at the end of the jetty on Yacht Road. Part musical instrument, part environmental sculpture, the Wave Organ is made of stones from a demolished cemetery and 25 PVC pipes submerged beneath the jetty. The organ creates music from the movement of the tides of San Francisco Bay.

Boating

The marina has 686 boat slips and houses the St. Francis Yacht Club, the Golden Gate Yacht Club, and City Yachts (10 Marina Blvd, 415-567-8880). At Mean Lower Low Water (MLLW), the depth of the west entrance channel is usually between 10 and 20 feet, while the MLLW in the east channel is between 10 and 15 feet.

The St. Francis Yacht Club (www.stfyc.com) offers guest docking facilities ranging in price from 35¢ to 50¢ per foot per day and $6.50–$26 extra for power hookups. Non-members must present a letter of introduction from their yacht club to gain entry. The VHF radio channels for the St. Francis Yacht Club dockmaster are 68 and 69.

The Golden Gate Yacht Club (www.ggyc.com) also offers reciprocal privileges to members of other yacht clubs. Call 415-346-2628 for info and reservations. Docking rates are $20 per calendar day plus 40¢ per foot over 30 feet. Power hookups cost $5 per day.

No Boat?

Then why not focus on your body? Exercise equipment and a parcourse stop are at the southeast corner of the Green. Good winds also make kite flying a popular activity.

Marina Green is a centerpiece of the chain of waterfront spaces that border the Bay. Fort Mason, a former military reservation, is at the east end and includes a youth hostel. There's a hill to climb and trails to explore before you end up at Aquatic Park and Ghirardelli Square. At the west end of the Green is Crissy Field and the brilliant/sublime Palace of Fine Arts, the only remnant of the Panama-Pacific Exposition. The Exploratorium is here along with a picturesque duck pond complete with swans, turtles, and the legions who feed them.

Amenities

Restrooms are located near the Harbormaster Building and in Marina Green Park.

The Safeway at the east end of the Green is, believe it or not, a popular singles pickup scene, and there are numerous restaurants and cafés five blocks south along Chestnut Street.

How to Get There

Public Transit: The Muni 22, 28, and 43 bus routes will get you where you want to go. Marina Green Park is located on Marina Boulevard between Scott and Webster streets.

You'll find ample weekday parking along the bay side except for the spaces marked "Permit Parking Only." Parking is hard to come by on weekends, so get to the lots early if you plan on making a day of it.

General Information

NFT Map: 4
Address: Beach St & The Embarcadero
San Francisco, CA 94119
Phone: 415-705-5500
Websites: www.pier39.com, www.pier39marina.com

Overview

Whether you're there to watch the sea lions, shop, or perhaps catch a ferry to attractions (like Angel Island or Alcatraz), or boats to nearby Sausalito and Tiburon, Pier 39 is your gateway to the San Francisco Bay. It's one of the most popular spots in the city and, on a nice day, a great place to stop as you walk from the Ferry Building and downtown to the wharf (or vice versa).

Keep in mind that Pier 39 is also perhaps the most touristy location in San Francisco. Tourists are a blessing to the city, but they tend to circulate in hermetically sealed environments that focus primarily on capturing their entertainment dollars. While commercialism and the scramble for tourist dollars is the overarching purpose for the 45-acre complex, locals often have opportunities to enjoy live music being performed along the Embarcadero outside the pier or one of the innumerable street performers that swarm the area.

Pier 39 does have something that can appeal to almost anyone. (anyone, that is, without an aversion to strong smells). An entire colony of sea lions has taken up near-permanent encampment on the West Marina side of the Pier 39 harbor atop the wooden floating K-Dock. Although their main activity is sleeping in the sun, there are always plenty of specimens awake and bickering, barking, playing king of the pallet, and otherwise carrying on in typical pinniped fashion. They're a pack of hams, and always draw a good crowd.

While the sea lion faction may dominate, Pier 39 does house a 300-berth marina with slips available for rent and guest docking. The Marina offers a variety of ways to experience the Bay. You can venture out on a sailboat or powerboat, or take a ride on one of the many tour boats that take off from the left side of the pier.

Boating Information

Boaters are welcome to use the guest slips for a few hours during the day, but must make overnight reservations, and pay the overnight price. You can make reservations by phone (415-705-5556) or marine radio (VHF channel 16). Same-day reservations are accepted, provided you call before 5 pm. Utilities include ice, water and electrical hookup, restrooms, six private shower rooms, laundry facilities, and pump-a-head. Check in is at noon and check out is at 11:30 am. A key deposit of a $50 credit card authorization is required, and overnight docking fees range from $40 to $50, depending on the size of your vessel.

Lease prices for permanent docking range between $338 a month for a 36′ x 13′ slip and $558 for a 60′ x 20′ slip. Visit www.pier39marina.com for more detailed docking information.

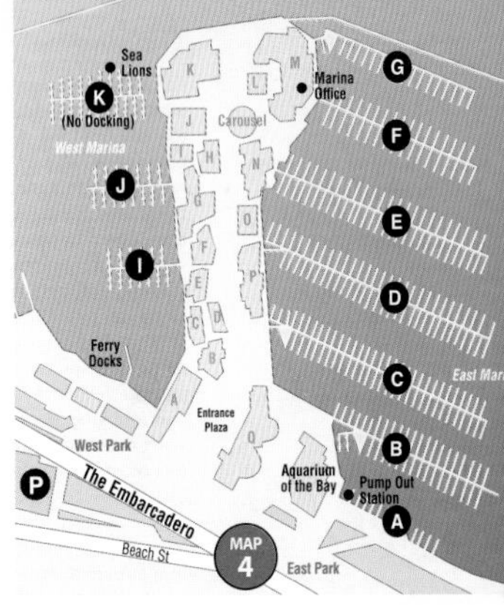

Getting There—Driving

The Pier 39 Marina is located on the San Francisco waterfront, between the two bridges, below Coit Tower. From the East Bay, take the Bay Bridge to SF, exit at Main Street/Embarcadero, turn right on Harrison, go three blocks to the Embarcadero, turn left. Pier 39 is on your right. Driving from the South Bay, take 101 N and follow the signs to the Bay Bridge. Exit at Fourth Street and turn left on Bryant Street to the Embarcadero. Driving from the North Bay, take 101 S, cross the Golden Gate Bridge, exit at Lombard Street, turn left on Van Ness Avenue and right on Bay Street to the Embarcadero.

Parking

Street parking is nearly nonexistent around the pier during the day. The Pier 39 Garage, open 24 hours a day, seven days a week, is located right across from the pier and works in collaboration with Pier 39's full-service restaurants to offer validation discounts for patrons who dine at any of the attraction's 14 major eateries. You can receive 1 hour of free parking at lunch time, and two free validated hours after 6pm for the dinner crowd.

Getting There—Mass Transit

Take BART to the Embarcadero Station. Go upstairs and cross the Embarcadero to the Ferry Building. Once you're in front of the Ferry Building, catch the F-line trolley to Pier 39. The Muni buses that serve the Pier are 10, 15, 39, and 47.

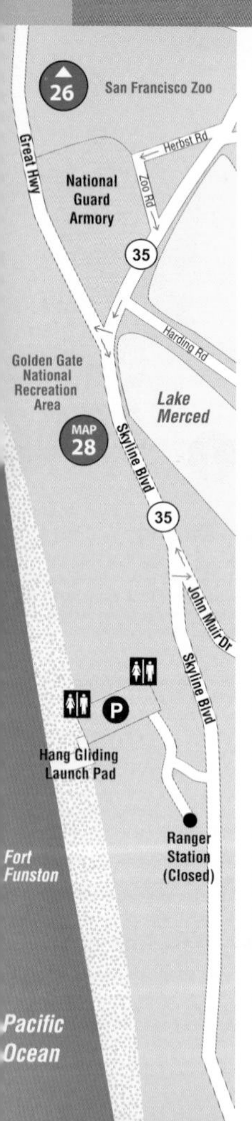

Overview

Fort Funston is named for Major General Frederick Funston of the US Army who, as Commandant of the Presidio, declared martial law and helped save the city from the great fire that followed the 1906 earthquake. The fort was originally a link in the fortifications surrounding San Francisco. The mortar batteries were decommissioned after WWII and, following a stint as a missile site, the area was handed over to the National Park Service. Today, the park sits on a large bluff overlooking the ocean, with a mile of beach stretching below. The site is largely undeveloped and includes a parking area, trails, dunes, derelict bunkers, and lots of coastal plant life.

The beach is extremely popular with dog owners. Drinking fountains are surrounded by public-use dog bowls and most dogs run off-leash, despite stringent leash laws. In fact, dog owners who frequent Fort Funston even have their own lobbying group, which has clashed with the National Park Service in recent years over enforcement of leash laws and the closure of some areas to protect coastal birds and plants. While enforcement seems lax (particularly on the beach), beware that you could be ticketed if caught letting your dog run free.

Hang gliders (and those of us who like to watch people jumping off cliffs into thin air) are another group of regulars at Fort Funston, as the strong coastal winds make the cliff a prime launching spot. If you want to spectate, the gliders jump off from a launch point near the observation deck by the parking lot, so grab a jacket (the strong winds here make the area chilly in all but the warmest weather) and a spot on the sand on one of the many primo viewing spots that line the ridge.

Amenities

Restrooms are located at the northwest and northeast corners of the parking area.

Activities

The beach is clean and pleasant, faced by 150-foot cliffs stretching from the far southern end of Ocean Beach. Most patrons are dog walkers, although families and sunbathers (occasionally nude) are also present, particularly on weekends. The track down to the beach is really a dune face, so be prepared for an arduous walk back up the shifting sands to paved trails on the bluff.

Hang gliders must be licensed and rated H3 to fly at Fort Funston. Access to the site is managed by the Fellow Feathers Hang Gliding Club (www.flyfunston.org); they provide the requisite helmet stickers as well as a mentor program for flyers new to the site.

How to Get There

The entrance to Fort Funston is off Skyline Boulevard (Route 35), half a mile south of John Muir Drive. There is a large parking area adjacent to the hang gliding launch point, observation deck, and trailheads. Some additional, unofficial parking is located along Skyline Boulevard at John Muir Drive, where stairs climb up the dunes and join the trails that lead to the beach. The Muni 18 bus circles Lake Merced, with a stop near the intersection of John Muir Drive and Skyline Boulevard. Look for parked cars and paths on the west side of the intersection before following the stairs up to the paved trails.

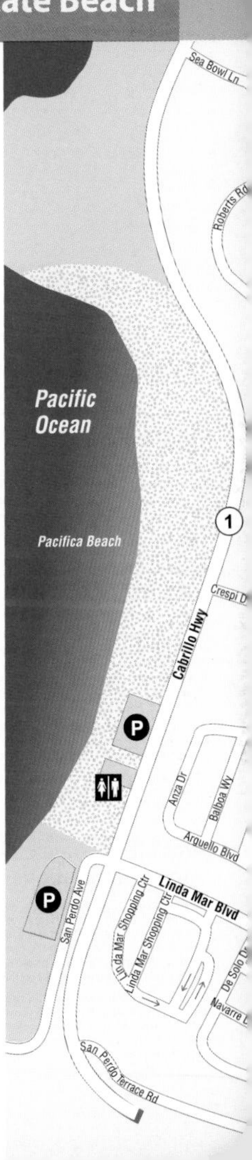

General Information

Phone:	650-738-7381
Website:	www.ci.pacifica.ca.us

Overview

A mile-long swath of beach running along Highway 1 from Rockaway Point in the north to San Pedro Point in the south, Pacifica State Beach (also called Linda Mar Beach) is as well known for its sunny days as its foggy ones. As the surfers and beachcombers who frequent this area know, there are plenty of both to go around. In general, the spring and summer months bring more fog-filled days, while autumn is the best season to find the sun. Whatever your preference is, check out http://surfline.com for live webcams and weather reports before you go.

In its former life, Pacifica Beach was the domain of the Ohlone Indians, a coastal group of Native Americans who inhabited the area for several thousand years before Spanish explorers arrived in the late 1700s. By 1800, many of the remaining Ohlone had converted to Christianity and gone to work for the missions dotting the California coast.

The area remained largely undeveloped until the Ocean Shore Railroad Company began building tracks to connect San Francisco with Santa Cruz in 1905. After damage from the infamous 1906 earthquake temporarily shut down railroad production, construction continued until the company went under in 1920. The railroad tracks were later paved over to create Highway 1. Even with the new highway in place, the area remained a scattered grouping of small communities until officially becoming a city in 1957. The name Pacifica, which means "peaceful" in Spanish, was chosen through a local contest.

Thanks to the efforts of the Pacifica Land Trust and local residents, Pacifica Beach has grown several acres in recent years. The trust first purchased private land near the beach in 2001. It has since removed houses, concrete, telephone poles, and other debris from the land to make way for landscaped dunes, native plants, and the snowy plover bird population.

In addition to attracting plenty of surfers (the world-famous Mavericks big wave surfing contest is located just south of the beach here), the beach is a favorite getaway for city-dwellers on warm days. Cold water and strong tides make it a less-than-ideal swimming spot, but you can usually see brave visitors taking the plunge anyway. A hiking trail up Pedro Point (look for the trailhead off the parking lot on the southern end of the beach) offers spectacular views, and fishing and clamming are permitted along the beach, as well as dogs on the leash. Facilities include restrooms, showers, and, oddly enough, a Taco Bell (undoubtedly one of the world's most scenic fast food joints).

Accommodations

- Pacifica Beach Resort & Restaurant • 525 Crespi Dr • 650-355-9999
- Best Western Lighthouse Hotel • 105 Rockaway Beach Ave • 650-355-6300
- Holiday Inn Express Pacifica • 519 Nick Gust Wy • 650-355-5000
- Howard Johnson Express Inn • 2160 Francisco Blvd • 650-359-9494

Activities

Plenty of hiking trails snake through the surrounding hills. Mountain biking, bird watching, running, canoeing, kayaking, paragliding, and golf are all popular activities in the area. The Pacifica Community Skatepark is located at 540 Crespi Drive. This new facility provides a much-needed practice space for skateboarders and inline skaters. There are also several additional beaches nearby, including Rockaway Beach, Sharp Park Beach, and Grey Whale Cove (nude sunbathing allowed).

How to Get There

Driving:
The beach is about 12 miles south of the city. From San Francisco, take 280 S past the Highway 35/Pacifica exit to the Highway 1/Pacifica exit. Continue five miles south on Highway 1. Go through the stoplight at Crespi Avenue and turn right into the north parking lot. To reach the south lot, continue along Highway 1 until you reach the Linda Mar Boulevard stoplight. There, turn right onto San Pedro Avenue and the lot will be on the right.

Mass Transit:
Take the Samtrans DX bus from the Transbay Terminal to the Crespi or Linda Mar Park & Ride stops in Pacifica. Alternatively, take the BART from San Francisco to the Colma Station and transfer to Samtrans CX. Get off at the Crespi or Linda Mar Park & Ride stops in Pacifica.

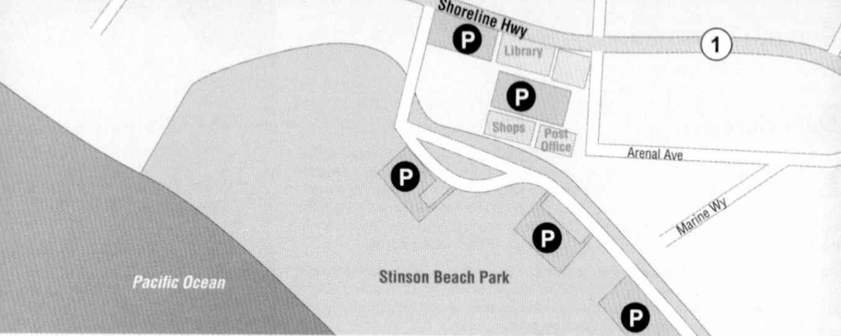

General Information

Website: www.nps.gov/goga/stbe.htm
Open: 9 am until sunset year-round

Overview

In the early 1800s, the area that is now Stinson Beach was a remote site used to raise milk cows. Before a dirt road was built in 1870 to connect the area to Sausalito, it was accessible only by schooner or horseback. Stinson Beach served as a much-needed shelter to refugees from the San Francisco earthquake of 1906. Ten years later, with the opening of the first post office, the area was named Stinson Beach in honor of the largest landowners. Stinson Beach saw an influx of new residents during World War II, and unused land was developed after the war, resulting in the recreation area we know and love today. The beach was incorporated into the Golden Gate Recreation Area in 1972.

Private cottages (some of which can be rented out for a weekend or more) border over half of the 3.5-mile-long beach, while the park itself lines the remainder in a grassy picnic and parking area. This is a family-friendly area, and the park is always filled with big groups combining beach time with BBQs. (Many of the picnic areas are equipped with grills.)

The public alarm system peals at noon and 5 pm daily. Two short blasts mean that everything is under control, and the ominous 15-second blast, roughly translated, means "Get the hell out of here!"

While nudity is accepted at many Bay Area beaches, Stinson isn't one of them, so keep your suit on. Dogs are not permitted on the beach at any time, but alcohol is—provided it is not in a glass bottle and you are over 21. Entrance to the beach is free, but parking is not.

Amenities/Practicalities/ Accommodations

The waterfront areas are manned by lifeguards May through October. Public showers and restrooms are located at the beach entrance. There is a café and grill at the southern end of the paved parking area, and a path near the center that leads out to the highway strip. There are busy picnic areas and BBQ pits in the parking area. Fires are prohibited on the public beach.

The town of Stinson Beach includes cafés with bars, outdoor seating, and sometimes live music. The usual assortment of surf shops, galleries, and trinket shops are packed into about two blocks. Good coffee and baked goods can be found at Greens Restaurant in nearby Fort Mason Center.

Lodging at Stinson Beach:

- The Sandpiper • 1 Marine Wy • 415-868-1632
- Ocean Court Motel • 18 Arenal Ave • 415-868-0212
- Stinson Beach Motel • 3416 State Rte 1 N • 415-868-1712
- Redwoods Haus B&B • Belvedere &Hwy 1 • 415-868-1034

Activities

Although sunbathing is hardly an athletic event, the Stinson Beach website lists it as a "sporting activity." For those who want to do more than lie down and bake in ultraviolet radiation, Stinson Beach offers hang-gliding, kayaking, and surfing. If you're more terrestrially-bound, there is plenty of hiking and biking to be done, and there are also volleyball nets. There is also a beautiful trail (of exactly 5 miles) that takes you from the Muir Woods parking area to the main parking lot of Stinson Beach.

As an alternative, the bohemian enclave of Bolinas sits across the lagoon inlet. There you'll find another impressive beach suitable for surfing and a small town area, but with fewer amenities than Stinson. One word of caution: the golden hills that surround here are alive with brambles of poison oak. Stay on the paths unless you're immune to this plant.

How to Get There—Driving

From the south, cross the Golden Gate Bridge and take 101 N about 3 miles to the Highway 1/Stinson Beach exit. Follow the signs and enjoy your drive down one of the most scenic highways in the nation. Stinson Beach is approximately 20 miles from San Francisco.

If you're after a more scenic route, look for signs to Muir Woods and Mt Tamalpais State Park while you're traveling along Highway 1. Turn right and take Panoramic Highway through the park. It will take you back to Highway 1 and ends only blocks south of Stinson Beach.

Please share the narrow shoulder-less roads with the cyclists. It is California law (and the nice thing to do).

How to Get There—Mass Transit

Take Golden Gate 10, 20, or 50 from Transbay Transit Terminal, Civic Center BART, or Golden Gate Bridge Toll Plaza to Marin City Transfer Center. Transfer to Golden Gate bus 63 (available weekends and holidays only).

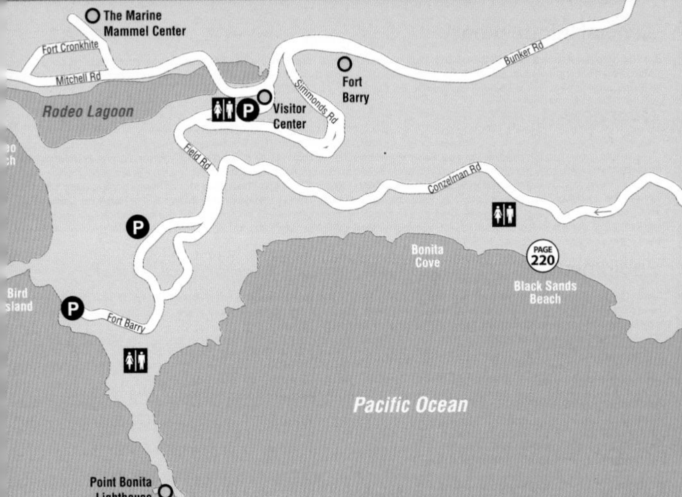

Overview

The best views of San Francisco are only minutes away—across the Golden Gate Bridge and up into the mountains of the Marin Headlands. It's definitely worth following the crowds up Conzelman Road to get an eyeful of San Francisco's spectacular skyline. If you don't keep driving up and over the hill you're missing the majority of what the Marin Headlands have to offer. Once home to the Miwok people, the land was later used by the military (like many of San Francisco's parks) before becoming a part of the Golden Gate National Recreation Area. Keep an eye out as you navigate the steep winding roads—it's not hard to spot the multitude of abandoned bunkers.

Activities

The area is host to numerous trails, suitable for an evening stroll or a grueling workout, depending on your preference. Most trails are open to travelers on foot or bike, and it's a good idea to stop by the ranger station to pick up a map before heading out. The park is home to numerous bird species, and if you keep your eyes peeled you might also catch a glimpse of some of the park's furry wildlife. If you have some time to spend exploring, you can tour the Point Bonita Lighthouse, check out Fort Baker, investigate the Bay Area Discovery Museum, volunteer with the Marine Mammal Center, or visit Muir Woods National Monument. Just don't try to do it all in one day. For more information on the Marin Headlands (including maps) check out www.nps.gov/goga/marin-headlands.htm, or stop by the Marin Headlands Visitor Center open 9:30 am–4:30 pm daily (closed Thanksgiving and Christmas Day).

Amenities/Practicalities

- Rangers and bathrooms are readily available in the Marin Headlands, but if you're looking for sandwiches or coffee your best bet is to cross back over to the other side of Hwy 101 into Sausalito.
- Trails can be very steep, and cliffs are prone to landslides. Use extreme caution if you decide to veer from the beaten path. That goes double if you are allergic to poison oak.
- Weather can change in a heartbeat. Dress in layers and keep an open mind—even the foggiest of days can be stunning.
- Swimming is not advised anywhere in the Marin Headlands as the currents are very strong and the tides bring drastic changes to shorelines.

How to get there

Take Hwy 101 North across the Golden Gate Bridge. The second exit after crossing the bridge is the Alexander Ave exit. Take Alexander Ave and follow signs to the Visitor's Center. For the best views, veer right on Conzelman Rd.

General Information

San Francisco Recreation & Parks Dept: 415-831-2700 • Courts List: http://sfrecpark.org/Rec-Tennis.aspx, http://sftenniscourts.com/ Golden Gate Park Saturday and Sunday Reservations call: 415-831-6301 on Wed 4–6 pm, Thurs and Fri 9 am–5 pm prior to the coming weekend. After noon on Fri, call Golden Gate Park Tennis Complex at 415-753-7001.

Overview

"Tenez!" ("hold" *en français*) or "Hang on to your racket, I'm about to serve!" (*en anglais*) was the pre-serve cry in royal tennis, and it gave the game its name. Though it seems like everyone in town tries to hold court at one of the 6 centrally-located courts in **Dolores Park (Map 10)**, San Francisco actually has 150 courts in nearly 70 locations around the city. Some of the small parks and hidden courts offer great city views (2 at **Buena Vista (Map 9)**, 2 at **Corona Heights (Map 10)**, 3 at **Alta Plaza (Map 5)**, 1 at **Alamo Square (Map 10)**), and some of the schoolyard parks let you play alongside a pickup basketball game (1 at **Hayes Valley (Map 10)**, 2 at **Hamilton Center (Map 5)**). Golden Gate Park (Page 188) is a safe bet with 21 courts (the most by far at any single location), but reservations are required for weekends. The Dolores Park courts are lamp-lit—perfect for short daylight in winter months, and if you can tough out the competition—are the most popular public courts in town.

Equipment

Super-sports stores like the Sports Basement (see shopping, Map 11 and the Presidio) or Sports Authority (Map 11) have everything you need to start out from rackets to balls to cute little tennis skirts. Extra balls can usually be found at any corner store (look somewhere in a corner behind the cleaning supplies, you may have to blow dust off the lid first).

Tennis Courts

All courts are hard, public, and outdoor, unless otherwise noted. [1]=indoor/outdoor; [2]=private; [3]=clay; [4]=lighted.

Courts	*Address*	*# of Courts*	*Map*
George Moscone	Chestnut St & Buchanan St	4	2
Alice Marble	Greenwich St & Hyde St	3	3
Helen Wills	Broadway & Larkin St	1	3
North Beach	Lombard St & Mason St	3	4
San Francisco Bay Club	150 Greenwich St	2[2,3]	4
Alta Plaza	Jackson St & Steiner St	3	5
Hamilton Recreation	1900 Geary Blvd	2[2]	5
Ella Hill Hutch Community Center	1050 McAllister St	4	6
Lafayette Square	Washington St & Laguna St	2	6
Margaret Hayward	Golden Gate Ave & Laguna St	2[2]	6
Chinese Playground	Sacramento St & Waverly Pl	1	8
Golden Gateway Fitness	370 Drumm St	9[2,3,4]	8
Buena Vista Park	Haight St & Buena Vista Ave	2	9
Grattan	Stanyan St & Alma St	1	9
Alamo Square Park	Hayes St & Steiner St	1	10
Corona Heights Park	States St, near Castro St	2	10
Eureka Valley	Collingwood St b/w 18th St & 19th St	1	10
Hayes Valley	Hayes St & Buchanan St	1	10
Mission Dolores Park	18th St & Dolores St	6[4]	10
Sidney Peixotto	15th St & Roosevelt Wy	2	10
Mission Playground	19th St & Linda St	2	11
Jackson	17th St & Carolina St	1	12
San Francisco Tennis Club	645 5th St	28[1,2,3,4]	13
Douglass Park	26th St & Douglass St	1	14
George Christopher	5210 Diamond Heights Blvd	1	14
Noe Valley Courts	24th St & Douglass St	1	14
Folsom	21st St & Folsom St	1	15
James Jr Rolph	Potrero Ave & Army St	2	16
Potrero Hill	22nd St & Arkansas St	2[4]	16
Cabrillo	38th Ave & Fulton St	1	19
Fulton	27th Ave b/w Fulton St & Cabrillo St	1	19
Margaret O Dupont	30th Ave b/w California St & Clement St	4	19
Rochambeau	24th Ave b/w Lake St & Calfornia St	1	19
Argonne	18th Ave b/w Geary Blvd & Anza St	1	20
Richmond	18th Ave b/w Lake St & California St	1	20
Angelo Rossi	Arguello Blvd & Edward St	3	21
Mountain Lake	12th Ave & Lake St	4	21
Julius Kahn	Spruce St & Pacific Ave	4	22
Laurel Hill	Euclid Ave & Collins St	1	22
West Sunset	39th Ave & Ortega St	4[4]	23
Sunset	28th Ave & Lawton St	2	24
Golden Gate Heights	12th Ave & Rockridge Dr	2	25
John P Murphy	1960 9th Ave	3	25
South Sunset	40th Ave b/w Wawona St & Vicente St	1	26
James B Moffet	26th Ave & Vicente St	4	27
Larsen Park	19th Ave & Vicente St	1	27
McCoppin Square	24th Ave & Taraval St	2	27
Stern Grove Annex	Sloat Blvd b/w 19th Ave & Crestlake Dr	2	27
Junipero Serra	300 Stonecrest Dr	1	28
Midtown Terrace	Clarendon Ave & Olympia Wy	4	29
Aptos	Aptos Ave & Ocean Ave	1	30
West Portal	Clarendon Ave & Olympia Wy	1	30
Miraloma	Omar Wy & Sequoia Wy	1	31
Sunnyside	Forester St & Melrose Ave	1	31
Peter Folger	Chenery St & Elk St	2	32
St Mary's	Murray St & Justin Dr	3	32
Upper Noe	Day St & Sanchez St	1	32
Merced Heights	Byxbee St & Shields St	1	33
Ocean View	Plymouth Ave & Lobos St	2[4]	33
Alice Chalmers	Brunswick St & Whittier St	1	34
Balboa	Ocean Ave & San Jose Ave	4	34
Cayuga Park	Cayuga St & Naglee Ave	1	34
Holly Park	Holly Park Cir & Highland Ave	1	35
Joseph Lee	Oakdale Ave & Mendell St	1	37
Youngblood Coleman	Galvez Ave & Mendell St	2	37
Crocker Amazon	Geneva Ave & Moscow St	3	38
Excelsior	Russia Ave & Madrid St	1	38
Francis J Herz	Visitacion Ave & Hahn St	1	39
Louis Sutter	University St & Wayland St	2	39
McLaren Park	Mansell St, near University St	6	39
Portola	Felton St & Holyoke St	2[4]	39
Silver Terrace	Thornton Ave & Bayshore Blvd	1	40
Golden Gate Park	John F Kennedy Dr & Middle Dr E	21[4]	GGP

Golf

From nondescript municipal courses to some of the country's most scenic and heralded links, San Francisco's got a course to suit every level of player, even those who don't want to use clubs. At the high end are two of the best courses in the nation—the **San Francisco Golf Club (Map 28)** and the **Olympic Club (Map 7)**. The SFGC claims only 250 members, which means you'd probably have better luck swimming to shore from Alcatraz than trying to get into this club. For those who do manage to obtain a tee time, it is a truly remarkable experience—the course offers a classic layout with empty fairways and pristine greens. (Yes, we wrote that as if we were one of the lucky few to get a tee time. We weren't.)

While the private courses are some of the most famous, there are numerous public options in and around San Francisco. **The Presidio Golf Course (The Presidio)** has hosted the US Open, and is a much-improved course since the Arnold Palmer Golf Company took over management. There are several interesting par threes on the course, and the 9th and 18th holes are great finishers. The food at the Presidio Café is also some of the best at any golf course in the area, particularly weekend brunch. If you want to play, call early, as tee times are hard to get. Be prepared for a five- to six-hour round on weekends.

Perhaps the most exciting development in San Francisco golf is the renovation of **Harding Park (Map 28)**. The course is ranked the second-best municipal course in the country. The course hosted the 2005 World Golf Championship (won by Tiger, of course). Harding is over 80 years old and, like many public courses, fell victim to overplay (160,000 rounds per year) under the management of the Parks & Recreation Department. Since 2002, however, various agencies have invested roughly $15 million to renovate the course to its former greatness.

There are also several options in San Francisco for golfers looking to save money or avoid crowds. **Lincoln Park (Map 19)** is an inexpensive municipal course boasting terrific views from several holes. Another economical choice is **Glen Eagles (Map 39)**, a nine-hole course that Lee Trevino once described as the hardest nine holes in golf. The course has several unique attributes, including a tree in a bunker on the sixth hole (a 600-plus-yard par five). You may also be treated to some bass-heavy music coming from the adjacent neighborhood on holes four and five.

At the local public courses, the rates for non-residents are roughly double what a resident pays. City residents must have a Resident Card in order to receive a discount. You can apply for a Resident Card at City Hall in room 140. Just take a valid form of ID (driver's license), a copy of a PG&E bill, and $90. Don't fear the bureaucracy; getting a resident card is worth it if you plan to do some golfing. City Hall works smoothly and you can be in and out in 15 minutes. The card pays for itself in a few rounds.

Another great resource for golfing around the bay is the *Golf Guide*, available free at courses and golf shops. It has maps, descriptions, green fees, and anything you want to know about any of the many courses in the region. Check out www.golfguide.org.

If you don't have clubs, take a stroll to the **Golden Gate Park Disc Golf Course (Golden Gate Park)** located along JFK Drive. The park district has recently expanded the course to a full 18-holes. It's free, just bring your Frisbee.

Golf Courses	*Address*	*Phone*	*Fees*	*Par*	*Map*
Lincoln Park Golf	34th Ave & Clement St	415-221-9911	$37 Mon–Thurs; $41 Fri–Sun	Par-68, Holes-18	19
Harding Park	99 Harding Rd	415-661-1865	$150 Mon–Thurs; $170 Fri–Sun	Par-72, Holes-18	28
San Francisco Golf Club	Junipero Serra Blvd & Brotherhood Wy	415-469-4122	$50 all times (membership req'd)	Par-71, Holes-18	28
Gleneagles GC	2100 Sunnydale Ave	415-587-2425	$17 Mon–Thurs; $20.50 Fri–Sun	Par-36, Holes-9	39
Golden Gate Park	970 47th Ave	415-751-8987	$15 Mon–Thurs; $19 Fri–Sun	Par-27, Holes-9	pg 188
Presidio Golf Course	300 Finley Rd	415-561-4663	$112 Mon–Thurs; $122 Fri–Sun	Par-72, Holes-18	pg 190
Mill Valley	280 Buena Vista Ave	415-388-9982	$17 Mon–Thur; $19 Fri–Sun	Par-33, Holes-9	pg 184
Tilden Park Golf Course	10 Golf Course Dr	510-848-7373	$45 Mon–Thurs; $55 Fri; $65 Sat–Sun	Par-70, Holes-18	pg 174
Lake Chabot Golf Course	11450 Golf Links Rd	510-351-5812	$$		pg 176
Metropolitan Golf Links	10051 Doolittle Dr	510-569-5555	$$$		pg 176
Montclair Golf Course	2477 Monterey Blvd	510-482-0422	$7 Mon–Thurs; $9 for 9 holes, Fri–Sun	Par-27, Holes-9	pg 176
Chuck Corica Golf Complex	1 Clubhouse Memorial Rd	510-747-7800	$28 Mon–Fri, $35 Sat–Sun		n/a
Cypress Golf	2001 Hillside Blvd, Colnia	650-992-5155	$14 Mon–Fri; $18 Sat–Sun	Par-37	n/a
Sharp Park Golf Course	Hwy 1, Sharp Park Rd, Pacifica	650-359-3380	$37 Mon–Thur; $41 Fri–Sat	Par-72	n/a

Note: Quoted fees are for non-residents.

General Information

San Francisco Bay Area hiking clubs: evbuck.weebly.com

Overview

Built on 42 hills, San Francisco is famous for its steep inclines and excellent vistas (a hill by definition is anything taller than 100 feet or 30 meters). The city's peaks serve as backdrops for car commercials and chase scenes; they fry transmissions and wear out brake pads; and they're the reason the avenues stay drenched in fog while sunbathers lounge in Dolores Park. On a more practical level, sometimes a 40-degree slope is all that stands between you and a clean load of laundry, the Muni stop, or a pint of ice cream from the corner store.

Built on a tumultuous network of fault lines, the hills and mountains give the Bay Area much of is romantic allure. Just outside the city offers an even wider array of hiking options from Mt. Tam to the unspoiled coast of Pt. Reyes and the rugged panoramas of Mt. Diablo and the East Bay Regional Park District.

Since hiking to your morning cup of coffee is an unavoidable fact of life for residents of this fair city, why would anyone deliberately seek out *other* places to break a sweat? Summits within city limits such as Twin Peaks and Inspiration Point actually require little exertion, and their vistas have a way of showing you the city in a whole new light. At Fort Funston, you can embrace your inner Californian and trek barefoot on the beach. And a walk through the redwood cathedral of Muir Woods will leave you feeling uplifted in a way that the Stairmaster or the Lyon Street steps just can't match.

The San Francisco Hiking Club offers regular group excursions. Route maps and detailed trail descriptions are available at www.bahiker.com.

Bay Trail

500 miles when completed, currently 290 miles—varied terrain

Once finished, the Bay Trail will extend over 500 miles through the Bay Area, covering nine counties and 47 cities. This massive route will weave through commercial, residential, rural, and coastal areas, creating scenic haven for bikers, joggers, rollerbladers, and walkers. Aside from the aesthetic appeal of the path, the Bay Trail will provide alternative commute routes for cyclists and link several public transportation systems. The majority of the trail will be paved. While some areas will overlap with city sidewalks, others will be more rustic. For more information, visit the official website http://baytrail.abag.ca.gov/.

Crissy Field

Presidio East Beach entrance • 1.65 miles • Easy—flat • Page 216

Formerly a major military post and landing strip, Crissy Field has long been one of the city's most popular recreation destinations. The main trail, which was restored in 1998, weaves through picturesque marshland, dunes, meadows, and shoreline peppered with native flora and fauna. At 3.3 miles out and back, the beautiful scenery and smooth, flat trail distinguish Crissy Field as an ideal place for walking, jogging, biking, rollerblading, and dog walking. But be prepared for gusty winds. Crissy Field can be reached by Muni bus lines 28-19th Ave, 29-Sunset, and 43-Masonic.

Fort Funston

Skyline Blvd & John Muir Dr • 1.52 miles • Easy—some elev. gain • Map 28

A favorite with Bay Area dog-walkers, Fort Funston offers beautiful ocean views, plentiful vegetation, and varied terrain. Sunset Trail, the main thoroughfare, is paved and wheelchair accessible, while other paths are sandy and more suited to sport sandals (or bare feet) than to hiking boots or sneakers. Most trails access the beach and involve some degree of scrambling on dunes (the aptly named Sand Ladder Trail provides steps). When wind conditions are right, Funston is a favorite launching spot for local hang-gliders, who swoop off the bluffs and over the surf below. If you're planning a long walk on the beach, check tide levels before setting out, as high tides can make parts of the beach impassable. To reach the park by car, take Highway 35 to John Muir Drive, and follows signs to the Fort Funston parking lot. For information about group walks, contact the Fort Funston Ranger Station at 415-561-4323.

Glen Canyon

Bosworth St & Elk St • 0.9 miles • Moderate—short but steep • Map 32

Positioned between Glen Canyon Park and Mount Davidson, the steep and gravelly trails in Glen Canyon are mostly used by nearby residents and dog-walkers. Although there is an entrance on Bosworth Street, the entrance off Diamond Heights Boulevard has better parking. Park in the Diamond Heights Shopping Center and enter the park through the Christopher Playground. The park may also be accessed by the 44-O'Shaughnessy bus (Elk Street stop) or the Glen Park BART station. The trails are short and riddled with poison oak, but the canyon is rarely crowded and offers some rewarding views. You'll find some of the best bouldering in San Francisco on the park's interesting rock formations. A hike to the bottom will make you forget that you are in the middle of the City.

Inspiration Point

Arguello Gate Presidio entrance • 1.78 miles • Easy—some hills • Page 190

Located in the Presidio, this trail offers yet another rustic escape from the sights and sounds of the city. Due to the surrounding non-native vegetation and urban development, this area has been dubbed an "ecological island." The Point houses the only serpentine grassland in the entire Golden Gate National Recreation area, in addition to many other native grasses. The flourishing plant life has much to do with an intensive three-year grassland restoration project which was completed in 1998.

The trail starts near Mountain Lake and continues for 1.78 miles. Yes, there are a few hills (this is San Francisco), but the path is not strenuous. Inspiration Point is dog-friendly, but be sure to observe the National Park Service's strict leash policy.

McLaren Park

Cambridge St & John F Shelly Dr • Easy • Map 39

McLaren is big—317 acres of out-of-the-way hilltop. This multi-faceted park has seven miles of paved trails, which are ideal for walking or jogging. Check out www.bahiker.com/sfhikes/mclaren.html for detailed hike directions in the park. By Muni take the *29 Sunset*, the *52 Excelsior*, or the *54 Felton*.

Mount Davidson Park

Lansdale Ave & Dalewood Wy • 0.5 miles • Easy • Map 31

At 927 feet, Mt Davidson is the city's highest point. The 40-acre park contains numerous paths, but the main trail to the top is short and moderately steep. Views from the top are obstructed by trees and a 103-foot tall concrete memorial cross to the Armenian genocide of 1915. The city of San Francisco was forced to sell the top of the park when residents complained that the gargantuan cross violated the separation of church and state. The peak was also the site of a famous scene from Clint Eastwood's *Dirty Harry* (1971). To get to the park from downtown, take 101 S to 280 W and exit at Monterey Boulevard. There is a small parking area on Portola Drive. Muni bus 36-Teresita conveniently stops right in front of the park. Dogs and bikes are allowed.

Muir Woods National Monument

Mill Valley • Page 184

This Marin County redwood preserve contains some of the most enchanting scenery in the country. Endowed with national monument status in 1908, today it is a quintessential San Francisco stop for tourists and locals alike, and is visited by more than a million people every year. Most visitors just ooh and ahh their way along the main trail, a one-mile wheelchair-accessible loop. Those who want a longer hike can link up with a large network of more strenuous trails (a great, full-day hike is a 5-mile, one-way trail to Stinson Beach). The best times to visit are on weekdays in the early morning, or after 4 pm. Parking at all other times will be an adventure in itself. Dogs, bikes, and picnics are not permitted within the park. To get there by car, cross the Golden Gate Bridge, get off at the first exit, and follow the signs for Muir Woods National Monument. For more information, visit the official website at www.nps.gov/muwo or call the information hotline on 415-388-2596.

Twin Peaks

Twin Peaks Blvd • 0.64 miles • Moderate—some hills • Map 29

Located at the center of the city, the 900-foot Twin Peaks afford incredible panoramic vistas, provided there's no fog creeping down the mountain. If you're seeking solitude, look elsewhere; this is a very touristy area. The entire trail through the hills is short and easily navigated, but some sections are very steep, so wear appropriate footwear. Bring an extra layer, too, since winds up on the peaks can be gusty and frigid. There's a portable toilet but no drinking water, and while there is handicapped parking, the peaks themselves are not wheelchair accessible. Dogs are allowed. To get to the trails, travel along Bosworth Street, which becomes O'Shaughnessy Boulevard, heading uphill. Follow O'Shaughnessy to its junction with Portola Drive at the top of the hill. Turn right, then quickly get into the left lane. Make a left turn at the light onto Twin Peaks Boulevard, then continue uphill and park at the first pullout on the left (immediately after the first sharp curve), or in the lot just past the north peak.

On the rare occasion that one actually needs to cool off in San Francisco, there is exactly one public outdoor swimming pool. **Mission Pool (Map 11)** is located at 19th St & Linda St, and is open primarily in the summer (which is a bit comical considering that the summer months are historically the coldest). For those less interested in the sun and more interested in the splashin', there are eight additional (indoor) public pools. Prices range between $1 and $5 depending on your age and whether you are signed up for one of the many swim lessons that are offered. For more information, visit sfrecpark.org/Rec-Aquatics.aspx or call 415-831-2747.

For the more serious swimmers, San Francisco offers a variety of experiences which far surpass the monotony of your basic lap swim. Aquatic Park, near Ghirardelli Square, is the spot for lap swimmers undeterred by the Bay's freezing waters, and the truly brave can check out the Alcatraz100 (www.alcatraz100.com). For a donation of just $135, you can get yourself a one-way ticket to Alcatraz Island. Also check out the Annual Alcatraz Invitational, or the Alcatraz Challenge (these and others are easily found through Google). What is it like to traverse this notorious 1.4 miles? In May 2006, Braxton Bilbrey described it as "pretty cool." He was only seven.

Swimming Pools	Address	Type	Fees	Map
North Beach Pool	1701 Lombard St	Indoor	Adults $5 / kids $1	4
San Francisco Bay Club	150 Greenwich St	Indoor	Membership required	4
Club One	1455 Fillmore St	Indoor	$20/day	5
Hamilton Recreation	1900 Geary Blvd	Indoor	Adults $5 / kids $1	5
Cathedral Hill Plaza Athletic Club	1333 Gough St	Indoor	$15/day	6
Club One	535 Mason St	Indoor	$20/day	7
Olympic Club	524 Post St	Indoor	Membership required	7
Club One	350 3rd St	Outdoor	$20/day	8
Embarcadero YMCA	169 Steuart St	Indoor	$15/day	8
Golden Gateway Fitness	370 Drumm St	Outdoor	Membership required	8
The Sports Club/LA	747 Market St	Indoor	Membership required	8
Boy's & Girl's Club	1950 Page St	Indoor	$3/day	9
24 Hour Fitness	1645 Bryant St	Indoor	$15/day	11
Mission Pool	19th St & Linda St	Outdoor	Adults $5 / kids $1	11
Mission Bay	1675 Owens St	Outdoor	$15/day	13
Garfield Pool	26th St & Harrison St	Indoor	Adults $5 / kids $1	15
Koret Gym at USF	2130 Fulton St	Indoor	$15/day	22
Rossi Pool	600 Arguello Blvd	Indoor	Adults $5 / kids $1	22
Herbst Natatorium	2001 37th Ave	Indoor	$4/day	23
Stonestown YMCA	333 Eucalyptus Dr	Indoor	$12/day	27
Sava Pool	19th Ave & Wawona St	Indoor	Adults $5 / Kids $1	27
24 Hour Fitness	1850 Ocean Ave	Indoor	$15/day	30
Balboa Pool	51 Havelock St	Indoor	Adults $5 / kids $1	34
City College Wellness Center	50 Phelan Ave	Indoor	Registration required	34
Coffman Pool	1701 Visitacion Ave	Indoor	Adults $5 / kids $1	39
MLK Jr Pool	5701 3rd St	Indoor	Adults $5 / kids $1	40
Letterman Pool	1151 Gorgas Ave	Indoor	$12/day	Presidio

All Things Skating

Looking to get outside? The 4.5-mile loop around lush Lake Merced, as well as several miles of pier shoreline along the Embarcadero and the Marina Green, is fairly flat and provides some fantastic views while you skate. For rolling hills and a cardio workout, check out six miles of windswept ocean vistas from the Cliff House to the Zoo (and back) on a paved path along the Great Highway at Ocean Beach. The Midnight Rollers, an organized group made up of hundreds of inline and roller city skaters, meet for their weekly event, known as Friday Night Skate, at 8:30 pm in front of the Ferry Building. From there they take off en masse for a long ride through the city streets to various sites throughout San Francisco. Interested in participating? Call the group's organizer, David Miles, at 415-752-1967 for more details. For other ideas, check out the California Inline Skating Guide (www.caskating.com) and California Outdoor Rollerskating Association (www.cora.org).

Of course, the all-time favorite is Golden Gate Park. Every Sunday, a two-mile section of JFK Boulevard, from Stanyan Street to 19th Avenue, is barricaded off for the exclusive use of pedestrians, skaters, and bikers. Let people roam around on what is usually car territory, and they will take full advantage. Nearly 75,000 people visit the park on the weekend, and a sizeable portion of them are on wheels—this makes navigation of the Park's main arteries that much easier and faster. It's your chance to let loose and roll on the main road as much as you please, but watch out for the speedsters on bikes, tour carriages, skateboarders, and little kids. The roller-dancing area, at JFK Boulevard and 6th Avenue, is a vision of neon spandex, rockin beats, and remarkably bedazzled roller skates. The regulars are welcoming and if you come at the right time on a Sunday afternoon, they will teach you the Thriller dance (RIP MJ). Turn to our Golden Gate Park (pg 188) for other exciting activities and happenings.

For the skateboarder, the cityscape offers a scrumptious plethora of hills, steps and curbs, to ollie, grind, and kick flip. There are a two free public skate parks. Potrero Del Dol (at Rolf park) which is located at 25th and Potrero and the skate park at Crocker-Amazon, (Geneva and Moscow). Both offer bowls, rails, and all the shindig.

Looking for something a little different and indoors? CELLspace, an alternative art and performance venue in the SOMA district, clears out its warehouse space for occasional "RollerJams," rollerskate dance parties with live music and cheap rental fees. The scene falls pretty high on the hippie spectrum and is far more raucous than your standard indoor rink. If you'd rather bring your own crowd, CELLspace can be rented out at dirt cheap rates for private parties (2050 Bryant St, 415-648-7562; www.cellspace.org).

The indoor ice rink in Yerba Buena Ice Skating and Bowling Center at 750 Folsom Street (415-820-3532; www.skatebowl.com) has a skating school and private lessons for figure skating and hockey year-round. If you're looking for something a little less structured, public ice skating sessions are offered daily (admission costs $8 for adults, $5.50 for seniors, and $6.25 for students and youths; $3 skate rental, rental free on Wednesday nights); visit the center's website for an up-to-date public skating schedule. From November to January, have some East Coast fun in a California climate on the outdoor holiday ice rink in the Embarcadero Center ($7.50 adults, $4 children; $3.50 skate rental). The Skating Club of San Francisco (www.scsf.org) is for the pros among you.

For skateboard or rollerblade gear, Skates on Haight is the place to go, and it's close to the Park (1818 Haight St, 415-752-8375; www.skatesonhaight.com). Also check out Purple Skunk (5820 Geary Blvd, 415-668-7905; www.purpleskunk.com) or DLX Skateboards & Clothing (1831 Market St, 415-626-5588; www.dlxsf.com). You can pick up ice skating gear at the fully-equipped Yerba Buena Pro Shop (750 Folsom St, 415-820-3521; www.skatebowl.com/proshop).

Bowling

Despite the proliferation of Lebowski-esque citizens, bowling options are slim pickings in San Francisco proper. After Japantown Bowl closed down a few years back, bowlers were left with only two options within the city. **Yerba Buena Ice Skating and Bowling Center (Map 8)** is the most accessible via public transportation. But the compact space has only 12 lanes and it fills up fast with teenagers on weekend nights. Another bummer is that they do not regularly serve alcohol or snacks—how the hell are you supposed to bowl without beer and nachos? Worse yet, the lanes are artificial, so you're bowling on plastic, not wood. The alley *does* have "Blacklight Bowling" on Friday and Saturday nights. But who doesn't? **Presidio Bowling Center (The Presidio)** located in Presidio Park, is equally small and family-oriented. Housed in the former Officer's Club, the Presidio can get packed around bowling hour so be prepared to wait for your lanes (or call ahead).

For a full-fledged bowling experience with beer and all the hullabaloo, you've got to head just outside the city. The closest option is **Serra Bowl** in Daly City. It offers ample parking, many lanes, air hockey, beer and every thing you need to start rolling. **Sea Bowl** is another old-school bowling operation located in the sleepy fog of Pacifica. **Albany Bowl** is perhaps the finest bowling alley but it is unfortunately located in the East Bay. Situated on San Pablo Avenue, this bowling alley remains popular with students, thugs, and anyone else looking to roll for $1.50/game on Tuesday nights. The place is jam-packed, so show up early unless you want to wait up to an hour for a lane. Pass the time eating in the café (which sells Thai dishes) or "prepping" at the bar.

If you're up for a longer drive outside of San Francisco or just happen to find yourself in Silicon Valley, check out **Palo Alto Bowl**, a classic 1970s-style bowling alley. Find your way to "Thirsty Thursdays" where after paying an $5 cover charge, sodas and beers are just 50 cents each. They also host "Planet Bowling" every Saturday, a similar deal to "AstroBowl." The Palo Alto alley has two sister operations: **Serra Bowl** in Daly City, which has disco bowling every Saturday and Sunday night, and **Bel Mateo Bowl** in San Mateo, where they rock out every Friday and Saturday night.

Bowling Alleys	*Address*	*Phone*	*Fees*	*Map*
Yerba Buena Ice Skating & Bowling Center	750 Folsom St	415-820-3532	Mon-Fri $5-6, Fri after 6 pm and weekends $35-40/lane/hr	8
Presidio Bowling Center	Moraga Ave & Montgomery St	415-561-2695	Weekdays $4.50-7.25/game, weekends $6-7.25/game, shoes $4	pg 190
Albany Bowl	540 San Pablo Ave, Albany	510-526-8818	Mon-Tue nights $1.50/game, Thur-Fri nights $1.25/game, Sun $2.50/game, all other times $4-5/game, shoes $4	n/a
AMF Southshore Lanes	300 Park St, Alameda	510-523-6767	$2–$3 / game; $4.50 for shoes	n/a
Bel Mateo Bowl	4330 Olympic Ave	650-341-2616	Weekdays until 5pm $5/game, weeknights and weekends $6/game, shoes $4	n/a
Country Club Bowl	88 Vivian Wy	415-456-4661	$4/game daytime, $5 at night, $5 on weekends. $3 for shoes.	n/a
Palo Alto Bowl	4329 El Camino Real	650-948-1031	Weekdays $4.50 / game, Weekends $29/lane/hour; $4 for shoes	n/a
Sea Bowl	4625 Coast Hwy	650-738-8190	Weekdays until 6pm $22/hr/lane, weeknights $27, weekends $29, shoes $4	n/a
Serra Bowl	3301 Junipero Serra Blvd	650-992-3444	Weekdays until 5pm $5/game, weeknights and weekends $6/game; shoes $4	n/a

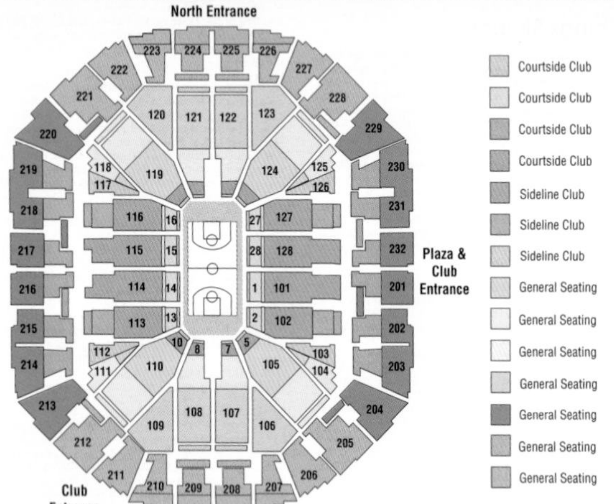

General Information

Address: 7000 Coliseum Wy
Oakland, CA 94621
Phone: 510-569-2121
Website: www.coliseum.com
Warriors: www.warriors.com

Overview

While the Oracle Arena plays host to a variety of sporting events and concerts, its full time tenant is the Golden State Warriors, the Bay Area's touch-and-go Cinderella of a basketball team.

The Golden State Warriors began as the Philadelphia Warriors, earning the honor of being the first NBA champions in the league's inaugural 1947 season. They moved to San Francisco in 1962 and changed their name to Golden State after relocating to Oakland in 1971. The Warriors can boast the NBA's first superstar in Joe Fulks, who averaged 23.2 points per game in the first season of the NBA (originally called the BBA). The only player to ever score 100 points in a single game was the Warriors' Wilt Chamberlain. One of the best free throw shooters ever was Rick Barry, whose underhanded tosses connected 89.3 percent of the time. Impressed yet?

How to Get There—Driving

Go east over the Bay Bridge to 880 S. Take the 66th Avenue exit. Turn left at the end of the ramp and follow signs to the Arena. The Arena is located right next door to McAfee Coliseum.

Parking

North and south parking lots open two hours prior to game time. Parking fees are $20 for cars and $50 for limos and buses.

How to Get There—Mass Transit

Take the Fremont BART to the Coliseum/Oakland Airport stop. AC Transit also runs buses 45, 46, 49, 56, 58, and 98 to the Coliseum BART stop.

How to Get Tickets

For Warriors season tickets, call 888-GSW-HOOP. For single game tickets or any other performances at the Arena, purchase your tickets from Ticketmaster—www.ticketmaster.com.

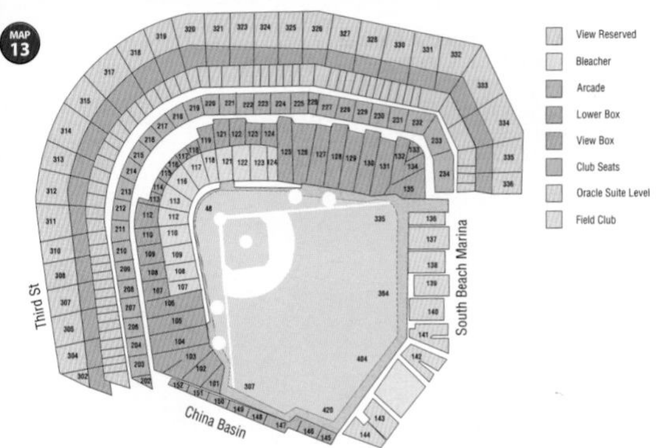

General Information

NFT Map:	13
Address:	AT&T Park 24 Willie Mays Plz San Francisco, CA 94107
Phone:	415-972-1800
Giants Website:	www.sfgiants.com

Overview

After playing at Seals Stadium and the much-maligned Candlestick Park, the San Francisco Giants got a home they could be proud of at AT&T Park, which opened in 2000 under the name Pacific Bell Park. This 41,503-seat jewel of a stadium is a glorious throwback to the intimate ball fields of yore, and the expansive views from the top levels take in the Bay and Treasure Island. Kayakers and other boaters forgo stadium views (and increasingly hefty ticket prices) and bob around McCovey Cove, drinking beers and waiting for splash four-baggers to drop from the sky. The park is emblazoned with giants nostalgia from the iconic statue of Wilie Mays to Orlando Cepeda's signature Cha Cha bowl located behind center field.

How to Get There—Mass Transit

Public transit is greatly encouraged when you're heading for the ballpark. Take the Muni Metro N Line inbound (or specially marked Metro trains on game days) directly to China Basin by getting off at the Second and King Muni Metro station. You can also catch regular Muni bus routes 10 (Townsend), 15 (Third Street), 30 (Stockton), 42 (Downtown Loop), 45 (Union), or 47 (Van Ness), which will drop you within one block of the park. If you're coming from the South Bay or the Peninsula and Caltrain is your mode of transportation, the San Francisco stop at Fourth and King Streets is one block from the ballpark. Or take BART from the Peninsula or the East Bay to downtown San Francisco and transfer to the Muni N Line at the Civic Center, Powell, Montgomery, or Embarcadero stations (or, better yet, stroll along the waterfront to the park, it's a local, albeit new, tradition). If sitting in game-day traffic is too daunting then leave your car in the East Bay and take the ferry from Alameda, Oakland, or Larkspur to the China Basin Ferry Terminal, right behind the park (and don't forget to enjoy the scenery on your way).

How to Get There—Driving

From the Peninsula/South Bay, take 1-280 N (or 101 N to I-280 N) to the Mariposa Street exit. Turn right on Mariposa Street, then left on Third Street.

From the East Bay, take I-80/Bay Bridge to the Fifth Street exit. Exit onto Harrison Street, then turn left onto Sixth Street and continue onto I-280 S. Take the first exit at 18th Street and turn left. Go over the freeway and turn left onto Third Street.

From the North Bay, take Highway 101 S/Golden Gate Bridge to the Marina Boulevard exit. Drive past Fort Mason and turn left onto Bay Street, then right onto the Embarcadero. Continue on the Embarcadero under the Bay Bridge until it turns into King Street. Turn left onto Third Street.

Parking

AT&T Park has over 5,000 parking spaces in Parking Lots A (Charter Seat Holder parking), B, and C. The lots are located on the south side of the China Basin Channel across the Lefty O'Doul Bridge from the ballpark. For season parking, call 415-972-2000.

How to Get Tickets

Individual tickets range in price from $10 to $90 and can be purchased through the Giants website.

If you're interested in season tickets, call 415-972-2298 or email seasontickets@sfgiants.com.

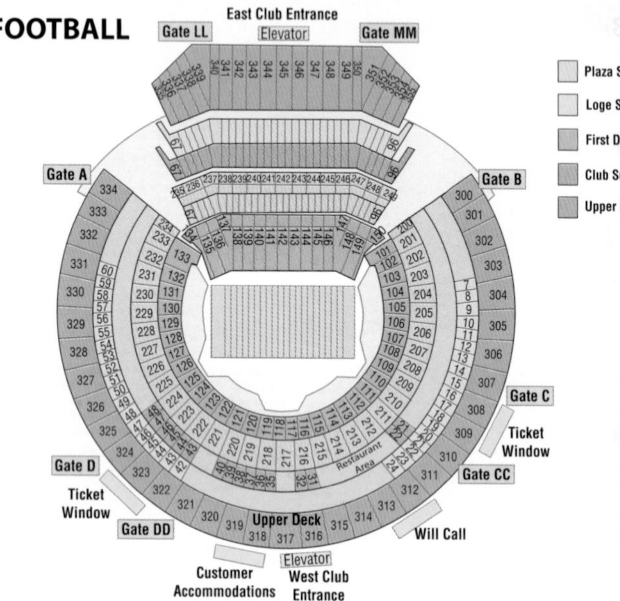

General Information

Address: 7000 Coliseum Wy
Oakland, CA 94621
Phone: 510-569-2121
Website: www.coliseum.com
A's Website: www.oaklandathletics.com
Raiders' Website: www.raiders.com

Overview

They used to call it the Oakland-Alameda County Coliseum. But we live in an age when corporate sponsorship dictates the majority of stadium names. So is it any surprise that Network Associates shelled out $5.8 million in 1998 to put their name on the stadium, then changed the company's name to McAfee in 2004, renaming the arena for the third time in seven years? But lo and behold, the recession took hold and now we're back to Oakland-Alameda County Coliseum. Built at an initial cost of $25.5 million in 1966, the 1996 renovation budget ballooned from $100 million to $200 million by the time it was complete. But hey, it was money well spent. After all, the renovated Coliseum lured the Raiders back from a 12-year stint in Los Angeles. The Coliseum also plays host to the Oakland Athletics, who began in 1901 as a franchise in Philly, moved to Kansas City in 1954, and then finally to Oakland in 1968. The A's have nine World Series wins to their name, four of them as the Oakland A's. Their next win, though, may be as the Fremont A's—recently, there's been talk that the team may relocate.

How to Get There—Driving

From San Francisco, take the Bay Bridge to I-580 E toward Hayward and exit at I-980 going toward downtown Oakland. Continue on I-980, which becomes I-880 S. Exit at 66th Avenue and follow signs to the Coliseum.

BASEBALL

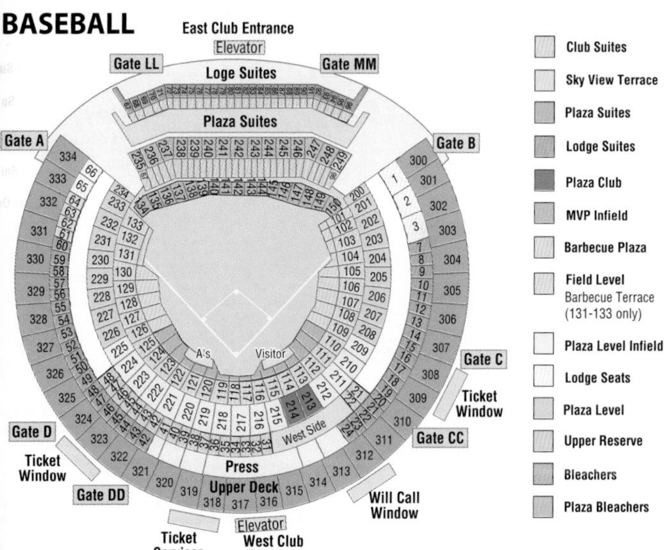

Parking

There is ample parking available for fans on all sides of the Coliseum. Bus and RV parking is located in a designated lot directly south of the stadium. Parking costs $15 for cars, $25 for limousines, and $25 for buses. Lots open 2.5 hours ahead of schedule for early birds and tailgaters. Fans can even reserve a tailgate space in advance for $85 by calling 510-638-4900 x2339. Amenities include portable bathrooms, charcoal bins, and garbage cans, with tables and chairs also available for rent.

How to Get There—Mass Transit

Take the Fremont BART to the Coliseum/Oakland Airport stop. AC Transit also runs buses 45, 46, 49, 56, 58, and 98 to the Coliseum BART stop.

How to Get Tickets

For Raiders season tickets, call 888-44-RAIDERS. For individual game tickets you can call the Box Office at 510-569-2121 or purchase them online from www.ticketmaster.com.

Athletics prices range from $9–$44 for individual game tickets and may be purchased through the team's official website, online at www.tickets.com, or by calling 510-762-BALL. If you're after season or group tickets, call 510-638-4627.

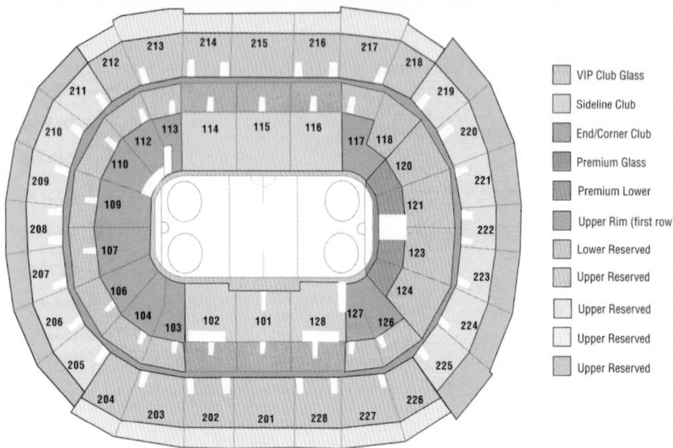

General Information

Address: 525 W Santa Clara St
San Jose, CA 95113
Phone: 408-287-9200
Website: www.hppsj.com
San Jose Sharks: www.sj-sharks.com

Overview

In 1991, the San Jose Sharks paid the $50 million entrance fee to the NHL. The construction of a brand new stadium soon followed, with the San Jose Sharks playing their first game in the San Jose Arena on September 30th, 1993. Since then, this 20,000-seat arena has undergone three name changes (San Jose Arena to Compaq Center at San Jose to HP Pavilion), yet remains known locally as the Tank. Ice skating events, boxing matches, and horse shows regularly make a spectacle of themselves here, and the arena was the site for the 2007 West Regional of the NCAA men's basketball tournament. Besides athletics, the Tank plays host to a wide variety of non-sporting entertainment acts. After a long week on the job, you can blow off steam and pump your fists in the general direction of the stage while catching Slayer or the Rock and Roll Visa Championships. Circuses abound at the Tank, with cirque de somethings and Ringlings on steady rotation. But before you grab your seats for Streisand, head down to the Club Level and sample the Oven Roasted Duckling with orange-lingonberry sauce and beluga lentil pilaf at The Grill at HP Pavilion. Regardless of your reason for visiting the Pavilion, please note that no one is allowed to throw objects onto the stage or playing surface or into the stands. However, there is one exception to the rule—"... when, during a hockey game, a player scores a 'hat trick' (three goals in a game); in this case, throwing of hats is customary and has been deemed appropriate." Keep in mind that HP Pavilion cannot return the hats.

How to Get There—Driving

Take the US-101 and exit at CA-87 Guadalupe Parkway. Bear right on Guadalupe Parkway and continue until the Julian Street exit. Turn right onto West Julian Street and left on Stockton Avenue. If you take 280, take the Bird Avenue exit and continue until it becomes Autumn Street. Follow the signs to the parking lots.

Parking

There are more than 6,000 parking spaces located within a 1/2-mile radius of the Pavilion. The charge for parking ranges from $10 to $15 for most events.

How to Get There—Mass Transit

Caltrain is the best public transportation option, with the San Jose Diridon stop located right across the street from the stadium. A one-way fare from any of the stations in Zone 1 to the San Jose Diridon station in Zone 4, costs $7. VTA bus lines 63, 64, 65, 68, 180, and the DASH all stop at the San Jose Diridon Station.

How to Get Tickets

For Sharks season passes, call 408-999-5757 or check their website for order form details. Single game tickets can be purchased via www.ticketmaster.com and all Ticketmaster outlets including Wherehouse Music, Tower Records, Ritmo Latino, and select Rite-Aid stores.

General Information

NFT Map: 40
Ticket Office: 415-656-4900
49ers Website: www.sf49ers.com

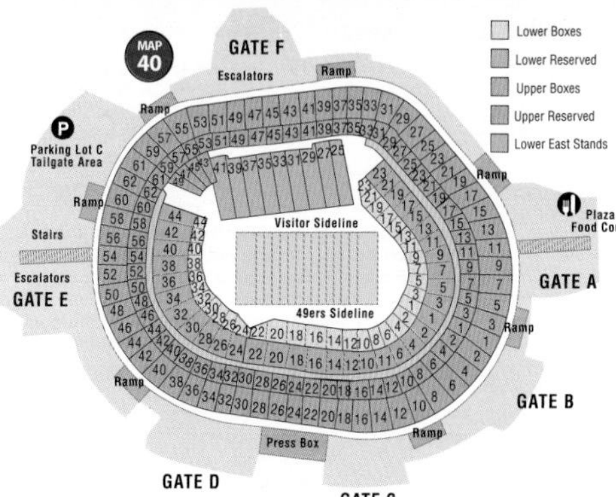

Overview

San Francisco 49ers fans are sometimes pegged a "wine and cheese" crowd, far more reserved than their rowdy Raider Nation counterparts across the Bay. While it is true the fans tailgate in style, this misnomer probably arises from jealousy over the 5 (count'em FIVE) Superbowl rings the Niners have amassed over the years. However, 49ers loyalists deserve a little more credit for withstanding foul weather. After all, they've remained steadfast fans through recent mediocre seasons, stadium name changes (ahem, just a few!), and even rumors of franchise movement. Monster Park is in need of a facelift, certainly, but that doesn't seem to deter fans. The 49ers consistently sell out every game in the 70,207-seat stadium.

The 49ers played their first game at the stadium in 1971 after moving from their previous field at Golden Gate Park's Kezar Stadium. All locals still use the original name (or just "The 'Stick" to natives) stems from Candlestick Point, a piece of land that juts into San Francisco Bay which used to maintain a long-billed curlew (or "candlestick bird") population. Candlestick was renamed 3Com Park in 1995, reverted back to Candlestick in 2002, and then became Monster Park in 2004 (when Monster Cable Systems signed a four-year deal with the team for naming rights, netting the city of San Francisco a cool $3 million as part of the deal). And now we're back to Candlestick. Maybe the city council should landmark it so the name never changes again. Since 1981, the team has won 13 division titles, five conference championships, and five Super Bowls.

How to Get There—Driving

The Candlestick Park exit from 101 N takes you directly to the park. During the two hours before a game, it is quicker to use the Third Street exit from the 101 instead of the Candlestick Park exit. Follow the detour signs to Salinas Avenue, and cross Third Street to Jameson Avenue. Coming from San Francisco and points north, take 101 S to the Third Street exit and continue on to Jameson Avenue. Be sure to enter the correct traffic lanes on Jameson for access to your parking lot. For Lots A, B, C, overflow C, or the TV lot, you must be in the far left lane closest to the fence. Enter the middle lane for Lot L, and the far right for the pre-paid parking lot.

Avoid post-game congestion on southbound 101 by taking Highway 280. Avoid post-game congestion on northbound 101 through downtown San Francisco by using Third Street or northbound Highway 280.

Parking

Parking is available in dirt lots just outside the stadium. Parking for cars and motorcycles costs $25. Bus parking costs $30, and bus drivers will need to take Third Street to Ingerson—entrance to the bus lot will be on the left. Limo and RV parking costs $40 and you enter the lot via Gilman Avenue.

How to Get There—Mass Transit

Direct bus service to the stadium is available on Muni, Santa Clara Valley Transportation Authority, or SamTrans buses.

For home games, the following express Muni services are offered: 9X from Sutter & Montgomery via Sutter, Stockton, Fourth to Folsom then express to Monster Park; 28X limited stop service from Funston & California to Monster Park via Funston, California, Park Presidio and regular route to 19th Avenue and Sloat, then via Sloat, Junipero Serra, Ocean, Geneva to Mission, then express to the park; 47X from California & Van Ness via Van Ness to South Van Ness & Mission, then express to Monster Park.

Adult fare for express service costs $10 round-trip ($7 for children ages 5–17 and seniors). Muni passholders pay $5. Muni also runs a $1.50 shuttle from Bacon & San Bruno via Paul and Third Streets (Caltrain) then express to the ballpark. SamTrans also runs bus lines 810, 820, 840, 850, 851, and 880 to the park on game days. A season pass will set you back $75, while a four-game pass costs $45. A single round-trip ticket costs $15.

How to Get Tickets

Single tickets can be purchased through Ticketmaster, with the usual "convenience fee" and a postage-and-handling fee. If you'd like to become a 49ers season ticket holder, you can do so online via the 49ers website, call 415-656-4900, or write to 49ers Ticket Office, Candlestick Park, Rm 400, San Francisco, CA, 94124.

Billiards

Billiards	Address	Phone	Fees	Map
King Kong	745 O'Farrell St	415-346-4645	$10/hr	7
Jillian's	101 4th St	415-369-6100	Before 4 pm: $8/table/hr After 4 pm: 12/table/hr.	8
Family Billiards	2807 Geary Blvd	415-931-1115	1 person: $7.25/hr:: 2 people: $12/hr.	22
Billiard Palacade	5179 Mission St	415-585-2331	1 person: $5.55/hr: 2 people: $10.75/hr.	34

Yoga

Vinyasa, Hatha, Iyengar, and Bikram. That's right, kids, yoga isn't just about saying "Omm" anymore. So many styles, so little time. Whether you are a yoga traditionalist, a novice, or someone contorting into an impossible pose at just this moment, the city has dozens of studios and schools for those learning to instruct others. **It's Yoga (Map 12)** has 11 instructors specializing in the Ashtanga variety of intense purification through 8 spiritual facets. They also train instructors. **The Mindful Body (Map 5)** teaches multiple styles of the breathing and muscle control technique. They have special prenatal classes and you can indulge in a deep tissue massage post-session as well.

Yoga	Address		Website	Map
Global Yoga	2425 Chestnut St	292-9774	www.globalyogasf.com	1
International Orange - Spa Yoga Lounge	2044 Fillmore St, 2nd Floor	800-387-7918	www.internationalorange.com	5
The Mindful Body	2876 California St	931-2639	www.themindfulbody.com	5
YogaWorks SF	1823 Divisadero St	292-5600	www.yogastudiomillvalley.com	5
Therapeia Yoga & Massage	1801 Bush St	885-4450	www.therapeiaspa.com	6
Funky Door Yoga Polk Street	1336 Polk St	673-8659	www.funkydooryoga.com	7
California Yoga Co	2410 California St	775-0570	www.yogicmotion.com	7
Satori Yoga Studio	40 1st St	618-0418	www.satoriyogastudio.com	8
Funky Door Yoga Haight Ashbury	1749 Waller St	668-2227	www.funkydooryoga.com	9
Kundalini Yoga Center	1390 Waloer St	863-0132	www.idoyoga.com	9
Yoga Tree Stanyan	780 Stanyan St	387-4707	www.yogatreesf.com	9
Yoga Tree Castro	97 Collingwood St	701-9642	www.yogatreesf.com	10
Yoga Garden of San Francisco	286 Divisadero St	552-9644	www.yogagardensf.com	10
Yoga Loft	321 Divisadero St	626-5638	www.theloftsf.com	10
Bikram Yoga in the Mission	2390 Mission St, 2nd Fl	401-9642	www.missionyoga.com	11
Yoga Tree Hayes	519 Hayes St	626-9707	www.yogatreesf.com	11
Pretzel's Yoga School	485 Carolina St	626-9642	www.pretzelsyoga.com	12
A Piece of Peace	3819 23rd St	647-2188	www.apieceofpeace.com	14
Bikram Yoga	301 Eureka St	821-9642	www.bikramyogacastro.com	14
Integral Yoga Institute	770 Dolores St	821-1117	www.integralyogasf.org	14
Yoga Society of San Francisco	2872 Folsom St	285-5537	www.yssf.com	15
Yoga Tree Valencia	1234 Valencia St	647-9707	www.yogatreesf.com	15
Elevation Pilates	3423 Balboa St	386-9008	www.elevationpilates.com	19
Bikram Yoga SeaCliff	6300 California St	751-6908	www.globalyogasf.com	19
SFA Yoga	701 11th Ave	221-9644	www.sfayoga.com	21
Bija Yoga	1348 9th Ave	661-9642	www.bijayoga.com	25
Bikram Yoga Inner Sunset	455 Judah St	753-8694	www.fluidyoga.biz	25
Iyengar Yoga Institute of San Francisco	2404 27th Ave	753-0909	www.iyisf.org	27
Sivananda Yoga Vedanta Center	1200 Arguello Blvd	681-2731	www.sfyoga.com	29
Abode of Iyengar Yoga	765 Monterey Blvd	469-9642	www.manouso.com	31
Kiki-Yo	605 Chenery St	587-5454	www.kiki-yo.com	32
Bernal Yoga	461 Cortland Ave	643-9007	www.bernalyoga.com	35
A Body of Work	569 Ruger St	561-3991	www.abodyofwork-sf.com	Presidio

If you're looking to add more cardiovascular activity to your life, a good place to start exploring your options is the San Francisco Recreation and Park Department webpage (sfrecpark.org). Here you will find information on all city-sponsored sports including tennis, volleyball, softball, lacrosse, football, and soccer. Of course, this fine city of ours prides itself on its diversity, so in addition to these more common sports, you will also find information on other activities such as bocce ball, badminton, lawn bowling, tai chi, public trampolines, and more. They've really got it all. Another semi-all inclusive website to check out is: www.playnotwatch.com, which isn't local but will help you find a team/league/facility in and around SF nonetheless. If you are looking to join a team, go to (the god of all things San Francisco) Craigslist and search the Community section for your particular sport. If you want to expand your team sports horizons even more, consider checking out some leagues in the East Bay. Since most games are once a week or less, it's worth the short commute and gives you a host of other options. Large workplaces are also apt to hosting softball teams. If you are a student, your school probably has intramural sports, but you're probably too busy drinking to be reading this page anyway.

One quick tip on joining any city league—it's about persistence, community, and timing. Many of the city's recreational leagues are run by the players in their spare time. If they are slow to return phone calls, or don't have a spot for you the first time you call—stick with it. The community you will find is worth the hassle of getting started.

Soccer

The San Francisco Soccer Football League (SFSFL) is one of the oldest semi-professional and amateur leagues in the nation. It is also one of the few venues in which the city's cultural diversity truly shines. Take a stroll through the Polo Fields at Golden Gate Park on a Saturday morning in July, and you'll feel like you've happened onto a World Cup opening ceremony. Games are played throughout Northern California between March and November. For more information call 415-863-8892 or visit www.sfsfl.com. Also check out All Power Indoor Soccer at 660 15th St in Oakland (510-452-1741).

Biking

Whether you prefer riding your bike on pavement or dirt, the Bay Area has what you're looking for. Even a short ride can traverse the entire city, and (depending on which route you take) will lead you up and over several challenging hills. Cross the Golden Gate for some spectacular views, and keep going into the Marin Headlands for even more great back roads and dirt trails. Not into Lycra shorts and toe clips? Pack yourself a cooler, grab some friends, and rent a bike for two, four, or even six people at Stow Lake Bike & Boat (415-752-0347) in Golden Gate Park.

Softball

With our mild climate, softball is one of the more popular league sports in the Bay Area, with leagues for every season. Activity levels range anywhere from those who bring a 6-pack to the game, to organized Sunday pick-up games, to a recreational high-level of competition. In addition to the above general info try www.sfsoftball.com for San Francisco, www.leaguelineup.com/oaklandsoftball for Oakland, 510- 981-5153 for Berkeley's softball league, and Daly City Softball at Daly City Parks and Rec 650-991-8001. You don't have to be a resident of any city to play in a league there. On a related note, check out Bay Area Vintage Baseball (www.eteamz.active.com/BAVBB). The league is dedicated to preserving the style of play that was in effect between 1880 and 1890, which includes regulations, uniforms, and style. Unfortunately that era excluded women players, as does this league.

Frisbee

Played that game in college to great success and want to rekindle that special feeling? You can find all your San Francisco Ultimate Frisbee needs at San Francisco Ultimate League (www.sful.org) or San Francisco Ultimate Club (www.sfuc.org.). Despite the often cold temps, work those calf muscles with a pick-up game of Beach Ultimate, played most weekends. Ultimate players are pretty hard-core and dedicated about their game, but that makes it all the more fun.

Frisbee Golf

If you are looking for a more beer-oriented Frisbee challenge, Disc Golf might be just the thing to float your boat. A world class (and non-profit) 18 hole course is located in GGP at Marx Meadow, deep in the Richmond between 25th and 30th Avenues.

Sports Arenas

If it's too foggy and cold out and/or you'd like to practice your skills, there are a few indoor arenas that have a variety of indoor team sports activities. You don't need to be a member to utilize the following places: Triple Play- 2055 Adams Ave, San Leandro, 510- 568-2255, www.tripleplayusa.com. Primarily softball and baseball batting cages as well as a small indoor basketball court and arcade games for the kid in you. Bladium Sports Complex- 800 West Tower Avenue, Alameda , 510- 814-4999, www.bladium.com. Best place for fun not under the sun. Indoor activities include basketball, soccer , football, inline hockey, lacrosse, volleyball, and climbing. You can also become a member for regular gym privileges. This place is in an old warehouse that used to be a Navy base, and while half of the base is still abandoned and unused, Bladium is hopping with action.

Gay Sports

No, not golf. We're referring to sports leagues for the LGBT community. Sports Complex (http://sportscomplex.org) organizes "Gay Games" of all kinds including swimming, cycling, softball, and track. Not only is their website a resource for finding teams and leagues, they also post news, events, and political actions affecting LGBT athletic folk.

No matter what you're into—football or badminton, SCUBA, diving, or hand gliding—the diverse topography combined with the adventurous spirit of the San Francisco people to guarantee almost anyone a good time in the great outdoors.

Airlines

	Phone	SFO	OAK	SJC
Aer Lingus	800-474-7424			
Aero Mexico	800-337-6639	■		
Air Canada	888-247-2262	■		
Air China	800-986-1985	■		
Air France	800-237-2747	■		
Air New Zealand	800-262-1234	■		
AirTran	800-247-8726	■		
Alaska Airlines	800-426-0333	■	■	■
Allegiant	702-505-8888		■	
American Airlines	800-433-7300	■		■
ANA	800-235-9262	■		
Asiana	800-227-4262	■		
British Airways	800-247-9297	■		
Cathay Pacific	800-233-2742	■		
China Airlines	800-227-5118	■		
Continental	800-525-0280	■		■
Delta	800-221-1212	■	■	■
Emirates	800-777-3999	■		
Eva Airways	800-695-1188	■		
Frontier Airlines	800-432-1359	■		
Hawaiian Airlines	800-367-5320	■	■	■
Iceland Air	800-223-5500	■		
Horizon Air	800-547-9308	■		■
Japan Airlines	800-525-3663	■		
Jet Blue	800-538-2583	■	■	■
KLM	800-447-4747	■		
Korean Air	800-438-5000	■		
LACSA	800-225-2272	■		
Lufthansa	800-645-3880	■		
Mexicana	800-531-7921	■		
Midwest Express	800-452-2022	■		
Philippine Airlines	800-435-9725	■		
Qantas	800-227-4500	■		
Singapore Airlines	800-742-3333	■		
Southwest	800-435-9792	■	■	■
Sun Country	800-359-6786	■		
TACA	800-535-8780	■		
Ted	800-225-5833			
United Airlines	800-241-6522	■	■	■
US Airways	800-428-4322	■	■	■
Virgin Atlantic	800-862-8621	■		
Virgin America	877-359-8474	■		
WestJet	888-937-8538	■		

Shuttle Services

	Phone	SFO	OAK	SJC
A-1 Shuttle Services	888-698-2663	■	■	
Acropolis Airport Shuttle & Limo	510-827-5894	■	■	■
Air-Transit Shuttle	510-568-3434	■	■	■
Alicia Shuttle	510-385-5513	■	■	■
Angel Express	866-295-3797	■	■	■
American Airport Shuttle	415-202-0733	■	■	■
Apollo Shuttle	925-676-9146	■	■	■
Atlas Shuttle Connection	888-467-0000	■	■	■
Avon Airporter Express	707-643-5778	■	■	■
B.A.B.E.S. Airporter	510-317-6983	■	■	
Bay Area Express	510-234-9759	■	■	
Bay Area Shuttle	510-324-3000	■	■	■
Bayporter Express	800-287-6783	■	■	
Bay Shuttle	415-564-3400	■	■	■
Best Way Shuttle	925-363-7711	■	■	
Bridge Airporter	510-867-1476	■	■	■
California Airporter	800-225-6316	■	■	
Chambers Airport Express	510-569-5445	■	■	■
City Express Shuttle & Limo	888-874-8885	■	■	■
Citywide Shuttle	510-336-0090	■	■	■
Comfort Shuttle	510-774-6833	■	■	■
Door-to-Door Express	415-775-5121	■		
East Bay Connection	800-675-3278	■	■	
E-Z Ride Airporter	510-393-5554	■	■	■
Fairfield Airporter	877-424-7767	■	■	■
Flying Eagle Shuttle	510-259-0095	■	■	
Lion Airport Shuttle	866-901-5466	■	■	■
Lorrie's Airport Shuttle	415-334-9000	■		
Lucky Shuttle	510-303-8772	■	■	■
Luxor Shuttle	510-562-7222	■	■	■
M&M Luxury Shuttle	415-552-3200	■	■	■
Pacific Airport Shuttle	415-681-6318	■		
Peter's Airport Shuttle	650-577-8858	■		
Pyramid Airporter	510-562-0822	■	■	■
Quake City Shuttle	415-255-4899	■	■	
Safety Express Shuttle	510-388-2029	■	■	
San Jose Express Shuttle	800-773-0039	■	■	■
Santa Clara Airporter	800-771-7794		■	■
SF City Shuttle	650-872-0440	■		
SFO Airporter (major hotels)	800-532-8405	■		
Shuttle Pro	866-499-2447	■	■	
South Bay Airport Shuttle	408-559-9477	■		■
South & East Bay Shuttle	408-225-4444	■		■
SuperShuttle	800-BLUE-VAN	■	■	■
Take Me Home Express	510-652-8700	■	■	■
The Shuttle	888-978-7379	■	■	■
Traveler Shuttle	510-909-0965	■	■	■
USA Shuttle & Charter	510-744-0222		■	■
VIP Airport Shuttle	408-885-1800	■	■	■
Yellow Express Shuttle	408-225-4937	■	■	■

General Information

Airport Information:	650-821-8211
Airport Website:	www.flysfo.com
Ground Transportation:	817-1717
(Bay Area only, no area code required)	
Lost & Found:	650-821-7014
Parking:	650-821-7900
Police (Non-Emergency):	650-821-7111
US Customs:	650-624-7200

Overview

This is fog city, baby, and airports and fog do not go hand in hand. With just two closely spaced runways, flights from SFO are particularly prone to weather-related delays. SFO is the fifth-largest airport in the US and the ninth-largest in the world, and serves over 40 million passengers per year. Eighty flights per day depart for Los Angeles, and 42 for New York. While other local airports have been giving SFO some stiff competition for popular destinations, SFO's streamlined security and baggage check make it far more user-friendly than Oakland's congested terminals. The newly-remodeled international terminal has earned rave reviews with its ultra-stylish design and art-filled space, and the BART connection to SFO has eased the commute for thousands of travelers.

New runways would ease congestion and delays, but the now eight-year-old runway expansion plan has been delayed. These runways would fill in 1.5 square miles of open water in the Bay—a prospect that has environmentalists worried (think churning mud, lots of nasty chemicals, dying fish). For now, the economic downturn and the resulting reduction in air traffic have the expansion on hold, but discussion is expected to heat up again when air travel increases.

How to Get There—Driving

If you're driving from San Francisco, take 101 S and get off at the SF International Airport exit. You can also take 280 south and connect to 101 via Highway 380, go south and take the SF International exit.

How to Get There—Mass Transit

There are three options for public transit to SFO, and the best option for you will depend on where you're going, how much baggage you have, and when you're leaving. BART is the most efficient, as the Millbrae line runs all the way to SFO (downtown SF to the airport is $8.10 one way), but you'll have to lug your bags. Also, the earliest train doesn't arrive at SFO until 5:30 am, which can be a problem, particularly for early morning international departures.

Caltrain runs a service from Millbrae Station to Fourth and King Streets ($4.25) and free shuttles run between the station and the airport approximately every 20–30 minutes, except on weekends. BART also offers a cross-platform transfer at Millbrae.

SamTrans runs a few bus routes out of SFO, including the KX Express bus, which provides service between San Francisco, SFO, and Palo Alto. You'd better be traveling light though, because the KX doesn't allow luggage! Route 292 is a local bus that makes many stops in the communities between San Francisco, SFO, and San Mateo. Route 397 runs an overnight "owl" service between San Francisco, SFO, and Palo Alto. Route 193 operates on a limited schedule between the Stonestown Galleria in San Francisco, Daly City BART Station, and SFO. KX Express will set you back $4, while the local buses cost $1.50.

How to Get There—Really

If you'd rather not drive and you don't relish the prospect of lugging your bags to the nearest BART station or bus stop, there are a number of shuttle services (Super Shuttle is a good one) that can get you to SFO from the city for around $20 (a bargain compared to the typical cab fare of $40). Most shuttles pick you up at your front door in plenty of time to make your flight—just be prepared to stop by a couple of other people's houses on your way to the airport.

Parking

For domestic flights departing from Terminal 1, park in Sections A/B, B, or C. Flights departing from Terminal 2 should head to Section D, and if you're going from Terminal 3, park in Sections E, F, or F/G. Rates for parking are $2 for 20 minutes, $33 maximum for the first 24 hours, and $35 maximum for each additional day.

If your destination is abroad, use Garage A for Air France, AirTran, Alaska Airlines (Mexico flights), British Airways, Cathay Pacific, China Airlines, Japan Airlines, KLM, Korean Air, LACSA, Northwest (International), Philippine Airlines, TACA, and Virgin Atlantic. Garage G serves AirChina, ANA, Asiana, EVA, Lufthansa, Mexicana, Singapore Airlines, and United (International). Parking costs $2 per 20 minutes and $20 per 24-hour period.

For two hours of free parking in any terminal garage, you need to spend $20 at participating shops and restaurants in the International Terminal to have your ticket validated. You can also print out discount parking coupons via the airport website at www.flysfo.com.

Parking—*continued*

If your budget doesn't cover long-term parking in the domestic lots, a cheaper alternative is the long-term lot located off the US 101/San Bruno Avenue-East exit. You can park there for up to 30 days and a free shuttle service to and from the terminals runs every few minutes. Parking costs $2 for each 20 minutes, $14 for 24 hours through day seven and $11 per 24 hours thereafter. The website offers a "seventh day free" coupon, so if you'll be there for a week, print it out and take it with you. If the long-term lot happens to be full, get a voucher to park right at the terminals for the same long-term rate!

Cabs

Typical fare from the airport to Cow Palace costs around $29. A cab from downtown will set you back roughly $37, and from the Wharf will be around $44.

Rental Cars

- **Alamo** • 650-616-2400
- **Avis** • 650-877-6780
- **Budget** • 650-877-0998
- **Dollar** • 866-434-2226
- **Enterprise** • 650-697-9200
- **Hertz** • 650-624-6600
- **National** • 650-616-3000
- **Thrifty** • 877-283-0898

Hotels

- **Best Western Grosvenor** • 380 S Airport Blvd, San Francisco • 650-873-3200
- **Clarion** • 401 E Millbrae Ave, Millbrae • 650-692-6363
- **Hampton Inn Airport** • 300 Gateway Blvd, San Francisco • 650-876-0200
- **Holiday Inn** • 373 S Airport Blvd, San Francisco • 650-589-0682
- **Hyatt Regency** • 1333 Bayshore Hwy, Burlingame • 650-347-1234
- **La Quinta Inn** • 20 Airport Blvd, San Francisco • 650-583-1431
- **North Travelodge** • 326 S Airport Blvd, San Francisco • 650-583-9600
- **Radisson San Francisco** • 5000 Sierra Point Pkwy, San Francisco • 415-467-4400
- **Sheraton Gateway** • 600 Airport Blvd, Burlingame • 650-340-8500
- **Staybridge Suites** • 1350 Huntington Ave, San Bruno • 650-588-0770

Terminal 1

Alaska Airlines (domestic & Canada flights)
Delta Airlines
Frontier Airlines
Hawaiian Airlines
Horizon
Midwest Airlines
Southwest
US Airways

Terminal 2

American Airlines
Virgin America

Terminal 3

Continental
United Airlines (domestic)
United Express

International Terminal

AeroMexico
Air Berlin
Air Canada
Air China
Air France
Air New Zealand
AirTran Airways
Alaska Airlines (Mexico flights)
ANA (All Nippon Airways)
Asiana
British Airways
Cathay Pacific
China Airlines
Delta (international)
Emirates
EVA Air
Japan Airlines
JetBlue
KLM
Korean Air
LACSA
LAN
Lufthansa
Philippine Airlines
Singapore Airlines
Sun Country
Swiss International Air Lines
TACA
United Airlines (international)
Virgin America (Mexico arrivals only)
Virgin Atlantic
WestJet

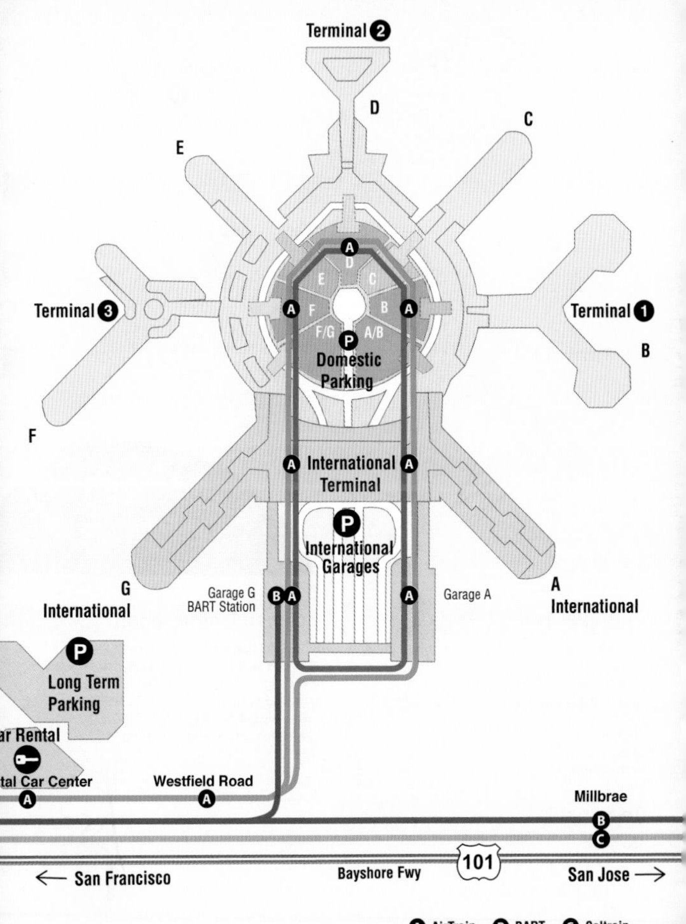

Terminal 2
D
C
E
Terminal 3
Terminal 1
B
F
D
E
C
F
B
F/G
A/B
Domestic Parking
International Terminal
International Garages
G
International
Garage G BART Station
Garage A
A
International
Long Term Parking
ar Rental
tal Car Center
Westfield Road
Millbrae
101
Bayshore Fwy
← San Francisco
San Jose →
A AirTrain
B BART
C Caltrain

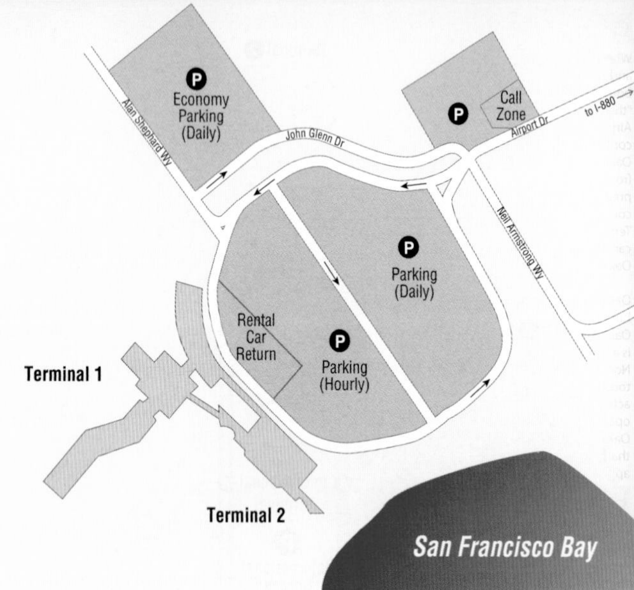

Terminal 1

Alaska Airlines
Allegiant
America West/US Airways
Delta/Delta Connection
Hawaiian
JetBlue
SATA
United/Express
Volaris

Terminal 2

Southwest

General Information

Airport Phone:	510-563-3300
Airport Website:	www.flyoakland.com
Parking:	1-888-IFLYOAK
Lost & Found:	510-563-3982
Friendly Cab Service:	510-536-3000
Veteran's Cab Service:	510-533-1900

Overview

When Gertrude Stein visited her Oakland birthplace and couldn't find her house, the famous quote was born: "There's no there there." Today, many people start "there" to get everywhere else. Oakland International Airport houses several low-fare carriers, and patronage continuously increases. However, while flights from Oakland are typically cheaper than those leaving from its higher-profile San Francisco counterpart, be prepared for the added toll on your sanity: chronically congested terminals (particularly Southwest Airlines Terminal 2), and security and baggage check lines can be over an hour long around the holidays. In fog, Oakland is always a faster landing than SFO.

Oakland might not be the biggest Bay Area airport, but it's rich in history. Amelia Earhart took off from Oakland on her ill-fated flight—thankfully navigation is a bit more reliable these days. The original airport at North Field was built in 1927 and is still in operation today for air cargo, general aviation, and corporate jet activities. Commercial passenger and cargo jet aircraft operate from South Field, which opened in 1962. Oakland Airport is a thriving business, handling more than 10 million passengers per year and employing approximately 10,700 airport-related workers.

How to Get There—Driving

If you're coming to Oakland from San Francisco, give yourself a little extra time for possible Bay Bridge delays, especially if you're traveling during the morning or evening rush hours. Travel south on 880 and exit at Hegenberger Road. Merge onto Hegenberger Road and continue straight ahead to the airport. Use the right lane for Terminal 1/ International, the economy parking lot, and cargo facilities. Use the left lane for Terminal 2, the hourly and daily parking lots, the new Park & Call Zone, and all rental car returns.

How to Get There—Mass Transit

The best way to get from San Francisco to the Oakland Airport is via the Fremont, Dublin/ Pleasanton (from points north), and Richmond (from points south) BART lines. Hours of operation to the Coliseum/Oakland Airport station are Monday–Friday, 4 am until midnight; Saturday, 6 am until midnight; Sunday, 8 am until midnight. From the Coliseum/Airport station, the airBART shuttle to the airport departs every 10 minutes and costs $3 for adults and $1 for those entitled to discounts. A BART extension from the Colisueum station to the airport is (and has been for several years) in the planning stages, but don't hold your breath.

If you're arriving to the area by Amtrak (Jack London Square Station), Alameda/Oakland Ferry, or BART, local AC Transit bus line N will take you right to the airport for $1.75 or 85¢ discounted fare.

How to Get There—Really

Avoid driving to Oakland Airport if you can—somewhat confusing signage and recent construction means about the only benefit is the view from the Bay Bridge. Instead, save yourself the money and hassle and take BART, or save yourself the hassle and time and call one of the many door-to-terminal shuttlebus services that will pick you up from anywhere in the Bay Area, usually for around $15–$20, like Supershuttle (1-800-BLUE-VAN) or BayPorter Express (1-877-467-1800).

Parking

Oakland Airport parking is logically organized by letter with Lot H accommodating hourly parking, Lot D housing daily parkers, and Lot E assigned for economy parking. All lots are $2 per 30 minutes for short-term parking; per day, Lot H is $32, Lot D is $22, and Lot E is $19. If you're picking someone up, the new Park & Call Zone offers 30 minutes free parking for those who connect with their passengers via cell phone. For real-time parking availability, call 510-633-2571

Rental Cars

- **Avis** • 510-577-6360 or 800-331-1212
- **Budget** • 800-527-0700
- **Dollar** • 866-434-2226 or 800-800-4000
- **Enterprise** • 510-567-1760 or 800-261-7331
- **Fox** • 800-225-4369
- **Hertz** • 510-639-0200 or 800-654-3131
- **National** • 510-632-2225 or 800-227-7368
- **Thrifty** • 877-283-0898 or 800-847-4389

Hotels

- **Best Western** • 170 Hegenberger Loop • 510-633-0500
- **Clarion Hotel** • 500 Hegenberger Rd • 510-562-5311
- **Comfort Inn and Suites** • 8452 Edes Ave • 510-568-1500
- **Courtyard by Marriott** • 350 Hegenberger Rd • 510-568-7600
- **Days Inn** • 8350 Edes Ave • 510-568-1880
- **Holiday Inn Express** • 66 Airport Access Rd • 510-569-4400
- **Hilton** • One Hegenberger Rd • 510-635-5000
- **La Quinta Inn** • 8465 Enterprise Wy • 510-632-8900

Terminal A

American/American Eagle
Continental
Hawaiian Airlines
JetBlue
United
US Airways
Volaris

Terminal B

Alaska Airlines
Delta Air Lines
Horizon Air
Southwest

General Information

General Airport Info:	408-277-4759
Airport Website:	www.flysanjose.com

Overview

Located two miles north of downtown San Jose, SJC is a completely self-supporting enterprise, owned and operated by the City of San Jose. Like Oakland Airport, with low-cost airlines like JetBlue and Southwest, SJC can sometimes offer more affordable flights than SFO (if you don't mind driving a while to get there). They're working on making SJC more accessible by adding freeway routes and new interchanges. It might be a tad messy right now, but it'll get better.

How to Get There—Driving

"Do You Know the Way to San Jose?" croons Dionne, but you might not be singing along if you're stuck in the morning commute to Northern California's biggest 'burb. Silicon Valley traffic can turn the trip from San Francisco into a two-hour plus affair, so if you have to drive to or from the city, particularly during rush hours, plan for the worst.

From San Francisco, begin on I-80 W, which eventually becomes US 101 S. Stay on US 101 S and take the Highway 87 exit on the right. Take the Skyport Drive exit to the airport. If you're coming down I-880, take the Brokaw Road exit. Drive along O'Toole Avenue and make a right on East Brokaw Road, which becomes Airport Parkway.

How to Get There—Mass Transit

There are a few public transportation options that will take you close to the airport, and then you'll need to take a bus or a shuttle to the terminals. Caltrain riders should get off at Santa Clara and take the VTA Airport Flyer (Route 10) to the airport. The Route 10 bus also makes a stop at the VTA Metro Light Rail Station. From there, it's a convoluted route to get to the BART. Other options: take the light rail to the Civic Center stop and board the VTA 180 Express Bus, which will take you right to the Freemont BART stop. If you're traveling from further afield, Greyhound and Amtrak both stop roughly three miles from the airport and then you can grab a cab.

Parking

There are only two options for parking at San Jose Airport—short-term or long-term parking. If you're going to Terminal A or International Arrivals, head to the short-term parking garage, and if Terminal C is your destination, try the short term parking lot across the roadway from the terminal. Short-term parking costs $1 per 20 minutes, with a maximum daily fee of $30. For longer stays, park in the long-term lot on Martin Avenue, which costs $15 per day. A free shuttle is provided to and from the terminals. Call 408-277-4759 for current parking availability.

Cabs

Yellow Cab (408-293-1234) departs from Terminal A and United Cab (408-971-1111) from Terminal C. Cab fare to San Francisco Airport will set you back $82, while a longer trip to downtown SF will cost you between $110 and $120.

Rental Cars

- **Alamo** • 408-327-9633
- **Avis** • 800-831-2847
- **Budget** • 800-527-0700
- **Dollar** • 800-800-4000
- **Enterprise** • 800-736-8222
- **Fox** • 800-225-4369
- **Hertz** • 800-654-3131
- **National** • 800-227-7368
- **Payless** • 800-729-5377
- **Thrifty** • 800-367-2277

Hotels

- **Adlon Hotel** • 1275 N Fourth St • 408-282-1000
- **Best Western Inn Airport South** • 2118 The Alameda• 408-243-2400
- **Courtyard by Marriott at the San Jose Airport** • 1727 Technology Dr • 408-441-6111
- **Crowne Plaza San Jose** • 282 Almaden Blvd • 408-998-0400
- **Hilton San Jose & Towers** • 300 Almaden Blvd • 408-287-2100
- **Holiday Inn Express Airport** • 1350 N Fourth St • 408-467-1789
- **Homestead Village Guest Studios** • 1560 N First St • 408-573-0648
- **Hotel De Anza** • 233 W Santa Clara St• 408-286-1000
- **Hyatt Saint Claire** • 302 S Market St • 408-295-2000
- **Radisson Plaza Hotel** • 1471 N Fourth St • 408-452-0200
- **Travelodge—San Jose Convention Center** • 1415 Monterey Hwy • 408-993-1711
- **Travelodge—San Jose Sports Arena** • 1041 The Alameda • 408-295-0159

Overview

Parking in San Francisco is a notoriously tricky game. Imagine you could get a half hour of your day back instead of circling the neighborhood for parking. Imagine you could get an extra $100 – 200 a month in spending money instead of giving it to the Department of Parking & Transportation. Imagine you didn't have to be outraged by the escalating gas prices. All that is more than a dream with car sharing. Use one when you need one, return it when you're done, and never worry about the inevitable costs and hassles that come with owning a car. It's like renting a car, but by the hour, and without trekking to the airport for cheap rates. Reserve your car online and pick it up in the designated lot in your 'hood where the cars live. It's great when you need that couch picked up from Ikea, or help a friend move, or go on a hike in Marin. For trips longer than two days, car-sharing is not as cost-efficient as renting a car the traditional way.

Car sharing's big two are **Zipcar** and **CityCar Share**. Both are constantly offering special deals, perks, and even social events as they expand their services. If you like new cars, these fleets change often and you can pick from a variety of economical models, with an emphasis on the hybrid. They are all better alternatives to having a car in the city, unless you have a really cool car and/or a good parking situation. Gas, insurance, and maintenance are always included in all of these company's fees, so you don't have to worry about the ever-increasing price of gas. But remember these are not your cars (and many people are sharing them), so pay attention to and respect the rules, otherwise you'll have to pay later (monetarily that is).

CityCar Share is a local company (founded in 2001 by transportation activists) and the most established operation with cars all over the Bay Area. Monthly membership fees are $45/month, and membership has its definite advantages.

Website: www.citycarshare.org
Phone: 415-995-8588 or 510-352-0323
Fees: Membership: $45/month.
One-time security deposit: $300.
Driving: $6.50/hour + 44¢/mile.

Zipcar is a national company trying to woo consumers with an $9.25 hourly, $0 per mile fee, as long as the mileage is "within reason." Zipcar offers two different plans, so be sure to do your research and assess your car needs before choosing one.

Website: www.zipcar.com
Phone: 415-495-7478
Address: 191 2nd Street
San Francisco, CA 94105
Fees: Occasional Driver: $50/yr and drive from $9.25/hr and $69/day weekdays, $9.75/hr and $74/day weekends.
Extra Value Plan: $50/month and drive from $8.33/hr and $62.10/day weekdays, $8.78/hr and $66.60/day weekends.
All Fees: 125 "free" miles per day (and then 20¢ for each extra mile). One-time application fee: $25

Taxis

OK, we're not Manhattan. It's not always easy to just walk outside and grab a cab, but taxis are still the most convenient way to get around the city if you're going out drinking, or if you're heading over to North Beach or Russian Hill, where it's notoriously difficult to park and walk. For some terrible reason, it seems to cost at least $10 to go anywhere in the city and usually more.

Cabs are a pricey way to get to the airport now that BART goes directly to the SFO and Oakland Airports. But if you've got lots of bags and don't want to park or take a shuttle, splurging on a cab is the way to go.

While there are a few spots around the city where you can reasonably expect to walk outside and hail a cab (16th and Valencia, Union Street, North Beach on a weekend), for the most part you're better off calling a cab company and having them pick you up. Here are a few numbers:

Alliance	415-285-3800
American	415-614-2000
Arrow	415-648-3181
Executive	415-401-8900
Luxor	415-282-4141
National	415-648-1313
Regents	415-487-1004
Town	415-401-8900
United	415-648-4444
Yellow	415-282-3737

Fares

San Francisco Taxicab Rates of Fare (Section 1135 San Francisco Municipal Police Code):

First 1/5th mile or flag	$3.10
Each additional 1/5th mile or fraction thereof	45¢
Each minute of waiting, or traffic time delay	45¢
Airport Exit Surcharge	$2.00

For out-of-town trips exceeding 15 miles beyond city limits, the fare will be 150% of the metered rate. For trips exceeding 15 miles from San Francisco International Airport and not terminating within the city limits of San Francisco, the fare will cost 150% of the metered rate except for those trips from San Francisco International Airport traversing San Francisco going to Marin County or to the East Bay—the 15-mile limit will apply from the city limits of San Francisco as set forth above.

If traditional car rental is more your style, or you need a rental for a longer period of time, try one of the many old-fashioned car rental places in San Francisco.

Map 3 • Russian Hill / Fisherman's Wharf

Avis	500 Beach St	415-441-4186
Budget	495 Bay St	415-292-3683
Electronic Time Car Rental	2800 Leavenworth St	415-674-8800
Hertz	500 Beach St	415-674-8330

Map 4 • North Beach / Telegraph Hill

Dollar	2500 Mason St	866-434-2226
Enterprise	350 Beach St	415-474-9600

Map 6 • Pacific Heights / Japantown

City Rent A Car	1500 Van Ness Ave	415-929-9025
Enterprise	1133 Van Ness Ave	415-441-3369
Hertz	1644 Pine St	415-923-1119

Map 7 • Nob Hill / Tenderloin

A-One Rent-A-Car	434 O'Farrell St	800-238-2663
Alamo	320 O'Farrell St	415-292-5353
Alamo	750 Bush St	415-693-0191
Avis	675 Post St	415-929-2555
Budget	321 Mason St	415-292-8981
Discount Rentals	349 Mason St	415-922-1994
Dollar	364 O'Farrell St	866-434-2226
Enterprise	222 Mason St	415-837-1700
Enterprise	819 Ellis St	415-441-2100
Hertz	335 Powell St	415-362-2780
Hertz	433 Mason St	415-771-2200
Hertz	500 Post St	415-771-8600
Hertz	55 4th St	415-957-9425
Hertz	55 Cyril Magnin St	415-392-8000
Hertz	950 Mason St	415-398-3944
National	320 O'Farrell St	415-292-5300
National	750 Bush St	415-693-0191
Reliable Rent-A-Car	349 Mason St	415-928-4414
Thrifty	350 O'Farrell St	415-788-8111

Map 8 • Financial District / SOMA

Alamo	687 Folsom St	415-882-9440
Budget	5 Embarcadero Ctr	415-433-3717
Enterprise	727 Folsom St	415-546-6777
Hertz	101 The Embarcadero	415-546-4480
National	687 Folsom St	415-882-9440

Map 10 • Castro / Lower Haight

Enterprise	2001 Market St	415-503-4131
Ford Rent-A-Car	2001 Market St	415-503-4131

Map 11 • Hayes Valley / The Mission

Alamo	150 Valencia St	415-701-7400
Enterprise	1480 Folsom St	415-487-2700
Enterprise	1600 Mission St	415-522-5900
Hertz	241 10th St	415-703-0205
National	150 Valencia St	415-701-1600
Specialty Car Rentals	150 Valencia St	415-701-1900

Map 12 • SOMA / Potrero Hill (North)

Avis	821 Howard St	415-957-9998
Enterprise	312 8th St	415-703-9000

Map 17 • Potrero Hill / Dogpatch

Rent-A-Wreck	2955 3rd St	415-282-6293

Map 21 • Inner Richmond

Enterprise	4250 Geary Blvd	415-750-2500
Hertz	3928 Geary Blvd	415-387-0136
Toyota	3800 Geary Blvd	415-750-8300

Map 27 • Parkside (Inner)

Enterprise	Winston Dr/ Stonestown Mall	415-337-9000
Enterprise	498 Winston Dr	415-242-5620

Map 33 • Ingleside

Enterprise	4050 19th Ave	415-406-1164

Map 36 • Bayview / Silver Terrace

Enterprise	445 Charter Oak Ave	415-330-0270

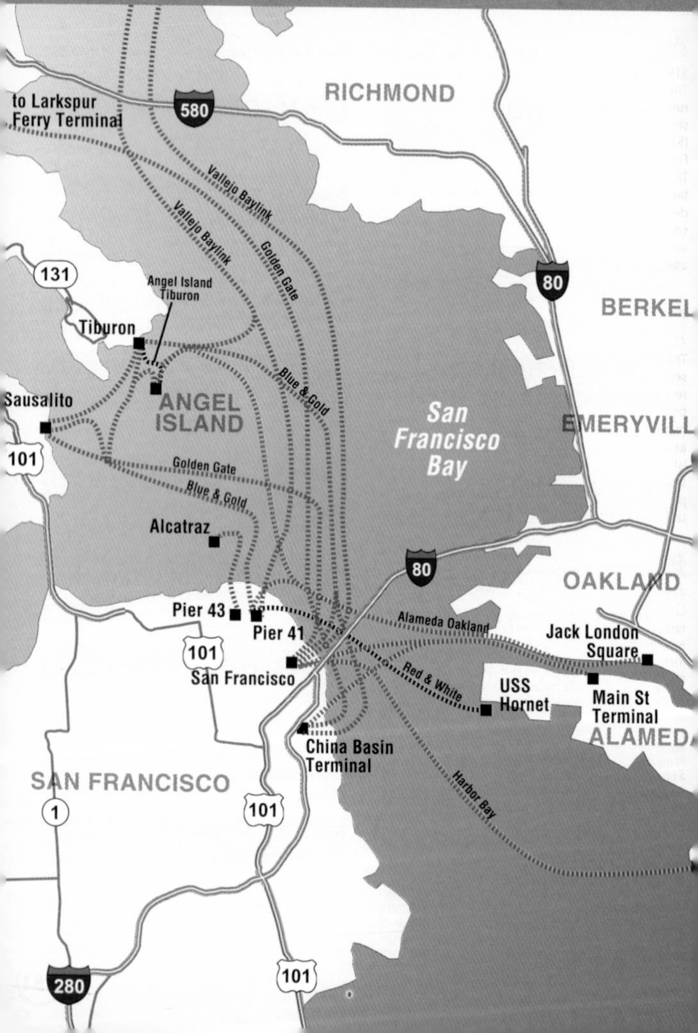

Transit • San Francisco Ferries

RICHMOND
to Larkspur Ferry Terminal
580
Vallejo Baylink
Vallejo Baylink
Golden Gate
131
Angel Island Tiburon
Tiburon
80
BERKEL
Blue & Gold
Sausalito
ANGEL ISLAND
San Francisco Bay
EMERYVILL
101
Golden Gate
Blue & Gold
Alcatraz
80
OAKLAND
Pier 43
Pier 41
Alameda Oakland
Jack London Square
101
San Francisco
Red & White
USS Hornet
Main St Terminal
ALAMEDA
China Basin Terminal
SAN FRANCISCO
Harbor Bay
1
101
101
280

Alameda/Oakland Ferry

510-749-5972 • www.eastbayferry.com

The Alameda/Oakland Ferry provides commuter routes from the East Bay to the city, as well as direct service from Pier 41 to AT&T Park for Giants games ($2.75–$5.50 one way). You can also take it from San Francisco direct to Jack London Square in Oakland. Tickets may be purchased on board and one-way fares vary from $1.25 to $5.50, depending on your destination. The Alameda/Oakland Ferry provides service to Angel Island on weekends during the summer ($8–$13.50 round trip, including park admission).

Angel Island-Tiburon Ferry

415-435-2131 • www.angelislandferry.com

This family-owned ferry offers an array of services, including sunset cruises (reservations recommended), whale watch cruises, and trips between Angel Island and Tiburon. These vessels may also be chartered for special occasions, such as weddings or birthday parties. Tickets from Angel Island to Tiburon cost $13.50 round trip for adults and $11.50 round trip for children 6–12 (includes park admission). Cash and checks only. The trip takes about ten minutes each way.

Blue & Gold Fleet

415-705-5555 • www.blueandgoldfleet.com

Located at Pier 41, Blue & Gold provides narrated historical tours of the Bay that last approximately one hour ($21), trips to Angel Island ($14.50 round trip, including park admission), ferry and bus shuttle to Six Flags Marine World ($60; includes park admission), and trips to Tiburon ($17 round trip).

Golden Gate Ferry

511, or 415-455-2000 • www.goldengate.org

Golden Gate Ferry serves Larkspur and Sausalito. The fare is $7.10 each way. Buy a frequent rider ticket book and ticket prices drop to $3.80 to Sausalito and $4.45 to Larkspur. The Larkspur ferry also goes to AT&T Park for Giants games ($7 one way). Great views of San Quentin too, if you're into prisons, that is.

Alameda Harbor Bay Ferry

510-769-5172 • www.alamedaharborbayferry.com

Alameda Harbor Bay Ferries provide convenient commuter service between San Francisco and Alameda. The fare is $6 one way, but commuter rates and monthly passes are available at discounted rates. The monthly pass ($165) includes free AC Transit and Muni transfers. Harbor Bay Ferry also offers a river cruise up the Sacramento Delta on weekends with lunch and no-host bar. All services leave from San Francisco's Ferry Plaza.

Red & White Fleet

415-673-2900 • www.redandwhite.com

This service offers tours of San Francisco Bay narrated in eight different languages. Tickets cost $21 but are usually offered at discounted prices if you buy them on the web. Ferries depart from Pier 43 1/2.

Vallejo Baylink Ferry

707-643-3779 • www.baylinkferry.com

Makes stops at Vallejo, Fisherman's Wharf (Pier 41), and the San Francisco Ferry Building. The fare is $12.50 each way for adults and $6.25 each way for students and seniors. Monthly passes are available for $270, which includes Baylink ferries and Vallejo Transit buses. A ten-ride punch ticket can be purchased for $78.

Fomalhaut Ferry

www.pkdpsychedelia.org

Currently, this one-way ferry to Fomalhaut is under major renovation, due to serious problems with the interstellar matter converters and the rear-window defroster. Both the Interstellar Rapid Transit Organization (IRTO) and Zetadyne, Inc. have promised to have it back in action within the next five parsecs.

SONOMA
Petaluma River
Black Point Rd
Sears Point Rd
Marine World Pkwy
SOLANO
Redwood Hwy
Novato
Vallejo
US Naval Res
Suisun Bay
MARIN
Carquinez Bridge
5
Benicia
Benicia-Martinez Bridge
6
Carquinez Strait
Martinez
San Pablo Bay
China Camp State Park
Hercules
John Muir Pkwy
San Rafael
San Pablo
Richmond
Concord
Richmond-San Rafael Bridge
4
San Pablo Reservoir
Briones Reservoir
Wildcat Canyon Park
Corte Madera
Redwood Hwy
Pleasant Hill
Shoreline Hwy
Walnut Creek
Tiburon
Albany
Berkeley
Mount Diablo State Park
Angel Island State Park
Golden Gate Nat'l Rec Area
Sausalito
Golden Gate Bridge
7
San Francisco
Oakland Bay Bridge
3
MacArthur Pkwy
Warren Fwy
Lake Merritt
Oakland
Danville
CONTRA COSTA
San Leandro Reservoir
Great Hwy
Sloat Blvd
Lake Merced
Alameda
Oakland Int'l Airport
Hegenberger
Mac Arthur Fwy
3rd St
Daly City
Lake Chabot
Dublin
South San Francisco
Pacifica
El Camino Real
Foothill Blvd
San Francisco Bay
San Francisco Int'l Airport
Skyline Blvd
Nimitz Fwy
ALAMEDA
Cabrillo Hwy
Bayshore Fwy
San Mateo Bridge
2
Hayward
San Andreas Lake
Junipero Serra Fwy
Union City
Niles Canyon
San Mateo
Foster City
Coyote Hills Park
Half Moon Bay Airport
Crystal Springs Reservoir
Fremont
Dumbarton Bridge
1
San Carlos Airport
El Camino Real
Newark
Half Moon Bay
Bayshore Fwy
Nimitz Fwy
Redwood City
Palo Alto Airport
Half Moon Bay
Oregon Expy
Palo Alto
Pacific Ocean
San Mateo
Cabrillo Hwy
El Camino Real
Alviso Fwy
Central Expy
Montague Expy

Bridges, in all their glory, are icons of San Francisco's romantic allure. The Golden Gate, the state's namesake and postcard darling, features in films from classics like *Vertigo* to sci-fi flicks like *The Core* (where it falls apart—let's not think about that one). In *So I Married an Axe Murderer*, sitting on the Bay Bridge in traffic after eating bran muffins was deemed worse than being electrocuted, and Dustin Hoffman drove across it to Berkeley (the wrong way on the upper deck!) in *The Graduate*. But don't let these star traffic conduits eclipse their lesser-known but no less hardworking counterparts: most of the seven bridges have claims to fame. The Dumbarton Bridge was the first vehicular crossing of the San Francisco Bay. The original San Mateo Bridge was the longest in the world when it was completed in 1929. Carquinez's new span is dedicated to Al Zampa, a construction worker who was instrumental in the building of four of the Bay Area bridges (and who was one of the first to have survived a fall off the Golden Gate).

The Golden Gate Bridge is California's only bridge that is not under state jurisdiction of Caltrans. It is left up to the folks at Golden Gate Bridge Highway and Transportation District to make sure the bridge's distinctive orange vermilion always sparkles. After the original coat of paint succumbed to corrosion and was replaced in 1965 by inorganic primer and acrylic topcoat, only touchups are needed once in a while. It's the most expensive bridge to cross—$6 cash or $5 if you use FasTrak. Aesthetics don't come cheap.

As Bay Area traffic balloons and overwhelms bridges built during the model T generation, most of the structures are going through rehab to incorporate the latest in steel and concrete bridge technology. The Carquinez Bridge welcomed the new westbound span in 2003, including a 12-foot-wide bike and pedestrian path (the old 1927 span will be demolished). The Benicia-Martinez Bridge is in the process of acquiring new 5-lane northbound digs by 2007, building just east of the existing one (the old structure will be converted to a 4-lane southbound span and incorporate a bike lane). The cantilever span between Oakland and Yerba Buena Island on the Bay Bridge is still under heavy construction, and will reincarnate as a suspension bridge in a few years.

FasTrack

www.bayareafastrak.org

If you own a car and drive at all, even if you only occasionally cross bridges (lets face it you'll have to eventually) it is worth getting a FastTrak. The device is free and automatically deducts from the account of your choosing as you zip past the other suckers stuck in the toll plaza traffic. Users of FasTrak also get a 15¢ discount at all other toll bridges.

		Toll	# of lanes	Bike Path?	# of vehicles/day (in thousands)	Cost in millions – original	Engineer	Length	Original Structure Completion Date
1	Dumbarton Bridge	$4	6	Yes	61	$2.5		1.6 mi	Jan 1927
2	San Mateo - Hayward Bridge	$4	6	Yes[1]	81	$70		7.0 mi	Oct 1967
3	SF - Oakland Bay Bridge	$4	10	Yes[2]	270	$77	Charles C. Purcell	8.4 mi	Nov 1936
4	Richmond - San Rafael Bridge	$4	4	No	59	$66	C. Derleth, Jr	5.5 mi	Sep 1956
5	Carquinez Bridge	$4	8	Yes	116	$4.6	Aven Hanford & Oscar Klatt	0.7 mi	May 1927
6	Benicia - Martinez Bridge	$4	6	No	94	$25		1.2 mi	Sep 1962
7	Golden Gate Bridge	$5	6	Yes	112	$35	Joseph Baermann Strauss	1.7 mi	May 1937

[1] Via AC Transit
[2] Bicycle Shuttle $1 each way
Check www.dot.ca.gov/dist4/shuttle.htm for bike shuttle schedules.

Web Resources

Bay Area Toll Authority: http://bata.mtc.ca.gov/bridges/
Department of Transportation (DOT): www.dot.ca.gov
Golden Gate Bridge: www.goldengatebridge.org

City of San Francisco Dept of Parking & Traffic

Address:	11 South Van Ness Ave San Francisco, CA 94103
Phone:	415-554-7275 (recorded info) 415-554-9805 (administration office)
Website:	www.sfgov.org www.sfbaytraffic.info www.sfgate.com/traffic

California Dept of Transportation (Caltrans)

Traffic Hotline:	800-427-7623
Outside CA:	916-654-5266
Website:	www.dot.ca.gov

Golden Gate Bridge

Phone:	415-921-5858

Bay Bridge Traffic:	www.dot.ca.gov/hq/roadinfo
Bay Area Traffic:	www.traffic.511.org

Radio Traffic Info:

KGO 810 AM
KQED 88.5 FM
KALW 91.7 FM

Orientation

San Francisco sits isolated on a peninsula, physically and ideologically separated from the rest of the country. It is a great city to walk, bike and bus in—that means driving can end up being a hectic conglomeration of bold pedestrians, honking commuters, and Critical Mass bikers.

Aside from the relatively orderly layout of the avenues out in the Sunset and the Richmond, the 46 square miles of streets, lanes, alleys, and winding roads that are crammed onto the tip of the San Francisco Peninsula make it look like Jackson Pollock was on the job when they were laying out the grid. Navigating a city seven by seven miles ought to be relatively easy, but there are too many pedestrians, cars, and hills to make driving here pleasant; rush hours (7 am to 10:30 am and 3:30 pm to 7 pm) can cause some gray hair (if you didn't know your usual lane is closed or left turns are illegal). And if there's a parade or construction going on—which happens frequently—forget about crossing Downtown, the Castro, the Mission, or any other central area for big gatherings. Icon signs and color-coded plaques mark famous tourist areas (map of Italy points to North Beach, a crab shows way to Fisherman's Wharf, and a pagoda is symbol for Chinatown).

Driving on the hills of San Francisco is a skill which takes years to master. If you drive a stick, be prepared for stop signs at the crest of very steep hills—the City will be the ultimate test of your mettle. Some intersections are so fierce you'll be airborne before you actually see the cross-street (Gough and Turk, middle lane, is a good one). And be mindful of the cable car and street car lines that run all over the City—there's plenty of pedestrian traffic as passengers board and disembark. And as long as you're staying polite, watch out for the bikers, if you cut them off don't be surprised when you hear an angry tirade of insults and a knock on the side of your car. (Conversely, if you are a biker, this increases your intimidation factor.) There are some designated bike lanes, but often they will be sharing lanes with you and your car. Remember, it's California law to share the road.

Bridges

The Golden Gate Bridge, which connects the city to Marin County in the north, and the Bay Bridge, which runs through Treasure Island and the into Oakland/Berkeley in the east, can be either smooth sailing or a grid-locked mess. With the ongoing Bay Bridge construction and new configuration of exits on the San Francisco side, there is almost always traffic, but on the off-chance that there's not, kick back and enjoy the views. On weekends, particularly if the weather is good, the Golden Gate is usually packed with residents fleeing the city for Marin. The Bay Bridge tends to back up most during weekday rush hours and Friday and Saturday nights. Check local traffic reports on www.511.org for up-to-the-minute bridge traffic updates.

Major Freeways

Hwy 101: Runs north to south from the Oregon border to Los Angeles.

I-280: Runs parallel and just to the west of Highway 101. This route tends to be less crowded than the 101, and the scenery is a bit easier on the eyes. On the south end, it becomes I-680 in San Jose as it wraps around the east side of the bay.

Hwy 1: Like a wayward lover, this pretty bit of road merges briefly with Highway 101 as they cross the Golden Gate Bridge together, then ambles off on its own again. Hwy 1's scenic, winding route is one of the prettiest in the nation—but don't drive it if you're in a hurry. Parts of the picturesque Pacific Coast Highway (PCH as they call it in LA) are treacherous, twisty and overlook some of the most iconic cliffs of the California the coast. The road is most often characterized by two snaking lanes, impressive vistas and double arched bridges.

I-80: Runs north-south through Berkeley and connects the East Bay with San Francisco via the Bay Bridge. Continues east to Sacramento and is a major thoroughfare to destinations in the Sierras.

I-580: Connects the East Bay with I-5 and I-80, which runs through the Central Valley and provides the fastest route south to Los Angeles. Be warned: the 390-mile, six-to-seven-hour drive isn't scenic (until you reach the grapevine which takes you into Los Angeles county), but it's the quickest and most direct way down. And you can always stop at Harris Ranch for a mid-trip burger (that is if the cow smell isn't too much to handle).

Major Construction Projects & Alternate Routes: The new six-lane Octavia Boulevard was completed in early 2006 and has been a blessing to anyone living west of Van Ness, providing a quick route off Oak and onto Fell. The new exit replaces the Fell Street off-ramp which closed some years back and forced Mission Street to function as the last Central Freeway exit. The area around the western end of the Bay Bridge is undergoing major exit reconfiguration, so watch out for signs or else you might easily be swept away onto the wrong off-ramp.

Drivers wishing to avoid Central Freeway congestion can use alternate surface street routes, or I-280. If you're coming into the city from the Bay Bridge (I-80), use the Harrison Street, Fremont Street, Fifth Street, or Ninth Street exits. Do not get off too early during rush hour or you'll hit downtown traffic, not to mention the one-way obstacles surrounding Market Street. If you're coming into the city from the Peninsula or the South Bay on Highway 101 and see a nasty-looking back-up, get off at Cesar Chavez or Vermont Street in Potrero Hill. Otherwise use the Ninth Street exit on US 101, or the Seventh Street exit on I-80 as alternatives to Mission Street. You can also take the I-280 and exit at Sixth Street to reach downtown San Francisco, the Richmond district, or the Western Addition.

Parking Stickers & Permits

If you live in an established Residential Permit Parking (RPP) area (identified by a sign displayed on your block), then you need a parking permit. The only catch is that even some metered streets are RPPs, and there aren't always signs posted. Your only real hope is to call one of the phone numbers listed below. If you reside in the area, you can get an application for a permit by calling 415-503-2020, by downloading it from www.sfgov.org, or by visiting the 1380 Howard Street office. (Unless you're in the business of wasting time, this should always be your last resort.)

Department of Parking & Traffic
Residential Parking Permit Office (RPP)
Address: 11 South Van Ness Ave
San Francisco, CA 94103
Phone: 415-503-2020 or 415-554-5000
(recorded info)

Enforcement Division
Address: 505 Seventh St
San Francisco, CA 94103
Phone: 415-553-1631

Traffic Engineering Division
Address: 25 Van Ness Ave, Ste 345
San Francisco, CA 94102
Phone: 415-554-2339

Tickets, Towing, and Other Bad Things

If your life suddenly turns into *Dude, Where's My Car?*, chances are you've been towed. Here are some phone numbers (and options) you need to know about:

Department of Parking & Traffic
Tow Line: 415-553-1235
(basic information)
Tow Desk: 415-553-1239 or 553-1240
(if you're not sure your car has been towed)
SF Police: 415-553-0123
(to report a stolen vehicle)
To protest a towing: 415-255-3967
(Hearing Division)
If the SFPD towed your car: 415-553-1619
If your car is booted: 415-553-1634
(Boot-removal fee is $75)

Getting Your Car Back
City Tow (Towing yard): 415-865-8200
Location of yard: 415 Seventh St, at Harrison
City Tow offices: 11 S Van Ness Ave
SFPD Towing: 850 Bryant St, Rm 154

For Parking Citations and Hearings
Address: 11 South Van Ness Ave
San Francisco, CA 94103
Phone: 415-255-3900 (citations/permits)
415-255-3964 (hearings)
415-255-3999 or 800-531-7357
(citation telephone payment)
Hours: Mon–Fri 8 am–5 pm

Parking Meters

Meters usually operate Monday–Saturday, 9 am–6 pm, but in some areas the hours start as early as 7 am and run to as late as 9 pm (just be sure you check your meter). On Port property (Including Fisherman's Wharf), meters also operate on Sundays and holidays. Remember that parking time limits are still enforced even if a meter is broken.

Hourly Rates for Selected Areas:
Downtown: $3.50 hourly/70¢ for motorcycles
Downtown Periphery: $3.00 hourly/60¢ motorcycles
Fisherman's Wharf: $3.00 hourly/60¢ motorcycles
All other areas: $3.00 hourly/60¢ motorcycles

Curb Colors

A handy guide to the curb palette:

Green: Limited time parking—ten minutes 9 am–6 pm, Mon–Sat.
Yellow: Commercial loading and unloading; vehicles with commercial plates may park up to 30 minutes from 9 am–6 pm Mon–Sat. Some yellow zones are restricted to trucks with commercial plates only. Violators will be towed. Usually accompanied by a sign; check for hours of enforcement.
Blue: Parking for vehicles with special disabled person plates or placards only. Always enforced; violators will be fined $275.
Red: No parking at any time. Vehicles in bus stops will be towed and subject to $250 additional fine.
White: Passenger loading zone (usually in front of churches, restaurants, hotels, etc.). Vehicles may not be left unattended for any length of time during enforcement hours; attended vehicles may stand for up to five minutes. Hours of enforcement may be painted on the curb or posted on a sign. If not, check to see if the business in front of the white zone appears to be in operation.
Brown: A dog just pooped here, so watch out when getting out of your car.

Street Cleaning

San Francisco streets are swept on a rotating weekly schedule between the hours of 6 am and 3 pm. Unless a posted sign says "Every day including holidays," the following holidays are exempt from street cleaning:

- New Years Day
- Martin Luther King Jr's Birthday
- Presidents' Day
- Memorial Day
- Independence Day
- Labor Day
- Columbus Day
- Veterans' Day
- Thanksgiving and Day after Thanksgiving
- Christmas Day

Transbay Terminal

Address: 425 Mission St
San Francisco, CA 94105
Phone: 415-495-1569, or 415-495-1575

The massive Transbay Terminal redesign project now underway is at once a utopian vision and an urban planner's nightmare. It's slated to cost billions and will attempt to tackle major structural issues, such as running transit lines under an already-developed city. But the new six-story modern building will, supposedly, become a center for a green transit system streaming into downtown from all corners of the Bay Area and even from the Central Valley, electrifying trains and cutting many commutes times nearly in half. For now, all we can do is hold our breath: it's not going to be affecting our lives for the better any time soon.

AC Transit

Phone: 510-891-4777
510-891-4706 (Lost & Found)
Website: www.actransit.org

Carrying 230,000 riders daily to and from 15 communities, the Alameda-Contra Costa Transit District runs a fleet of 700 buses. Most of the vehicles can accommodate two bikes on a front-mounted rack, and all are wheelchair-accessible. AC Transit operates more than 70 local East Bay routes, as well as almost 30 transbay lines, which offer a convenient ground alternative to commuting into the city by BART. From East Bay destinations to the Transbay Terminal, the fare is $3.50 with a free transfer. Within the East Bay, you'll want to save your quarters to pay $2.00 (and 25¢ for a transfer good for 1.5 hours). Frequent riders can buy a monthly pass for $80 and then swipe on board (the pass costs just $15 for riders under 17). NextBus Internet and satellite tracking technology is supposedly on the way, so you'll know when the next bus will arrive. For routes and schedules, AC Transit website and TripPlanner (www.transitinfo.org) are both very useful. Fun places to go on AC Transit from SF: the 19th-century estate Ardenwood Historic Farm in Fremont, where you can learn about the horse-to-mechanic power agricultural transition, or a planetarium show at the Lawrence Hall of Science in Berkeley.

Golden Gate Transit

Phone: 415-455-2000;
415-257-4476 (Lost & Found, buses)
415-925-5565 (Lost & Found, ferries)
Website: www.goldengate.org

Golden Gate Transit serves the North Bay passage from San Francisco into Marin and Sonoma counties by land (bus) and water (ferries), and operates using ten fare zones. The cash-only fares range from $3.15 to $8.40, depending how many zones you cross in your commute. Commuters can purchase a ticket book for up to 20% discount (25% youth and 50% seniors discounts also exist). Transfers from bus to ferry are free, and you can even ride Muni for free with a transfer from a GGT ferry (but not from a GGT bus). Bikes are welcome on front-mounted racks, available on most buses. Special event and discount purchase locations can be found on the GGT website. Fun places to go on GGT from SF: Muir Woods on a free "route 66" shuttle departing Marin City on weekends between Memorial Day and Labor Day; Stinson Beach/Bolinas and Point Reyes via the West Marin Stagecoach departing Marin City; back to the North Bay by ferry after music and sports events at AT&T Park.

SamTrans

Phone: 800-660-4287
Website: www.samtrans.org

San Mateo County Transit District is mostly for travel within the county, but also serves destinations around Palo Alto and San Francisco, including a special service for wheelchairs. SamTrans fares range from $1.50 for local travel to $4 for express commuter service. Monthly passes for unlimited travel can be as expensive as $132.50. But, for traveling locally only, monthly passes cost $80. All SamTrans buses with front-mounted racks can carry two bikes, and can take on two more inside the bus (if it is not crowded). Special event and discount purchase locations can be found on the SamTrans website. Fun places to go on SamTrans from SF: back to the Peninsula from Bay2Breakers on a special "participant bus" that holds your stuff during the race; or to Año Nuevo State Reserve near Santa Cruz during seal mating season.

Greyhound

Phone: 415-495-1569
415-495-1555 (Baggage)
Website: www.greyhound.com

Never taken Greyhound? It's exactly what you've heard it to be: sporadically on time, habitually uncomfortable, and always an "interesting" ride. Seating is on a first-come, first-served basis, so if you don't hurry to get that window seat next to the little Southern lady with '50s-style hair, you might end up next to another colorful character or two. In comparison, you'll probably appreciate the old lady's perfume over other scents for the duration of your ride. Greyhound offers service between major cities and goes through little towns on the way. Nonetheless, most of us prefer other modes of transportation, and in 2004 Greyhound cut service to over 60 destinations across California, rural and suburban both, due to decreasing revenues.

A standard one-way fare from San Francisco to Los Angeles costs around $50, which is cheaper than flying on most days, but it is also about a ten-hour bumpy ride. The cheap fares also explain the clientele. If you think a cool beer will make the ride more bearable, so does everyone else. Though alcohol is not allowed on the bus, many patrons take care of the matter prior to boarding. A pillow and earplugs can become more precious than gold if you board a bus from San Francisco to Seattle, after paying the $82 fare by credit card online or at the station's ticket office (save more when you reserve seven days in advance): Greyhound will creep up the coast for one day and eight hours straight.

Still excited about traveling America's scenic highways and country by-ways by Greyhound? Head over to the Bay Area hub at the Transbay Terminal or find out about select buses that stop at the Ferry Building, Caltrain depot, and the Airport from the website. And don't forget the TP.

Greyhound also provides a Package Express service for commercial and personal shipping needs from the Transbay Terminal (so while your college textbook collection travels securely by bus to your parents' basement in Minnesota, you can enjoy the comfort of staying home in San Francisco).

Green Tortoise Adventure Travel

www.greentortoise.com

Green Tortoise Adventure Travel offers another option for long-distance bus travel for college kids and adults who don't mind an alternative experience. The company has been transporting folks to exciting destinations like Mardi Gras, Burning Man, and the Mayan trail in Mexico, among others, for many years, and having fun on the way. They also run hostels in San Francisco and Seattle, and are devoted to bringing together "beautiful places, great food, and sociable people" for a gratifying traveling experience.

San Pablo Bay
Benicia
Carquinez Strait
Hercules
John Muir Pkwy
San Rafael
RICHMOND
El Cerrito del Norte
El Cerrito Plaza
Wildcat Canyon Park
San Pablo Reservoir
Briones Reservoir
North Berkeley
Downtown Berkeley
Ashby
Rockridge
Orinda
Lafayette
Walnut Creek
Pleasant Hill
Concord
North Concord/Martinez
PITTSBURG/BAY POINT
Tiburon
Angel Island State Park
Sausalito
CONTRA COSTA
MACARTHUR (transfer station)
19th St/Oakland
OAKLAND CITY CENTER/12th ST (transfer station)
Oakland
Danville
Embarcadero
Montgomery St
San Francisco
West Oakland
Lake Merritt
Fruitvale
Powell St
Civic Center
16th St Misson
24th St Mission
Coliseum/ Oakland Airport
Glen Park
Balboa Park
DALY CITY
Colma
Oakland Int'l Airport
San Leandro
Castro Valley
BAY FAIR
South San Francisco
(Peak Only)
San Bruno
San Francisco Bay
San Francisco International Airport
(Peak Only)
MILLBRAE
Hayward
South Hayward
Union City
Skyline Blvd
Junipero Serra Fwy
Nimitz Fwy
San Mateo Bridge
San Mateo
Foster City
Coyote Hills Park
Dumbarton Bridge
San Carlos Airport
El Camino Real
Bayshore Fwy
Palo Alto Airport
FREMONT
TRANSFER STATION
Regular Station

General Information

Mailing Address: PO Box 12688
Oakland, CA 94604
Phone: 415-989-2278
Website: www.bart.gov
Hours: Mon–Fri: 4 am–midnight;
Sat: 6 am–midnight;
Sun: 8 am–midnight.

Overview

The Bay Area Rapid Transit system (BART) evolved in order to ease congestion on the Bay Bridge that followed the post-war influx of people and automobiles to the Bay Area. The proposed solution was an underwater tube devoted solely to high-speed electrical trains. After years of researching, planning, and gaining public approval, the Transbay Tube structure was completed in August 1969. Constructed in 57 sections and sitting as deep as 135 feet beneath the surface on the bay floor, the $180 million structure took six years to design and less than three years to construct. Today, the BART system provides efficient train transit between San Francisco and the East Bay cities and suburbs of Contra Costa and Alameda counties.

Tickets & Fares

BART fares are calculated based on distance traveled. You can determine the cost of your trip by using the BART Fare Calculator or one of the fare charts located at each station. The minimum is $1.75 and the maximum is $7.65. Children under four ride for free. All vending machines accept nickels, dimes, quarters, $1, $5, and $10 bills. If you place more money on the ticket than is needed for the ride, the ticket can be used for several trips. Discount tickets for seniors, children, students and persons with disabilities are sold online, through the mail, and at select retail vendors throughout the San Francisco Bay Area. Check online for vendor locations and discount rates. Participate in the re-chargeable ticket EZ Rider program, and never buy another BART ticket at the machines again!

To enter the BART system, insert your ticket into the fare gate. The ticket will be returned to you, and then the fare gate will open. Use the same ticket when you exit the station. The correct fare will automatically be deducted, and a ticket with any remaining value will be returned to you. Money can be added to your card using the Addfare machines.

Lost & Found

The Lost & Found office is located at the 12th Street City Center Station in Oakland near the 14th Street exit. Hours: Mon, Wed, Fri: noon–2 pm and 3 pm–6 pm. Call 510-464-7090 for more information.

Parking

Customers parking at Daly City, Colma, South San Francisco, San Bruno, and Millbrae Stations will be required to pay a daily ($1–$2) or monthly parking fee (between $30 and $84 dollars depending on the station). There is a 24-hour limit to all parking, but Daly City and all East Bay BART stations offer additional long-term parking.

Seniors & People with Disabilities

All BART stations have escalators and elevators. All trains have a sign located above some seats suggesting that passengers make those seats available to seniors and persons with disabilities. Specific C2 cars have flip-up seats, which are near each set of doors, to allow room for wheelchairs. All restrooms are designed to be wheelchair accessible.

Bicycles & Pets

Bikes abide by enforced rules on the trains: no bikes in packed commuter rush hour trains, no bikes in the the first car of any train, no bikes on moving escalators; no riding in the station. Otherwise, bikes can be taken on any train — and the newly updated BART schedule in all stations indicates which trains are off-limits. Also no gas-powered vehicles (mopeds, scooters) are permitted. If you chain your bike to a pole, fence, or railing in any BART station, it'll probably be removed while you're gone — use the bike parking cages inside the station.

Pets are only allowed if they are in carrying cases, but service animals (guide dogs, police dogs, magician's assistant, etc.) can always ride, especially if they can talk.

3rd Street Light Rail & BART Expansion

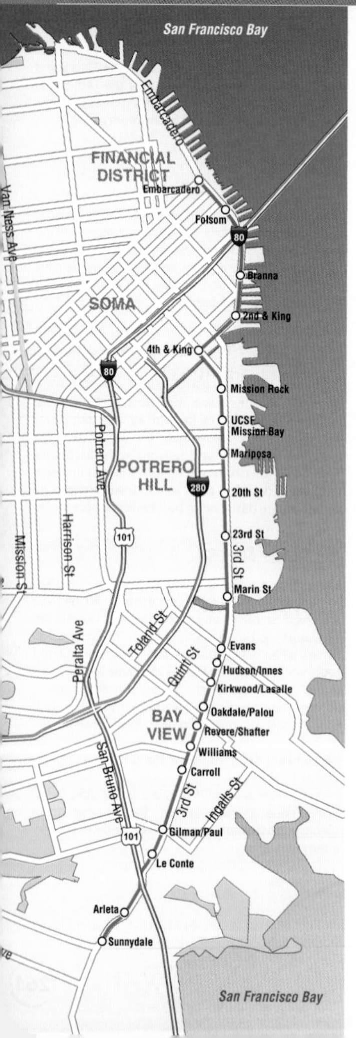

Third Street Light Rail

In 2006, a new, extensive line known as the Third Street Light Rail Project opened running south from the current Caltrain depot station along 3rd Street. It is a modern light rail line, like the Embarcadero extension, and runs all the way to the south border of the city. At its north end, the line passes through older industrial areas that have become more residential in the aftermath of the city's late-90s real estate boom; at its center, it runs through some of San Francisco's most economically depressed areas, and planners hope that it will improve the prospects of those neighborhoods. This extension is served by a new line, the T-Third. After initial mechanical complications and scheduling mishaps which often screamed "debacle" in newspaper headlines, Muni has supposedly brought the T-Third up to a serviceable level. It is still affectionately called the "T-Turd" by patrons, a colloquialism which needs no explanation.

Expansion

The recession has hit public transit hard. The glories of new downtown stations have be trumped by the realities of a huge budget shortfall. In classic Muni fashion, the result has effected service—there are fare hikes and undisclosed service cuts slated for late 2009, which will make buses run less frequently and eliminate some lines all together.

Federal funding has been secured for an ambitious new project dubbed the Central Subway. This line will head north and west from the Caltrain depot and quickly pass underground into a new subway tunnel. The line will pass under the current Metro tunnel, with a transfer station at Montgomery, then turn due north with stops at Union Square and Chinatown. Though the line would be relatively short, it would provide service to areas of downtown currently somewhat isolated from the Metro network, as well as a springboard for future expansion. Planners hope that the Central Subway will be completed by 2010.

Construction on a sixth light rail line from the Caltrain Depot to Visitacion Valley (and Bayview/Hunter's Point) is expected to be completed by December 2006. The new line will consist of new 19 street-level high platform stations, including at least one within walking distance of Monster Park. The line was supposed to connect the Bayshore Caltrain station with light rail, but Caltrain failed to notify Muni about a reconfiguration it did to the Bayshore station that would have resulted in a modification to the new light rail line. This will force the light rail line to have its current terminus at Sunnydale Avenue for a few years, but it's hoped that the new Muni line will connect to the Bayshore station in the near future.

A further underground expansion for this line is being planned. Four proposed new underground stations at Moscone Center, Market Street and Stockton Street, Union Square, and Chinatown are being studied for a possible target date of 2009. Two more underground stations at North Beach and Fisherman's Wharf may be built in a third phase.

Many activists have sharply criticized these long-term plans as catering to the needs of visitors at the expense of city residents, asserting that Muni's resources would be better spent on a seventh light rail line running along (or under) Geary Boulevard into the densely populated Richmond District. Well, something is better than nothing, folks—just ask the people in places like LA and Dallas.

The Owl

The Muni system operates 24 hours a day with the aid of its late-night Owl service. After the stations close, the Owl takes flight from 1 am to 5 am every thirty minutes on 10 lines throughout the city, replacing Muni streetcar service with a fleet of buses. It sounds like a good idea in theory, 24-hour bus service all over the city. But nightrider beware…waits between these buses are frequently well over what the hypothetical 30 minute schedule predicts. The buses run on lines 5, 14, 22, 24, 38, and 108 (Treasure Island and Yerba Buena Island), and duplicate service along the L and N lines as well. The 90 and 91 Owl lines are night-only; the 91-Owl is actually the longest route in the Muni system at 24.1 miles one-way, combining several other routes into one looping and winding trip through late-night SF's variegated display.

SAN FRANCISCO
4th & King
22nd St
Bayshore
South San Francisco
San Bruno
Millbrae
Broadway (Weekends only)
Burlingame
San Mateo
Hayward Park
Bay Meadows (race days only)
Hillsdale
Belmont
San Carlos
Redwood City
Atherton (weekends only)
Menlo Park
Palo Alto
California Ave
San Antonio
Mountain View
Sunnyvale
Lawrence
Santa Clara
College Park
San Jose Diridon
Tamien
Capitol

San Francisco Oakland Bay Toll Bridge
OAKLAND
Alameda
Oakland Int'l Airport
CONTRA COSTA
Danville
San Leandro Reservoir
Lake Chabot
San Francisco Bay
San Mateo Toll Bridge
San Mateo
Hayward
Foster City
Union City
ALAMEDA
Coyote Hills Park
Dumbarton Toll Bridge
Fremont
Newark
Half Moon Bay
Redwood City
Palo Alto
Stanford Univ
SAN MATEO
San Jose Int'l Airport
SAN JOSE
Cupertino
Saratoga

Warren Fwy
Mac Arthur Fwy
Hegenberger Rd
Foothill Blvd
Nimitz Fwy
El Camino Real
Junipero Serra Fwy
Bayshore Fwy
Cabrillo Hwy
Page Mill Rd
Alviso Fwy
Central Expy
Lawrence Expy
Foothill Expy

Zone 1
Zone 2
Zone 3
Zone 4
Zone 5

General Information

Mailing Address: 1250 San Carlos Ave
PO Box 3006
San Carlos, CA 94070-1306
Phone: 800-660-4287
Website: www.caltrain.com

Overview

Caltrain provides a fast, reliable alternative to one of the Bay Area's most stressful activities—driving. The system runs local and express trains between 31 stations along the peninsula from San Francisco to Gilroy, with connections to San Francisco and San Jose International Airports. Free shuttles are also available between several stations and surrounding office and residential areas—the Caltrain website provides links to detailed schedules and maps. Caltrain is also the best way to get to Giants games—the San Francisco station at Fourth & King is just one block from AT&T Park. Extra trains run before and after baseball games.

Schedules & Fares

Caltrain offers daily service between San Francisco and San Jose, with extended service to Gilroy during peak weekday commute hours. During these times, Caltrain runs only "Baby Bullet" express and limited-stop trains on a staggered schedule, with timed connections to all other stations. Baby Bullet trains travel from San Francisco to San Jose in one hour, limited-stop trains in just over an hour; specific stops for either line vary according to departure time. Local trains make all stops and operate during non-peak hours and on weekends.

Fares range from $2.25 to $11.00 depending on distance traveled, and must be paid before boarding. Conductors check for tickets frequently, so fare-jumping is never advisable. All stations have ticket vending machines, which take cash and major credit cards. Monthly, daily, and 10-ride passes are available.

Airport Connections

Connections are available from Caltrain to both San Francisco and San Jose International Airports. BART operates a shuttle train every 15 minutes between Caltrain's Millbrae station and SFO. Tickets for the shuttle cost $1.50 and must be purchased before boarding.

The SJC Airport Flyer (Rte 10) shuttles passengers between the Santa Clara Caltrain Station and San Jose International Airport. The Airport Flyer is free and operates daily between 5:30 am and midnight. Buses operate every ten minutes on weekdays and every fifteen minutes on weekends.

Parking

All-day parking (24-hour limit) is available at most Caltrain stations for $2.00. Stations south of San Jose Diridon offer free parking. Palo Alto, San Jose Diridon, and other select stations charge higher rates on some evenings. The Millbrae Station lot is reserved for customers with a monthly parking permit until 10 am. After 10 am, anyone can pay to park. Monthly parking permits may be purchased along with monthly train tickets from ticket vending machines, at staffed stations, or through the Ticket-By-Mail program (forms available online).

Lost & Found

The San Francisco and San Jose Diridon stations collect lost articles. To check for an item, call 415-546-4482 for San Francisco or 408-271-4980 for San Jose.

Seniors and People with Disabilities

Discounts on one-way tickets and monthly and 10-day passes are offered to seniors and the disabled. Most, but not all, Caltrain stations are wheelchair-accessible. Check the website for a list of accessible stations. All trains offer priority seating for seniors and people with disabilities, and parking fees at Caltrain stations are waived for vehicles displaying DMV-issued Disabled Person (DP) plates.

Bicycles

Bikes are allowed on all trains at all times, provided there is enough space. The regular trains can accommodate up to 32 bikes, and some are equipped to handle 64 bikes if a second bike car is added; Baby Bullet trains have limited space, and allow only 16 bikes on board per car. The bike car on each train is located at the northern-most end of the train (the end closest to San Francisco) and is clearly marked with a black and yellow bike sticker. Bike lockers are available at 27 Caltrain stations, and cost $33 per six-month rental term, plus a $25 refundable key deposit. Fridays, the 5:48pm train from Mountain View station is the Bike Party Car. Bring snacks and drinks to share! TGIF.

Transit • Muni Metro (Surface)

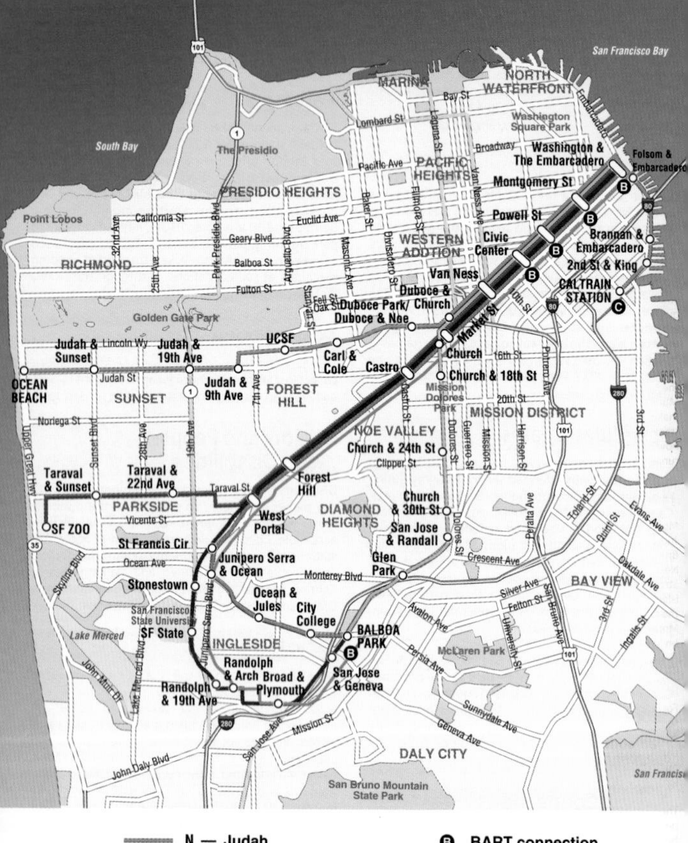

General Information

Website: www.sfmuni.com
Mailing Address: 949 Presidio Ave, #243
San Francisco, CA 94115
Phone: 415-554-6999 (recorded hotline)
415-673-6864 (voice operator)
Lost & Found: 415-923-6168

Overview

Muni mirrors the the city it serves. Unfortunately, "boisterous individualism" isn't necessarily a good thing when it comes to public transportation. However, steps have recently been made to get Muni running a little bit better. Digital scrolls at the major stops that tell you when the next train or bus will arrive make the ride more predictable. You can also time your morning walk by checking www.nextbus.com before you leave the house. This feature is still working the kinks out, but in general it is accurate within a few minutes before actual arrival. Would-be Muni riders who don't have this GPS technology at hand should know that it is not uncommon for buses to be 10–20 minutes late in off-peak hours. In peak hours, the system works. The five train lines (J,K,L,M,N) of the Muni Metro are more reliable than the numbered buses. Muni will always get you there eventually, but be wary when making plans that include this sometimes ornery player in the transportation scene. A new line of hybrid electric buses is now servicing Haight-Sunset part of the city: though diesel-run, they have fewer emissions and consume 19% less fuel.

Hours

Muni operates 24 hours on the following lines: L Taraval, N Judah, 5 Fulton, 14 Mission, 24 Divisadero, 38 Geary, 90 San Bruno Owl (a combination of routes 9 San Bruno and 47 Van Ness), 91 Owl (a combination of routes K Ingleside, 15 Third Street, 30 Stockton, and 28 19th Avenue), and 108 Treasure Island. All night "owl" services operate every 30 minutes, with the exception of route 108. All other Muni lines run 5 am–1 am Monday through Friday. On these lines, service begins at 6 am on Saturdays, and 8 am on Sundays.

Fares & Tickets

For buses, Metro, and historic streetcars, adults pay $2.00, seniors and youth pay 75¢, and children four and under ride free. Exact fare is always required, as drivers cannot provide change. Transfers are available and are generally good for 90 minutes from time of issue. Monthly passes are also available for $55 (ages 18–64) and $15 (everyone else).

There are three cable car lines still running. The two most popular are the Powell-Mason and the Powell-Hyde. They both start at Hallide Plaza (Powel and Market) and go to Mason and Hyde at the waterfront, respectively. The third line runs up California Street from Market to Van Ness. The fare is $5 each way. Transfers are not given or accepted on cable cars, so flash your fast pass for a free ride.

Speed up your trip by boarding at any door of any Metro streetcar with your proof of payment. Your valid Muni pass, passport, ticket, or transfer is your proof of payment. Keep it for your entire ride on all five Muni Metro lines, including anywhere inside the fare gates and on the platforms at the Muni Metro subway stations, from the Embarcadero Station to the West Portal Station. Muni Fare Inspectors may ask you for proof of payment and if you don't have it, you risk getting a citation for up to $500.

Safety

Smoking, eating, drinking, littering, or playing sound equipment without earphones is not allowed on Muni vehicles or at Metro stations. Under Muni regulations, passengers are not allowed to put their feet on the seats and children (and adults) are not allowed to stand on the seats.

Between 8:30 pm and 6:30 am, additional passenger stops will be made for people waiting for a transit vehicle, or for passengers on a transit vehicle at their request, at the nearside corner of any street intersection located between the regular stops.

Working dogs, including guide dogs, signal dogs, and service dogs may ride free at any time. These dogs do not have to be muzzled, but must be leashed. People boarding with an animal that is not a working dog must pay the same fare for the animal as they do for themselves. Non-service animals are allowed to ride on Muni vehicles from 9 am to 3 pm and between 7 pm and 5 am on weekdays, and all day on Saturdays, Sundays, and holidays. Only one animal may ride per vehicle. Dogs must be muzzled and on a short leash or in a closed container, and all other animals must be carried in closed containers.

Airport Connections

Muni does not serve the San Francisco International Airport. The airport is located 14 miles south of downtown San Francisco, in San Mateo County. For public transit information to the airport, check out our BART and Caltrain pages.

Seniors and People with Disabilities

Most Muni vehicles are fully accessible to the elderly and handicapped. Cable cars are not wheelchair accessible. All of the underground stations are easy to get to by elevator, escalator (except for Forest Hill, which has no escalators, and West Portal, which has ramps), or stairs. If you're using Muni elevators, you might want to wear a surgical mask—the lifts are not always clean, and the aroma inside the elevators can be less than welcoming.

Bicycle Rules

All newer trolley and diesel Muni buses are equipped with bike racks. The only lines that might not have a bike rack are the 6-Parnassus and 41-Union vehicles, though on other routes, if an older vehicle is used, you might have to wait for the next bus to load up your bike. There are racks on the front of the buses that fit two bikes per bus. If a Muni vehicle does not have a bike rack, then bikes are not allowed. Metro vehicles, historic streetcars, and cable cars do not have bike racks.

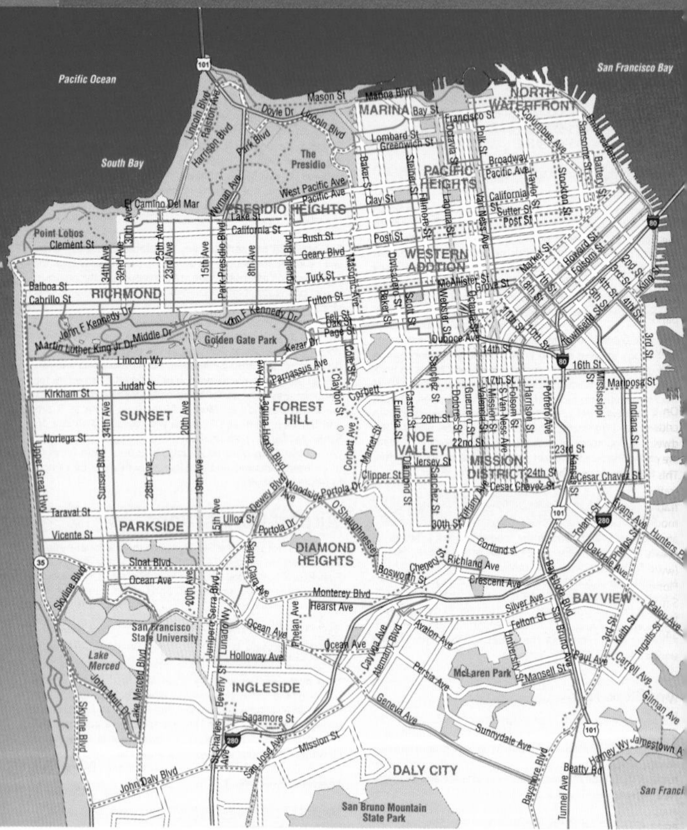

bike path

wide road

bikes and cars share road

bike lane

Biking Information

San Francisco's many bicycle subcultures all have one thing in common: the hills, the hills! Whether you're a messenger who rides for a living, a cyclist who rides for distance, a commuter who rides for exercise, or if you're just taking your vintage cruiser out for a spin on the weekends, we all have to do the climbs. The city's landscape profile bestows grueling physical trials, like fighting gravity on a fixie out of the Presidio. Sharing the road can also be a challenge: weaving through the morning rush hour commute along Market Street is reminiscent of a videogame (except for the multiple lives part). Many San Franciscans do it every day. The non-profit Bike Coalition (SFBC for short: 415-431-BIKE, www.sfbike.org) has been working for more than two decades to improve cycling conditions. Among other things, it's achieved legislation for mandatory bike racks in parking garages, as well as new bike lanes all over town, and a citywide marked bike route system that makes it easy to get around even without a map. Its "Bike to Work Day" event strives to promote commuting by bicycle, and makes converts of many drivers each May.

On the last Friday of every month, Critical Mass (www.critical-mass.org) takes over the streets. Downtown dwellers in the know are aware that to get to where they are going, they should cross Market Street before 6:30 pm. This is when hundreds of bikers assert the right of way in traffic (letting buses get through), as the fifteen year-old tradition celebrates alternative, environmentally-friendly modes of transportation (and not mayhem, as some angered drivers assume). Your bike needs help? Thrifty bikers or fans of DIY should check out the Bike Kitchen (www.bikekitchen.org), in their new space at 19th and Florida, repair co-op on Tuesday and Thursday nights and Saturday afternoons: the volunteer mechanics won't fix it for you, but they'll show you how to do it ($5 per visit or $40 per year membership for use of tools and services).

Where to Ride Bikes

Within city limits, scenic rides abound. The best route to the beach is "The Wiggle", which skirts around the grades and provides a hill-free ride to Golden Gate Park. Email bicycle@sfgov.org for a free bike map and know which routes are for you, based on hill grade and bike route signs. Some bike shops in town host monthly or weekly rides, a great opportunity to adopt new routes and meet like-minded folk. Favorites remain the city loop, encompassing the Embarcadero, Ocean Beach, and the Daily City border; Golden Gate Park loop; and the classic ride over the Golden Gate Bridge to destinations in Marin County. A great resource with maps is the SF Mountain Biking website (www.sfmtb.com). Check our Buses pages (p. 258) for bikes onboard rules for mass transit systems—almost every bus in the Bay Area now has bike racks on the front. Just remember that for every short-of-breath climb, there will be a downhill you'll descend with wind in your helmeted hair. Have fun! Rider beware: it is known that people steal bikes off of the front of buses at red lights, lock up and keep an eye out.

Beyond city limits, hundreds of miles of bike-friendly roads weave a network through the North and the East Bay, uncovering gorgeous views and sunny skies, a welcome escape from city fog. If you can't ride out there, take public transit. BART-accessible mountain biking is at Joaquin Miller Park near Fruitvale Station or Mount Diablo near Walnut Creek and Pleasant Hill Stations. BART-accessible road biking is in the Berkeley and Oakland hills and around Mount Diablo off the Walnut Creek Station. Check the Bicycle Rules section on our BART pages and be aware of the regulation prohibiting bikes on BART during rush hour. To get to South Bay's regional parks, take Caltrain: it has room for 32 bikes per train, but only 16 on the Baby Bullet Express trains. Blue & Gold, Alameda/Oakland, Golden Gate, and Vallejo/Baylink ferries accommodate bikes onboard.

Bike Shops

- **American Cyclery** • 510 Fredrick St • 415-664-4545
- **American Cyclery Too** • 858 Stanyan St • 415-876-4545
- **Avenue Cyclery** • 756 Stanyan St • 415-387-3155
- **Big Swingin' Cycles** • 2260 Van Ness Ave • 415-441-6294
- **Bike & Roll** • 899 Columbus Ave • 415-229-2000
- **The Bike Hut** • Pier 40 Embarcadero & Townsend • 415-543-4335
- **The Bike Kitchen** • 650H Florida Street • 415-255-2453
- **Bike Nook** • 3004 Taraval St • 415-731-3838
- **Blazing Saddles Bike Rental** • 2715 Haight St • 415-202-8888
- **City Cycle** • 3001 Steiner St • 415-346-2242
- **DD Cycles** • 4049 Balboa St • 415-752-7980
- **Fresh Air Bicycles** • 1943 Divisadero St • 415-563-4824
- **Freewheel Bicycle Shop** • 914 Valencia St • 415-643-9213
- **Freewheel Bicycle Shop** • 1920 Hayes St • 415-752-9195
- **Noe Valley Cyclery** • 4193 24th St • 415-647-0886
- **Nomad Cyclery** • 2555 Irving St • 415-564-2022
- **Ocean Cyclery** • 1935 Ocean Ave • 415-239-5004
- **Pedal Revolution** • 3085 21st St • 415-641-1264
- **Roaring Mouse Cycles** • 1352 Irving St • 415-753-6272
- **Road Rage Bicycles** • 1063 Folsom St • 415-255-1351
- **Sports Basement** • 1415 16th St • 415-437-0100
- **Sports Basement** • 610 Mason Str (the Presidio) • 415-437-0100
- **Valencia Cyclery** • 1065 and 1077 Valencia St • 415-550-6600

Overview

Just when you thought it was safe to pencil in that all-important date, check again because San Franciscans can almost always find an excuse to celebrate. Taking cues from many different ethnic and cultural sectors of the community, the next 365 days are chock full of events dedicated to voices mingling, laughter erupting, minds overflowing, and booties shaking. The arts often motivate the annual festivals, but revelry for the hell of it never hurt anyone, either. Wherever your merrymaking takes you throughout town, good food and drink are sure to be close by. So party on!

January

- **San Francisco Sketchfest** • www.sfsketchfest.com • Improv, stand-up, one-man shows, and musical comedy from a mix of amateurs and comic celebrities.

February

- **Chinese New Year Celebration & Parade** • www.chineseparade.com • The largest and longest-running Chinese Parade in the country. Sponsored by Southwest Airlines.
- **San Francisco Bluegrass & Old Time Festival** • www.sfbluegrass.org • Break out your banjo.

March

- **St. Patrick's Day Parade** • www.uissf.org •158-years-old and still getting drunk with the best of us.
- **San Francisco International Asian American Film Festival** • http://festival.asianamericanmedia.org • Showcasing one of the Bay Area's most vibrant ethnic communities.
- **Noise Pop** • www.noisepop.com • The most promising independent and local musicians take over the city's venues.

April

- **Cherry Blossom Festival** • www.nccbf.org • Celebrating nature and Japanese culture.
- **International Beer Festival** • www.sfbeerfest.com • If the neighborhood bars don't cut it anymore, sample over 300 brews from around the world instead.
- **San Francisco International Film Festival** • www.sffs.org • The stars come out for this one…get your tickets early.

May

- **Cinco de Mayo Celebration** •www.sfcincodemayo.com • See the Mission in all of its glory. Most definitely not to be missed.
- **ING Bay to Breakers** • www.baytobreakers.com • Run the 12K naked or strap a keg to your back. Either way, you won't be alone. Better yet, watch the insanity from the sidelines.
- **Carnaval Celebration** • www.carnavalsf.com • Cinco de Mayo with a lot more skin and sin.
- **KFOG KaBoom** • www.kfog.com • Waterfront concert and extravagant (and alarmingly loud) fireworks show.
- **Mission Creek Music & Arts Festival** • www.mcmf.org • Multi-venue indie music and experimental art explosion.

June

- **Escape from Alcatraz Triathlon** • www.escapefromalcatraztriathlon.com • Grueling 1.5-mile swim, 18 mile bike ride, and 8 mile run—all commencing in the frigid waves surrounding the Rock.
- **Haight Ashbury Street Fair** • www.haightashburystreetfair.org • Haight. Hemp. Hippies. Hordes.
- **San Francisco Gay & Lesbian Film Festival** • www.frameline.org/festival • Queer cinema at its most intriguing. Just in time for Pride.
- **San Francisco Gay Pride Week** • www.sfpride.org • Somewhere over the rainbow is here. Come see for yourself.
- **Stern Grove Festival** • www.sterngrove.org • Free live music and performances throughout the summer. Jam among the redwoods.

July

- **SF Silent Film Festival** • www.silentfilm.org • Check out the festival at the Castro Theatre, built in 1922 to screen silent films.
- **Fillmore Jazz Festival** • www.fillmorejazzfestival.com • Everybody likes jazz, especially when it's free.
- **San Francisco Jewish Film Festival** • www.sfjff.org • Thirty years and running. You'd really have to be meshuga to miss it.
- **Up Your Alley Fair** • www.folsomstreetfair.com/alley • Warning: the alley party makes the Folsom Street Fair seem PG.
- **North Beach Jazz Fest** • www.nbjazzfest.com • Cool neighborhood. Cool music.

August

- **Nihonmachi Street Fair** • www.nihonmachistreetfair.org • Celebration of the Asian and Pacific American community in Japantown.
- **Outside Lands Festival** • www.sfoutsidelands.com • Massive music and arts festival with headliners reminiscent of Lollapalooza's glory years.
- **San Francisco Zine Fest** • www.sfzinefest.com • Two-day conference for do-it-yourself publishers.

September

- **Comedy Day** • www.comedyday.com • Five hours, 30 comedians, all free, some funny. Have a hoot in Golden Gate Park.
- **San Francisco Fringe Festival** • www.sffringe.org • Release your inner freak (or at least see what some of the best freaky artists are up to). If you've got time on your hands, they're always looking for volunteers.
- **Opera at the Ballpark** • www.sfopera.com/simulcast • Arias aplenty, and a blanket for two.
- **San Francisco Blues Festival** • www.sfblues.com • Bring your own shades. Lost-love-induced angst included.
- **Folsom Street Fair** • www.folsomstreetfair.com • Not your mother's street fair—this is all whips, chains, and leather, baby.

October

- **Castro Street Fair** • www.castrostreetfair.org • Shop in the sun under the Big Rainbow flag.
- **Marin Italian Film Festival** • www.italianfilm.com • A bit of recent Italian cinema across the Golden Gate every Saturday night through October (and a little bit of November, too).
- **San Francisco Open Studios** • www.artspan.org • A scavenger hunt for the best local artists. Bring your street map (or your NFT, silly).
- **Exotic Erotic Ball** • www.exoticeroticball.com • Inhibitions be damned! One of the Bay Area's hottest parties.
- **Fleet Week** • www.military.com/fleetweek • Spectacular weekend event celebrating the armed forces, featuring the Navy's famous Blue Angels.
- **Litquake** • www.litquake.org • Get a dose of SF's literary scene. Advisors include Dave Eggers and Lawrence Ferlinghetti.
- **San Francisco LovEvolution** • www.sflovevolution.org • The spirit of Berlin's Love Parade unleashed at the Civic Center and streets of downtown.

November

- **Dia de los Muertos (Day of the Dead)** • www.sfmission.com/dod • Come purge all your Catholic demons.

Monthly

- **Critical Mass** • www.critmasssf.tribe.net • Mobs of cyclists show support for their eco-friendly mode of transportation the last Friday of each month.

Overview

The roughly 47 square miles that comprise the city of San Francisco contain a collection of diverse and lively neighborhoods—not to mention people. Now that you're here, there are some things you should know. Although many of the city's nicknames annoy residents, you'll still hear the following used from time to time: Fog City, Frisco (mostly from out-of-towners), Baghdad By the Bay, San Fran Disco, Sam Clam's Disco, the City by the Bay, Ess Eff, Golden Gate City, and often simply the City. The city counts 43 hills with names—and a whole lot more without. The official flower is the dahlia, the city's namesake is St. Francis of Assisi, the city colors are black and gold, and the tallest building is the 853-foot Transamerica Pyramid. We could go on and on with the mindless trivia, but we know you're busy. We'll just stick to the stuff every San Franciscan should have at their fingertips. With so much juicy history and cultural intrigue, it's hard to reduce San Francisco to facts and figures, but what the hell—we're going to try.

Population

San Francisco city population:		808,977
Area (square miles):		46.69
(source: U.S. Census Bureau, State and County QuickFacts)		
Gender		
Male:	362,869	50.5%
Female:	356,208	49.5%
Age		
Median:	39.4 years	
Under 18:	108,695	14.7%
Ages 18–64:	610,407	84.9%
Age 65 and Over:	105,176	14.6%
Race		
One race:	699,514	97.3%
Caucasian:	382,220	53.2%
Asian:	238,133	33.1%
African-American:	46,779	6.50%
American Indian/Alaskan Native:	2,098	0.30%
Native Hawaiian/Pacific Islander:	2,726	0.40%
Hispanic or Latino:	98,891	13.8%
Two or more races:	19,563	2.7%
Some other race:	27,558	3.8%

*All numbers from U.S. Census Bureau, 2005 American Community Survey, unless otherwise noted

Useful Phone Numbers

Emergencies	911
Traffic Information	511
PG&E	800-743-5000
Comcast Cable	800-266-2278
AT&T	800-228-2020
City Hall	415-554-4933
Police Department (Non-Emergencies)	415-553-0123
Fire Department	415-558-3200
Department of Elections	415-554-4375
Department of Motor Vehicles	800-777-0133
Department of Parking & Traffic	415-554-9811
Department of Public Works	415-554-6920
SF Rent Board	415-252-4600

Essential San Francisco Movies

Greed (1925)
The Thin Man (1934)
San Francisco (1936)
The Maltese Falcon (1941)
Dark Passage (1947)
The House on Telegraph Hill (1951)
Vertigo (1958)
Flower Drum Song (1961)
Point Blank (1967)
The Graduate (1967)
Bullitt (1968)
Dirty Harry (1971)
Harold and Maude (1971)
Play Misty for Me (1971)
The Towering Inferno (1974)
The Conversation (1974)
High Anxiety (1977)
Invasion of the Body Snatchers (1978)
Foul Play (1978)
Time After Time (1979)
Chan Is Missing (1982)
Presidio (1988)
So I Married an Axe Murderer (1993)
Mrs. Doubtfire (1993)
The Joy Luck Club (1993)
The Rock (1996)
Romeo Must Die (2000)
Haiku Tunnel (2001)
The Wedding Planner (2001)
Pursuit of Happyness (2006)
Zodiac (2007)
Milk (2008)
Star Trek (2009)

Essential San Francisco Songs

"I Left My Heart in San Francisco" — Tony Bennett
"San Francisco" — Judy Garland
"Dock of the Bay" — Otis Redding
"Frisco Blues" — John Lee Hooker
"San Francisco Days" — Chris Isaak
"Lights" — Journey
"San Francisco" — Scott McKenzie
"We Built This City" — Starship
"San Francisco (You've Got Me)" — Village People
"Little Boxes (Ticky, Tacky)" — Pete Seeger

Essential San Francisco Books

The Maltese Falcon, by Dashiell Hammet. Sam Spade, in perhaps the most famous noir detective story.

Tales of the City, by Armistead Maupin. Seven-volume series about San Francisco in the 1970s and beyond.

The Works of Philip K. Dick, by Philip K. Dick. The man who gave us Blade Runner set nearly all his novels and stories in the Bay Area.

Flower Drum Song, by C.Y. Lee. A young Chinese immigrant strives to make it in San Francisco's Chinatown.

McTeague, by Frank Norris. An unnerving, realistic portrayal of a crazed dentist in 19th-century San Francisco.

Our Lady of Darkness, by Fritz Leiber. Wonderfully creepy supernatural thriller that pays loving homage to the city.

Bombardiers, by Po Bronson. Perhaps "the" novel of the dot-com boom.

Lonesome Traveler, by Jack Kerouac. The famous Beat wanders around San Francisco, and elsewhere.

The Mayor of Castro Street, by Randy Shilts. Novelistic report about the assassinations of Mayor George Moscone and Supervisor Harvey Milk.

Golden Gate, by Vikram Seth. A novel set in verse about the lives and loves of '80s-era San Francisco singles.

The Joy Luck Club, by Amy Tan. Four immigrant families mingle generations of memories.

A Rush of Dreamers, by John Cech. A novel based on the life of real-life eccentric Joshua "Emperor" Norton in 19th-century San Francisco.

A Heartbreaking Work of Staggering Genius, by Dave Eggers. A cult hit based on the author's life in San Francisco during the 1990s.

Daughter of Fortune, by Isabel Allende. Largely set in the Gold Rush era, this tale of entwined lives paints a portrait of San Francisco in its infancy.

China Boy, by Gus Lee. Semi-autobiographical account of growing up Chinese American in the 1950s.

The Confessions of Max Tivoli, by Andrew Sean Greer. Musings of love, time, and humanity at the turn of the 20th century.

San Francisco Timeline

A timeline of significant events in San Francisco's history (by no means complete).

Circa 1000 BC: Ohlone people construct villages in marshlands and along creeks, where they live until Spanish explorers arrive.

1542: Juan Rodriguez Cabrillo discovers the Farallones.

1575: Sebastian Rodriguez Cermeno claims Drake's Bay for Spain and names it Puerto de San Francisco.

1579: Sir Francis Drake claims Drake's Bay for England and names it Nova Albion.

1769: The Golden Gate is discovered by Jose Francisco Ortega and Don Gaspar de Portola.

1776: The Presidio and Mission Dolores are founded.

1835: Yerba Buena is founded.

1846: Yerba Buena is renamed San Francisco by Washington A. Bartlett, Chief Magistrate.

1848: Gold is discovered!

1850: San Francisco County is officially created.

1850: The City of San Francisco is incorporated.

1850: Transbay ferry service begins.

1852: Domingo Ghirardelli opens his chocolate company.

1853: California Academy of Sciences is founded.

1856: The Consolidation Act of 1856 combines the City and County of San Francisco.

1858: Sutro & Co. is founded by Gustav, Charles, and Emil Sutro. It is the oldest investment banking firm in San Francisco.

1859: The highly eccentric Joshua A. Norton declares himself Emperor of the United States.

1861: Fort Point is completed.

1864: Mark Twain visits San Francisco and writes for *San Francisco Daily Morning Call.*

1865: San Francisco is hit with a great earthquake on October 8th.

1868: San Francisco is damaged by another severe earthquake on October 22nd at 7:53 am.

1868: Charles and M.H. De Young launch *The Daily Morning Chronicle.*

1868: The San Francisco SPCA is founded.

1869: The first westbound train reaches San Francisco on September 6th.

1870: California Legislature creates Golden Gate Park.

1873: Jacob Davis and Levi Strauss patent and begin selling jeans.

1873: Andrew S. Hallidie's cable car system begins public service.

1875: Pacific Stock Exchange opens.

1880: The highly eccentric Joshua A. Norton drops dead on California Street. Between 10,000 and 30,000 people reportedly attended his funeral.

San Francisco Timeline

1883: The infamous Black Bart (Charles Boles) is arrested and sentenced to 6 years at San Quentin for robbing Wells Fargo stagecoaches.
1892: The Sierra Club is founded and John Muir is elected president.
1892: US Quarantine Station opened on Angel Island.
1898: The Ferry Building is built.
1906: The Great Earthquake strikes on April 18 at 5:12 am, magnitude 8.25, and lasts 49 seconds. The Great Fire that follows destroys 28,000 buildings, killing 3,000, and leaving 225,000 homeless.
1910: Angel Island opens.
1915: Bernard Maybeck's Palace of Fine Arts is built to host the Panama Pacific International Exposition.
1915: James Rolph dedicates the new City Hall.
1923: Lombard, "the crookedest street in the world," is built.
1923: Golden Gate Park and the Steinhart Aquarium open to the public.
1929: The Great Highway and Ocean Beach Esplanade are completed.
1933: Coit Tower on Telegraph Hill is completed.
1933: The San Francisco Ballet is founded.
1935: The San Francisco Museum of Art opens.
1936: The Bay Bridge officially opens to the public on November 12th.
1937: The Golden Gate Bridge officially opens to pedestrian traffic on May 27, and to vehicular traffic the next day.
1945: World War II ends.
1954: San Francisco International Airport opens.
1955: Allen Ginsberg reads "Howl" at the Six Gallery.
1960: Candlestick Park opens.
1966: Beatles play last live concert at Candlestick Park.
1967: The Summer of Love draws thousands to Haight-Ashbury.
1968: Zodiac Killer kills first victim in the Bay Area.
1968: Alcatraz occupied by Native Americans.
1970: Jim Jones starts People's Temple in San Francisco.
1972: The Transamerica Pyramid officially opens.
1972: BART carries first passengers.
1976: George Moscone elected mayor.
1977: Harvey Milk is elected supervisor and becomes the country's first openly-gay elected official.
1978: Supervisor Dan White assassinates Mayor George Moscone and Supervisor Harvey Milk. Dianne Feinstein becomes mayor.
1979: White Night Riots erupt after Dan White's sentencing.
1988: Art Agnos elected mayor.
1989: A severe earthquake (the Loma Prieta, also known as the World Series Quake) hits the San Andreas fault on October 17 at 5:04 pm, causing extensive damage in and around San Francisco and the collapse of part of the Bay Bridge.
1992: Frank Jordan elected mayor.
1995: The Grateful Dead's Jerry Garcia dies.
1996: Willie Brown elected mayor.
2000: SBC Park (originally Pacific Bell Park) opens.
2001: The dot com investment bubble bursts, severely damaging San Francisco's economy and thousands lose their jobs.
2004: Gavin Newsom elected mayor.
2004: San Francisco becomes the first city to issue same-sex marriage licenses.
2005: SBC Park changes its name, once again, to AT&T Park.
2008: Controversial Proposition 8 passes, eliminating same-sex couples' right to marry.
2010: Judge overturns Proposition 8.

Overview

According to San Francisco's Animal Care and Control Department, there were an estimated 120,000 dogs in the city in 2007. In the city's upscale Marina neighborhood, for instance, where pooches outnumber strollers, dogs have free reign of its streets and waterfront parks. And it makes sense, too: living in San Francisco is pricey, so raising a pooch is much easier than a kid—and perhaps more fashionable. With their ability to accompany you on your morning coffee run, or wait patiently for you at home while you're hittin' the bar, dogs are where it's at. Boasting trendy dog hotels, established pet cemeteries and services, and an eco-friendly plan to convert pet waste into fuel, San Francisco is simply an urban playground for canines. The San Francisco Recreation and Park Department is in the midst of a 10-year, $400 million capital plan for the development and renovation of the city's parks. And thanks to the growing strength and influence of pet-owning communities and an approved dog policy recommended by the Dog Advisory Committee in 2002, considerations are underway to include more off-leash dog facilities. More informally, dogs are welcome at many restaurants and cafés with outdoor seating areas, in many stores, and can even be seen at a bar (with its drinking owner, of course). Decent, often hip pet stores are easily found in most neighborhoods. If you're looking to adopt a new poochie, contact a shelter or one of the many local dog rescue organizations: www.hopalong.org, www.badrap.org, www.homeatlastrescue.org, www. smileydogrescue.org, www.milofoundation.org.

For questions regarding off-leash dog policy, contact the San Francisco Recreation and Park Department at 415-831-2700 or www.parks.sfgov.org. Other good local dog websites include www.sfdog.org, www.d5dog.org, and www.sfspca.org.

Alamo Square Park

Along Scott Street between Hayes and Fulton Streets. The western half of the park is an open playground for dogs to romp off-leash. Come see the Victorian houses known as the "Painted Ladies" with your little tramp.

Alta Plaza Park

Bordered by Jackson, Clay, Steiner, and Scott Streets. This on-leash dog park with some designated off-leash areas hosts the Original Pug Sunday in San Francisco on the first Sunday of every month at the top of the park's hill. At these gatherings, which take place between 1 pm and 4 pm, there can be up to 50 pugs in the park at one time. When it comes to pugs, it seems these pups prefer the Alta Plaza Park.

Bernal Heights

At the top of the hill bounded by Bernal Heights Boulevard, there's a doggie utopia of off-leash frolicking. The park is such a haven for canines that humans without puppy pals are a rare breed indeed.

Buena Vista Park

Located at Buena Vista Avenue and Central Avenue, Buena Vista is Spanish for "great view." This park truly does offer a spectacular view of the city for the many dog-walkers who swarm the park, with some off-leash areas.

Corona Heights

Field area next to Randall Museum at Roosevelt Way and Museum Way. The Randall Museum Dog Run is taken over by smaller, off-leash dogs for the Chihuahua Cha Cha held on the first Sunday of every month at noon. It's the only time that Corona and Chihuahuas should ever be mixed.

Dolores Park

The off-leash doggie area is located south of the tennis courts between Church and Dolores Streets. This beautifully renovated park is actually built on top of a cemetery, but don't worry about your dog digging up any bones. Nobody's been buried there since 1894.

Glen Canyon

Hiking with your dog has never been easier. Many residents are amazed to discover that they can roam freely with their canine companions along scenic trails, past jutting rock outcroppings and little streams—all without leaving the city. Dogs are allowed off-leash. The park's main entrance is at Bosworth Street and O'Shaughnessy Boulevard in the Glen Park neighborhood, but you can also pick up trails at the back of Christopher Playground Park, which is behind the Diamond Heights shopping center (the one with the Safeway). The trails down to the canyon's floor are steep and narrow at times, but offer a gorgeous view that's well worth the knee strain.

Golden Gate National Recreation Area

Starting at the coastline south of San Francisco and stretching for 76,500 acres to the area north of the Golden Gate Bridge, this dog-friendly recreation area includes many San Francisco parks and beaches, some with off-leash areas. In June 2005, a San Francisco judge affirmed off-leash rights in certain sections of the GGNRA. Visit http://www.nps.gov/goga/planyourvisit/pets.htm for complete, updated information about where your pooch can roam free.

Golden Gate Park Dog Runs

Golden Gate Park has four off-leash areas: a southeast section bounded by Lincoln Way, King Drive, and 2nd and 7th Avenues; a northeast section at Stanyan and Grove Streets; a south-central area bounded by Kind Drive, Middle Drive, and 34th and 38th Avenues; and a fenced training area in the north-central area near 38th Avenue and Fulton Street.

Lafayette Park

The off-leash dog section is located on the corner of Gough and Sacramento. This area is unfenced and bordered by busy streets, so be careful with that long-distance tennis ball fetch.

Lake Merced

This lake is San Francisco's largest body of water and an oasis for large dogs to cool down. The official off-leash area is at the North End, at Lake Merced and Middlefield Drive. However, not all of the area is open to doggies. The area to the south by the cement bridge is where your furry friend can take a dip.

McLaren Park

This is a nicely wooded park popular with children and picnickers, so you may not want to let your dog wander off. The official off-leash area is at the top of the hill bounded by Shelly Drive and Mansell Avenue.

Mountain Lake Park

8th Avenue and Lake Street. A strong, local dog community utilizes this off-leash park, which features a canine water fountain at 9th Avenue.

Panhandle

Though those driving past the panhandle see it as the beginning of Golden Gate Park, it is a haven for those who live in the nearby neighborhoods. The park, which is one block wide between Fell and Oak Streets and almost eight blocks long (between Baker and Stanyan), is a great place to exercise yourself or your dog. While it's not a sanctioned off-leash area, you can find dogs roaming free of their leashes at any given time. If your dog likes to chase bicycles or runners, stay clear of the two paths on either side of the park.

Pine Lake Park

Adjacent to Stern Grove, this park has a small lake at the west end of the park. Swimming is not allowed, but there's always the muddy shore for wallowing. This is supposed to be an on-leash park, but you'll notice quite a few puppies roaming free.

St Mary's Park

Located at Murray Street and Justin Drive. This park has a recreation center with a fenced-in dog park on the lower tier below the playground, including canine water fountains.

Walter Haas Playground

A fenced-in, double-gated dog park with doggie drinking fountains sits at the top of this Diamond Heights park and playground area. Located at the intersection of Diamond Heights Boulevard and Gold Mine Drive, the park is moderate in size and, consequently, a popular choice for smaller dogs, though larger dogs are also frequent visitors. This is a good park to choose if you need an after-dark option. It's clean, safe, and outfitted with a red, sandy base instead of grass or dirt.

Beaches

San Francisco has a handful of dog-friendly beaches. However, owners should be aware that most of the time dogs are required to remain on their leashes, unless signs specify otherwise.

Baker Beach, which is located in the Golden Gate National Recreation Area between Lincoln Boulevard and Bowley Street, has a great view of the Golden Gate Bridge. Baker Beach is dog-friendly and is one of the areas recently designated an off-leash beach in a June 2005 court decision.

Crissy Field, another area recently confirmed as an off-leash frolicking ground, is one of the most picturesque beaches in the city. Located in the Presidio at 603 Mason Street at Halleck Street, Crissy Field has panoramic views of the Golden Gate Bridge, Alcatraz, and Marin County. Water dogs can paddle far in the usually calm waters, while non-swimmers can trot down the coastline from the East Beach to Fort Point leash-free. The grass field is also leash-free as long as dogs are under voice control.

Fort Funston/Burton Beach is very popular with dogs and their owners. This beach features trails that run through the dunes, and a water faucet/trough for thirsty K-9s at the Skyline Boulevard and John Muir Drive parking lot. Though you'll probably see many dogs running off-leash, beware that you will be ticketed if caught by the authorities.

Ocean Beach is 4 miles long and runs parallel to the Great Highway. The beach has a mix of off-leash and leash-required areas. Dogs must be on-leash on Ocean Beach between Sloat Boulevard and Fulton Street. Dogs may be off-leash north of Fulton to the Cliff House and south of Sloat for several miles.

Other Dog Play Areas to Explore

Douglass Park • 26th St & Douglass St
Duboce Park • Steiner St & Duboce Ave
Eureka Valley Park •19th St & Collingwood St, east of the baseball diamond
McKinley Square Park • San Bruno Ave & 20th St, on the western slope
Potrero Hill Mini-Park • 22nd St & Arkansas St
Upper Noe Park • Day St & Sanchez St

Overview

If there was an unofficial gay capital of the world, San Francisco rivals all major cities for such a title. In 2004, Mayor Gavin Newsom allowed more than 4,000 gay and lesbian couples to legally wed, transforming the steps of City Hall into an altar and turning the Civic Center into a place of celebration. The State Supreme Court eventually nullified the marriage licenses, but the act of the mayor reminded the rest of the world that the City by the Bay has remained a leader in the fight for equal rights. And although the gay rights movement suffered a major defeat as California voters passed Prop 8—approving a ban on same-sex marriages—the community continues to fight for equality. Recent films such as Milk, the biopic about Harvey Milk, the openly gay politician and city's champion of gay rights in the 1970s, reflect the pride and spirit of San Francisco's LGBT community, which continues to grow strong.

Sunny weekends on Castro Street are alive with buff, tanned men in tank tops, while the Mission is home to the girls. While the Castro is man-ville and the Mission might be girl-ville, LGBT families gravitate towards Noe Valley and Bernal Heights in San Francisco, and the Rockridge, Piedmont Ave, and Laurel districts of Oakland. Make no mistake, the queers are not somewhere, they are everywhere, as are bi-sexual, bi-curious, transsexual, and outside-the-box gender creative folks. The only thing you can be sure of is that every bar or club is "mixed." If you can think of it, you can find it in San Francisco. Don't be afraid to ask.

Annual Events

- **San Francisco Pride**, end of June—www.sfpride.org, 415-864-0831
- **Lesbian and Gay Film Festival**, usually held in June each year—www.frameline.org/festival/, 415-703-8650
- **National Queer Arts Festival**, June—www.queerculturalcenter.org
- **Up Your Alley Fair**, end of July—www.folsomstreetfair.com/alley, 415-777-3247
- **Drag King Contest**, usually August—www.sfdragkingcontest.com
- **Castro Street Fair**, usually in October—www.castrostreetfair.org, 415-841-1824
- **Folsom Street Fair**, usually in September—www.folsomstreetfair.com, 415-777-3247

Bookstores

- **A Different Light**, 489 Castro Street, 415-431-0891—www.adlbooks.com. An extensive selection of gay, lesbian, bisexual, and transgender literature since 1979. The bookstore hosts excellent readings; check their website for upcoming events.
- **Books Inc**, 2275 Market Street, 415-864-6777—www.booksinc.net. This general bookstore is located in the Castro and has a decent selection of gay and lesbian books.
- **Modern Times**, 888 Valencia Street, 415-282-9246—www.mtbs.com. In the Book Buzz section of their website, Seeley's Starter List for Transgender and Queer Issues sits comfortably amongst Monthly Staff Picks, Children's Books, and Ideal Books for a Lazy Sunday. Located in the Mission.
- **City Lights Bookstore**, 261 Columbus Avenue at Broadway, 415-362-8193—www.citylights.com. In North Beach, Lawrence Ferlinghetti's City Lights Bookstore has an excellent selection of fiction, including many foreign titles. Queer beats include Ginsberg, Kerouac, Burroughs, Orlovsky, and bi-fave Diane DiPrima.

Websites

- **Craigslist**—www.craigslist.org
  General community site with heavily trafficked "men seeking men" and "women seeking women" sections, as well as "casual encounters" for those who need it now and "missed connections" if you are intent on chasing fate.
- **Hillgirlz**—www.hillgirlz.com
  If you can excuse the usage of the "z," the calendar page is helpful.
- **Bay Area Bisexual Network**—www.babn.org
  An online resource and network for the multicultural bisexual community.
- **Betty's List**—www.bettyslist.com
  Betty's List is the one-stop web resource for all things LGBT in the Bay Area.
- **Dykealicious**—www.dykealicious.com
  Blog, calendar, and listings for upcoming lesbian-related events.
- **TransBay**—www.transbay.org
  Everyone means everyone. Bay Area resource for those who transcend the gender assigned at birth.
- **Out in San Francisco**—www.outinsanfrancisco.com
  Read your homoscope (ugh, sorry) and plan accordingly.
- **SFGate**—www.sfgate.com/eguide/gay
  The gay and lesbian section of the sfgate.com website with local stories and extensive reviews of nightlife venues.
- **SF Gay**—www.sfgay.org
  Powered by the popular website SF Station, this online resource lists events and news for the entire LGBT community.
- **SF Queer**—www.sfqueer.com
  Queer event listings, Tweets, and a sampling of LGBT-related links.

Publications

- **The Bay Area Reporter**—www.ebar.com
  Weekly newspaper for San Francisco's lesbian, gay, bisexual, transgender, queer, and questioning community. Look for it on Thursdays.
- **The Bay Times**— www.sfbaytimes.com
  Free weekly newspaper with extensive arts and entertainment listings.
- **The Bay Guardian**—www.sfbg.com
  SF's major (and free) alternative weekly with all of the news, entertainment, and events the Gay, er, Bay Area has to offer.
- **Frontiers Magazine**—www.frontierspublishing.com
  Biweekly publication for the LGBT community. Based in Southern California, but relevant for all California readers.
- **Girlfriends Magazine**—www.girlfriendsmag.com
  Lesbian culture, politics, and entertainment.
- **Odyssey Magazine**—www.odysseymagazine.net
  Online source for gay nightlife, news, entertainment, and celebrity gossip.
- **San Francisco Spectrum**—www.sfspectrum.org
  Offers community news and entertainment listings, as well as columns for specific LGBT communities (bears, leather, etc.).
- **Passport Magazine**—www.passportmagazine.com
  Gay and lesbian travel magazine.
- **Gaypocket San Francisco**—www.gaypocketusa.com
  A small, free quarterly available at gay-frequented businesses.

Health Centers and Support Organizations

- **Asian & Pacific Islander Wellness Center,** 730 Polk St, 4th Fl, San Francisco, CA 94109, 415-292-3400—www.apiwellness.org. HIV-related and general health services for the Asian LGBT community.
- **California AIDS Hotline**—800-367-AIDS—www.aidshotline.org
- **CUAV (Community United Against Violence**), 170A Capp St, San Francisco, CA 94110 , 415-777-5500, 24-hour support line: 415-333-HELP—www.cuav.org. CUAV offers counseling and legal assistance for victims of hate crimes and domestic violence, as well as education programs and programs for queer youth.
- **Gay and Lesbian Medical Association**, 459 Fulton St, Ste 107, San Francisco, CA 94102, 415-255-4547—www.glma.org. A 501(c)3 non-profit organization working to end homophobia in health care. If you're looking for a gay, lesbian, bisexual, transgender, or LGBT-friendly chiropractor, dentist, therapist, or doctor, they have an online referral service and will point you in the right direction.
- **Gay Health Care in San Francisco**, 45 Castro Street, Ste 402, San Francisco, CA 94114, 877-693-6633—www.owenmed.com. Bill Owen, MD's practice places emphasis on the primary health care of adults. As a gay doctor, Bill has a special focus on primary care of gay men and lesbians, including patients with HIV/AIDS.
- **San Francisco LGBT Community Center**, 1800 Market St, San Francisco, CA 94102, 415-865-5555—www.sfcenter.org. The 35,000-square-foot facility is referred to simply as the Center, and supports the needs of all LGBT individuals. Health, wellness, arts, culture, social activities, job skill development, events, and resources. Very community-oriented, staffed with more than 100 volunteers.
- **LYRIC (Lavender Youth Recreation and Information Center**), 127 Collingwood St, San Francisco, CA 94114, 415-703-6150—www.lyric.org. Youth Talkline: 800-246-PRIDE. Peer-based education, advocacy, recreation, information, and leadership for queer youth, 23 and under.
- **Rainbow Flag Health Services**, 510-521-7737—www.gayspermbank.com. A bank that provides known-donor insemination, Rainbow Flag Health Services actively recruits gay and bisexual sperm donors.
- **Pacific Reproductive Services**, 444 De Haro St, #222, San Francisco, CA 94107, 415-487-2288—www.pacrepro.com —Fertility center for women planning alternative families.
- **San Francisco AIDS Foundation**, 995 Market St, #200, San Francisco, CA 94103, 415-487-3000—www.sfaf.org—A leader in the fight against AIDS, the foundation seeks to educate and provide services for people living with the disease. Co-produces the AIDS Ride from SF to LA every June.
- **New Leaf**, 103 Hayes St, San Francisco, CA 94102, 415-626-7000—www.newleafservices.org. Providing mental health and substance abuse counseling, as well as social support for LGBT individuals and families.
- **National Center for Lesbian Rights**, 870 Market St, Suite 370, San Francisco, CA 94102, 415-392-6257—www.nclrights.org. NCLR is a non-profit law firm headquartered in San Francisco. Offers free legal advice.
- **Team San Francisco**, www.teamsf.org. Find a recreational league or participate in an upcoming athletic event.

Places of Interest

- **Castro Theatre** • 429 Castro St, 415-621-6120 • Built in 1922, this is a historic movie palace that shows popular, special interest flicks and is home to the gay and lesbian film festival. www.thecastrotheatre.com
- **Dolores Park** • Dolores St (between 18th and 20th) • With one of the city's warmest microclimates, the park is also known as Dolores Beach. Gaze at the boys on Speedo row or take a cute dog to spark conversation. The Dyke March during Pride starts here, and there are often speakers and activities.
- **Good Vibrations** • 603 Valencia St, 415-522-5460 • Co-operatively owned sex toy institution. www.goodvibes.com
- **North Baker Beach** • Sunbathe naked or simply avoid shrinkage from the freezing winds off of the Bay.
- **Q Comedy** • 1519 Mission St, 415-541-5610 • 2nd Mondays at the LGBT center showcase queer comedy. And yes, gay stand-up is funnier than straight humor. www.qcomedy.com
- **QCC** (The Center for Lesbian, Gay, Bi, Transgender Art and Culture) • Queer comedy event listings in San Francisco.
- **Rainbow Grocery** • 1745 Folsom St, 415-863-0620 • While not all lesbians are granola-crunching, soy-slurping vegans who shop at co-ops, many are. The best place in the city for natural, organic, and healthy food at reasonable prices. www.rainbowgrocery.org
- **White Horse Inn** • 6551 Telegraph Ave, 510-652-3820 • This spot is the second oldest gay bar in the nation. It may be in the East Bay, but its history is reason enough to make the trek across the bridge. www.whitehorsebar.com
- **The Women's Building** • 3543 18th St, 415-431-1180 • One stop shop for women gay and straight to tap into the best resources San Francisco has to offer. This place is practically a landmark. You'll be smarter leaving than when you arrived. www.womensbuilding.org

Venues

Lesbian	*Address*	*Phone*
El Rio (4th Saturday)	3158 Mission St	415-282-3325
Endup (Saturday)	401 6th St	415-357-0827
Harveys (2nd and 4th Tuesday)	500 Castro St	415-431-4278
Lexington Club	3464 19th St	415-863-2052
Medjool	2522 Mission St	415-550-9055
Wild Side West	424 Cortland Ave	415-647-3099

Gay	*Address*	*Phone*
440 Castro	440 Castro St	415-621-8732
1015 Folsom	1015 Folsom St	415-431-1200
Asia SF	201 Ninth St	415-255-2742
Aunt Charlie's Lounge	133 Turk St	415-441-2922
Cinch Saloon	1723 Polk St	415-776-4162
Divas	1081 Post St	415-928-6006
Edge	4149 18th St	415-863-4027
Endup (Asian LGBT, Saturday)	401 6th St	415-357-0827
Esta Noche	3079 16th St	415-861-5757
Harvey's (Gay comedy, Tuesday)	500 Castro St	415-431-4278
Hole in the Wall Saloon	1360 Folsom St	415-431-4695
Pink	2925 16th St	415-431-8889
Lone Star Saloon	1354 Harrison St	415-863-9999
The Lookout	3600 16th St	415-703-9750
Marlena's	488 Hayes St	415-864-6672
Martuni's	4 Valencia St	415-241-0205
Midnight Sun	4067 18th St	415-861-4186
Moby Dick	4049 18th St	415-861-1199
Mix	4086 18th St	415-431-8616
N Touch Bar	1548 Polk St	415-441-8413
Powerhouse	1347 Folsom St	415-552-8689
SF Badlands	4121 18th St	415-626-9320
Twin Peaks Tavern	401 Castro St	415-864-9470

Mixed	*Address*	*Phone*
The Café	2367 Market St	415-861-3846
Café Du Nord	2170 Market St	415-861-5016
Club Eight	1151 Folsom St	415-431-1151
The Deco Lounge	510 Larkin St	415-346-2025
Eagle Tavern	398 12th St	415-626-0880
El Rio	3158 Mission St	415-282-3325
Lucky 13	2140 Market St	415-487-1313
Lush Lounge	1092 Post St	415-771-2022
The Mint	1942 Market St	415-626-4726
Pilsner Inn	225 Church St	415-621-7058
Phone Booth	1398 S Van Ness Ave	415-648-4683
Sadie's Flying Elephant	491 Potrero Ave	415-551-7988
Stray Bar	309 Cortland Ave	415-821-9263
The Stud Bar	399 9th St	415-252-7883
Trax	1437 Haight St	415-864-4213
Truck	1900 Folsom St	415-252-0306

Overview

Raising your kids in San Francisco gives them—and you—boundless opportunities for learning and playing. Or learning while playing. Or learning about playing (after all, it's a lost art). Whatever—the point is that the city offers enough interesting educational, cultural, and just plain fun options that you'll never be at a loss for things to do.

The Best of the Best

- **Coolest Place to Cool Down:**
  Toy Boat Dessert Café (401 Clement St, 415-751-7505) So maybe we don't get your typical summer weather. That doesn't mean you can't take your kids out for a cool treat. The walls of this ice cream parlor are lined with little plastic cartoon toys, and a coin-operated horse ride will distract the antsy ones while you wait in line.

- **Spookiest Hike:** Lands End
  (El Camino del Mar, 415-561-4323) If your kids have a "been there, done that" attitude about the 4.5-mile Coastal Trail, spice things up with a "Shipwrecks of the Golden Gate" tour. Park rangers lead visitors on monthly hikes when low tide allows a glimpse at the remains of the unfortunate, resting in the murky waters below. Call the Visitor's Center for times. Yaaaar.

- **Funnest Park:** Adventure Playground
  (160 University Ave, Berkeley Marina, Berkeley, 510-981-6720) Kids hammering on everything in the house? See a future architect in your Lego maker?

Take them to this fenced-in, carpentry fun-for-all to exorcise those demons. They can check out tool and wood to add to the existing kid-built shacks in the park or start their own. It's free for four children or less if they are accompanied by an adult, while groups must make reservations. Don't forget to wear sturdy shoes!

- **Neatest Museum:** Zeum
  (221 Fourth St, 415-820-3320, www.zeum.org) One of the coolest muZeums in town, this space inside Yerba Buena Gardens is an interactive arts mecca that imaginative kids and their families will enjoy. Children are encouraged to try their hand at such jobs as television producer and cartoon animator, as well as experiment with other art media. There's also a 200-seat theater for live performances organized by the American Conservatory Theater. And if the kids run out of ideas, you can hop over to the bowling alley or ice-skating rink. (Adults: $10; kids 3–18: $8; students/seniors: $8)

- **Funniest Store:** Tutti Frutti
  (718 Irving St, 415-661-8504) Giggles abound in this funky gag-gift emporium. From fake mustache kits to whoopee cushions, this tiny, overstocked store is chock full of stuff that your kids (and you) will get a real kick out of.

- **Best Out-of-the-Way Place to Find Project Goodies:**
  Scroungers Center for Reusale Art Parts (SCRAP) (801 Toland St, 415-647-1746 www.scrap-sf.org) Fabric, wood, plastic, glass, cardboard and tile—you can find the weird and wonderful in this bargain-hunter's treasure trove that will inspire your children's creativity and teach a great lesson in recycling while they're at it.

- **Brainiest Place to Expand Your Mind:**
  San Francisco Public Library (415-557-4400, http://sfpl4.sfpl.org) There's always something exciting going on at one of the 27 branch libraries and the expansive Main Library downtown, from magic shows and opera to art exhibits and readings. Or just get lost in the stacks. It's free! It's educational!

Parks for Playing

Oh plaaaaaymate, come out and play with me…

- **Bernal Heights Playground and Recreation Center**
  (Cortland St & Moultrie St) This playground features updated equipment with benches and picnic tables nearby for the weary. A rec center next to the park has programs for tots, teens, and adults.

- **Cow Hollow Playground**
  (Baker St & Miley St) This small, sand-covered, fenced-in park is ideal for babies to 6-year-olds and is just a short walk from Union Street shopping if anyone (say, you) is getting restless.

- **Crocker Amazon Playground**
  (Geneva Ave & Moscow St) A large play area with updated, brightly colored plastic equipment. If yours are more inclined towards organized sports, you'll find six ball fields, tennis courts, and a bocce court nearby.

- **Duboce Park**
  (Duboce Ave & Scott St) Perched on one end of a grassy knoll, this recently renovated fenced-in playground provides kids ages 3 to 9 with a balance beam, climbing wall, slides, and fountain. The surrounding field is great for flying kites, playing tag, and watching the dog people.

- **Garfield Playground & Pool**
  (26th St & Harrison St) A large playground for kids 2 & up replete with the regular sandbox and climbing structures, plus a public pool (adults: $4, kids: $1, call for schedule: 415-695-5001) for those hot summer days. There's also a ball field and game courts nearby.

- **Golden Gate Park**
  (Fulton St & Lincoln Wy) Within more than 1,000 acres of parkland are tennis courts, casting ponds, the Conservatory of Flowers, boating, and a carousel ($2/ride). The city's biggest playground is also here, the recently remodeled (and aptly named) Children's Playground, off Kezar Drive, with a huge concrete slide and climbing structures for those 3 & up.

- **Hamilton Pool/Raymond Kimball Playground** (Geary Blvd & Steiner St) This playground provides a sand play area, a gym, green space, a pool (adults: $4, kids: $1, call for schedule: 415-292-2001), climbing structures, and ball fields for children aged 2 to 12.
- **Holly Park** (Park St) The wooden-structured playground is fun for kids of all ages, and the nearby tennis court, ball field, and basketball court provide something for everyone to enjoy. Steep, grassy hills give ample opportunity for rolling down and climbing back up.
- **Julius Kahn Park** (W Pacific Ave & Maple St) Known as "JK," this park has a well-maintained playground for well-maintained children featuring two fenced-in sandy areas: one for babies and toddlers, the other for older kids. Both feature climbing structures, swings, and slippery slides.
- **McKinley Square** (20th St & Vermont St) A park on Potrero Hill with great views, a playground, and sandbox (bring your own buckets). There's also a grassy area where you can run around and kick a ball. The weather is usually sunny here, so don't forget a hat and sunscreen.
- **Moscone Recreation Center** (Chestnut St & Laguna St) A small park full of activity: four baseball diamonds, two tennis and basketball courts, a gym, two putting greens, and a shiny new playground for kids up to 12 years old.
- **Mountain Lake Park** (Lake St & 8th Ave) Great for kids of all ages, this park provides a sandy play area with two slides, swings, climbing structures, hiking trails, and a small beach with assorted (and sometimes cranky) fowl for feeding. Basketball and tennis courts, as well as soccer/baseball fields are also close by.
- **West Portal Playground** (Lenox Wy & Ulloa St) A newly refurbished rec center and added picnic tables put the perfect touches on this park above the Muni tunnel (a great diversion for young trainspotters). Climbing structures, swings, and an adjacent playing field almost make kids forget about the fog rolling through.

Museums with Kid Appeal

- **Asian Art Museum** (200 Larkin St, 415-581-3500, www.asianart.org) One of the largest collections in the West dedicated to Asian art and culture, this museum next to the public library's main branch offers interactive family programs, from storytelling, performances, yoga, and art projects. Family activities are free with museum admission, while kids 12 and under are always free.
- **Exploratorium** (3601 Lyon St, 415-561-0360, www.exploratorium.com) Hands-on exhibits that encourage children and their parents to explore the natural and scientific world around them make this one of the best science museums in the world. Make a reservation for the Tactile Dome, a network of tunnels and slides that you must crawl through in complete darkness. (Adults: $14; students, seniors, and kids 13–17: $11; kids 4–12: $9; free the first Wednesday of the month; Tactile Dome: $17)
- **California Academy of Sciences / Steinhart Aquarium** (55 Music Concourse Dr, 415-379-8000, www.calacademy.org) The newly reopened Academy, in a state-of-the-art sustainable facility, is the greenest museum in the world. Located across from the DeYoung Museum, it offers the whole universe under one roof: an aquarium, planetarium, rainforest, coral reef, and living roof. (Adults: $24.95; students/kids 12-17: $19.95; kids 7-11: $14.95; kids 6 and under: free; free the third Wednesday of the month)
- **Bay Area Discovery Museum** (East Fort Baker, 557 McReynolds Rd, Sausalito, 415-339-3900, www.baykidsmuseum.org) Located just across the Golden Gate Bridge, this museum for younger kids lets them play and use their bodies to their heart's content. In addition to changing exhibits, kids love Lookout Cove—it's got a shipwreck, Crow's Nest, tidepools, and a model of the Golden Gate Bridge to play on. All hands-on fun! (Adults: $10; kids 1 and up: $8)
- **Musee Mecanique** (Pier 45, The Embarcadero & Taylor St, 415-346-2000 www.museemecanique.org) If it's tough dragging your kids out of the video arcade, take them to see the largest private collection of antique carnival coin-operated machines, including the spooky old fortune-teller booths and the landmark "Laffing Sal." Admission is free, but don't forget the quarters.
- **Randall Museum** (199 Museum Wy, 415-554-9600, www.randallmuseum.org) This small, city-run, interactive museum with a focus on area wildlife offers several affordable art and science classes for kids and their families, weekly art programs, and a theater that features family-friendly films and live performances. All exhibits—including a small room with 100 rescued wild animals—are free.
- **Ripley's Believe It or Not Museum** (175 Jefferson St, 415-202-9850, http://sanfrancisco.ripleys.com) Features a walk-through kaleidoscope tunnel and such oddities as a shrunken human torso once owned by Ernest Hemingway. If your child is into the weird and occasionally grotesque, they'll take to this place. (Ages 13 and up: $14.99; kids 5–12: $8.99)
- **USS Pampanito** (Pier 45, 415-775-1943, www.maritime.org) A WWII fleet sub built in 1943, the *USS Pampanito* sank six Japanese ships, damaged four others, and narrowly escaped destruction twice herself. A self-guided audio tour takes you from the gun decks and periscope all the way down to the torpedo room, where some men had to sleep. Not for the claustrophobic or very young. (Adults: $9; kids 6-12: $4; kids under 6: free; self-guided tour: $2)

And Some Other Distractions

- **Jewish Community Center of San Francisco** (3200 California St, 415-292-1200, www.jccsf.org) The center provides educational, social, cultural, and fitness programs to the community and is open to all; it has wonderful programs for kids. Choose from art, music, theater, gymnastics, dance, yoga, and sports of all types. The JCC will keep you and your kids busy and healthy. Class schedules and costs are on their website.
- **Yerba Buena Ice-Skating Center** (750 Folsom St, 415-820-3532, www.skatebowl.com) An NHL-sized ice skating rink in Yerba Buena Gardens where your children can live out their hockey and figure skating fantasies. The center offers skating events, parties, and instruction. (A bowling alley is also part of the complex.) Check website for public session schedules. (Adults: $8; kids up to age 12: $6.25 seniors (over 55):$5.50; skate rental: $3)

Outdoor *and* Educational

It's time for some outside stimulation—the Learning Channel isn't quite cutting it anymore.

- **San Francisco Zoo** (1 Zoo Rd, 415-753-7080, www.sfzoo.org) The Zoo houses more than 250 species of animals and birds on its grounds. Exhibits not to miss: the Australian Walkabout full of kangaroos and koalas, the Lemur Forest with an elevated walkway that puts you on eye-level with the animals, and the Hearst Grizzly Gulch with its 20,000-gallon pool and heated rocks. (Adults: $12/locals, $15/non-locals; kids 4–14: $5.50/locals, $9/non-locals; kids 3 and underfree; free the first Wednesday of the month)
- **San Francisco Fire Engine Tours & Adventures** (415-333-7077, www.fireenginetours.com) Aspiring firefighters will absolutely love this tour, seated high atop a classic red 1955 Mack Fire Truck. The open-air expedition requires all participants to dress in an authentic fireman's uniform (provided) and lasts 75 minutes, taking guests on a ride throughout the city. The tour ends back at the century-old firehouse with a talk on fire safety and the history of the SFFD. The tour leaves from the Cannery on Beach Street and Columbus Avenue. Call for current rates and to make a reservation. (Adults: $45; teens 13–17: $30; kids under 12: $25)

Some Great Places to Make Art

- **Sharon Art Studio** (Golden Gate Park, 415-753-7004, www.sharonartstudio.org) Located in Golden Gate Park, next to Children's Playground and opposite the carousel, the Sharon Art Studio is one of the city's best deals, offering affordable art classes for children 5 and up. Check the website for class schedules, and register early because they fill up quickly!
- **Center for Creative Exploration** (300 Chenery St, 415-333-9515, www.ccesf.org) Come paint! Providing a nonjudgmental environment where curiosity and exploration can flourish, the Center offers weekly painting classes where children 6 and up can get their creative juices flowing. Check the website for class schedules and costs; scholarships are available.
- **San Francisco Children's Art Center** (Fort Mason, Bldg C, 415-771-0292, www.childrensartcenter.org) Empowering children through creative exploration! Put on your smock and get messy. Art and painting classes for kids ages 2 to 10 taught in an open studio environment where creativity and visual expression are encouraged. Call ahead for a drop- in class to see what it's all about. You can have an ARTrageous birthday party here, too.
- **Stretch the Imagination** (2509 Bush St, 415-922-0104, www.stretchtheimagination.com) Kids can express their inner creativity with art, yoga, and music.
- **SFMOMA** (151 Third St, 415-357-4000, www.sfmoma.org) Help your child find his inner Cubist! This world-class museum offers Target Family Days three times a year, as well as Family Studio programs, where kids and adults explore connections between art and their own creative genius. Activities such as book readings, film screenings, gallery tours, and hands-on art projects are included. Held on the first and third Sunday of every month.

Best Places to Spin Your Wheels

- **Golden Gate Park** (415-831-2700, www.parks.sfgov.org/) JFK Drive in the park is closed to cars on Sundays, so put on your helmet and ride your bike, or lace up those skates and go, go, go.
- **Golden Gate Promenade** (Marina/Presidio, www.nps.gov/goga) Right along the water in the Marina, this is a beautiful place to take the kids to bike, skate, or scooter. The 3.5-mile path goes from Aquatic Park through Crissy Field to Fort Point. You can stop and play on the beaches or grassy meadows, or have a snack at one of the many beautifully landscaped picnic areas.

Where to go for additional information:
www.gocitykids.com

Television

2	KTVU	(FOX)	www.ktvu.com
4	KRON	(Independent)	www.kron.com
5	KPIX	(CBS)	www.kpix.com
7	KGO	(ABC)	www.abc7news.com
9	KQED	(PBS)	www.kqed.org
11	KNTV	(NBC)	www.kntv.com
14	KDTV	(Univision)	www.univision.net
20	KOFY	(Independent)	www.yourtv20.com
26	KTSF	(Independent)	www.ktsf.com
28	KFTL	(HSN)	www.kftl.com
44	KBCW	(CW)	http://cwbayarea.com
48	KSTS	(Telemundo)	www.telemundo.com
50	KFTY	(Clear Channel)	www.kfty.com
54	KTEH	(PBS)	www.kteh.org
60	KCSM	(PBS)	www.kcsm.org
65	KKPX	(i)	www.ionmedia.tv

AM Stations

560	KSFO	Talk
610	KEAR	Religious
680	KNBR	Sports
740	KCBS	News
810	KGO	News/Talk
910	KNEW	Talk
960	KKGN	Liberal Talk
1010	KIQI	Spanish Talk
1050	KTCT	Sports
1100	KFAX	Religious
1260	KSFB	Religious
1450	KEST	Personal Growth, Multicultural
1550	KYCY	Talk, Sports

FM Stations

88.5	KQED	News/Public Radio/NPR
89.5	KPOO	Variety
90.1	KZSU	Eclectic/Independent
90.3	KUSF	Alternative Music
91.1	KCSM	Jazz
91.7	KALW	News/Public Radio/NPR
92.7	KNGY	Dance Top 40
93.3	KRZZ	Spanish
94.1	KPFA	Community/Variety
94.9	KYLD	Urban top 40/Commercial Hip-hop
95.7	KBWF	Country
96.5	KOIT	Light Rock
97.3	KLLC	Adult Contemporary
98.1	KISQ	R&B/Classic Soul/Disco
99.7	KMVQ	Urban Top 40/Pop/R&B
101.3	KIOI	Adult Contemporary
102.1	KDFC	Classical
103.7	KKSF	Smooth Jazz
104.5	KFOG	Adult Contemporary Rock
105.3	KITS	Modern Rock
106.1	KMEL	Urban contemporary/Hip-hop
106.9	KFRC	Oldies/Classic Hits
107.7	KSAN	Classic Rock

Magazines

7x7 • www.7x7sf.com • Monthly glossy with coverage on food, design, and fashion in the Bay Area.

Bark • www.thebark.com • Bi-monthly magazine of musings on modern dog culture.

Bitch • www.bitchmagazine.org • Print magazine and evolving website devoted to feminist analysis and media and pop culture criticism.

Common Ground • www.commongroundmag.com • Publication focused on alternative health, social consciousness, and sustainable living.

Curve • www.curvemag.com • Nationally distributed, cutting-edge lesbian culture magazine printed 10 times a year.

Dwell • www.dwell.com • Glossy focused on fresh, contemporary home architecture and design printed 10 times a year.

Earth Island Journal • www.earthisland.org/journal • Quarterly magazine devoted to environmental activism, sustainability, and grassroots campaigns. Based in Berkeley.

Edible San Francisco • www.ediblesanfrancisco.net • Quarterly rag dedicated to the finest local food and drink.

Edutopia • www.edutopia.org • The George Lucas Educational Foundation's publication on innovation and trends in K-12 public education.

Hyphen • www.hyphenmagazine.com • Nonprofit, all-volunteer-staff magazine on Asian American culture, politics, and social issues.

Mother Jones • www.motherjones.com • Progressive, investigative, and social justice reporting on news, politics, and culture. National bi-monthly magazine and comprehensive website.

Nob Hill Gazette • www.nobhillgazette.com • Monthly magazine with a focus on local charity and society events for the city's upscale Nob Hill neighborhood.

PLANET • www.planet-mag.com • Independent culture and lifestyle mag of art, fashion, music, travel, and design with a global slant.

ReadyMade • www.readymademag.com • The DIY lifestyle magazine for the hip, resourceful, and crafty. Published six times a year.

Red Herring • www.redherring.com • Reflective of the Silcon Valley set, the publication covers trends and innovation in technology and business.

San Francisco Downtown • www.sfdowntown.com • Free lifestyle, business, and entertainment monthly.

San Francisco Magazine • www.sanfran.com • Monthly city-centric glossy.

Sierra • www.sierraclub.org • Sierra Club's bi-monthly magazine.

SOMA • www.somamagazine.com • Glossy monthly featuring high-end fashion, art features, and interviews.

Thrasher • www.thrashermagazine.com • The authority on skateboarding culture. Monthly.

Wired • www.wired.com • Conde Nast's monthly glossy on technology, science, and intelligent pop culture.

Newspapers

Asian Week • www.asianweek.com • News for SF's Asian community.

Bay Area Business Woman • www.babwnews.com • Business and lifestyle newspaper for female professionals and business owners.

Bay Area Reporter • www.ebar.com • News for gay and lesbian community.

Central City Extra • www.studycenter.org/test/cce • Progressive community news for the Tenderloin, Civic Center, and Sixth Street neighborhoods.

East Bay Express • www.eastbayexpress.com • East Bay version of the *Guardian* and the *Weekly*.

El Tecolote • www.eltecolote.org • Bi-weekly, bilingual newspaper for the Mission District.

Frontlines • www.sf-frontlines.com • Progressive news

Haight-Ashbury Beat • www.haightbeat.com • Independent neighborhood publication distributed to Upper Haight residents and businesses.

J • www.jewishsf.com • News for Bay Area Jewish community.

Marina Times • 2161 Union St • 415-931-0515 • Independent community newspaper.

Mission Dispatch • www.missiondispatch.com • Community news for the Mission District.

The New Fillmore News • www.newfillmore.com • Independent community newspaper.

The Noe Valley Voice • www.noevalleyvoice.com • Independent community newspaper.

North Beach Journal • Independent community newspaper.

The Oakland Tribune • www.oaklandtribune.com • Daily covering general news for Oakland, Berkeley, Richmond, and the surrounding areas.

Potrero View • www.potreroview.net • Independent community newspaper.

Richmond Review/Sunset Beacon • www.sunsetbeacon.com • Community publications serving the Richmond and Sunset districts on the west side of SF.

San Francisco Bay Guardian • www.sfbg.com • Alternative, progressive news and features.

San Francisco Bay View • www.sfbayview.com • National newspaper for the African American community.

San Francisco Business Times • http://sanfrancisco.bizjournals.com • Bay Area business news.

San Francisco Chronicle • www.sfgate.com • Major daily newspaper.

San Francisco Examiner • www.sfexaminer.com • Free, daily, tabloid-format newspaper.

San Francisco Weekly • www.sfweekly.com • Alternative, progressive news and features.

San Jose Mercury News • www.mercurynews.com • Major daily newspaper of San Jose and Silicon Valley.

San Francisco Spectrum • www.sfspectrum.com • Online newspaper for LGBT readers

Street Sheet • www.cohsf.org/streetsheet • Publication of the Coalition on Homelessness.

Western Edition • www.thewesternedition.com • Community news for Alamo Square, Hayes Valley, the Fillmore, Japantown, and the Panhandle.

Websites

www.notfortourists.com—THE San Francisco source. Mmhmm, that's right.

www.onlyinsanfrancisco.com—The official Convention & Visitors Bureau site—loads of useful information.

www.craigslist.org—Easily the most popular site for hooking up in San Francisco, whether that means hooking yourself up with a new job, a new apartment, news about what's going on, or a hot, new date.

www.sfstation.com—An entertainment-oriented city guide that offers a calendar of events, info on clubs, music, film, special events, literary happenings, and the like.

www.sfgate.com—The *San Francisco Chronicle's* site—news about San Francisco and the Bay Area, as well as national news, classifieds, weather and traffic updates.

www.sanfrancisco.com—Guide to hotels, restaurants, events, nightlife, jobs, and real estate.

www.sanfrancisco.citysearch.com—Comprehensive, up-to-date listings of restaurants, clubs, and other entertainment venues. Includes ratings of popular hot spots, photos of each venue, and links to related sites.

http://sanfrancisco.going.com—Social networking fused with Bay Area event listings.

http://cityguide.aol.com/sanfrancisco—AOL's City Guide to San Francisco. Coverage of select events, music, arts, restaurants, and bars in the Bay Area.

www.sfist.com—Bay Area news and gossip blog.

www.sfusualsuspects.com—Daily political news and analysis.

http://sf.flavorpill.net—Weekly selection of off-beat, artsy shows, music events, and literary readings chosen by its staff.

www.yelp.com—Popular site with peer reviews on just about every restaurant, bar and business in town.

Reference Books

Herb Caen's San Francisco: 1976-1991, by Herb Caen and Irene Mecchi (Chronicle Books, 1992) The late *Chronicle* columnist's best pieces about the city he loved.

San Francisco Then & Now, by Bill Yenne (Thunder Bay Press, 2003) Collection of historical and contemporary photographs of the city's neighborhoods and landmarks.

Streets and San Francisco: The Origins of Street and Place Names, by Louis K. Loewenstein and Penny Demoss (Wilderness Press, 1996) The stories behind the city's streets and landmarks.

The Barbary Coast: An Informal History of the San Francisco Underworld, by Herbert Asbury (Thunder's Mouth Press, 2002) San Francisco has always had its share of sin—here's a tour of the city's darker side.

Stairway Walks in San Francisco, by Adah Bakalinsky (Wilderness Press, 2006) The sixth edition of this popular guidebook lists just about all of the city's stairway walks, from the well-known to the hard-to-find.

Imperial San Francisco: Urban Power, Earthly Ruin, by Gary A. Brechin (University of California Press, 2001) A study of the rich and powerful who helped make San Francisco.

Reclaiming San Francisco History: History, Politics, Culture: A City Lights Anthology, edited by James Brook, Chris Carlsson, and Nancy J. Peters (City Lights Books, 1998) A collection of essays about San Francisco's history.

San Francisco Secrets: Fascinating Facts about the City by the Bay, by John Snyder (Chronicle Books, 1999) A collection of city factoids perfect for the trivia-obsessed.

San Francisco Bizarro, by Jack Boulware (St. Martin's, 2000) An insider's guide to some of the strangest incidences in SF's counterculture history.

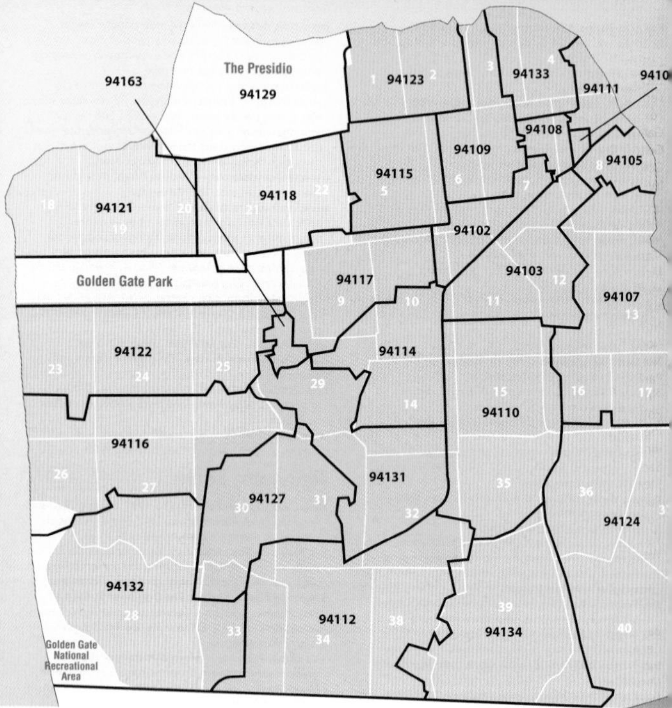

Post Offices

Post Offices	Address	Phone	Map
18th Street Station	4304 18th St	415-431-2701	10
Bayview Station	2111 Lane St	415-822-7157	40
Bernal Heights Finance Station	189 Tiffany Ave	415-550-7538	35
Brannan Street Finance	460 Brannan St	415-536-6413	8
Bryant Street Station	1600 Bryant St	415-431-3720	11
Chinatown Station	867 Stockton St	415-433-1202	7
Civic Center Box Unit / Pacific Center	101 Hyde St	415-563-7284	7
Clayton Street Station	554 Clayton St	415-621-5816	9
CPU University of SF	2299 Golden Gate Ave	415-462-2525	22
CPU World Pioneer	2830 24th St	415-282-6838	15
Diamond Heights Carrier Annex	151 Mendell St	415-641-0183	37
Diamond Heights Finance	5262 Diamond Heights Blvd	415-641-0158	32

Post Offices—*continued*

Post Offices—*continued*	*Address*	*Phone*	*Map*
Embarcadero Postal Center	226 Harrison St	415-536-6412	8
Excelsior Finance Station	15 Onondaga St	415-334-1057	38
Federal Building	450 Golden Gate Ave	415-487-8981	7
Fox Plaza Finance Station	1390 Market St	415-931-1053	11
Gateway Station	1 Embarcadero Ctr	415-956-5296	8
Geary Station	5654 Geary Blvd	415-665-1355	20
Golden Gate Station	3245 Geary Blvd	415-751-9739	22
Irving Street Postal Store	821 Irving St	415-759-6652	25
Lakeshore Plaza Station	1543 Sloat Blvd	415-564-0258	27
Macy's Union Square Station	170 O'Farrell St	415-956-0131	7
Marina Green Retail Store	3749 Buchanan St	415-440-4390	2
Marina Station	2055 Lombard St	415-351-1875	2
McLaren Station	2755 San Bruno Ave	415-467-5026	39
Mission Station	1198 S Van Ness Ave	415-648-0155	15
Napoleon Street Carrier Complex	180 Napoleon St	415-285-4647	36
Noe Valley	4083 24th St	415-821-3863	14
North Beach (Carrier) Station	2200 Powell St	415-986-3494	4
North Beach (Finance) Station	1640 Stockton St	415-362-3128	4
Parkside Station	1800 Taraval St	415-759-0150	27
Pine Street Station	1400 Pine St	415-351-2435	7
Potrero Retail Store	1655 Bryant St	415-861-8130	11
Presidio Station	950 Lincoln Blvd, Bldg 210	415-563-0126	pg 191
Rincon Finance	180 Steuart St	415-896-0762	8
San Francisco P+DC	1300 Evans Ave	415-550-5005	37
Steiner Street Station	1849 Geary St	415-931-1053	5
Sunset Finance Station	1314 22nd Ave	415-759-6381	24
Sutter Street Postal Store	150 Sutter St	415-765-1761	8
Visitacion Station	68 Leland Ave	415-333-4629	39
West Portal Station	317 West Portal Ave	415-759-0158	30

Police

Police	*Address*	*Phone*	*Map*
Bayview Police Station	201 Williams Ave	415-671-2300	40
Central Police Station	766 Vallejo St	415-315-2400	4
Ingleside Police Station	1 John Young Ln	415-404-4000	34
Mission Police Station	630 Valencia St	415-558-5400	11
Northern Police Station	1125 Fillmore St	415-614-3400	5
Park Police Station	1899 Waller St	415-242-3000	9
Richmond Police Station	461 6th Ave	415-666-8000	21
Southern Police Station	850 Bryant St	415-553-1373	12
Taraval Police Station	2345 24th Ave	415-759-3100	27
Tenderloin Police Station	301 Eddy St	415-345-7300	7

Hospitals

From the top-ranked **UCSF Medical Center at Parnassus (Map 29)** to the smaller, community-based facilities like **Chinese Hospital (Map 7)**, San Francisco is a good place to get sick or hurt yourself, if you insist.

If you have to visit a hospital in a hurry, it's obviously best to know where to go. As a quick reference, this is a list of the largest hospitals with ERs open to the general public. We recommend going to the map page for your neighborhood to see the location of these and all hospitals in your area.

Emergency Rooms	*Address*	*Phone*	*Map*
California Pacific Medical Center California Campus	3700 California St	415-600-6000	22
California Pacific Medical Center Davies Campus	Castro St & Duboce St	415-600-6000	10
California Pacific Medical Center Pacific Campus	2333 Buchanan St	415-600-6000	6
Chinese Hospital	845 Jackson St	415-982-2400	7
Kaiser Permanente Medical Center	2425 Geary Blvd	415-833-3300	5
San Francisco General	1001 Potrero Ave	415-206-8000	16
San Francisco VA Medical Center	4150 Clement St	415-221-4810	18
St Francis Memorial	900 Hyde St	415-353-6000	7
St Luke's	3555 Cesar Chavez St	415-647-8600	35
St Mary's Medical Center	450 Stanyan St	415-668-1000	9
UCSF Medical Center at Parnassus	505 Parnassus Ave	415-476-1000	29

Other Hospitals	*Address*	*Phone*	*Map*
Laguna Honda Hospital and Rehabilitation Center	375 Laguna Honda Blvd	415-759-2300	25

Libraries

While the Main branch in Civic Center has a good reference section, thousands of tomes, and a bookstore and a café, the local neighborhood branches hold many of the literary treasures themselves. For special collections, check out Chinatown branch for titles in Asian languages, and the Eureka Valley branch for LGBT literature. : But running all over town is unnecessary: the online catalog and request system allows you to transfer an item from one library to the branch in your neighborhood.

Library	*Address*	*Phone*	*Map*
Anza Branch Library	550 37th Ave	415-355-5717	19
Bayview - Anna E Waden	5075 3rd St	415-355-5757	36
Bernal Heights Branch Library	500 Cortland Ave	415-355-2810	35
Chinatown Branch Library	1135 Powell St	415-355-2888	7
Eureka Valley / Harvey Milk Memorial Library	1 José Sarria Ct	415-355-5616	10
Excelsior Branch Library	4400 Mission St	415-355-2868	38
Foundation Center, San Francisco	312 Sutter St	415-397-0902	8
Glen Park Branch Library	2825 Diamond St	415-337-4740	32
Golden Gate Valley Library	1801 Green St	415-355-5666	2
Helen Crocker Russell Library	9th Ave & Lincoln Wy	415-661-1316	25
Ingleside Branch Library	1298 Ocean Ave	415-355-2898	33
Library & Center for Knowledge	530 Parnassus Ave	415-476-2334	29
Marina Branch Library	1890 Chestnut St	415-355-2823	2
Mechanics' Institute Library	57 Post St	415-393-0114	8
Merced Branch Library	155 Winston Dr	415-355-2825	30
Mission Bay Branch Library	960 4th St	415-355-2838	13
Mission Branch Library	300 Bartlett St	415-355-2800	15
Noe Valley Branch Library	451 Jersey St	415-695-5095	14
North Beach Branch Library	2000 Mason St	415-355-5626	4
Ocean View Branch Library	345 Randolph St	415-355-5615	33
Ortega Branch Library	3223 Ortega St	415-504-6053	23
Park Branch Library	1833 Page St	415-355-5656	9
Parkside Branch Library	1200 Taraval St	415-355-5770	27
Portola Library	2450 San Bruno Ave	415-355-5660	39
Potrero Library	1616 20th St	415-355-2822	16
Presidio Branch Library	3150 Sacramento St	415-355-2880	5
Richmond Branch Library	351 9th Ave	415-355-5600	21
San Francisco Law Library	401 Van Ness Ave	415-554-6821	7
San Francisco Law Library Branch	685 Market St	415-882-9310	8
San Francisco Main Library	100 Larkin St	415-557-4400	7
Sunset Branch Library	1305 18th Ave	415-355-2808	25
Sutro Library	480 Winston Dr	415-731-4477	27
United Irish Cultural Center	2700 45th Ave	415-661-2700	26
Visitacion Valley Library	45 Leland Ave	415-355-2848	39
West Portal Branch Library	190 Lenox Wy	415-355-2886	30
Western Addition Library	1550 Scott St	415-355-5727	5

All times shown are for last pick-up.

Map 1 • Marina / Cow Hollow (West)

The Postal Chase	3053 Fillmore St	5 pm

Map 2 • Marina / Cow Hollow (East)

FedEx Kinko's	3225 Fillmore St	5 pm
Self-Service	3225 Fillmore St	5 pm
Self-Service	2750 Van Ness Ave	5 pm
Self-Service	2055 Lombard St	5 pm
Self-Service	3749 Buchanan St	5 pm
Mailbox & Company	1517 North Point St	4:45 pm
Self-Service	2001 Union St	4:45 pm
Self-Service	1300 Columbus Ave	5:15 pm

Map 3 • Russian Hill / Fisherman's Wharf

Mailboxes & Company	792 Bay St	4:45 pm

Map 4 • North Beach / Telegraph Hill

Postal Annex	350 Bay St	5 pm
Self-Service	1005 Sansome St	5 pm
Self-Service	80 Francisco St	5 pm
Self-Service	55 Francisco St	4:15 pm
Self-Service	1849 Geary Blvd	4:45 pm
Self-Service	2404 California St	4:30 pm

Map 5 • Pacific Heights / Western Addition

Jet Mail	2130 Fillmore St	4:15 pm

Map 6 • Pacific Heights / Japantown

FedEx Kinko's	1 Daniel Burnham Ct	5:15 pm
Self-Service	1 Daniel Burnham Ct	5:15 pm
Self-Service	1255 Post St	5:15 pm
Self-Service	1700 California St	5:10 pm
Self-Service	727 Van Ness Ave	5 pm
Self-Service	1388 Sutter St	5 pm
Self-Service	2333 Buchanan St	4:30 pm
Mail Box Plus	1450 Sutter St	4 pm
Jna Tall	2115 Van Ness Ave	4 pm
Self-Service	500 Van Ness Ave	3:30 pm
Self-Service	870 Market St	5:15 pm
Self-Service	1 Hallidie Plaza	5:15 pm
Self-Service	455 Golden Gate Ave	5:15 pm
Self-Service	1355 Market St	5:15 pm
Self-Service	490 Post St	5:10 pm
Self-Service	360 Post St	5:10 pm
Mailbox 4u	1230 Market St	5 pm
Self-Service	291 Geary St	5 pm
Self-Service	450 Golden Gate Ave	5 pm
Self-Service	909 Hyde St	5 pm
Self-Service	1400 Pine St	4:45 pm

Map 7 • Nob Hill / Tenderloin

Cyber Copy	272 O'Farrell St	4:30 pm
Self-Service	450 Golden Gate Ave	4:30 pm
FedEx Kinko's	3 Embarcadero Ctr	5:30 pm
FedEx Kinko's	120 Bush St	5:30 pm
FedEx Kinko's	555 California St	5:30 pm
FedEx Kinko's	127 Kearny St	5:30 pm
FedEx Kinko's	71 Spear St	5:30 pm
FedEx Kinko's	724 Battery St	5:30 pm

Map 8 • Financial District / SOMA

Federal Express	350 Sansome St	5:30 pm
FedEx Kinko's	50 Fremont St	5:30 pm
FedEx Kinko's	100 California St	5:15 pm
FedEx Kinko's	303 2nd St	5:15 pm
Self-Service	100 California St	5:15 pm
Self-Service	685 Market St	5:15 pm
Self-Service	655 Montgomery St	5:15 pm
Self-Service	303 2nd St	5:15 pm
Self-Service	703 Market St	5:15 pm
Self-Service	705 Market St	5:15 pm
Self-Service	301 Howard St	5:15 pm
Self-Service	631 Howard St	5:15 pm
Self-Service	246 1st St	5:15 pm
Self-Service	180 Steuart St	5:15 pm
Self-Service	201 Spear St	5:15 pm
Self-Service	303 2nd St	5:15 pm
Self-Service	501 2nd St	5:15 pm
Self-Service	333 3rd St	5:15 pm
Self-Service	650 California St	5:15 pm
Self-Service	785 Market St	5:10 pm
Self-Service	71 Stevenson St	5:10 pm
Self-Service	90 New Montgomery St	5:10 pm
Self-Service	530 Bush St	5:10 pm
Self-Service	1 Maritime Plaza	5:05 pm
Self-Service	550 Montgomery St	5:05 pm
Self-Service	221 Main St	5:05 pm
Postal Annex	100 1st St, Ste 100	5 pm
FedEx Kinko's	369 Pine St	5 pm
Self-Service	44 Montgomery St	5 pm
Self-Service	225 Bush St	5 pm
Self-Service	550 California St	5 pm
Self-Service	580 California St	5 pm
Self-Service	120 Montgomery St	5 pm
Self-Service	433 California St	5 pm
Self-Service	456 Montgomery St	5 pm
Self-Service	351 California St	5 pm
Self-Service	333 Market St	5 pm
Self-Service	595 Market St	5 pm
Self-Service	605 Market St	5 pm
Self-Service	525 Market St	5 pm
Self-Service	1 California St	5 pm
Self-Service	111 Pine St	5 pm
Self-Service	100 Pine St	5 pm
Self-Service	388 Market St	5 pm
Self-Service	101 California St	5 pm
Self-Service	1 Ferry Plaza	5 pm
Self-Service	1 Embarcadero Ctr	5 pm
Self-Service	444 Market St	5 pm
Self-Service	600 Montgomery St	5 pm
Self-Service	369 Pine St	5 pm
Self-Service	50 Fremont St	5 pm
Self-Service	760 Market St	5 pm
Self-Service	201 3rd St	5 pm
Self-Service	201 Sansome St	5 pm
Self-Service	101 2nd St	5 pm
Self-Service	135 Main St	5 pm
Self-Service	100 Spear St	5 pm
Self-Service	120 Howard St	5 pm
Self-Service	140 2nd St	5 pm
Self-Service	33 New Montgomery St	5 pm
Self-Service	345 Spear St	5 pm
Self-Service	201 Mission St	5 pm
Self-Service	160 Spear St	5 pm
Self-Service	139 Townsend St	5 pm
Self-Service	475 Brannan St	5 pm
Self-Service	600 Harrison St	5 pm
Self-Service	475 4th St	5 pm
Self-Service	222 Kearny St	5 pm
Self-Service	600 California St	5 pm
Self-Service	601 California St	5 pm
Self-Service	88 Kearny St	5 pm
Self-Service	768 Sansome St	5 pm
Self-Service	560 Davis St	5 pm
FedEx Kinko's	726 Market St	4:45 pm
Self-Service	726 Market St	4:45 pm
Unionpostsf	237 Kearny St	4:30 pm
Self-Service	150 Sutter St	4:30 pm
Self-Service	460 Brannan St	4:15 pm
The Postal Chase	912 Cole St	4:30 pm

Map 9 • Haight Ashbury / Cole Valley

FedEx Authorized ShipCenter	1388 Haight St	4:30 pm
Haight Natual Foods & Mail	1621 Haight St	4 pm

Map 10 • Castro / Lower Haight

FedEx Kinko's	1967 Market St	5:10 pm
FedEx Kinko's	1967 Market St	5:10 pm
Self-Service	1967 Market St	5:10 pm
PO Plus	584 Castro St	5 pm
Mail Access	2261 Market St	4:45 pm
Post All Center	530 Divisadero St	4:30 pm
Self-Service	4304 18th St	4:15 pm
Self-Service	2336 Market St	4 pm

Map 11 • Hayes Valley / The Mission

Print & Ship	1586 Market St	5:15 pm
Self-Service	1750 Harrison St	5:15 pm
Self-Service	1540 Market St	5:15 pm
Self-Service	1390 Market St	5:15 pm
Self-Service	2300 Harrison St	5 pm
Self-Service	1550 Bryant St	4:45 pm
Self-Service	100 Van Ness Ave	4:30 pm
Self-Service	1655 Bryant St	4:30 pm
Self-Service	2169 Folsom St	4:30 pm
Self-Service	555 Florida St	4 pm

Map 12 • SOMA / Potrero Hill (North)

FedEx Kinko's	1155 Harrison St	5:30 pm
Self-Service	1155 Harrison St	5:30 pm
Self-Service	200 Kansas St	5:15 pm
Self-Service	1000 Brannan St	5:15 pm
Self-Service	2 Henry Adams St	5:15 pm
Self-Service	965 Mission St	5:10 pm
The Packaging Store	1255 Howard St	5 pm
Self-Service	600 Townsend St	5 pm
Self-Service	101 Henry Adams St	5 pm
Self-Service	90 7th St	5 pm
Self-Service	888 Brannan St	5 pm
Self-Service	555 De Haro St	4:40 pm
Self-Service	550 15th St	4:30 pm
Self-Service	651 Bryant St	4:30 pm
Self-Service	1111 8th St	4:15 pm
Self-Service	444 De Haro St	4 pm
Post & Parcel	1459 18th St	5 pm
Self-Service	185 Berry St	5 pm
Self-Service	330 Townsend St	5 pm

Map 13 • Mission Beach

Aim Mail Center #92	221 King St	4:45 pm
Self-Service	600 16th St	4 pm
Self-Service	1550 4th St	4 pm
Mail Boxes Etc	4104 24th St	5 pm
Self-Service	4083 24th St	4:15 pm

Map 14 • Noe Valley

Jensen's Mail & Copy	5214-F Diamond Heights Blvd	4 pm
The Mail Carrier Etc	3288 21st St	4:30 pm

Map 15 • Mission (Outer)

Golden Express	2390 Mission St, Ste 103	4:30 pm
Self-Service	1198 S Van Ness Ave	4 pm

Map 16 • Potrero Hill (Southwest)

Self-Service	1001 Potrero Ave	5 pm

Map 17 • Potrero Hill / Dogpatch

Self-Service	2343 3rd St	5:15 pm

Map 19 • Outer Richmond (East) / Seacliff

Media Pro	3739 Balboa St	4 pm

Map 20 • Richmond

Rn Union Post	5432 Geary Blvd	4 pm
Self-Service	5654 Geary Blvd	4 pm

Map 21 • Inner Richmond

Box Brothers	4644 Geary Blvd	4:30 pm
Lph Shipping & Bus Service	4338 California St	4 pm
Self-Service	3700 Geary Blvd	4 pm
Post & Parcels	3450 Sacramento St	5 pm
Lph Shipping & Business	3701 Sacramento St	4:30 pm

Map 22 • Presidio Heights / Laurel Heights

FedEx Kinko's	25 Stanyan St	4:30 pm
Self-Service	25 Stanyan St	4:30 pm
Self-Service	3333 California St	4 pm
Self-Service	3245 Geary Blvd	4 pm

Map 24 • Sunset

Postal Depot	2636 Judah St	4 pm
Self-Service	1314 22nd Ave	4 pm

Map 25 • Inner Sunset / Golden Gate Heights

Self-Service	821 Irving St	4:15 pm

Map 27 • Parkside (Inner)

FedEx Kinko's	1597 Sloat Blvd	5 pm
Self-Service	1597 Sloat Blvd	5 pm
Self-Service	1800 Taraval St	4:45 pm
Self-Service	3251 20th Ave	4 pm
Parkside Postal	945 Taraval St	3:45 pm

Map 28 • SFSU / Park Merced

Self-Service	1600 Holloway Ave	4:30 pm

Map 29 • Twin Peaks

Self-Service	350 Parnassus Ave	5 pm
The Postal Chase 3	58 West Portal Ave	5 pm

Map 30 • West Portal

Self-Service	2499 Ocean Ave	5 pm
Self-Service	317 West Portal Ave	4:45 pm

Map 32 • Diamond Heights / Glen Park

Glen Park Mail Depot	2912 Diamond St	4:45 pm
Year Round Tax Accounting	1601 Ocean Ave	4:30 pm

Map 33 • Ingleside

PostNet	3931 Alemany Blvd, Ste 2002	4 pm

Map 35 • Bernal Heights

Copy Central Mission	3181 Mission St	4:30 pm
Federal Express	1875 Marin St	5:50 pm
Self-Service	1875 Marin St	5:30 pm
Self-Service	20 Dorman Ave	4:45 pm
Self-Service	2200 Jerrold Ave	4:45 pm

Map 36 • Bayview / Silver Terrace

Baycopy Plus	3801 3rd St	4:30 pm

Map 37 • India Basin / Hunters Point

Self-Service	50 Mendell St	5 pm
Self-Service	5 Thomas Mellon Cir	5 pm
Self-Service	250 Executive Park Blvd	5 pm
Self-Service	150 Executive Park Blvd	5 pm

Map 40 • Bayview / Candlestick Point

Self-Service	1485 Bay Shore Blvd	4:30 pm

The Presidio

Self-Service	1012 Lincoln Blvd	4 pm
Self-Service	215 Lincoln Blvd	3:30 pm
Self-Service	39 Mesa St	3:30 pm

Overview

There is no shortage of landmarks in San Francisco, from the very recognizable sights to the tucked-away treasures known only to locals. On any day, you can find something new to explore, whether you want to be in the center of the action or away from the commotion.

Great Architecture

The **Sentinel Building (Map 8)**, a.k.a. the Coppola Building, is a beautiful and distinctive green copper Flatiron. The ultra-modern design of the new **DeYoung Museum in Golden Gate Park (Golden Gate Park)**, seems to inspire either love or hate from city residents-—stroll around the copper-skinned walls and twisting observation tower and decide for yourself. The **Roos House (Map 22)** in Pacific Heights shows off Bernard Maybeck's style. For a touch of modernism, check out **St. Mary's Cathedral (Map 6)** with its washing machine component-shaped cross. More churches in classic styles include the grand **Grace Cathedral (Map 7)** and **St. Peter and Paul's Church (Map 4)**. Moreover, the city's trademark is its ornate Victorian and Edwardian homes from the early 20th century that can be found all over town. The **Transamerica Pyramid (Map 8)** defines our skyline and we'd love to get access to the little room on top one day.

Great Public Buildings

The **Palace of the Legion of Honor (Map 18)**, in its breathtaking setting overlooking the **Golden Gate Bridge (The Presidio)**, is a beautiful Beaux Arts copy of its namesake in Paris at 3/4-scale. **City Hall (Map 7)** also belongs with Beaux Arts French Renaissance architecture and is arguably one of the finest public buildings in the world.

Great Outdoor Spaces

The Presidio (The Presidio), is an entryway to the vast expanse of Marin County over the Golden Gate Bridge, complete with a chapel, a bowling alley, and a campground. Angel Island is a nice way to get out on the Bay by ferry—you can even take your bike. **Alamo Square (Map 10)** has postcard-worthy views of Victorian homes juxtaposed against the backdrop of skyscrapers, and **Dolores Park (Map 10)** is perfect for people and their dogs; enjoy a game of tennis in both spaces. Favorite neighborhood hilltop parks with amazing views include **Alta Plaza Park (Map 5)** in Pacific Heights, **Buena Vista Park (Map 9)** in the Haight, and **Corona Heights (Map 10)** in the Castro. **Crissy Field's (The Presidio)** beaches, running trail, and picnic areas make it a beautiful place to escape the hustle and bustle of our amazing city. But of course, there is no contest with **Golden Gate Park (Golden Gate Park)**, with its 1,013 acres of verdant green space built on what were barren sand dunes only 100 years before. Along with miles of bike trails and acres of sports fields, it is home to the De Young Museum, the Conservatory of Flowers, and the Japanese Tea Gardens.

Great Obscure Landmarks

Visit the **Official City Tree (Golden Gate Park)**, the **Golden Gate Fortune Cookie Company (Map 7)**, or the **"Shoe Garden" (Map 10)** in Alamo Square for a dose of the random historic. Roam around town and discover the dozens of murals by local artists depicting city history and culture—**Balmy Alley in the Mission (Map 15)** is a good place to start.

Overrated Landmarks

Ghirardelli Square (Map 3) and the old brick **Del Monte Cannery (Map 3)** environs are basically crowded malls chock full of tourist shops. **Fisherman's Wharf (Map 3)** is, without a doubt, the city's most popular tourist trap. But, if you've never had clam chowder in a bread bowl there, be a tourist for an hour and enjoy a bowl with some people-watching on the pier.

Map 1 • Marina / Cow Hollow (West)

Exploratorium	3601 Lyon St • 415-561-0360	Experimental hands-on museum of science, art, and human perception at the Palace of Fine Arts. Check out the Tactile Dome.
Marina Green	Marina Blvd b/w Scott St & Webster St	Fly a kite with the Golden Gate in the background.
Palace of Fine Arts	3301 Lyon St • 415-567-6642	Designed for the 1915 World's Fair by Bernard Maybeck, the Roman ruin's grandeur is strikingly beautiful.
Wave Organ	Yacht Rd	Trippy ocean-powered musical instrument and sculpture created by artists in the '80s.

Map 2 • Marina / Cow Hollow (East)

Fort Mason Center	Buchanan St & Marina Blvd • 415-441-3400	Former military base. Now houses small galleries, museums, and restaurants.
Octagon House	2645 Gough St • 415-441-7512	Fengshui a la Orson Fowler in 1861: octagonal houses provide a healthful living environment. Now a museum for colonial decorative arts.

Map 3 • Russian Hill / Fisherman's Wharf

Alice Marble tennis court	Greenwich St & Hyde St	Russian Hill-top courts named after the 1930s US tennis star.
Bimbo's 365 Club	1025 Columbus Ave • 415-474-0365	Plush music venue with a swanky vibe. Topless mermaids.
Del Monte Cannery	2801 Leavenworth St • 415-771-3112	What was once the biggest peach cannery in the world is now a big ol' tourist trap.
Fisherman's Wharf	Embarcadero b/w Aquatic Park & Pier 39	Tacky tourist trap, but the sea lions love it. Historic boats, fresh crabs, the ferry to Alcatraz, etc.
Ghirardelli Square	900 North Point St • 415-775-5500	Site of the original Ghirardelli chocolate factory; touristy shops and cafés.
Lombard Street	Lombard St b/w Hyde St & Leavenworth St	Known as "the world's crookedest street," it is packed with tourist cars on weekends, but fun to ride down on a bike!
Macondray Lane	Jones St b/w Green St & Union St	Hidden gem on Russian Hill. Influenced Armistead Maupin's "Barbary Lane" in *Tales of the City*. No cars allowed.
Musee Mecanique	Fisherman's Wharf • 415-346-2000	Fun and nostalgic. Old arcade games and carnival attractions. Take lots of quarters.
National Maritime Museum	900 Beach St • 415-561-6662	Museum of everything seaworthy—ship models, figureheads, maritime paintings, photos, and artifacts. Free.
San Francisco Art Institute	800 Chestnut St • 415-771-7020	Spanish mission-style building with Diego Rivera mural.
Vallejo Steps	Vallejo St & Mason St	Sweat the 167 steps and 45-degree slope, and you will be rewarded with views of Coit Tower and Bay Bridge.
The Balclutha	Pier 41 • 415-561-6662	Over one hundred years old, and still a beaut.

Map 4 • North Beach / Telegraph Hill

Coit Tower	1 Telegraph Hill Blvd • 415-362-0808	Built in 1933 for the city"s firefighters, still our favorite... pole joke.
Condor Club	560 Broadway • 415-781-8222	Birthplace of world's first topless and bottomless entertainment.
Filbert Steps	Filbert St & Sansome St	Telegraph Hill stairway amidst gardens and residences. A flock of wild parrots lives in the trees here.
Joe DiMaggio Playground	651 Lombard St	The playground where the Yankee Clipper learned to play ball.
Sts. Peter and Paul	666 Filbert St • 415-421-0809	Church where Joe DiMaggio's funeral was held, also featured in Dirty Harry.
Teatro ZinZanni	The Embarcadero & Pier 5 • 415-438-2668	Five-course dinner and an evening of European cabaret and cirque in a luxurious waterfront tent.

Map 5 • Pacific Heights / Western Addition

Alamo Square	Fulton St & Scott St	One of the most picture-perfect sights in the city.
Alta Plaza Park	Clay St & Steiner St	Tennis courts top this park terrace with several steep staircases leading up from the street.
The Fillmore	1805 Geary Blvd • 415-346-6000	Part of Bill Graham's entertainment empire. Have a red apple from the bucket at the entrance, it's a Fillmore tradition.
KPOO Mural	Post St & Steiner St	Tribute to one of the first Black non-commercial radio stations.
Lyon Street Stairs	Lyon St & Broadway St	Scenic flight of stairs guaranteed to make you sweat.
Mrs. Doubtfire House	2640 Steiner St	The house where the 1993 comedy hit was filmed.
The Painted Ladies	720 Steiner St	Famous row of Victorian houses in pastel colors juxtaposed against the SF cityscape.
St John Coltrane African Orthodox Church	1286 Fillmore St • 415-673-7144	Jazz-inspired services and a John Coltrane memorial.

Map 6 • Pacific Heights / Japantown

Haas-Lilienthal House	2007 Franklin St • 415-441-3004	Queen Anne classic with added turrets and towers for extravagant ornamentation. Tour the grand Victorian home which survived the earthquake of 1906.
Japan Center Peace Pagoda	Geary Blvd & Webster St	Five-tiered structure designed by Yoshiro Taniguchi.
Sarcophagus of Thomas Starr King	Geary Blvd & Franklin St	The only public sarcophagus in the city.
Spreckels Mansion	2080 Washington St	1912 Spreckels family home, an example of a shift from late Victorian to Neoclassical. Now owned by Danielle Steele.

St Mary's Cathedral	1111 Gough St • 415-567-2020	Modern funky-looking cathedral with a hyperbolic paraboloid that forms a cross. Designed by Peter Luigi Nervi in 1971.
War Memorial Opera House	401 Van Ness Ave • 415-621-6600	Magnificent performances amidst French Renaissance design. Also, birthplace of the UN.

Map 7 • Nob Hill / Tenderloin

450 Sutter Medical Building	450 Sutter St	26-story Art Deco masterpiece by renowned architect Timothy Pfleuger.
Asian Art Museum	200 Larkin St • 415-581-3500	Extensive Asian art collection in the old Beaux Arts style library building—a little claustrophobic in the galleries, but well worth your time.
Bohemian Club	624 Taylor St	Club for rich republicans who like to get freaky-deaky in the woods.
Chambord Apartments	1298 Sacramento St	James Francis Dunn's 1921 Gaudi-esque building evokes the art and design of fin-de-siecle Paris.
City Hall	1 Dr Carlton Goodlet Pl • 415-701-2311	Administrative offices and art exhibits inside. The most earthquake-retrofitted National Landmark.
Civic Center	Grove St b/w Franklin St & Leavenworth St • 415-904-7100	Includes City Hall, Court House, state and federal buildings, the main library, Asian Art Museum, Davies Symphony Hall, War Memorial Opera House, Bill Graham Civic Auditorium. Whew!
Civic Center Farmers Market (Wed & Sun, 7am-5:30pm)	Market St b/w 7th & 8th St • 415-558-9455	Shopping for cheap fruits and veggies alongside crazies on Wednesdays and Sundays at the UN Plaza.
Fleur De Lys	777 Sutter St • 415-673-7779	High-end French cuisine in one of the most romantic dining rooms in SF.
Glide Memorial United Methodist Church	330 Ellis St • 415-674-6000	Uplifting all-inclusive Sunday services led by Reverend Cecil Williams and a full chorus.
Golden Gate Fortune Cookie Company	56 Ross Aly • 415-781-3956	Dimly-lit business in the oldest alley in SF. A bag of 40 cookies is a bargain at $3, or buy the "unfortunate" flat disks.
Grace Cathedral	1100 California St • 415-749-6300	Grand Episcopalian cathedral on Nob Hill.
Great American Music Hall	859 O'Farrell St • 415-885-0750	Grand, ornate venue in a gritty neighborhood.
Heart Sculpture	Post St & Powell St	The heart Tony Bennett left in San Francisco.
The Huntington Hotel	1075 California St • 415-474-5400	Old luxury hotel reminiscent of a bygone era of San Francisco.
Masonic Auditorium	1111 California St • 415-776-4702	Theater on top of Nob Hill, seats about 2,000. Excellent acoustics. Exhibits downstairs.
Melvin M Swig Interfaith Memorial Labryinth	California St & Taylor St	Tune out the trolly bells at this circular labyrinth at Grace Cathedral, which offers a place for rest and meditation.
Ocean Aquarium	120 Cedar St • 415-771-3206	For piranhas go elsewhere; these are friendly fish to look at and purchase.
Pacific Union Club	1000 California St • 415-775-1234	Private men's club. Former home to James C. Flood. Brownstone built in 1885 and survivor of the 1906 earthquake and fire.
Powell St Cable Car Turn Around	Powell St & Market St	Gawk at the tourists who think you have to stand in line to take a cable car.
San Francisco Main Library	100 Larkin St • 415-557-4400	Very modern, very organized public library.
Union Square	Powell St & Geary St	The epicenter of downtown shopping, anchored by department giant Macy's.

Map 8 • Financial District / SOMA

555 California	555 California St	Formerly the Bank of America Building, this structure features in the Towering Inferno, back when OJ was cool.
City Lights	261 Columbus Ave • 415-362-8193	Ferlinghetti's baby and a mecca for 1950s Beat scene. Check out the poetry room upstairs.
Cupid's Span	Embarcadero & Folsom St	The giant bow and arrow on the Embarcadero by Claes Oldenburg and Coosje van Bruggen.
Embarcadero Center	301 Clay St • 415-772-0700	Fancy-pants retail and office district.
Ferry Building	Embarcadero & Market St • 415-693-0996	Gathering of local farmers and artisan producers, creating a foodie community in the 1850s-erected building.
Hallidie Building	130-150 Sutter St	Early Modern architecture; first glass-curtain wall building in America, 1918.

Historic Interpretive Signage Project	Embarcadero & King St	Twenty-two bronze plaques tell the story of the waterfront in a span of 2.5 miles.
Hunter-Dulin Building	111 Sutter St (at Montgomery)	The city's most gorgeous Deco skycraper. Check out the lobby.
Justin Herman Plaza	Market St & Embarcadero	A good place to meet for a protest, or better yet Critical Mass. Downtown types rendezvous here for lunch.
Lotta's Fountain	Kearny St b/w Geary Blvd & Market St	Meeting point for separated families during the 1906 eathquake.
One Rincon Hill	511 Harrison St	Tallest residential structure west of the Mississippi.
Portsmouth Square	Kearny St b/w Clay & Washington St	Chinatown's living room and center of social activity. Also the site of California's first public school.
Rincon Center	101 Spear St • 415-777-4100	Controversial California history depicted in nearly thirty murals at this post office-turned-popular downtown lunch spot.
Sea Change Sculpture	Townsend St & 2nd St	Bright-red stainless steel sculpture on the Embarcadero by abstract expressionist Mark di Suvero.
Sentinel Building	916 Kearny St	Francis Ford Coppola bought this 1905 green copper flatiron from the Kingston Trio in the 1970s, and has used it for his film company since.
SFMOMA	151 3rd St • 415-357-4000	Mario Botta-designed modern art museum. Check out the new rooftop sculpture garden.
Sing Chong and Sing Fat Buildings	Grant St & California St	Great examples of Chinese pagoda-style architecture, built in 1908.
South Park	2nd St & Brannan St	Local riche in the 1870s and dotcom royalty in the 1990s live around this oval SOMA park.
Spec's Twelve Adler Museum Cafe	12 William Saroyan Pl • 415-421-4112	Eclectic, bohemian bar hidden in a tiny nook off Columbus.
Transamerica Pyramid	600 Montgomery St	San Francisco's tallest (853') and most distinctive building, built by William Pereira in 1972.
Transamerica Redwood Park	600 Montgomery St	Relax among cute, baby redwoods.
Tree Sculpture	747 Howard St • 415-974-4000	Hand-carved from a single NoCal redwood tree, this sculpture scales the staircase of Moscone Center West.
Vaillancourt Fountain	4 Embarcadero Ctr	It's that weird fountain sculpture thing at Embarcadero 4. Herb Caen hated it and most of San Francisco still does.
VC Morris Building (Circle Gallery)	140 Maiden Ln	1948 Frank Lloyd Wright-designed building with interior spiral.
Vesuvio	255 Columbus Ave • 415-362-3370	Old Beat hang-out.
Yerba Buena Center for the Arts	701 Mission St • 415-978-2787	Fumikiko Maki-designed exhibition and performance meditation.

Map 9 • Haight Ashbury / Cole Valley

Buena Vista Park	Haight St & Buena Vista Ave	A labyrinth of paved paths in SF's oldest park.
Charles Manson's House	636 Cole St	SF "family" recruiting grounds.
Grateful Dead House	710 Ashbury St	Corner of Haight and Ashbury, circa-1890s Cranston-Keenan building. We miss you Jerry.
Haight-Ashbury	Haight St & Ashbury St	1960s hippie haven and early home to the Grateful Dead. Great Victorians, cool shops, disillusioned youth, and drugs.

Map 10 • Castro / Lower Haight

Abner Phelps House	1111 Oak St	Oldest house in SF, built by Colonel Phelps in 1850 and since relocated three times.
Café du Nord	2170 Market St • 415-861-5016	Though it gets big musical acts, it still maintains a lounge atmosphere. Also check out the Swedish American Club upstairs.
Castro Theatre	429 Castro St • 415-621-6120	Beautiful old-fashioned Art Deco theater for movies and special programs.
Corona Heights	Roosevelt Wy & Museum Wy	Hilltop park dominated by native chert formations and 360-degree views.
DMV	1377 Fell St • 800-777-0133	Good spot to mention while giving directions.
Dolores Park	Dolores St b/w 18th St & 20th St • 415-554-9529	The sunniest spot in the city (and great tennis courts!).
Duboce Bikeway Mural	Duboce b/w Market St & Church St	Celebrates the car-free public space of bikeway behind the "super" Safeway, sponsored by the SF Bicycle Coalition.
Harvey Milk Memorial Plaza	400 Castro St	Castro Street plaza built in memory of Harvey Milk.
Harvey's	500 Castro St • 415-431-4278	Bar and Castro Street institution at the former site of the Elephant Walk and the 1979 White Night riots.

Market St Railway Mural	300 Church St	Depicts sweeping birds-eye view of Market Street through different eras and historical events in harmonious colors.
Mission Dolores	3321 16th St • 415-621-8203	1776 Spanish mission and Catholic church.
Randall Museum	199 Museum Wy • 415-554-9600	Petting zoo, earthquake exhibit, and model trains!
Randall Museum Dog Run	Roosevelt Wy & Museum Wy	Home of the Chihuahua Cha Cha.
Shoe Garden	Steiner St & Grove St	Old abandoned shoes get a new life with plants with help from Alamo Square's gardener.

Map 11 • Hayes Valley / The Mission

The Armory	1800 Mission St • 415-677-0456	Former military base, now the HQ for fetish company Kink.
Bike Kitchen	650 Florida St • 415-647-2453	A do-it-yourself bicycle repair and resource shop run entirely by volunteers.
Clarion Alley	17th St & Valencia St	Alley of vibrant, socially conscious community street art. Bring your camera.
Global Exchange	2017 Mission St • 415-255-7296	Activism headquarters for fair trade. Volunteers always needed, and rooftop has great views on Friday beer day.
Hayes Green	Octavia Blvd b/w Hayes & Fell St	Newest green area to go along with Octavia Boulevard freeway exit in the heart of Hayes Valley.
Maestrapeace Mural	18th St & Valencia St	Mural by 7 women painters depicting women at work, play, etc. on the side of the Women's Center Building.
Mission Police Station	630 Valencia St • 415-558-5400	Seven Dancing Stones in the lobby are arranged in form of Pleiades constellation, telling myths of the native Oholone Indians.
San Francisco Opera	301 Van Ness Ave • 415-864-3330	Second largest opera company in America.
San Francisco Symphony	201 Van Ness Ave	Seen the likes of Stravinsky and Metallica.

Map 12 • SOMA / Potrero Hill (North)

Anchor Brewing Company	1705 Mariposa St • 415-863-8350	Call for info about the free brewery tours of this SF institution.
Defenestration	6th St & Howard St	That great empty building south of Market with furniture and home appliances stuck all over the outside of it. Brian Goggin created it in 1997.
Flower Mart	640 Brannan St • 415-392-7944	The best place to buy flowers—open to the public after 10 am.
Marriott View Lounge	55 4th St • 415-896-1600	The steep drink prices you're paying at the roof lounge are really for the magnificent 180-degree view.
The Metreon	101 4th St • 415-369-6000	Shopping complex frequented for movies and virtual bowling.
Mint Plaza	Jessie St & Mint St	A new public open space, the plaza is an urban haven for art exhibits, live music and small festivals.

Map 13 • Mission Beach

AT&T Park	24 Willie Mays Plaza	Ball games and concerts. Best place to catch a homerun: on the bay in a kayak.
House featured in the movie Pacific Heights	1243 19th St	Film location of the 1990 movie with Michael Keaton and Melanie Griffith

Map 14 • Noe Valley

Sparky	20th St & Church St	From this hydrant "came a stream of water allowing the firemen to save the Mission district" in 1906. Annually painted gold by admirers.

Map 15 • Mission (Outer)

Balmy Alley	Balmy St b/w 24th & 25th St	Every garage door in this narrow passage is an artistic statement.

Map 16 • Potrero Hill (Southwest)

Potrero del Sol/ La Raza Skatepark	25th St & Utah St	SF's newest skatepark.
Potrero Hill Recreation Center	801 Arkansas St	See the old OJ Simpson mural, where as a kid The Juice once ran loose.
Vermont St	20th St & Vermont St	The actual crookedest street in SF; steeper than Lombard!

Map 18 • Outer Richmond (West) / Ocean Beach

Camera Obscura	1096 Point Lobos Ave • 415-750-0415	Based on a 15th-century Da Vinci invention. Giant camera provides 360-degree views of Seal Rock.
Cliff House	1090 Point Lobos Ave • 415-386-3330	Originally built in 1863, then again in 1896,1909, and 2005, it currently houses touristy restaurants and bars with great ocean views.
Fort Miley	El Camino Del Mar & Clement St • 415-556-8371	SFSU Adventure Rope Courses at the ruins of old defense batteries.
Lands End	El Camino del Mar & Seal Rock Dr	Walk from Ocean Beach to Golden Gate Bridge along the shoreline on a lush hiking path.
Palace of the Legion of Honor	Clement St & 34th Ave • 415-750-3600	Our prettiest museum. Ancient, European, and decorative arts.
Sutro Baths	Point Lobos Ave & 48th Ave	Ruins of Mayor Alfred Sutro's clifftop mansion.

Map 19 • Outer Richmond (East) / Seacliff

Lincoln Park Golf Course	300 34th Ave • 415-750-4653	Public golf course, built in 1908. Stellar views.

Map 21 • Inner Richmond

Temple Emanu-El	2 Lake St • 415-751-2535	Jewish temple built in a Byzantine-Roman fusion style.

Map 22 • Presidio Heights / Laurel Heights

Blood Centers of the Pacific Fountain	270 Masonic Ave	Most consistently-flowing, unnaturally-blue fountain in the city.
Bridge Theater	3010 Geary Blvd • 415-267-4893	1939 Art Deco theater showing indie and foreign films.
Jefferson Airplane House	2400 Fulton St	Mortuary turned music mansion.
Roos House	3500 Jackson St	Classic Bernard Maybeck house in Pacific Heights.
San Francisco Columbarium	1 Loraine Ct • 415-771-0717	Neoclassical building and repository of burial ashes, including remains of prominent San Francisco figures.
St Ignatius Church	650 Parker Ave • 415-422-2188	Jesuit Baroque architecture parish in its fifth incarnation, now on University of San Francisco campus.

Map 26 • Parkside (Outer)

San Francisco Zoo	1 Zoo Rd • 415-753-7080	An infant gorilla named Hasani is among the newest residents of the zoo, which is home to more than 250 animals.

Map 27 • Parkside (Inner)

Sigmund Stern Grove	19th Ave & Sloat Blvd • 415-252-6252	Free concerts in the summer, Sundays at 2.
Stonestown Galleria	3251 20th Ave • 415-759-2626	Large shopping center.

Map 28 • SFSU / Park Merced

Fort Funston	Skyline Blvd & John Muir Dr • 415-239-2366	Cliffside view of coast—excellent hang-gliding and hiking.

Map 29 • Twin Peaks

Seward Street Slides	Douglass St & Seward St	Make like you're 12! Bring some cardboard.
Sutro Tower	250 Palo Alto Ave	Giant antenna in a wealthy 'hood.
Tank Hill	Twin Peaks Blvd & Crown Ter	Hilltop park. Look into people's backyards 300' below, and view both bridges.
Twin Peaks	Twin Peaks Blvd	The geographical center of the city. Arguably the best panoramic views, particularly at night.
UCSF's Kalmanovitz Library	530 Parnassus Ave • 415-476-2334	Best views of any university library in the world (from the ocean to downtown). Public admission.

Map 31 • Mt Davidson

Mt Davidson Cross	Dalewood Wy & Myra Wy	Controversial symbol embodied in a 103' concrete and steel structure inaugurated by FDR.

Map 32 • Diamond Heights / Glen Park

Children's Art at Glen Canyon	Glen Canyon	Freaky public art
Sunnyside Conservatory	236 Monterey Blvd	Nature unleashed on an old Victorian.

Map 33 • Ingleside

Ingleside Terraces Sundial	Borica St & Entrado Ct	Massive 28' white sundial erected in 1913 to lure young families to developments south of the city center commotion.

Map 35 • Bernal Heights

Alemany Farmers Market (Sat, dawn to dusk)	100 Alemany Blvd • 415-647-9423	Oldest in town. Mixed crowd on Saturdays in the sunny colorful parking lot supporting family-owned farms.

Map 36 • Bayview / Silver Terrace

Bayview Opera House	4705 3rd St • 415-824-0386	Performing arts training for kids.
Flora Grubb Gardens	1634 Jerrold Ave • 415-626-7256	8,000-square foot, solar-paneled building housing many a flowering plant.

Map 37 • India Basin / Hunters Point

Hilltop Park Skatebowl	Hilltop Park	"The Dish." Classic 70s skateboard saucer.

Map 38 • Excelsior / Crocker Amazon

Crocker Amazon Skatepark	1600 Geneva Ave	Single, large skateboard bowl.

Map 40 • Bayview / Candlestick Point

Candlestick Point Recreation Area	1150 Carroll Ave • 415-671-0145	Windsurfing, picnicking, community gardens.

Golden Gate Park

Buffalo Paddock	John F Kennedy Dr (West of Spreckels Lake)	Chill-out zone for local bison.
California Academy of Sciences	55 Music Concourse Dr • 415-321-8000	Natural history museum and planetarium, new location. They even have live alligators. Free on first Wednesdays.
Conservatory of Flowers	100 John F Kennedy Dr • 415-666-7001	Temple of photosynthesis.
de Young museum	50 Hagiwara Tea Garden Dr	Major fine arts museum; 360-degree views from tower.
John McLaren Statue	John F Kennedy Dr & Conservatory Dr W • 415-831-2701	Statue of former park superintendent John McLaren.
Official City Tree	JFK Dr near Fell St	The official city tree is the 100' Monterey Cypress in front of McLaren Lodge.
Queen Wilhelmina Tulip Gardens	JFK Dr & Great Hwy	Lovely tulip garden by the windmill at the ocean. Best time: early spring.

The Presidio

Andy Goldsworthy Spire	Arguello Blvd	Goldsworthy brilliance amongst (and with) the trees.
Crissy Field	Mason St	Incredible shoreline access and views of the bay.
Fort Point	Long Ave & Marine Dr • 415-556-1693	Anybody see *Vertigo*? Fort built during the Civil War, historic site since 1970. Popular destination for runners along the Marina.
Golden Gate Bridge	US Hwy 101	The one and only. Sublime beyond all accounting.
Presidio Golf Course	300 Finley Rd • 415-561-4663	Great public golf course founded in 1895, formerly operated by the military.
The Presidio (Visitor's Center)	50 Moraga Ave • 415-561-4323	1776 Spanish military post; 1,480 acres of buildings and grounds.
Rob Hill Campground	Harrison Blvd & Central Magazine Rd • 415-561-5444	Camping in the city? The Presidio has it all. Rob Hill will reopen for the 2010 season; call after January 2010 to reserve a space.

Mill Valley

Old Mill Park	Throckmorton Ave & Old Mill St	The reason why the quaint town of Mill Valley has its name.
Outdoor Art Club	1 W Blithedale Ave • 415-388-9886	Conservation and civic duty are the foundation here.

Berkeley (West)

Berkeley Marina	University Ave & Frontage Ave • 510-981-6740	Sweeping views of the bay, the city, and the GG Bridge Check out the historic, and long, Berkeley pier.
Berkeley Skatepark	5th & Harrison St	First-rate Bay Area skatepark.

Berkeley (East)

Berkeley Iceland	2727 Milvia St • 510-647-1606	Classic skating rink closed in March 2007.
Berkeley Rose Garden	1200 Euclid Ave	3,000 bushes and more than 250 varieties.
People's Park	2556 Haste St	Site of contention between the University and activists since the '60s.

Oakland

Morcom Rose Garden	600 Jean St	Eight acres of rose gardens.
Peralta Hacienda Historical Park	2465 34th Ave	A 6-acre park in the heart of Oakland.

Downtown Oakland / Lake Merritt

African-American Museum and Library	659 14th St	Sharing historical and cultural experiences of African Americans.
Cathedral of Christ the Light	180 Grand Ave • 510-271-1928	Internationally renown modern cathedral design. Redefines Oakland's lakefront.
Children's Fairyland	699 Bellevue Ave • 510-452-2259	Magical fantasy amusement park.
Creative Growth Art Center	355 24th St • 510-836-2340	Serves disabled adult artists.
Malonga Casquelourd Center for the Arts	1428 Alice St • 510-238-7219	Formerly Alice Art Center. Great classes, performances, and more.
The Museum of African-American Technology Science Village	408 14th St	Atmosphere of an African village.
Museum of Children's Art	538 9th St • 510-465-8770	Expressive exhibits and workshops for kids.
Oakland Asian Cultural Center	388 9th St • 510-637-0455	The only Pan-Asian Cultural Center in the Bay Area.
Oakland Museum of California	1000 Oak St • 510-238-2200	History, art, and natural sciences of California.
Oakland Public Library - Main Branch	125 14th St • 510-238-3134	The public library.
The Paramount Theatre	2025 Broadway St • 510-465-6400	Grand music and entertainment hall.
Pro Arts	Clay St & 2nd St • 510-763-4361	The region's primary visual arts venue.

North Oakland / Emeryville

Mountain View Cemetery	5000 Piedmont Ave • 510-658-2588	Large and impressive burial grounds.

Sausalito

Battery Spencer	Hwy 101, Marin side of Golden Gate Bridge	Best views of the GG Bridge and the city.
Bay Model Visitor Center	2100 Bridgeway • 415-332-3871	Huge scale model of San Francisco Bay.

As a major destination for both business and pleasure, San Francisco has a wide range of hotels to choose from. Obviously, these listings will be of limited use to San Franciscans, but knowing a thing or two about the local hotel scene can be useful, indeed.

With this knowledge you can weigh in on cocktail conversations about trendy hotspots such as **Hotel Vitale (Map 8)** and steer visiting friends, family, and colleagues into accommodations that match their budgets and sensibilities. After all, you wouldn't want to land your 85-year-old auntie from Cowtown, USA smack dab in the middle of the Tenderloin and your party-hearty younger bro in a buttoned-up hotel in Pacific Heights. 'Nuff said.

For the high rollers in your life, classic luxury resides at the **Palace (Map 8), Ritz-Carlton (Map 7)**, **Four Seasons (Map 8), Mandarin Oriental (Map 8)**, and **Hotel Nikko (Map 7).** Upscale accommodations steeped in local history abound on Nob Hill, where you'll find the **Fairmont (Map 7),** a favorite lodging option among US presidents; the **Huntington Hotel (Map 7)**, home of the famous Big 4 Restaurant; and the **Intercontinental Mark Hopkins (Map 7)**, with its Top of the Mark lounge offering unparalleled city views. When your jet-setting, trend-watching friends descend upon the city, send them to the **W (Map 8)** just south of Market, or to Ian Schrager's **Clift Hotel (Map 7)**, where the visually arresting Redwood Room lounge draws many a well-heeled San Franciscan on weekend nights. If they're hip but slightly grungy, the **Phoenix Hotel (Map 7)** or the **The Hotel Tropicana (Map 11)** should fit the bill. If their main place of interest is the Castro, try the classic **Beck's Motor Lodge (Map 10)**.

The city also plays host to a bevy of boutique hotels and bed and breakfasts, each with their own unique style and offerings. Love art? Downtown's **Hotel Triton (Map 8)** and **Hotel Des Arts (Map 8)** feature permanent and temporary art installations from local and well-known artists. **Hotel Monaco (Map 7)** welcomes guests with pets, and will even provide a goldfish companion for visitors who've left their furry friends at home. Other top boutique hotels include **Hotel Majestic (Map 6)** and **Hotel Drisco (Map 5)** in Pacific Heights, as well as downtown's **Campton Place (Map 7)**, **Harbor Court (Map 8)**, and **Prescott (Map 7)** hotels. San Francisco, the land of the Victorian, also has a number of beautiful, quaint, well-placed bed and breakfasts. Two fine B&B choices are: the undiscovered **'A Country Cottage' (Map 11)** and the historic **Red Victorian Bed and Breakfast (Map 9)**. Do your own searching at www.bedandbreakfast.com for the plethora of other B&B's in this city.

For the budget-conscious, the **Holiday Inn Golden Gateway (Map 6)**, **Marriott's Courtyard Downtown (Map 8)**, and **Hyatt Fisherman's Wharf (Map 3)** offer solid accommodations and amenities. And for your granola-eatin' cousin backpacking across the country, hostel choices include **the Green Tortoise (Map 8)** and **Hostelling International (Map 7)** with locations downtown, at the Civic Center, and at Fisherman's Wharf. Whatever you choose, remember that the rates indicated here are estimates and subject to change. For deals, check out one of the many hotel accommodation websites (Hotels.com, Priceline, Hotwire, Travelocity, Kayak.com, etc.) to get the best rates. Prices are generally highest during holidays, summer months, and special events like the Gay Pride Parade (June). Not all hotels have star ratings, and those that do are sometimes inaccurate. Room rates are usually a pretty good indication of hotel quality. Be aware that overnight parking fees at many city hotels can exceed $30/day. Lastly—if you are looking for good rates, great amenities and the best locations, try Craigslist's 'Vacation Rentals' section. Normal people like you and me will rent their apartment out by the night/week/month if they know they are going to be out of town and sometimes these are the best kinds of housing situations as long as there is a smidgen of mutual trust between both parties.

Like most cities, San Francisco has an over-abundance of S.R.O hotels—this stands for Single Room Occupancy, otherwise known as a residential hotel. Some are totally respectable places to live if you can't afford an apartment, some have vibrant communities, some are owned and re-habbed by non-profit organizations to make them livable places for seniors and those with life-challenges, and some are bathroom-down-the-hall-dimly-lit places where people on the fringes of society go to die. Chances are that you, Not For Tourist reader, probably do not want to be living in one or sending your friends/parents/relatives to stay in one. Thankfully, most of the places listed in this guide are not SRO hotels. The most concentrated area of these are in the Tenderloin and South of Market area. You can tell by the per week/per month offers and also by the kind of people who hang out outside, or the kinds of things hanging in the windows. Since we can't spend a month going to every single one of these places, we'll leave it up to you to decide for yourself.

Map 1 • Marina / Cow Hollow (West)

		Phone	Price
Alpha Inn & Suites	2505 Lombard St	415-921-2505	74
Chelsea Motor Inn	2095 Lombard St	415-563-5600	79
Country Hearth Inn	2707 Lombard St	415-567-2425	79
Days Inn Lombard	2358 Lombard St	415-922-2010	100
Economy Inn	2630 Lombard St	415-922-0810	85
Edward II Inn and Suites	3155 Scott St	415-922-3000	89
Greenwich Inn	3201 Steiner St	415-921-5162	93
Marina Motel	2576 Lombard St	415-921-9406	85
Pacific Motor Inn	2599 Lombard St	415-346-4664	79
Presidio Inn	2361 Lombard St	415-931-7810	79
Sea Captain Motel	2322 Lombard St	415-921-4980	80
Super 8 Motel	2440 Lombard St	415-922-0244	99
Surf Motel	2265 Lombard St	415-922-1950	55
Travelodge	2755 Lombard St	415-931-8581	99
Travelodge Golden Gate	2230 Lombard St	415-922-3900	94

Map 2 • Marina / Cow Hollow (East)

America's Best Inns & Suites	2850 Van Ness Ave	415-776-3220	99
Buena Vista Motor Inn	1599 Lombard St	415-923-9600	134
Comfort Inn by the Bay	2775 Van Ness Ave	415-928-5000	179
Coventry Motor Inn	1901 Lombard St	415-567-1200	79
Cow Hollow Motor Inn	2190 Lombard St	415-921-5800	96
Francisco Bay Motel	1501 Lombard St	415-474-3030	166
Heritage Marina Hotel	2550 Van Ness Ave	415-776-7500	99
Hostelling International- Fisherman's Wharf	240 Ft Mason	415-771-7277	25
Hotel Del Sol	3100 Webster St	415-921-5520	144
Lombard Motor Inn	1475 Lombard St	415-441-6000	72
Lombard Plaza Motel	2026 Lombard St	415-921-2444	79
Marina Inn	3110 Octavia St	415-928-1000	115
Motel Capri	2015 Greenwich St	415-346-4667	99
Pacific Heights Inn	1555 Union St	415-776-3310	79
Ramada Limited	1940 Lombard St	415-775-8116	99
Redwood Inn	1530 Lombard St	415-776-3800	90
SF Motor Inn	1750 Lombard St	415-921-1842	57
Star Motel	1727 Lombard St	415-346-8250	99
Town House Motel	1650 Lombard St	415-885-5163	90
Travelodge by the Bay	1450 Lombard St	415-673-0691	54
Union Street Inn	2229 Union St	415-346-0424	179

Map 3 • Russian Hill / Fisherman's Wharf

Argonaut Hotel	495 Jefferson St	415-563-0800	269
Bayside Inn at the Wharf	1201 Columbus Ave	415-776-7070	99
Columbus Motor Inn	1075 Columbus Ave	415-885-1492	90
Courtyard San Francisco Fisherman's Wharf	580 Beach St	415-775-3800	180
Fairmont Heritage Place, Ghirardelli Square	900 North Point St	888-991-4300	339
Hilton San Francisco Fisherman's Wharf	2620 Jones St	415-885-4700	237
Holiday Inn Express Fisherman's Wharf	550 North Point St	415-409-4600	182
Holiday Inn Fisherman's Wharf	1300 Columbus Ave	415-771-9000	170
Hyatt Hotels & Resorts	555 North Point St	415-563-1234	289
San Francisco Marriott Fisherman's Wharf	1250 Columbus Ave	415-775-7555	229
Suites at Fisherman's Wharf	2655 Hyde St	415-771-0200	170

Map 4 • North Beach (East) / Telegraph Hill

Best Western Tuscan Inn at Fisherman's Wharf	425 North Point St	415-561-1100	179
Castle Inn Motel	1565 Broadway St	415-441-1155	109
Castro Hotel	705 Vallejo St	415-788-9709	165 per week
Entella Hotel	905 Columbus Ave	415-929-7195	35
Europa Hotel	310 Columbus Ave	415-391-5779	55
Golden Eagle Hotel	402 Broadway	415-781-6859	52
Hotel Boheme	444 Columbus Ave	415-433-9111	174
Il Triangolo Hotel	524 Columbus Ave	415-433-5122	54
Radisson Hotel Fisherman's Wharf	250 Beach St	415-392-6700	99
Royal Pacific Motor Inn	661 Broadway	415-781-6661	95
San Remo Hotel	2237 Mason St	415-776-8688	65
Sheraton	2500 Mason St	415-362-5500	189
Washington Square Inn	1660 Stockton St	415-981-4220	159
Wharf Inn	2601 Mason St	415-673-7411	139

Map 5 • Pacific Heights / Western Addition

Best Western Hotel Tomo	1800 Sutter St	415-921-4000	109
Chateau Tivoli Bed & Breakfast	1057 Steiner St	415-776-5462	99
Hotel Drisco	2901 Pacific Ave	415-346-2880	209
Laurel Inn	444 Presidio Ave	415-567-8467	199
Monte Cristo Hotel	600 Presidio Ave	415-931-1875	109

Map 6 • Pacific Heights / Japantown

Artists Inn	2231 Pine St	415-346-1919	195
Broadway Manor Inn	2201 Van Ness Ave	415-776-7900	90
Cathedral Hill Hotel	1101 Van Ness Ave	415-776-8200	99
Circa 1870-B&B	2119 California St	415-928-3224	189

Holiday Inn Golden Gateway	1500 Van Ness Ave	415-441-4000	143
Inn at the Opera	333 Fulton St	415-863-8400	169
Jackson Court San Francisco	2198 Jackson St	415-929-7670	180
Kenmore Hotel	1570 Sutter St	415-776-5815	210 weekly
Majestic Hotel	1500 Sutter St	415-441-1100	139
Monroe Hotel	1870 Sacramento St	415-474-6200	190 weekly
Oasis Inn	900 Franklin St	415-885-6865	99
Opal	1050 Van Ness Ave	415-673-4711	109
Queen Anne Hotel	1590 Sutter St	415-441-2828	99
Radisson Miyako Hotel	1625 Post St	415-922-3200	98
Red Coach Motor Lodge	700 Eddy St	415-771-2100	89
Rodeway Inn Civic Center	860 Eddy St	415-474-4374	79
Sonoma Inn	1485 Bush St	415-928-8540	50

Map 7 • Nob Hill / Tenderloin

Adante Hotel	610 Geary St	415-673-9221	89
Adelaide Hostel	5 Isadora Duncan Ln	415-359-1915	25 dorm, 75 private
Admiral Hotel	608 O'Farrell St	415-885-4989	250 weekly
Albergo Hotel Verona	317 Leavenworth St	415-775-1641	57
Aldrich Hotel	439 Jones St	415-885-6604	60
Alexis Park Hotel	825 Polk St	415-673-0411	99
The Andrews Hotel	624 Post St	415-563-6877	$89
Balmoral Residence Club	1010 Bush St	415-673-5070	$40
Bel Air Hotel	344 Jones St	415-771-3460	$50
Beresford Arms	701 Post St	415-673-2600	119
Biltmore Hotel	735 Taylor St	415-673-4277	89
Budget Inn	1139 Market St	415-864-9343	66
Cable Car Court	1499 California St	415-346-5219	290 weekly
California Hotel	910 Geary St	415-440-4775	256 weekly
Campton Place Hotel	340 Stockton St	415-781-5555	340
Cartwright Hotel	524 Sutter St	415-421-2865	159
Chancellor Hotel	433 Powell St	415-362-2004	148
Civic Center Inn	790 Ellis St	415-775-7612	99
Clift Hotel	495 Geary St	415-775-4700	375
Cornell Hotel de France	715 Bush St	415-421-3154	100
Cova Hotel	655 Ellis St	415-771-3000	108
Crescent	417 Stockton St	415-400-0500	$95
Dakota Hotel	606 Post St	415-931-7475	70
Donatello Hotel	501 Post St	415-441-7100	209
Donnelly Hotel	1272 Market St	415-552-3373	160 weekly
Edgeworth Hotel	770 O'Farrell St	415-931-0723	50
Embassy Suites Hotel	610 Polk St	415-673-1404	109
Executive Vintage Court Hotel	650 Bush St	800-654-1100	119
Fairmont San Francisco	950 Mason St	415-772-5000	299
Fitzgerald Hotel	620 Post St	415-775-8100	89
Garland Hotel	505 O'Farrell St	415-771-0525	50
Gateway Inn	438 O'Farrell St	415-749-1888	275 weekly
Gaylord Suites	620 Jones St	415-673-8445	650 weekly
Golden Gate Hotel	775 Bush St	415-392-3702	95 shared, 150 private
Grand Hyatt San Francisco	345 Stockton St	415-398-1234	199
Grant Hotel	753 Bush St	415-421-7540	72
Grosvenor Suites	899 Pine St	415-421-1899	149
Halcyon Hotel	649 Jones St	415-929-8033	$79
Handlery Union Square Hotel	351 Geary St	415-781-7800	135
Harcourt Hotel	1105 Larkin St	415-673-7721	200 weekly
Herbert Hotel	161 Powell St	415-362-1600	105
Hilton San Francisco Union Square	333 O'Farrell St	415-771-1400	220
Hostelling International	685 Ellis St	415-474-5721	29 dorm, 85 private
Hotel 480	480 Sutter St	415-398-8900	189
Hotel Adagio	550 Geary St	415-775-5000	229
Hotel Aida	1087 Market St	415-863-4141	66
Hotel Beresford	635 Sutter St	415-673-9900	109
Hotel Bijou	111 Mason St	415-771-1200	139
Hotel California	580 Geary St	415-441-2700	139
Hotel Carlton	1075 Sutter St	415-673-0242	119
Hotel Diva	440 Geary St	415-885-0200	139

Map 7 • Nob Hill / Tenderloin—*continued*

Hotel King George	334 Mason St	415-781-5050	149
The Hotel Mayflower	975 Bush St	415-673-7010	70
Hotel Metropolis	25 Mason St	415-775-4600	129
Hotel Monaco	501 Geary St	415-292-0100	319
Hotel Nikko San Francisco	222 Mason St	415-394-1111	229
Hotel Palomar	12 4th St	415-348-1111	209
Hotel President	935 Geary St	415-885-0123	725 monthly
Hotel Rex	562 Sutter St	415-433-4434	207
Hotel Serrano	405 Taylor St	415-885-2500	209
Hotel Union Square	114 Powell St	415-397-3000	179
The Huntington Hotel	1075 California St	415-474-5400	300
Inn at Union Square	440 Post St	415-397-3510	209
JW Marriott San Francisco Union Square	500 Post St	415-771-8600	329
Kensington Park Hotel	450 Post St	415-788-6400	169
Layne Hotel	545 Jones St	415-922-3568	90
Luz Hotel	725 Geary St	415-928-1917	75
Marilyn Inn	27 Dashiell Hammett St	415-392-6102	60
Marines' Memorial Club	609 Sutter St	415-673-6672	199
Mark Hopkins Inter-Continental	1 Nob Hill	415-392-3434	309
Mark Twain Hotel	345 Taylor St	415-673-2332	89
Maxwell Hotel	386 Geary St	415-986-2000	99
Mithila Hotel	972 Sutter St	415-441-9297	69
Monarch Hotel	1015 Geary St	415-673-5232	99
Monticello Inn	127 Ellis St	415-392-8800	139
Motel 6	895 Geary St	415-441-8220	102
Nob Hill Hotel	835 Hyde St	415-885-2987	149
Nob Hill Inn	1000 Pine St	415-673-6080	165
Nob Hill Motor Inn	1630 Pacific Ave	415-775-8160	124
Olympic Hotel	140 Mason St	415-982-5010	69
Orchard Hotel	665 Bush St	415-362-8878	199
Parc 55 Hotel	55 Cyril Magnin St	800-468-3571	135
Petite Auberge	863 Bush St	415-928-6000	139
Phoenix Hotel	601 Eddy St	415-776-1380	119
Post Hotel	589 Post St	415-749-1285	79
Powell Hotel	28 Cyril Magnin St	415-398-3200	119
Prescott Hotel	545 Post St	415-563-0303	179
Ramada Plaza	1231 Market St	415-626-8000	89
Renoir Hotel	45 McAllister St	415-626-5200	85
Ritz-Carlton San Francisco	600 Stockton St	415-296-7465	429
San Francisco Marriott Marquis	55 4th St	415-896-1600	145
Sheldon Hotel	629 Post St	310-385-7685	700 monthly
Shirley Hotel	1544 Polk St	415-928-3353	175 weekly
Sir Francis Drake Hotel	450 Powell St	415-392-7755	179
Spaulding Hotel	240 O'Farrell St	415-397-4924	72
St Moritz Hotel	190 Ofarrell St	415-397-4639	57
Stanford Court Renaissance Hotel	905 California St	415-989-3500	143
Stratford Hotel	242 Powell St	415-397-7080	129
Super 8	415 O'Farrell St	415-928-6800	100
Taylor Hotel	615 Taylor St	415-775-0780	59
Touchstone Hotel	480 Geary St	415-771-1600	99
Union Square Back Packers Hostel	70 Derby St	415-775-7506	24 dorm, 30 private
Union Square Plaza Hotel	432 Geary St	415-776-7585	79
USA Hostel	749 Taylor St	415-440-5600	24 dorm, 48 private
Vantaggio Suites	580 O'Farrell St	415-614-2400	425 Weekly
Villa Florence Hotel	225 Powell St	415-397-7700	116
Warwick Regis Hotel	490 Geary St	415-928-7900	85
Westin St Francis	335 Powell St	866-500-0338	179
White Swan Inn	845 Bush St	415-775-1755	159
Winton Hotel	445 O'Farrell St	415-885-1988	165 weekly
York Hotel	940 Sutter St	415-885-6800	109

Map 8 • Financial District / SOMA

Argent Hotel San Francisco	50 3rd St	415-974-6400	179
Baldwin Hotel	321 Grant Ave	415-781-2220	99
Balmoral Hotel	706 Kearny St	415-956-8858	175 weekly
Courtyard San Franisco Downtown	299 2nd St	415-947-0700	134

Four Seasons Hotel SF	757 Market St	415-633-3000	475
Galleria Park Hotel	191 Sutter St	415-781-3060	209
Grant Plaza Hotel	465 Grant Ave	415-434-3883	75
Green Tortoise Hostel	494 Broadway St	415-834-1000	25 dorm, 60 private
Harbor Court Hotel	165 Steuart St	415-882-1300	119
Hilton	750 Kearny St	415-433-6600	188
Hotel Des Arts	447 Bush St	415-956-3232	109
Hotel Griffon	155 Steuart St	415-495-2100	249
Hotel North Beach	935 Kearny St	415-986-9911	39
Hotel Vitale	8 Mission St	415-278-3700	369
Hyatt Regency Hotel	5 Embarcadero Center	415-788-1234	269
Le Meridien San Francisco	333 Battery St	415-296-2900	439
Mandarin Oriental Hotel	222 Sansome St	415-276-9888	460
Omni San Francisco Hotel	500 California St	415-677-9494	189
Orchard Garden	466 Bush St	888-717-2881	
Palace Hotel	2 New Montgomery St	415-512-1111	149
Park Hotel	325 Sutter St	415-956-0445	100
St Regis San Francisco	125 3rd St	415-284-4000	389
SW Hotel	615 Broadway St	415-362-2999	159
Triton Hotel	342 Grant Ave	415-394-0500	159
W San Francisco	181 3rd St	415-777-5300	199

Map 9 • Haight Ashbury / Cole Valley

Baby Bear's House	1424 Page St	415-255-9777	75
Carl Hotel	198 Carl St	415-661-5679	78
Inn 1890	1890 Page St	415-386-0486	99
Red Victorian Bed, Breakfast & Art	1665 Haight St	415-864-1978	149
Stanyan Park Hotel	750 Stanyan St	415-751-1000	135

Map 10 • Castro / Lower Haight

Beck Motor Lodge	2222 Market St	800-227-4360	124
Country Cottage	5 Dolores Terrace	415-899-0060	79
Grove Inn	890 Grove St	415-929-0780	95
Inn on Castro	321 Castro St	415-861-0321	125
Metro Hotel	319 Divisadero St	415-861-5364	76
Perramont Hotel	2162 Market St	415-863-3222	50
Twin Peaks Hotel	2160 Market St	415-863-2909	49
Willows Bed & Breakfast Inn	710 14th St	415-431-4770	95

Map 11 • Hayes Valley / The Mission

Ascot Hotel	1657 Market St	415-864-9034	55
Days Inn Downtown Civic Center	465 Grove St	415-864-4040	90
Edwardian San Francisco Hotel	1668 Market St	415-864-1271	121
Hayes Valley Inn	417 Gough St	415-431-9131	73
Hotel Mirabelle	1906 Mission St	415-377-4170	255 weekly
Hotel Sunrise	447 Valencia St	415-431-2211	65
The Hotel Tropicana	659 Valencia St	415-701-7666	299
San Francisco Central Travelodge	1707 Market St	415-621-6775	54
Sleep Over Sauce	135 Gough St	415-252-1423	125
Villa Soma	1554 Howard St	415-348-1562	150 weekly

Map 12 • SOMA / Potrero Hill (North)

Bay Bridge Inn	966 Harrison St	415-397-0657	100
Best Western Americania	121 7th St	415-626-0200	149
Best Western Carriage Inn	140 7th St	415-552-8600	149
Best Western Civic Center Inn	364 9th St	415-621-2826	94
Best Western Flamingo Inn	114 7th St	415-621-0701	99
Clebia's Place	767 San Bruno Ave	415-648-0135	170
European Guest House	761 Minna St	415-861-6634	29 dorm, 60 private
Haveli Hotel	37 6th St	415-957-9900	45
Holiday Inn Civic Center	50 8th St	415-626-6103	93

Map 12 • SOMA / Potrero Hill (North)—*continued*

Hotel Milano	55 5th St	415-543-8555	219
Howard Johnson Inn Express	385 9th St	415-431-5131	89
Mosser	54 4th St	415-986-4400	75
Orlando Hotel	995 Howard St	415-495-9706	900
Pickwick Hotel	85 5th St	415-421-7500	121
Pontiac Hotel	509 Minna St	415-863-7775	35
Ramada Inn	240 7th St	415-861-6469	89
Rodeway Inn Downtown	101 9th St	415-621-3655	105

Map 15 • Mission (Outer)

El Capitan Hotel	2361 Mission St	415-695-1597	40
Inn San Francisco	943 S Van Ness Ave	415-641-0188	175
Noe's Nest	1257 Guerrero St	415-821-0751	159

Map 17 • Potrero Hill / Dogpatch

Balmoral Hotel North	730 22nd St	415-956-8858	150

Map 18 • Outer Richmond (West) / Ocean Beach

Seal Rock Inn	545 Point Lobos Ave	415-752-8000	99

Map 21 • Inner Richmond

Geary Parkway Motel	4750 Geary Blvd	415-752-4406	80

Map 23 • Outer Sunset

Beach Motel	4211 Judah St	415-681-6618	75
Oceanview Motel	4340 Judah St	415-661-2300	65

Map 26 • Parkside (Outer)

Days Inn at The Beach	2600 Sloat Blvd	415-665-9000	90
Ocean Park Motel	2690 46th Ave	415-566-7020	85
Roberts-at-the-Beach-Motel	2828 Sloat Blvd	415-564-2610	69

Map 32 • Diamond Heights / Glen Park

Arlington Street Urban Inn	562 Arlington St	415-286-3217	79

Map 34 • Oceanview

Amazon Motel	5060 Mission St	415-334-1533	75
Mission Inn	5630 Mission St	415-584-5020	75

Map 40 • Bayview / Candlestick Point

Franciscan Motel	6600 3rd St	415-467-9710	50

Golden Gate Park

Great Highway Inn	1234 Great Hwy	415-731-6644	99

Self-Storage

Self-Storage	Address	Phone	Map
Storagepro - Fort Knox Self Storage	370 Turk St	415-775-1195	7
City Storage	144 Townsend St	415-495-2300	8
Public Storage	611 2nd St	415-495-2760	8
Storagepro	135 Townsend St	415-777-0463	8
Attic Self Storage	2440 16th St	415-626-0800	11
Extra Space	1400 Folsom St	415-626-6665	11
Public Storage	190 10th St	415-621-3346	11
Public Storage	99 S Van Ness Ave	415-863-2903	11
Security Public Storage	43 Page St	415-861-5100	11
Self Storage 1	190 Otis St	415-552-5751	11
Soma Self Storage	1475 Mission St	415-861-5500	11
Storage Land	1855 Mission St	415-252-9821	11
Auto Storage	980 Folsom St	415-863-8882	12
City Storage	500 Indiana St	415-436-9900	13
Cor-O-Van Moving & Storage	901 16th St	415-934-1600	13
One Big Man & One Big Truck Moving Company	401 Terry Francois St	415-777-3250	13
Emerald Moving & Storage	974 Valencia St	650-342-0177	15
Extra Space Storage	2501 Cesar Chavez St	415-643-8400	16
Affordable Self Storage	901 Illinois St	415-822-4444	17
Army Street Mini Storage	1100 26th St	415-282-0200	17
California Mini Storage	790 Pennsylvania Ave	415-826-7900	17
Golden Bay Relocation	3024 Fulton St	415-668-9562	21
Public Storage	2690 Geary Blvd	415-923-0280	22
Celtic Moving & Storage	2434 45th Ave	415-822-0564	26
19th Avenue Self Storage	4050 19th Ave	415-333-3192	33
Public Storage	2587 Marin St	415-821-1224	35
A Olympic Moving & Storage	2450 Newcomb Ave	415-647-4040	36
Bay City Movers	1569 Custer Ave	415-970-0299	36
Jack TRUX Moving Specialist	660 Toland Place	415-821-4755	36
Kennedy Van & Storage	2015 McKinnon Ave	415-826-5605	36
Public Storage	2090 Evans Ave	415-550-6922	36
Shamrock Moving & Storage	3830 3rd St	415-731-2777	36
Stop N Store Mini Storage	2285 Jerrold Ave	415-970-3300	36
American Storage	600 Amador St	415-824-2338	37
A-1 Transfer Moving & Storage	1290 Egbert Ave	415-822-3900	40
All Aboard Mini Storage	1700 Egbert Ave	415-467-4600	40
Saagan Moving & Storage	5501 3rd St	415-822-7200	40
Searles Van & Storage	1301 Donner Ave	415-822-5330	40
Self Storage 1	1828 Egbert Ave	415-508-1000	40
U-Haul Self-Storage	1575 Bayshore Blvd	415-467-3830	40
Vector A Move Ahead	1480 Carroll Ave	415-822-2377	40

Van & Truck Rental

Van & Truck Rental	Address	Phone	Map
Budget Truck Rental	SF Mini Storage, 1000 7th St	415-252-0400	12
Budget Truck Rental	Army Street Mini Storage, 1100 26th St	415-285-2493	17
Coast Truck Rental	2955 3rd St	415-282-6200	17
Grant's Auto Repair	5500 Mission St	415-584-5072	34
Penske	Crocker's Lockers, 1400 Folsom St	415-775-4269	11
Penske	640 Cesar Chavez St	415-970-9000	17
Penske	Public Storage, 2690 Geary Blvd	415-923-1341	22
Postal Depot	2636 Judah St	415-661-1506	24
Ryder Truck Rental	2700 3rd St	415-285-0700	17
U-Haul	Stewart's Market, 2498 Sutter St	415-776-0301	5
U-Haul	McAllister Market, 136 McAllister St	415-255-0502	7
U-Haul	1525 Bryant St	415-252-0133	11
U-Haul	City Storage, 500 Indiana St	415-467-3830	13
U-Haul	1575 Bayshore Blvd	415-467-3830	40

Bail Bonds

Bail Bonds	Address	Phone	Map
De-Soto Bail Bonds	855 Bryant St	415-626-7290	12
Puccininelli Bail Bonds	879 Bryant St	415-863-1440	12

Car Rental

Car Rental	Address	Phone	Map
Avis	780 McDonnell Rd, SFO Airport	650-877-6780	n/a
Budget	780 McDonnell Rd	650-877-0998	n/a
Hertz	780 McDonnell Rd	650-624-6600	n/a
National Car Rental	780 McDonnell Rd, SFO Airport	650-616-3016	n/a

Car Wash

Car Wash	Address	Phone	Map
American Legal Copy	28 2nd St	415-777-4449	8
Capitol Reprographics	500 Sansome St	415-362-1200	8
Midnight Run Copy	98 Battery St	415-989-7922	8
San Francisco Legal Copy	100 California St	415-392-2900	8

Delivery and Messengers

Delivery and Messengers	Phone		Phone
Express Delivery	800-400-7874	Sunny Express	888-786-6939
Professional Messenger	415-957-9600	Western Messenger Services	415-487-4100
Silver Bullet	415-777-5100		

Gyms

Gyms	Address	Phone	Map
24 Hour Fitness	3741 Buchanan St	415-563-3535	2
24 Hour Fitness	350 Bay St	415-395-9595	4
24 Hour Fitness	2434 California St	415-929-2424	5
24 Hour Fitness	1200 Van Ness Ave	415-776-2200	6
24 Hour Fitness	100 California St	415-434-5080	8
24 Hour Fitness	303 2nd St	415-543-7808	8
24 Hour Fitness	45 Montgomery St	415-623-2424	8
24 Hour Fitness	2145 Market St	415-864-0822	10
24 Hour Fitness	1645 Bryant St	415-437-4188	11
24 Hour Fitness	1850 Ocean Ave	415-334-1400	30

Locksmith

Locksmith	Phone
Academy Locksmith	415-285-7000
All City Locksmith	415-495-7217
Castro Locksmiths	415-386-1774

Plumbers

Plumbers	Phone
AAA Discount Rooter	415-550-0356
Bell Plumbing	415-550-0777
Economy Rooter	415-337-7070
Roto-Rooter Plumbers	415-221-2710

Pharmacies

Pharmacies	Address	Phone	Map
Walgreens	3201 Divisadero St	415-931-6417	1
Safeway	15 Marina Blvd	415-563-4986	2
Safeway	2020 Market St	415-861-7660	10
Walgreens	498 Castro St	415-861-3136	10
Safeway	2300 16th St	415-575-1120	11
Walgreens	1189 Potrero Ave	415-647-1397	16
Safeway	850 La Playa St	415-387-4664	18
Rite Aid	5280 Geary Blvd	415-668-2041	20
Walgreens	5411 Geary Blvd	415-752-8370	20
Safeway	4950 Mission St	415-587-7200	38

Private Investigator

Private Investigator	Address	Phone	Map
JE Gann Investigations	2194 Edison Ave	510-568-1465	7
Denver B Moore	588 Sutter St	415-978-9755	8

Video Rental

Video Rental	Address	Phone	Map
Video Café	5700 Geary Blvd	415-387-3999	20

Internet Access

Since his election in 2003, San Francisco mayor Gavin Newsom has been talking up his plan to blanket the entire city with free, wireless Internet access. But don't hold your breath. It would take a Google and a miracle to make it happen. In the meantime, you'll have to settle for one of the many cafés that offer free wireless with a purchase, stores like FedEx or the Apple Store, or some of the downtown hotels that offer Internet kiosks. Your best option though, is to drop by any branch of the city's public library, all of which offer wireless and computer terminal access for free.

Internet	*Address*	*Phone*	*Map*
FedEx Office	3225 Fillmore St	415-441-2995	2
Notes from Underground	2399 Van Ness Ave	415-775-7638	2
FedEx Office	1800 Van Ness Ave	415-292-2500	6
Cup a Joe Coffee House	896 Sutter St	415-563-7745	7
H20 Café	1330 Polk St	415-929-6880	7
Quetzal	1234 Polk St	415-673-4181	7
FedEx Office	100 California St	415-834-0240	8
FedEx Office	303 2nd St	415-495-8880	8
FedEx Office	369 Pine St	415-834-1053	8
FedEx Office	50 Fremont St	415-512-7766	8
Golden Gate Perk Internet Café	401 Bush St	415-362-3929	8
Cup a Joe Coffee House	1901 Hayes St	415-221-3378	9
Rockin' Java Coffee House	1821 Haight St	415-831-8842	9
Sacred Grounds Coffee House	2095 Hayes St	415-387-3859	9
FedEx Office	1967 Market St	415-252-0864	10
H Café	3801 17th St	415-487-1661	10
Oakside Café	1195 Oak St	415-437-1985	10
Brainwash Café & Landromat	1122 Folsom St	415-431-9274	12
Muddy's Coffee House	1304 Valencia St	415-647-7994	15
Javacat Coffee	5549 Geary Blvd	415-933-8465	20
FedEx Office	25 Stanyan St	415-750-1193	22
Nani's Coffee	2739 Geary Blvd	415-928-8817	22
FedEx Office	1597 Sloat Blvd	415-566-0572	27
Java on Ocean	1700 Ocean Ave	415-333-6075	33
Maggie Mudd	903 Cortland Ave	415-641-5291	35

San Francisco has long been hip to an electric art scene. Even back in the dusty days of the Gold Rush, there was a strong arts tradition among pioneering groups like the **San Francisco Women Artists (Map 22)**, an organization that has managed its own gallery in Hayes Valley since the 1880s. Today the city is stocked with small art galleries that attract the diverse crowds San Francisco is known for. These galleries support the cutting-edge creations of local and emerging artists working in every medium.

Sutter and Geary Streets, near Union Square, have one of the larger concentrations of commercial art galleries in the city, and the plethora of exhibition spaces in 49 Geary are definitely worth a visit, especially the first Thursday evening of each month, when "First Thursdays" features gallery openings, free wine and cheese, and throngs of artsy SF folks to gawk at. If you're in the market, be sure to stop by the **Stephen Wirtz Gallery (Map 8)** or **Gregory Lind Gallery (Map 8)**, and the nearby **HANG** and **HANG Annex (Map 7)** at 556 & 567 Sutter Street. The more quirky, nonprofit, contemporary spots like **New Langton Arts (Map 12)** on Folsom Street and **Southern Exposure (Map 11)** in the Mission District are not to be missed. Edgier pieces depicting chaotic urban scenes and graffiti art come out of the **Tenderloin's White Walls Gallery (Map 7)**. Just next door is a sister art space, the **Shooting Gallery (Map 7)**, where tattoo art, erotic photography, and Japanimation are all celebrated in contemporary renderings.

Some other highlights include the new **Superfrog Gallery (Map 6)**, showcasing Japanese pop culture-inspired art at New People, an arts, shopping and entertainment center for Japanese pop culture. **111 Minna Gallery (Map 8)** is a large studio that fuses fine art and local music with a nightclub atmosphere. Housed within California College of the Arts, a forerunner in art, architecture, and design, the **CCA Wattis Institute (Map 12)** (on Wisconsin and Eighth Streets) has a reputation for putting on some of the most interesting contemporary exhibitions. The **San Francisco Center for the Book (Map 12)** on De Haro Street is also another local treasure.

All area codes are 415 unless otherwise noted.

Map 2 • Marina / Cow Hollow (East)

Hourian Fine Art Gallery	1843 Union St	346-6400

Map 3 • Russian Hill / Fisherman's Wharf

Franklin Bowles Gallery	765 Beach St	441-8008
Martin Lawrence Galleries	747 Beach St	229-2784

Map 4 • North Beach / Telegraph Hill

Charles Campbell Gallery	647 Chestnut St	441-8680
Le Trianon Gallery	706 Sansome St	544-0780
Paul Thiebaud Gallery	645 Chestnut St	434-3055

Map 5 • Pacific Heights / Western Addition

Thomas Reynolds Gallery	2291 Pine St	441-4093

Map 6 • Pacific Heights / Japantown

Anthony Meier Fine Arts	1969 California St	351-1400
San Francisco Arts Commission Gallery	401 Van Ness Ave	554-6080
African American Art & Culture Complex	762 Fulton St	922-2049

Map 7 • Nob Hill / Tenderloin

Alliance Francaise	1345 Bush St	775-7755
Axelle Fine Arts Galerie De l'Europe	434 Post St	434-4341
Braunstein/Quay Gallery	430 Clementina St	278-9850
California Modern Gallery	1035 Market St	716-8661
Christopher Clark Fine Art	377 Geary St	397-7781
Cohen Rese Gallery	432 Suttter St	781-6440
Frey Norris Gallery	456 Geary St	346-7812
Gallery 444	444 Post St	434-4477
HANG	567 Sutter St	434-4264
Hosfelt Gallery	430 Clementina St	495-5454
Jenkins Johnson Gallery	464 Sutter St	677-0770
Jewett Gallery	100 Larkin St	557-4277
John Pence Gallery	750 Post St	441-1138
The Luggage Store	1007 Market St	255-5971
Meridian Gallery	535 Powell St	398-7229
Pasquale Iannetti Art Gallery	500 Sutter St	433-4105
The Shooting Gallery	839 Larkin St	931-8035
Velvet da Vinci	2015 Polk St	441-0109
Weinstein Gallery	383 Geary St	362-8151
White Walls	835 Larkin St	931-1500

Map 8 • Financial District / SOMA

111 Minna Gallery	111 Minna St	974-1719
Aftermodern	445 Bryant St	512-7678
Andrea Schwartz Gallery	525 2nd St	495-2090
Brian Gross Fine Art	49 Geary St	788-1050
Caldwell Snyder Gallery	341 Sutter St	392-2299
Camerawork Gallery & Bookstore	657 Mission St	863-1001

Catharine Clark	150 Minna St	399-1439
Chandler Fine Art	170 Minna St	546-1113
The Clay Studio	61 Bluxome St	777-9080
Crown Point Press	20 Hawthorne St	974-6273
Dolby Chadwick Gallery	210 Post St	956-3560
871 Fine Arts Gallery and Bookstore	20 Hawthorne St	543-5812
Elins Eagles Smith	49 Geary St	981-1080
FiftyCrows Gallery	49 Geary St	391-6300
Fraenkel Gallery	49 Geary St	981-2661
Gallery 16	501 3rd St	626-1616
Gallery Paule Anglim	14 Geary St	433-2710
George Krevsky Gallery	77 Geary St	397-9748
Gregory Lind Gallery	49 Geary St	296-9661
Hackett-Freedman Gallery	250 Sutter St	362-7152
Haines Gallery	49 Geary St	397-8114
Hespe Gallery	251 Post St	776-5918
John Berggruen Gallery	228 Grant Ave	781-4629
Larry Evans	333 Grant Ave	215-9016
Marx & Zavattero	77 Geary St	627-9111
Meyerovich Gallery	251 Post St	421-7171
Micaela Gallery	49 Geary St	551-8118
Modernism Inc	685 Market St	541-0461
Montgomery Gallery	406 Jackson St	788-8300
Patricia Sweetow Gallery	77 Geary St	788-5126
Rena Bransten Gallery	77 Geary St	982-3292
Robert Koch Gallery	49 Geary St	421-0122
Scott Nichols Gallery	49 Geary St	788-4641
Serge Sorokko Gallery	231 Grant Ave	421-7770
Shapiro Gallery	49 Geary St	398-6655
Stephen Wirtz Gallery	49 Geary St	433-6879
Steven Wolf Fine Arts	49 Geary St	263-3677
Toomey-Tourell Fine Art	49 Geary St	989-6444
Xanadu Gallery	140 Maiden Ln	392-9999
Yerba Buena Center for the Arts	701 Mission St	978-2787

Map 9 • Haight Ashbury / Cole Valley

Giant Robot	618 Shrader St	876-4773

Map 10 • Castro / Lower Haight

Edo Salon	601 Haight St	861-0131
Ruby's Clay Studio & Gallery	552 Noe St	558-9819

Map 11 • Hayes Valley / The Mission

CELLspace	2050 Bryant St	648-7562
City Art Cooperative Gallery	828 Valencia St	970-9900
Creativity Explored	3245 16th St	863-2108
Fecal Face Dot Gallery	66 Gough St	255-6479
Glama-rama	417 S Van Ness Ave	861-4526
Intersection for the Arts	446 Valencia St	626-2787
Jack Hanley Gallery	395 Valencia St	522-1623
The Lab	2948 16th St	864-8855
LGBT Community Center	1800 Market St	865-5555
Lincart	1 Otis St	503-1981
Micaela Gallery	333 Hayes St	551-8118
Mina Dresden Gallery	312 Valencia St	863-8312
Mission 17	2111 Mission St	861-3144
Octavia's Haze	370 Hayes St	255-7283
Paxton Gate	824 Valencia St	824-1872
Start Soma	672 S Van Ness Ave	505-4734
Vista Point	405 Florida St	215-9073

Map 12 • SOMA / Potrero Hill (North)

CCA Wattis Institute	1111 8th St	551-9210
New Langton Arts	1246 Folsom St	626-5416
San Francisco Center for the Book	300 De Haro St	565-0545

Map 13 • Mission Beach

Limn	290 Townsend St	543-5466

Map 15 • Mission (Outer)

Artists' Television Access	992 Valencia St	824-3890
Galleria de la Raza	2857 24th St	826-8009
Mission Cultural Center for Latino Arts	2868 Mission St	643-2785
Precita Eyes Mural Arts Center	2981 24th St	285-2287
Triple Base Gallery	3041 24th St	643-3943

Map 17 • Potrero Hill / Dogpatch

Ampersand International Arts	1001 Tennessee St	285-0170

Map 21 • Inner Richmond

Table Asia Gallery	1101 Lake St	750-9955

Map 22 • Presidio Heights / Laurel Heights

San Francisco Women Artists Gallery	3489 Sacramento St	440-7392
Thatcher Gallery	2130 Fulton St	422-5762

The Presidio

Gallery at Thoreau	1016 Lincoln Blvd	561-6300

Downtown Oakland/Lake Merritt

Mama Buzz	2318 Telegraph Ave	465-4073
Rock, Paper, Scissors	2278 Telegraph Ave	238-9171

North Oakland/Emeryville

ABCo	3135 Filbert St	n/a

From the strange to the bold, San Francisco's museums are on the cutting edge. The city has several major destination museums, plus smaller ones devoted to single, sometimes peculiar, subjects (think tattoos and cartoons). In addition to museums focusing on ethnic cultures and art, the city has several interactive museums where tactile experience is as important as the objects on display. Of the art museums, the four "biggies" are the **San Francisco Museum of Modern Art (SFMOMA) (Map 8)**, the **California Palace of the Legion of Honor (Map 18)**, the **De Young (Golden Gate Park)**, and the **Asian Art Museum (Map 7)**. In addition to the "big four," the **Yerba Buena Center for the Arts (Map 8)**, in close proximity to **SFMOMA**, has hosted an increasing number of significant exhibits in the last several years.

SFMOMA began its life in 1935 as the first museum on the West Coast dedicated solely to 20th-century art. Back then, it was known as the San Francisco Museum of Art, and it was not until 1975 that the word "modern" was added to its name. In the late '80s the museum began expanding its exhibitions program. Today it offers a wealth of exhibits and public programs. When you visit, you can do it on the cheap by going on Thursdays from 6 pm and 9 pm when admission is half-price, or on the first Tuesday of each month when admission is free.

The **Legion of Honor**, is a gorgeous Beaux-Arts building located within a picturesque setting in the Richmond District's Lincoln Park. Funded by Alma de Bretteville Spreckels to honor the soldiers who died in World War I, the museum is a three-quarter-scale copy of the Palais de la Légion d'Honneur in Paris and was completed in 1924. Today it houses Rodin sculptures, including "The Thinker", European decorative arts and paintings, ancient art and artifacts spanning 4,000 years, and a large prints and drawing collection. Admission is free every Tuesday. When you go, consider adding a hike through the neighboring golf course out to Lands End. The ocean views are not to be missed.

Founded in 1895, the **de Young** in Golden Gate Park is the city's oldest museum. Its collection includes American painting, decorative arts and crafts, arts from Africa, Oceania, and the Americas, and Western and non-western textiles. The museum recently underwent major renovations that returned 88,000 square feet to green space. The state-of-the-art facility, with a stunning Post-Modern design by Herzog & de Meuron (check out the observation level) is covered in a copper façade intended to gain a patina, and thus a natural look, over time. For an evening excursion try the Friday Night series which features lectures, live music, and happy-hour with a cash bar.

The **Asian Art Museum** opened in 1966 in a wing of the de Young to house part of Avery Brundage's vast collection of Asian art. Featuring nearly 15,000 objects, the museum is the largest Asian art museum in the country. In 2003, the museum moved to its current home in the former Main Library in the Civic Center. The Asian Art Museum holds an enormous collection that spans 6,000 years and covers the major traditions of Asian art and culture. Admission is half-price on Thursdays after 5 pm and free on the first Sunday of every month.

The Asian Art Museum may be the largest city museum devoted to one cultural diaspora, but it's certainly not the only one. Founded in 1975, the **Mexican Museum (Map 2)** at Fort Mason Center has a permanent collection of over 12,000 Mexican, Mexican-American, Chicano, and Latino art and cultural objects. When construction of the museum's new building in the Yerba Buena Center for the Arts is complete, the museum will relocate to the SOMA neighborhood. Call first to make sure it's open.

San Francisco is also home to the **Museo Italo Americano (Map 2)** in Fort Mason, the only museum in the country devoted exclusively to Italian and Italian-American arts and artists. The **Museum of the African Diaspora (Map 8)** examines the origins, movement, adaptation, and transformation of people of African descent. The museum showcases the works of African-American artists and features exhibits on Africa, African culture, and the African-American experience. The stylish interior coupled with interactive exhibits make this one of the most exciting recent addition to the city's museum circuit. The **Chinese Historical Society of America Museum and Learning Center (Map 7)** offers exhibits, library facilities, and programs on Chinese history and culture in America. **The Contemporary Jewish Museum**'s Daniel Libeskind designed space **(Map 8)** presents exhibitions and programs that explore contemporary perspectives on Jewish culture, history, art, and ideas.

For a museum trek that's a little out of the ordinary, consider visiting the **Cartoon Art Museum (Map 8)** or the **Tattoo Art Museum (Map 4).** If you dare, you can brave Fisherman's Wharf for several museums popular with tourists but still worth a visit. The **Musee Mecanique (Map 7)** at Pier 45 houses one of the world's largest collections of antique arcade machines, hand-cranked music boxes, and other mechanical musical instruments, plus rare finds like toothpick art made by inmates at San Quentin. The nearby **Ripley's Believe It or Not! (Map 3)** museum offers 11 galleries and over 10,000 square feet of weird, mind-bending illusions and unbelievable exhibits such as the Shrunken Torso and the Two-Headed Calf. Also at the Wharf, the **Wax Museum (Map 4)** is filled with eerily lifelike versions of your favorite celebs, like Nicole Kidman, Angelina Jolie, and Lance Armstrong.

For lessons in San Francisco's history, there are several museums document elements of the city's past. Check out the **Fire Museum (Map 5)** for papers and artifacts detailing San Francisco fires, firefighters, and tools from 1849 onward. Tour restored ships and speak with knowledgable National Park Service employees at the **Maritime Museum (Map 3)** at Fisherman's Wharf. **The Cable Car Museum (Map 7)**, the **Wells Fargo Museum (Map 8)**, and the **San Francisco Museum & Historical Society** exhibition spaces in City Hall's South Light Court **(Map 7)** and at Pier 45 **(Map 3)** are also good places to brush up on city history. Perhaps San Francisco's most spectacular history museum will be the one set to open in 2010 in **The Old Mint (Map 12)**.

Take a kid or be one at Dr. Frank Oppenheimer's **Exploratorium (Map 1)**. The museum has hands-on exhibits and demonstrations focusing on science, art, and human perception—you can touch and play with everything. Don't miss the Tactile Dome (make a reservation), where you crawl around in total darkness using only your sense of touch to guide you. Pack a picnic and enjoy the fairytale-like building and lush gardens. Another science-friendly city favorite is the **California Academy of Sciences (Map 25)**. Cal Academy houses a natural history museum, the Steinhart Aquarium, and the Morrison Planetarium. Be sure to explore Cal Academy's Living Roof, a 2.5 acre rooftop designed by Renzo Piano to accommodate a living tapestry of native plant species. The rooftop's seven undulating green hillocks pay homage to the iconic topography of San Francisco. The free **Randall Museum (Map 10)** offers a hands-on approach to exploring the sciences with both indoor and outdoor exhibits on nature, the environment, and live animals. Another fun place to take the kids is **Zeum (Map 12)**, an art and technology center in Yerba Buena Gardens. Exhibits allow kids to work with computer programs, sound equipment, and other tools to produce their own creations.

For everything you ever wanted to know about San Francisco, check out the Virtual Museum of the City of San Francisco at www.sfmuseum.org.

Museum	*Address*	*Phone*	*Map*
Asian Art Museum	200 Larkin St	415-581-3500	7
The Beat Museum	540 Broadway St	800-537-6822	4
California Academy of Sciences	55 Music Concourse Dr, Golden Gate Park	415-379-8000	25
Cartoon Art Museum	655 Mission St	415-227-8666	8
Chinese Culture Center of San Francisco	750 Kearny St, 3rd Fl	415-986-1822	8
Chinese Historical Society of America	965 Clay St	415-391-1188	7
The Contemporary Jewish Museum	736 Mission St	415-355-7800	8
De Young	50 Hagiwara Tea Garden Dr	415-750-3600	pg 189
Exploratorium	3601 Lyon St	415-397-5673	1
Gay, Lesbian, Bisexual, Transgender Historical Society Museum	657 Mission St, Ste 300	415-777-5455	8
Haas-Lilienthal House	2007 Franklin St	415-441-3004	6
Legion of Honor	100 34th Ave	415-750-3600	18
Mexican Museum	Ft Mason Ctr, Bldg D	415-202-9700	2
Mission Dolores	3321 16th St	415-621-8203	10
Musee Mecanique	Pier 45 at the end of Taylor St	415-346-2000	3
Museo Italo Americano	Ft Mason Ctr, Bldg C (entrance at Marina Blvd & Buchanan St)	415-673-2200	2
Museum of Craft & Folk Art	51 Yerba Buena Ln	415-227-4888	8
Museum of the African Diaspora	685 Mission St	415-358-7200	8
Museum of Vision	655 Beach St	415-561-8502	3
National Japanese American Historical Society	1684 Post St	415-921-5007	6
National Maritime Museum	900 Beach St	415-561-6662	3
North Beach Museum	1435 Stockton St	415-391-6210	4
Octagon House	2645 Gough St	415-441-7512	2
Randall Museum	199 Museum Wy	415-554-9600	10
Ripley's Believe It or Not! Museum	175 Jefferson St	415-771-6188	3
Russian Center	2450 Sutter St, 4th Fl	415-921-7631	5
San Francisco Fire Museum	655 Presidio Ave	415-563-4630	5
San Francisco Museum of Craft & Design	550 Sutter St	415-773-0303	7
San Francisco Performing Arts Library & Museum	401 Van Ness Ave	415-255-4800	6
San Francisco Railway Museum	77 Steuart St	415-974-1948	8
Sculpture Garden at SF Recycling & Disposal	501 Tunnel Ave	415-330-1415	40
SFMOMA	151 3rd St	415-357-4000	8
Society of California Pioneers	300 4th St	415-957-1849	12
The Wax Museum	145 Jefferson St	800-439-4305	4
Wells Fargo History Museum	420 Montgomery St	415-396-2619	8
Yerba Buena Center for the Arts	701 Mission St	415-978-2787	8
Zeum	221 4th St	415-820-3320	12

General Information

NFT Map:	8
Address:	151 Third St (between Mission and Howard Sts) San Francisco, CA 94103
Phone:	415-357-4000
Website:	www.sfmoma.org
Hours:	Mon–Tues & Fri–Sun: 11 am–5:45 pm; Thurs 11 am–8:45 pm. Closed Wednesdays, Thanksgiving, Christmas, Fourth of July, & New Year's Day. Open from 10 am Memorial Day through Labor Day.
Entry:	$18 for adults, $12 for seniors, $11 for students, free for children 12 and under, free admission on the first Tuesday of each month, half-price admission Thursday evenings 6 pm–8:45 pm. Note that the museum stops selling tickets 45 minutes prior to closing.

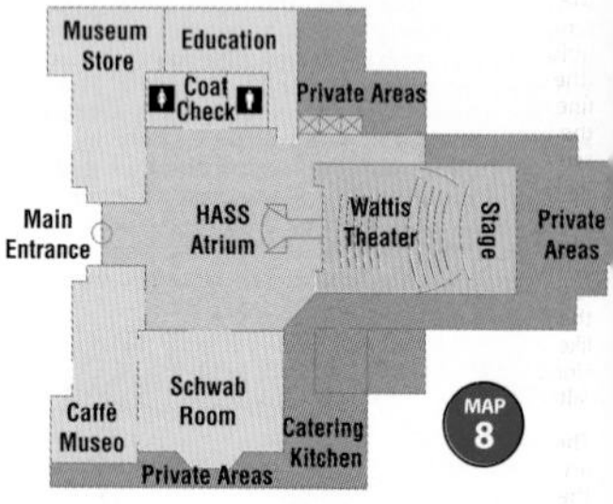

Overview

How about sharing your midday with Mondrian? Or taking an afternoon break with Diebenkorn? For those who work downtown, the San Francisco Museum of Modern Art (SFMOMA) offers an easy-to-reach oasis of calm and creativity. When it opened in 1935 (in another location and without the "modern" in its name) under the direction of Grace L. McCann Morley, it was the first museum on the West Coast devoted solely to 20th-century art. In January 1995, SFMOMA opened a new museum facility in the burgeoning South of Market district, designed by renowned Swiss architect Mario Botta. Across the street from Yerba Buena Center, the SFMOMA is the centerpiece of a growing cluster of downtown and SOMA-area museums, with a permanent collection of more than 26,000 works.

The extensive painting and sculpture collection contains creations by distinguished artists such as Jackson Pollock and Henri Matisse and includes genres such as American Post-Minimalism, German Expressionism, and Fauvism. It also showcases the work of San Francisco Bay Area artists such as David Park and Wayne Thiebaud. More than 50 years ago, the museum was one of the first to recognize photography as an art form. Today, its Department of Photography has international stature. SFMOMA has a state-of-the-art education center adjacent to the permanent collection galleries on the second floor. Alongside the permanent collection, SFMOMA's temporary exhibitions often draw both crowds and accolades (check website for current and upcoming exhibitions). The SFMOMA library, open by appointment only, comprises more than 60,000 catalogued items, including monographs, exhibition catalogues, and 1,890 periodical titles.

Be sure to check out SFMOMA's new Rooftop Garden, a 14,400 square-foot multifunctional open-air space designed by Jensen Architects, where you can ogle well-known and rare large-scale sculpture, sip a Blue Bottle Coffee latte, and take in the San Francisco skyline.

How to Get There—Driving

From the East Bay, take I-80 and exit at Fremont Street. Take an immediate left from Fremont onto Howard Street and get into the right lane. Go two blocks and turn right onto Third Street. From the Peninsula, take US 101 until it connects to I-80 and exit at Fourth Street; Fourth immediately leads onto Bryant Street. Take a left from Bryant onto Third Street and follow it until you reach the museum. From the North Bay, take US 101 to Lombard Street. Follow Lombard to Van Ness Avenue and turn right; follow Van Ness until you reach Golden Gate Avenue and turn left. Follow Golden Gate as it crosses Market Street onto Sixth Street. Turn left from Sixth Street onto Folsom Street and follow Folsom up to Third Street; turn left onto Third. Once you've arrived, you can park at the SFMOMA garage located behind the museum on Minna between Third and New Montgomery Streets or at the 5th and Mission garage.

How to Get There—Mass Transit

BART will take you to either the Montgomery Street or Powell Street Stations; both are within walking distance of SFMOMA.

Muni bus lines 9 San Bruno, 14 Mission, 15 Third, 30 Stockton, 38 Geary, and 45 Union run near the museum, and Muni Metro lines J-Church, K-Ingleside, L-Taraval, M-Oceanview, and N-Judah will take you to either Montgomery Street or Powell Street Stations.

Golden Gate Transit buses 10, 20, 50, 60, 70, and 80 stop on Mission and Third Streets in front of the Yerba Buena Center for the Arts, and Caltrain will get you to the San Francisco station at Fourth and Townsend Streets.

While over 35 smaller theaters have disappeared from the San Francisco cinema scene in the past 20 years, the remaining contingent still stands strong in the face of the ubiquitous multiplex. **The Clay (Map 5)** in Pacific Heights (the oldest continually operated theater in town) shows a fine variety of international and specialty films. Although the Inner Richmond's historic **Bridge (Map 22)** has small screens and higher prices, it is a bastion for good foreign features and hosts Peaches Christ's Midnight Mass in the summer. The Outer Richmond's **Balboa (Map 19)** shows both first-run art films and special programs on its two screens, offering a bargain matinee and occasional double features. The tiny **Four Star Theater (Map 20)** caters to the large Chinese community in Outer Richmond—just like a neighborhood theater should—with weekend Hong Kong cinema, and it also offers double features and "alternative world cinema."

The three-screen **Lumiere (Map 7)** in Russian Hill plays art films you may never see anywhere else (check out the original main room; the newer two are cramped). The two-screen **Roxie (Map 11)** in the Mission wishes to remain the last gritty stronghold of independent documentaries and local shorts. The classy organ-clad **Castro Theatre (Map 10)** in the heart of the Castro prefers vintage classics to woo patrons under its 1920s-style gilded cupola. (It even has the occasional sing-along showing of the *Sound of Music*, when fans costume up to fa-so-la-ti the night away.)

The **Embarcadero (Map 8)** and **Opera Plaza (Map 6)** have a great selection of first-run international, arty, and specialty flicks. If you are looking for Hollywood blockbusters, opt for the **UA Metro (Map 2)** in Cow Hollow (remodeled, including plush couches in the ladies' room). Originality and charm aside, for the cineplex experience, head to the **Metreon (Map 12)** south of Market (for big and comfortable everything and an IMAX screen), the multitiered **AMC Van Ness 14 (Map 6)** (housed in an old Cadillac dealership), **VIZ Cinema (Map 5)**, San Francisco's (and the country's) only venue featuring strictly Japanese films, located in the basement of New People, a J-Pop culture shopping and entertainment destination, or the **Century San Francisco Centre 9 (Map 7)** inside the new downtown Westfield mall. Just outside the city's borders is the **Century 20 Daly City**. Fandango (www.fandango.com) or Moviefone (777-FILM; www.moviefone.com) can help you beat the weekend crowds by reserving tickets in advance.

Besides the ordinary showcases, the city is home to many annual film festivals, from Jewish to LGBT, Asian to underground—even bicycle! These festivals present some of the best contemporary cinematic work year-round. Finally, let's not overlook some greats in the nearby East Bay: learn something new and culturally enriching at the **Pacific Film Archive** in Berkeley, or check out the **Elmwood Theatre**, Berkeley's best neighborhood theater, for new indie films and real butter on your popcorn.

Movie Theater	*Address*	*Phone*	*Map*
4-Star Theatre	2200 Clement St	415-666-3488	20
AMC Bay Street 16	5614 Shellmound St	510-457-4AMC	North Oakland
AMC Van Ness 14	1000 Van Ness Ave	415-922-4AMC	6
Balboa Theater	3630 Balboa St	415-221-8184	19
Bridge Theater	3010 Geary Blvd	415-267-4893	22
California Theater	2113 Kittredge St	510-464-5980	Berkeley (East)
Castro Theatre	429 Castro St	415-621-6120	10
Century Empire 3	85 West Portal Ave	415-661-2539	30
Century San Francisco Centre 9	845 Market St (5th Fl of Westfield)	415-538-8422	7
CineArts at Sequoia	25 Throckmorton Ave	415-388-4862	Mill Valley
Clay Theatre	2261 Filmore St	415-267-4893	5
Elmwood Theatre	2966 College Ave	510-649-0530	Berkeley (East)
Embarcadero Theater	1 Embarcadero Ctr	415-267-4893	8
Foreign Cinema	2534 Mission St	415-648-7600	15
Four Star Theater	2200 Clement St	415-666-3488	20
Grand Lake Theater	3200 Grand Ave	510-452-3556	Downtown Oakland
Jack London 9 Cinemas	100 Washington St	510-433-1320	Downtown Oakland
Lowes Theater/IMAX at Metreon	101 4th St	415-369-6201	12
Lumiere Theater	1572 California St	415-267-4893	7
Marina Theatre	2149 Chestnut St	415-345-1323	1
Oaks	1875 Solano Ave	510-526-1836	Berkeley (West)
Opera Plaza Cinemas	601 Van Ness Ave	415-267-4893	6
Parkway Speakeasy Theater	1834 Park Blvd	510-814-2400	Downtown Oakland
Pacific Film Archive	2575 Bancroft Wy	510-642-0808	Berkeley (East)
Piedmont Cinemas	4186 Piedmont Ave	510-464-5980	North Oakland
Presidio Theatre	2340 Chestnut St	415-776-2388	1
Red Vic	1727 Haight St	415-668-3994	9
Roxie	3117 16th St	415-863-1087	11
San Francisco Cinematheque	145 9th St	415-552-1990	12
Shattuck Cinemas	2230 Shattuck Ave	510-843-3456	Berkeley (East)
Sundance Kabuki Cinema	1881 Post St	415-929-4650	5
UA Emerybay 10	6330 Christie Ave	800-326-3264	North Oakland
UA Stonestown Twin	501 Buckingham Wy	800-326-3264	28
UA Vogue	3290 Sacramento St	415-221-8183	5
United Artists Cinemas 7	2274 Shattuck Ave	510-486-1852	Berkeley (East)

In search of the printed word? Although you can find your typical big-box behemoths sprinkled here and there, the city is better known for its independently owned and operated bookstores, which give personality to the many neighborhoods they serve. Their loyal clientele will argue the merits of their favorite ones, so we'll leave it up to you to choose your own bookstore focus and vibe.

General

Famed for its connection to the Beat movement during the 1950s, **City Lights (Map 8)** is often pegged as the city's best-known literary landmark. Located in the lively North Beach neighborhood, the store was opened in 1953 by poets Lawrence Ferlinghetti and Peter D. Martin, and quickly became a hub for progressive political thinkers, poets, and novelists, from Allen Ginsberg to Frank O'Hara. Today, it regularly features readings by alternative authors and poets. Be sure to visit the downstairs. Another popular venue for readings by well-known authors is **Booksmith (Map 9)** on Haight Street, with an excellent assortment of new books and a reputation for scheduling cult-hit authors and respected musicians-turned-writers. According to many in the city, the best general new and used bookstore around is Clement Street's **Green Apple Books (Map 21)**. The large store is famous for its bargain books from publisher overstock. Sadly, the oldest and largest independent bookstore in San Francisco, Stacey's, closed in 2009 due mostly to competition from the Interweb and big-box bookstores.

New & Used

Just about every neighborhood in San Francisco has a used bookstore or two, but some of our favorites are **Phoenix Books & Records (Map 14)**, **Bookshop West Portal (Map 30)**, **Red Hill Books (Map 35)**, and **Black Oak Books (Map 25)**. The Mission has several independent bookstores worth visiting, including **Valencia Books (Map 11)** and **Dog Eared Books (Map 15)**. Down at Fort Mason Center is the **Book Bay Bookstore (Map 2)**, stocked with remainders and used books; sales support the city's public library system.

Art & Architecture

For books on art and design, San Francisco's museum bookstores are virtual goldmines. Not surprisingly, the **SFMOMA Bookstore (Map 8)** has an extensive collection of new art and art-related books, as does the **Asian Art Museum (Map 7)** store. At the brilliant **William Stout Architectural Books (Map 8),** aesthetics are the raison d'etre. Titles range from the instructional to the theoretical, and span a vast array of architecture, design, and decorative arts subjects, including interior design, landscaping, textiles, furniture, and urban planning. **Foto-Grafix Books (Map 8)** (formerly the Friends of Photography bookstore) has what many consider the best selection of photography books in the city.

Specialty

Niche bookstores also abound. Whether you're looking for Japanese comics or highly technical design books, you'll be sure to find them. **Borderlands (Map 11)** is a favorite destination among science fiction, fantasy, and horror aficionados. **Fields Book Store (Map 7)** specializes in the metaphysical, if that's your thing.

Given the city's large number of residents whose first language is something other than English, it's no surprise that there are plenty of foreign-language bookstores around. The largest Japanese bookstore in San Francisco, **Kinokuniya (Map 6)** in Japantown, carries tons of Japanese-language books and magazines, as well as a number of English-language Japanese periodicals, comics, and novels. The **European Book Company (Map 7)** emphasizes French and German texts, while **Arkipelago Philippine Books (Map 12)** stocks Filipino and Asian-language books.

If you're into Eastern thought and Buddhism, try **Eastwind Books (Map 4)** for classic and recently published new age books. Seekers of the spiritual and philosophical realms will find reading materials at **Vedanta Society Bookshop (Map 2)**, the **Zen Center Bookstore (Map 11)**, and **Browser Books (Map 5)**.

For a wide selection of politically and culturally progressive books, head to **Modern Times (Map 15)**. **Bound Together (Map 9)** has all of your anarchist and subversive literary needs. **Bolerium Books (Map 11)** stocks rare and out-of-print books, posters, and ephemera on social movements.

Old sea salts love the **Maritime Bookstore (Map 3)** at the Hyde Street Pier for new nautical books. Rare book collectors can be found browsing **Thomas A. Goldwasser (Map 7)**. Two stores in the city are known for their immense inventory of African-American and black history books: **Marcus Books (Map 5)** and **Alexander Book Company (Map 8)**. **Dandelion (Map 11)** is a well-known destinations for children's books. Find books about science and the natural world at the **California Academy of Sciences Bookstore (Map 25)** as well as the **Exploratorium Store (Map 1)**. If you're looking for books about California and its history, the **California Historical Society (Map 8)** store is where it's at. **A Different Light (Map 10)** in the Castro has books for the LGBT reader.

Happy reading!

Map 1 • Marina / Cow Hollow (West)

Books Inc	2251 Chestnut St	931-3633	General new.
Exploratorium Store	3601 Lyon St	397-5673	Museum gift shop.

Map 2 • Marina / Cow Hollow (East)

Book Bay	Ft Mason Ctr #C	771-1076	Used general donated books, nonprofit.
The Collectors Cave	2072 Union St	929-0231	Comics, cards, collectibles.
Vedanta Society Bookshop	2323 Vallejo St	922-2323	Spiritual, metaphysical books.

Map 3 • Russian Hill / Fisherman's Wharf

Maritime Store	2905 Hyde St	775-2665	Maritime, historical, nature, non-fiction.
Russian Hill Bookstore	2234 Polk St	929-0997	General used.

Map 4 • North Beach / Telegraph Hill

Cavalli Cafe & Imports	1441 Stockton St	421-4219	Italian books.
Eastwind Books & Arts	1435A Stockton St	772-5877	Chinese and Asian culture and medicine books.
Golden Gate National Park Store	Pier 39	433-7221	Guidebooks, travel, educational books.

Map 5 • Pacific Heights / Western Addition

Browser Books	2195 Fillmore St	567-8027	General.
Marcus Books	1712 Fillmore St	346-4222	African-American books.

Map 6 • Pacific Heights / Japantown

Alan Wofsy Fine Arts	1109 Geary Blvd	292-6500	Used and out-of-print art books.
Kinokuniya Bookshop	1581 Webster St	567-7625	Japanese books, English books, Asian culture, and history.

Map 7 • Nob Hill / Tenderloin

Argonaut Book Shop	786 Sutter St	474-9067	California history, the West, and Americana.
Asian Art Museum Store	200 Larkin St	581-3500	Museum gift shop.
Book Bay	30 Grove St	557-4238	Used general donated books, non profit.
European Book Co	925 Larkin St	474-0626	French, German, Spanish.
Fields Book Store	1419 Polk St	673-2027	Metaphysical, mind-body-spirit, world religion.
Islamic Bookstore	20 Jones St	863-8005	Islamic books.
Kayo Books	814 Post St	749-0554	Vintage paperbacks from the '40s to the '70s and esoteric books of all persuasions.
Magazine	920 Larkin St	441-7737	Magazines, out-of-print, and used only.
Thomas A Goldwasser Rare Books	486 Geary St	292-4698	Rare books.
World Books	824 Stockton St	397-8473	Chinese books.

Map 8 • Financial District / SOMA

Alexander Book Co	50 2nd St	495-2992	General new.
The Book Passage	Embarcadero & Market St	835-1020	General new.
Brick Row Book Shop	49 Geary St, #230	398-0414	Rare 18th and19th-century lit.
California Historical Society Store	678 Mission St	357-1860	California history.
Camerawork Gallery & Bookstore	657 Mission St	863-1001	Photography books.
Chronicle Bookstore	680 2nd St	369-6271	Only books published by Chronicle.
City Lights	261 Columbus Ave	362-8193	General new.
Discovery Channel Store	4 Embarcadero Ctr	956-4911	General, science.
871 Fine Arts Gallery and Bookstore	20 Hawthorne St	543-5812	Art books only.
Foto-Grafix Books	655 Mission St	495-7242	Photography books.
Jeffrey's Toys	685 Market St	546-6551	Children's books.
John Windle Antiquarian Bookseller	49 Geary St, #233	986-5826	Old and rare.
Johns Western Gallery	250 Sutter St	308-5566	Specializes in Western Americana.
Louie Brothers Book Store	754 Washington St	391-8866	Chinese books.
New China Book Store	642 Pacific Ave	956-0752	Chinese books.
Pacific Book Auction Galleries	133 Kearny St	989-2665	Book auctions of rare books, maps, manuscripts, photos.
Salve Regina Books	728 Pacific Ave	989-6279	Chinese culture and religious books.
SFMOMA Museum Store	151 3rd St	357-4035	Art, architecture, painting, photography, design.
Sino-American Books & Arts	751 Jackson St	421-3345	Chinese books.
William Stout Architectural Books	804 Montgomery St	391-6757	Architecture, design, art, landscape.

Map 9 • Haight Ashbury / Cole Valley

Booksmith	1644 Haight St	863-8688	General new.
Bound Together Anarchist Collective Bookstore	1369 Haight St	431-8355	Anarchist books.
Recycled Records	1377 Haight St	626-4075	Music, entertainment, movie books.

Map 10 • Castro / Lower Haight

A Different Light Bookstore	489 Castro St	431-0891	Gay and lesbian.
Aardvark Books	227 Church St	552-6733	Primarily used.
Bolerium Books	2141 Market St	863-6353	Rare and out-of-print books on social movements.
Books Inc	2275 Market St	864-6777	General new.
Comix Experience	305 Divisadero St	863-9258	Comics… Only comics.
Crystal Way	2335 Market St	861-6511	Spiritual, metaphysical, recovery, yoga.

Map 11 • Hayes Valley / The Mission

Adobe Book Shop	3166 16th St	864-3936	General used, specialize in philosophy and Greek and Roman literature.
Al's Comics	1803 Market St	861-1220	Al Comics "al" the time.
Bolerium Books	2141 Mission St, #300	863-6353	Mostly used. American social movements.
Borderlands	866 Valencia St	824-8203	Sci-fi, fantasy, horror, new/used.
California Institute of Integral Studies Bookstore	1453 Mission St	575-6100	Textbooks, spiritual-books.
Dandelion	55 Potrero Ave	436-9500	Gift shop with an extensive collection of children's books.
Forest Books	3080 16th St	863-2755	General used, poetry, eastern religion, art.
Isotope	326 Fell St	621-6543	Comics.
Meyer Boswell Books	2141 Mission St, #302	255-6400	History of law.
Symposium	325 Hayes St	437-0400	Classic books from around the world.
Valhalla Books	2141 Mission St, #202	863-9250	General literature, first editions.
Zen Center	300 Page St	255-6524	Buddhist books.

Map 12 • SOMA / Potrero Hill (North)

Arkipelago Philippine Books	1010 Mission St	553-8185	Filipino books.

Map 13 • Mission Beach

Christopher's Books	1400 18th St	255-8802	Neighborhood bookshop.

Map 14 • Noe Valley

Omnivore Books on Food	3885 Cesar Chavez St	282-4712	Haven of foodie booklovers.
Phoenix Books & Records	3957 24th St	821-3477	General new and used.

Map 15 • Mission (Outer)

Dog Eared Books	900 Valencia St	282-1901	General new and used.
Modern Times Bookstore	2919 24th St	282-9246	Progressive bookstore.
Nueva Libreria Mexico	2886 Mission St	642-0759	Spanish only.
Promesa Christian Bookstore	2862 Mission St	641-3131	Spanish Christian books.
Scarlet Sage Herb Co	1173 Valencia St	821-0997	Healing books.

Map 19 • Outer Richmond (East) / Seacliff

Educational Exchange	600 35th Ave	752-3302	Educational materials for the classroom.

Map 20 • Richmond

Arlekim Russian Bookstore	5909 Geary Blvd	751-2320	Russian books.
Cards and Comics Central	5424 Geary Blvd	668-3544	Comic books, collectibles.

Map 21 • Inner Richmond

Green Apple Books & Music	506 Clement St	387-2272	General interest.
Pacific Books & Arts	524 Clement St #A	751-2238	General Chinese bookstore.

Map 22 • Presidio Heights / Laurel Heights

Books Inc	3515 California St	221-3666	General new.
Dayenu Judaica	3220 California St	563-6563	Jewish books, music, and art.
USF Campus	2130 Fulton St	422-6493	General.

Map 25 • Inner Sunset / Golden Gate Heights

Amazing Fantasy	650 Irving St	681-4344	Comics
Archangel Bookstore	1352 9th Ave	242-9698	Religious bookstore.
Black Oak Books	630 Irving St	564-0877	New and used books.
Botanical Garden Bookstore	9th Ave & Lincoln Wy	661-1316	Plant books.
California Academy of Sciences Store	55 Music Concourse Dr	379-8000	Museum gift shop.
Elsewhere Books	260 Judah St	661-2535	Mystery and science-fiction.
The Great Overland Book Company	345 Judah St	664-0126	General used, California history.

Map 28 • SFSU / Park Merced

SFSU Bookstore	1650 Holloway Ave	338-2665	Textbooks, general books.

Map 29 • Twin Peaks

UCSF Bookstore	500 Parnassus Ave	476-1666	Medical, general.

Map 30 • West Portal

Bookshop West Portal	80 West Portal Ave	564-8080	General.
Comic Outpost	2381 Ocean Ave	239-2669	Comic books, collectibles.
Mark Post, Bookseller	2555 Ocean Ave, #101	586-2363	Literature, history, art, Scottish studies. Mostly used.

Map 32 • Diamond Heights / Glen Park

Bird & Beckett Books & Records	653 Chenery St	586-3733	General new and used.

Map 35 • Bernal Heights

Red Hill Books	401 Cortland Ave	648-5331	New and used books to buy or trade.

Berkley (East)

Moe's Books	2476 Telegraph Ave	849-2087	Four stories of new and used books, academically inclined..

Berkley (West)

Black Oak Books	2618 San Pablo Ave	486-0698	Berkeley independent bookseller.

The Presidio

Crissy Field Warming Hut	983 Marine Dr	561-3040	Environmental/nature.

San Francisco is a drinkin' kind of town—has been since the Gold Rush, when a raucous drinker could end up falling through a trap door and into the the clutches of a crimp, a nefarious type who specializes in kidnapping drunks and selling them to ships in need of sailors, a practice known as Shanghaiing. Though the drunken pirate fights have calmed down over the years, if you're looking for trouble, you can find it here. Nightlife is dynamic: old places close down, new ones pop up. Niche markets are both plentiful and eclectic here, and San Francisco has a huge assortment of bars to fulfill your every desire. Here we selected a few choice destinations to fit some of your basic bar variables.

Dive Bars

San Francisco is full of more dive bars than you can shake a broken pool cue at. We like **Trad'r Sam (Map 19)** for a grungy Richmond tiki bar, the **500 Club (Map 11)** in the Mission for shooting pool and soaking up diversity on a foggy summer night, **Mr. Bing's (Map 8)** where you can play liar's dice (at your own risk) with Mr. Bing himself, and **Skip's Tavern (Map 35)** if you find yourself parched in Bernal Heights. Other good bets are the **Latin American Club (Map 15)** and Chinatown's **Buddha Bar (Map 8)**. The East Bay is also a dive bar haven, with **George Kaye's (Downtown Oakland/Lake Merritt)**, **Merchant's (Oakland)** which resides largely in a hole in Jack London Square, and Club Mallard (752 San Pablo Ave in Albany 510-524-8450) topping our list.

Best Beer Selection

Without a doubt, Lower Haight's **Toronado (Map 10)** wins the category prize. They pour 50 beers on tap and double that number in bottled brews. **The Mad Dog in the Fog (Map 10)** across the street has a great selection of English beers, try them out over Thursday Quiz Night. There are no shortage of great Irish bars (and Irish beers) in San Francisco, such as **Kate O'Brien's (Map 8)**, **O'Reilly's Irish Bar (Map 4)**, and **Ireland's 32 (Map 21)**. We also should mention Oakland's favorite Irish pub **McNally's (North Oakland/Emeryville)** with a solid beer selection, and the recently opened **The Trappist (Downtown Oakland/Lake Merritt)** boasting one of the finest selection of Belgian brew in the Bay Area. And of course there are the locally-brewed favorites—**Gordon Biersch (Map 8)**, **Speakeasy (Map 37)**, and the **SF Brewing Company (Map 8)**.

Outdoor Spaces

Nothing beats those beautiful San Francisco days when the fog hasn't made it over Twin Peaks yet and you're having drinks outside on the sunny side of town. We love **The Ramp (Map 13)** and **Pier 23 (Map 4)** on the Embarcadero for their cocktails, burgers, seafood, and salads on fabulous waterfront decks. The rooftop bar at **Medjool (Map 15)** in the Mission certainly doesn't suck, and you can always catch an old movie outside at **Foreign Cinema (Map 15)**, or get drunk and eat BBQ in a gritty old junkyard turned beer garden at **Zeitgeist (Map 11)**, which, on nice days, is packed with patrons from before happy hour to the wee hours of the morning. On the other side of the Bay, **Raleigh's (Berkeley East)** on Telegraph features an expansive outdoor beer garden, as well Alameda's Lucky 13 (1301 Park St, 510-523-2118) is a popular outdoor spot rain or shine for cocktails and BBQ.

Best Décor

For class and sophistication, newly opened **Slide (Map 7)** is a large, ultra-hip speakeasy with an actual slide and posh ambiance for folks who don't mind waiting in line, or try **Matrix Fillmore (Map 2)** and the **Nectar Wine Bar (Map 1)**. For funky and simple, check out the space at the **Knockout (Map 35)** or **Madrone (Map 10)**. For funky and nautical, **Spec's (Map 8)** is the place for lovers of maritime décor. For cozy and comfortable, visit **Liverpool Lil's (Map 1)** or **Balboa Café (Map 2)** (midweek only, it's anything but cozy on the weekends). For dark and romantic, try the bar at **The Big Four (Map 7)** in the Huntington Hotel, **The Redwood Room (Map 7),** or **XYZ (Map 8)** in the W Hotel. For something completely different, **Etiquette Lounge (Map 7)** is what would happen if the Barbarella character, Duran Duran, got it on with the New Wave band, Duran Duran, had a love child and that child went into bar decorating.

Best Jukebox

Dalva (Map 11) and **Argus Lounge (Map 35)** both have great all-around jukeboxes. Rocker types have perennially awarded **Lucky 13 (Map 10)** with 'best jukebox' awards in local publications. For Louis Prima swing-era music hit **La Rocca's Corner (Map 3)** in North Beach or for Italian opera hit the **Tosca Café (Map 8)**. **Mucky Duck's (Map 25)** selection is also impressive (especially if you actually make it to the Sunset), and in addition to quirky live music, **Hemlock Tavern (Map 7)** has one of the more awesome indie and shoe-gazer jukes in the city.

Live Music

For live music there are historic heavy-hitters such as **The Warfield (Map 7)**, **Great American Music Hall (Map 7)**, **Bimbo's 365 (Map 3)**, **Slim's (Map 11)**, and, of course, **The Fillmore (Map 5)**—the only place where you can still get a free apple before the show and often a free poster after the show. Other venues to check out are **The Boom Boom Room (Map 5)**, **DNA Lounge (Map 11)**, **The Independent (Map 10)**, **Café Du Nord (Map 10)**, **The Elbo Room (Map 11)**,

Rickshaw Stop (Map 11), **12 Galaxies (Map 15)**, **Annie's Social Club (Map 7)**, **Bottom of the Hill (Map 13)**, and the **Hotel Utah (Map 12)**. **The Saloon (Map 4)** has free live blues, and **Hemlock Tavern (Map 7)** and **Edinburgh Castle (Map 7)** are great spots for cheap to free local indie acts of all sorts.

If you are feeling like tapping your foot along some sit-down jazz, the best of the best come to **Yoshi's (Downtown Oakland/Lake Merritt)** in Oakland. **Rasselas (Map 5)** and **Savannah Jazz (Map 15)** are also havens for that great local sound. Also across the Bay, the Paramount Theatre (see Landmarks for Downtown Oakland/Lake Merritt) is one of the most historic and beautiful venues around that's grabbing some huge names of late, and **Uptown (Downtown Oakland/Lake Merritt)** is a notable new venue for various live music most nights of the week.

Sheik Yerbouti

When you're ready to get your groove on in big-n-swanky club-style, hit **Ruby Skye (Map 7)**, **1015 Folsom (Map 12)**, and **Fluid (Map 8)** are big with the kids who like to wait in line for the traditional mega-club experience. Be sure to verify that the turntablist du jour fits your personal taste because the DJ scene here goes beyond subculture all the way to individual ecosystems. More eclectic dance hotspots include **Club 6 (Map 7)**, **Mezzanine (Map 7)**, **Milk (Map 9)**, **111 Minna (Map 8)**, **Mighty (Map 12)**, and **Luka's Taproom (Downtown Oakland/ Lake Merritt)** is taken over by DJ's most nights after the dinner crowds departs. For salsa, hit **Roccapulco (Map 35)** or **Café Cocomo (Map 13)**—they offer lessons three times a week for the novice. **Little Baobab (Map 11)** offers African music and cocktails made with exotic mixers like hibiscus, ginger and tamarind. And when you feel like partying after everything else shuts down, you'll probably end up at the **EndUp (Map 12)**.

Map 1 • Marina / Cow Hollow (West)

Bin 38	3232 Scott St	415-567-3838	Comfy new wine bar.
The Final Final	2990 Baker St	415-931-7800	Sports bar off the beaten path.
Gravity Room	3251 Scott St	415-776-1928	Sleek bar and dancing.
Liverpool Lil's	2942 Lyon St	415-921-6664	Quiet, comfy little pub tucked away by the Presidio. NFT fave.
Marina Lounge	2138 Chestnut St	415-922-1475	Marina dive.
Nectar Wine Lounge	3330 Steiner St	415-345-1377	Stylish wine bar. Flights and small bites.

Map 2 • Marina / Cow Hollow (East)

Balboa Cafe	3199 Fillmore St	415-921-3944	Historic upscale pub.
Bar None	1980 Union St	415-409-4469	Union Street pub with beer pong.
Black Magic Voodoo Lounge	1400 Lombard St	415-931-8711	The voodoo that they do so well is a spell made with Absinthe.
The Brazen Head	3166 Buchanan St	415-921-7600	Low-key marina bar serving food 'til late.
Bus Stop	1901 Union St	415-567-6905	Casual Cow Hollow hangout.
City Tavern	3200 Fillmore St	415-567-0918	Good for afternoon sidewalk drinkin'.
Comet Club	3111 Fillmore St	415-567-5589	Good spot for the last round.
Hi Fi	2125 Lombard St	415-345-8663	Marina club with velvet paintings and disco balls.
Horseshoe Tavern	2024 Chestnut St	415-346-1430	Sports bar.
Kelley's Tavern	3231 Fillmore St	415-567-7181	Chic Irish pub, if that's possible.
Matrix Fillmore	3138 Fillmore St	415-563-4180	Shiny happy people doing key bumps in the bathroom.
MatrixFillmore	3138 Fillmore St	415-563-4180	Cool Marina lounge. Originally opened in 1965 for the psychedelic '60s scene.
Mauna Loa	3009 Fillmore St	415-563-5137	Low-key dive, with a pool table.
Ottimista Enoteca Café	1838 Union St	415-674-8400	European wine bar. Serves brunch.
Silver Cloud	1994 Lombard St	415-922-1977	The regular drunken Marina crowd, only singing.

Map 3 • Russian Hill / Fisherman's Wharf

Bimbo's 365 Club	1025 Columbus Ave	415-474-0365	Topless mermaids.
The Buccaneer	2155 Polk St	415-673-8023	Arrrr! Free pool and cheap prices.
The Buena Vista Cafe	2765 Hyde St	415-474-5044	The "inventors" of the Irish Coffee.
Cresta's 2211 Club	2211 Polk St	415-673-2211	Friendly and cozy neighborhood saloon.
Fiddler's Green	1333 Columbus Ave	415-441-9758	Irish bar, tiny downstairs, dance area on second floor.
The Greens Sports Bar	2239 Polk St	415-775-4287	Great sports bar with tons of TVs.
Kennedy's Irish Pub & Indian Curry House	1040 Columbus Ave	415-441-8855	Hookahs and Tandoori and Foosball and Guiness, oh my.
La Rocca's Corner	957 Columbus Ave	415-674-1266	Old Italian bar. Louis Prima-era jukebox.
Tonic	2360 Polk St	415-771-5535	Dim corner lounge fit for happy hour in Russian Hill.

Map 4 • North Beach / Telegraph Hill

15 Romolo	15 Romolo Pl	415-398-1359	Blue velvet and candlelight. Tiny. Great jukebox.
Bamboo Hut	479 Broadway St	415-989-8555	Tiki bar amongst the strip clubs.
Broadway Studios	435 Broadway	415-291-0333	Everything from blues to burlesque.
Dragon Bar	473 Broadway	415-834-9383	Excellent beats and cool bartenders.
Fuse	493 Broadway	415-788-2706	Trendy retro cocktails.
Gino and Carlo	548 Green St	415-421-0896	1940s bar in the heart of North Beach. Pool table, pinball, serves Italian food.
Grant & Green Saloon	1371 Grant Ave	415-693-9565	North Beach classic, good live blues.
Hawaii West	729 Vallejo St	415-362-3220	North Beach island dive.
La Trappe	800 Greenwich St	415-440-8727	Over 200 beers and tasty, Belgian food.
Northstar Café	1560 Powell St	415-397-0577	Free popcorn and 80s music on the jukebox.
O'Reilly's	622 Green St	415-989-6222	Traditional Irish pub.
Pier 23 Café	Pier 23	415-362-5125	Live music, great deck, on the water.
The Red Jack Saloon	131 Bay St	415-989-0700	New England-style bar.
Rogue Ales Public House	673 Union St	415-362-7880	If 44 ales on tap doesn't grab you, the menu is enormous and very tasty.
Rosewood	732 Broadway	415-951-4886	A gem of a hideaway in burnished wood.
The Saloon	1232 Grant Ave	415-989-7666	North Beach institution, great live music.
Savoy Tivoli	1434 Grant Ave	415-362-7023	Good for an afternoon beer or wine, or pool game, in a touristy setting.
SIP Bar & Lounge	787 Broadway	415-699-6545	Chill spot to sip and quip. Don't forget to tip.
Steps of Rome Caffe	348 Columbus Ave	415-397-0435	Euro-scene.
Suede	383 Bay St	415-399-9555	Decent dance club.
Tony Nik's Café	1534 Stockton St	415-693-0990	Cool retro cocktail lounge.

Map 5 • Pacific Heights / Western Addition

Bar 821	821 Divisadero St	N/A	The bubbles tickle my nose.
Boom Boom Room	1601 Fillmore St	415-673-8000	Great live music every night, mostly blues.
The Fillmore	1805 Geary Blvd	415-346-6000	Legendary music venue. Purple chandeliers and free apples.
Fly Bar	762 Divisadero St	415-931-4359	Sake cocktails.
Frankie's Bohemian Café	1862 Divisadero St	415-921-4725	Beer bar, pub food.
Harry's Bar	2020 Fillmore St	415-921-1000	Neighborhood fare.
Lion Pub	2062 Divisadero St	415-567-6565	Free appetizers and great music.
Rassela's Jazz Club	1534 Fillmore St	415-346-8696	A Jazz club. On Fillmore. And all is right with the Universe.
Solstice	2801 California St	415-359-1222	Restaurant with a lively bar.
Yoshi's Jazz Club & Japanese Restaurant	1330 Fillmore St	415-655-5600	Nothing says jazz like Japanese fusion.

Map 6 • Pacific Heights / Japantown

Crimson Lounge	687 McAllister St	415-673-9353	Dark, red, and sexy for your next private party.
Koko Cocktails	1060 Geary St	415-885-4788	Hip and low-down. Cheap drinks, samurai films.
Route 101	1332 Van Ness Ave	415-474-6092	Decent jukebox, a motley crowd and two pool tables.

Map 7 • Nob Hill / Tenderloin

222 Hyde	222 Hyde St	415-345-8222	Counter-culture canvases and turbulent turntables enliven this cavernous artsy speak-easy.
Aunt Charlie's Lounge	133 Turk St	415-441-2922	Gay drag shows.
Big 4 Restaurant	1075 California St	415-771-1140	Classy, clubby, elegant San Francisco.
Bigfoot Lodge	1750 Polk St	415-440-2355	Find your inner cub scout over campground-themed cocktails.
Blur	1121 Polk St	415-567-1918	Laid back boozin'. Unlimited lollipops on the house.
Bourbon & Branch	501 Jones St	415-346-1735	Speakeasy where the entrance is clandestine and requires a password.
Bourbon and Branch	501 Jones St	415-346-1735	An old speakeasy. Sh. Let"s not tell them prohibition is over.
The Brown Jug Saloon	496 Eddy St	415-441-8404	Mellow Tenderloin dive. Pool table, pinball, jukebox.
Cantina	580 Sutter St	415-398-0195	Pisco sours, caipirinhas, other great cocktails.
The Cellar	685 Sutter St	415-441-5678	Hip-hop and '80s tunes.
Chelsea Place	641 Bush St	415-989-2524	Darts, jukebox, fireplace.
The Cinch	1723 Polk St	415-776-4162	Gay and western.
Club Six	60 6th St	415-863-1221	Duck off seedy 6th Street and dance.
Diva's Nightclub and Bar	1081 Post St	415-474-3482	Lots of lovely special ladies at this 3-story nightclub.
Edinburgh Castle	950 Geary St	415-885-4074	Great divey Scottish bar.
Etiquette Lounge	1108 Market St	415-869-8779	New downtown bar with Karaoke, DJs and Barbarella"s decorator.
Great American Music Hall	859 O'Farrell St	415-885-0750	Grand, ornate venue in a gritty neighborhood.
Ha-Ra Club	875 Geary St	415-673-3148	Tenderloin dive. Pool table.
Harry Denton's Starlight Room	450 Powell St	415-395-8595	Swanky cocktails and dancing with a view.

Hemlock Tavern	1131 Polk St	415-923-0923	Live music.
The Hidden Vine	620 Post St	415-674-3567	Delightful little wine bar with an unusual selection.
High Tide	600 Geary St	415-771-3145	You've been here before, you just don't remember.
The Hyde Out	1068 Hyde St	415-441-1914	Dive. Sit upstairs by the window. Eat free popcorn.
Kimo's	1351 Polk St	415-885-4535	Polynesian décor and drag shows upstairs.
Le Colonial	20 Cosmo Pl	415-931-3600	Vietnamese restaurant and bar. Hit the upstairs lounge.
Lefty O'Doul's	333 Geary St	415-982-8900	Hofbrau, baseball and AM Gold: The Holy Trinity of piano bars.
Lush Lounge	1221 Polk St	415-771-2022	Cool mixed crowd, good happy hour, and oatmeal cookie martinis.
Mezzanine	444 Jessie St	415-625-8880	New huge dance club, DJs can be hit or miss.
Mr Smith's	34 7th St	415-355-9991	Three-level club with DJs.
Owl Tree	601 Post St	415-359-1600	Who, who decorated this place? Hmm.
R Bar	1176 Sutter St	415-567-7441	Neighborhood watering hole.
Red Devil Lounge	1695 Polk St	415-921-1695	Popular Russian Hill bar. Live music.
Redwood Room	495 Geary St	415-929-2372	Upscale trendy hotel bar for the beautiful people.
Rrazz Room	222 Mason St	415-394-1189	Shine up your spats. This place is classy up the assy.
Ruby Skye	420 Mason St	415-693-0777	Terribly hip and trendy dance club.
Shanghai Kelly's	2064 Polk St	415-771-3300	Laid back Russian Hill saloon.
Slide	430 Mason St	415-421-1916	Speakeasy style, nightclub lines, and an actual slide.
Soluna	272 McAllister St	415-621-2200	Great food and drink, reasonably priced.
Suite One8one	181 Eddy St	415-345-9900	Semi-cheesy commuter dance spot, but open til 4 am.
Swig	561 Geary St	415-931-7292	LOTS of whiskey. Emerge Art on Wednesdays.
Tonga Room & Hurricane Bar	950 Mason St	415-772-5278	Tiki bar with dancing and thunderstorms. You can't beat it.
Top of the Mark	1 Nob Hill	415-616-6916	Swanky drinkin' and dancin'. Expensive and touristy.
Tunnel Top	601 Bush St	415-722-6620	Perched above the Stockton Tunnel, good mojitos.
The Warfield	982 Market St	415-345-0900	Legendary live music venue.
Whiskey Thieves	839 Geary St	415-409-2063	Kleptomaniac smoker's bar stocks a zillion whiskeys.
Zeki's Bar	1319 California St	415-928-0677	Cozy pub near Fillmore. Fireplace and pool table.

Map 8 • Financial District / SOMA

111 Minna Gallery	111 Minna St	415-974-1719	Bar-cum-gallery. It's all about Wednesday after work.
Azul	1 Tillman Pl	415-362-9750	Cool blue interior with good weekend DJs.
Bacar	448 Brannan St	415-904-4100	Great wine selection. Noisy.
Bix	56 Gold St	415-433-6300	Remarkable martinis, beautiful bar.
The Bubble Lounge	714 Montgomery St	415-434-4204	Our outpost of the New York champagne bar.
Buddha Bar	901 Grant Ave	415-362-1792	Chinatown classic.
The Cigar Bar and Grill	850 Montgomery St	415-398-0850	Feels like Havana circa 1945–or at least how we imagine it.
Club NV	525 Howard St	415-339-8686	Ultra-swanky SOMA dance club.
The Cosmopolitan	121 Spear St	415-543-4001	After work suit set martini bar.
Dave's	29 3rd St	415-495-6726	Quite possibly the diviest dive that ever dived.
Eddie Rickenbacker's	133 2nd St	415-543-3498	It's run by one of the guys from Deliverance. Squeal, little piggies.
EZ5	684 Commercial St	415-362-9321	Hip Chinatown meets Pac-Man. DJs spin house to hip-hop.
Fluid Ultra Lounge	662 Mission St	415-615-6888	Stylish, modern, state of the art dance club and lounge.
Fourth Street Bar and Deli	55 4th St	415-442-6734	The place to stop in on your way home from work, and check the score.
Glas Kat	520 4th St	415-495-6620	Supper club, live music, dancing.
Gordon Biersch	2 Harrison St	415-243-8246	Brew pub, good patio, financial district and bridge and tunnel crowd.
Harrington's Bar & Grill	245 Front St	415-392-7595	Stop here for snacks and a pint after work.
House of Shields	39 New Montgomery St	415-975-8651	Financial crowd decompressor.
The Irish Bank	10 Mark Ln	415-788-7152	Financial district watering hole.
Jillian's	101 4th St	415-369-6100	Play some pool after a flick at the Metreon.
Kate O'Briens	579 Howard St	415-882-7240	Average busy Irish pub.
L'Amour Nightclub	600 Jackson St	415-781-5224	Chinese karaoke, gold-digging cocktail waitreses, spotty service. Awesome.
Li Po Cocktail Lounge	916 Grant Ave	415-982-0072	Cool Chinatown dive.
The Lusty Lady	1033 Kearny St	415-391-3991	The girls in this peep show are unionized, like Norma Rae, only naked.
Mr. Bing's	201 Columbus Ave	415-362-1545	Liar's dice is not a game for pussies.
The Pied Piper Bar & Maxfield's	2 New Montgomery St	415-512-1111	Maxfield Parrish's Pied Piper mural dominates this lush,
The Punch Line	444 Battery St	415-397-4337	Top-notch comedy in Embarcadero Center.
Rickhouse	246 Kearny St	415-398-2827	Big, crowded, and actually pretty good.
Royal Exchange	301 Sacramento St	415-956-1710	Financial district pub.
San Francisco Brewing Company	155 Columbus Ave	415-434-3344	North Beach beer bar, grab a table on the sidewalk.
Seasons Bar & Lounge	757 Market St	415-633-3000	$15 cocktails and worth every penny.
Specs' Twelve Adler Museum	12 William Saroyan Pl	415-421-4112	Eclectic, bohemian bar hidden in a tiny nook off Columbus.
Sugar Cafe	679 Sutter St	415-441-5678	This schizophrenic little minx is coffee by day and booze at night.

Sutter Station	554 Market St	415-434-4768	The ultimate commuter dive bar.
Temple Nightclub	540 Howard St	N/A	White lounge, dimlit dining, dancing in the dark, and Buddha.
Thirsty Bear	661 Howard St	415-974-0905	Brew pub and tapas by Moscone.
Tosca Cafe	242 Columbus Ave	415-986-9651	Italian opera on the juke, Tom Waits sightings, classic red booths...pretty much heaven.
Vesuvio	255 Columbus Ave	415-362-3370	North Beach literati bar.
XYZ	W Hotel • 181 3rd St	415-817-7836	If you're stuck at the Moscone Center. In the W Hotel.
Zeke's	600 3rd St	415-392-5311	Have a beer before they charge you double at the ball park.

Map 9 • Haight Ashbury / Cole Valley

The Alembic Bar	1725 Haight St	415-666-0822	Home crafted cocktails (try a Ladyslipper) and local brews.
Club Deluxe	1511 Haight St	415-552-6949	Art deco swing-era lounge.
Finnegan's Wake	937 Cole St	415-731-6119	Cole Valley dive with ping-pong.
Gold Cane Cocktail Lounge	1569 Haight St	415-626-1112	Cheapest drinks in town and bartenders as toasted as you.
Hobson's Choice	1601 Haight St	415-621-5859	Victorian décor and rum drinks.
Kezar Pub	770 Stanyan St	415-386-9292	Sports bar.
Magnolia Pub and Brewery	1398 Haight St	415-864-7468	Quality handmade beers with hippie names. Kitchen open late.
Martin Macks	1568 Haight St	415-864-0124	Haight Street pub showing Gaelic futbol in the early mornings.
Milk Bar	1840 Haight St	415-387-6455	DJs spin hip-hop, funk, and retro grooves.
Murio's Trophy Room	1811 Haight St	415-752-2971	Great rock and roll dive.
Persian Aub Zam Zam	1633 Haight St	415-861-2545	Funky stylish interior. Crowded on weekends.
Trax	1437 Haight St	415-864-4213	Gay and straight in the Haight.

Map 10 • Castro / Lower Haight

The Bar on Church	198 Church St	415-861-7499	Former seedy Transfer transformed into a trendy gay hangout.
Blackbird	2124 Market St	415-503-0630	Thank you Blackbird, caw caw!
Café du Nord	2170 Market St	415-861-5016	Excellent live music, pool tables. Former speakeasy.
Café Flore	2298 Market St	415-621-8579	Open air café. Great for an afternoon beer or wine and Castro people watching.
Club Waziema	543 Divisadero St	415-346-6641	Stiff drinks and Ethiopian food.
Harvey's	500 Castro St	415-431-4278	A Castro institution. Considered touristy by the locals.
The Independent	628 Divisadero St	415-771-1421	Ideal live music venue. Great staff and stiff drinks.
Last Call Bar	3988 18th St	415-861-1310	A row of bar stools complete this local gay dive.
Lime	2246 Market St	415-621-5256	Trendy bar and tapas.
Lucky 13	2140 Market St	415-487-1313	Rocker bar. Great beer selection. Award winning jukebox and pool table.
Mad Dog in the Fog	530 Haight St	415-626-7279	Great beer bar. Your dog is welcome on the patio.
Madrone Lounge	500 Divisadero St	415-241-0202	Chill neighborhood art lounge.
The Midnight Sun	4067 18th St	415-861-4186	Gay bar with big TVs and sitcoms.
The Mint	1942 Market St	415-626-4726	Karaoke! Gay and straight.
Mojo Bicycle Cafe	639 Divisadero St	415-440-2370	Get your bike fixed while you swill a brew.
Molotov's	582 Haight St	415-558-8019	The quintessential dive of Lower Haight, punk rockers and all.
Nickies	466 Haight St	415-255-0300	Dancing, DJ, food and drink - no mixed drinks
The Page	298 Divisadero St	415-255-6101	Young, hip crowd with a neighborhood bar feel.
Pilsner Inn	225 Church St	415-621-7058	Gay bar with a pool table, darts, and pinball.
Q Bar	456 Castro St	415-864-2877	Castro Street bar with small dance floor and front patio smoking.
San Francisco Badlands	4121 18th St	415-626-9320	Gay dance bar.
Toad Hall	4146 18th St	415-621-2811	Like a nightly gay fiesta with Top 40 music and a happening back patio.
Toronado	547 Haight St	415-863-2276	THE BEST beer selection in the city.
Twin Peaks Tavern	401 Castro St	415-864-9470	One of the oldest gay bars in the Castro.
Uva Enoteca	568 Haight St	415-829-2024	All Italian wine bar, an instant classic.

Map 11 • Hayes Valley / The Mission

500 Club	500 Guerrero St	415-861-2500	Fine Mission dive. We love the sign.
Absinthe	398 Hayes St	415-551-1590	Have a minty Ginger Rogers with your fries.
Amnesia	853 Valencia St	415-970-0012	Beer, wine, and lots of red light.
Beauty Bar	2299 Mission St	415-285-0323	Be beautiful or get beautiful after a couple of drinks.
Bender's Bar and Grill	806 S Van Ness Ave	415-824-1800	Weird Fish, PBR and punk rock. Bring your Taz tat.
Blondie's Bar and No Grill	540 Valencia St	415-864-2419	Big blondes and even bigger...martinis.
Butter	354 11th St	415-863-5964	House music, PBR, WWF on big screen, and tater tots.
Casanova Lounge	527 Valencia St	415-863-9328	Swanky lounge with cozy couches and dim red lighting.
Cav Wine Bar & Kitchen	1666 Market St	415-437-1770	400+ wines and delicious small plates.

Dalva	3121 16th St	415-252-7740	Nice Mission lounge. Candlelight and sangria. Check out the jukebox!
Delirium	3139 16th St	415-552-5525	Pokey, punky, pukey party.
DNA Lounge	375 11th St	415-626-1409	ABC wants to shut them down for lewd behavior. Yeah lewd behavior.
Double Dutch	3192 16th St	415-503-1670	Post-modern old-school hip-hop vibe.
Double Play	2401 16th St	415-621-9859	Old time San Francisco sports bar. Giants and Seals memorabilia.
The Eagle Tavern	398 12th St	415-626-0880	Lots of leather dads, bears, and an outdoor fire pit.
Elbo Room	647 Valencia St	415-552-7788	Legendary alternative live music joint.
Elixir	3200 16th St	415-552-1633	Corner pub with lots of beers on tap.
Esta Noche	3079 16th St	415-861-5757	Bisexuals and drag queens.
Gestalt Haus	3159 16th St	415-560-0137	Pork, beef AND vegan sausages with your massive beer. Yes!
Homestead	2301 Folsom St	415-282-4663	Ask the bartender to play Yahtzee.
Kilowatt	3160 16th St	415-861-2595	Great trashy place to get trashed. Dogs allowed.
Lexington Club	3464 19th St	415-863-2052	Cozy lesbian bar.
Little Baobab	3388 19th St	415-643-3558	Hybrid nightclub and Caribbean-Creole restaurant.
Marlena's	488 Hayes St	415-864-6672	Drag queens and transvestites.
Martuni's	4 Valencia St	415-241-0205	Show tunes anyone? Great piano bar, mostly gay crowd.
The Monk's Kettle	3141 16th St	415-865-9523	Gastropub with over 100 bottled and 20 draft beers.
Nihon Whiskey Lounge	1779 Folsom St	415-552-4400	For well-heeled lovers of the brownest of the brown liquors.
Orbit Room	1900 Market St	415-252-9525	Café atmosphere, great Mojitos.
Parea Wine Bar and Cafe	795 Valencia St	415-255-2102	Good selection of wine and small plates.
Phoenix Bar	811 Valencia St	415-695-1811	Irish bar and restaurant.
Place Pigalle	520 Hayes St	415-552-2671	Low-key watering hole for the locals of Hayes Valley.
Rickshaw Stop	155 Fell St	415-861-2011	Eclectic live music, cheap eats, and real rickshaws.
Rite Spot Cafe	2099 Folsom St	415-552-6066	Funky piano bar/grub pub that is Rite, tight and out of sight.
Roxie Theater	3117 16th St	415-863-1087	Get out of the multiplex and into this charismatic theater.
Skylark	3089 16th St	415-621-9294	Mission watering hole.
Slim's	333 11th St	415-552-0333	Big name live music.
Sugar Lounge	377 Hayes St	415-255-7144	Happy hour cocktails and food for free - - enough said.
Thieves Tavern	496 14th St	415 252 9082	Beers, bicycle enthusiasts and (pool) balls.
Truck	1900 Folsom St	415-252-0306	Rough and scruff live up to this LGBT pit-stop.
Uptown	200 Capp St	415-861-8231	Cool Mission dive.
Wish Bar & Lounge	1539 Folsom St	415-278-9474	Intimate lounge.
Zeitgeist	199 Valencia St	415-255-7505	Biker bar with a big yard.

Map 12 • SOMA / Potrero Hill (North)

1015 Folsom	1015 Folsom St	415-431-7444	Club scene.
Annie's Social Club	917 Folsom St	415-974-1585	Upscale/ridiculous karaoke with Brit-pop dance marathons.
Asia SF	201 9th St	415-255-2742	Gender illusionists. Go for the entertainment.
Brainwash Cafe & Laundromat	1122 Folsom St	415-861-3663	Laundry, cocktails, live music.
Cat Club	1190 Folsom St	415-703-8964	DJ dance club.
The Chieftain Irish Pub	198 5th St	415-615-0916	Irish pub. 20 beers on tap.
The City Beer Store & Tasting Bar	1168 Folsom St	415-503-1033	The proverbial candy store for kids who like to drink beer and wine.
Club 93	93 9th St	415-522-0200	You're a long way from home, yuppie boy.
Connecticut Yankee	100 Connecticut St	415-552-4440	New England-style sports bar.
The Endup	401 6th St	415-896-1095	An institution and notorious for the Sunday T dance. Watch for theme nights.
Hole in the Wall Saloon	1369 Folsom St	415-431-4695	Neighborhood SoMa gay dive with cheap drinks and horny daddies.
Hole in the Wall Saloon	289 8th St	415-431-4695	Self-explanatory. Super-sketchy crowds make great people-watching.
Holy Cow	1535 Folsom St	415-621-6087	Holy Cow! There are a lot of bridge and tunnelers here.
Hotel Utah Saloon	500 4th St	415-546-6300	Serving up suds since 1908. Intimate live music venue.
Il Pirata	2007 16th St	415-626-2626	Italian restaurant and bar. Mermaid murals.
Mars Bar & Restaurant	798 Brannan St	415-621-6277	Jetsons-like lounge.
Mighty	119 Utah St	415-762-0151	Spacious dance club with rotating DJs.
Shine	1337 Mission St	415-255-1337	House music and free photo booth shots at this dive bar.
The Stud	399 9th St	415-863-6623	Infamous gay club.
Thee Parkside	1600 17th St	415-252-1330	Punk garage haven. Good bloody Marys.

Map 13 • Mission Beach

Bottom of the Hill	1233 17th St	415-621-4455	Great live music of all kinds.
Café Cocomo	650 Indiana St	415-410-4012	Salsa club with thrice-weekly dance lessons.
The Ramp	855 Terry Francois St.	415-621-2378	Hit the deck on Saturday/Sunday afternoons.

Map 14 • Noe Valley

Bliss Bar	4026 24th St	415-826-6200	Crimson walls and DJ grooves.
The Dubliner	3838 24th St	415-826-2279	Casual local Irish bar.
Noe's Bar	1199 Church St	415-282-4007	Sports bar.
Valley Tavern	4054 24th St	415-285-0674	Check out the beer garden in back.

Map 15 • Mission (Outer)

The Attic Club	3336 24th St	415-643-3376	Mellow hole in the wall.
Bruno's	2389 Mission St	415-643-5200	Old-time Mission supper club. Live music.
Dirty Thieves	3050 24th St	415-401-8474	It used to be Treat St. It"s still awesome.
Doc's Clock	2575 Mission St	415-824-3627	Mission hipster bar with shuffle board.
Dovre Club	1498 Valencia St	415-285-4169	Outer Mission dive bar.
Foreign Cinema	2534 Mission St	415-648-7600	Cool outdoor (and indoor) dining and cocktails where you can catch a talkie in the courtyard.
Latin American Club	3286 22nd St	415-647-2732	Kick back Mission bar. Pool table.
The Liberties	998 Guerrero St	415-282-6789	Neighborhood Irish pub and grub.
Lone Palm	3394 22nd St	415-648-0109	Laid back sleek Mission dive.
Make-Out Room	3225 22nd St	415-647-2888	Great divey local, alternative live music.
Medjool	2522 Mission St	415-550-9055	Nice outdoor space for those rare warm evenings.
Mission Bar	2695 Mission St	415-647-2300	The sign says it all: BAR.
The Napper Tandy	3200 24th St	415-550-7510	Irish dive pub with Wednesday quiz night and Saturday karaoke.
The Phone Booth	1398 S Van Ness Ave	415-648-4683	All the popcorn and hipsters you can sink your teeth into.
Pop's	2800 24th St	415-401-7677	Pacman, pool, friends, and the neighborhood sketchballs.
The Red Poppy Art House	2698 Folsom St	415-826-2402	Artists' studios, gallery, classroom, performance space. Small and unpretentious.
Savanna Jazz	2937 Mission St	415-285-3369	New jazz club in the Mission with Afro-Caribbean food.

Map 17 • Potrero Hill / Dogpatch

Dogpatch Saloon	2496 3rd St	415-643-8592	Comfy bar. Beers on tap.
Yield Wine Bar	2490 3rd St	415-401-8984	Don't it make your red wine green.

Map 19 • Outer Richmond (East) / Seacliff

Tee Off Bar & Grill	3129 Clement St	415-752-5439	Dive bar with strong drinks and pool table.
Trad'r Sam	6150 Geary Blvd	415-221-0773	Unpretentious tiki bar.

Map 20 • Richmond

Blarney Stone	5625 Geary Blvd	415-386-9914	Irish sports bar. Darts.
Tommy's Mexican Restaurant	5929 Geary Blvd	415-387-4747	Legendary margaritas!

Map 21 • Inner Richmond

540 Club	540 Clement St	415-752-7276	Classic local dive showcasing art, DJs, and irreverent theme parties.
Abbey Tavern	4100 Geary Blvd	415-221-7767	Irish pub and sports bar. Live music and TVs.
The Bitter End	441 Clement St	415-221-9538	Cozy, neighborhood Irish bar. Fireplace, pool tables, pinball, darts.
Buckshot Restaurant, Bar and Gameroom	3848 Geary Blvd	415-831-8838	Get shots and play some shuffleboard!
Dirty Trix	408 Clement St	415-752-1452	Pub.
Ireland's 32	3920 Geary Blvd	415-386-6173	Irish pub and live music.
The Plough and-- the Stars	116 Clement St	415-751-1122	More Irish than a head of cabbage...and the body of potato.
Rockit Room	406 Clement St	415-387-6343	Live music for a fratty crew.
Would You Believe?	4652 Geary Blvd	415-752-7444	A bit weird. Not as weird as the name, but still...weird.

Map 22 • Presidio Heights / Laurel Heights

The Pig & Whistle	2801 Geary Blvd	415-885-4779	Cozy pub where Guiness is poured the right way.

Map 23 • Outer Sunset

Flanahan's Pub	3805 Noriega St	415-665-2424	Serious dive bar for serious drinkers who get seriously drunk.
Pittsburgh's Pub	4207 Judah St	415-664-3926	The single most frightening bar ever. You MUST go.

Map 24 • Sunset

Dubliner	1849 Lincoln Way	415-242-9930	Have a hankering for an easy lay? Check out the Dub.
Durty Nelly's Irish Pub	2328 Irving St	415-664-2555	Irish pub with a fireplace.
The Taco Shop at Underdogs	1824 Irving St	415-566-8700	Because watching sports without tacos would be stupid.

Map 25 • Inner Sunset / Golden Gate Heights

Blackthorn Tavern	834 Irving St	415-564-6627	Cozy Irish pub. Darts.
Fireside Bar	603 Irving St	415-731-6433	Yes, this dive bar does have a working fireplace.
The Little Shamrock	807 Lincoln Way	415-661-0060	Must love Guinness and Darts.
Mucky Duck	1315 9th Ave	415-661-4340	Ugly people and dartboards. England in SF.
Yancy's Saloon	734 Irving St	415-665-6551	Sports-y Sunset bar.

Map 26 • Parkside (Outer)

Riptide	3639 Taraval St	415-681-8433	Last great bar before the ocean.

Map 27 • Parkside (Inner)

Costello's Four Deuces	2319 Taraval St	415-566-9122	Your wild Irish rose is here, drunk off her ass, singing Karaoke.
Grandma's Saloon	1016 Taraval St	415-665-7892	Local dive for those seeking to destroy their livers.
Shannon Arms	915 Taraval St	415-665-1223	Fog, fights, frat boys, and fiddles.

Map 30 • West Portal

Joxer Daly's	46 W Portal Ave	415-564-1412	Irish pub.
Philosopher's Club	824 Ulloa St	415-753-0599	After a few drinks all the women look like Simone de Beauvoir.
Portals Tavern	179 W Portal Ave	415-731-1208	Neighborhood bar.
Que Syrah	230 W Portal Ave	415-731-7000	A place you can imagine even Doris Day getting drunk.

Map 32 • Diamond Heights / Glen Park

Glen Park Station	2816 Diamond St	415-333-4633	Neighborhood bar.
O'Greenberg's	1600 Dolores St	415-695-9216	Sports bar.

Map 33 • Ingleside

The Ave	1607 Ocean Ave	415-587-6645	Proudly serving The Champagne of Beers for 2 bucks a pop.

Map 35 • Bernal Heights

3300 Club	3300 Mission St	415-826-6886	Poetry readings.
Argus Lounge	3187 Mission St	415-824-1447	Great jukebox.
El Rio	3158 Mission St	415-282-3325	Latin dive, racially and sexually mixed.
The Knockout	3223 Mission St	415-550-6994	Pretty people, cheap drinks… "Let the good times roll!"
Roccapulco	3140 Mission St	415-648-6611	One of the oldest Latin clubs in town, great for salsa.
Skip's Tavern	453 Cortland Ave	415-282-3456	Exceptional dive with live music.
Stray Bar	309 Cortland Ave	415-821-9263	The make-out room is in back. Own it.
Vino Rosso	629 Cortland Ave	415-647-1268	Mama mia! That's a spicy meatball.
The Wild Side West	424 Cortland Ave	415-647-3099	Western and Victorian, but not country. Fireplace. Check out the backyard.

Map 36 • Bayview / Silver Terrace

Space 550	550 Barneveld Ave	n/a	Depends on the night, but mostly techno or hip-hop.

Map 37 • India Basin / Hunters Point

Speakeasy Ales & Lagers	1195 Evans Ave	415-642-3371	Independent microbrewery.

Map 38 • Excelsior / Crocker Amazon

The Broken Record	1166 Geneva Ave	415-963-1713	Outer Mission chill spot with great food.
Geneva Pub	1196 Geneva Ave	415-452-9913	Comfy smoky vibe, mostly Asian crowd.

Map 40 • Bayview / Candlestick Point

Monte Carlo	1705 Yosemite Ave	415-822-7338	Mardi Gras year round.

Sausalito

No Name Bar	757 Bridgeway	415-332-1392	Friendly bar with frequent live music from Dixieland jazz to folk and everything in between.
Paterson's Bar	739 Bridgeway	415-332-1264	Scottish pub with sports on TV and a large selection of single malts.
Smitty's Bar	214 Caledonia St	415-332-2637	This local joint brings in all types. The only pool table in town.

Mill Valley

2 AM Club	380 Miller Ave	415-388-6036	Always a good idea, no matter what the time.

Berkeley (West)

924 Gilman	924 Gilman St	510-525-9926	Punk rock landmark.
Albatross Pub	1822 San Pablo Ave	510-843-2473	Check out board games at the bar. Endless popcorn for 25 cents!
Ashkenaz	1317 San Pablo Ave	510-525-5054	Multicultural dance and performance center. A staple of Berkeley flare.
Lanesplitter	2033 San Pablo Ave	510-845-1652	Excellent vegan pizza, great late-night 'n grab-a-bite hangout.
Missouri Lounge	2600 San Pablo Ave	510-548-2080	Drink Fernet and Maker's with the local art & music scenesters.
Pyramid Alehouse & Brewery	901 Gilman St	510-528-9880	Summertime movies in the parking lot. Bring your couch!

Berkeley (East)

Beckett's Irish Pub	2271 Shattuck Ave	510-647-1790	Open mics during the week. Steady acts return.
Blakes on Telegraph	2367 Telegraph Ave	510-848-0886	Drinks upstairs, bands downstairs. Caters to the college crowd.
Epic Arts	1923 Ashby Ave	510-644-2204	Sweet and cozy performance space. Live music, art, and more every night.
Jupiter	2181 Shattuck Ave	510-843-8277	The beer garden is fabulous on a warm evening.
La Peña Cultural Center	3105 Shattuck Ave	510-849-2568	Hispanic cultural arts center. Live music, open mics.
Shattuck Down Low	2248 Shattuck Ave	510-548-1159	(Literally) An underground nightclub and hip hop venue.
The Starry Plough	3101 Shattuck Ave	510-841-2082	Irish pub with poetry slam on Wednesdays.
Triple Rock Brewery	1920 Shattuck Ave	510-843-2739	Microbrews from micro-dudes.
Thalassa Bar & Billiards	2367 Shattuck Ave	510-848-1766	Huge pool hall and underwater-themed second room.

Oakland

Kingman's Lucky Lounge	3332 Grand Ave	510-465-5464	DJ's, eclectic crowd, fine drinks.

Downtown Oakland / Lake Merritt

@Seventeenth	510 17th Ave	510-433-0577	This dance club caters to the upscale hip-hop set.
Air Lounge	492 9th St	510-444-2377	Wednesday night open mics always draw a crowd.
Baggy's by the Lake	288 E 18th St	510-763-5721	Comfortable dive, just like home.
Café Van Kleef	1621 Telegraph Ave	510-763-7711	Pan progenitor barfs up hipsters.
EASY	3255 Lakeshore Ave	510-338-4911	Cocktails with fresh farmer's market fruit. Diverse crowd.
Heinold's First and Last Chance Bar	48 Webster St	510-839-6761	Since 1883 exclamation point.
Kincaid's	1 Franklin St	510-835-8600	Waterfront surf, turf, and libations.
La Estrellita	446 E 12th St	510-465-7188	Margaritas, margaritas, margaritas.
Luka's Taproom & Lounge	2221 Broadway	510-451-4677	Live music/DJ's nightly, pool room, funky jukebox.
Radio Bar	435 13th St	510-451-2889	Ruby Room's grown up sister art bar.
The Ruby Room	132 14th St	510-444-7224	50s-style lounge with dancing.
Stork Club	2330 Telegraph Ave	510-444-6174	Christmas lights, Barbie collection, local bands on tinsel lined stage.
The Trappist	460 8th St	510-238-8900	The finest selection of Belgian beer in the Bay Area.
Uptown Nightclub	1928 Telegraph Ave	510-451-8100	Music venue at the heart of the downtown Oakland renaissance.
Yoshi's	510 Embarcadero W	510-238-9200	World class jazz and sushi.

North Oakland / Emeryville

Ben & Nick's	5612 College Ave	510-923-0327	Neighborhood spot: pub grub, microbrews and cocktails-best crowds on College Ave.
Bill McNally's Irish Pub	5352 College Ave	510-654-9463	Drink a pint and watch soccer.
Cato's Ale House	3891 Piedmont Ave	510-655-3349	Brewpub and burgers.
Conga Lounge	5422 College Ave	510-463-2681	Retro '50s tiki lounge.
Egbert Souse's	3758 Piedmont Ave	510-658-4740	Every 'hood dive should have a screen door.
George and Walt's	5445 College Ave	510-653-7441	Classy dive.
George Kaye's	4044 Broadway	510-547-9374	Dive.
Kerry House	4092 Piedmont Ave	510-652-4032	Smokey dive bar and hangout. Thank God for the jukebox.
Kona Club	4401 Piedmont Ave	510-654-7100	Cozy and spacious. Kitsch galore. Yummy drinks. Not too hipster.
The White Horse Inn	6551 Telegraph Ave	510-652-3820	Gay and lesbian hangout.

Eating out is an intrinsic part of San Francisco living. For some, it's an obsession. For others, it's an art form. We can't wait to try a new restaurant (when we can get in) or a new type of food, and while we don't mind spending a fortune (sometimes) in the city's sleekest dining rooms, we're also down to gobble cheap grub in places that would alarm most tourists—it's all part of eating out San Francisco-style. With so many distinct neighborhoods, ethnicities, and cultures, it's no surprise that San Francisco brims with just about every kind of restaurant and cuisine imaginable. Eritrean? You got it. Afghan? It's here. Finding gastronomic pleasures in this city is easy. It's choosing among them that's tricky.

Eating Fresh

Patronizing and assessing new restaurants is practically a competitive sport in San Francisco. Everyone wants to stumble upon the next big culinary treasure before word hits the streets. Take **farmerbrown (Map 7)**, for example. This destination for "neo" soul food now attracts everyone from hipsters who've come for the swanky scene to organic foodies who appreciate the restaurant's reliance on small, local farms. **Alive! (Map 2)** features an exclusively raw menu, while **Minako (Map 11)** offers organic Japanese to patient diners. **Joe DiMaggio's Italian Chophouse (Map 4)** in North Beach wows patrons with its hefty steaks, **Zuni Café (Map 11)** is famous for its roast chicken, while across the Bay **Doña Tomas (North Oakland/Emeryville)** continues to impress critics and patrons alike with south of the border cuisine. Reservations at **NOPA (Map 10)** are hard to come by, at **Home (Map 10)** in the Castro business folk and bike messengers line up to feast on simple, organic contemporary American fare and slurp down after-work cocktails, and **Coi's (Map 4)** 4- and 11-course tasting menus have foodies all a-flutter.

Eating Cheap

Can you really do this here? Most definitely! Chow pizza, noodles, burritos, naan…go ethnic! Hey, it's what we survive on. For pizza, check out **Golden Boy (Map 4)** in North Beach, **Giorgio's (Map 21)** in the Richmond area, and the venerable **Escape From New York Pizza (Map 9)** on Haight. There's cheap Chinese, in almost every neighborhood, but we recommend **Ton Kiang (Map 20)** in Richmond, **R & G Lounge (Map 8)** near North Beach, and **Tai Chi (Map 7)** in upscale Russian Hill. Possibly the greatest—if weirdest—Chinese experience in all the land is **Sam Wo (Map 8)** in Chinatown, which is open til' the wee hours. Down by the ballpark, **Primo Patio (Map 13)** is a reliably cheap and awesome Caribbean lunch spot. There is also an endless supply of Thai—try **Manora (Map 11)** South of Market or **Thep Phanom (Map 10)** in the Lower Haight. You can also get just about any type of Southeast Asian food in the Richmond area. One of our favorites is **Burma SuperStar (Map 21)** on Clement Street, not far from a handful of Vietnamese Pho cafés. For tasty Indian on a shoestring budget, hit the popular **Naan-N-Curry** chain, **Shalimar (Map 7)**, or **Udupi Palace (Map 15)**.

Best burrito? After decades of research, we're still trying to figure that one out. But the Mission is a gold mine for Mexican and, with so many taquerias, you'll find fresh tacos and bulging burritos on every block. **Papalote (Map 15)**, **El Toro (Map 11)**, **La Taqueria (Map 15)**, and **El Farolito (Map 15)** are city favorites.

Mediterranean fare is another way to save a buck or two. Stop by **Ali Baba's (Map 10)** for a falafel with fries wrapped up inside tasty flatbread or try **Truly Mediterranean (Map 11)**. For poultry fans, **Goood Frikin' Chicken (Map 35)** (yes, that's three O's) serves up yummy bird and American sides with Middle Eastern flair.

Eating Hip

To see and be seen by San Francisco's beautiful people while indulging in a truly fabulous meal, we've got a few suggestions. Hot new spots include **Nopalito** on Lower Haight **(Map 10)**, **Dosa on Fillmore (Map 5)** and Noe Valley Catalan restaurant **Contigo (Map 14)**. If you find yourself in the chi-chi Marina, try **Betelnut (Map 2)** for swanky Asian small plates or make a beeline for **Mamacita (Map 1)**. Just be prepared to suck down a few cocktails while you wait for tables. In the Mission, **The Blue Plate (Map 35)**, **Foreign Cinema (Map 15)** and **Luna Park (Map 11)** are constant favorites, while bold new ice-cream parlor **Humphry Slocombe (Map 15)** offers startling ice-cream scoops—brown bag it with the bourbon-flavored Secret Breakfast. In the Lower Haight, check out **RNM (Map 10)** for a steady stream of hungry hipsters. In the financial district, you can mingle with businessmen and locals for chic Northern Italian hotshot **Perbacco (Map 8)**. Across the Bay, the Oakland renaissance continues with **Wood Tavern (North Oakland/Emeryville)**, **Flora (Downtown Oakland/Lake Merritt)**, and **Tamarindo (Downtown Oakland/Lake Merritt)**. For whiskey cocktails as dressy as its diners, line up for **Picán (Downtown Oakland/Lake Merritt)**, or try **Luka's Taproom (Downtown Oakland/Lake Merritt)**, where the Belgian fries are not to be missed.

Eating Brunch

Saturdays and Sundays are *eggfests* in the city, and there's no shortage of restaurants and cafés to choose from. So sleep late, call some friends, and step out for the best first meal of the day. Down home diners like **Chow (Map 10)** in the Castro, while **Dottie's True Blue Café (Map 7)** and the **Pork Store Café (Map 11)** are jumping almost every day of the week. Weekend warriors are willing to wait at constant favorites like **Mama's (Map 4)** on Washington Square in North Beach, Noe Valley's **Chloe's Café (Map 14)**, **Ella's (Map 5)** in Laurel Heights, and Cole Valley's **Zazie (Map 9)**. Castro residents rush to **Tangerine (Map 10)** for omelets with international flare, **Brenda's French Soul Food (Map 7)** wows the Tenderloin with beignets, while **Outerlands (Map 23)** attracts early birds for Dutch Pancakes in the Sunset district. Further afield, **Fred's Coffee Shop (Sausalito)** serves good French toast, **Mama's Royal Café (Downtown Oakland/Lake Merritt)** hashipsters out the door on weekends, while **Somerset (North Oakland/Emeryville)** draws chic crowds to its wisteria crowned patio for mango mimosas.

Eating Old

Even though restaurant turnover continues at an astonishing rate, there are some old San Francisco eateries worth checking out, including 1867 relic **Sam's Grill (Map 8)**, **The Big Four (Map 7)** at the Huntington Hotel, the **Tadich Grill (Map 8)**, and **Swan Oyster Depot (Map 7)**. **Alfred's (Map 8)** serves up steaks and **Sears Fine Foods (Map 7)** still plates a mighty good breakfast. **Art's Crab Shack (Downtown Oakland/Lake Merritt)** still kicks it old-school across the Bay.

Eating Meat

As much as we love our locally grown, organic veggies, sometimes nothing will do but a thick slab of rare beef. Van Ness Avenue is home to several, including **Harris' (Map 6)**, **Ruth's Chris (Map 6)**, and **House of Prime Rib (Map 6)**, which has been there forever and serves up good martinis and huge portions. Also worth mention on Van Ness is **Tommy's Joynt (Map 6)** which dishes up carved turkey and roast beef to locals, tourists and the occasional celebrity (previous diners include Metallica and the late Hunter S. Thompson). Nearby, you'll find **Boboquivari's (Map 2)**, a crab and steak joint with carnival-esque décor. If you want to bring it down a notch, hit **Izzy's (Map 1)** in the Marina (order the creamed spinach and Izzy's potatoes). For upscale diners, **5A5 Steak Lounge (Map 8)** offers Japanese steaks at blue-chip prices in a Vegas-style setting. For the best BBQ, go to the East Bay, where the venerable **Everett & Jones (Downtown Oakland/Lake Merritt)** leads the pack, and **T-Rex (Berkeley West)** sends em' home lickin' their fingers.

Eating Meatless

Pretty much every San Francisco restaurant offers vegetarian options, but there are some places that cater strictly to the greens-only crowd, from **Millennium (Map 7)**, San Francisco's high-end organic vegan restaurant (even the wine is organic), to tiny **Lucky Creation (Map 7)** in Chinatown Vegan chain **Herbivore (Map 15)** offers soups, salads, and wraps at three locations around the Bay Area, while at vegan **Café Gratitude (Map 15)** in the Mission, even the menu is life-affirming. How can anyone forget they're in San Francisco, with the 'I Am Eternally Youthful' vanilla shake? **Greens (Map 2)** is a city favorite for its gentle food and beautiful Bay views, while the veggie burgers at **Houston's (Map 4)** are always popular. Fans of Asian cuisine will find many options for meatless fare. Head to **Shangri-La (Map 24)** in the Sunset, **New Ganges (Map 29)** in the Upper Haight, and **Cha-Ya (Map 11)** in the Mission.

Eating Your Wallet

If you can afford it, this is possibly the best (and easiest) way to spend your time in San Francisco. Living in this city is not cheap and neither are some of the most delicious restaurants. The following all cost a fortune, so when you get there the best thing to do is sit back with your glass of Pinot and lap up the indulgence. **Gary Danko (Map 3)** is the best of the best. You'll have to call at least a month before to get a reservation, but the experience is well worth the wait. **Masa's (Map 7)**, **Quince (Map 6)**, **Spruce (Map 22)**, **Fleur de Lys (Map 7)**, **Campton Place (Map 7)**, **Boulevard (Map 8)**, **La Folie (Map 3)**, and **Michael Mina (Map 7)** are just a handful of the others where you can empty your bank account, fill your belly, and enjoy every minute of it. Happy eating!

Eating Small

While few wallets stretch as far as the fanciest restaurants, most folk can afford an egg custard tart. That's why we've gone small, for specialty dishes like the famous tarts at **Golden Gate Bakery (Map 8)**, or the fried chicken sandwich at **Bakesale Betty (North Oakland)**. Think of these as urban orienteering, as foodies map their way around the city bite by bite: breakfast beignets from **Just For You Café (Map 17)**, tamales from the Tamale Lady at **Zeitgeist (Map 11)**, or banana cream pie at **Mission Pie (Map 15)**. Some people rave about the XLB at **Shanghai Dumpling King (Map 19)**, others swear by the pollo pibil at **Poc Chuc (Map 11)**. Whatever your tastes, San Francisco has something tasty awaiting you, from the good—crab salad at **Swan Oyster Depot (Map 7)**—to the bad, cream puffs at **Beard Papa (Map 7)**, to the just plain strange: octopus lolly-pop at **Lalola (Map 7)**. Continue the culinary treasure hunt across the Oakland Bay Bridge with the huge bhatura cholle breads at **Vik's Chaat (Berkeley West)**, pork leg stew at **Chai Thai Noodle (East Oakland)** and lemon icebox pie at **Lois the Pie Queen (North Oakland/Emeryville)**.

Eating By the Bay

Surrounded by sea on three sides, San Francisco is a wonderful place for waterfront dining. Start out west with a view of the Pacific at **Cliff House (Map 18)** or swap silverware for sandwiches at nearby **Louis' (Map 18)**, where the outlook is higher but the prices are lower. Go east for Golden Gate snapshots and vegetarian fare at **Green's (Map 2)** or order crab fresh off the boat at **Scoma's (Map 3)**, one of Fisherman's Wharf's better options. The Ferry Building is a foodie mecca—especially with its farmers market on Saturday—try Vietnamese at **The Slanted Door (Map 8)** or rotisserie sandwiches at newcomer **Cane Rosso (Map 8)**. Further down the Embarcadero, in the shadow of the Bay Bridge, splurge on steaks at **Epic Roasthouse (Map 8)** or kick back with chili cheese fries and burgers at **Red's Java House (Map 8)**. Past the ballpark to the south, **The Ramp (Map 13)** offers beer, brunch and burgers a stone's throw from the ship yards. Elsewhere around the Bay, there are options aplenty, from **Fish.** in Sausalito to **Sam's Anchor Café** in Tiburon, a popular joint where the seafood is secondary to the skyline view across the water.

Key: $: Under $10 / $$: $10–$20 / $$$: $20–$30 / $$$$: $30–$40 / $$$$$: $40+
** : Does not accept credit cards. / † : Accepts only American Express. / †† : Accepts only Visa and MasterCard*
Time refers to kitchen closing time on Friday night.

Map 1 • Marina / Cow Hollow (West)

A16	2355 Chestnut St	415-771-2216	$$$$	11 pm	Rustic Italian, great pizzas, vintage foosball table. Nice wines.
Ace Wasabi's Rock and Roll Sushi	3339 Steiner St	415-567-4903	$$$$	11 pm	Lively sushi bar. Bingo at 6:30.
Amici's East Coast Pizzeria	2200 Lombard St	415-885-4500	$$	11 pm	Thin crust pizzas, with vegan and gluten-free options.
Baker Street Bistro	2953 Baker St	415-931-1475	$$$	10:30 pm	Casual, quaint, French.
Barney's Gourmet Hamburger	3344 Steiner St	415-563-0307	$$	10 pm	Good burgers. Take the kids.
Bechelli's Coffee Shop	2346 Chestnut St	415-346-1801	$$	4 pm	Coffee shop. Excellent breakfast. Open for breakfast and lunch only.
Bistro Aix	3340 Steiner St	415-202-0100	$$$$	11 pm	Mediterranean- and French-inspired bistro with a cozy heated patio.
Blue Barn	2105 Chestnut St	415-441-3232	$$	7:00 pm	Cozy spot with carefully-sourced salads and sandwiches, popular but pricey.
Chilayo	2150 Chestnut St	415-674-1814	$$		Pricey Marina Mexican, decent salsa bar.
Circa	2001 Chestnut St	415-351-0175	$$$	11 pm	Popular, LOUD bar and grill.

Key: $: Under $10 / $$: $10–$20 / $$$: $20–$30 / $$$$: $30–$40 / $$$$$: $40+
** : Does not accept credit cards. / † : Accepts only American Express. / †† : Accepts only Visa and MasterCard*
Time refers to kitchen closing time on Friday night.

Dragon Well	2142 Chestnut St	415-474-6888	$$$††	10 pm	Cheap modern Chinese.
E'Angelo	2234 Chestnut St	415-567-6164	$$$*	10:30 pm	Old-fashioned Italian.
Grove Cafe	2250 Chestnut St	415-474-4843	$$	11 pm	Cozy, laptop-friendly café.
Home Plate	2274 Lombard St	415-922-4663	$††	4 pm	Complimentary scones. The only Marina freebie.
International House of Pancakes	2299 Lombard St	415-921-4004	$$		Where else can you get pancakes and eggs at 3am?
Isa	3324 Steiner St	415-567-9588	$$$$$	10:30 pm	Excellent small plates and charming heated patio.
Izzy's Steak and Chops	3345 Steiner St	415-563-0487	$$$$	11 pm	Casual steakhouse. Don't miss the creamed spinach and Izzy's potatoes.
Liverpool Lil's	2942 Lyon St	415-921-6664	$$	1 am	Quiet, comfy little pub tucked away by the Presidio.
Los Hermanos	2026 Chestnut St	415-921-5790	$*		Simple, friendly, unfussy tacos and burritos.
Mamacita	2317 Chestnut St	415-346-8494	$$	10 pm	Mexican for the trendy set.
Mel's Drive-In	2165 Lombard St	415-921-2867	$$	24-hrs	Diner food, great for kids. Anybody see *American Graffiti*?
Mezes	2373 Chestnut St	415-409-7111	$$$†	10 pm	Popular Marina Greek.
Original Buffalo Wings	2499 Lombard St	415-931-8181	$	3 am	Lunchtime specials are reasonable value for the Lombard motel crowd.
Pluto's	3258 Scott St	415-775-8867	$$	10 pm	Made-to-order salads are the key attraction.
Ristorante Parma	3314 Steiner St	415-567-0500	$$$	10:30 pm	Casual Italian. Try the carbonara.
Rose's Café	2298 Union St	415-775-2200	$$$	11 pm	Charming Italian-style café. Breakfast, lunch, and dinner. Great for sidewalk dining.
Squat and Gobble	2263 Chestnut St	415-441-2200	$$		Sizeable menu and a nice patio out back.
Terzo	3011 Steiner St	415-441-3200	$$$	12 am	Ever-changing, always-enticing menu of Mediterranean small plates.
Yukol Place Thai Cuisine	2380 Lombard St	415-922-1599	$$††	10:30 pm	Neighborhood Thai.

Map 2 • Marina / Cow Hollow (East)

Abigail's	2120 Greenwich St	415-929-8889	$	5:00 pm	Friendly café serving brunch, gelato, and delicious flaky pastries.
Alegrias Spanish Restaurant	2018 Lombard St	415-929-8888	$$$	10:30 pm	Specialities from Campania; great pizza.
Balboa Cafe	3199 Fillmore St	415-921-3944	$$$$	11 pm	Fresh California fare in a clubby setting. Owned by Mayor Gavin Newsom.
Betelnut Pejiu Wu	2030 Union St	415-929-8855	$$$$	12 am	Popular contemporary Asian cuisine. Prepare to wait.
Boboquivari's	1450 Lombard St	415-441-8880	$$$$$	11 pm	Steak and crab. Outlandish décor.
The Brazen Head	3166 Buchanan St	415-921-7600	$$$$*	1 am	Low-key Marina bar serving food til' late.
Eastside West	3154 Fillmore St	415-885-4000	$$$	11 pm	Seafood, live music, and swanky bar scene.
Greens Restaurant	Ft Mason	415-771-6222	$$$$	9 pm	Imaginative vegetarian cuisine; great views.
Helmand Palace	2424 Van Ness Ave	415-345-0072	$$	11 pm	Pleasant Afghan restaurant - order the kaddo, baked pumpkin.
Jake's Steaks	3301 Buchanan St	415-922-2211	$	10 pm	Artery-busting cheesesteaks with onion rings and waffle fries.
La Boulange at Union	1909 Union St	415-440-4450	$*	7 pm	Exceptional French bakery.
La Cucina	2136 Union St	415-921-4500	$$	4 pm	Diner. Great for breakfast.
Mas Sake Freestyle Sushi	2030 Lombard St	415-440-1505	$$	11 pm	California-influenced sushi; party atmosphere.
Matterhorn Swiss Restaurant	2323 Van Ness Ave	415-885-6116	$$$$	9 pm	Fondue!…and other Swiss goodies.
Pacific Catch	2027 Chestnut St	415-440-1950	$$	10 pm	The wasabi bowls are worth a try.
Pane e Vino	1715 Union St	415-346-2111	$$$$	9:30 pm	A new location for an old favorite. Italian.
Perry's	1944 Union St	415-922-9022	$$	12 am	An institution and classic bar and grill. Go for brunch!
What's Up Dog!	2211 Filbert St	415-776-3647	$	2 am	Go for Chicago-style, then add the works.
Zushi Puzzle	1910 Lombard St	415-931-9319	$$$	10:30 pm	Immaculate sushi, best enjoyed at the bar.

Map 3 • Russian Hill / Fisherman's Wharf

Ana Mandara	891 Beach St	415-771-6800	$$$$$	10:30 pm	Upscale, French-influenced Vietnamese with great cocktail lounge.
Aux Delices	2327 Polk St	415-928-4977	$$††	10 pm	Consistently good, budget-friendly Vietnamese.
Boudin	160 Jefferson St	415-928-1849	$$	11 pm	Watch the bakers kneading dough, or try clam chowder in sourdough bowls.
Boulange de Polk	2310 Polk St	415-345-1107	$$*	7 pm	Exceptional French bakery.
Buena Vista	2765 Hyde St	415-474-5044	$	12 am	Sometimes you need a view with your Irish coffee.

Frascati	1901 Hyde St	415-928-1406	$$$$	9:45 pm	Neighborhoody and friendly.
Gary Danko	800 North Point St	415-749-2060	$$$$$††	10 pm	The best of the big names. Sophisticated California cuisine.
Grandeho's Kamekyo	2721 Hyde St	415-673-6828	$$$$	10 pm	Great sushi.
In-N-Out Burger	333 Jefferson St	800-786-1000	$*	1:30 am	Legendary fast food burgers. Double double with cheese, please.
Kara's Cupcakes	900 North Point St	415-351-2253	$	8 pm	Frosted cupcakes, beautifully presented.
La Folie	2316 Polk St	415-776-5577	$$$$$	10:30 pm	One of the greats. California-French.
Lemongrass Thai Cuisine	2348 Polk St	415-346-1818	$$	10:30 pm	Order the prawn pumpkin curry in this cozy Thai joint.
Luella	1896 Hyde St	415-674-4343	$$$$$	10 pm	Sleek but cozy interior showcases Mediterranean flavors.
Nick's Crispy Tacos	1500 Broadway	415-409-8226	$*	9 pm	Fabulous fresh fish tacos, but burritos are sub-par.
Okoze Sushi	1207 Union St	415-567-3397	$$$	11 pm	A stylish, cozy neighborhood spot for slightly pricey fish.
Pesce	2227 Polk St	415-928-8025	$$$$	11 pm	Venetian-style small plates.
Polker's	2226 Polk St	415-885-1000	$††	10:30 pm	Gourmet burgers and weekend brunch.
Rex Cafe	2323 Polk St	415-441-2244	$$		Lively weekend brunch spot for Russian Hill residents.
Scoma's	Pier 47	415-771-4383	$$$$	10:30 pm	Classic touristy San Francisco seafood. Try the crab sandwich.
Sushi Groove	1916 Hyde St	415-440-1905	$$$$	10:30 pm	Small and swanky destination for picky sushi eaters.
Swensen's Ice Cream	1999 Hyde St	415-775-6818	$*	11 pm	Landmark ice cream shop right off the cable car route.
Yabbies Coastal Kitchen	2237 Polk St	415-474-4088	$$$$	11 pm	Pricey seafood.
Za Pizza	1919 Hyde St	415-771-3100	$	11 pm	Great hole-in-the-wall thin crust pizza place. They deliver, too.
Zarzuela	2000 Hyde St	415-346-0800	$$$	10:30 pm	Authentic Spanish tapas.

Map 4 • North Beach / Telegraph Hill

Burgermeister	759 Columbus Ave	415-296-9907	$$*	12 am	Juicy half-pound Niman Ranch burgers. Fine onion rings.
Buster's	366 Columbus Ave	415-776-7100	$*	3 am	Cheesesteaks for the midnight munchies.
Butterfly	Pier 33 & Bay St	415-864-8999	$$$$	11 pm	Trendy average tapas.
Café Jacqueline	1454 Grant Ave	415-981-5565	$$$$$	9 pm	Romantic… and they only serve souffle.
The Caffe Sport	574 Green St	415-981-1251	$$*	10:30 pm	Classic Sicilian.
Caffe Sport	574 Green St	415-981-1251	$$*		Old school Sicilian, family style and family run.
Capp's Corner	1600 Powell St	415-989-2589	$$	11 pm	Bare-bones Italian.
Cavalli Cafe & Imports	1441 Stockton St	415-421-4219			
Coi	373 Broadway	415-393-9000	$$$$	10 pm	Inventive global cuisine in four or eleven courses.
Da Flora	701 Columbus Ave	415-981-4664	$$††	9:30 pm	Beautifully crafted Italian soul food; meltingly good gnocchi.
El Raigon	510 Union St	415-291-0927	$$$	10:30 pm	Traditional Argentine grilled meats.
Enrico's Sidewalk Café	504 Broadway St	415-982-6223	$$$$	7 pm	Broadway fixture. Great live music and people-watching.
Firenze by Night	1429 Stockton St	415-392-8585	$$$	11 pm	Old-school Italian by day.
Fog City Diner	1300 Battery St	415-982-2000	$$$	11 pm	Yes, it's touristy, but we still love it!
Forbes Island	Forbes Island	415-951-4900	$$$	9:30 pm	Nemo-esque island getaway a few yards off Fisherman's Wharf.
Golden Boy Pizza	542 Green St	415-982-9738	$$*	2 am	Great cheap pizza.
Henry's Hunan	924 Sansome St	415-956-7727	$$	9:30 pm	Get Diana's Meat Pie - gloriously greasy!
The House	1230 Grant Ave	415-986-8612	$$$	11 pm	Asian fusion extraordinaire in a North Beach nook.
Houston's	1800 Montgomery St	415-392-9280	$$	11 pm	Nice American grill. Great cocktails.
Il Fornaio	1265 Battery St	415-986-0100	$$$$	11 pm	Italian. Shhh, don't tell anyone about the patio for brunch.
Il Pollaio	555 Columbus Ave	415-362-7727	$$	9:00 pm	Neighborhood nook with roast chicken and carafes of red wine.
Iluna Basque	701 Union St	415-402-0011	$$$$	11:30 pm	Spanish-French small plates.
Impala	501 Broadway	415-982-5299	$$$	11 pm	Deluxe Mexican restaurant and lounge.
International House of Pancakes	200 Beach St	415-837-0221	$		Breakfast 24/7 for the Fisherman's Wharf crew.
Joe DiMaggio's	601 Union St	415-421-5633	$$$	11 pm	Swanky chophouse pays homage to the famous ballplayer.
L'Osteria del Forno	519 Columbus Ave	415-982-1124	$$$*	10:30 pm	Tiny and everything is cooked in the wood oven.

Key: $: Under $10 / $$: $10–$20 / $$$: $20–$30 / $$$$: $30-$40 / $$$$$: $40+
** : Does not accept credit cards. / † : Accepts only American Express. / †† : Accepts only Visa and MasterCard*
Time refers to kitchen closing time on Friday night.

La Boulange	543 Columbus Ave	415-399-0714	$††	4 am	Ahhh...Paris.
La Trappe	800 Greenwich St	415-440-8727	$$	12am	Over 200 beers and tasty, Belgian food.
Mama's on Washington Square	1701 Stockton St	415-362-6421	$$*	3 pm	Outstanding breakfast. Go early.
Mario's Bohemian Cigar Store Cafe	566 Columbus Ave	415-362-0536	$	10:00 pm	Focaccia sandwiches, Italian sodas and a Washington Square view.
Mo's Grill	1322 Grant Ave	415-788-3779	$$††	11:30 pm	Really good burgers.
North Beach Pizza	Pier 39	415-433-0400	$$	10 pm	Good local chain pizza.
North Beach Pizza	1462 Grant Ave	415-433-2444	$$	3 am	Good local chain pizza.
North Beach Restaurant	1512 Stockton St	415-392-1700	$$$$	11:45 pm	Authentic Italian fare. Watch for mob-esque clientele and proprietors.
Panta Rei	431 Columbus Ave	415-591-0900	$$$	12:30 am	Italian.
Pasta Pomodoro	655 Union St	415-399-0300	$$	11 pm	Fast cheap pasta.
Pier 23 Café	Pier 23	415-362-5125	$$	10 pm	Seafood, margaritas, music, and an outdoor patio overlooking the bay.
Piperade	1015 Battery St	415-391-2555	$$$$	10:30 pm	Really good Basque.
Ristorante Ideale	1315 Grant Ave	415-391-4129	$$$$	11 pm	Modern Roman trattoria.
Rose Pistola	532 Columbus Ave	415-399-0499	$$$$$	12 am	Popular family-style Ligurian.
Steps of Rome Caffe	348 Columbus Ave	415-397-0435	$$	3 am	Lively spot to drink a bottle of wine with some friends and have a good, basic Italian meal.
The Stinking Rose	325 Columbus Ave	415-781-7673	$$$	11 pm	Garlic everything, including the ice cream.
Sushi Hunter	1701 Powell St	415-291-9268	$$	11 pm	Great all-you-can-eat sushi.
Trattoria Contadina	1800 Mason St	415-982-5728	$$$$	11 pm	More good, basic Italian.
Victoria Pastry Co	1362 Stockton St	415-781-2015	$	9 pm	One of the city's oldest bakeries. Try the cakes and tiramisu.
Washington Square Bar & Grill	1707 Powell St	415-433-1188	$$$$	11 pm	The old Washbag is back again. The bar is better than the food.

Map 5 • Pacific Heights / Western Addition

Blue Jay Café	919 Divisadero St	415-447-6066	$$	10 pm	Down-home comfort food for ersatz Confederates.
Café Abir	1300 Fulton St	415-567-6503	$$*	10 pm	Classy renovation includes new menu items.
Candybar	1335 Fulton St	415-673-7078	$$	12 am	Wine and desserts. Pricier than the name would suggest.
The Cheese Steak Shop	1716 Divisadero St	415-346 3712	$	10 pm	Outstanding cheese steaks. Philly's best export since Rocky Balboa.
Dino's Pizzeria	2101 Fillmore St	415-922-4700	$††	11 pm	Tasty Pac Heights pizza joint.
Dosa	1700 Fillmore St	415-441-3672	$$$	12:00 am	South Indian crepes and a Mark Bright wine list.
Elite Café	2049 Fillmore St	415-673-5483	$$$$	11 pm	Cajun and Creole food with a great bar.
Eliza's	2877 California St	415-621-4819	$$$	9:30 pm	Healthy modern Chinese.
Ella's	500 Presidio Ave	415-441-5669	$$$	2 pm	A weekend brunch institution. Prepare to wait.
Florio	1915 Fillmore St	415-775-4300	$$	11 pm	Cozy French/Italian. Great atmosphere.
Fresca	2114 Fillmore St	415-447-2668	$$$$	11 pm	Tasty Peruvian.
Garibaldi's on Presidio	347 Presidio Ave	415-563-8841	$$$$$	10:30 pm	California Cuisine and an upscale local crowd.
Godzilla Sushi	1800 Divisadero St	415-931-1773	$$	10:30 pm	Packed place for sushi in Pac Heights.
The Grove	2016 Fillmore St	415-474-1419	$$	11:45 pm	Cozy, laptop-friendly café.
Jackson Fillmore	2506 Fillmore St	415-346-5288	$$$$	10:30 pm	A Pac Heights favorite for casual Italian.
King Lee's Chinese	1426 Fillmore St	415-563-8882	$	10 pm	Good delivery option.
La Mediterranee	2210 Fillmore St	415-921-2956	$$	11 pm	Cozy Middle Eastern.
Little Star Pizza	846 Divisadero St	415-441-1118	$$	11 pm	SF-specialized versions of both thick and thin crust; good jukebox.
Noah's Bagels	2213 Fillmore St	415-441-5396	$	6:30 pm	To go with your Saturday morning coffee.
Osaka	1923 Fillmore St	415-346-6588	$$	11:30 pm	Casual neighborhood sushi and Japanese fare.
SPQR	1911 Fillmore St	415-771-7779	$$$	11:00 pm	Roman inspired osteria for the upper-Fillmore set.
Stelladoro Pizza	808 Divisadero St	415-928-4454	$*	11 pm	Decent slice near The Independent.
Takara	22 Peace Plaza	415-921-2000	$$$	9:45 pm	Great bet for standard Japanese.
Ten-Ichi	2235 Fillmore St	415-346-3477	$$$	10 pm	Homestyle Japanese and sushi.
Tony's Cable Car Restaurant	2500 Geary Blvd	415-931-2416	$*	9:45 pm	Great signage, outdoor seating, cheap prices, and Tony himself.
Tortilla Heights	1750 Divisadero St	415-346-4531	$$	2 am	Best (and cheapest) of the upscale taquerias in the neighbhorhood.
Woodhouse Fish Company	1914 Fillmore St	415-437-2722	$$	9:30 pm	It's crabtastic.

Map 6 • Pacific Heights / Japantown

Harris'	2100 Van Ness Ave	415-673-1888	$$$$$	10 pm	Steak house serving California-grown beef.
House of Prime Rib	1906 Van Ness Ave	415-885-4605	$$$$$	10 pm	Beef and martini fest.
Iroha	1728 Buchanan St	415-922-0321	$$	10 pm	Small, busy Japanese.
Juban	1581 Webster St	415-776-5822	$$$	9:30 pm	Grill it yourself Japanese.
Korea House	1640 Post St	415-563-1388	$$$	12 am	Popular Korean.
May's Coffee Shop	1737 Post St	415-346-4020	$*	6 pm	Japanese tea, pastries, and sweets.
Mel's Drive-In	1050 Van Ness Ave	415-292-6358	$$	4 am	Diner food, great for kids. Anybody see *American Graffiti*?
Mifune	1737 Post St	415-922-0337	$$	10 pm	Casual Japanese noodles.
Sapporo-ya	1581 Webster St	415-563-7400	$$	10:30 pm	Ramen noodles.
Tommy's Joynt	1101 Geary Blvd	415-775-4216	$*	1:45 am	Carved meats, Buffalo meatball sandwiches and beer on tap. SF institution.

Map 7 • Nob Hill / Tenderloin

A La Turca	869 Geary St	415-345-1011	$$	11 pm	Turkish delights, bare-bones décor.
Acquerello	1722 Sacramento St	415-567-5432	$$$$$	10:30 pm	Good, swanky Italian.
Allegro Romano	1701 Jones St	415-928-4002	$$$$	10 pm	Simple, neighborhood, tablecloth Italian.
Ananda Fuara	1298 Market St	415-621-1994	$*	8 pm	Veggie/vegan menu, sarong-wearing staff.
The Bagelry	2139 Polk St	415-441-3003	$*	2:30 pm	Local fresh-baked bagels.
The Bell Tower	1900 Polk St	415-567-9596	$$	12 am	Friendly neighborhood grub and cocktails. Seats outside when sunny.
Big 4 Restaurant	1075 California St	415-771-1140	$$$$$	9:30 pm	Classy, clubby, elegant San Francisco.
Biscuits and Blues	401 Mason St	415-292-2583	$$$	11 pm	Southern cookin' and live music nightly.
Brenda's French Soul Food	652 Polk St	(415) 345-8100	$$	3 pm	Gumbo"s great, but beignets are better. Worth the wait.
Campton Place	340 Stockton St	415-955-5555	$$$$$	11 pm	Fancy Union Square dining for the ladies who lunch, or a romantic date.
Canteen	817 Sutter St	415-928-8870	$$$$	10 pm	Bijou space, creative Californian menu.
Chutney	511 Jones St	415-931-5541	$*	12 am	Best Indian food around. Don't go for the atmosphere.
Colibri	438 Geary St	415-440-2737	$$$	12 am	Mexican tapas and fruity margaritas.
Crustacean	1475 Polk St	415-776-2722	$$$$$	10:30 pm	Vietnamese roasted crab and garlic noodles.
Dining Room at the Ritz-Carlton	600 Stockton St	415-296-7465	$$$$	9:30 pm	Memorable Japanese-influenced French creations in a dazzlingly sumptuous setting.
Dottie's True Blue Café	522 Jones St	415-885-2767	$$	3 pm	Even Mark Ruffalo eats breakfast here. Seriously. We ate next to him.
Farallon	450 Post St	415-956-6969	$$$$$	11 pm	Superb seafood and a cool aquatic décor.
farmerbrown	25 Mason St	415-409-3276	$$	12 am	Neo-soul food with a hip vibe and ingredients from local farmers.
Fifth Floor	12 4th St	415-348-1555	$$$$$	11 pm	Fancy and elegant.
Fleur De Lys	777 Sutter St	415-673-7779	$$$$$	10:30 pm	High-end French cuisine in one of the most romantic dining rooms in SF.
Golden Era	572 Ofarrell St	415-673-3136	$$††	9 pm	Vegetarian and vegan Asian dishes on the cheap.
Grand Café	501 Geary St	415-292-0101	$$$	11 pm	French fare in Belle Epoque surroundings at the Monaco Hotel.
Hana Zen	115 Cyril Magnin St	415-421-2101	$$$	12 am	Straightforward sushi and solid bento boxes are great for lunch.
Hyde Street Bistro	1521 Hyde St	415-292-4415	$$$$	10:30 pm	Casual neighborhood French.
Hyde Street Seafood House & Raw Bar	1509 Hyde St	415-931-3474	$$	10:30 pm	Oysters at happy hour... where do we sign?
Indonesia Restaurant	678 Post St	415-474-4026	$$	3 am	Friendly Indonesian; killer roti and beef rendang.
Jai Yun	923 Pacific Ave	415-981-7438	$$$$$*	9:30 pm	Wonderful Chinatown dive. No menu, let the chef choose your meal.
Katana-Ya	430 Geary St	415-771-1280	$	6 pm	A bowl of bliss in a bustling downtown spot.
Kuleto's	221 Powell St	415-397-7720	$$$$	11 pm	Perfect Northern Italian after the theater or shopping in Union Square.
Lalola Bar de Tapas	1358 Mason St	415-981-5652	$$	11 pm	Lively tapas bar with $2 sangria at happy hour.
Le Colonial	20 Cosmo Pl	415-931-3600	$$$$	11 pm	Upscale, trendy, Vietnamese.
Lotta's	1720 Polk St	415-359-9039	$††	7 pm	Great all-American bakery. Try the gingerbread.
Lucky Creation	854 Washington St	415-989-0818	$*	9:30 pm	Very small, family-owned and operated all-vegetarian Chinese.
Mangosteen	601 Larkin St	(415) 776-3999	$$		Popular garlic noodle and bun dishes in Little Saigon.
Masa's	648 Bush St	415-989-7154	$$$$$	9:30 pm	Classic San Francisco. Another one of the greats.

Key: $: Under $10 / $$: $10–$20 / $$$: $20–$30 / $$$$: $30–$40 / $$$$$: $40+
** : Does not accept credit cards. / † : Accepts only American Express. / †† : Accepts only Visa and MasterCard*
Time refers to kitchen closing time on Friday night.

Michael Mina	335 Powell St	415-397-9222	$$$$$	10 pm	New American cuisine from famed chef. Inside St Francis Hotel.
Millennium	580 Geary St	415-345-3900	$$$$$	10 pm	Fancy vegan and organic everything.
Morty's	280 Golden Gate Ave	415-567-3354	$	8 pm	UC Hastings law students munch sandwiches while dodging Tenderloin transients.
Nook	1500 Hyde St	415-447-4100	$$	10:30 pm	Café by day. Lounge by night.
Olive Bar and Restaurant	743 Larkin St	415-776-9814	$$*	12 am	Artsy lounge serving tasty small plates and gourmet pizzas.
Ozone Thai	1160 Polk St	415-440-9663	$$††	1 am	Thai fusion.
Pakwan	653 Clay St	415-776-0160	$	11 pm	Indian. Bare bones, cheap, and good.
Pearl's Deluxe Burgers	708 Post St	415-409-6120	$	10 pm	Burgers, fries, and milkshakes. Deluxe and delightful.
Persimmon	582 Sutter St	415-433-5525	$$	11 pm	Yummy hummus.
Piccadilly Fish & Chips	1348 Polk St	415-771-6477	$*	11 pm	Oy mates! Bloody good fish-and-chips.
Postrio	545 Post St	415-776-7825	$$$$$	10.30 pm	Wolfgang Puck's place. Still going after more than a decade.
Ristorante Milano	1448 Pacific Ave	415-673-2961	$$$$	10:30 pm	The gnocchi here has its own fan club.
Rotunda	150 Stockton St	415-362-4777	$$$$	5 pm	Grab a cocktail at the bar to ease your shopping pain.
Rue St Jacques	1098 Jackson St	415-776-2002	$$$	10 pm	Authentic French atop Nob Hill has the locals saying 'bon.'
Saha	1075 Sutter St	415-345-9457	$$$	11 pm	Outstanding Arabic fusion inside the Carlton hotel.
Saigon Sandwich Shop	560 Larkin St	415-474-5698	$*	6 pm	Wallet-friendly French-Vietnamese sandwiches bursting with flavor and spice.
Scala's Bistro	432 Powell St	415-395-8555	$$$$$	12 am	Classic Union Square bistro…and it's open late! Great atmosphere.
Sears Fine Food	439 Powell St	415-986-0700	$$	10 pm	A Union Square breakfast institution.
Shalimar	532 Jones St	415-928-0333	$$*	11:30 pm	Excellent, cheap, bare bones Indian.
Straits Restaurant	845 Market St	415-668-1783	$$$	10:30 pm	High-end Singaporean in the giant Westfield. Atmosphere a bit busy, loud.
Street	2141 Polk St	415-775-1055	$$$$	11 pm	Sturdy food, real drinks. No reservations.
Sushi Rapture	1400 Leavenworth St	415-359-1388	$$	10:00 pm	Rapturously good tiny sushi spot atop Nob Hill.
Swan Oyster Depot	1517 Polk St	415-673-1101	$$*	5:30 pm	A tiny seafood and oyster institution. Seats 18 at the counter. Open 8-5:30, closed Sundays.
Tai Chi Restaurant	2031 Polk St	415-441-6758	$	10 pm	Delicious. Healthy. Chinese. Take Out. Crazy-ass cheap.
Taqueria CanCun	1003 Market St	415-864-6773	$*	1:45 am	Gigantic burritos.
Thai Spice	1730 Polk St	415-775-4777	$	11 pm	One of the better Thai places on Polk Street.
Tu Lan	8 6th St	415-626-0927	$$*	9:30 pm	Good Vietnamese in a seedy 'hood.
Turtle Tower	631 Larkin St	415-409-3333	$*	7:30 pm	Popular and packed place for pho.
U-Lee Restaurant	1468 Hyde St	415-771-9774	$*	9 pm	Don't leave without trying the potstickers.
Venticello	1257 Taylor St	415-922-2545	$$$$$	10 pm	Italian. Oozes Nob Hill charm.
Victor's Pizza	1411 Polk St	415-885-1660	$	12:30 am	New York-style pizza and calzones. One of the best.

Map 8 • Financial District / SOMA

21st Amendment	563 2nd St	415-369-0900	$$$	10 pm	Grab a microbrew and a burger before the game.
5A5 Steak Lounge	244 Jackson St	415-989-2539	$$$	1:30 am	Expensive steaks in a Vegas-style setting.
Alfred's Steak House	659 Merchant St	415-781-7058	$$$$$	10 pm	Great, old-world steakhouse.
Americano	8 Mission St	415-278-3777	$$$$	11 pm	Enjoy Italian while gazing at the Bay Bridge. In the Hotel Vitale.
B44	44 Belden Pl	415-986-6287	$$$$	11 pm	Catalan and great paella.
Bacar	448 Brannan St	415-904-4100	$$$$$	12 am	Amazing wine list (loads by the glass, too). Upscale and trendy.
Baladie Gourmet Café	337 Kearny St	415-989-6629	$	8 pm	Delicious, huge pita pockets; you can eat one for lunch AND dinner.
Banana House	321 Kearny St	415-981-9090	$$	9:30 pm	Thai for lunch. Try the pumpkin curry with tofu.
Birley's Sandwiches	4 Embarcadero Center	415-318-1800			Myriad mayo options.
Bix	56 Gold St	415-433-6300	$$$$$	12 am	First-rate martinis. The food's OK.
B & M Mei Sing Restaurant	62 2nd St	415-777-9530	$	-	Whole fried fish includes tasty intact eyeballs.
Bocadillos	710 Montgomery St	415-982-2622	$$	11 pm	Delicious, moderately priced Basque restaurant.
Boulevard	1 Mission St	415-543-6084	$$$$$	10:30 pm	Wonderful, classic, San Francisco institution.

Boxed Foods	245 Kearny St	415-981-9376	$	3 pm	Fresh. Organic-oriented. Not too cheap. Decent eats.
Brandy Ho's Hunan Food	217 Columbus Ave	415-788-7527	$$$	12 am	Popular Hunan Chinese restaurant.
Brickhouse Café and Bar	426 Brannan St	415-369-0222	$††	10 pm	Fresh, casual, American fare from friendly folks.
Brindisi Cucina di Mare	88 Belden Pl	415-593-8000	$$$$	11:30 pm	Southern Italian.
The Butler And The Chef Bistro	155 S Park St	415-896-2075	$$	3:00 pm	An unexpected Gallic treat in SOMA—delicious Croque Monsieurs.
Café Bastille	22 Belden Pl	415-986-5673	$$$	10:30 pm	Popular French bistro downtown with outdoor seating.
Cafe Claude	7 Claude Ln	415-392-3505	$$	10:30 pm	Live jazz on weekends, fabulous fries, full bar.
Cafe Venue	218 Montgomery St	415-989-1144	$	3:30 pm	Quick service and a wide array of sandwich and salad options.
Cafe Venue	70 Leidesdorff St	415-576-1144	$	3:30 pm	Quick service and a wide array of salad and sandwich options.
Cafe Venue	215 Fremont St	415-357-1144	$		Quick service and a wide array of salads and sandwiches.
Caffe Centro	102 S Park St	415-882-1500	$	5 pm	Popular coffee and lunchspot for nearby businesses.
Caffe Macaroni Sciue Sciue	124 Columbus Ave	415-217-8400	$$	11 pm	Authentic Neapolitan restaurant-trattoria.
Cane Rosso	1 Ferry Building	415-391-7599	$$	9 pm	Sandwiches from the rotisserie.
Chaat Café	320 3rd St	415-979-9946	$$††	9:30pm	Lunch-counter Indian.
Chaya Brasserie	132 The Embarcadero	415-777-8688	$$$	10:30 pm	Trendy Franco-Japanese fusion. Good drinks and sushi, too.
Chef Jia's	925 Kearny St	415-398-1626	$	10 pm	Avoid the line next door and check this place out.
Ciao Bella Gelato	1 Ferry Building	415-834-9778	$	8 pm	From Cabernet to Amaretto, these sweet flavors are sensational.
Crossroads Café	699 Delancey St	415-836-5624	$	10 pm	Part café, part bookstore; serves thick sandwiches and eclectic tapas.
Delica	Market St & The Embarcadero	415-834-0344	$$	6 pm	Sleek Japanese deli. Take-out only.
Globe	290 Pacific Ave	415-391-4132	$$$$	1 am	Casual California cuisine. Open late.
Golden Flower Vietnamese Restaurant	667 Jackson St	415-433-6469	$*		A decent bowl of pho in Chinatown.
Golden Star Vietnamese Restaurant	11 Walter U Lum Pl	415-398-1215	$*	9 pm	Best spot to get pho'ed up near Chinatown.
Gott's Roadside	1 Ferry Building	866-328-3663	$$	10 pm	Classic burgers with an eco-friendly recycling policy.
Henry's Hunan	110 Natoma St	415-546-4999	$$	9 pm	Get Diana's Meat Pie—gloriously greasy!
Hog Island Oyster Company	1 Ferry Building	415-391-7117	$$$	6 pm	Excellent oyster bar with a view.
House of Nanking	919 Kearny St	415-421-1429	$$	10 pm	Legendary cheap Chinese.
Jai Yun	680 Clay St	415-981-7438	$$$$$	9.30 pm	Wonderful Chinatown dive. No menu, let the chef choose your meal.
Koh Samui and the Monkey	415 Brannan St	415-369-0007	$$	10 pm	Thai. No monkey meat.
Kokkari Estiatorio	200 Jackson St	415-981-0983	$$$$$	11 pm	Comfortable, glamorous Greek.
Kyo-Ya	2 New Montgomery St	415-512-1111	$$$$$	10 pm	Top-drawer Japanese.
Le Central Bistro	453 Bush St	415-391-2233	$$$$	10 pm	Clubby lunch scene.
Local Kitchen and Wine Merchant	330 1st St	415-777-4200	$$	10:30 pm	Wood-fired pizzas and a Mark Bright wine list.
MarketBar	Market St & Embarcadero	415-434-1100	$$$$	10 pm	California cuisine, great cocktails, huge sidewalk patio.
Maya	303 2nd St	415-543-2928	$$$$	10 pm	High-end Mexican.
Mel's Drive-In	801 Mission St	415-227-0793	$$	24-hrs	Diner food, great for kids. Anybody see *American Graffiti*?
Mijita	Market St & The Embarcadero	415-399-0814	$$		Una cocina mexicana - get the queso fundido!
Mixt Greens	560 Mission St	415-296-8009	$	3 pm	Save the world. Eat a salad.
MoMo's	760 2nd St	415-227-8660	$$$$	10 pm	Fun American grill across form the ballpark. Great bar.
Naan-N-Curry	533 Jackson St	415-693-0499	$$	11:30 pm	Indian on the cheap.
One Market	1 Market St	415-777-5588	$$$$$	9 pm	Consistently good.
Out the Door	Market St & Embarcadero	415-321-3740	$	10:30 pm	Slanted Door's take-out counter.
Ozumo	161 Steuart St	415-882-1333	$$$$$	10:30 pm	High-end Japanese fare overlooking the waterfront. Excellent sake selection.
Paladar Cafe Cubano	329 Kearny St	415-398-4899	$$	4 pm	Excellent lunch option for downtown office slaves.
Pazzia Caffe & Pizzeria	337 3rd St	415-512-1693	$$$	10:30 pm	Homeade pasta down the street from SF MOMA.
Perbacco	230 California St	415-955-0663	$$$$	11 pm	Hip Northern Italian perfect for a date or party.

Key: $: Under $10 / $$: $10–$20 / $$$: $20–$30 / $$$$: $30-$40 / $$$$$: $40+
** : Does not accept credit cards. / † : Accepts only American Express. / †† : Accepts only Visa and MasterCard*
Time refers to kitchen closing time on Friday night.

Plouf	40 Belden Pl	415-986-6491	$$$$	11 pm	French cuisine. Try the mussels.
R&G Lounge	631 Kearny St	415-982-7877	$$$	10 pm	Cantonese favorite of in-town Hong Kongers.
Red's Java House	Pier 30 & Bryant St	415-777-5626	$*	4 pm	Cheap burgers and dogs by the bay.
Salt House	545 Mission St	415-543-8900	$$$$	11pm	Superb contemporary cuisine.
Sam Wo Restaurant	813 Washington St	415-982-0596	$$*	2 am	Late-night wonton soup that will save your soul. Much character, much food.
Sam's Grill & Seafood Restaurant	374 Bush St	415-421-0594	$$$$	9 pm	Classic American grill since 1867.
San Buena Taco Truck	375 Pacific Ave	N/A	$*		Tacos de lengua rock!
The Sentinel	37 New Montgomery St	415-284-9960	$	2:30 pm	FiDi lunch fave—must try the meatball sandwich!
Slanted Door	Market St & Embarcadero	415-861-8032	$$$$$	10 pm	First-rate Vietnamese. Make a reservation.
South Park Café	108 S Park St	415-495-7275	$$$$	10 pm	Distinguished, casual French.
Sweet Joanna's Café	101 Howard St	415-974-6822	$	4 pm	Tasty sandwiches and macaroons.
Tadich Grill	240 California St	415-391-1849	$$$$	9:30 pm	Legendary old-world seafood.
The Toaster Oven	145 2nd St	415-243-0222	$	7 pm	Warm toasty goodness!
The Toaster Oven	201 Spear St	415-537-1111	$	7 pm	Warm toasty goodness!
The Toaster Oven	3 Embarcadero Center	415-421-0111	$	7 pm	Warm toasty goodness!
Tommaso's	1042 Kearny St	415-398-9696	$$$	10:30 pm	Best pizza in North Beach since 1935.
Tommy Toy's Cuisine Chinoise	655 Montgomery St	415-397-4888	$$$$$	9:30 pm	Fancy, expensive Chinese.
Town Hall	342 Howard St	415-908-3900	$$$$$	11 pm	Wildly popular modern American food.
Tres Agaves	130 Townsend St	415-227-0500	$$	11 pm	Casual, hip spot for Mexican with top-notch tequila menu. Good for groups.
Tropisueño	75 Yerba Buena Lane	415-243-0299		10 30 pm	Chic Mission style burritos if that makes any sense.
What's Up Dog!	28 Trinity Pl	415-821-9886	$*	4 pm	Hot dog stand with mini-donuts for the lunchtime crowd.
Yank Sing	101 Spear St	415-957-9300	$$$$	3 pm	Terrific dim sum.
Zare	606 Folsom St	415-243-0580	$$$$	10:30 pm	Northern Italian and Southern French.

Map 9 • Haight Ashbury / Cole Valley

All You Knead	1466 Haight St	415-552-4550	$††	10:30 pm	Legit diner. Greasy eggs and free-flowing coffee.
Best of Thai Noodle	1418 Haight St	415-552-3534	$*	1:30 am	Sticky rice with mangos fulfills any late night sweets craving.
Blue Front Café	1430 Haight St	415-252-5917	$††	11 pm	Middle Eastern café with killer lemonade.
Boulange de Cole Valley	1000 Cole St	415-242-2442	$$*	7 pm	Café with excellent baked goods.
Burgermeister	86 Carl St	415-566-1274	$$*	11 pm	Large burgers, also hot dogs and cheesesteaks. Cash only.
Cha Cha Cha	1801 Haight St	415-386-5758	$$$	11:30 pm	Popular Caribbean-style tapas. Be ready to wait.
Citrus Club	1790 Haight St	415-387-6366	$$	11 pm	Popular Asian noodle dishes with California twist. Try the chicken noodle soup.
El Balazo	1654 Haight St	415-864-2140	$	10:30 pm	Haight Street Mexican. Mole, fish tacos, burritos, Grateful Dead!
Eos Restaurant & Wine Bar	901 Cole St	415-566-3063	$$$$$	11 pm	Asian fusion, nice wines.
Escape From New York Pizza	1737 Haight St	415-668-5577	$*	12 am	Big, cheap slices not just to soak up the booze.
Grandeho's Kamekyo	943 Cole St	415-759-8428	$$$$	11 pm	Great sushi.
Hama-Ko Sushi	108 Carl St	415-753-6808	$$$	9 pm	Sushi for the hardcore—follow the rules and you're golden.
Home Service Market	1700 Hayes St	415-346-7000	$	-	Off-the-radar spot serves off-the-hook sandwiches.
Kan Zaman	1793 Haight St	415-751-9656	$$$	12 am	Smoke the hookah, eat some hummus.
North Beach Pizza	800 Stanyan St	415-751-2300	$$	2 am	Good local chain pizza.
Panhandle Pizza	2077 Hayes St	415-750-0400	$$$	10 pm	Eclectic toppings such as soy cheese, clams, and eggplant.
Parada 22	1805 Haight St	415-750-1111	$$	-	One of the only Puerto Rican restaurants in SF.
People's Cafe	1419 Haight St	415-553-8842	$	10 pm	Spacious, mellow space for coffee and casual meals.
Ploy II	1770 Haight St	415-387-9224	$$	10:30 pm	A second floor Thai secret.
Pork Store Café	1451 Haight St	415-864-6981	$$	4 pm	Greasy breakfast joint.
Red Victorian Peace Café	1665 Haight St	415-864-1978	$	10:30 pm	Reminisce about the summer of love while eating quiche.
Squat and Gobble	1428 Haight St	415-864-8484	$$		Eggs, omelettes, crepes, sandwiches.
Zazie	941 Cole St	415-564-5332	$$$	10 pm	Brunch is a Cole Valley tradition here.

Map 10 • Castro / Lower Haight

2223 Restaurant	2223 Market St	415-431-0692	$$$$	11 pm	Cuisine from around the globe served in a hip setting.
Alamo Square Seafood Grill	803 Fillmore St	415-440-2828	$$$	10 pm	Carefully prepared seafood, no corkage fee on Weds.
Ali Baba's Cave	531 Haight St	415-255-7820	$$	11 pm	It's all about the shawarma.
Anchor Oyster Bar	579 Castro St	415-431-3990	$$$††	10 pm	Get the crab cakes.
Axum Café	698 Haight St	415-252-7912	$$	10:30 pm	Ethiopian. Eat with your fingers.
Bar Crudo	655 Divisadero St	415-409-0679	$$$	11 pm	Amazing raw bar that never disappoints.
Bi-Rite Creamery	3692 18th St	415-626-5600			Gourmet ice cream. Long lines. High prices. Worth every penny.
Burgermeister	138 Church St	415-437-2874	$$*	11 pm	Two-hand burgers, a little pricey.
Café du Soleil	200 Fillmore St	415-934-8637	$	10 pm	Charming, rustic French café.
Café Flore	2298 Market St	415-621-8579	$	11:30 pm	Great people-watching.
Catch	2362 Market St	415-431-5000	$$$$	11 pm	Seafood and California-style cuisine. Live piano and a patio.
Cathay Express Restaurant	720 14th St	415-431-3229	$††	9.30 pm	Cheap bastards chow down on chow mein.
Chilli Cha Cha	494 Haight St	415-552-2960	$$	12 am	Good, cheap Thai.
Chow	215 Church St	415-552-2469	$$$	12 am	Good, affordable home-cookin'.
Club Waziema	543 Divisadero St	415-346-6641	$$		Stiff drinks and Ethiopian food.
Crepevine	216 Church St	415-431-4646	$	10 pm	Fresh food and big selection, but the items add up.
Cuco's	488 Haight St	415-863-4906	$*	9 pm	Salvadorean, only plantain burrito in town.
Da Pitt	705 Divisadero St	415-440-7427	$$	10:30 pm	Solid ribs from the smoker. Pay cash.
Eiji	317 Sanchez St	415-558-8149	$$	10 pm	Cute, tiny, yummy spot. Get the homemade tofu.
El Castillito	136 Church St	415-621-3428	$*	12 am	Substitute fresh avocado for guac.
Estela's Fresh Sandwiches	250 Fillmore St	415-864-1850	$*	6 pm	Homemade smoothies and sandwiches to go.
Frances	3870 17th St	415-621-3870	$$$	10:15pm	Exceptional Cal cuisine in casual setting.
Home	2100 Market St	415-503-0333	$$$	12 am	Comfy home-cookin'. Great patio in the back.
Indian Oven	233 Fillmore St	415-626-1628	$$$	11 pm	Above-average Indian.
Jay's Cheesesteak	553 Divisadero St	415-771-5104	$	11 pm	Philly-style cheesesteaks.
Kate's Kitchen	471 Haight St	415-626-3984	$$*	3:45 pm	Breakfast and lunch with a Southern edge.
La Fajita	2312 Market St	415-593-0031	$*	12 am	Lesser known, but solid Mexican. Great chips.
La Mediterranee	288 Noe St	415-431-7210	$$	11 pm	Cozy Middle Eastern.
The Little Chihuahua	292 Divisadero St	415-255-8225	$	11 pm	Health conscious Mexican using Niman Ranch and Petaluma Poultry products.
Love N Haight Deli & Café	553 Haight St	415-252-8190	$*	2 am	Vegetarian deli sandwiches, some with fake meat.
M&L Market	691 14th St	415-431-7044	$	4 pm	Choose your bread first: a.k.a Mae's Sandwich Shop.
Marcello's Pizza	420 Castro St	415-863-3900	$	12 am	A quick slice across from the Castro Theater.
Memphis Minnie's BBQ Joint	576 Haight St	415-864-7675	$$	10 pm	Casual barbecue and sake menu (seriously).
Metro Caffe	247 Fillmore St	415-621-9536	$*	10 pm	Pint-sized joint for good, greasy cheesesteaks and burgers.
Nickies	466 Haight St	415-255-0300	$$	2 am	Dancing, DJ, food and drink - no mixed drinks
Nizario's Pizza	4077 18th St	415-487-0777	$††	2 am	Decent, at least when you're drunk.
NOPA	560 Divisadero St	415-864-8643	$$$	1 am	Airy, sexy room serves late.
Nopalito	306 Broderick St	415-437-0303	$$	10 pm	Mexican kitchen serving totopos (terrific!) and house-made popsicles.
Oakside Cafe	1195 Oak St	415-437-1985	$*		Open super early, great space for studying.
Orphan Andy's	3991 17th St	415-864-9795	$	24-hrs	Burgers, scrambles, and drag queens 24 hours a day.
Red Jade Restaurant	245 Church St	415 -621-3020	$$	9 pm	Indulge in hot crab rangoons and generous Chinese dishes.
RNM	598 Haight St	415-551-7900	$$$$	11 pm	Hip and trendy in the Lower Haight (lock the car).
Rosamunde Sausage Grill	545 Haight St	415-437-6851	$*	10 pm	Gourmet sausage joint.
Rotee	400 Haight St	415-552-8309	$	10:30 pm	Tucked at the end of the Lower Haight strip, it's fast and good Indian food.
Samovar Tea Lounge	498 Sanchez St	415-626-4700	$$	9 pm	Tea lounge that also serves breakfast.
Sausage Factory	517 Castro St	415-626-1250	$$	12 am	Hearty Italian in the Castro.
Sparky's	242 Church St	415-626-8666	$††	24-hrs	Open 24 hours for all your alcohol absorbing needs.
Starbelly	3583 16th St	415-252-7500	$$	11.30 pm	Taking Cali comfort food to new levels with Mediterranean flourishes.
Tangerine	3499 16th St	415-626-1700	$$$	10 pm	Gourmet Pacific Rim cuisine. The brunch menu is recommended.
Thep Phanom Thai Cuisine	400 Waller St	415-431-2526	$$	10:15 pm	Thai food at its finest.
Woodhouse Fish Company	2073 Market St	415-437-2722	$$	9:30 pm	It's crabtastic.
Ziryab	528 Divisadero St	415-522-0800	$$	1 am	Good Middle Eastern food and desserts.

Key: $: Under $10 / $$: $10–$20 / $$$: $20–$30 / $$$$: $30–$40 / $$$$$: $40+
** : Does not accept credit cards. / † : Accepts only American Express. / †† : Accepts only Visa and MasterCard*
Time refers to kitchen closing time on Friday night.

Map 11 • Hayes Valley / The Mission

Absinthe	398 Hayes St	415-551-1590	$$$$$	12 am	French brasserie with great cocktails. Open late.
Andalu	3198 16th St	415-621-2211	$$$$	12:30 am	Eclectic small plates.
Arinell Pizza	509 Valencia St	415-255-1303	$*	12 am	Thin-crust New York-style pizza with punk rock atmosphere.
Bar Jules	609 Hayes St	415-621-5482	$$$	11 pm	Menu changes every day, has brunch.
Bar Tartine	561 Valencia St	415-487-1600	$$	11 pm	Upscale spin-off of popular French bakery.
Basil Canteen	1489 Folsom St	415-552-3963	$$	10:30 pm	Atypical Thai restaurant, serving fusion dishes and cocktails.
Big Lantern	3170 16th St	415-863-8100	$$	10 pm	Specializes in dim sum and mock meats.
Big Nate's Barbeque	1665 Folsom St	415-861-4242	$$	9:30 pm	Memphis pork from owner and former NBA star Nate Thurmond.
Blowfish Sushi	2170 Bryant St	415-285-3848	$$$$	12 am	Upscale sushi, cocktails, and electronic beats.
Blue Muse	370 Grove St	415-701-9888	$$$	12 am	Reopened in new location, popular with opera crowd
Bodhi Vietnamese Cuisine	211 Valencia St	415-626-7750	$	10 pm	Prices that have resisted Mission gentrification.
Burger Joint	807 Valencia St	415-824-3494	$$*	11 pm	*Jetsons*-like burger joint.
Caffe Delle Stelle	395 Hayes St	415-252-1110	$$$	10 pm	Cozy, simple Italian.
Canto do Brasil	41 Franklin St	415-626-8727	$$	-	Brazilian ambience in the heart of SF.
Cav Wine Bar & Kitchen	1666 Market St	415-437-1770	$$$	-	400+ wines and delicious small plates.
Cha Cha Cha	2327 Mission St	415-824-1502	$$$	1 am	Caribbean-style tapas.
Cha-Ya Vegetarian Japanese Restaurant	762 Valencia St	415-252-7825	$$$$*	10 pm	Not just vegetarian, it's vegan too.
Charanga	2351 Mission St	415-282-1813	$$$	11 pm	Caribbean-style tapas.
Chez Spencer	82 14th St	415-864-2191	$$$$	10:30 pm	Pricey French.
Christopher Elbow Chocolates	401 Hayes St	415-355-1105	$$$	10 pm	Gourmet chocolate, need we say more?
Delfina	3621 18th St	415-552-4055	$$$$$††	11 pm	Exceptional Italian. If we ever get in we'll like it.
DeLessio Market	1695 Market St	415-552-5559	$$	7.30 pm	Bakery, buffet and hot lunch by the pound
Destino	1815 Market St	415-552-4451	$$$$	11 pm	Nuevo Latino bistro.
Domo	511 Laguna St	415-861-8887	$$	10 pm	Very very very tiny. Great sushi.
Double Decker	465 Grove St	415-552-8042	$*	10 pm	Spicy chicken wings are a big hit
El Toro Taqueria	598 Valencia St	415-431-3351	$$	10 pm	Fantastic tacos and burritos.
Espetus Churrascaria	1686 Market St	415-552-8792	$$$$$	11 pm	Brazilian steakhouse, all-you-can-eat roasted meats served on swords.
Farina	3560 18th St	415-565-0360	$$	10 pm	Interesting decor, solid Italian food, but early close hours for dinner on weekends
Flipper's	482 Hayes St	415-552-8880	$	10 pm	Neighborhood favorite with outdoor seating.
Frjtz	581 Hayes St	415-864-7654	$$	12 am	Chimay, Belgian fries, and nouveau dips.
Go Getters Pizza	69 Gough St	415-621-1401	$	1 am	Go Get 'Em! Em=shitty pizza.
Hayes Street Grill	320 Hayes St	415-863-5545	$$$$	10:30 pm	Good, basic seafood–popular with the symphony crowd.
Hotel Biron	45 Rose St	415-703-0403	$$	12 am	Get a cheese platter and an unusual grape wine by the glass.
Irma's Pampanga Restaurant	2901 16th St	415-626-6688	$*	8 pm	Cafeteria-style Filipino restaurant made with love.
It's Tops Coffee Shop	1801 Market St	415-431-6395	$$††	3 am	Basic greasy spoon that's great for breakfast.
Jardiniere	300 Grove St	415-861-5555	$$$$$	11:30 pm	High-end California-French fare.
Kenny's Restaurant	518 S Van Ness Ave	415-621-8902	$*		Greasy spoon, with breakfasts as cheap as chips.
La Cumbre	515 Valencia St	(415) 863-8205	$	2 am	Classic longstanding taqueria.
La Oaxaquena	2128 Mission St	415-621-5446	$	-	Try the tlayuda--a large tortilla slathered in toppings.
Limon	524 Valencia St	415-252-0918	$$$$	11 pm	Modest, popular Peruvian. Try the ceviche.
Little Star Pizza	400 Valencia St	415-551-7827	$$	11 pm	Deep dish or thin crust and a variety of toppings.
Luna Park	694 Valencia St	415-553-8584	$$$	11:30 pm	Casual, moderately-priced American food. Try the make-your-own 'smores for dessert!
Manora's Thai Cuisine	1600 Folsom St	415-861-6224	$$$	10:30 pm	Above average Thai.
Maverick	3316 17th St	415-863-3061	$$	11 pm	Southern comfort food.
Minako	2154 Mission St	415-864-1888	$$	9:30 pm	Homey Japanese.
Moisehe's Pippic	425 Hayes St	415-431-2440	$$*	4 pm	Jewish-style deli.
The Monk's Kettle	3141 16th St	415-865-9523	$$	1 am	Tasty, filling pub grub.
Momi Toby's Revolution Café	528 Laguna St	415-626-1508	$*	10 pm	Great spot for an afternoon Chimay or coffee.
Pakwan	3182 16th St	415-255-2440	$$*	11 pm	Indian. Bare bones, cheap, and good.

Paramount Piroshki	585 Potrero Ave	415-552-5475	$	5 pm	Takeout piroshkis made on site
Patxi's Chicago Pizza	511 Hayes St	415-558-9991	$$	10 pm	They let you order while you wait.
Pancho Villa Taqueria	3071 16th St	415-864-8840	$	12 am	Try the prawn quesadilla.
paul k	199 Gough St	415-552-7132	$$$$	11 pm	Mediterranean, open late.
Pauline's Pizza and Wine Bar	260 Valencia St	415-552-2050	$$	10 pm	Wild and wonderful California 'za.
Picaro	3120 16th St	415-431-4089	$	12 am	Authentic Spanish tapas. Good sangria.
Pizzeria Delfina	3611 18th St	415-437-6800	$$††	11 pm	Absurdly popular. Absurdly tasty.
Poc Chuc	2886 16th St	415-558-1583	$$	-	Mayan fusion in the heart of the Mission.
Pork Store Café	3122 16th St	415-626-5523	$$	4 pm	Greasy breakfast joint.
Puerto Alegre Restaurant	546 Valencia St	415-255-8201	$$	11 pm	Popular standard Mexican.
Range	842 Valencia St	415-282-8283	$$$††	11 pm	Inventive California cuisine.
The Sage Cafe	340 Grove St	415-252-9887	$	8 pm	Best watermelon juice in town
Samovar Tea Lounge	297 Page St	(415) 861-0303	$$	10 pm	A (pricey) assortment of teas in a cozy atmosphere.
Slow Club	2501 Mariposa St	415-241-9390	$$$$††	11 pm	Cool supper-club vibe.
Stacks'	501 Hayes St	415-241-9011	$$	2:30 pm	Don't hate it because it's a chain - the pancakes are great.
Sunflower Restaurant	3111 16th	415-626-5022	$	11:30 pm	Two locations with an attached kitchen, Vietnamese food.
Suppenkuche	525 Laguna St	415-252-9289	$$$	10 pm	Authentic German food and great beers.
Suriya Thai Restaurant	1532 Howard St	415-355-9999	$$	11 pm	Former Mission restaurant brings classic Thai to SoMa.
Sushi Groove South	1516 Folsom St	415-503-1950	$$$$	11:30 pm	Hip sushi.
Taqueria Cancun	2288 Mission St	415-252-9560	$*	2:45 am	Gigantic burritos.
Taqueria El Buen Sabor	699 Valencia St	415-552-8816	$	10 pm	Good tofu burritos, but otherwise average.
Tartine Bakery	600 Guerrero St	415-487-2600	$$	8 pm	Great French café.
Tartine Cafe Francais	244 Gough St	415-553-4595	$	6 pm	Good pastries, nothing to do with Tartine Bakery, however
Thrill Of The Grill	535 Valencia St	415 776 7100	$	2:30 am	Late night, greasy food, drunk clientele (ex-Cable Car pizza).
Tokyo Go Go	3174 16th St	415-864-2288	$$$$	11 pm	Handroll happy hour. Super yummy. Cucumber gimlet. Creative Sushi.
Truly Mediterranean	3109 16th St	415-252-7482	$	12 am	Quick Mediterranean take-out. Falafel, shawarma, hummus, and baba ghanoush.
Universal Café	2814 19th St	415-821-4608	$$$$	10:30 pm	Warm, sleek, California cuisine. Excellent for brunch.
Walzwerk	381 S Van Ness Ave	415-551-7181	$$$	10 pm	Hearty German grub and excellent beer.
What's Up Dog!	1599 Howard St	415-861-5366	$$	8 pm	If Costco dogs don't do it, who ya gonna call?
Woodward's Garden	1700 Mission St	415-621-7122	$$$$$	8:30 pm	Cozy and discreet.
Yamo	3406 18th St	415-553-8911	$	9.30 pm	Friendly, raucous, cheap, and tasty.
Zuni Café	1658 Market St	415-552-2522	$$$$$	12 am	An institution… and there's so much more than the sublime roasted chicken.

Map 12 • SOMA / Potrero Hill (North)

54 Mint	16 Mint Plaza	415-543-5100	$$$	-	Warm welcome, wow wine list, pretty people, perfect pasta!
AK Subs	397 8th Street	415-241-9600	$	10 pm	SoMa sub-sandwich shop serving delicious deli meats.
Asia SF	201 9th St	415-255-2742	$$$$	10 pm	Anything but a "drag," the waitstaff are as stunning as they are entertaining.
Axis Café & Gallery	1201 8th St	415-437-2947	$	6 pm	Sunny patio, yummy salads.
Basil Thai	1175 Folsom St	(415) 552-8999	$$	10 pm	A taste of Thailand in SOMA.
Brainwash Cafe & Laundromat	1122 Folsom St	415-861-3663	$	11 pm	Eat food, drink coffee, and do laundry.
Cafe Venue	67 5th St	415-546-1144	$		Quick service and a wide array of salads and sandwiches.
Chez Maman	1453 18th St	415-824-7166	$$$	11 pm	Casual French brunch in a charming, pocket-sized space.
Chez Papa	4 Mint St	415-546-4134	$$$$	11 pm	French bistro that's quickly becoming a city favorite.
The Chieftain Irish Pub	198 5th St	415-615-0916	$$	10 pm	Classic Irish pub with food to match.
Custom Burger	121 7th St	415-252-2634	$$	9:30 pm	Pick your own meat and toppings at this contemporary burger joint.
Dos Pinas	251 Rhode Island St	415-252-8220	$	9 pm	Loud and lively taqueria with $2 Coronas on Fridays.
Goat Hill Pizza	300 Connecticut St	415-641-1440	$$	11 pm	Monday neighborhood night in P-hill: $8 AYCE.
Grab 'N Go	480 6th St	415-553-6666	$	8 pm	Vietnamese done fast 'n cheap.
Heaven's Dog & Noodle Shop	1148 Mission St	415-863-6008	$$$	1 am	Enjoy a Chinese fusion meal as dog portraitures hover over your shoulder.

Key: $: Under $10 / $$: $10–$20 / $$$: $20–$30 / $$$$: $30–$40 / $$$$$: $40+
** : Does not accept credit cards. / † : Accepts only American Express. / †† : Accepts only Visa and MasterCard*
Time refers to kitchen closing time on Friday night.

Henry's Hunan	1016 Bryant St	415-861-5808	$	9 pm	Get Diana's Meat Pie - gloriously greasy!
Orson	508 4th St	(415) 777-1508	$$$	11 pm	Refreshingly unique (and decidedly pricey) small plates.
Out the Door	865 Market St	415-541-9913	$$	9 pm	The Slanted Door, mall-style.
Restaurant LuLu	816 Folsom St	415-495-5775	$$$$	11 pm	Wood-fired oven and grill fare served family-style.
Sally's	300 De Haro St	415-626-6006	$††	5 pm	Honkin' big omelets, strong coffee.
Triptych	1155 Folsom St	415-703-0557	$$$	10:30 pm	Mediterranean with California twist in artsy, industrial setting.
What's Up Dog!	300 De Haro St	415-241-9400	$*	5:30 pm	Hot dog stand: chili cheese, Chicago, veggie.
Wolfe's Lunch	1220 16th St	415-621-3684	$	4:30 pm	Korean BBQ, omelets, burgers and sushi. Located at the corner of a three-way intersection.

Map 13 • Mission Beach

Aperto	1434 18th St	415-252-1625	$$$	10 pm	Cute, unpretentious Italian.
Chez Papa Bistrot	1401 18th St	415-824 -8205	$$	11pm	Where the homesick French dine.
Fringale	570 4th St	415-543-0573	$$$$	10:30 pm	Excellent French.
Hazel's Kitchen	1319 18th St	415-647-7941	$*	4 pm	Tiny sandwich joint with a couple of streetfront tables.
Moshi Moshi	2092 3rd St	415-861-8285	$$††	10 pm	Hidden sushi place with tangy miso dressing.
Primo Patio Cafe	214 Townsend St	415-957-1129	$	4 pm	Great, affordable local hole-in-the-wall Caribbean food.
The Ramp	855 Terry Francois St.	415-621-2378	$$	8 pm	Simple food with a great deck. Go on a sunny day.

Map 14 • Noe Valley

Barney's Gourmet Hamburger	4138 24th St	415-282-7770	$$	10 pm	Good burgers. Better onion rings. Take the kids.
Chloe's Café	1399 Church St	415-648-4116	$$*	3:30 pm	Popular Noe Valley brunch spot.
Eric's Restaurant	1500 Church St	415-282-0919	$$	10 pm	American-Chinese joint serving up fresh dishes, fast.
Fattoush	1361 Church St	415-641-0678	$$$	10 pm	Hearty, authentic Middle eastern grub in low-key setting.
Firefly	4288 24th St	415-821-7652	$$$$	10 pm	Fantastic, warm, and cozy home-style restaurant.
Fresca	3945 24th St	415-695-0549	$$$$	11 pm	Tasty Peruvian.
Hamano Sushi	1332 Castro St	415-826-0825	$$$$	10:30 pm	Neighborhood Japanese.
Happy Donuts	3801 24th St	415-285-5890	$*	24-hrs	Bear claws rule.
Incanto	1550 Church St	415-641-4500	$$$$$	10 pm	Fantastic neighborhood Italian.
Le Zinc	4063 24th St	415-647-9400	$$$$	10 pm	Parisian-style bistro.
Lovejoy's Tea Room	1351 Church St	415-648-5895	$$††	6 pm	Classic British tearoom.
Pasta Pomodoro	4000 24th St	415-920-9904	$$	11 pm	Fast cheap pasta.
Ristorante Bacco	737 Diamond St	415-282-4969	$$$$	10 pm	Cozy neighborhood Italian.
Savor	3913 24th St	415-282-0344	$$††	11 pm	Crepes, omeletes, frittata, and sandwiches. A brunch favorite.

Map 15 • Mission (Outer)

Atlas Café	3049 20th St	415-648-1047	$*	8 pm	Hipster café with soups, sandwiches, and wireless access.
Big Mouth Burger	3392 24th St	415-821-4821	$		Solid burgers cooked to order. Good fries too.
Boogaloo's	3296 22nd St	415-824-4088	$$††	3 pm	Breakfast joint for the hip and hungover.
Café Gratitude	2400 Harrison St	415-830-3014	$††	10 pm	Eclectic vegan menu served by friendly, blissed-out staff.
Dosa	995 Valencia St	415-642-3672	$$	11 pm	South Indian fare. Mostly vegetarian.
Dynamo Donuts	2760 24th St	415-920-1978	$	5 pm	Three words: maple bacon donuts.
El Farolito	2779 Mission St	415-824-7877	$*	4 am	Looks like a dive, but the tacos and burritos taste like a dream.
El Mahajual	1142 Valencia St	415-821-7514	$	9 pm	Family run Salvadorian-Colombian restaurant.
El Metate	2406 Bryant St	415-641-7209	$*	10 pm	Neighborhood gem. Fresh grilled veggie tacos.
El Nuevo Fruitilandia	3077 24th St	415-648-2958	$$††	9:30 pm	Zesty Cuban and Puerto Rican. A portal to the Carribean.
El Tonayense	3150 24th St	415-550-9192	$*	12 am	Tortas beat burritos.

El Valenciano Restaurant and Bar	1153 Valencia St	415-826-9561	$$	2 am	Salsa dancing, Spanish food, and a ginormous tequila selection.
flour + water	2401 Harrison St	415-826-7000	$$$	12 am	Modern and classic interpretations to pasta and pizza in the Italian bistro.
Foreign Cinema	2534 Mission St	415-648-7600	$$$$	11 pm	Cool outdoor (and indoor) dining where you can catch a talkie in the courtyard.
Garcon	1101 Valencia St	415-401-8959	$$$	10:30 pm	Friendly French bistro.
Herbivore	983 Valencia St	415-826-5657	$$††	11 pm	Good, clean, cheap vegetarian.
Jay's Cheesesteak	3285 21st St	415-285-5200	$*	10 pm	Philly-style cheesesteak.
La Taqueria	2889 Mission St	415-285-7117	$$*	9 pm	Good tacos, burritos.
La Taqueria Guadalajara	3146 24th St	415-642-4892	$*		Skip the lines, savor the flavor. Home of atomic habanero salsa.
Lolo	3230 22nd St	415-643-5656	$$	10 pm	Turkish-Mexican.
Los Jarritos	901 S Van Ness Ave	415-648-8383	$$	10 pm	Popular Mexican brunch.
Medjool	2522 Mission St	415-550-9055	$$$$	11 pm	Mediterranean restaurant and club. Sweet rooftop bar.
Mission Pie	2901 Mission St	415-282-1500	$	10 pm	Sustainable responsibly produced pies and social change.
Old Jerusalem Restaurant	2976 Mission St	415-642-5958	$$	10 pm	Tasty falafel served by stylish Israeli guys.
Papalote	3409 24th St	415-970-8815	$	10 pm	Vegetarian-accommodating Mission taqueria.
Pete's Barbeque	2399 Mission St	415-826-1009	$*		Reliable rotisserie chicken and baked potatoes.
Phat Philly	3388 24th St	415-550-7428	$	11 pm	Cheesesteaks with Kobe beef and Amoroso rolls. Regular is 7", Phat is 12".
Revolution Café	3248 22nd St	415-642-0474	$††	1 am	Bohemian-style cafe/bar with sidewalk patio and live music.
Roosevelt's Tamale Parlor	2817 24th St	415-824-2600	$$	11 pm	Recent make over has dulled the spice.
Schmidt's	2400 Folsom St	415-401-0200	$$*	3 pm	A delicious new German place for lunch in the Mission.
Serrano's Pizza	3274 21st St	415-695-1615	$*	1 am	Fresh-made slices, so call ahead.
Sidewalk Juice	3287 21st St	415-341-8070	$*	7 pm	Smooth Travels.
St Francis Fountain	2801 24th St	415-826-4200	$††	10 pm	Good sundaes but no more homemade candy.
Tao Café	1000 Guerrero St	415-641-9955	$$$	10 pm	Vietnamese.
Udupi Palace	1007 Valencia St	415-970-8000	$$*	10:30 pm	Huge dosas; delicious South Indian food at equally tasty prices.
Velvet Cantina	3349 23rd St	415-648-4142	$††	11 pm	Clever desserts.

Map 16 • Potrero Hill (Southwest)

Jay's Deli	501 Connecticut St	415-824-5297	$	7 pm	Popular corner deli on Potrero Hill.

Map 17 • Potrero Hill / Dogpatch

Hard Knox Café	2526 3rd St	415-648-3770	$††	9 pm	Simple, cheap soul food.
Just for You Café	732 22nd St	415-647-3033	$*	3 pm	All the breakfast standards, plus beignets.
Piccino	801 22nd St	415-824-4224	$$	9 pm	Excellent flatbread style pizza, salads, and cafe fare. Great for lunch. Miniscule seating.

Map 18 • Outer Richmond (West) / Ocean Beach

Al-Masri Egyptian Restaurant	4031 Balboa St	415-876-2300	$$$$	10 pm	Authentic Egyptian.
Beach Chalet Brewery	1000 Great Hwy	415-386-8439	$$$	11 pm	Brewpub with a view of Ocean Beach.
Hunan Cafe #2	4450 Cabrillo St	415-751-1283	$	10 pm	Great neighborhood Chinese with delivery
Louis' on Sutro Baths	902 Point Lobos Ave	415-387-6330	$$*	8 pm	Cheaper breakfast and better view than Cliff House next door.
Seal Rock Inn	545 Point Lobos Ave	415-752-8000	$$	6 pm	"Friendly underwater theme" and view make up for so-so food.

Map 19 • Outer Richmond (East) / Seacliff

Bill's Place	2315 Clement St	415-221-5262	$††	11 pm	Big burgers, sit at the bar with locals.
Chino's Taqueria	3416 Balboa St	415-668-9956	$*	10 pm	Good burrito.
Drunken Sushi	2311 Clement St	415-876-2311	$$	2 am	Open late, cute servers, pretty sushi.
El Mansour	3119 Clement St	415-751-2312	$$$	10 pm	Moroccan cuisine mixed with belly dancing in the Outer Richmond.
Mayflower	6255 Geary Blvd	415-387-8338	$$$	10 pm	Hong Kong-style seafood.
Oyaji Restaurant	3123 Clement St	415-379-3604	$$	10pm	Very good sushi.
Pacific Café	7000 Geary Blvd	415-387-7091	$$$	10:30 pm	If there's a wait they'll give you a free glass of wine.
Pagan Restaurant	3199 Clement St	415-751-2598	$	10 pm	Separate Thai and Burmese menus.

Key: $: Under $10 / $$: $10–$20 / $$$: $20–$30 / $$$$: $30–$40 / $$$$$: $40+
** : Does not accept credit cards. / † : Accepts only American Express. / †† : Accepts only Visa and MasterCard*
Time refers to kitchen closing time on Friday night.

Pizzetta 211	211 23rd Ave	415-379-9880	$*	9 pm	Vera pizza napolitana.
Simple Pleasures Café	3434 Balboa St	415-387-4022	$*	11 pm	Have a cup of joe, play a game, argue politics.
The Sweet House	3512 Balboa St	415-876-1388	$*	7 pm	Bubble tea, taro smoothies.
Zephyr Caffe	3643 Balboa St	415-221-6063	$*	11 pm	Huge coffeehouse, low on atmosphere.

Map 20 • Richmond

Aziza	5800 Geary Blvd	415-752-2222	$$$$	10:30 pm	Modern versions of Moroccan classics.
Creations Dessert House	5217 Geary Blvd	415-668-8812	$*	2 am	Mmmm… I want some glutinous rice balls.
Kabuto Sushi	5121 Geary Blvd	415-752-5652	$$$$††	10:30 pm	Fresh, consistent sushi.
Khan Toke Thai House	5937 Geary Blvd	415-668-6654	$$$	10:30 pm	Thai with a garden.
Kitaro	5723 Geary Blvd	415-386-2777	$$††	10:30 pm	Satisfies the sushi craving. Go for the rolls.
La Vie	5830 Geary Blvd	415-668-8080	$$$	10:30 pm	Tasty Vietnamese.
Mescolanza	2221 Clement St	415-668-2221	$$$††	10 pm	Wonderful neighborhood Italian.
Tia Margarita	300 19th Ave	415-752-9274	$$$	11 pm	Traditional Northern Mexican food.
Tommy's Mexican Restaurant	5929 Geary Blvd	415-387-4747	$$$	9 pm	Terrific tequila, fair food.
Ton Kiang	5821 Geary Blvd	415-387-8273	$$$	9:30 pm	Authentic Chinese and good dim sum.
Yet Wah	2140 Clement St	415-387-8040	$$	10 pm	Great authentic Chinese and dim sum.

Map 21 • Inner Richmond

B Star Bar	127 Clement St	415-933-9900	$$$	9:30pm	Burma Superstar offshoot, takes reservations.
Bella Trattoria	3854 Geary Blvd	415-221-0305	$$$	10:30 pm	Friendly neighborhood Italian.
Brother's Korean BBQ	4128 Geary Blvd	415-387-7991	$$$	12 am	Cook-it-at-your-table Korean.
Burma Superstar	309 Clement St	415-387-2147	$$	10 pm	OMG! The hype is totally justified.
Chapeau!	126 Clement St	415-387-0408	$$$	10:30 pm	Excellent neighborhood French.
Cinderella Russian Bakery and Café	436 Balboa St	415-751-9690	$$	8 pm	Yummy desserts and traditional Russian dishes.
Coriya Hot Pot City	852 Clement St	415-387-7888	$$††	11 pm	More cook-it-at-your-table Korean.
Giorgio's Pizza	151 Clement St	415-668-1266	$$††	11 pm	Great pizza.
Katia's Russian Tea Room	600 5th Ave	415-668-9292	$$$	10 pm	Traditional Russian tea room and restaurant.
King of Thai	346 Clement St	415-831-9953	$$*	2:30 am	Standard neighborhood Thai.
King of Thai	639 Clement St	415-752-5198	$$*	1:30 pm	Standard neighborhood Thai that sets the standard.
Le Soleil	133 Clement St	415-668-4848	$$$	10:30 pm	Casual, clean-tasting Vietnamese.
Little Vietnam Café	309 6th Ave	415-876-0283	$*	7 pm	Cheap and tasty sandwiches.
Mandalay	4348 California St	415-386-3895	$$	10 pm	Southeast Asian cuisine.
Q	225 Clement St	415-752-2298	$$$	11 pm	Funky American comfort food.
The Richmond	615 Balboa St	415-379-8988	$$$		Cozy local spot offering attentive service and top-notch food.
Spices I	294 8th Ave	415-752-8884	$$*	11 pm	Stinky tofu, flaming red oil = yum.
Spices II	291 6th Ave	415-752-8885	$††	12 am	Funky little Szechuan café. Good chow, cheap.
Star India	3721 Geary Blvd	415-668-4466	$$	11 pm	Great buffet.
Sushi Bistro	445 Balboa St	415-933-7100	$$	10:30 pm	Mellow vibe, amazing combos, decent service.
Tawan's Thai	4403 Geary Blvd	415-751-5175	$	9 pm	When they say "hot," take them seriously.
Tong Palace	933 Clement St	415-668-3988	$$††	10 pm	Cantonese standby.
Toy Boat Dessert Café	401 Clement St	415-751-7505	$	12 am	25-cent rocking horse and vintage toys keep kiddies busy.
Velo Rouge Café	798 Arguello Blvd	415-752-7799	$	10 pm	Biker-friendly café along the Arguello bike path.
Wing Lee Bakery	503 Clement St	415-668-9481	$*	9 pm	Dim sum.

Map 22 • Presidio Heights / Laurel Heights

Asqew Grill	3415 California St	415-386-5608	$	9 pm	Skewers of grilled meat, tofu or veggies over starch and salad.
Lucky Penny	2670 Geary Blvd	415- 921-0836	$		If you weren't already going to barf at 3 AM...
Mel's Drive-In	3355 Geary Blvd	415-387-2255	$$	3 am	Diner food, great for kids. Anybody see *American Graffiti*?
Pancho's Salsa Bar & Grill	3440 Geary Blvd	415-387-8226	$*	11 pm	Really good non-authentic Mexican food.
Papalote	1777 Fulton St	415-776-0106	$	10 pm	Healthy enough burritos.
Rigolo	3465 California St	415-876-7777	$$††	9 pm	French bakery café with great breakfast menu.
Sociale	3665 Sacramento St	415-921-3200	$$$$	10 pm	Upscale, casual patio dining.
Twilight Cafe	2600 McAllister St	415-386-6115	$	7 pm	The BEST hummus and super-friendly service.

Map 23 • Outer Sunset

El Beach Burrito	3914 Judah St	415-731-2004	$††	9 pm	Burritos.
Golden Gate Pizza and Indian Cuisine	4038 Judah St	415-564-5514	$$††	11:30 pm	Proof that Indian and Italian people should not mate.
Java Beach Café	1396 La Playa St	415-665-5282	$††	11 pm	Beachfront café with strong coffee and large subs. Bring a windbreaker.
Outerlands	4001 Judah St	(415) 661-6140	$$	10 pm	A warm oasis of bread and soup.
Pisces	3414 Judah St	415-564-2233	$$$	10 pm	Cheaper than downtown food, better than SOMA food.
The Pizza Place on Noriega	3901 Noriega St	415-759-5752	$	10 30 pm	Surfside pies: The Spicoli comes with double-cheese and sausage.
Polly Ann Ice Cream	3138 Noriega St	(415) 664-2472	$	10 pm	Asian-themed frozen fare. Try the Durian, if you dare.
Sea Biscuit Café	3815 Noriega St	415-661-3784	$*	10 pm	Surfer café with laid-back vibe–reeeeal laid back.
Sea Breeze Café	3940 Judah St	415-242-6022	$††	9 pm	Almost perfect neighborhood diner.
Thanh Long	4101 Judah St	415-665-1146	$$$$$	10:30 pm	Vietnamese roasted crab and garlic noodles.

Map 24 • Sunset

Café Bakery	1365 Noriega St	415-661-6116	$*	7 pm	Hungry and poor? Get a bbq pork bun.
Marnee Thai	2225 Irving St	415-665-9500	$$$	10 pm	Above-average Thai.
Micado	2126 Irving St	415-564-1122	$$$††	10 pm	Good sushi.
Shangri-La	2026 Irving St	415-731-2548	$$††	8:45 pm	Vegetarian Chinese.
Sunrise Deli & Café	2115 Irving St	415-664-8210	$††	7 pm	Homey Palestinian deli. Really fresh falafel.

Map 25 • Inner Sunset / Golden Gate Heights

Arizmendi Bakery	1331 9th Ave	415-566-3117	$*	7 pm	Fresh bread and gourmet pizza. Cheeseboard's sister co-op.
Art's Cafe	747 Irving St	415-665-7440	$$	3 pm	The hashbrown sandwich will cure any hangover.
Crepevine	624 Irving St	415-681-5858	$††	12 am	Crepes for any time of day.
Ebisu	1283 9th Ave	415-566-1770	$$$$	11 pm	Quality sushi.
Enjoy Vegetarian Restaurant	754 Kirkham St	415-682-0826	$$	9 pm	Unpretentious Chinese for herbivores.
Gordo Taqueria	1239 9th Ave	415-566-6011	$††	10 pm	Rock-solid burritos, fantastic take-out salsa.
Hahn's Hibachi	535 Irving St	415-731-3721	$$††	10 pm	Pile o' Pork and Meat Mountain say it all.
Hotei	1290 9th Ave	415-753-6045	$$	10 pm	Friendly Japanese with great soba and udon noodles.
Irving Street Cafe	716 Irving St	415-664-1366	$*		Cheap breakfasts, good hash browns.
Kiki	1269 9th Ave	415-661-5522	$	10 pm	Cheap sushi that will make you smile.
L'Avenida	511 Irving St	415-681-1246	$††	9:30 pm	Fast, cheap, neighborhood Mexican joint.
Marnee Thai	1243 9th Ave	415-731-9999	$$$	10 pm	This location is roomier and the food's just as good.
Milano Pizzeria	1330 9th Ave	415-665-3773	$*	1 am	Pizza place for pizza placeophiles.
Naan-N-Curry	642 Irving St	415-664-7225	$	12 am	Indian on the cheap.
New Eritrea Restaurant	907 Irving St	415-681-1288		11 pm	Warm and friendly staff.
Pacific Catch	1200 9th Ave	415-504-6905	$$	12 am	Try the Hawaiian Poke and sweet potato fries.
Park Chow	1240 9th Ave	415-665-9912	$$	11 pm	American comfort food with a great atmosphere.
Peasant Pies	1039 Irving St	415-731-1978	$	7:30 pm	Fresh hand-held pies. Savory and sweet. Meal + dessert.
Pluto's	627 Irving St	415-753-8867	$$	10 pm	Made-to-order salads are the key attraction.
San Tung Chinese Restaurant	1031 Irving St	415-242-0828	$$		Sino chicken wings.
Wing Sing Bakery	339 Judah St	415-681-5798	$*	9 pm	Ridiculously cheap dim sum a' plenty.
Yumma's	721 Irving St	415-682-0762	$$*	10 pm	Fast Mediterranean-gyros, shawarma, hummus, etc.

Map 26 • Parkside (Outer)

Bashful Bull Too!	3600 Taraval St	415-759-8112	$††	10 pm	Breakfast basics.
North Beach Pizza	3054 Taraval St	415-242-9100	$$	1 am	Good local chain pizza.
Old Mandarin Islamic	3132 Vicente St	415-564-3481			Muslim Chinese food, specializing in hot pot.

Key: $: Under $10 / $$: $10–$20 / $$$: $20–$30 / $$$$: $30–$40 / $$$$$: $40+
** : Does not accept credit cards. / † : Accepts only American Express. / †† : Accepts only Visa and MasterCard*
Time refers to kitchen closing time on Friday night.

Map 27 • Parkside (Inner)

Eight Immortals	1433 Taraval St	415-731-5515	$$††	9:30 pm	Good neighborhood Chinese restaurant.
El Burrito Express	1601 Taraval St	415-566-8300	$*	9 pm	Small burrito shop.
King of Thai	1541 Taraval St	415-682-9958	$$*	1 am	Standard neighborhood Thai.
Ming's Diner	2129 Taraval St	415-242-0811	$$††	10 pm	Chinese.
Shin Toe Bul Yi	2001 Taraval St	415-566-9221	$††	9:30 pm	Friendly neighborhood Korean place.

Map 29 • Twin Peaks

Lime Tree	450 Irving St	415-665-1415	$	9:30 pm	It's cheap and good, but don't come here in a hurry.
New Ganges Restaurant	775 Frederick St	415-681-4355	$$	10 pm	100% vegetarian Indian using all fresh ingredients.
Pomelo	92 Judah St	415-731-6175	$$$	10 pm	Rice, noodle, and grain dishes with global flair.
Yellow Submarine	503 Irving St	415-681-5652	$*	8:30 pm	Very decent East-Coast-style subs.

Map 30 • West Portal

Ambrosia Bakery	2605 Ocean Ave	415-334-5305	$	6 pm	Princess cake and mousse cake–next question?
Bulls Head Restaurant	840 Ulloa St	415-665-4350	$$	10 pm	The buffalo head over the door should give you a clue.
Bursa	60 W Portal Ave	415-564-4006	$$††	9:30 pm	Turkish food makes you glad for meat.
Café for All Seasons	150 W Portal Ave	415-665-0900	$$	9:30 pm	Popular home-style American food. Burgers, pastas, etc.
El Toreador	50 W Portal Ave	415-566-2673	$$	10 pm	Standard Mexican, very friendly.
Fresca	24 W Portal Ave	415-759-8087	$$$$	10 pm	Tasty Peruvian.
Manor Coffee Shop	321 W Portal Ave	415-661-2468	$$*	8 pm	Diner food, good for breakfast.
Mozzarella di Bufala	69 W Portal Ave	415-661-8900	$$	12 am	Pizza and Brazilian food, together at last.
Raintree Café	118 W Portal Ave	415-242-9000	$$††	9 pm	Standard café menu. No frills, no crowds.
Submarine Center	820 Ulloa St	415-564-1455	$*	7 pm	Best sandwiches in town.

Map 32 • Diamond Heights / Glen Park

Alice's	1599 Sanchez St	415-282-8999	$$	10 pm	Chinese. Similar to Eric's.
Chenery Park	683 Chenery St	415-337-8537	$$$$	10 pm	Chic American food.
Eggettes	2810 Diamond St	415-839-5282	$	12:30 am	Relive your magical Hong Kong childhood.
Joe's Cable Car	4320 Mission St	415-334-6699	$$$	11pm	"Joe grinds his own fresh chuck daily".
La Ciccia	291 30th St	415-550-8114	$$††	10 pm	Sardinian take on Italian fare.
La Corneta Taqueria	2834 Diamond St	415-469-8757	$$*	10 pm	Great tacos and burritos.
Le P'tit Laurent	699 Chenery St	415-334-3235	$$$	10 pm	Classic French bistro.
Pomelo	1793 Church St	415-285-2257	$$$	10 pm	Rice, noodle, and grain dishes with global flair.
Regent Thai	1700 Church St	415-643-5893	$$††	10 pm	Above average Thai at ridiculously cheap prices.
Tyger's	2798 Diamond St	415-239-4060	$*	3:30 am	Busy breakfast joint on the weekends.

Map 33 • Ingleside

Ocean Taqueria	1941 Ocean Ave	415-586-7013	$*	10 pm	Décor is plain, but the burritos are plump and lovely.
Yama Sushi	850 Holloway Ave	415-333-2889	$$	10 pm	This corner's been cursed before, but we've got a winner.

Map 34 • Oceanview

Beep's Burgers	1051 Ocean Ave	415-584-2650	$$	10 pm	Throwback drive-in with meaty burgers and thick-cut fries.
Java Creperie	1125 Ocean Ave	415-333-3771	$	10 pm	Great coffee and sandwiches near City College.
Reinas Restaurant	5479 Mission St	415-585-7694	$	5:45 pm	Great pupusas, crappy service.

Map 35 • Bernal Heights

Angkor Borei	3741 Mission St	415-550-8417	$$	10:30 pm	Neighborhood Cambodian.
Baby Blues BBQ	3149 Mission St	415-896-4250	$$		Order the Mason-Dixon, chicken and Memphis ribs.
Blue Plate	3218 Mission St	415-282-6777	$$$$	10:30 pm	Great, cozy, American food.
El Patio	3193 Mission St	415-641-5056	$	12 am	Salvadoran pupusas.

El Zocalo	3230 Mission St	415-282-2572	$	3.45 am	Edible flowers, plantains times infinity.
Emmy's Spaghetti Shack	18 Virginia Ave	415-206-2086	$$$*	12 am	The specialty is spaghetti and meatballs, just like it sounds.
The Front Porch	65 29th St	415-695-7800	$$$††	10:30 pm	Gastropub simple fare with Caribbean influence.
Goood Frikin' Chicken	10 29th St	415-970-2428	$††	12 am	Yummy chicken and mac 'n' cheese.
Jasmine Tea House	3253 Mission St	415-826-6288	$$	10 pm	Nothing fancy, but you'll crave it later.
Liberty Café	410 Cortland Ave	415-695-8777	$$$	9:30 pm	Wonderful neighborhood restaurant serving home-style food.
Little Nepal	925 Cortland Ave	415-643-3881	$$$	10 pm	Go crazy with Tandoori at this Nepali café.
Mitchell's Ice Cream	688 San Jose Ave	415-648-2300	$*	11 pm	City favorite. Scooping exotic flavors since the '50s.
Moki's Sushi & Pacific Grill	615 Cortland Ave	415-970-9336	$$$	10:30 pm	Creative sushi with a Hawaiian twist.
Nervous Dog Coffee	3438 Mission St	415-282-4364	$	11 pm	Coffee, art, and free wireless.
Taqueria Cancun	3211 Mission St	415-550-1414	$*	2:45 am	The food here's good.
Zante's Indian Cuisine & Pizza	3489 Mission St	415-821-3949	$$	11 pm	Naan bread pizzas with Indian toppings.

Map 36 • Bayview / Silver Terrace

La Laguna	3906 3rd St	415-401-9420	$*	3 pm	Cavernous taqueria with extensive menu.
Old Clam House	299 Bayshore Blvd	415-826-4880	$$$	10pm	Old School Seafood. Est. 1861
Soo Fong	3801 3rd St	415-285-2828	$	8 pm	Decent Chinese in Bayview Plaza shopping center.

Map 37 • India Basin / Hunters Point

Evans Street Post Office Cafeteria	1300 Evans Ave	415-641-0177	$††	24-hrs	How often do you get to eat in a post office.
Wok-In Cafeteria	50 Mendell St	415-550-7200	$††	9 pm	Cheap, all-you-can-eat Chinese buffet open for lunch only.

Map 38 • Excelsior / Crocker Amazon

North Beach Pizza	4787 Mission St	415-586-1400	$$	12 am	Good local chain pizza.

Map 39 • Visitacion Valley

Cafe and Restaurant Montecristo	2101 Geneva Ave	415-334-2326	$$*	9pm	Authentic El Salvadorian. Near Cow Palace.

Map 40 • Bayview / Candlestick Point

B&J 1/4 lb Burgers	6202 3rd St	415-467-4560	$*	3 pm	Former drive-in with handmade no-swearing signs.
El Azteca Taqueria	5298 3rd St	415-822-1460	$*	8 pm	Heaviest burritos in town. Try the steak and ham.

The Presidio

Crissy Field Warming Hut	983 Marine Dr	415-561-3040	$	5 pm	Classic Crissy Field retreat serving coffee and snacks.

Sausalito

Avatars	2656 Bridgeway	415-332-8083	$$††	9 pm	Interesting Indian-Mexican fusion cuisine, such as curry enchiladas and tostadas.
Feng-Nian Chinese Restaurant	2650 Bridgeway	415-331-5300	$$$	10 pm	Excellent Chinese that's lighter than most, and many fresh seafood options.
Fish.	350 Harbor Dr	415-331-3474	$$$*	8 pm	Freshest seafood expertly prepared, and a great location on the waterfront to watch the boats come and go.
Fred's Coffee Shop	1917 Bridgeway	415-332-4575	$$††	3 pm	Deep-fried french toast—need we say more?!?
Paradise Bay	1200 Bridgeway	415-331-3226	$$$$	10:30 pm	Grab a drink and enjoy the view; the New American fare leaves something to be desired.
Poggio Ristorante	777 Bridgeway	415-332-7771	$$$$	11 pm	Top-rated Italian, worth the splurge.
Saylor's Landing	305 Harbor Dr	415-332-6161	$$$	10 pm	Popular with the local marina crowd, boasting an outdoor patio and fresh seafood.
Sushi Ran	107 Caledonia St	415-332-3620	$$$$	11 pm	Crowded, but worth the wait for some of the best sushi in the Bay Area.

Key: $: Under $10 / $$: $10–$20 / $$$: $20–$30 / $$$$: $30–$40 / $$$$$: $40+
** : Does not accept credit cards. / † : Accepts only American Express. / †† : Accepts only Visa and MasterCard*
Time refers to kitchen closing time on Friday night.

Mill Valley

Avatars Punjab Burritos	15 Madrona St	415-381-8293	$*	8 pm	How can you not be curious?
Buckeye Roadhouse	15 Shoreline Hwy	415-331-2600	$$$	11 pm	Martinis, Brutus salad (Caesar with chili), and serious meat dishes.
Bungalow 44	44 E Blithedale Ave	415-381-2500	$$$$††	11 pm	Latest offering in a well-known spot, causing a stir.
ino	25 Miller Ave	415-383-7180	$$$††	9:30 pm	A favorite sushi bar.
Joe's Taco Lounge	382 Miller Ave	415-383-8164	$$	10 pm	Great, reliable Mexican.
La Ginestra	127 Throckmorton Ave	415-388-0224	$$$	10 pm	What they call "homestyle" Italian cucina in America.
Mama's Royal Café	393 Miller Ave	415-388-3261	$††	3 pm	For the breakfast craving.
Pearl's Phatburgers	8 E Blithedale Ave	415-381-6010	$	9 pm	Chi-chi burgers. This is Mill Valley after all.
Piazza D'Angelo	22 Miller Ave	415-388-2000	$$$	11 pm	Busy, upscale Italian that's been around for some years.

Berkeley (West)

900 Grayson	900 Grayson St	510-704-9900	$$	3 pm	Foodie food.
Bacheeso's Garden	2501 San Pablo Ave	510-644-2035	$$	9:30 pm	Unbelievable fusion brunch buffet for cheap. Get there early.
Bette's Oceanview Diner	1807 4th St	510-644-3230	$$††	2:30 pm	Never ordinary. Always delicious.
Cactus Taqueria	1881 Solano Ave	510-528-1881	$	9 pm	Mexican with the choice of whole wheat tortillas.
Cafe M	1799 4th St	510-526-4429	$$	4 pm	Scrumptious brunch sans line.
Café Rouge	1782 4th St	510-525-1440	$$$	10 pm	Fancy schmancy meat market.
Everett and Jones in Berkeley	1955 San Pablo Ave	510-548-8261	$$	10 pm	Awesome downhome East Bay BBQ, hot, medium or mild?
Fellini	1401 University Ave	510-841-5200	$	10 pm	No lines, great brunch, vegan menu, pizza at night.
Gioia Pizzeria	1586 Hopkins St	510-528-4692			New York thin with Cali toppings.
Gregoire	2109 Cedar St	510-883-1893	$$	9 pm	Crispy Potato Puffs. Get 'em while they're deep-fried.
Juan's Place	941 Carleton St	510-845-6904	$$	10 pm	Super-friendly feels like family. Sit-down or take out. Mexican food.
The Kabana	1106 University Ave	510-845-3355	$$††	9:30 pm	Enjoy great Pakistani food while watching the latest Bollywood hits.
King Tsin	1699 Solano Ave	510-525-9890	$$	3:30 pm	Berkeley dim sum. Jazz on Thursday nights.
Picante Berkeley	1328 6th St	510-525-3121	$	10 pm	Straight-up Mexican food. High quality.
Spenger's Fresh Fish Grotto	1919 4th St	510-845-7771	$$$	11 pm	Plenty of fresh fish for the connoisseurs. $1.95 happy hour menus, too.
Tacubaya	1788 4th St	510-525-5160	$	9 pm	Taqueria. From the people who brought you Dona Tomas.
T-Rex Barbecue	1300 10th St	510-527-0099	$$	12:30 am	Warehouse-turned-restaurant serves 'em likes they advertises 'em.
Vanessa's Bistro	1715 Solano Ave	510-525-8300	$$	9:30 pm	Fancy French-Vietnamese tapas sans exorbitant price.
Viks Chaat Corner	726 Allston Wy	510-644-4432	$††	6 pm	Street-stand-style authentic Indian. Spice shop next door.
Zachary's Pizza	1853 Solano Ave	510-525-5950	$$*	10:30 pm	Hands down, best deep-dish pizza anywhere around the bay!
Zaki Kabob	1101 San Pablo Ave	510-527-5452	$$	-	Scrumptious rotisserie chicken and Palestinian specials.

Berkeley (East)

Blondie's Pizza	2340 Telegraph Ave	510-548-1129	$	2 am	All the fatty cheese you can handle on the go.
Brazil Café	1983 Shattuck Ave	510-845-1056	$*	9 pm	Food stand-turned-restaurant makes good.
Cancun Taqueria	2134 Allston Wy	510-549-0964	$††	10:30 pm	Fantabulous salsa bar. Good Mexican food.
César	1515 Shattuck Ave	510-883-0222	$$$	11 pm	Hip yet casual restaurant/bar.
Cha Am Thai	1543 Shattuck Ave	510-848-9664	$$	10 pm	Adequate Thai. Back room for big dinner parties.
The Cheese Board	1512 Shattuck Ave	510-549-3055	$$††	8 pm	A multitude of cheeses, bread, and pizza delights. Gets happily packed.
Chez Panisse	1517 Shattuck Ave	510-548-5525	$$$$$	11:30 pm	Mondays are prix-fixe. Famous and delicious, for a price.

Crepes A Go-Go	2125 University Ave	510-841-7722	$	10 pm	Endless sweet or savory crepe variety for those on the go. Yum.
Fat Apples	1346 Martin Luther King Jr Wy	510-526-2260	$$	9 pm	Cute neighborhood breakfast place.
House of Curries	2984 College Ave	510-841-1688	$	10:30 pm	Affordable, solid Indian and Pakistani cuisine-great naan and tandoori.
Jayakarta	2026 University Ave	510-841-0884	$*	10 pm	Exotic flavors and spices you never knew existed.
Joshu-ya Sushi	2441 Dwight Way	510-848-5260	$$	10 pm	Big rolls. Funny names (Zoolander, et al.).
Kirala	2100 Ward St	510-549-3486	$$$	9:30 pm	Sushi and bar. Wasabi goodness.
La Burrita	1832 Euclid Ave	510-845-9090	$	9:30 pm	Cheap and quick, the super veggie burrito is awesome.
La Cascada	2164 Center St	510-704-8688	$	9 pm	Cali-Mexican taqueria. A little pricey, but what isn't!
La Note	2377 Shattuck Ave	510-843-1535	$$$††	n/a	Culinary portal to Provence.
Long Life Vegi House	2129 University Ave	510-845-6072	$$	10 pm	Vegetarian Chinese, yummy fake meats galore.
Manpuku	2977 College Ave	510-848-2536	$$	10 pm	Poor but dying for sushi? Eat here.
Mitama	3201 College Ave	510-652-6157	$$	10 pm	New kid sushi on the block- Morimoto of Iron Chef endorsed.
Revival Bar + Kitchen	2102 Shattuck Ave	510-549-9952	$$$	-	Thoughtful food and cocktails.
Saul's Deli and Restaurant	1475 Shattuck Ave	510-848-3354	$$††	9:30 pm	Classic NY-style deli with a catch…it's all organic, fair trade, etc.
Shen Hua	2914 College Ave	510-883-1777	$$	10 pm	Authentic and fabulous regional Chinese cuisine with a full bar.
The Smokehouse	3155 Telegraph Ave	510-845-3640	*$$	9 pm	Perfect late night munchies option.
Sushi Ko	64 Shattuck Sq	510-845-6601	$$	9 pm	Many veggie sushi options
Top Dog	2534 Durant Ave	510-843-5967	$*	3 am	Libertarian wieners.
Udipi Palace	1901 University Ave	510-843-6600	$*	10 pm	Great vegetarian Indian food.
Yogurt Park	2433 Durant Ave	510-549-2198	$*	12 am	You can even call in advance for flavors of the day!

Oakland

Camino	3917 Grand Ave	510-547-5035	$$$	10 pm	New restaurant from Chez Panisse alums.
El Farolito	3646 International Blvd	510-533-9194	$††	12 am	East Oakland branch of the Mission Street spot.
El Taco Zamorano	4345 International Blvd	510-261-9125	$††	11 pm	Great taqueria.
Jalisco	1721 International Blvd	510-436-8696	$*	6 pm	Best carnitas ever!
Los Cocos	1449 Fruitvale Ave	510-536-3079	$*	8:30 pm	El Salvadorean fare, pupusas rule.
Powderface Café	3411 E 12th St	510-536-3223	$††	7 pm	Specializes in New Orleans-style beignets.
Quinn's Lighthouse	1951 Embarcadero	510-536-2050	$$	10 pm	Go to hear pirate songs, eat peanuts, and have food/beer.

Downtown Oakland / Lake Merritt

Arizmendi	3265 Lakeshore Ave	510-268-8849	$*	7 pm	Populist bakery co-operative, try the cherry-corn scones.
Battambang	850 Broadway St	510-839-8815	$	10 pm	Authentic Cambodian cuisine.
BC Deli Sandwiches	818 Franklin St	510-286-9978	$	-	Dirt-cheap Vietnamese in Oakland Chinatown.
Flora	1900 Telegraph Ave	510-286-0100	$$$	11 pm	Hipper than Berkeley for gourmet, organic cuisine while Downtown.
Golden Lotus	1301 Franklin St	510-893-0383	$	10 pm	Affordable vegan staple of DTO.
Holy Land Kosher	677 Rand Ave	510-272-0535	$*		Israeli food. Low key. Excellent hummus.
House of Chicken 'n Waffles	444 Embarcadero W	866-421-1482	$	4 am	Diner-style soul food.
Le Cheval	1007 Clay St	510-763-8495	$$	9:30 pm	Great French-Vietnamese food.
Luke's Taproom & Lounge	2221 Broadway	510-451-4677	$$	12 am	Fusion restaurant/nightclub, hugely popular in both incarnations.
Lynn and Lu's	3353 Grand Ave	510-835-5705	$$††	4 pm	A relaxed breakfast/brunch favorite with cozy outdoor seating.
Pho Ga Huong Que Café	1228 7th Ave	510-835-8488	$	6 pm	-
Smart Alec's Intelligent Food	2355 Telegraph Ave	510-704-4000	$	10 pm	Healthy, fresh fast food. Air-baked garlic fries.
Tamarindo Antojera	468 8th St	510-444-1944	$$	10 pm	Contemporary Mexican small plates, outstanding cocktails and sangria.
Yoshi's	510 Embarcadero W	510-238-9200	$$$	10 pm	World class jazz and sushi.

Key: $: Under $10 / $$: $10–$20 / $$$: $20–$30 / $$$$: $30–$40 / $$$$$: $40+
** : Does not accept credit cards. / † : Accepts only American Express. / †† : Accepts only Visa and MasterCard*
Time refers to kitchen closing time on Friday night.

North Oakland / Emeryville

Art's Crab Shak	4031 Broadway	510-654-2864	$$$	11 pm	Crabtastic institution since '63.
Asmara	5020 Telegraph Ave	510-547-5100	$$	11 pm	Fine Ethiopian cuisine.
A Cote	5478 College Ave	510-655-6469	$$$	12 am	French inspired small plates, extensive wine list- known for outstanding service.
Bakesale Betty's	5098 Telegraph Ave	510-985-1213	$	7 pm	Rave reviews. Sandwiches and baked goods. Holy shit good!
Barney's Gourmet Burgers	5819 College Ave	510-601-0444	$$	10 pm	Burgers galore, accounts for your vegan friends with tofu burgers.
Ben & Nick's	5612 College Ave	510-923-0327	$	2 am	Classic pub grub with contemporary Cali twists- great specials daily.
Bucci's	6121 Hollis St	510-547-4725	$$$	9:30 pm	Spacious patio is an urban sanctuary in nice weather.
Burma Superstar	4721 Telegraph Ave	510-652-2900	$$		You can never go wrong with this superstar.
Café Colucci	6427 Telegraph Ave	510-601-7999	$$††	10 pm	Ethiopian cuisine, no forks.
César	4039 Piedmont Ave	510-985-1200	$$$	11:30 pm	Tapas.
Crepevine	5600 College Ave	510-658-2026	$$	11 pm	Open sun up to midnight, cafeteria style.
Dona Tomas	5004 Telegraph Ave	510-450-0522	$$$	10 pm	Hyper-Authentic contemporary Mexican food, insane margaritas, always packed.
Dopo	4293 Piedmont Ave	510-652-3676	$$	11 pm	Contemporary Italian with an emphasis on rustic pizzas—quite popular.
Fentons Creamery	4226 Piedmont Ave	510-658-7000	$$	12 am	Old-fashioned handmade ice cream.
Genova Delicatessen and Ravioli	5095 Telegraph Ave	510-652-7401	$††	7 pm	Panino is Italian for sandwich.
J's Mexican American Food	4063 Piedmont Ave	510-655-7429	$	11 pm	A greasier, cheaper place to go for Mexican/American brunch.
La Calaca Loca	5199 Telegraph Ave	510-601-8226	$††	9 pm	The crazy female skeleton taqueria.
Lanesplitter's	4799 Telegraph Ave	510-653-5350	$$	1:30 am	Burning man, bikes, beer, and pizza.
Little Shin Shin	4258 Piedmont Ave	510-658-9799	$*	10 pm	Greasy, awesome, cash only. Crab in black bean sauce.
Lois the Pie Queen	851 60th St	510-658-5616	$$*	3 pm	Soul + pie = !!!
Los Cantaros	5412 San Pablo Ave	510-601-1653	$††	6 pm	Rad taqueria con flavor.
Mama's Royal Café	4012 Broadway St	510-547-7600	$*	4 pm	Popular breakfast joint.
Nan Yang	6048 College Ave	510-655-3298	$$††	10 pm	Eclectic Burmese.
Noodle Theory	6099 Claremont Ave	510-595-6988	$$	9:30 pm	Asian fusion involving noodles.
Oliveto Café and Restaurant	5655 College Ave	510-547-5356	$$$	10 pm	Home-made pastas, wood-fired pizzas and tapas.
Pizzaiolo	5008 Telegraph Ave	510-652-4888	$$	10 pm	Trendy gourmet pizza. Worth the long wait.
Sabuy Sabuy	5231 College Ave	510-653-8587	$$	9:30 pm	Solid, authentic and affordable neighborhood Thai food.
Shangri-La Vegan Restaurant	4001 Linden St	510-985-8386	$$††	9 pm	Yuppie-hippie macrobiotic fare.
Soi 4	5421 College Ave	510-655-0889	$$	10 pm	Cheeky northern Thai fusion, high modern concepts—occasionally brilliant.
Somerset	5912 College Ave	510-428-1823	$$$	10 pm	Popular for brunch and eclectic mimosas, gorgeous patio dining.
Sura	4869 Telegraph Ave	510-654-9292	$$	10 pm	Whole lotta Korean. Loads on the kimchee small plates.
Tropix	3814 Piedmont Ave	510-653-2444	$$	10 pm	Modernity in the Caribbean.
Wood Tavern	6317 College Ave	510-654-6607	$$$	10:30 pm	Very, very good.
Xyclo	4218 Piedmont Ave	510-654-2681	$$	10 pm	Asian Fusion with fancy martinis. Not your neighborhood pho joint.
Zachary's Pizza	5801 College Ave	510-655-6385	$*	10:30 pm	Chicago deep-dish pizza done California-style. Ack.

San Francisco is a city where you can find anything and everything—literally. Sure, the boutiques, thrift and specialist clothing stores are outstanding, but even you folk with a passion for taxidermy, pirate supplies, gigantic bongs and doggie shoes are catered for too. So here, for your delectation, are the best places to find the basics and not-so basics, plus some ideas of what neighborhoods to walk in if you're just looking to stroll, window shop, and find a bargain.

Clothing

Fashionistas could be lost for days inside of the trendy boutiques in town. Small boutiques, such as **Ooma (Map 4)** and **Ambiance (Map 2)**, glitter at the Fillmore and Marina. And the Mission is full of independent designs—check out **Studio 3579 (Map 15)**, **The Mission Statement (Map 15)** and **Weston Wear (Map 15)** for high end, and **Clobba (Map 9)** and **Dema (Map 15)** for smaller budgets. For more mainstream tastes, head to Union Square. Just be prepared for the hordes of tourists.

For vintage clothing head to the Haight and check out **La Rosa Vintage (Map 9)**, **Buffalo Exchange (Map 9)**, **Villain's (Map 9)**, and **Wasteland (Map 9)**. In the Mission, stop by **Idol Vintage (Map 11)**, **Shauplatz (Map 11)**, **Thrift Town (Map 11)**, and **Clothes Contact (Map 11)**, where you can buy clothes by the pound. For thrift store junkies with a conscience, check out any of the three locations of **Out of the Closet (Maps 7, 9, 12)**, where threads are sold to benefit AIDS research. For more eclectic desires try **Foot Worship (Map 7)** and **Camper (Map 8)** for your feet, and **Dark Garden (Map 11)** to squeeze your waist with a custom corset, followed by **Stormy Leather (Map 12)**—an institution specializing in the city's own special brand of kinky. **Zoe Bikini (Map 11)** in the Mission is turning heads with custom bikini designs. Accessorize with the hip custom messenger bags at **Timbuk2 (Map 11)**. If you want to get noticed, try wearing the fancy homemade jewelry at **Therapy (Map 15)**, **Claudia Kussano (Map 15)** and **Artist Xchange (Map 11)** where you can also pick up some reasonably priced art and Bay Area-pride t-shirts.

Sports

Skates on Haight (Map 9) sells and rents rollerblades, scooters, and skateboards. **FTC (Map 9)** on Haight has a great selection of skateboard gear and clothing. If you're into snowboarding and surfing when you're not on your skateboard, then check out **Purple Skunk (Map 20)** on Geary or **SFO Snowboard Shop (Map 9)** on Shrader. Bicyclists should check out **Freewheel (Map 9)** where you can fix up your bike, **Valencia Cyclery (Map 15)**, **Box Dog Bicycles (Map 15)** or the **Missing Link Bike Co-op (Berkeley East)**. Rustic camper types should try finding outdoor gear at the **North Face Outlet (Berkeley West)**, **REI (Map 12)**, and **Patagonia (Map 3)**. **Lombardi's (Map 7)** in Russian Hill provides a broad range of affordable sports clothing, shoes, and goods.

Houseware

If you're looking for modern, traditional and unusual furniture, try **Artesanias Unique Home Furnishings (Map 2)**, **Monument (Map 15)** and **Harrington's Antiques (Map 15)** Try hitting up some of the shops around 9th Street and Folsom and be sure to stop by **Limn (Map 13)** and **Propeller (Map 11)** for modern designs. If you are looking for a nice mattress, price the one you want at one of the chain stores, then head down to **Bedroom Outlet (Map 22)**, where the family-run store will beat any other price and give you a sweet deal and excellent service. **Cliff's Variety Store (Map 10)** is good for design savvy, space saving, household basics. For cheap kitchen outfitters, try **City Discount (Map 7)** on Polk, where you can find everything you need to equip your kitchen without breaking the bank. If you're on a low-budget and you want something new, try many of the 'junk' stores on Clement Street in the Inner Richmond or Mission Street in the Mission where you can find anything you might ever need for your home, including sushi dishes, tortilla makers, and those lucky cats that wave at you for good luck. If you aren't that picky and you are looking for a deal, check out the plethora of thrift stores for cheap anything-you-need-in-your-household-items. Lastly, for those with money to burn and the taste to match, head for the East Bay to Berkeley's posh 4th Street shopping district, which features numerous high-end home furnishing and kitchen supply stores.

Food

San Francisco is gourmet, but in simplicity and extravagance. This goes beyond restaurants and into the ubiquitous specialty food shop. For healthy eating, **Bi-Rite (Map 11)**, **Harvest Market (Map 10)**, **Valencia Whole Foods (Map 15)** and **Real Food (Maps 2 & 7)** are good neighborhood choices, as are the larger spots such as **Trader Joe's (Maps 12 & 22)** and vegan favorite, **Rainbow Grocery (Map 11)**, with fresh produce, bulk foods, and local products. **Berkeley Bowl (Berkeley East)** is one of the original large-scale health food and organic produce grocery outlets. For those not so concerned with calories, try gourmet ice-cream at **Bi-Rite Creamery (Map 15)**, or the unique flavors of **Bombay Creamery (Map 11)** If you still have a sweet tooth when you're finished, try the chocolates and sweets at **Joseph Schmidt Confections (Map 10)** or **Tartine (Map 15)**. **Boulangerie Bay Bread (Map 5)**, **Acme Bread (Map 8)**, **Thorough Bread And Pastry (Map 14)**, and **Noe Valley Bakery (Map 14)** all have great loaves. Top them with slices and spreads from the **24th Street Cheese Company (Map 14)** or the **Cowgirl Creamery Artisan Cheese (Map 8)** in the Ferry Building. Also head to the Ferry Building on weekends for the Bay Area's more notable farmers market and **Stonehouse California Olive Oil (Map 8)** where tastings are free. At the **Bargain Bank (Map 21)** you can find slightly expired food products, including Hershey's candy and international products at rock bottom prices. It's worth a stop if you are on Clement Street.

Art & Photography Supplies

Running low on Cadmium Red? Use your last stick of charcoal drawing a nude? The best art stores are scattered all over the city, but **Flax (Map 11)** is the most well-known. Located on Market Street, it is the size of a small city and sells every type of art and framing supply you can imagine. **Blick Art Materials (Map 7)** is nearby and sells a variety of materials with a good paint and brush selection—they also feature an East Bay location. You can find the best selection of paper at **Paper Source (Map 5)** on Fillmore or go to **Kozo (Map 2)** on Union for fine, handmade Japanese papers. If you're looking for photography supplies, try **Adolph Gasser (Map 8)** on Second Street, **North Bay Photographer's Supply (Map 8)**, **Discount Camera (Map 8)**, or **The Looking Glass (Berkeley East)**. **Pro Camera (Map 17)** on Minnesota Street is great for rental equipment. **Arch (Map 13)** in Potrero Hill is great for graphic design supplies, portfolios, and gifts. For wearable art, try **Imaginit (Map 10)** or **Article Pract (North Oakland/Emeryville)** for yarn.

Music

From Billie Holliday through the Grateful Dead and all the way to Green Day, the San Francisco music scene has been legendary. Accordingly, there are music shops with rare finds, nostalgia producing hits, and up and coming underground artists.

Hit up **Amoeba Music (Map 9)** on Haight for everything from new and used CDs to 78s—it's down the street from the former pads of several sixties bands and is a must for a dazed afternoon in the Haight. It's also the size of a bowling alley. Speaking of large record stores, **Rasputin (Map 8 and Berkeley East)** on Telegraph Avenue offers three stories and two storefronts of new and used tunes. **Streetlight Records (Map 10)** is another good resource for new and used music. For rare vinyl, stop by **Open Mind Music (Map 10)** and **Jack's Record Cellar (Map 10)** in the Lower Haight. The smaller stores carry more eclectic selections and, more often than not, the staff can help you out with musical queries. Try indie shop **Aquarius (Map 15)** for a good selection and **Thrill House Records (Map 15)** for all your punk rock needs.

Books

San Francisco is one of the great literary cities. **City Lights (Map 8)** is the beatnik throwback essential bookstore and they'll let you have your mail sent there if you're drifting. Specialty books can be found at **Kinokuniya (Map 6)** (Japanese), **A Different Light (Map 10)** (LGBT), **Get Lost (Map 11)** (Travel) and **Needles And Pens (Map 15)** (Art and graphic novels). The **SF Mystery Bookstore (Map 14)** is a must for the noir inclined. Continue on in the Mission to **Borderlands (Map 11)**, where you can indulge in Fantasy and Sci-Fi. **Modern Times (Map 15)** holds readings and has a large local section. Down the street is **826 Valencia (Map 11)**, a spot for writing workshops that includes a pirate-themed gift store and a full collection of McSweeneys-related material. In Berkeley try the famous **Cody's Books (Berkeley West)** whose main location on Telegraph closed after 40 years, or the academically inclined **Moe's (Berkeley East)** for four stories of new and used books. **Oakland's Diesel (North Oakland/Emeryville)** not only has a great selection and a good atmosphere, but also hosts book and Spanish language groups. While used books stores abound, you can often find the best (if not most refreshed) selection and price at **Community Thrift Store (Map 11)**.

Pets

Where pets are more populous than kids, you can also find more pet stores than kid's stores. Most of them cater to the pampered pooch as well as having standard fare of collars, food, and the like. **The Bernal Beast (Map 35)** is less pretentious than many such shops and has a good selection at decent prices. **Best in Show (Map 10)** has a cherry-picked toy selection to keep your pup occupied and the ritzy-est of clothing to keep your little ms. or mr. in fashion, even in the Castro. Aside from designer pooch sweaters, **George Shop (Map 5, Berkeley West)** even has a selection of fancy baked-good items like birthday cake, donuts, etc. for your pup's special day or just for a treat.

Gifts

With neighborhoods full of boutique-y shops, you might think that any store can qualify as a gift store. Here are a few where you'll be able to find something unique. **Artist XChange (Map 11)** hosts an excellent variety of well-made arts and crafts, and **Bell Jar (Map 15)** and **The Curiosity Shoppe (Map 15)** have a grand selection of gorgeous and unusual nick-nacks, as does **Paxton Gate (Map 15)**, although it is dominated by long-expired, stuffed creatures, For letterpress cards, vintage stationery, calendars, hip notebooks, pens, and laptop holders, try **Piedmont Stationers & Office Supply (North Oakland/Emeryville)**, an old-fashioned, independent stationery store, where the staff will help you find exactly what you are looking for. **Good Vibrations (Map 11, 7)** is the best place to buy your significant other a sex toy, or shop for one together as a gift for your 3-month anniversary. Don't be shy. If you're looking for a classy or fun gift and want to support a good cause, try **Under One Roof (Map 10)**. Every donation or purchase goes to support 35 local AIDS service organizations. If you need to go to therapy, but don't want to deal, at least you can find some retail therapy at the store with the same name (**Therapy (Map 11)**), that also has a host of gifts like cat-butt magnets and retro-vintage signs. On weekends Telegraph Avenue near the UC Campus **(Berkeley East)**—already well-endowed with shops of all sorts—is packed with street vendors selling all manner of eclectic crafts, t-shirts, and jewelry. Or, of course, you can go to your neighborhood box store and just ask for a gift certificate.

Neighborhood Shopping

Most neighborhoods have some shopping, but here are some ideas for half-day trips in the following neighborhoods where you can satisfy your need for additional therapy. **Clement Street (Map 21)** in the Inner Richmond is great for the host of junk stores, where you can find cheap gloves, bags, and soap as well as restaurant supplies and sushi platters, plus **Green Apple Bookstore (Map 21)** makes it all worthwhile. **Mission Street (Map 15)** is much the same with pseudo-hardware stores, thrift stores, and household goods, cheap but often not of the best quality. **Valencia Street (Map 15)** has recently been transformed into a mecca for hip young designers, curiosity shops and boutiques. **Fillmore Street** in Pacific Heights **(Map 5)**, **Hayes Street** in Hayes Valley **(Map 11)**, and **4th Street** in West Berkeley **(Berkeley West)** offer the higher-end of neighborhood shopping and great window shopping. Try **Cortland Ave** in Bernal Heights **(Map 35)**, **24th Street** in Noe Valley **(Map 14)**, and **Piedmont Avenue (North Oakland/Emeryville)** for shopping in neighborhoods with a nice mix of book, stationery, gift, pet stores, and cafés. The same can be said for the **Rockridge District** of Oakland/Berkeley along College Avenue in either direction from the Rockridge BART Station **(North Oakland/Emeryville)**.

Map 1 • Marina / Cow Hollow (West)

Benefit	2219 Chestnut St	415-567-1173	Cosmetics galore.
Books Inc	2251 Chestnut St	415-931-3633	Books and magazines.
Chadwick's of London	2068 Chestnut St	415-775-3423	Lingerie.
City Optix	2154 Chestnut St	415-921-1188	Cool eyewear.
Fiori	2314 Chestnut St	415-346-1100	Beautiful flowers.
Fleet Feet	2076 Chestnut St	415-921-7188	Running shoes and clothes.
Lucca Delicatessen	2120 Chestnut St	415-921-7873	Good Italian deli and staples.
Lucky Brand	2301 Chestnut St	415-749-3750	Jeans and casual wear.
Miette	2109 Chestnut St	415-359-0628	Indulgent baked treats.
Pure Beauty	2085 Chestnut St	415-922-2526	The 411 on beauty products.
Rabat	2080 Chestnut St	415-929-8868	Women's urban wear, shoes, and accessories.
Red Dot Chestnut	2176 Chestnut St	415-346-0606	Affordable clothes, sportswear, and accessories.
Smash	2030 Chestnut St	415-673-4736	Hip shoes.

Map 2 • Marina / Cow Hollow (East)

Ambiance	1864 Union St	415-923-9797	All the hip local girls shop here.
Artesanias Unique Home Furnishings	1711 Greenwich St	415-922-2783	Excellent furniture store. Locally owned. Owners extremely helpful.
The Bar Method	3333 Fillmore St	415-441-6333	A workout like no other.
Canyon Beachwear	1728 Union St	415-885-5070	All bikinis, all the time.
Chan's Trains & Hobbies	2450 Van Ness Ave	415-885-2899	Model trains and all the fixings for the kid in all of us.
Cocoa Bella Chocolates	2102 Union St	415-931-6213	Fabulous compendium of world-wide designer chocolates.
Enchanted Crystal	1895 Union St	415-885-1335	Exquisite jewelry, art, and crystal.

Jest Jewels	1869 Union St	415-563-8839	Accessories and gifts for girls.
Kozo Arts	1969A Union St	415-351-2114	Fancy and beautiful paper. Handmade books.
Krimsa	2190 Union St	415-441-4321	Beautiful handmade rugs, from one-of-a-kind Oriental to modern.
Lush	2116 Union St	415-921-5874	Funky and fresh handmade soaps.
MetroSport	2198 Filbert St	415-923-6453	Running, biking, and swimming gear.
Mingle	1815 Union St	415-674-8811	Women's and men's clothing from emerging designers.
Mudpie	1694 Union St	415-771-9262	Nice clothes for kids.
PlumpJack Wines	3201 Fillmore St	415-346-9870	Great wines at great prices.
Real Food Company	3060 Fillmore St	415-567-6900	Neighborhood market for organic foods.
Wonders of Tibet	1771 Union St	415-409-2994	For those with expensive spiritual taste.

Map 3 • Russian Hill / Fisherman's Wharf

Aimee, Andrew & Company	2238 Polk St	415-447-4094	Upscale deli, dinners to go.
Atelier des Modistes	1903 Hyde St	415-775-0545	Custom-made evening and bridal gowns. By appointment only.
The Candy Store	1507 Vallejo St	415-921-8000	Quality chocolate and old-fashioned jars of candy. Very sweet indeed.
Lavande Nail Spa	2139 Polk St	415-931-7389	Spa pleasure in grand style without the huge price.
Patagonia	770 N Point St	415-771-2050	Adventure gear for outdoor enthusiasts or fakers.
Russian Hill Bookstore	2234 Polk St	415-929-0997	Greeting cards for every occasion. Used books too.
Smoke Signals	2223 Polk St	415-292-6025	International magazine stand.
Swallowtail	2217 Polk St	415-567-1555	Quirky objects that attract stylists and designers.
William Cross Wine Merchants	2253 Polk St	415-346-1314	Great little wine shop on Russian Hill. Don't miss the tasting bar in the back.

Map 4 • North Beach / Telegraph Hill

101 Music	1414 Grant Ave	415-392-6369	Vintage vinyl for serious collectors.
AB Fits	1519 Grant Ave	415-982-5726	Jeans from all over the world.
Alla Prima	1420 Grant Ave	415-397-4077	Dreamy lingerie.
Biordi Arts Imports	412 Columbus Ave	415-392-8096	Imported Italian handmade Majolica pottery.
Eastwind Books & Trading	1435 Stockton St	415-772-5888	Chinese and Asian culture and medicine books.
Goorin Hats Shop	1612 Stockton St	415-402-0454	Add some style to your noggin.
Graffeo Coffee Roasting Co	735 Columbus Ave	415-986-2420	The coffee that makes North Beach smell so good.
Liguria	1700 Stockton St	415-421-3786	Focaccia!
Lola of North Beach	1415 Grant Ave	415-781-1817	Cute cards, quirky gifts, and custom printing.
Mee Mee Bakery	1328 Stockton St	415-362-3204	Ask nicely, and they"ll show you the old fortune cookie machine. Very cool.
Ooma	1422 Grant Ave	415-627-6963	Carrie Bradshaw would shop here.
Schein & Schein	1435 Grant Ave	415-399-8882	Fabulous den of curiosities.

Map 5 • Pacific Heights / Western Addition

Benefit	2117 Fillmore St	415-567-0242	Cosmetics galore.
Betsey Johnson	2031 Fillmore St	415-567-2726	Fun(ky) women's clothing.
Crossroads Trading Company	1901 Fillmore St	415-775-8885	Used clothes.
Divine Girls	340 Presidio Ave	415-409-4901	Great selection of designers at this chic women's boutique.
The Firm	2999 Washington St	415-409-0214	Women's shop in converted Victorian.
George	2411 California St	415-441-0564	Privileged pet supplies.
Gimme Shoes	2358 Fillmore St	415-441-3040	Top-notch, hip shoes.
HeidiSays Collections	2426 Fillmore St	415-749-0655	Friendly designer boutique.
In Water Flowers	2132 Fillmore St	415-359-1232	Flowers.
Juicy News	2453 Fillmore St	415-441-3051	Newsstand and smoothies.
Jurlique	2136 Fillmore St	415-346-7881	Gorgeous Australian skincare.
Kiehl's	2360 Fillmore St	415-359-9260	Skin-care nirvana!
L'Occitane	2207 Fillmore St	415-563-6600	Wonderful French soaps.
La Boulange	2325 Pine St	415-440-0356	Excellent breads, pastries, and desserts.
Marcus Books	1712 Fillmore St	415-346-4222	African-American history, culture and thought.
Margaret O'Leary	2400 Fillmore St	415-771-9982	Rustic, urban, locally-made clothes.
Mrs Dewson's Hats	2050 Fillmore St	415-346-1600	Stylish chapeaux for men and women.
Narumi	1902 Fillmore St	415-346-8629	Decoratives and gifts from Japan.
Nest	2300 Fillmore St	415-292-6199	French-inspired gifts and things.
Paper Source	1925 Fillmore St	415-409-7710	All kinds of paper for all kinds of things.
Shu Uemura	1971 Fillmore St	415-395-0953	Popular Japanese skin care boutique.
Sue Fisher King	3067 Sacramento St	888-811-7276	Top-notch bath, bedroom, tabletop, and home furnishings.
Toujours	2484 Sacramento St	415-346-3988	Entertain your lingerie fantasy.
Winterbranch Gallery	2119 Fillmore St	415-673-2119	Handpainted scarves, artsy jewlery, and handblown glassware.
Zinc Details	1905 Fillmore St	415-776-2100	Clean, contemporary home furnishings.

Map 6 • Pacific Heights / Japantown

Kinokuniya Bookshop	1581 Webster St	415-567-7625	75,000 Japanese and English books and mags.
Rosebowl Florist & Wine Shop	601 Van Ness Ave	415-474-1114	Offerings from boutique wineries and custom arrangements, too.
Whole Foods Market	1765 California St	415-674-0500	Great produce, meats, fish, and cheese.

Map 7 • Nob Hill / Tenderloin

Alessi	424 Sutter St	415-434-0403	Playful Italian housewares.
Apple Store	1 Stockton St	415-392-0202	The building looks like an iBook.
Argonaut Book Shop	786 Sutter St	415-474-9067	California history, the West, and Americana.
Betsey Johnson	160 Geary St	415-398-2516	Fun(ky) women's clothing.
Cheese Plus	2001 Polk St	415-921-2001	Cheese and hard-to-find specialty gourmet foods.
City Discount	1542 Polk St	415-771-4649	Affordable kitchen and housewares.
Clarion Music Center	816 Sacramento St	415-391-1317	Array of quality exotic musical instruments.
Cocoa Bella Chocolates	865 Market St	415-896-5222	Coo coo for Cocoa…
Cris	2056 Polk St	415-474-1191	Top-drawer consignment shop.
DSW Shoe Warehouse	111 Powell St	415-445-9511	Pile 'em high, sell 'em cheap.
European Book Co	925 Larkin St	415-474-0626	European language and travel.
Foot Worship	1214 Sutter St	415-921-3668	Kinky shoes for all of your desires.
Ghirardelli	44 Stockton St	415-397-3030	Site of the West Coast chocolate empire's original factory.
Good Vibrations	1620 Polk St	415-345-0400	A clean, well-lighted place for sex toys.
Kayo Books	814 Post St	415-749-0554	Vintage paperbacks from the '40s through the '70s and esoteric books of all persuasions.
L'Occitane	865 Market St	415-856-0213	Wonderful French soaps.
The Levi's Store	300 Post St	415-501-0100	Flagship store with design your own jeans technology.
Lombardi's Sports	1600 Jackson St	415-771-0600	Basic sporting goods.
Lush	240 Powell St	415-693-9633	Funky and fresh handmade soaps.
The North Face	180 Post St	415-433-3223	High-performance outdoor gear.
One Half	1837 Polk St	415-775-1416	Books, dinnerware, cosmetics, and everything in between at half the retail price.
Out of the Closet	1498 Polk St	415-771-1503	Great thrift store benefiting AIDS research.
Pink	255 Post St	415-421-2022	Beautiful button-downs.
Public Barber Salon	571 Geary St	415-441-8599	Affordable and awesome cuts.
Rasputin Music	69 Powell St	800-350-8700	New and used music.
Real Food	2140 Polk St	415-673-7420	Neighborhood market for organic foods.
Velvet da Vinci	2015 Polk St	415-441-0109	Exquisite collectors' jewelry and art.
Westfield San Francisco Centre	865 Market St	415-512-6776	The beautiful old facade hides the mallrats from view.

Map 8 • Financial District / SOMA

Acme Bread	1 Ferry Building, Shop #15	415-288-2978	Premier high-end bakery.
Adolph Gasser	181 2nd St	415-495-3852	One of the best camera stores in town.
Ambassador Toys	2 Embarcadero Ctr	415-345-8697	Great toys and books for junior.
Camper	39 Grant Ave	415-296-1005	Funky urban shoes.
Candelier	33 Maiden Ln	415-989-8600	Candles, candles, candles.
City Lights	261 Columbus Ave	415-362-8193	Ferlinghetti's store with fab poetry section.
Container Store	26 4th St	415-777-9755	Organizational superstore.
Cowgirl Creamery Artisan Cheese	1 Ferry Building	415-362-9354	Yummy, stinky cheese.
Discount Camera	33 Kearny St	415-392-1100	One of the other best camera stores in town.
Eastern Bakery	720 Grant Ave	415-433-7973	Moon cakes and BBQ pork buns. If they"re good enough for Bill Clinton...
Far West Fungi	Embarcadero & Market St	415-989-9090	Mushrooms. (Not the magic kind.)
Ferry Plaza Wine Merchant	Embarcadero & Market St	415-288-0470	Wine and spirits.
Filippa K	66 Kearny St	415-951-0210	Sleek Swedish styles for men and women.
Fiona's Sweetshoppe	214 Sutter St	415-399-9992	The British (candy makers) are coming!
Frette	124 Geary St	415-981-9504	Bedding heaven.
Frog Hollow Farm	Embarcadero & Market St	415-445-0990	Organic urban farmstand.
Golden Gate Bakery	1029 Grant Ave	415-781-2627	The best egg tarts.
Gump's	135 Post St	800-766-7628	Very upscale home décor.
Hermes	125 Grant Ave	415-391-7200	Loud scarves and Birkin bags.
Hog Island Oyster Company	1 Ferry Building	415-391-7117	Look for a pearl.
Indie Industries	218 Columbus Ave	415-986-7043	Tiny clothing boutique on North Beach"s busiest drag.
Japonesque	824 Montgomery St	415-391-8860	Authentic Japanese art and antiques.
Jeremy's	2 S Park St	415-882-4929	Cheap designer clothing.
Jeffrey's Toys	685 Market St	415-546-6551	No. Not the Giraffe. This is an independent joint for kids of all ages.
John Walker & Co	175 Sutter St	415-986-2707	Top-drawer liquor store.
Loehmann's	211 Sutter St	415-395-0983	Designer clothes at a deep discount.

Ma Maison	592 3rd St	415-777-5370	Francophlic trove of imported dinnerware and household knicknacks.
Marina Morrison	30 Maiden Ln	415-984-9360	Quintessential bridal salon.
Miette	1 Ferry Building	415-837-0300	Sweet pastries.
North Bay Photographer's Supply	436 Bryant St	415-495-8640	Not quite B&H, but good.
Recchiuti	1 Ferry Building	415-834-9494	Carefully crafted chocolate and confections you"ll crave.
Red Blossom Tea Company	831 Grant Ave	415-395-0868	Assortment of premium teas from the Far East.
Stonehouse California Olive Oil	1 The Embarcadero	415-765-0405	Olive oil plus tasting rooms!
Sur La Table	Embarcadero & Market St	415-262-9970	Remarkable kitchen stuff.
Teuscher Chocolate	307 Sutter St	415-834-0850	Celebrated Swiss chocolate store speciallizing in truffles.
Torso Vintages	272 Sutter St	415-391-3166	Luxury vintage that you can afford.
William Stout Architectural Books	804 Montgomery St	415-391-6757	Architecture, art, furniture, and landscaping books.
Yves Saint Laurent	166 Maiden Ln	415-837-1211	Hoity-toity haute couture.

Map 9 • Haight Ashbury / Cole Valley

Ambiance	1458 Haight St	415-552-5095	All the hip local girls shop here.
American Apparel	1615 Haight St	415-431-4028	Brightly colored sweatshop-free threads.
Amoeba Music	1855 Haight St	415-831-1200	Huge music store, new and used. Frequent free live shows!
Aqua Surf Shop	1742 Haight St	415-876-2782	Like totally awesome dude.
Ashbury Tobacco Center	1524 Haight St	415-552-5556	Water pipe is the legal term.
Buffalo Exchange	1555 Haight St	415-431-7733	Vintage wear.
Cal Surplus	1541 Haight St	415-861-0404	Patches with your name on it and army surplus kinds of things.
Ceiba	1364 Haight St	415-437-9598	Future fashions, digital arts, and music.
City Optix	1685 Haight St	415-626-1188	Cool eyewear.
Cold Steel America	1783 Haight St	415-933-7233	Glow-in-the-dark nipple ring anyone?
Cole Hardware	956 Cole St	415-753-2653	For all your hardware needs, shop local.
Crossroads Trading Company	1519 Haight St	415-355-0555	Used clothes.
Daljeets	1773 Haight St	415-668-8500	Funky, kinky clothes and shoes.
Discount Fabrics	2315 Irving St	415-564-7333	A little dingy, but fabric people go nuts for this place.
Egg	85 Carl St	415-564-2248	Eclectic gifts and housewares.
FTC	1632 Haight St	415-626-0663	Skateboards and clothes.
Giant Robot	618 Shrader St	415-876-4773	Japanese-American goodies from t-shirts to toys.
Haight Ashbury Music Center	1540 Haight St	415-863-7327	Guitars, drums, flutes, and all your music needs.
Haight Ashbury Tattoo and Piercing	1525 Haight St	415-431-2218	Tattoos, body manipulation, and general oddness…
Held Over	1543 Haight St	415-864-0818	Add it to the vintage store loop.
Ideele	1600 Haight St	415-431-8836	Cool cute clothes on the (fairly) cheap.
Isabel Shoes	1529 Haight St	415-252-7065	Ultra-sexy to ultra-comfy shoes at ultra-good prices.
John Fluevog	1697 Haight St	415-436-9784	Crazy. Comfy. Cool.
Kidrobot	1512 Haight St	415-487-9000	Funky, Asian pop-inspired toys.
La Rosa Vintage	1711 Haight St	415-668-3744	Fine vintage clothing.
Loyal Army Clothing	1728 Haight St	415-221-6200	Cutest comfiest clothes ever!
Luichiny	1529 Haight St	415-252-7065	Shoes as art. Beautiful Italian shoes bordering on outlandish.
Mendel's Art Supplies	1556 Haight St	415-621-1287	Art supplies and far out fabrics.
New York Apparel	1772 Haight St	415-786-8076	Strippers get dancer discounts on all foxy 'fits.
Occasions Boutique	858 Cole St	415-731-0153	Beauty products, candles, and scents.
Piedmont Boutique	1452 Haight St	415-864-8075	The ultimate source for custom-made hats, feather boas, wigs, and other fancy trashy stuff.
Positively Haight	1400 Haight St	415-252-8747	Steal Your Faces sold here!
Say Cheese	856 Cole St	415-665-5020	One of the best specialty cheese shops in the city. Wine and other epicurean delights as well.
SFO Snowboard Shop	1630 Haight St	415-626-1141	Rip the pow-pow.
Shoe Biz II	1553 Haight St	415-861-3933	Hard to find and alternative-style shoes. Yes, there really are three on Haight.
Skates on Haight	1818 Haight St	415-752-8375	Skate gear.
Super Shoe Biz	1420 Haight St	415-861-0313	Hard to find and alternative-style shoes. Yes, there really are three on Haight.
Villains	1672 Haight St	415-626-5939	Urban chic institution.
Villains Vault	1653 Haight St	415-864-7727	Upscale urban chic housed in an old bank.
Wasteland	1660 Haight St	415-863-3150	Super cool vintage clothes.
X Generation 2	1401 Haight St	415-863-6040	Hip, trendy, sparkly T's and sexy little dresses.

Map 10 • Castro / Lower Haight

A Different Light	489 Castro St	415-431-0891	Gay, lesbian, and bisexual books.
AG Ferrari Foods	468 Castro St	415-255-6590	Italian foods and wine and wonderful deli items.
Alabaster	90 Buena Vista Terrace	415-864-604	High-end, upscale alabaster everything. Great lamps, vessels, urns, and more.
Backspace	351 Divisadero St	415-355-1051	Amazing jackets, jewelry and jeans.
The Bead Store	417 Castro St	415-861-7332	All your basic beading supplies plus exotics and handblown glass.
Citizen	536 Castro St	415-575-3560	Hip men's clothes.
Cliff's Variety Store	479 Castro St	415-431-5365	Excellent hardware store.
Comix Experience	305 Divisadero St	415-863-9258	Comic books.
Cookin'	339 Divisadero St	415-861-1854	Huge, disorganized selection of professional cookware.
Costumes on Haight	735 Haight St	415-621-1356	Huge and funky selection of costumes for all budgets, all the time.
Country Cheese, Inc.	415 Divisadero St	415-621-8130	Friendly service, bulk food options galore, good cheese.
Crossroads Trading Company	2123 Market St	415-552-8740	Used clothes.
De La Sole Footwear	549 Castro St	415-255-3140	Foot wear from the basics to sexy uber funky—it's all here.
Delessio Market	302 Broderick St	415-552-8077	Fancypants market sells wonderful prepared food.
Doe	629 Haight St	415-558-8588	The cutest little things at the cutest little department store.
Edo Salon	601 Haight St	415-861-0131	Hair salon. Straight out of Tokyo (Edo).
Faye's Video & Espresso Bar	3614 18th St	415-522-0434	Small, cool, video joint that also serves coffee.
Furlong Castro	572 Castro St	415-864-2262	Wine shop.
Gamescape	333 Divisadero St	415-621-4263	All kinds of board games.
Golden Produce	172 Church St	415-431-1536	The name says it all.
Groove Merchant	687 Haight St	415-252-5766	Lots of vinyl.
Harvest Ranch Market	2285 Market St	415-626-0805	Amazing soup and salad bar. Vegetarian-friendly.
Imaginknit	3897 18th St	415-621-6642	Get your yarn, fancy and plain. Helpful staff!
Jack's Record Cellar	254 Scott St	415-431-3047	Rare 78s and offbeat vinyl.
Karizma	213 Church St	415-861-4515	Get your hippie on at this beads/ crystals/ jewelry mecca.
Katz Bagels	663 Haight St	415-621-5183	Dense and chewy bagels, chive spread is amazing.
L'Occitane	556 Castro St	415-621-4668	Wonderful French soaps.
Life	604 Haight St	415-252-9312	Lovely assortment of fragrant oils, candles and incense.
Mickey's Monkey	218 Pierce St	415-864-0693	Used furniture and knick knacks.
Needles and Pens	3253 16th St	415-255-1534	Zines and other punk rock things.
Other Shop Li	327 Divisadero St	415-621-5424	Retro furnishings.
Out of the Closet	100 Church St	415-252-1101	Great thrift store benefiting AIDS research.
Plant'It Earth	661 Divisadero St	415-626-5082	Pretty plants and gobs of garden goods.
Rolo	2351 Market St	415-431-4545	Hip men's clothes.
Salon Baobao	2041 Market St	415-626-6806	Ask for the latest haircut in this mod salon.
Sam's Smoke Shop	250 Divisadero St	415-626-7173	Family-owned head shop.
Stem	3690 18th St	415-861-7836	Funky florist with cards and kids' gifts to boot.
Streetlight Records	2350 Market St	888-396-2350	New, used, and rare music.
Studio 3579	499 Dolores	415-626-2533	Assorted hipster ephemera (read: lots of silk-screened t-shirts, pillows, and even panties).
Tan Bella	2185 Market St	415-522-1234	Award-winning spray and UV tanning from friendly, stylish salon.
Thorough Bread And Pastry	248 Church St	415-558-0690	Adorable bakery; tasty treats.
Three Twins Ice Cream	254 Fillmore St	415.ITS.TWIN	Three green twins.
Tim's Market	667 Fillmore St	415-552-6830	Smokes, nutter butters, and alcohol.
Under One Roof	518 Castro St	415-503-2300	Support a good cause by buying that special something.
Upper Playground	220 Fillmore St	415-861-1960	Gallery, Fifty24SF, urban clothing, and used music.
Venus Superstar	351 Divisadero St	415-749-1978	Edgy, underground clothing and accessories for men and women.
Wak Shack Salon	782 Haight St	415-255-8554	Never hard to get an appointment.
Zip Zap Hair	245 Fillmore St	415-621-1671	Super stylists and service.

Map 11 • Hayes Valley / The Mission

826 Valencia	826 Valencia St	415-642-5905	It's a pirate supply store AND classroom. Pretty darn amazing.
Abandoned Planet Books	518 Valencia St	415-861-4695	Get lost for hours in this amazing old bookstore.
ADS Hats	418 Valencia St	415-503-1316	Fedoras, berets, caps, and more.
Adobe Book Shop	3166 16th St	415-864-3936	Best place to lose time browsing.
Alla Prima	539 Hayes St	415-864-8180	Dreamy lingerie.
Amore Animal Supply	696 Valencia St	415-436-9788	Goods for cats, dogs, smaller furry friends and birds.
The Apartment	3469 18th St	415-255-1100	Eclectic, interesting furniture; vintage artefacts; awesome exterior mural.
Arlequin Wine Merchant	384 Hayes St	415-863-1104	Specialty wine shop.
Artist Xchange	3169 16th St	415-864-1490	A gallery...a store. It's both! Browse and buy!
Azalea Boutique	411 Hayes St	415-861-9888	Eclectic boutique and nail bar for men and women.
Bell Jar	3187 16th St	415-626-1749	Darling items for your home and body. Fall in love.
Bi-Rite Market	3639 18th St	415-626-5600	Small, good, old grocery store.

Black And Blue Tattoo	381 Guerrero St	415-626-0770	Impressive, female-centric tattoo, cutting and branding shop.
Bombay Ice Creamery	552 Valencia St	415-861-3995	Indian ice cream flavors such as almond, saffron, pistachio, and rose.
Borderland Books	866 Valencia St	415-824-8203	Sci-fi, fantasy, and horror.
Botanica Yoruba	998 Valencia St	415-826-4967	Fulfilling your Santeria, Lucumi, Palo, and Ifa needs.
British American Imports	726 15th St	415-863-3300	Find crumpets, Cadbury, and other imports in this teeny underground Brit shop.
Bulo	418 Hayes St	415-255-4939	Fashionable footwear for women.
Candy Store	3153 16th St	415-887-7637	Quirky designer clothes and accessories, created with love.
Chamalyn	3491 19th St	415-850-9955	Japanese cuteness overload! With specialty tea and candy treats!
Claudia Kussano	591 Guerrero St	415-671-076	Unique, contemporary jewelry from local designer.
Clothes Contact	473 Valencia St	415-621-3212	Vintage clothing sold by the pound.
Community Thrift Store	623 Valencia St	415-861-4910	Proceeds go to the charity of your choice.
The Curiosity Shoppe	855 Valencia St	415-671-5384	Gorgeous, crafty items for your home or artsiest loved one.
Currents	911 Valencia St	415-648-2015	Soap and stuff.
Dark Garden	321 Linden St	415-431-7684	Custom-made corsets, bridal gowns, and bras.
Density	593 Valencia St	415-552-2220	Hipster threads for men and women, with great service.
Discount Fabrics	201 11th St	415-495-4201	A little dingy, but fabric people go nuts for this place.
Dish	541 Hayes St	415-252-5997	Women's clothing with simple, feminine styles.
Evelyn's	381 Hayes St	415-255-1815	Antique Chinese furniture.
Five and Diamond	510 Valencia St	415-255-9747	Like stepping onto the set of a Western movie with Malcolm McLaren as art director.
Flax	1699 Market St	415-552-2355	Excellent art and craft supplies for all kinds of projects.
Flight 001	525 Hayes St	415-487-1001	Hip travel store with everything you need to carry everything you want, everywhere you go.
Gimme Shoes	416 Hayes St	415-864-0691	Top-notch, hip shoes.
Good Vibrations	603 Valencia St	415-522-5460	A clean, well-lit place for sex toys.
Harrington's Antiques	599 Valencia St	415-861-7300	Vast space full of unusual old and new home furnishings.
Haseena	526 Hayes St	415-252-1104	Stylish women's boutique.
Hideo Wakamatsu	563 Valencia St	415-255-3029	Suitcases so divine, you won"t want to check them.
Idol Vintage	3162 16th St	415-255-9959	Vintage clothing store, specializing in the '60s, '70s, and '80s.
Katz Bagels	3147 16th St	415-552-9050	Dense and chewy bagels, chive spread is amazing.
La Library	380 Guerrero St	415-558-984	This "friendly socialist boutique" offers shabby chic and vintage bargains.
Lava9	542 Hayes St	415-552-6468	Animal coats.
Lavish	540 Hayes St	415-565-0540	Vintage décor, home, bath, jewelry, women's clothing, and baby gifts.
Little Otsu	849 Valencia St	415-255-7900	Artist-made paper goods and vegan products.
Lost Art Salon	245 Van Ness Ave	415-861-1530	Like prowling through an eccentric aunt's private gallery.
Martin's 16th Street Emporium	3248 16th St	415-552-4631	Leave with lots of (pirate) booty.
Miette Confiserie	449 Octavia St	415-626-6221	Old-fashioned sweet shop in Hayes Valley.
The Mission Statement	3458 18th St	415-255-7457	New co-op featuring clothing from up-and-coming SF designers.
Mission Thrift	2330 Mission St	415-821-9560	Keep this one on the DL.
Monument	572 Valencia St	415-861-9800	High class and high priced gorgeous furniture designs.
Multikulti	539 Valencia St	415-437-1718	Hotbed of kooky accessories, including the best tights in town!
Nomads	556 Hayes St	415-864-5692	Trendy men's clothing.
Oxenrose	448 Grove St	415-252-9723	Haven for hipsters and fresh haircuts in Hayes Valley.
The Painted Lady	491 Guerrero St	415 552 5778	Sharp artists, fine lines, attitude-free, top tattoo talent.
Paxton Gate	824 Valencia St	415-824-1872	Taxidermy, fossils, and other things once living.
Paxton Gate's Curiosities For Kids	766 Valencia St	415-252-999	Ignite your kids' imaginations with old fashioned 'n' fun delights.
Propeller	555 Hayes St	415-701-7767	Innovative furniture and home accessories.
RAG	541 Octavia St	415-621-7718	Clothing by young designers.
Rainbow Grocery	1745 Folsom St	415-863-0620	Best natural, organic, vegetarian-focused food market in town, not just for hippies anymore.
The San Francisco Chocolate Factory	286 12th St	888-732-4626	Free samples!
Schauplatz	791 Valencia St	415-864-5665	Reasonably priced, colorful, vintage awesomeness. Great finds galore.
Self Edge	714 Valencia St	415-558-065	Denim specialists with a global eye and designer prices.
Seventh Heart	1592 Market St	415-431-1755	Clothing loved by indie rockers and art students.
Shoe Biz	877 Valencia St	415-550-8655	Their shoes are the business!
Sports Authority	1690 Folsom St	415-734-9373	Sports apparel and gear.
Sports Basement	1590 Bryant St	415-575-3000	Warehouse sporting goods at outlet prices.
Stitch Lounge	182 Gough St	415-431-3739	Lounge, boutique, and classes. So hip, sew urban.

Sunhee Moon	3167 16th St	415-355-1800	A clothing boutique almost too chic for the Mission District.
Therapy	545 Valencia St	415-861-6213	Hip clothing and magnets of cat butts.
Thrift Town	2101 Mission St	415-861-1132	Thift-y emporium.
Timbuk2	506 Hayes St	415-252-9860	Not for your average bike messenger.
Trout Farm Retrospect Fine Furniture	1649 Market St	415-863-7414	Fine vintage furniture.
True Sake	560 Hayes St	415-355-9555	Sake shop.
Weston Wear	569 Valencia St	415-621-1480	Smart clothes for smart women.
Z-Barn	560 Valencia St	415-864-5800	Modern, stylish and classic furniture for your entire home.
Zeni	567 Hayes St	415-864-0154	Hip boutique for men and women.
Zoe Bikini	3386 18th St	415-621-4551	The latest and greatest in custom Bikinis.

Map 12 • SOMA / Potrero Hill (North)

Flower Mart	640 Brannan St	415-392-7944	THE wholesale flower market. Opens to the public at 10:00 am.
General Bead	637 Minna St	415-255-2323	Beads, beads, beads. Best selection in town.
Off the Wall	281 9th St	415-863-8170	Ready-to-hang posters and prints, as well as custom framing.
Out of the Closet	1295 Folsom St	415-558-7176	Great thrift store benefiting AIDS research.
Podesta Baldocchi	410 Harriet St	415-346-1300	A San Francisco institution for elegant flowers.
REI	840 Brannan St	415-934-1938	Outdoor gear co-op.
SF Design Center	2 Henry Adams St	415-490-5800	Browse contemporary furnishings from top designers.
Stormy Leather	1158 Howard St	415-626-1672	Animal skins for sex play.
Trader Joe's	555 9th St	415-863-1292	Affordable specialty foods.

Map 13 • Mission Beach

Arch	99 Missouri St	415-433-2724	They sell cool quirky gifts, too.
Bell and Trunk Flowers	1411 18th St	415-648-0519	Spectacular blooms by the stem.
Christopher's Books	1400 18th St	415-255-8802	Neighborhood bookshop.
Collage Gallery	1345 18th St	415-282-4401	Crafts for the home by Bay Area artists.
K&L Wine Merchants	638 4th St	415-896-1734	The best wine shop in town. Great selection, including old and rare wines.
Limn	290 Townsend St	415-543-5466	Modern furniture.
Ruby Wine	1419 18th St	415-401-7708	Wine, beer, and gourmet treats.
Stem	1411 18th St	415-648-0519	Spectacular blooms by the stem.

Map 14 • Noe Valley

24th Street Cheese Company	3893 24th St	415-821-6658	Gourmet cheese shop.
Ambiance	3985 24th St	415-647-7144	All the hip local girls shop here.
Apple Blossom	1303 Castro St	415-401-0602	Hip, pretty, women's clothes.
Astrid's Rabat Shoes	3909 24th St	415-282-7400	Go see Ronnie if you need some comfort (shoes).
Church Nail	1211 Church St	415-826-6207	No frills service; bank balance-friendly.
Flowers of the Valley	4077 24th St	415-970-0579	Flowers.
French Tulip	3903 24th St	415-647-8661	Lovely, lush bouquets, great gifts, and stellar service.
Gypsy Honeymoon	3599 24th St	415-821-1713	Beautiful, vintage, unique furniture, nick-nacks and oddities.
Holey Bagel	3872 24th St	415-647-3334	For non-New York bagels, Holey"s are damn decent.
Joshua Simon	3915 24th St	415-821-1068	Women's clothes. Normal to plus sizes.
Lehr's German Specialties	1581 Church St	415-282-6803	All things German.
Noe Valley Bakery	4073 24th St	415-550-1405	Artisan breads, tasty pastries, and seasonal loaves.
Noe Valley Pet	1451 Church St	415-282-7385	Only the best for your pup.
PlumpJack Wines	4011 24th St	415-282-3841	Great wines at great prices.
Rabat	4001 24th St	415-282-7861	Women's urban wear, shoes, and accessories.
Scribbledoodles / Just for Fun	3982 24th St	415-285-4068	Whimsical gifts and stationery.
See Jane Run	3910 24th St	415-401-8338	Women's athletic gear.
Shoe Biz	3810 24th St	415-821-2528	Their shoes are the business!
Wink SF	4107 24th St	415-401-8881	Quirky gifts from around the globe.
Xela Imports	3925 24th St	415-695-1323	Super selection of sterling silver jewelry.

Map 15 • Mission (Outer)

Aquarius Records	1055 Valencia St	415-647-2272	Independent record shop with all types of music.
Back To The Picture	934 Valencia St	415-826-2321	Custom picture framing for locals in the know.
Casa Bonampak	1051 Valencia St	415-642-4079	Traditional Mexican arts and crafts celebrated in this colorful store.
Casa Lucas Market	2934 24th St	415-826-4334	Latino produce market.
Dema	1038 Valencia St	415-206-0500	60s-inspired threads.
Dianda's Italian American Pastry Co	2883 Mission St	415-647-5469	Sicilian cookies.
Dog Eared Books	900 Valencia St	415-282-1901	New and used books, with good local zines.
Encantada	908 Valencia St	415-642-3939	Stunning arts and crafts, keeping Latin lusciousness alive on Valencia.
Fabric 8	3318 22nd St	415-647-5888	Rad urban art, plus hip-hop stylings from independent designers.
Ginger Rubio	600 Shotwell St	415-829-7750	Sleek, stylish, bright and modern hair salon.
Hair Candy	3387 22nd St	415-550-8238	Cosy, creative and (literally) cutting edge.
House Of Hengst	924 Valencia St	415-642-0841	Cutting edge but low key designer chic.
Humphry Slocombe	2790 Harrison St	415-550-6971	Breakfast done right: (ice) cream (and bourbon) with your cornflakes.
Janet Moyer Landscaping	1031 Valencia St	415-821-3760	By appointment only, high end garden landscaping.
Laku	1089 Valencia St	415-695-1462	Oddball collection of old-timey clothes, nick-nacks and oddities.
Lucca Ravioli	1100 Valencia St	415-647-5581	Old-fashioned Italian deli.
Modern Times Bookstore	2919 24th St	415-282-9246	Progressive bookstore.
Retro Fit	910 Valencia St	415-550-1530	Vintage used clothes and remakes of old t-shirts.
Room 4	904 Valencia St	415-647-2764	Hand-picked, charismatic, vintage goodies for you and your home.
Ruby	3602 20th St	415-550-8052	This cute boutique, named after owner"s dog, has gifts galore.
Saffron	949 Valencia St	415-648-8990	Providers of vanilla and saffron-related products for 30 years!
The Touch	956 Valencia St	415-550-2640	Mid-century furniture with random curiosities and a retro vibe.
Valencia Whole Foods	999 Valencia St	415-285-0231	Pricey but delicious organic produce, salads, snacks and frozen meals.

Map 16 • Potrero Hill (Southwest)

Good Life Grocery	1524 20th St	415-282-9204	Friendly neighborhood market.

Map 17 • Potrero Hill / Dogpatch

Crushpad	2573 3rd St	415-864-4232	Make your own wine.
Pro Camera	1405 Minnesota St	415-282-7368	Camera rentals.

Map 19 • Outer Richmond (East) / Seacliff

AK Meats	2346 Clement St	415-933-6328	Butcher shop with cracking pastrami sandwiches.
Gaslight & Shadows Antiques	2335 Clement St	415-387-0633	Rare yet affordable antiques.

Map 20 • Richmond

Blackwell's Wines	5620 Geary Blvd	415-386-9463	Best Scotch/bourbon selection around.
Hobby Company of San Francisco	5150 Geary Blvd	415-386-2802	Independent source for craft and hobby supplies.
Kawaii Corner	5406 Geary Blvd	415-666-3826	Sanrio and San-X cuteness.
Purple Skunk	5820 Geary Blvd	415-668-7905	Skate, surf, and snowboard gear.
San Francisco Brewcraft	1555 Clement St	415-751-9338	Everything you need to make beer!

Map 21 • Inner Richmond

April in Paris	55 Clement St	415-750-9910	Leather goods and purses by appointment only.
Arguello Super Market	782 Arguello Blvd	415-751-5121	Must get a fresh-roasted turkey sandwich.
Green Apple Books & Music	506 Clement St	415-387-2272	Get lost in here for hours, literally.
Heroes Club	840 Clement St	415-387-4552	Sci-fi and anime action figures.
Kamei Kitchen Wares	547 Clement St	415-666-3699	Cheap things for the chef.
Kumquat	147 Clement St	415-752-2140	Local art and jewelry.
New May Wah	707 Clement St	415-221-9826	Large Asian grocery saves a scouring of Chinatown.
Richmond New May Wah Supermarket	707 Clement St	415-221-9826	Asian supermarket selling everything from frozen potstickers to pineapples.
Schubert's Bakery	521 Clement St	415-752-1580	Exquisitely crafted cakes.
Sloat Garden Center	327 3rd Ave	415-752-1614	All kinds of plants and gardening supplies.
Super Tokio	251 Clement St	415-668-1118	Your source for Asian junk food.

Map 22 • Presidio Heights / Laurel Heights

AG Ferrari Foods	3490 California St	415-923-4470	Italian food and wine and wonderful deli items.
Bedroom Outlet	2901 Geary Blvd	415-387-7892	Need a mattress? Friendly service, family run, great prices.
Bryan's Quality Meats	3473 California St	415-752-3430	Best place to buy meat, fish, and poultry in San Francisco.
Button Down	3415 Sacramento St	415-563-1311	Beautiful and pricey clothing for men and women.
Day One	3490 California St	415-440-3291	Strollers, slings, books, bottles, breastpumps, and parent classes.
The Grocery Store	3625 Sacramento St	415-928-3615	High-end casual women's clothes.
Kendall Wilkinson Home	3419 Sacramento St	415-409-1966	Upscale homewares and furniture.
Kindersport	3655 Sacramento St	415-563-7778	Kids ski and sport outfitters.
Mom's the Word	3385 Sacramento St	415-441-8261	Funky maternity clothes.
The Ribbonerie	3695 Sacramento St	415-626-6184	Absolutely every kind of ribbon ever.
Threshold	3419 Sacramento St	415-409-1966	Upscale homewares and furniture.
Trader Joe's	3 Masonic Ave	415-346-9964	Affordable specialty foods.

Map 23 • Outer Sunset

Other Avenues	3930 Judah St	415-661-7475	Highest concentration of hippies outside the Haight.

Map 24 • Sunset

The Hard Wear Store	2401 Irving St	415-682-9565	Ocean Beach hoodies and Sunset tee-shirts. Represent.
Jazz Quarter	1267 20th Ave	415-661-2331	Music store-cum-esoterica extravaganza.
Sunset Music Company	2311 Irving St	415-731-1725	Everything a brilliant musician needs, and lessons for the not-so brilliant.
Sunset Soccer Supply	3401 Irving St	415-753-2666	Everything soccer.
Wonderful Foods Co	2035 Irving St	415-731-6889	Snack foods, candy, and tapioca drinks here.
Yes Variety	2345 Irving St	415-242-5170	Everything the modern chinese kitchen needs...and at a good price.

Map 25 • Inner Sunset / Golden Gate Heights

Amazing Fantasy	650 Irving St	415-681-4344	Comic books.
Andronico's	1200 Irving St	415-661-3220	Another good spot for fancy groceries.
Cheese Boutique	1298 12th Ave	415-566-3155	Nice little cheese shop.
Crossroads Trading Company	630 Irving St	415-681-0100	Mecca of re-sale clothing.
Great Stuff	1377 9th Ave	415-681-7696	Eclectic gifts, kitchenware, and garden goods.
Holy Gelato!	1392 9th Ave	415-681-3061	Biodegradable containers!
Irving Variety	647 Irving St	415-731-1286	Endearing garage-sale charm.
Le Video	1231 9th Ave	415-566-3606	Offers a huge selection of eclectic movie rentals.
Misdirections Magic Shop	1236 9th Ave	415-566-2180	All the magic anyone needs.
On the Run	1310 9th Ave	415-682-2042	Running shoes.
Paragraph	1234 9th Ave	415-753-0700	Hip clothes for the whole family.
Tutti Frutti	718 Irving St	415-661-8504	Gifts, cards, t-shirts. Kitsch and toys for all ages.
Wishbone	601 Irving St	415-242-5540	Eclectic items for personal and home use.

Map 26 • Parkside (Outer)

Aqua Culture Surf & Snowboard Shop	2830 Sloat Blvd	415-242-9283	Boards and gear.
Sloat Garden Center	2700 Sloat Blvd	415-566-4415	All kinds of plants and gardening supplies.
Sunset Supermarket	2801 Vicente St	415-504-8188	Quintessential Asian supermarket.

Map 27 • Parkside (Inner)

Apple Store	3251 20th Ave	415-242-7890	NFT app for SF now available on the iPhone or iPod Touch!
L'Occitane	3251 20th Ave	415-665-2863	Wonderful French soaps.
Marco Polo	1447 Taraval St	415-731-2833	Tropical flavors.
Stonestown Galleria	3251 20th Ave	415-759-2626	120 stores in this urban mall.

Map 30 • West Portal

Ambassador Toys	186 West Portal Ave	415-759-8697	Global games for kids.
Goodwill Boutique	61 West Portal Ave	415-665-7291	Isn't that an oxymoron?
Growing Up	240 West Portal Ave	415-661-6304	Books and toys for kids.
Little Fish Boutique	320 W Portal Ave	415-681-7242	Chic boutique for the sippy-cup set.

Map 32 • Diamond Heights / Glen Park

Artesanias Unique Home Furnishings	1747 Church St	415-643-6309	Excellent furniture store. Locally owned. Owners extremely helpful.
Canyon Market	2815 Diamond St	415-586-9999	Gourmet supermarket with prices to match.
Cheese Boutique	666 Chenery St	415-333-3390	Cheese, cheese, cheese!
Destination Bakery	598 Chenery St	415-864-5800	Local, seasonal ingredients; warm service.
Manila Oriental Market	4175 Mission St	415-337-7272	Buy live frogs, fresh fish, and oriental treats in this Outer Mission Asian.
Modernpast	677 Chenery St	415-333-9007	Danish modern, classic, eclectic, museum-worthy furnishings.
Thrill House Records	3422 Mission St	N/A	Non-profit, volunteer-run, punk rock record and "zine store.

Map 35 • Bernal Heights

Bernal Beast	509 Cortland Ave	415-643-7800	Pet supplies and grooming.
Chloe's Closet	451 Cortland Ave	415-642-3300	Hand-me downs for the only child.
Heartfelt	436 Cortland Ave	415-648-1380	Cute and gifty things you don't really need.
Red Hill Books	401 Cortland Ave	415-648-5331	New and used books to buy or trade.

Map 36 • Bayview / Silver Terrace

San Francisco Wholesale Produce Market	2095 Jerrold Ave	415-550-4495	More than 30 vendors on a 25-acre facility.

Map 37 • India Basin / Hunters Point

Building Resources	701 Amador St	415-285-7814	Non-profit building salvage emporium.
Casa Lucas Market	4555 Mission St	415-334-9747	Cheap produce, cheeses, etc. in this Latin American market.

Map 38 • Excelsior / Crocker Amazon

El Chico Produce No 2	4600 Mission St	415-587-6025	Fresh and cheap Mexican produce and groceries.

Map 40 • Bayview / Candlestick Point

Leeling Imports & Exports	5534 3rd St	415-822-4082	Underground oil painting shop with an abundance of deals. Owner paints as you browse.

The Presidio

Sports Basement	610 Old Mason St	415-437-0100	Warehouse sporting goods at outlet prices.

Sausalito

Great Overland Book Co	215 Caledonia St	415-332-1532	Used bookshop; lots of nautical books.
Heath Ceramics	400 Gate 5 Rd	415-332-3732	Beautiful modern ceramics made on-site.
Pinestreet Papery	42 Caledonia St	415-332-5458	High-quality paper goods.
Sausalito Ferry Company	688 Bridgeway	415-332-9590	Paul Frank merchandise, and other hipster-wanna-be paraphernalia.

Mill Valley

Alphadog	6 Miller Ave	415-389-6500	Because dogs must look good in Mill Valley, too.
Benefit Cosmetics	35 Throckmorton Ave	415-383-5577	Waxing and girlie makeup.
The Depot Bookstore & Café	87 Throckmorton Ave	415-383-2665	Browse the books then read your purchase over a sandwich.
Mill Valley Cycleworks	357 Miller Ave	415-388-6774	Products and advice on how to tackle Mt Tam's trails.
Mill Valley Hat Box	118 Throckmorton Ave	415-383-2757	A true milliner.
Mill Valley Market	12 Corte Madera Ave	415-388-3222	The town market gone gourmet. Good deli and wine sections.
Mill Valley Vintage Wine & Spirits	67 Throckmorton Ave	415-388-1626	Thorough and helpful wine shop.
Pharmaca	230 E Blithedale Ave	415-388-7822	Natural medicine pharmacy, supplements, and pure skincare products.
Strawbridges	86 Throckmorton Ave	415-388-0235	Stationery, cards, and leather-bound photo albums.
Tea Garden Springs Day Spa	38 Miller Ave	415-389-7123	Beautiful and serene retreat. Stellar massages and treatments.
Tony's Shoe Repair	38 Corte Madera Ave	415-388-5935	Much-loved Tony keeps all of Mill Valley shod.
Two Neat	111 Throckmorton Ave	415-381-4222	Subversive films, cards, and t-shirts. The way Marin used to be.
Village Music	31 Sunnyside	415-388-7400	For vinyl nostalgia.
Whole Foods Market	414 Miller Ave	415-381-1200	When you need lots of gourmet groceries.

Berkeley (West)

Acme Bread	1601 San Pablo Ave	510-524-1327	The best bread in Berkeley.
Berkeley Horticultural Nursery	1310 McGee Ave	510-526-4704	Plants.
Chocolat	1485 Solano Ave	510-528-2462	Chocolate sale!
Cody's Books	1730 4th St	510-559-9500	Great discounted books galore. Last remaining location of the venerable Berkeley book seller.
Fourth Street Shopping District	Cedar St & 4th St	n/a	Boutiques and unobtrusive chains, good for stuff for your home.
George Shop	1844 4th St	510-644-1033	Pet shop caters to pampered pets of fancy 4th Street shoppers.
La Farine Bakery	1820 Solano Ave	510-528-2208	Stop the suffering from Paris withdrawal.
Magnet	2508 San Pablo Ave	510-848-1966	Indie couture shopping outside of LA, NYC, London.
Monterey Foods	1550 Hopkins St	510-526-6042	Great produce.
The North Face Outlet	1238 5th St	510-526-3530	Discount North Face gear: cheap(er) packs, fleece and boots!
Ohmega Salvage	2407 San Pablo Ave	510-204-0767	Architectural salvage specializing in Victorian through 1950s products.
Pegasus & Pendragon Books	1855 Solano Ave	510-525-6888	General Interest. New and used, foreign and domestic.
Photolab	2235 5th St	510-644-140	Get the most out of your art and photography.
Sketch	1809 4th St	510-665-5650	Excellent gelateria.
Sweet Adeline Bakeshop	3350 Adeline St	510-985-7381	Gorgeous pastries.
Urban Ore	900 Murray St	510-841-7283	A yard sale for the home improvement crowd.

Berkeley (East)

Amoeba Music	2455 Telegraph Ave	510-549-1125	Indie music. Awesome selection.
Annapurna	2416 Telegraph Ave	510-841-6187	Fun adult gifts.
Berkeley Bowl	2020 Oregon St	510-843-6929	Independent grocery.
Berkeley Flea Market	1937 Ashby Ave	510-644-0744	Saturday and Sunday.
Buffalo Exchange	2585 Telegraph Ave	510-644-9202	Used clothing store. Buy and sell.
The Cheese Board	1512 Shattuck Ave	510-549-3055	A multitude of cheeses, bread, and pizza delight. Gets happily packed.
Crossroads Trading Company	2338 Shattuck Ave	510-843-7600	Used clothing store. Buy and sell.
Jeremy's	2967 College Ave	510-849-0701	This branch usually has clearance items.
Looking Glass Photo	2848 Telegraoh Ave	510-548-6888	Everything photography store.
Mars Mercantile	2398 Telegraph Ave	510-843-6711	Vintage clothing.
Moe's Books	2476 Telegraph Ave	510-849-2087	Four stories of new and used books, academically inclined.
Pegasus & Pendragon Books	2349 Shattuck Ave	510-649-1320	General Interest. New and used, foreign and domestic.
Rasputin Music	2401 Telegraph Ave	800-350-8700	New and used music, performances.
What the Traveler Saw	2999 College Ave	888-339-8162	Travel gift shop.
Whole Foods Market	3000 Telegraph Ave	510-649-1333	Duh, great organic groceries.

Oakland

The Food Mill	3033 MacArthur Blvd	510-482-3848	Health market with a million grains and nuts.
Nuherbs	3820 Penniman Ave	510-534-4372	Chinese herbs.
Walden Pond Books	3316 Grand Ave	510-832-4438	Support your local radical bookstore. Like coming home.

Downtown Oakland / Lake Merritt

AK Press	674 23rd St	510-208-1700	Radical and independent books and other media.
Bibliomania	1816 Telegraph Ave	510-835-5733	Out-of-print and obscure books.
Country Cheese	2101 San Pablo Ave	510-841-0752	Great cheese varieties, cozy general store.
Fiveten Studio	831 Broadway	510-451-9900	Local artist designs for interesting home furnishings and decor.
Juniper Tree	3303 Lakeshore Ave	510-444-4650	Funky, fun, affordable.
Karibu	427 Water St	510-444-6906	International craft art and gifts.
Mannequin Madness	2020 Dennison St.	510-444-0650	Buy, sell, trade, or rent mannequins (by appointment only).
Mignonne	1000 Jefferson St	510-444-5288	Homebound antiques from France with love.
Rock, Paper, Scissors	2278 Telegraph Ave	510-238-9171	Radical artisan and craftiness collective.
Verse	461 9th St	510-663-4400	Limted edition sneakers in gallery setting.

North Oakland / Emeryville

Ancient Ways	4075 Telegraph Ave	510-653-3244	Occult, pagan, and herbcraft supplies.
Apple Store	5656 Bay St	510-350-2400	Smaller than the one in the city, but still has a good selection and free internet.
Article Pract	5010 Telegraph Ave	510-595-7875	Hip yarn and knitting store.
Atomic Garden	5453 College Ave	510-923-0543	Eco-everything clothing outlet.
Café Mariposa & Bakeshop	5427 Telegraph Ave	510-595-0955	Environmentally-committed bakery!
Crossroads Trading Company	5636 College Ave	510-420-1952	Used clothing. Buy and sell.
Diesel	5433 College Ave	510-653-9965	Bookseller with couches.
Fenton's Creamery	4226 Piedmont Ave	510-658-7000	Old-fashioned handmade ice cream.
Issues	20 Glen Ave	510-601-7800	Hot new store. Magazines, newspapers, music, great local treat.
Itsy Bitsy	5520 College Ave	510-428-1651	Rare handmade Asian imported goods.
Maison d'etre	5640 College Ave	510-658-2801	Quirky, fancy home goods. Bring your wallet.
Pendragon Books	5560 College Ave	510-652-6259	Local independent bookseller.
Rockridge Market Hall	5655 College Ave	510-250-6000	Specialty fresh food merchants.
Rockridge Rags	5711 College Ave	510-655-2289	Contemporary clothing on consignment.
Saturn Records	1501 Powell	510-407-0358	Specialty and hard-to-find vinyl.
Siobhan Van Winkel	6371 Telegraph Ave	510-652-1415	Creative and unique children's clothing and toys.
Teacake Bake Shop	5615 Bay St	510-655-0865	Red velvet cupcakes. Perfection.
Trader Joe's	5700 Christie Ave	510-658-8091	Affordable specialty foods.

Overview

Theater in San Francisco can mean anything from lavish productions straight off Broadway stages to more interactive, handcrafted performances from one artist's soul to yours. The Holy Trinity of playhouses in San Francisco may as well be represented by the **Curran (Map 7)**, **Golden Gate (Map 7)**, and **Orpheum Theaters (Map 7)**. The theaters all opened in the 1920s and are each architecturally individual examples of the grandiose theater environment. Current and future schedules and ticket sales for these theaters are available through www.bestofbroadway-sf.com.

Long-Running Shows

Not all big productions in San Francisco are touring shows. At North Beach's **Club Fugazi (Map 4)**, *Beach Blanket Babylon* (with its ever-evolving send-ups of current events and pop culture) has been running right here in the city for over 30 years. Experiencing the wacky musical performance, complete with actors in over-the-top costumes and towering hats, is almost a rite of passage for any San Franciscan. This famous production is billed as the longest running musical revue in theater history.

The Mix

Theater-goers will find that most city theaters stage a mixture of time-honored productions and new plays. Since 1974, the **Geary Theater (Map 7)** has been owned by the American Conservatory Theater (ACT), San Francisco's highly acclaimed training institute and regional theater. ACT productions, also showcased at the **Zeum Theater (Map 8)** in Yerba Buena Gardens, include classics such as *Cat on a Hot Tin Roof*, as well as new works. Expect plays from playwrights like Tom Stoppard, David Mamet, and Eugene O'Neill. Known for embracing diversity and fostering youth empowerment, the **New Conservatory Theatre Center (Map 11)** houses three theaters: **The Decker (Map 11)**, **The Walker (Map 11)**, and **Theatre Three (Map 11)**. Through its Pride Season program, the center stages multiple LGBT-themed productions each year. Other productions include solo performances, musicals, and even a few classics.

Performing Arts

The **Palace of Fine Arts Theatre (Map 1)** can hold 1,000 patrons and hosts concerts, comedy shows, and lectures in a structure that started out as a temporary structure built for the 1915 Panama Pacific Exposition. Made of wood and plaster, it began to deteriorate after the Expo. In the late 1950s, a restoration movement began, and the building was reconstructed using concrete castings. Today, the theater plays host to performance groups, concerts, film festivals, and lectures. Part of the War Memorial and Performing Arts Center in San Francisco's Civic Center area, the stage at the ornately decorated **Herbst Theatre (Map 6)** is home to a variety of annual musical productions and choral concerts, including the San Francisco Jazz Festival, as well as City Arts & Lectures presentations with authors and artists of the moment. While perhaps not as grand as the Palace of Fine Arts Theatre or the Herbst, there are many city theaters that embrace much more than staged productions. You'll find combinations of multi-disciplinary performance spaces, acting workshops, classes, youth programs, and rental space at theaters such as **The Marsh (Map 15)**, **Next Stage (Map 6)**, **ODC Theater (Map 11)**, **Intersection for the Arts (Map 11)**, **Yerba Buena Center for the Arts Theater (Map 8)**, **Victoria Theatre (Map 11)** (which happens to be the oldest operating theater in San Francisco), and **Shotwell Studios (Map 11)**.

Smaller Theaters

The city is full of small theatrical outfits boasting unique programs. Within Fort Mason Center, one can find five different venues, each catering to distinct patrons and art forms. At **Bayfront Theater (Map 2)**, you'll find the BATS improv troupe making it up as they go along. Recitals and classes for budding musicians take place at the **Blue Bear School of Music Performance Hall (Map 2)** and original plays are acted upon the stages of the **Cowell Theater** and **Magic Theatre (Map 2)**. Even kids get in the act inside the **Young Performers Theater (Map 2)**.

You'll find more small-run, off-Broadway performances, improv, one-act plays, and even some stand-up comedy at the **The Custom Stage (Map 12)**, **Shelton Theater (Map 7)**, **Phoenix Theater (Map 7)**, **EXIT Theater (Map 7)** (host of the annual San Francisco Fringe Festival), and **Eureka Theatre (Map 8)**, which puts an emphasis on local talent and productions with social messages. Tony Kushner's *Angels In America* premiered here in 1992.

Cultural Theater

San Francisco has a variety of theaters that focus on performances of interest to specific cultural groups. Located in the Mission District, the **Brava Theatre Center (Map 15)** is the only women-owned theater in San Francisco. The primary purpose of Brava! for Women in the Arts is to produce outstanding world premieres by women of color as well as lesbian playwrights. The first US theater devoted to productions addressing LGBT issues, **Theater Rhinoceros (Map 11)** stages a five-play season each year on its main stage and maintains a smaller studio for emerging artists, workshops, and solo performances. The **Buriel Clay Theatre (Map 6)**, located inside the African-American Cultural Complex, and the **Lorraine Hansberry Theatre (Map 7)** emphasize African-American theater, artists, and performances. Other culturally-based theater organizations include the **Bindlestiff Studio (Map 12)** for budding Filipino artists and **El Teatro de la Esperanza (Map 11)**. Begun as a student theater in 1970, this Mission haunt produces bilingual plays focused on Latino mythology and culture.

Getting Tickets

If you're short on cash, one of the best places to find advance tickets is through Goldstar Events, www.goldstar.com. This online service offers deeply discounted tickets to local events and theatrical performances. For other affordable ticket options, check out Brown Paper Tickets, at www.brownpapertickets.com, a fair-trade ticketing company with the lowest service fees in the industry, at which many smaller venues sell their tickets. If you're killing time in the city and want to see a show, visit the TIX Bay Area walk-up box office, which sells half-price tickets on the day of performance; they now accept cash AND credit cards. The TIX Pavilion is located in Union Square on Powell Street, between Geary and Post. Half-price tickets go on sale at 11 am each day, and tickets for Sunday and Monday are sold on Saturday and Sunday respectively. To check which shows are discounted each day, visit www.theatrebayarea.org/tix/halfprice.jsp. TIX Bay Area is a program of Theatre Bay Area, a nonprofit organization serving over 300 theater and dance companies in the 9-county Bay Area. Check out their website at www.theatrebayarea.com for a comprehensive list of shows playing throughout the area. You'll also discover on their website an abundance of information about arts education, applying for CA$H grants, costume rental, auditions, publications, and anything else related to the Bay Area theater scene.

Theater	Address	Phone	Map
Actor's Theatre of San Francisco	855 Bush St	415-296-9179	7
Alcazar Theatre	650 Geary St	415-441-6655	7
Audium	1616 Bush St	415-771-1616	6
Bayfront Theater	350 Fort Mason	415-474-6776	2
Bayview Opera House	4705 3rd St	415-824-0386	36
Bill Graham Civic Auditorium	99 Grove St	415-974-4060	7
Bindlestiff Studio	505 Natoma St	415-255-0440	12
Blue Bear Performance Hall	Fort Mason	415-673-3600	2
Brava Theatre Center	2781 24th St	415-647-2822	15
Buriel Clay Theatre	762 Fulton St	415-922-2049	6
CELLspace	2050 Bryant St	415-648-7562	11
Climate Theater	285 9th St	415-978-2345	12
Club Fugazi	678 Green St	415-421-4222	4
Cowell Theater	Fort Mason	415-441-3400	2
Curran Theater	445 Geary St	415-551-2000	7
Dance Mission	3316 24th St	415-826-4441	15
Davies Symphony Hall	201 Van Ness Ave	415-864-6000	11
Decker Theater	25 S Van Ness Ave	415-861-8972	11
Eureka Theater	215 Jackson St	415-788-1125	8
Exit on Taylor	277 Taylor St	415-673-3847	7
EXIT Theater	156 Eddy St	415-931-1094	7
Geary Theater	405 Geary St	415-749-2228	7
Golden Gate Theatre	1 Taylor St	415-551-2000	7
Herbst Theatre	401 Van Ness Ave	415-392-4400	6
The Hypnodrome	575 10th St	415-248-1900	11
Intersection for the Arts	446 Valencia St	415-626-2787	11
Last Planet Theatre	351 Turk St	415-440-3505	7
Le Palais Nostalgique	Piers 27–29	415-438-2668	4
Lorraine Hansberry Theatre	620 Sutter St	415-474-8800	7
Magic Theatre	Fort Mason	415-441-8001	2
The Marsh	1062 Valencia St	415-826-5750	15
McKenna Theatre/SFSU Campus	1600 Holloway Ave	415-338-2467	28
Mission Cultural Center for Latino Arts	2868 Mission St	415-821-1155	15
Museum of Performance and Design	401 Van Ness Ave	415-255-4800	6
New Conservatory Theatre Center	25 S Van Ness Ave	415-861-8972	11
The Next Stage	1620 Gough St	415-826-6505	6
ODC Theater	3153 17th St	415-863-9834	11
Off-Market Theatres	965 Mission St	415-896-6477	12
Orpheum Theatre	1192 Market St	415-551-2000	7
Palace of Fine Arts	3301 Lyon St	415-567-6642	1
Phoenix Theatre	414 Mason St	415-989-0023	7
The Playhouse	533 Sutter St	415-677-9596	7
The Purple Onion	140 Columbus Ave	415-956-1653	8
Shelton Theater	533 Sutter St	415-433-1226	7
Shotwell Studios	3252-A 19th St	415-920-2223	11
Theatre 3	25 S Van Ness Ave	415-861-8972	11
Theatre 39 at Pier 39	2 Beach St (at Embarcadero)	415-433-3939	4
Theater Rhinoceros	2926 16th St	415-861-5079	11
Theatre of Yugen at NOHspace	2840 Mariposa St	415-621-7978	11
Theatre on the Square	450 Post St	415-433-9500	7
Thick House	1695 18th St	415-401-8081	12
Victoria Theatre	2961 16th St	415-863-7576	11
Walker Theater	25 S Van Ness Ave	415-861-8972	11
War Memorial Opera House	301 Van Ness Ave	415-621-6600	11
The Xenodrome	1320 Potrero Ave	415-285-9366	16
Yerba Buena Center for the Arts	701 Mission St	415-978-2787	8
Young Performers Theater	Fort Mason	415-346-5550	2
Z Space Studio	131 10th St	415-626-0453	12
Zeum Theater	221 4th St	415-820-3220	8

WHAT IS *THAT?!*

HUH? OH, IT'S WWW.NOTFORTOURISTS.COM

NFT
BUT WHY?! WHY WOULD YOU USE ANYTHING OTHER THAN ME?

WELL, THE WEBSITE JUST OFFERS A FEW THINGS THAT YOU DON'T: DAILY CONTENT, FUN PHOTOS, SEARCHABLE DATABASE... COOL STUFF LIKE THAT.

DEVASTATED

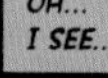
OH...
I SEE...

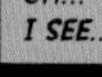

BUT I FIT IN YOUR POCKET.
YOU CAN TAKE ME ANYWHERE.
SWOOP!
OH!
TUCK
TUCK
OH PLEASE. THE WEBSITE COULD NEVER
REPLACE YOU. I NEED YOU BOTH TO GET
THE MOST OUT OF MY CITY!

MUNI LINE F
Historic Streetcar
Embarcadero & Mark
Ferry Building
SPECIAL
496

Street Index

Street Index

Street Index

Street Index

D

G

H

I

Street Index

M

Street Index

Y

Z

Customize your NFT.

We can put **your organization's logo or message** on NFT using custom foil stamps of your (or our) design. Not For Tourists Guidebooks make **great gifts** for employees, clients, and promotional events.

For more information, call us at 212-965-8650, or visit www.notfortourists.com/corporatesales.aspx